D0931632

1000
PERFECT
WEEKENDS

White rhinos graze in front of Mount Kenya (p. 298) at sunrise.

1000
PERFECT
WEEKENDS

Great Getaways Around the Globe

NATIONAL
GEOGRAPHIC

WASHINGTON, D.C.

The Space Needle towers over Seattle's skyline (p. 209).

CONTENTS

Plant yourself on the beach (chapter one) for a weekend escape.

"THE BOOK YOU HOLD IN YOUR HANDS IS
ENTIRELY DEDICATED TO THE BEAUTY
AND POSSIBILITIES OF THE PERFECT
WEEKEND—1,000 OF THEM TO BE EXACT."

INTRODUCTION

The Endless Weekend Possibilities

All it takes is one weekend to fall in love with a place. I discovered this firsthand on a trip to Israel. After a week touring the country, experiencing the beauty of Tel Aviv's beaches and the grandeur of Jerusalem's walls, we took a weekend side trip to Haifa. The port city still has the strongest hold in my memory. In just 48 hours we explored the historic temples and sites, the terraced landscapes. When I close my eyes, I can still smell the sea breeze and see the colorful town stretched below me.

As life got busier with work demands and family obligations, I came to rely on the miracle of a weekend vacation again and again. I took on the challenge of eating my way through Charleston, South Carolina (p. 446), from its Michelin-starred restaurants to beachfront taco stands in just 72 hours. On a long-weekend trip to Park City, Utah (p. 65), I found that a laid-back mountain culture blends perfectly with top-of-the-line ski runs. Then there was the weekend beach trip to Canoa, Ecuador—a quick jump from Quito—where I learned to surf and tried my first caipirinha. And when I added a weekend in Bangkok (p. 197) to a longer vacation in Thailand, I threw myself into temple hopping and the city's celebrated night markets.

The book you hold in your hands is entirely dedicated to the beauty and possibilities of the perfect weekend—1,000 of them to be exact. (To help with the math, that comes out to more than 19 years of weekend exploration!) On every page you'll find an opportunity to discover a new place in 36 to 72 hours, or make the most of a hard-earned longer vacation by tacking on an extra weekend excursion. And with so many wide-ranging options, it's safe to say that there is a trip for everyone here: sandy beach escapes (p. 8), modern city excursions (p. 202), adventures for adrenaline junkies (p. 590), and family-friendly getaways (p. 282), to name a few. And our top 10 lists will help you curate a bucket list built to your interests, from museums (p. 220) and hotels of a lifetime (p. 360) to national parks (p. 406) and theme parks (p. 290).

Carefully curated by our own National Geographic expert travelers, each weekend in this vivid treasury offers an opportunity to explore the world around you, or to unplug after a busy week. Under six hours from their starting hubs, each destination provides an easy, accessible escape.

I hope these pages will ignite your wanderlust, entice you to explore places near and far, and encourage you to make your own perfect weekend—wherever that may be.

—Allyson Johnson, *Travel Editor, National Geographic Books*

CHAPTER ONE

BEACH ESCAPES

Sand, surf, and sun from Nantucket, Massachusetts, to Thonga Beach, South Africa

Enjoy clear water and palm tree-shaded beaches in Phú Quoc, Vietnam (p. 36).

The Finest Coastline

Block Island, Rhode Island, U.S.

Quaint 10-square-mile (25 sq km) Block Island is a microcosm of coastal New England. There are boutique shops, historic inns, two picturesque lighthouses, and a ton of seafood joints. Summer is the best time to visit the 17 miles (27.33 km) of beach on offer here, with golden sands and swimmable water. Highlights of a weekend on Block Island include Fred Benson Town Beach, an amenity-rich subsection of Crescent Beach that faces the Atlantic and is close to town. Then there's Charleston Beach, a great spot for good fishing and spectacular sunsets. Beyond town, crowds thin. Stroll to spot shorebirds or dig for clams (licenses available at New Harbor) at Andy's Way on the inland Great Salt Pond. Mohegan Bluffs is undoubtedly the most scenic and secluded spot: The architecturally stunning redbrick Southeast Light towers atop dune grass–covered 200-foot-tall (61 m) clay cliffs that back the swimmable beach. Long Island's Montauk, 14 miles (23 km) away, is visible from the overlook on clear days. A car ferry connects Block Island to the commercial fishing town of Point Judith in under an hour.

HUB | *Northeastern United States*

"BLOCK ISLAND IS A MICROCOSM OF COASTAL NEW ENGLAND. THERE ARE BOUTIQUE SHOPS, HISTORIC INNS, TWO LIGHTHOUSES, AND A TON OF SEAFOOD JOINTS."

The North Lighthouse sits on the grassy, northern tip of Block Island.

Hateruma's white-sand coast melts into the turquoise waters of the Philippine Sea.

A Far-Flung Treasure

Hateruma, Taketomi, Japan

Hateruma, a tiny island in the Yaeyama archipelago, is a tropical treasure at roughly the same latitude as northwestern Hawaii. Far closer to Taiwan than Japan's larger islands, you'll have to fly to larger Ishigaki Island—Tokyo, Kyoto, and Haneda all have direct flights—then take an hour-long ferry to reach it. The journey is worth it. White-sand beaches meld into crystal blue waters that stretch in all directions. Rent a bike to make the two-hour circumnavigation of the island, crossing inland fields of sugar cane en route to northerly Nishihama Beach. The calm blue waters of "Nishi" offer some of the country's best swimming and snorkeling—near-shore coral mounds swarm with colorful reef fish. Be sure to stay overnight to check out the Southern Cross—visible between April and June—with the aid of the island's 20-millimeter refracting telescope at the observation tower near the monument marking Japan's southernmost point.

HUB | *Tokyo, Kyoto, or Haneda, Japan; Taiwan*

Take a two-hour bike ride around the entire island.

"MOST HEAD TO VIÑA DEL MAR FOR SUN WORSHIPPING."

Artistic Fishing Village

Valparaíso, Chile

Urban Valparaíso, with its containership-filled harbor and crane-dominated waterfront, is hardly a dream beach getaway. Yet the hilly former fishing village boasts an endearing, if gritty, artists' vibe with bold street murals, colorful houses, and a UNESCO-recognized historic quarter that visitors won't want to miss. Less than a half-hour north by public transit, the neighboring resort town of Viña del Mar has a handful of the fine sandy beaches that Valparaíso's coast lacks. Make a weekend on the central coast of Chile for the best of both worlds.

Aside from a few wetsuit-clad bodyboarders, most head to Viña del Mar for sun worshipping; the Pacific here is typically too chilly for more than quick dips. Hunker down on the less than half-mile (450 m) strip at Caleta Abarca on the Valparaíso side of the artificially created Estero Viña del Mar estuary. Close to downtown, it has showers and lockers, but can be jam-packed. The larger stretch—backed by high-rise apartment towers, restaurants, and a promenade that spans the length of downtown along San Martin Avenue—offers much more space to spread out. It's so long that it has three different names as you move along its sandy stretch. A late 19th-century industrial pier divides Acapulco Beach from Playa del Sol. Near its north end, old military weapons front a section called Playa Los Cañones (Cannons Beach). The most secluded is a tiny berm-backed crescent, Playa Las Salinas, with a small cluster of tide pools on the other side of the rocky point from Los Cañones.

After your beach stroll head to Valparaíso, take an interpretive street art tour, including a stop at the multistory building-spanning "Mural de Valparaiso" by Inti Castro, a renowned artist and Valparaíso native son. Also visit La Sebastiana, the hilltop former residence of poet Pablo Neruda featuring sweeping views of the colorful houses and the harbor below. To fully embrace Valparaíso's charm, get there the old-fashioned way, via Ascensor Espíritu Santo, one of the city's historic hillside ascensor remnants of late 19th-century industrial infrastructure.

HUB i *Santiago, Chile*

The colorful historic city of Valparaíso is a UNESCO World Heritage site.

A young girl plays with her beach toys on the sandy shores of Destin.

Emerald Paradise

Destin, Florida, U.S.

This panhandle paradise has been a regional retreat for hardworking families for decades. Part of Florida's Gulf-facing Emerald Coast, Destin's calm, green, and warm shallow waters are perfect for swimming, and its wide berths of fine ivory sand are excellent for sandcastle building. The beach here stretches straight and virtually uninterrupted to Panama City Beach some 45 miles (72 km) east. A strip of hotels spills patrons from lobbies right onto the shore, and eight public thoroughfares afford access to those staying farther inland. While several dune-backed sections, including 1.2-mile-long (1.9 km) Henderson Beach east of town, sport fewer beach umbrellas and offer a quieter scene, most visit Destin for the camaraderie of the quintessential American beach vacation. Prop planes advertise crab dinner specials on aerial signs, Jet Ski and paddleboard rentals are plentiful, and parasailing, waterskiing, and fishing charter companies compete for business. There's a water park, museums, a downtown boardwalk, and of course miniature golf.

HUB | *Southeastern United States*

Boulders front the Lake Michigan beach at Wind Point in Racine.

Lakeshore Treats

Racine, Wisconsin, U.S.

North Beach's palm-dotted golden sands spill into an infinite horizon of calm blue waters. No, it's not the ocean. As souvenir shirts proudly proclaim: "This is shark-free, salt-free Lake Michigan. The palms are potted." Just a half-hour drive south of Milwaukee, this half-mile (0.8 km) stretch of lakeshore is one of the top freshwater beaches in the country. It has all of the best summer weekend amenities: lifeguards, volleyball courts, a snack bar, picnic areas, a large playground, and regular live music. In the broader town and county of Racine, there's a charming downtown thoroughfare, a quirky fine art museum, inland lakes, a canoe-able river filled with trout, lakeside butterfly gardens with a native plant nature trail, bike paths, a bakery that makes 36 flavors of Danish Kringle pastries, and eight publicly accessible golf courses (six have 18-plus holes). Don't miss a visit to Wingspread, the largest of Frank Lloyd Wright's prairie-style homes.

HUB | *Milwaukee, Wisconsin, U.S.; Midwestern United States*

A kayaker paddles the waters of Lake Champlain at sunset.

Natural Wonders

Milton Island and Grand Isle, Vermont, U.S.

On the peaceful, forested shores of Lake Champlain, long summer days are best spent at the beach. Book a campsite, lean-to, or cabin on Grand Isle's southeastern shore, often referred to as South Hero Island. Then spend the weekend grilling picnics, tromping down forest trails, and splashing in cool lake waters. A mile-long (1.6 km) road-topped sand berm connects South Hero to Milton, where popular Sand Bar State Park has a long, shady stretch of golden sand and a huge area of shallow water perfect for families. Rent a stand-up paddleboard to ply the waters and take in views of Hero Island and the Green Mountains beyond the lakeshore. The mouth of the Lamoille River, whose sediments formed the natural bridge, spills into a 1,500-acre (607 ha) protected marsh south of the park that's meant for wildlife-watching. The nutrient-rich region is a nursery for lake fish and home to everything from herons and beavers to spiny softshell turtles and the occasional moose.

| HUB | Burlington, Vermont, U.S.; Northeastern United States; Montréal or Québec City, Canada |

Palms hang over the sandy
shores of One Foot Island
in the Cook Islands.

Beaches

These top swaths of surf and sand—from Western Australia
to the Cook Islands—offer the ultimate watery getaways.

1. PLAYA DEL AMOR, MARI-ETAS ISLANDS, MEXICO

You have to hire a tour operator—and swim through a nearly invisible cave opening—for access to "Love Beach," a hidden cove encircled by a rock ring formation with an opening to the sun and sky. Only six people are allowed on the beach at a time.

2. ANSE SOURCE D'ARGENT, LA DIGUE, SEYCHELLES

Giant boulders pepper the white-sand beaches on this Indian Ocean escape. This palm tree–lined oasis offers turquoise waters and a postcard-perfect setting.

3. ONE FOOT ISLAND, AITUTAKI, COOK ISLANDS

Survivor once filmed on this atoll, and for good reason. The crystal clear lagoon offers a prime snorkeling opportunity, and the palm-lined shore can be circled in just a 15-minute jaunt. Don't forget to have your passport marked with the footprint-shaped stamp before leaving the island.

4. BOWMAN'S BEACH, SAN-IBEL ISLAND, FLORIDA, U.S.

Bowman's is mecca for shell collectors. On the shores of the Gulf of Mexico, currents wash up conchs, coquinas, and sand dollars, among other beachy treasures. For a day collecting your own, stock up on supplies at Bailey's General Store, a local favorite.

5. SHELL BEACH, SHARK BAY, AUSTRALIA

On the Western side of Australia, white cockleshells, instead of sand, make up miles of shore in this portion of the Shark Bay UNESCO World Heritage site. In some parts, the shells are piled up to 30 feet (9.1 m) deep.

6. CANNON BEACH, OREGON, U.S.

Haystack Rock, an Oregon icon, looms offshore from this public beach. The rock, a seasonal nesting spot for tufted puffins, is just one draw—you'll also find sweeping, misty ocean views and hidden coves. Dogs are most welcome on the beach, too—in fact, the Surf-sand Resort hosts an annual dog show every October.

7. NOORDWIJK BEACH, THE NETHERLANDS

Dog lovers should make their way to this seaside town, where beach trails are pup friendly, as are designated stretches of its sandy shores. There are even dog-friendly restaurants (try Bubbels Beach) near the beach.

8. REYNISFJARA BEACH, ICELAND

Not a warm weather beach, Reynis-fjara is worth a visit for its black sand and basalt sea stacks. The inky scene is even more mesmerizing after a light snowfall. Be careful on your visit here—the waves are powerful and known to knock people right off of their feet.

9. PINK BEACH, GREAT SANTA CRUZ ISLAND, ZAM-BOANGA, THE PHILIPPINES

Crushed red organ-pipe coral has turned the sand here a stunning pink hue. To protect this beloved spot, visitors to the island are regulated and must book a visit through the tourist office in Zamboanga in advance.

10. CORNICHE BEACH, LA TESTE-DE-BUCH, FRANCE

Corniche Beach, on the Atlantic, is backed by the massive Dune of Pilat, a haven for paragliders and sandboarders. Climbing on the 357-foot-tall (108.8 m) dune is an adventure in itself, too—and makes for fun sliding down. The pine forest behind the dunes doesn't hurt this picturesque setting, either.

Postcard Perfect

Andaman Islands, India

The mysterious tropical archipelago of the Andamans is chock-full of postcard-perfect beaches and unspoiled reefs. Hundreds of uninhabited islands fringe 36 inhabited ones that divide the Bay of Bengal and the Andaman Sea between India, Myanmar, and Indonesia. Interiors overflowing with banana and coconut groves, dense mahua, and palm jungle are home to native birds, wild elephants, and some of the world's last remaining uncontacted tribes. The Andamans sit some 850 miles (1,370 km) east of mainland India, admittedly a long haul, but you'd be remiss to miss the beaches on Swaraj Dweep (Havelock Island), so tack on a long weekend here if you're already touring the country. The islands' handful of named stretches each has something different to offer: Snorkelers love Elephant Beach while Radhanagar is widely regarded as one of the world's most gorgeous. Kayak coastal mangroves at sunset to see bioluminescent plankton echo a profusion of emerging stars. Direct flights to the capital run regularly from Mumbai, Kolkata, and Chennai; it's another 2.5-hour ferry ride to Swaraj Dweep.

HUB | Southern India

"INTERIORS OVERFLOW WITH BANANA AND COCONUT GROVES, DENSE MAHUA, AND PALM JUNGLE, HOME TO NATIVE BIRDS AND WILD ELEPHANTS."

A couple pauses to capture an oceanfront picture on Radhanagar Beach.

Walk the rocky coastline of Dahab's shores to take in ruins and sea views.

Big Blue in the Red Sea

Dahab, Egypt

This mountain foothill fishing village has become a bona fide bucket list destination in recent years. There's a sugary sand stretch around a protected lagoon, but for the real flavor of Dahab, find a spot on the mostly rocky shores to soak everything in. Numerous resorts, including glamping-style Bedouin camps, hug the coast, but taking a dip requires the aid of a snorkeling or diving charter. And you'll definitely want to get wet. This stretch of the clear Red Sea's big blue is within Ras Abu Galum National Park, where elaborate near-shore fringing reefs are home to some of the world's most colorful, healthy, and resilient underwater scenery. One of the most popular offshore locales, the Blue Hole, is 5 miles (8 km) north of Dahab. There, a massive sinkhole plummets beyond recreational scuba depths. Underwater exploration here has been described as reverse skydiving, with coral and fish for company.

HUB | *Cairo, Egypt; Jerusalem, Israel; Middle East*

Dive or snorkel with colorful reef fish in Ras Abu Galum.

A colorful dhow is moored on the shore of Paradise Island.

Sunny Mozambique

A Wistful Voyage of Discovery to Faraway Isles

I've come to Mozambique to test the waters of this rapidly changing African nation. Only 40 years ago it declared independence after almost five centuries as a Portuguese colony. Twenty years ago, ravaged by years of Marxist misrule and a brutal civil war, it was one of the poorest lands on Earth. Today it tends one of the world's fastest-growing economies and is framing itself as southern Africa's beach destination.

I want to experience the southern part of the coast, known for the seaside town of Vilankulo and the five islands that form Bazaruto Archipelago National Park, recognized by the World Wildlife Fund as a "Gift to the Earth." Until recently a crumbling port, Vilankulo now is popular for its seafood eateries, budget lodgings, diving, and dhow safaris to the archipelago, where three of the islands—Magaruque, Benguerra, and Bazaruto—have seen a slate of resorts and hotels open. But it's the small jewel of an island named Santa Carolina that holds particular allure for me. Santa Carolina is where my parents honeymooned, back when it was known as Paradise Island, at the Hotel Santa Carolina—and where a young Bob Dylan is said to have stayed in the 1970s, inspiring his song "Mozambique."

I drive from my parents' home in Zimbabwe. I reach Vilankulo at dusk and check into a beach resort called Archipelago. I awake at dawn to an ancient sight: fishermen in dhows—traditional wooden vessels powered by billowing cloth sails. Arab traders sailed dhows to these shores more than a thousand years ago, as they trafficked slaves, pearls, and ivory. These days, dhows ferry visitors to the islands.

The next morning is drizzly and windswept, and I am one of two passengers on Sailaway Dhow Safaris' *Adriana*. The vessel is a piece of work, made with three types of wood and painted in tropical greens and purples. Seating is on benches under an angled boom. *Adriana* is not built for comfort, but she is sturdy as an ocean liner. I love every second of our four-hour sail.

The Bazaruto Archipelago was declared a marine reserve in 1971 and today is home to many rare species, including the last viable population of manatee-like dugongs in East Africa. These draw visitors to locally flavored resorts, such as &Beyond's Benguerra Lodge, where I'm staying on Benguerra Island.

I expect a tropical paradise of sand, palm trees, and coconuts. Instead, the interior reminds me of inland savanna, a landscape of grasses and freshwater lakes filled with Nile crocodiles. A flock of flamingos has turned the water in one secluded cove a fluorescent red; around them, green-and-red Narina trogon birds dart among ironwood trees.

I wake before dawn and barrel north to beat the sunrise. Reaching Inhassôro, I spot a band of burly South African travelers strapped into life jackets and piling into a pair of rubber dinghies. I join them, we gun the engines, and the blue waters of the Indian Ocean froth under us. As we approach Santa Carolina, there's not a soul to be seen. We pull into a cove with sand so white, it hurts my eyes.

I head into the dense island scrub. Twenty minutes of walking on spiky casuarina cones brings me to a potholed airstrip. Just beyond, I push away some palm fronds and spot it: the ruins of Hotel Santa Carolina, where my newlywed parents began their life together. I feel as though I've stumbled on a lost city.

I make my way to the sprawling concrete shell, which fronts the island's eastern shore. Finding stairs, I climb up one flight, turn right, and step into a room. Hundreds of tiny pink tiles lie scattered across the floor. I pick a few up as mementos, then look out from the balcony toward a chapel, its roof swooping like some Palm Springs modern masterpiece, perched on nearby rocks.

I continue to the top floor, and into the ballroom. Its walls and windows long since shattered by waves and cyclones, the space is open to the elements. But in its middle is a spectacular sight: a pillar inlaid with thousands of tiny blue tiles painstakingly pieced together by artisans half a century ago. Even more unbelievable to me is a piano, leaning against the back wall, the ivories long since pilfered.

Did Bob Dylan compose his song "Mozambique" on it? The lyrics come to me on the wind:

I like to spend some time in Mozambique
The sunny sky is aqua blue
And all the couples dancing cheek to cheek

I flash to one couple in particular. It's 1963. My parents, full of youthful optimism, are dancing on this very floor.

I reach for my cellphone and make a call. My mother's voice comes on the answering machine. "Mom," I say. "I'm here on Paradise Island, at the Santa Carolina Hotel. Tell Dad."

—**Douglas Rogers** is the author of *The Last Resort: A Memoir of Zimbabwe.*

Something Magical

Road's End State Recreation Site, Oregon, U.S.

There's something magical about the Road's End State Recreation Site, a protected beach just 2.5 hours from Portland. Visitors frequent its scenic sands even in windswept winter months. It's not just its rocky miniature islands or secret beach; there's also hope of finding treasure. Fifteen- to 20-million-year-old volcanic and sandstone berms back the beach, filled with colorful minerals, petrified wood, and ancient whale bones that break free with stormy waves. The community also injects "random acts of findness": For 20 years, a local artists' collective has hidden kaleidoscopic handblown glass floats between Road's End and Siletz Bay 7.5 miles (12 km) away, an homage to coveted Japanese fishing floats that once washed ashore. The new floats can be found anywhere from the high tide line to the grassy embankments. If you're not lucky in your "Finders Keepers" search, bring a bag of gathered beach trash to the Visitor Center for a monthly drawing entry to win one.

HUB | *Pacific Northwest United States*

Waves crash onto Road's End Beach on a stormy day.

Play back-to-back greens on the Jack Nicklaus Four Seasons Golf Course at Punta Mita, Mexico.

Golf Courses

The top links to play from every corner of the world include courses played by presidents, fairways made for championship rounds, and oceanside scenic greens.

1. ST. ANDREWS LINKS, SCOTLAND

The so-called home of golf—where the game has been played since the 15th century—the Old Course at St. Andrews is reportedly the world's oldest and, arguably, Scotland's most iconic (the Royal & Ancient Clubhouse doesn't hurt).

2. TORREY PINES GOLF COURSE, LA JOLLA, CALIFORNIA, U.S.

Nodding to golf's motherland, the doormen wear kilts at this legendary La Jolla, California, course, where you'll play the same fairways that hosted the U.S. Open—and President Obama, who crashed a wedding photo session on the 18th green.

3. THE OMNI HOMESTEAD RESORT, HOT SPRINGS, VIRGINIA, U.S.

Having hosted more U.S. presidents than any other public golf course, the Old Course at this mountainous Virginia retreat is reportedly home to the nation's oldest first tee in continuous use.

4. PEBBLE BEACH, MONTEREY, CALIFORNIA, U.S.

If there's one American public course that's most widely beloved—by presidents, golf pros, and everyone in between—it's this stunner on California's Monterey Peninsula, home to more U.S. Opens than any other course over the past 50 years.

5. TROMSØ GOLF CLUB, NORWAY

This Arctic Circle hub is remarkably accessible—and even more remarkably, golf friendly (come summer, anyway). In fact, the world's northernmost 18-hole course offers around-the-clock golfing in June against a backdrop of forest and mountains.

6. FANCOURT, SOUTH AFRICA

This resort along the vineyard- and beach-blessed Garden Route is home to three Gary Player–designed golf courses that rank among the continent's best, plus a golf academy for good measure.

7. THE BROADMOOR, COLORADO SPRINGS, COLORADO, U.S.

For golf geeks, it doesn't get better than the course where Jack Nicklaus won the 1959 U.S. Amateur (his "most important putt," he said). For others, two stellar courses backed by the Cheyenne Mountains are reason enough to visit.

8. AMANERA, DOMINICAN REPUBLIC

The first golf-equipped resort by cult favorite Aman Resorts International Luxury group, this Dominican retreat boasts more oceanside holes than any other in the Western Hemisphere. You have golf course architect Rees Jones to thank for that—and for the stunning clifftop course in general.

9. COEUR D'ALENE RESORT, COEUR D'ALENE, IDAHO, U.S.

Perhaps the world's most famous 14th hole, the Floating Green is a boat-accessible movable island in Idaho's Lake Coeur d'Alene. *Golf Magazine* once described it as "America's Most Beautiful Resort Golf Course," and for good reason: A mahogany boat delivers you across the lake to the manicured fairways, with lakeviews from nearly every hole.

10. PACIFICO GOLF COURSE, FOUR SEASONS PUNTA MITA, MEXICO

The Tail of the Whale, or "3B," is the only natural island that doubles as a hole. Accessible by foot during low tide and amphibious cart otherwise, the feature has made Jack Nicklaus's work on this lush Mexican peninsula nothing short of legendary.

Sardinian Tahiti

Cala Coticcio Beach, Italy

Below interior pine forest and amid an arid shrub-dotted hillscape, the eye-popping electric blues of tiny Cala Coticcio Beach helped earn it the nickname "Sardinian Tahiti." To get to these gorgeous sandy shores, fly into one of Sardinia's three main airports or take the ferry from Rome, Milan, or Naples to the Sardinian island of La Maddalena. It's a short bridge crossing from there to Isola Caprera. Beach access requires a hike down a boulder-strewn trail or a less taxing boat charter. It's nestled in a protected marine park filled with Mediterranean denizens such as starfish, flying fish, rays, and skates. Other island beaches are worth a visit too: On the northern coast, the similarly secluded and picturesque Cala Garibaldi, named for the 19th-century Italian general who retired here, and the pink sand Cala Serena are alternative options. You'll have to return to La Maddalena in the evening; Isola Caprera is blissfully undeveloped.

HUB | *Rome, Italy*

> "IN A PROTECTED MARINE PARK FIND MEDITERRANEAN DENIZENS SUCH AS STARFISH, FLYING FISH, RAYS, AND SKATES."

Take in the rays laid out in a cove on Cala Coticcio Beach.

Étretat's white cliffs border and protect its sandy shores, adding to its stunning beach landscape.

Seascapes on the Cliffs

Étretat, Normandy, France

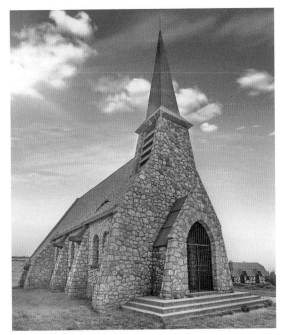

The white pebble beach and dramatic striated sea cliffs at the northerly French village of Étretat are so captivating that when Claude Monet visited in 1883, he painted 20 different views of them in an attempt to capture how light morphed their appearance. The beauty of the 230-foot-high (70 m) chalk cliffs, carved over millennia by wind and waves, endures, even as they are subject to slow but constant change.

Base your weekend at the Dormy House, which sits on 10 clifftop acres (4 ha) with sea views from its restaurant and rooms. For sea-level views, make your way to one of the many beaches, or to Chapelle Notre-Dame-de-la-Garde, a triangular stone chapel with epic views from atop Porte d'Amont in the north. Above Port d'Aval in the south, a trail winds near the cliff edge with views of Manneporte, the thickest and largest of Étretat's three sea arches, and passes the remains of 18th-century oyster beds.

HUB | Paris, France

A stone church sits in the medieval village of Étretat.

> ## "ITS NAME STEMS FROM THE WORDS FOR 'FARAWAY LAND.'"

Empty & Calm

Nantucket, Massachusetts, U.S.

While New England's beaches surge with crowds in summer, it's still possible to find long, empty stretches along the 82 miles (132 km) of pale sand shores ringing the former world whaling capital. Thirty miles (48 km) south of Cape Cod and reachable only by plane or boat, Nantucket's relative remoteness has long been a draw for escape seekers; even the island's name is said to stem from the words for "faraway land" in the native Wampanoag dialect.

With dozens of named beaches (seven under the watchful eye of lifeguards in summer), there's one for every mood and every beachgoer. North shore stretches like Children's or popular Jetties—just east of the Nantucket Harbor channel and walkable from downtown—tend to have calmer seas and Nantucket Sound views. South shore beaches like Tom Nevers, Miacomet, Cisco, and Nobadeer are wilder, in terms of offshore activity—larger waves and rip currents are more common here—and patrons. Nobadeer is a renowned party beach, and Cisco is home to one of the island's most popular surfing schools. East and west coast beaches, with a few notable exceptions like swimmable Sconset, are great places to stroll and spot coastal wildlife when sunny skies are obscured by the island's notorious gray fog. Don't miss the lighthouse at easterly Great Point or sunset with a picnic on far west Madaket.

It's not just the variety and quantity of great beaches that make Nantucket a perfect weekend getaway. Protected from the wider Atlantic by Nantucket Sound and tempered by the Gulf Stream, summer days are cooler and winter days are milder than their Cape Cod counterparts. There's lots to do inland as well: A whaling museum open since 1930 showcases artifacts from the area's glory days; quaint cobblestoned streets sport boutiques proffering antiques, souvenirs, and beach reads; and nearly half of the island's interior, including a huge cranberry bog, is undeveloped open space.

A boardwalk leads to Steps Beach on Nantucket Island.

The sun sets over
the beach at Cape May.

Garden State Variety

More Than a Shore Thing: There's a Lot to Love About New Jersey

We're treating our kayaks like floating La-Z-Boy recliners, the three of us leaning back, legs stretched out on the decks. Here on the Delaware River, New Jersey lies to our left, Pennsylvania to our right. It's been several minutes since we've needed to paddle. As Interstate 80 comes into view, we dip our paddles into the water to guide our boats around one of the thick concrete pillars of the highway overpass. "It's all right here," says my friend Leslie.

Indeed. That is the best and worst of New Jersey summed up. With 39,000 miles (62,764 km) of public roadway paving the 8,723-square-mile (22,592 sq km) state, it's easy to get everything and, it can seem, hard to get away from anything. Though the Garden State ranks 46th by size, it is No. 11 in population. It bests Wyoming's resident count 15 to 1.

After an 8-mile (12.8 km) float, we pull the kayaks out of the water near the Kittatinny Point Visitor Center in the Delaware Water Gap National Recreation Area. Families crowd the beach. Kids in the river blast each other with water cannons.

I drive 4 miles (6.4 km) up Old Mine Road, trees thick on either side of the road that's at times barely paved. At my campsite in Worthington State Forest, I'm suddenly immersed in a quieter New Jersey, the only human sounds coming from two campsites away and the late afternoon kayakers drifting by on the water below.

Camping doesn't mesh with the Jersey I grew up in: the malls, beach houses, highways, and 16-plex movie theaters. It's hard to push away the thought of all those houses and people in nearby towns.

Relaxing into my chair by the campfire, I look up at the night sky. The stars poke through the darkness. Bullfrogs provide the evening's soundtrack and, later, the light of my headlamp catches the evening's final entertainment—tiny frogs hopping around, no bigger than my thumbnail. Camping in New Jersey starts to make sense.

The next morning, 30 miles (48.2 km) from Worthington, on State Highway 94, the landscape opens up to fields, houses here and there, a baseball diamond in the distance. There's room to breathe. I'm moving along steadily when, finally, the stream of farm stands proves too difficult to resist, and I stop at Lentini's. The baskets around the stand overflow with local corn and tomatoes.

My passenger seat piled with produce, I drive on. By the time I get to High Point, my steering wheel is sticky with cherry juice. I park in the lot and make the short walk up the road to High Point Monument, a 220-foot (67 m) obelisk that honors war veterans. There's no use trying to see past the day's fog out to the Pocono Mountains or the Wallkill River Valley. Instead I focus on some bright pink wildflowers. After yesterday's heat, the rain-day air comforts me. I get to my car just as it starts to pour.

The next morning, after several stops on Route 31—including a spur-of-the-moment paddle on a reservoir—a familiar bridge welcomes me to the Garden State Parkway. On this July day, I luck out. Cars move along, unsnarled by summer beach traffic. Blue skies accented by fluffy clouds tempt me to drive barefoot.

A few hours later I check into the Hotel Tides in Asbury Park. I slip on flip-flops and walk down to the boardwalk.

The unexpected sounds of drums and tambourines hit my ears, getting louder with every step. It doesn't take long to find the source: a weekly music gathering of the town's finest hippies, misfits, and parents with toddlers.

I'm craving a touch of my Jersey Shore childhood, an arcade. My old pal, the KISS-themed machine, doesn't hold up to memory, but I still can't resist Galaga, my favorite video game from the 1980s. The next 40 minutes disappear.

After the arcade's bells and whistles, the boardwalk is steeped in quiet. I look down to see a crab slowly sidestepping along the beach.

One final stop. At long last it's time to forgive my parents for our decades-ago move to Jersey. I drive south—as far south as Jersey goes—to Cape May Point, where my mom meets me at my beach house rental.

Sitting at a picnic table on the deck of H&H Seafood, the basin in front of us loaded with crabs, I'm rambling on and on about the past days. About the sour cherries and the diners and a storm that soaked me while I was kayaking on a quiet reservoir the day before. My brain is in a New Jersey whirlwind. This change—my new, true love of the place—shocks my mom and me.

—**Jenna Schnuer** lives in Alaska and has written for *National Geographic Traveler*, among other publications.

A great egret perches above a wetland pond.

Swim, Golf & Bobcats
Kiawah Island, South Carolina, U.S.

Exclusive Kiawah, a barrier coast island in the Atlantic connected by causeway to Charleston, boasts 10 miles (16 km) of beautiful beaches. Not only is it a great place for swimming and lounging, it's also a vital nesting habitat for vulnerable loggerhead sea turtles. Outsiders can explore the island by day, including the gorgeous strip of alabaster sand at Beachwalker Park, but you'll need to rent a house or book a room at the Sanctuary at Kiawah Island Golf Resort to see much of Kiawah's private spoils. The five-star property has hosted PGA Golf Championships and boasts five seaside courses. If you need a break from the course, kayak inland ponds and marshes that are home to seabirds and alligators or look for bobcats, shy and about twice the size of a house cat. Kiawah tracks some 35 of the felines, more than double typical mainland concentrations, which keep the island's deer and mice populations in check.

HUB | *Charleston, South Carolina, U.S.; Southeastern United States*

Take a boat out on the blue waters of St. Kitts.

Uncrowded Caribbean Waters
Saint Kitts, Saint Kitts & Nevis

With regular direct flights from New York and Atlanta, it's easy to make a weekend getaway to Saint Kitts. One of the Caribbean's lesser visited islands, you'll get the same sparkling seas without the chaotic beach atmosphere. Get to limin' (local parlance for hanging out, drinking, and talking) on the warm curve of Cockleshell Bay, backed by forested volcanic hills home to vervet monkeys. You can see smaller Nevis island across the Narrows channel. If you feel summoned, take a short water taxi to Nevis's, a popular snorkeling beach. Also on offer on Saint Kitts are the explorable rusty remains of an old fishing boat near Majors Bay; a slave-built British military fortress used to fend off pirate attacks; rainforest bat caves; the Atlantic-facing, reef-protected strip of sand at North Frigate Bay Beach; and restaurants serving up conch fritters, a local delicacy.

HUB | *East Coast United States*

Tropical plants border
the white sands of
South Shore Park.

Easy Beach Access

Bermuda

Electric teal and cerulean seas envelop Bermuda, an island more than 800 miles (1,325 km) into the North Atlantic off South Carolina's coast. The remote 20-square-mile (52 sq km) British island territory sports so many tantalizing strips of peach-sand beach (a combo of crushed white coral and pink foraminifera), you could explore one a day for weeks and still have options. But if you're fitting as much into a weekend as possible, start with the highlights: the much lauded stretch at Horseshoe Bay; Church Bay with its nearshore snorkeling reef; the tiny, secret Jobson's Cove protected from ocean surge by a ring of natural slanted rocks; and the hike-in-only uncrowded Astwood Cove. Or opt to stay put at a peaceful toes-in-the-sand resort like southwesterly Pompano Beach Club or the luxe Elbow Beach Hotel. Bermuda is often overlooked in favor of Caribbean islands far to the south but access is easy: Numerous U.S. East Coast cities offer two- to three-hour direct flights or three-night cruises to the island.

HUB | *East Coast United States*

"THE PARK OFFERS NATURE
TRAILS, TIDE POOLS,
AND HISTORY."

Sea Dragons & Tides

Kamay Botany Bay National Park, Kurnell
Peninsula, Australia

Sydney has no shortage of delightful beaches within easy
reach for a weekend escape. Case in point: the Kurnell
Peninsula, home to Kamay Botany Bay National Park. Less
than an hour's drive from famous Bondi Beach, the park offers
nature trails, tide pools, and history; Cronulla Beach, the city's
longest stretch of golden sand; plus windsurfing, paddleboarding, swimming, and diving in the peninsula's protected coves.

Base yourself in Cronulla for a visit to the national park, which
juts out into Botany Bay, named for the numerous plants gathered here and brought aboard the *Endeavor* when James Cook's
crew became the first Westerners to set foot on Australia in 1770.
Take the short Burrawang trail to see the memorial marking their
landing spot; then follow the longer Cape Bailey Coast Trail
through sand dunes and bushlands for a sense of how the region
may have appeared before first contact. Be sure to watch for
whales spouting offshore. Across the bay, the first French visitors
landed at La Perouse in 1788. Today, scuba divers can head
beneath the waves at Barre Island just offshore to spot endemic
weedy sea dragons camouflaged in the seagrass.

When you're ready for the beach, choose between Towara,
with its secluded white sands that merge into mangrove forest
and skyline views, and the long, quiet, neighborhood-backed
stretch at Silver Beach.

On day two, after some beach time at Cronulla, take the ferry
to Bundeena, gateway to Royal National Park, for more nature
hiking and 1,000-year-old Aboriginal petroglyphs at Jibbon.
When you get back to Cronulla, cap off your weekend escape
with a surfing lesson or some tide pool exploration if the waves
are kicking.

Sandstone cliffs face the Pacific in Kamay Botany Bay National Park.

Red mangroves grow throughout Biscayne National Park.

A One-of-a-Kind Park
Biscayne National Park, Florida, U.S.

There are few proper beaches at Biscayne National Park, save for the thin crescent across the boat channel from its visitor center. That's for the best. This aquatic Arcadia begs you to brush the sand off your bum and explore the 270-square-mile (700 sq km) park, 95 percent of which is water. Just offshore, and still within ogling distance of Miami skyscrapers, dip below the surface and you'll see coral cities teeming with reef traffic. There are some 600 fish species in the park—butterflyfish, stingrays, grouper, moray eels, cowfish, pufferfish, and sharks among them—all with a role to play. The mangrove-lined coast and offshore island lagoons are perfect for a paddle, and tree roots transition to underwater meadows that conceal seahorses, turtles, and manatees. And then there's the area's rich maritime history. Pirates once prowled these waters, and six wooden and steel shipwrecks, accessible at snorkeling or scuba diving depths, lie on the sea floor.

HUB | *Miami, Florida, U.S.; Southeastern United States*

Palm-Lined White Sand
Phú Quoc, Vietnam

Until recently the island of Phú Quoc was a locals-only vacation destination. Today, international tourists flock here in search of stunning beaches—some of the few white sand stretches in the country—with easy access. The large island near the Cambodian border is much closer to the mainland and a much shorter ferry ride than many other Gulf of Thailand island locales. Sao Beach, southeast of Duong Dong (the island's largest city), is the place to be. Its palm-lined white stretch has in-water swings, Jet Ski rentals, boat tours, massage cabanas, and numerous small restaurants. Those seeking a quieter scene can venture beyond to the uninterrupted forests that spill onto abandoned stretches of sand to both the north and south. Or head to the aptly named Long Beach, which runs along nearly the entire southwestern coast and at parts is within walking distance of Duong Dong's popular night food market.

Explore Phú Quoc's pristine shores, like Sao Beach.

HUB | *Ho Chi Minh City, Vietnam; Southeast Asia*

Find charm and fun on the Brighton Marine Palace and Pier.

Britain's Jersey Shore
Brighton, England

If your British beach vacation fantasies include quaint cottages, empty beaches, and dune grasses swaying in the wind, you're better off heading to quiet Climping, 25 miles (40 km) east of raucous Brighton. This wild urban beach is like an artsy older brother to the U.S. Jersey Shore. Sure, you can dine on fish and chips, soak in the sun, play seaside bocce, and rent a brightly colored beach hut, but you can also wander through outdoor shopping malls to the tunes of buskers, play arcade games atop the Brighton Palace Pier, dance in a club until dawn, and ride the 530-foot-high (162 m) British Airways i360 for views that tower above even the tallest beach-backing high-rise. Don't miss Brighton Pride, the beach's largest annual party thrown by its splashy LGBTQ community every August; hundreds of thousands of people come out for the parade, and past years' concert headliners include Britney Spears and Kylie Minogue.

HUB | *London, England*

Traditional watercrafts
line the beaches of
Huanchaco.

"ON THE WATERFRONT, WITNESS A CLASHING OF WORLDS."

Surfing Ancient Watercraft

Huanchaco, Peru

An ancient tradition is alive and well on the sandy beaches of Huanchaco: surfing. No, this isn't Polynesia, but the desert-backed northern Peruvian coastline, where the custom of building watercraft specifically for riding waves seems to have evolved independently and perhaps many centuries earlier than in the South Pacific.

Head to the waterfront to witness a clashing of worlds on the popular left-hand point break off the town's center. *Caballito de totora* (little reed horses) are ancient watercraft that have been used by fishermen in Peru for more than 2,500 years. Made from native wetland grasses, they resemble a cross of a paddleboard, kayak, and longtail boat. Lounge under an umbrella and watch the scene as these authentic vessels share the 3- to 6-foot (1 to 3 m) waves with modern surfers. Or join in yourself. Numerous schools offer surfing lessons and rentals, and some companies combine caballito de totora building lessons with excursions.

On land, dine on fresh ceviche before heading off to learn more about the region's ancient cultures. The UNESCO-protected Chan Chan archaeological site just outside town was the Chimu capital from A.D. 800 until it was abandoned under Inca domination around 1470. Protected for centuries by the desert sand and sun, the ruins comprise one of the world's largest adobe complexes. Farther afield are the pyramid sites at Huacas del Sol y de la Luna, built by the Moche, predecessors of Chimu who flourished here between the first and seventh centuries. Colorful friezes are still visible in situ. Plus, you'll spot the resident viringos, a revered Peruvian hairless dog.

HUB | *Lima, Peru*

Paddle through mangroves in Sarasota Bay.

"ITS WHITE QUARTZ SAND FEELS LIKE
COOL POWDERED SUGAR BENEATH
OUR FEET, ITS CLEAR BLUE WATER
IS WARM AND INVITING."

PERSPECTIVE

Beaches & Beyond

From Mangroves and Palm Trees to Rooftop Bars and Drum Circles, Sarasota, Florida, Offers the Perfect Weekend Escape

My husband and I were searching for sunshine in the Sunshine State, somewhere between Tampa and Fort Myers on Florida's central west coast, when we happened upon Sarasota. It was here the unrelenting rain gave way to a brilliant blue sky and warm golden rays, inviting us to explore this waterfront wonderland. With six barrier islands (known as keys) separating Sarasota County from the Gulf of Mexico, over 35 miles (56.3 km) of white-sand beaches, abundant outdoor activities, and a vibrant cultural scene, we ebb and flow between relaxation and recreation all weekend.

Friday afternoon is spent at Ted Sperling Nature Park, on the southern end of Lido Key, where we rent kayaks and paddle out to the mangroves. We're searching for bottlenose dolphins and manatees when a playful black diving bird, known as a cormorant, pops up between us and plunges beneath our boats, becoming our unofficial escort across the bay. Once we reach the mangroves, narrow tunnels transport us to a hidden world within its twisted roots and branches. Skittish crabs and slow-moving starfish hint at a thriving ecosystem.

We return to civilization on the western shore of Lido Beach, right in time to watch the sun set over the Gulf, a nightly spectacle that draws people to the water's edge. Once the last light is gone, we walk to St. Armands Circle, a posh shopping roundabout, where we dine beneath palm trees and window-shop with ice-cream cones in hand.

On Saturday morning, we follow the smell of sweet pastries and savory empanadas to the Sarasota Farmer's Market on Lemon Street. Here local merchants sell everything from culinary creations to handmade arts and crafts. By afternoon we're seeking sun and solitude and find both on Longboat Key. The northernmost and longest of Sarasota's barrier islands, Long-

boat has 12 miles (19.3 km) of pristine coastline with a dozen beach access points. Conveniences like restrooms are rare, but shorebirds outnumber sunbathers, offering a more secluded beach experience.

At night, downtown Sarasota comes to life, its after-dark activities as plentiful as its daytime options. We drink in panoramic views of Sarasota Bay and city lights from the Westin's rooftop bar on the 19th floor and dine beneath a trellis of purple flowers at Clasico Italian Chophouse, on the corner of Main and Palm, as live music drifts down the street. After dinner, performance venues throughout town open their doors to a variety of shows, from Broadway to ballet to the blues and beyond.

On Sunday morning, we cast lines at Shell Beach on Siesta Key's north shore, catching and releasing black-and-white striped sheepshead and yellow-bellied pompano. When our stomachs rumble, we head to Siesta Village and split an aptly named Paradise Pizza from Ripfire and people-watch on the patio. At the end of the street is Siesta Beach, regularly voted the number one beach in the United States by travelers and coastal experts alike. It's not hard to understand why; its white quartz sand feels like cool powdered sugar beneath our feet, its clear blue water is warm and inviting, and a modern pavilion puts concessions and restrooms within easy reach.

As the sun sets on our weekend in paradise, a drum circle forms on the beach. Some people dance, others Hula-Hoop, and newcomers, like us, simply watch as the rhythm becomes a collective heartbeat paying tribute to the final rays of warmth and light until they disappear beyond the blue horizon.

—**Erika Liodice** is a Sarasota-based writer and author of the novel *Empty Arms* and the children's series High Flyers.

A boat anchors above a coral reef and tropical fish in the Caribbean Sea.

Underwater Adventures

Scuba or snorkel among the world's most colorful reefs, largest schools of fish, and impressive wrecks.

1. LAGOA AZUL, ILHA GRANDE, BRAZIL

Easily accessible from São Paolo or Rio de Janeiro, Lagoa Azul (the Blue Lagoon) offers a chance to dive with seahorses, turtles, angelfish, and more as you work your way through warm water and hidden coves. Stop for lunch in the small village on Japariz Beach to dine with views of dolphins splashing in the sea.

2. KEALAKEKUA BAY STATE HISTORICAL PARK, BIG ISLAND, HAWAII, U.S.

Full of snorkeling hot spots, there may be none better than Kealakekua Bay State Historical Park, the spot where explorer Captain Cook arrived in 1779. The park's bay boasts beautiful coral and fish just steps from the shore. Make your way to Captain Cook Monument, and you may be lucky enough to spot dolphins.

3. SILVER BANK, DOMINICAN REPUBLIC

If you've dreamed of swimming with humpback whales, Silver Bank offers you the chance. From December to April, thousands of North Atlantic humpback whales pass through the sanctuary (declared in 1986) every year, delighting snorkelers.

4. ISLA HOLBOX, MEXICO

Often thought of as Mexico's best-kept secret, this small island to the north of the Yucatán Peninsula offers the best chance to swim with whale sharks that glide near the surface to feast on plankton during the summer (mid-May to September). The island itself is worth a visit too—no cars are allowed to protect its natural habitats.

5. SILFRA GAP, ÞINGVELLIR NATIONAL PARK, ICELAND

Want to float between two continental plates? Dry suits are required to dive in Iceland's Silfra fissure, but it's worth bracing the cold for crystal clear water and watching geothermal chimneys. While there is not much marine life to speak of, there are caverns, tunnels, and plenty of rocky underwater terrain to explore in this remarkable fissure.

6. ALMIRANTE BAY, BOCAS DEL TORO, PANAMA

There are very few waves in Almirante Bay, making it a calm and easy place to swim in crystal clear waters and take in the protected coral reefs. Great snorkel spots with plenty to see include Hospital Point and Solarte Island.

7. S.S. *THISTLEGORM*, RED SEA, EGYPT

Sunk in 1941, the British *Thistlegorm* (Blue Thistle) is a wreck worth diving for. You can still see its war supplies, including rifles, motor bikes, train carriages, and trucks.

8. KAILUA-KONA, HAWAII, U.S.

Every night off the coast of Kona, Hawaii, huge manta rays circle the waters to feed on plankton. Watch as they glide past, illuminated by underwater lights on a night snorkel with one of the many local outfitters. Do your research to choose a guide that follows animal-safety practices.

9. NAVY PIER, AUSTRALIA

You can spend a whole week diving Western Australia's Navy Pier, but on a weekend dive or snorkel you can spot nudibranchs, flatworks, eels, wobbegong and white-tipped sharks, scorpion fish, and more.

10. USTICA, ITALY

The island's pristine, clear waters are draw enough for divers and snorkelers, but a chance to swim through underwater trails highlighting Ustica's volcanic history is even more worth the trip.

"AN EASY-TO-REACH VILLAGE WITHOUT THE FUSS."

For the Jet-Set Crowd
Sperlonga, Italy

A parade of beige and tan buildings jut from a vegetated hilltop headland in Sperlonga, the historic center of a sleepy Tyrrhenian seaside city halfway between Rome and Naples. The buildings' colors blend in with the scrubby Apennine foothills beyond and look like a blocky forest in reverse—a vertical village of trunks resting on its canopy. Two golden crescents of sand below arc into the distance on either side of the city's base.

Popular with mid-20th-century jet-setters for its picturesque charm, Sperlonga is largely overlooked today in favor of splashier scenes and modern luxury. The result is an easy-to-reach village without the fuss, where downtown shops in narrow block-paved alleys sell staples and souvenirs within view of a cyan sea. This is a place where it is still possible to find empty beach chairs and umbrellas on the shore, an unheard-of luxury in almost any other Italian beach town.

The modern city of Sperlonga has expanded along its western beach, Riviera di Ponéte. But on its eastern side, tucked into a rocky promontory at the Riviera di Levante, are the first-century ruins of the summer villa of Tiberius, second emperor of Rome. The secluded spot was so rarely visited that the home was lost for centuries—rediscovered and properly identified only in the late 1950s. Bathing suit–clad visitors can stroll right up to its short walls, natural ponds, and a connected seaside grotto right from the beach. A nearby museum houses artifacts, including ornate sculptures that seem to show scenes from the *Odyssey*, that were found in the sea cave where it's believed Tiberius entertained guests.

At the end of a languid day, order some *vino* and *fruti del mare* (fruit of the sea) and watch the moonlight bounce off the waves.

HUB | *Rome or Naples, Italy*

Turglia Tower on the
Sperlonga shore overlooks
the Tyrrhenian Sea.

Coveted Mediterranean

Cyprus

A coveted site of Mediterranean cultures since the Neolithic, Cyprus is steeped in a tumultuous history. It's also fringed by turquoise waters that stay warmer longer than their mainland counterparts. And its more than 50 named beaches are some of the Mediterranean's best. With a weekend based on the western side of the Greek Cypriot–controlled south, it's easy to worship the sun and sneak in some culture too. North of the Baths of Aphrodite (a natural grotto with clear, fig-shaded pools) on the undeveloped Akamas Peninsula is the secluded Blue Lagoon—a beach worthy of its proximity to mythical beauty. The short coastal cliffs that cuff the beach seem to continue underwater in darker shades of blue. On the peninsula's opposite side, an expansive horseshoe bay fronts the empty golden sands of Lara Beach, a historical haunt of nesting loggerhead and green sea turtles. En route to southerly Petra tou Romiou, a beach with a legend-steeped offshore rock, stop at the UNESCO-lauded Tombs of the Kings, an ancient necropolis carved into solid rock that contains burial sites dating from the fourth century B.C.

HUB | *Beirut, Lebanon; Middle East*

> "ITS MORE THAN 50 NAMED BEACHES ARE SOME OF THE MEDITERRANEAN'S BEST."

Rock sculptures dot Lara Beach on the Akamas Peninsula.

Deluxe suites at the Thonga Beach Lodge feature private plunge pools with optimal views.

Remote & Unspoiled

Thonga Beach, iSimangaliso Wetland Park, South Africa

The coastal dunes are home to birds and small antelope.

Secreted in a sandy milkwood forest atop coastal dunes and accessible only by a 4x4 vehicle, 12 luxury grass-thatched bungalows afford guests of Thonga Beach Lodge in northern KwaZulu-Natal the full run of one of the continent's most unspoiled beaches. The sun-toasted pink sands reach for uninterrupted stretches from the lodge nearly all the way to the Mozambique border in the north. All of this is just one small part of the massive iSimangaliso Wetland Park. Spend early mornings kayaking Lake Sibhayi among fish eagles and hippos, followed by afternoons snorkeling or scuba diving in the warm Indian Ocean—domain of the coelacanth, the world's oldest fish. You may also spot electric rays, dolphins, octopus, and whale sharks. Between November and January, rare loggerhead sea turtles fill their beach nests with hopes for the next generation. Naturally, meals and massages are alfresco.

HUB | *Johannesburg, South Africa*

The sun sets over the
Blue Ridge Mountains in
North Carolina (p. 52).

CHAPTER TWO

MOUNTAIN RETREATS

Escape to the great outdoors with abundant options for skiing, hiking, biking, and relaxing.

The outdoor pool at Rigi Kaltbad Spa overlooks the Alps.

Take the Plunge
Rigi Kaltbad, Lucerne, Switzerland

Rejuvenate body, mind, and spirit by practicing a centuries-old Swiss tradition: plunging into the mineral-rich waters of Three Sisters Springs in the Mount Rigi resort town of Rigi Kaltbad. The community's natural spring isn't geothermally heated, so the original tradition involved chilly and invigorating *chalet bad* (cold baths). With the opening of the subterranean Rigi Kaltbad Mineral Baths & Spa in 2012, located directly under the Giardino Minerale (Mineral Garden) town square, the same healing waters are warmed to a soothing 95°F (35°C).

Soar up to Rigi Kaltbad from Lucerne via the Weggis cable car, soaking in awe-inspiring aerial views of the snow-capped Alps on the way. Then buy a day pass or "Spoil and Pamper" package to luxuriate in the heated, spring-fed pools in two separate areas: the mineral baths (indoor and outdoor) and the serene crystal spa (ages 16 and up). Hotel Rigi Kaltbad offers weekend packages that include free use of the mineral baths and spa.

HUB | *Zurich, Switzerland*

Traditional red roofs pepper the hillside village of Metsovo.

A Step Back in Time
Metsovo, Greece

Starting in Athens, take an hour-long flight to Ioannina, followed by a similar-length drive, to be transported back a few hundred years in the village of Metsovo. Perched high in the Pindus range of northwestern Greece near the Albanian border, Metsovo is famous for its narrow, cobbled lanes lined with stone houses, regional folk art like wood carvings and embroidery, and metsovone, a flavorful smoked cheese you likely haven't tried before but will want to bring home in bulk.

This is an Aromanian, or Vlach, village, culturally rooted in the language and traditions of an ancient Balkan people. Learn about the heritage at the Metsovo Folk Art Museum, established by politician and author Evangelos Averoff-Tossizza, the visionary benefactor who helped preserve Metsovo's original stone architecture and folk traditions. He also planted the high-altitude vineyards that grew into Katogi Averoff, a winery and boutique hotel scenically positioned on the steep slopes outside town.

HUB | *Athens, Greece*

An Enchanted Village

Hallstatt, Austria

Pocket-size Hallstatt is neatly tucked away on the western shore of Lake Hallstatt, one of 75 bodies of water in Upper Austria's lake country, the Salzkammergut. Part of the World Heritage site Hallstatt-Dachstein/Salzkammergut Cultural Landscape east of Salzburg, Hallstatt enchants with its fairy-tale Alpine architecture, flower-filled window boxes, and wooden boathouses. Adding to the authentic charm are the lederhosen- and dirndl-wearing locals—a common sight since the Salzkammergut is an Austrian *tracht* (traditional clothing) production hub.

Hallstatt, bordered on three sides by steep slopes, is also considered one of Austria's oldest settlements, with salt production there dating back to the Middle Bronze Age. Savor the salty flavor by feasting on salt brine–soaked lake fish smoked over a beechwood fire. For breathtaking village, lake, and Alpine views, ride the Salzberg (salt mine) funicular up to the Skywalk, the 360-degree observation deck jutting out 1,148 feet (350 m) in the air above the village.

HUB | *Salzburg, Austria*

At dusk, Hallstatt's old-world charm is even more vibrant.

> "A LESS CROWDED AND
> PEACEFUL SLICE OF
> MOUNTAIN PARADISE"

Small-Town Charms

Jackson County, North Carolina, U.S.

Stretching from the southern edge of Great Smoky Mountains National Park down to the South Carolina border, Jackson County often gets overshadowed by Asheville, its artsy neighbor to the east. Being out of the limelight is just fine with the people who've already discovered this less crowded and peaceful slice of western North Carolina mountain paradise.

Encompassing part of the Qualla Boundary, owned by the Eastern Band of Cherokee Indians, Jackson County is relatively undeveloped and ready-made for relaxation. The county's main small towns—Cashiers, Dillsboro, and Sylva—are home to farmers markets, art galleries, resplendent spas, and charming inns and lodges.

Jackson's main attraction is the great outdoors: miles of hiking trails, dozens of waterfalls, spectacular mountain vistas, and the wide-open rivers and crystal clear trout streams of the Western North Carolina Fly Fishing Trail. Even if you never catch a brook, brown, or rainbow trout, spending a couple of hours silently casting in a secluded fishing hole is pure bliss. The fishing trail is entirely in Jackson County, and guides and gear are readily available.

To tap the full restorative power of nature, spend a couple of hours forest bathing in Sylva's Pinnacle Park with Pinnacle Forest Therapy. More than a slow walk through the woods, forest bathing (known as *shinrin-yoku* in Japan, where the mindfulness practice originated) is a meditative exercise focused on experiencing nature through the five senses. In keeping with shinrin-yoku tradition, the practice closes with a ceremony featuring tea brewed from white pine or another foraged plant.

Jackson County boasts a bounty of independent farm-to-fork restaurants like Sylva's Guadalupe Café, where the house specialty is tropical-fusion anything. Try the blackened plantain stuffed with salsa, tofu, gorgonzola, and vegetables, or the curried goat, from Dark Cove Farm in nearby Cullowhee.

Sunlight shines through evergreen trees in the Great Smoky Mountains.

Georgia Gold
Dahlonega, Georgia, U.S.

In 1829, prospectors struck it rich in the foothills of the Blue Ridge Mountains near Dahlonega, site of the nation's first major gold rush and only an hour north of Atlanta via GA-400. The gold is mostly gone, save for panning for flecks in rivers and creeks, but the gold-era buildings from the 1800s lining historic Dahlonega Square remain and are home to thriving restaurants, shops, studios, and wine tasting rooms. Saturday afternoons from April to October, pickers and other mountain music players gather at the historic courthouse in the center of the square for a toe-tappin' Appalachian jam session.

In the bucolic hills beyond downtown, relax at the 72-acre (29 ha) Dahlonega Resort and Vineyard, hike to a few of north Georgia's more than 120 waterfalls, and responsibly sip your way around the 39-mile (62.8 km) Dahlonega Wine Trail. Looping through "the Heart of Georgia Wine Country," the trail features seven unpretentious and undeniably fun (think red wine paired with Cheetos) wineries.

HUB | *Atlanta, Georgia, U.S.; Southeastern United States*

> "A LOOP THROUGH THE HEART OF GEORGIA WINE COUNTRY IS UNDENIABLY FUN (THINK RED WINE PAIRED WITH CHEETOS)."

Taste local reds and whites with a flight in one of Dahlonega's wineries.

Come autumn, the Berkshires' famed woodlands turn hues of gold and amber.

Mass Escape

The Berkshires, Massachusetts, U.S.

A painter works at the Tanglewood Music Center.

It's fitting that the Norman Rockwell Museum is in Berkshire County. Not only did the iconic artist, creator of a record 321 cover illustrations for the *Saturday Evening Post*, spend the last 25 years of his life here in Stockbridge, his Americana images capture the quintessential New England charms of this westernmost slice of Massachusetts.

Sandwiched between Vermont to the north and Connecticut to the south, with a side of New York State to the west, the Berkshires, as the county is best known, is the bucolic counterpart to bustling Boston, 130 miles (209.2 km) east. Unplug year-round at one of the many romantic, Gilded Age estate inns like Blantyre or Wyndhurst Manor & Club in Lenox. In summer, catch a concert on the lawn at Tanglewood, the summer home of the Boston Symphony Orchestra. Any season, indulge in a pampering spa weekend at the Inn at Canyon Ranch in Lenox.

HUB | *Boston, Massachusetts, U.S.; Northeastern United States*

The North Branch Inn

·EST 1868·

NORTH BRANCH INN

New York's North Branch
Inn offers 19th-century
charm with modern luxuries.

Bed & Breakfasts and Inns

Charming, cozy, and homey, these quaint bed and breakfasts and inns will be more than just a place to rest your head on your next adventure.

1. CANYON VILLA BED & BREAKFAST INN, SEDONA, ARIZONA, U.S.

With views of Sedona's famous Bell Rock and Courthouse Butte from virtually every room, this cozy B&B offers daily breakfast (don't miss the cinnamon rolls), nightly appetizers, and a friendly staff who can guide you to the best hiking trails. An outdoor fireplace makes for cozy stargazing at night, and the pool offers a welcome retreat from Arizona's summer heat.

2. CLIFFSIDE LUXURY INN, BUZIOS, BRAZIL

Choose a garden suite with a private patio or the presidential suite's view over the sea in this hip resort town. The five-room inn offers an infinity pool and quick access to Geriba and Ferradura beaches.

3. RAFIKI SAFARI LODGE, SANTO DOMINGO SAVEGRE, COSTA RICA

Tucked away in the lush jungle along Costa Rica's Savegre River, the lodge offers 10 luxury, safari-style tents on 843 acres (341.2 ha) of private reserve. Don't miss the guided horseback ride to waterfalls or a float down the Savegre River. The lodge also offers guided birding and nature hikes.

4. NORTH BRANCH INN, NEW YORK, U.S.

Two hours north of New York City, this 19th-century property offers vintage delights—a two-lane wooden bowling alley and theater seats from Radio City Music Hall—with all modern amenities.

5. BIRDS OF A FEATHER VICTORIA OCEAN LAGOON B&B, BRITISH COLUMBIA, CANADA

Located on a coastal lagoon, this B&B offers luxury amenities (think heated floors and a waterfront hot tub) and a chance to spot sea otters while paddling one of the property's free-to-use kayaks. Voted the "Most Loved" B&B in Victoria, British Columbia, Birds of a Feather offers three condo-style suites and plenty of attractions nearby.

6. SNAPDRAGON INN, VERMONT, U.S.

Nine guest rooms and a cozy library are just some of this cozy inn's charms. Located in Windsor, it also offers access to the town's eclectic Main Street and walks around Lake Runnemede. Explore everything the Upper Valley has to offer, including Mount Ascutney, picturesque Woodstock, Vermont, and Dartmouth across the river.

7. BENTWOOD, JACKSON HOLE, WYOMING, U.S.

At this upscale, 6,000-square-foot (557.4 sq m) lodge, start the day with a homemade breakfast before setting out to explore the great American West. The log-built, rustic inn offers easy access to the Snake River, Grand Teton National Park, and natural hot springs.

8. TO SØSTRE GUESTHOUSE, BERGEN, NORWAY

Tucked away on a charming cobblestone street, this family-operated inn offers only three Scandinavian-style guest rooms. You'll feel spoiled by the homemade breakfast and easy walk to the Fløibanen funicular.

9. HAKONE AIRU, HAKONE, JAPAN

This lavish *ryonkan,* or inn, features balconies overlooking the mountains in every room, hot spring baths, breakfast, and, a Japanese kaiseki multi-course dinner.

10. THE GRANGE, FORT WILLIAM, SCOTLAND

With views of the Scottish Highlands and Loch Linnhe, this Victorian town house offers luxurious suites and room service breakfast delivered to you each morning.

> ## "STOWE HASN'T STRAYED FAR FROM ITS CLASSIC NEW ENGLAND SKI TOWN ROOTS."

Stowe Away

Stowe, Vermont, U.S.

When the singing von Trapp family of *The Sound of Music* fame decided to build a guest lodge in the United States in the late 1940s, it's no wonder that they chose a hilltop farm overlooking the village of Stowe. The surrounding Green Mountains of northern Vermont could pass for lower-elevation versions of the Alps in the von Trapps' native Austria, and an alpine ski culture was already in place. Vermont's first purpose-built ski trail was constructed on Stowe's Mount Mansfield in 1933; the following year, the fledgling ski area introduced the nation's first ski patrol.

Stowe hasn't strayed far from its classic New England ski town roots. The idyllic setting that attracted the von Trapps remains, as does their Austrian-inspired Trapp Family Lodge, rebuilt after a fire in 1980. And even though Vail Resorts acquired Stowe Mountain Resort (home to two ski mountains, Mansfield and Spruce Peak, which are connected by a gondola) in 2017, the village and the resort exude a local, small-town community vibe. People gather on the Village Green at Spruce Peak to ice skate in winter and, in warmer months, listen to live music and shop at the Friday artisans' market. The Green is also the open-air dining room for Friday's Spruce Peak Farm Table Dinner Series, serving seasonal family-style meals sourced from local products.

Winter is peak season, yet even then, the charms of cozy inns, horse-drawn sleigh rides, and crackling fireplaces compensate for the extra foot traffic in village shops and brewpubs like the Alchemist and Idletime. The fall colors blaze brilliantly too, making autumn a glorious, albeit more crowded, time. If total relaxation is the goal, ensconce yourself in the Lodge at Spruce Peak and indulge in a Stowe Cider Uber Scrub, which pairs local Stowe cider (in an exfoliating scrub and to drink afterward) and massage.

The Lodge at Spruce Creek lights up as the sun sets over Stowe Mountain.

Le Village Windigo private balconies look out over water views.

Inland Sea
Le Village Windigo, Québec, Canada

Known as Montréal's playground, Québec's Laurentians region is a four-season destination for weekend escapes. The iconic resort town, Mont Tremblant, buzzes with activity year-round, which is why it's worth driving an extra 90 minutes northwest to secluded and serene Le Village Windigo.

Situated on the Baskatong Reservoir, a man-made inland sea, and bordering densely wooded Devil's Mountain Regional Park, Windigo is designed for unplugging. Power down the electronics (cell coverage is spotty anyway) and tune into nature on the sandy beach and wooded walking trails. Guest lodging—condos, cottages, two bubble spheres, and a transparent dome—are tucked in the trees or along the water. Rates include access to the sauna and whirlpool and use of equipment for seasonal activities, such as snowshoeing and skating in winter and kayaking and biking in summer. Condos and cottages have kitchens, and there's a cozy log cabin restaurant and bar, Les Berges du Windigo.

HUB | *Montréal or Québec City, Canada; Northeastern United States*

Thermal baths at Bains du Rocher steam in the cool winter air.

Healing Waters
Cauterets, Occitanie, France

Being only 18 miles (29 km) south of the famed pilgrimage site of Lourdes (and its purportedly miracle-working waters) bodes well for the therapeutic potential of the thermal springs in Cauterets. The ski-and-spa resort town in Pyrénées National Park, which extends along France's mountainous, southwestern border with Spain, has been a hotbed of healing since Roman times. The mountain community gained celebrity status in the 19th and early 20th centuries when novelist Victor Hugo and King Edward VII soaked in Cauterets' naturally hot, sulfur-rich waters.

Local spas, such as Les Bains du Rocher and Les Thermes de Cauterets, incorporate the water into relaxation and medical treatments, such as thermal mud wraps and therapies for respiratory conditions and autoimmune diseases. From Cauterets, you can also ride the cable car up to Cirque du Lys ski area for a Pyrenees panorama, deep-powder skiing in winter, and hiking in summer.

HUB | *Toulouse, France; Barcelona, Spain*

Mist covers
Quiraing on the
Isle of Skye.

Into the Mist

Isle of Skye, Scotland

Connected to Scotland's northwest coast by a bridge, the Isle of Skye is a mist-shrouded and mystical place. Famous for its otherworldly landscapes—including the bare rock summits of the Cuillin mountain range, the jagged cliffs of the Quiraing, and the inexplicable conical hills and stone circles of Fairy Glen—the island is a favorite of photographers and moviemakers. *Macbeth* and *Snow White and the Huntsman* are among the more recent films with scenes shot here.

Mel Gibson's Scottish epic *Braveheart* was mainly filmed in Ireland, but it's easy to channel your inner Scots warrior on Skye. Pass surreal rock formations, stone walls, and ancient castles as you walk across foggy moors, through verdant glens, and along the coastal cliffs and beaches. As you go, scan the skies for Skye's legendary white-tailed eagles, Scotland's largest bird of prey with a wingspan of up to 8 feet (2.4 m).

HUB | *Glasgow, Scotland*

Downtown Oslo has seen
a modern revival for
tourists and locals alike.

"FLANKED ON THREE SIDES BY THE WOODED HILLS AND ON ONE BY OSLOFJORD, NORWAY'S CAPITAL IS AN IDEAL DESTINATION FOR LOVERS OF THE OUTDOORS."

PERSPECTIVE

An Ode to Oslo

Oslo Serves Up Scandinavian Cool With Heartwarming Enthusiasm

Oslo defines Nordic cool. Once a seat of the Viking empire, Norway's capital was shaped by centuries of maritime culture. Visitors today can take a bite out of a thriving food scene and discover a new breed of young designers and quirky drinking dens.

Natural features—forests, valleys, island-studded inlets—distinguish this Scandinavian metropolis. Flanked on three sides by the wooded hills of the Marka region and on one by the 62-mile (99.8 km) inlet known as Oslofjord, Norway's capital is an ideal destination for lovers of the outdoors—which describes most of the city's 600,000 residents. Stay at one of the hotels in the Holmenkollen district, Oslo's leafy playground, and you may find yourself hiking, biking, or, weather permitting, cross-country skiing before dinner. A 20-minute metro ride from this verdant outer borough sits Oslo's center, founded some 1,000 years ago and pulsing with museums and galleries, world-class restaurants, and fun-loving nightlife. For recreation, head to Frogner Park, where locals promenade, skateboard, and sunbathe among 212 statues by Norwegian artist Gustav Vigeland.

For the best impression of Oslo, experience it from the water. Catch one of the hop-on, hop-off sailboats for a cruise that takes in the reenergized Aker Brygge area, City Hall (home to the Nobel Peace Prize awards ceremony), and the medieval Akershus Fortress. A particular draw is the waterfront Opera House, completed in 2007 and shaped like an ice floe; its sloping marble-clad roof lures walkers at all hours.

For a nation with a small population, Norway has produced a surprising number of world-class chefs, including four Bocuse d'Or gold medalists. You will find one of them, Bent Stiansen, at his restaurant, Statholdergaarden. Other worthy culinary emporia include Eik and Maaemo, the latter the only Nordic restaurant to receive two Michelin stars on its first attempt.

Classic Norwegian fare fills the menu at Grand Café, where smørbrød (open-faced sandwiches) and prawn mayonnaise are perennial favorites. One of Oslo's most popular lunch spots for 120 years, the Viennese-style Theatercaféen, across from the National Theater, also serves smørbrød, along with reindeer and seafood (try the lutefisk) entrées.

Norwegians drink more coffee than anyone else, which is reflected in Olso's trove of independent coffee shops. Many double as nighttime cocktail bars, such as LaWo, Café Con Bar, and Fuglen, where the vintage furniture is for sale.

In Grünerløkka you'll find such fun venues as the 1950s-style Bar Boca (fabulous mojitos in summer) and the industrial-chic club Blå. For creative cocktails and one of the best vistas of Oslo, ascend to 34 SkyBar, atop Norway's tallest hotel, the Radisson Blue Plaza. And for performances—on stage and on a plate—head to the coolest venue in town, the Oslo Opera House, where the arts are complemented by some creative cooking in the winter-themed Argent Restaurant and the glass-walled Sanguine Brasserie.

—**Anne-Sophie Redish** has lived in Norway. This is an adaptation of a story that ran in the U.K. edition, *National Geographic Traveller.*

A ride down Telluride's slopes offers skiers and boarders winter wonderland vistas.

Ski Resorts

Hit the slopes and then enjoy a scenic après-ski in these mountain towns meant for skiers and snowboarders.

1. PARK CITY, UTAH, U.S.

Not only are there three resorts within 10 minutes of each other—Park City, the Canyons, and Deer Valley—but Park City also provides easy access (under an hour) to other top-notch mountains, including Snow Basin, Alta, and Brighton. Both Park City and the Canyons are owned by Vail Resorts, so one Epic pass gets you access to both mountains.

2. CHAMONIX, FRANCE

Known for its ski terrain—one lift gives you access to 11 ski areas and challenging backcountry—Chamonix also offers a cobblestoned main street with plenty of bars to warm up après-ski. For a bonus, take a break from the slopes to ride the famous rack and pinion railway to the Grotte de Glace (Ice Cave) and take in views of the imposing Mer de Glace glacier.

3. INTERLAKEN, SWITZERLAND

On and off the slopes, Interlaken is a fairy tale. From its web of trails that overlook Lake Thun and Lake Brienz to its lively bar scene, there is plenty to entertain everyone from beginners to experts. In mid-December, non-skiers can delight in Interlaken's Ice Magic—five interconnected skating rinks.

4. BOZEMAN, MONTANA, U.S.

There's a reason this place is called Big Sky Country, and the skiing is even bigger. Options are plentiful at Bridger Bowl and Big Sky resorts, just north of Yellowstone National Park. Bridger Bowl is a nonprofit, community ski area, so you'll find cheaper lift tickets. But the price is worth it at Big Sky, too, where you'll ski one of North America's largest terrains—and ride America's first eight-seat chairlift.

5. WHISTLER BLACKCOMB, CANADA

The largest winter sports area in North America, the two mountains of Whistler Blackcomb offer more than 200 runs and 37 lifts for skiers of all levels, not to mention views of the Pacific Ocean from the peak.

6. SUN VALLEY, IDAHO, U.S.

The world's first chairlift was built here, but that was just the beginning for this family-friendly resort, which offers more than 70 runs and stunning mountain scenery.

7. ZERMATT, SWITZERLAND

You might recognize this mountain next time you bite into a Toblerone, but it is more iconic for its year-round skiing. Don't miss a ride on the Gornergrat Bahn, a train that takes you up the mountain when your ski legs are tired.

8. CERRO CASTOR, USHUAIA, ARGENTINA

At the southernmost tip of South America, you will find the southernmost ski resort in the world. With deep snow and icy temperatures, you won't even need the stunning glacier views to persuade you to ski these slopes.

9. TELLURIDE, COLORADO, U.S.

There are more than 2,000 acres (809.4 ha) of skiable terrain at Colorado's most popular ski resort. With hike-to-ski options and a ski-in, ski-out base area connected by gondola, this is a mountain everyone can enjoy. Off skis, the resort also offers fat-tire bike rides—on bikes outfitted with big tires that can handle the snow—and winter fly-fishing.

10. KITZBÜHEL, AUSTRIA

This picturesque Alpine ski town (its medieval center is car-free) offers luxury hotels, fashionable boutiques, and gourmet restaurants at the base of its epic ski resort, which includes a legendary 85 percent vertical descent.

"JAW-DROPPING SCENERY, MINERAL HOT SPRINGS, AND PAMPERING SPA RESORTS"

Oh, Canada

Banff–Lake Louise, Alberta, Canada

Located only 80 miles (128.7 km) west of Calgary in southwestern Alberta, Banff National Park puts the jaw-dropping scenery, soothing mineral hot springs, and pampering spa resorts of the Canadian Rockies within easy reach. The park, a UNESCO World Heritage site, encompasses the pedestrian-friendly town of Banff and the quiet hamlet of Lake Louise, 25 miles (40.2 km) to the northwest. Various shuttles and Roam Transit, Banff's ecofriendly public transit system, make it possible to get to Banff and Lake Louise from the Calgary airport and explore several areas in the park without a car.

Banff offers a wide selection of accommodations with spa services, such as therapeutic and relaxation massage therapy, body wraps, and restorative soaks in rooftop hot tubs. Splurge on the royal treatment by staying at the landmark Fairmont Banff Springs, opened in 1888 and nicknamed Canada's "Castle in the Rockies." The luxury resort's award-winning Willow Stream Spa, renovated and expanded in late 2019, is a tranquil sanctuary centered around an indoor mineral pool. Expansive windows add calming mountain vistas to indoor spa services, and the outdoor whirlpool and terraces are blissful spaces in which to soak in the views and the fresh alpine air.

Whether you stay in Banff or Lake Louise, you'll have access to some of the national park's more than 1,000 miles (1,609 km) of trails. The easy Lake Louise Lakeshore Trail is ideal for a leisurely, 1.2-mile (1.9 km) stroll and leads to a milky blue-green creek, source of the lake's surreal turquoise color. In Banff, the trailhead to the easy Fenlands Trail is less than 1 mile (1.6 km) from downtown. Walk the level 1.3-mile (2.1 km) loop through old-growth spruce to experience the serenity of the forest without venturing far from your hotel. For sky-high views of the Rockies, ride the Banff–Lake Louise sightseeing chairlifts and gondolas, open mid-May or June to early October.

HUB | *Western Canada; Mountain West United States*

At the Banff Springs Hotel, guests relax poolside with epic views.

Californian Alps

Lake Arrowhead, California, U.S.

If jetting to Switzerland for a weekend isn't in your budget, Lake Arrowhead is an attractive alternative for Golden State residents and visitors alike. Sometimes called the Alps of Southern California, the lofty mountain lake resort town sits at an elevation of 5,174 feet (1,577 m) in the San Bernardino Mountains, a 90-minute drive west of Los Angeles.

Close proximity has made Lake Arrowhead a four-season weekend escape for well-heeled Angelenos since the 1920s. Lodging, restaurants, and shops are concentrated in and around Bavarian-style Lake Arrowhead Village, which hosts a free Center Stage Summer Concert Series Fridays, Saturdays, and holiday nights from mid-May to Labor Day. Stay lakeside at the upscale Lake Arrowhead Resort and Spa, a short walk from the village. From the resort's private beach and dock in summer, you can fish, kayak, paddleboard, and take boat tours of the lake. During any season, relax in the pool and spa or go hiking or mountain biking on pine-scented forest trails.

> "SOMETIMES CALLED THE ALPS OF SOUTHERN CALIFORNIA, THE LOFTY MOUNTAIN LAKE RESORT TOWN IS JUST A 90-MINUTE DRIVE WEST OF LOS ANGELES."

HUB | *Los Angeles, California, U.S.*

Lake Arrowhead sits below the San Bernardino Mountains.

There are plenty of options for relaxation in the Yamashiro Onsen hot springs resort district.

Hot Spring City

Kaga Onsen, Japan

Kaga, a city in the mountainous Chubu region of Honshu, is well known for its traditional arts. Brightly colored *Kutaniyaki* pottery originated here in the 1600s, and today visitors can tour ceramics, wood turning, lacquerware, and papermaking studios. Thanks to a wealth of *onsen*, or hot springs, however, relaxation may be the city's most famous art form.

Located within Kaga are four hot springs villages: Yamashiro Onsen, site of the world's oldest Kutani kiln; Yamanaka Onsen, located along Kakusenkei Gorge; Awazu Onsen, home to one of the world's oldest operating hotels, Hoshi Ryokan, opened in A.D. 718; and Katayamazu Onsen, on the shores of Lake Shibayama. Collectively, the villages are called Kaga Onsen. They're accessible via public transportation, convenient for soaking in the healing waters of all four over one blissful weekend. All the villages have public baths and *ryokans* (traditional Japanese inns) with private baths for guests.

Two women in traditional dress walk along the city's streets.

Painted storks perch in a
tree in Keoladeo National
Park in Rajasthan, India.

Bird-Watching Destinations

Birds of a feather flock to these prime destinations for spotting species from Malaysian rail babblers to African violet-backed starlings.

1. JAMAICA BAY WILDLIFE REFUGE, NEW YORK, U.S.

For the sheer novelty of birding in New York City—with the Empire State Building for a backdrop—this refuge is a must. Expect any of 330 or so species—not least, masses of high-drama snow geese (if you go in winter).

2. PANTI FOREST RESERVE, MALAYSIA

This Malaysian peat swamp forest is home to a rainbow of winged wonders—violet cuckoos, red-crowned barbets, banded kingfishers, rufous-tailed shama, grey-chested jungle-flycatchers—but the reason birders peregrinate here from all over the world is the ground-dwelling rail babbler, which is on the reserve in high density and easy to spot given the sparse undergrowth in the area.

3. AVALON MARSHES, SOMERSET, UNITED KINGDOM

One of winter's craziest spectacles, thousands of starlings periodically fill the night sky here with their impossibly synchronized aerobatics, called murmurations. You never know when the birds will show, but they're worth trying for. (For your best chance at seeing them, consult the update hotline: +44-786-655-4142.)

4. TIRITIRI MATANGI OPEN SANCTUARY, NEW ZEALAND

A renowned conservation project on reclaimed farmland outside Auckland, this sanctuary is now home to a bird population people travel for, including the rare flightless takahe and the adorable morepork.

5. CELESTÚN, MEXICO

Dazzling quantities of flamingos in the local biosphere reserve bring enthusiasts from around the globe to this sleepy Yucatán fishing village near Merida. Book an early morning boat tour for the best viewing—ideally November to mid-March.

6. BHARATPUR, RAJASTHAN, INDIA

Flamingos are just a part of a whole striking ensemble cast in this corner of Rajasthan. Think sarus cranes (the tallest flying bird), painted storks, purple herons—and about 395 other species.

7. KRUGER NATIONAL PARK, SOUTH AFRICA

Granted, most travel here for the Big Five. But it's the little things that make birders ecstatic. In fact, Kruger packs so many shimmering, color-saturated birds—southern carmine bee-eaters, lilac-breasted rollers, violet-backed starlings—it's like a giant, open-air jewelry box.

8. CARONI BIRD SANCTUARY, TRINIDAD AND TOBAGO

As the sun sets over a swamp outside Port of Spain, thousands of fire-engine-red scarlet ibises swoop in to roost in the mangroves—a hallucinatory scene you'll want to take in from a boat.

9. MAINE, U.S.

The only U.S. state with puffin colonies, Maine becomes a birding pilgrimage site in the summer. Between April and August, the Eastern Egg Rock colony is visible by boat. There's even an Acadia Birding Festival the last weekend of May, when you'll find birding walks, talks, and cruises.

10. TAMBOPATA, PERU

This Peruvian reserve is home to countless macaws and parrots that all love a good clay lick in the morning. Watching from behind a blind as they zealously stake out their turf—the rising sun hitting their kaleidoscopic plumage just so—you'll wonder if someone slipped you some ayahuasca.

"SEDONA'S RED ROCKS CAN
HELP REJUVENATE THE
BODY AND SPIRIT."

On the Rocks

Sedona, Arizona, U.S.

With its soaring red-rock monoliths and steep-walled canyons, Sedona isn't the archetypal mountain retreat. The enchanting town, perched in the high desert midway between Phoenix and Grand Canyon National Park, is internationally famous for its vortexes, the enhanced energy sites thought to swirl among the red-rock buttes, pinnacles, and spires. The ubiquitous red rocks and universal awareness of the Earth's energy make Sedona a magnet for artists, creative spirits, and practitioners of all sorts of health, wellness, spiritual development, and self-discovery techniques, from aura photography to Zen meditation.

Treat your senses to Sedona's restorative energy at one of the many luxury spas, like L'Auberge de Sedona, whose holistic practices include sound healing and guided forest-bathing sessions. To experience the natural beauty and tranquility of a vortex on your own, pick up a map at the Visitor Center for directions to iconic sites like Bell Rock and Boynton Canyon. Or go with a guide to learn the science and hear the legends of the unseen power source.

Simply standing among Sedona's red rocks can help rejuvenate the body and spirit, particularly at sunrise and sunset. For an easy hike to a magnificent vista, follow the paved Centennial Trail (1 mile/1.6 km round-trip) with views across Mingus Mountain, Cockscomb, Doe Mountain, and Bear Mountain; or take the half-mile (0.8 km) Yavapai Vista Trail. The trail links to a wider network of hiking and mountain biking trails in the Coconino National Forest if you want closer views of the red-rock escarpments, such as Sedona's signature monolith, Cathedral Rock.

Cobblestone paths lead through the sycamore-shaded Tlaquepaque Arts & Crafts Village, a Sedona fixture since the 1970s. Visit the area to see working artists and browse more than 50 galleries and specialty shops.

HUB | *Phoenix, Arizona, U.S.; Southwestern United States*

As the sun falls on Cathedral Rock, the monolith is reflected in Oak Creek.

The healing Riverbend Hot Springs offers Rio Grande views.

Soaking It All In
Truth or Consequences, New Mexico, U.S.

Quirky-cool Truth or Consequences gets its name from the iconic 1950s TV quiz show and its fame from the area's thermal waters. According to legend, soaking in the hot waters–temperatures range from 98°F (37°C) to 115°F (46°C)–three times daily for 21 days could cure anything that ails you.

From the 1920s to the 1940s, health seekers flocked to the high-plateau town (named Hot Springs until 1950, when the name was changed to win a contest). Spas and bathhouses sprouted up downtown in what's been revitalized as the Hot Springs Bathhouse Historic District. The district has 10 retro motels and spas evoking the charm of the town's health resort heyday. Some are walk-ins, others have lodging with in-room baths for unlimited soaking, and at least one, Charles Motel & Spa, has rooftop hot tubs and views of nearby Turtleback Mountain. Visit on your birthday to enjoy a free soak at La Paloma Hot Springs & Spa.

HUB | *Southwestern United States*

Historic buildings make up the scene in Dunton Hot Springs.

Modern Ghost Town
Dunton Hot Springs, Colorado, U.S.

Secluded and scenic, Dunton Hot Springs is an abandoned southwestern Colorado mining settlement reborn as a luxurious hideaway. Two hours from Telluride, guests stay in 13 meticulously restored and exquisitely appointed miners' cabins (book the Well House for the private hot spring pool), hand-hewn in the 19th century. Large cabin windows welcome in stunning vistas of the surrounding San Juan Mountains.

The cabins are positioned in a circle around the mining settlement's original Saloon and Dance Hall. Here, guests gather for communal meals and adult beverages, both included in the nightly rates. Menus showcase local and regional specialties, such as fresh-caught trout and beer from the Dolores River Brewery in nearby Dolores (35 miles/56.3 km away).

Since the enclave is remote, has indoor and outdoor options for soaking in natural hot springs, and offers seasonal activities—like guided hikes with llamas, ice climbing, and snowmobiling—plan to stay put during the whole weekend.

HUB | *Telluride, Colorado, U.S.*

The Quiet Season

Jackson Hole, Wyoming, U.S.

Surrounded by mountains, the 48-mile-long (77.2 km) Jackson Hole, or valley, is best known as a summer stopover on the way to Grand Teton and Yellowstone National Parks, and for skiing and snowboarding at Jackson Hole Mountain Resort, Grand Targhee, and Snow King. In between the busy summer parks and winter snow-play seasons, the focus in Jackson Hole shifts to quieter pursuits such as wildlife-watching, art festivals, and pampering wellness treatments at destination spas like the three-story SpaTerre at Teton Mountain Lodge & Spa.

Fewer visitors, groves of golden aspen and cottonwood trees, and the music of bugling bull elks make the fall shoulder season one of the most relaxing times to spend a weekend in Jackson Hole. To walk to restaurants, shops, and galleries, stay in Jackson, the historic town at the southern end of the valley. For easy access to hiking trails or for a spa weekend, lodge in Teton Village at the base of Jackson Hole Mountain Resort.

HUB | *Mountain West United States*

A bull moose eats from Oxbow Bend in Grand Teton National Park.

A dusting of snow turns
Prague into a real-life
snow globe.

Winter Wonderlands

When the temperatures plunge, escape to snowy capitals of the world
where Christmas markets, tasty hot cocoa, and magical ice sculptures await.

1. VIENNA, AUSTRIA

It's worth bundling up to stroll Vienna's historic Old Town's snowflake-covered baroque palaces and twinkling lights. Don't miss a cup of Viennese hot chocolate (made with egg yolk, semisweet cocoa, and whipped cream).

2. BANFF NATIONAL PARK, CANADA

Once glacial Lake Louise freezes over, this already dazzling park shines even brighter with its surrounding snowcapped Canadian Rockies, frosted trees, and regular wildlife. In fact, winter may be the best time of year to spot some of the local species, including elk, bighorn sheep, deer, moose, coyotes, wolves, and numerous species of birds including Clark's nutcrackers, falcons, and white-tailed ptarmigans.

3. BRYCE CANYON NATIONAL PARK, UTAH, U.S.

Most visitors visit from spring to fall, but come winter, you can take part in ranger-led snowshoe hikes to see snow-covered hoodoos and winter astronomy programs. It's easy to navigate the park from the road along the canyon's rim, which is paved and plowed regularly, as are viewpoint parking lots.

4. SHIRAKAWA-GO AND GOKAYAMA, JAPAN

Covering more than 170 acres (68.8 ha) in central Japan, the thatched cottages of UNESCO-protected Shirakawa-go and Gokayama could be mistaken for Santa's village when covered in snow. The Gassho-style houses (*gassho* is Japanese for pressing hands together in prayer) are steep and designed to withstand heavy snow.

5. CENTRAL PARK, NEW YORK, U.S.

It's fun to roam Manhattan's famous green space any time of year, but in winter you'll find the beloved Wollman Rink, a quintessential ice-skating spot opened in 1949 with the city's skyline for views. Winter park goers can also cross-country ski or snowshoe through Central Park's meadows, wander the Arthur Ross Pinetum featuring 17 different species of pine trees, or go sledding down Pilgrim or Cedar Hill (open with six inches of snow).

6. PRAGUE, CZECH REPUBLIC

The baroque architecture and historic pubs that make Prague so beloved are even better with snow. Grab a glass of warm mulled wine as you explore the city's Christmas villages.

7. NEUSCHWANSTEIN CASTLE, GERMANY

The inspiration behind Disney's Sleeping Beauty Castle, this clifftop palace gets an extra dose of magic during the winter, when regular snow tops its turrets with glittery fluff. Visitors can roam the castle's interior on a 30-minute guided tour, available in English and German.

8. GOTHENBURG, SWEDEN

Sweden's largest Christmas market takes place here from November to the end of the year in Liseberg amusement park. What you'll see with your coffee and fresh pastries: five million lights and 700 decorated Christmas trees.

9. JUKKASJÄRVI, SWEDEN

What says "winter wonderland" more than an ice hotel? In this town of 500, beds of ice come second only to the northern lights, amusing reindeer, and the hotel's other ice sculptures.

10. BLED, SLOVENIA

Surrounded by tree-covered mountains and a glacial lake, Bled Island, with its 17th-century church, becomes more spectacular with the annual snowfall. For the best view, visit the 12th-century Bled Castle, which towers over the lake.

The pedestrian Liberty Bridge in Falls Park allows passersby to linger above downtown waterfalls.

"A COLLEAGUE DESCRIBED THE SUNNY HILLS OF THE SURROUNDING COUNTRYSIDE AS THE TUSCANY OF THE SOUTH."

PERSPECTIVE

Going Greenville

Start-Ups and a Fresh Look Transform a Sleepy South Carolina Town

In a black-and-white sheath dress and sporting a pixie haircut, Cherington Love Shucker emanates the no-nonsense cool you'd expect from a former New Yorker. Then she breaks into a warm smile that's unmistakably southern. We're at the old Brandon Mill, in Greenville, in the northwestern corner of South Carolina. A native who returned last year after two decades away, Shucker now serves as executive director of the new Greenville Center for Creative Arts.

"People in Greenville love ideas," says Shucker. Over the past decade, the three-day, juried Artisphere festival put her hometown on the national art map, and, on a personal level, helped persuade her and her artist husband to relocate from Manhattan.

Ideas are what got me here, too—not just to this town of some 61,000 in the foothills of the Blue Ridge Mountains but to the South. When my 30s brought a shift in priorities, friends began to eye suburbia, but my husband and I found ourselves dreaming instead of a place with room for ambitions to grow.

Our horizons expanded south. Make that the New South, to rising cities where a start-up culture has replaced industry, forging new, more inclusive paths along the way. Soon after moving to Asheville, North Carolina, we kept hearing about nearby Greenville. A colleague described the sunny hills of the surrounding countryside as the Tuscany of the South. *Fast Company* magazine dubbed Greenville "the knowledge economy's next big thing." I needed to see for myself what was happening.

I meet walking guide John Nolan at Greenville's nucleus: Falls Park, where a nearly 40-foot (12.2 m) natural waterfall churns just off Main Street. A pedestrian-only bridge curves overhead. It's a bright spring day, and locals and tourists line up under the suspension cables.

Much credit for Greenville's new groove goes to five-term Mayor Knox White, who has spent the past two decades showing how to turn an idea—make Greenville "the most beautiful and livable city in America"—into a movement. White persuaded officials to tear down a heavily used, four-lane bridge that for decades blocked the falls. The city cleaned up the long-ignored Reedy River and built Falls Park, which became an instant community gathering space when it opened in 2004. Five years later, the Swamp Rabbit Trail transformed an old railroad bed. Packed with cyclists and runners year-round the 18.7-mile (30.1 km) paved path connects Falls Park north to the 19th-century stagecoach stop of Travelers Rest.

Perhaps the biggest revelation is Greenville's urbane downtown. On Main Street you're as likely to hear a southern drawl as you are to catch snippets of French or German. The blocks around the thoroughfare hum with scores of restaurants and bars, serving Persian *mezze* and lamb shank, Belgian Trappist beer, and southern novelties like fried green tomatoes dipped in pimento cheese fondue.

Back at the Brandon Mill, Shucker recalls a conversation with her three-and-a-half-year-old daughter. "I recently asked her, 'Do you love living in Greenville?' She said, 'Yes, because I can take my shoes off and run in the grass.'"

I know the feeling. This place makes me want to kick off my heels and stay awhile too.

—**Katie Knorovsky** is the managing editor of *Smoky Mountain Living* magazine.

> **"THERE IS A SOFTER, SLOWER PACED SIDE OUTSIDE OF SKI SEASON."**

Provincial Mountains
South Tyrol, Italy

Part of the Austro-Hungarian Empire until the end of World War I, the province of South Tyrol in northernmost Italy is a slice of Austria and Switzerland, its northern neighbors. Nestled at the foot of the World Heritage site Dolomites, the area (officially South Tyrol/Alto Adige) is home to Italian, German, and Ladin (an ancient Romance language) speakers. Signs are commonly written in all three languages, and the efficient public transportation network, which makes it easy to arrive by train and get around without a car, runs with Swiss precision.

The mountains naturally make South Tyrol an outdoor adventure destination, but there is a softer, slower paced side, particularly outside of the busy winter ski season. From the provincial capital, Bolzano, you can hop between some or all of the 16 wine villages on the Alto Adige Wine Road. The 93-mile (150 km) route features 70 wineries and a wide variety of lodging, such as Alpine chalets surrounded by apple orchards and vineyards, historic villas and manor homes, and wellness-themed hotels with saunas and pools, like Parc Hotel Am See on the shores of Lake Caldaro.

To totally immerse yourself in the South Tyrolean wellness scene, stay in the province's second largest city, Merano, tucked in a basin bordered by both snowcapped peaks and palm trees, and famous for its thermal springs. There are 25 spring-fed pools, as well as saunas and steam rooms inside the glass-and-steel bathing hall, thermal park, and spa at Merano's redeveloped thermal baths, Terme Merano.

Whatever South Tyrol town or village you select for your stay, be sure to try a traditional Tyrolean wellness treatment, such as a rejuvenating, warm-water hay bath (*alpenbadl*) or a purifying, hot-water apple bath. Continue the wellness tradition at home by bringing back locally produced skin care products made with oil from Swiss mountain pines native to South Tyrol's Val Sarentino (Sarntal Valley).

HUB | *Milan, Italy; Zurich, Switzerland*

Old cabins sit below the rocky Dolomites in South Tyrol.

Two safari guides discuss the history of a cave in the reserve.

A Spot in the Wild
Grootbos Private Nature Reserve, Gansbaai, South Africa

Drive just two hours southeast of Cape Town and you'll arrive in the natural nirvana that is Grootbos. Named for the Afrikaans word meaning "big forest," Grootbos Private Nature Reserve overlooks Walker Bay, famous for frequent sightings of the "marine big five": great white sharks, southern right whales, seals, penguins, and dolphins.

The luxury ecotourism resort's 27 rooms and suites are in sea-facing lodges and private villas, tucked among ancient milkwood trees. Guests sustainably share the forest with the reserve's permanent residents, including 21 amphibian species, 29 mammal species, 118 bird species, and 800 plant species. Blanketing the reserve in a tapestry of colors is blooming fynbos, or "fine bush," vegetation, which is unique to the Cape Floral Region, a UNESCO World Heritage site located at the southwestern tip of South Africa. See and learn about the fynbos on a Grootbos 4x4 botanical safari.

HUB | *Cape Town, South Africa*

Musicians perform in the city's Independence Day parade.

Ex-Pat Enclave
San Miguel de Allende, Mexico

The Spanish founded San Miguel de Allende in the 16th century, but it was an influx of U.S. World War II veterans that established this colonial charmer as an artsy, ex-pat enclave. In the late 1940s, hundreds of American vets used GI Bill stipends to study fine arts here at the Escuela de Bellas Artes. So although the old-world town, a UNESCO World Heritage site, is off the beaten path in Mexico's northern central highlands, the prevalence of U.S. ex-pat cafés and guesthouse owners makes English speakers quickly feel at home.

Spend a leisurely weekend walking the cobblestone streets lined with brightly colored colonial facades and a captivating mix of architectural styles: baroque colonial next door to neo-Gothic. Many of the historic buildings house art spaces, such as Fabrica La Aurora, a former factory that is now an artist studio collective, or eateries like the Restaurant, featuring the global comfort food of celebrity chef Donnie Masterton.

HUB | *Mexico City, Mexico*

Serene Scene

Whistler, British Columbia, Canada

Home to North America's largest ski area, 8,171-acre (3,307 ha) Whistler Blackcomb is packed with powder hounds in the winter. But from late spring to early fall, this classic Coast Mountain resort town has a more serene outdoor scene. Slowing down is easy in Whistler, where you can leave your car parked (or take a direct shuttle from the Vancouver airport) and get around on foot or by bike. A cobblestone Village Stroll path winds through pedestrian-only Whistler Village, the charming dining, shopping, and lodging hub.

Escape to the edge of Lost Lake Forest for a massage and traditional Finnish hydrotherapy cycle—hot, cold, rest, repeat—at the silent (no phones, no talking) Scandinave Spa. Take leisurely bike rides and walks among ancient cedar trees and along glacier-fed lakes—always with snowcapped peaks in the distance. Spend a magical evening at Vallea Lumina, a multisensory, forest walk experience featuring twinkling lights, holograms, and other special effects.

HUB | *Vancouver, Canada; Pacific Northwest United States*

The sun sets over Canada's Coast Mountain range.

Take in the views from
Capilano Suspension Bridge
Park in North Vancouver.

PERSPECTIVE

Northern Exposure

Canada's *Rocky Mountaineer* Train Explores How a Country Came to Be

Sir John Macdonald, Canada's beloved first prime minister, built the Canadian Pacific Railway (CPR) in the 1880s to turn Canada into a unified, transcontinental nation. Eventually it spawned the country's national park system, opened up the mountains to tourism, and led to the development of Canada's first luxury hotels. The only way to traverse the historic railway's most rugged stretches is the *Rocky Mountaineer*, a luxury excursion train from Seattle to Banff, with overnight stops in Vancouver and Kamloops. That gives plenty of opportunity to consider the essences of Canada. Oh, yes, and dine on three-course meals while sipping Okanagan Valley wines.

U.S. and Canadian flags stand on either side of the *Rocky Mountaineer's* eight cars in Seattle, as I—and about 150 others—board the train. Soon the rails take us alongside Puget Sound, where we pass stacks of crab pots on the water and barns labeled "APPLE" and "CIDER."

We have a full day to explore Vancouver, so in the morning I hop on a free shuttle to the Capilano Suspension Bridge, Vancouver's most popular attraction. It was built from hemp rope and cedar shortly after the railway reached town. First Nations groups called it the "laughing bridge" for the sounds the wind made whipping through the loose planks. It's sturdier now, running 450 feet (137.2 m) above a canyon and leading to elevated walkways between 250-year-old Douglas firs.

Later, from the former CPR train station, a neoclassic building now serving as a SeaBus ferry terminal, I cab it to Yaletown. It's there I find a 19th-century roadhouse, constructed to service trains. It's home to Engine 374, the first train to pull into town (in 1887).

Early the next morning, the *Rocky Mountaineer* has expanded into a 23-car train for more than 600 passengers. A bagpiper, dutifully kilted, offers a brief sign-off, as we all board and head east into a scene that looks like an ending shot of an early *Lord of the Rings* film: an impossible barrier of rocky peaks. Over the next two days, we will take them, and many more, as we cross the girth of British Columbia's canyons, cliffs, snowy summits, and green meadows of sedge where, we're told, black bears like to dine in full view of the passing train.

A half hour out of Vancouver, the sun streams through the clear roof of the top-deck panorama car. I watch as we pass cranberry farms and raw logs stored on rivers, while the vista gradually narrows, with spruce and pine trees and exposed rock walls edging closer to our windows. At Yale, I search for—and miss—a diminutive memorial to the thousands of Chinese workers who helped build the railway.

After an overnight stop in Kamloops, a historic trading town on the Thompson River, we're off again. At Craigellachie, I spot the marker for the last spike, marking the end of the CPR construction in 1885.

But it's the last five hours of the three-day ride that steal the show. Wide patches of woods climb in green waves up rocky bluffs whose mountaintops are coated in snow. Soon we enter a tunnel, looping on a dark path shaped like a cursive *L*, then pop out again to find the familiar mountain landmarks have been inverted. We enter another tunnel and reappear in British Columbia, near the Continental Divide. Rolling under mountain peaks, the train cuddles up alongside the delicious banks of the blue-green Bow River. I join others in the open-air vestibule, snapping photos, until we pull into Banff. It's been a 28-hour ride from Seattle.

The Banff Springs Hotel is a castle-style hotel that dates to 1888, when rail execs set up railway hotels like this. The next day, visiting Banff's Whyte Museum, I read that the second CPR president, William Cornelius Van Horne, said, "If we can't export the scenery, we'll import the tourists."

Photos there also show early surveyors with pickaxes who climbed peaks to plot the future course of the CPR. Eventually they discovered the springs that made Banff Springs famous and spawned the Alpine Club of Canada, founded in 1906 and run by Swiss guides. So all of this started with bearded men in suspenders climbing mountains. I hate heights, but I had to try. Chucky Gerard, wearing a sprout of red hair dangling off his chin, teaches mountaineering classes and leads first-timers like me up Mount Norquay, a ski mountain that opened the *via ferrata* (a course of bolted steel cables) last summer. He's also something of a psychologist, with his words of affirmation and encouragement.

Whatever. They work, and he gets me to cross the feared chasm. At the top, the wind whips around in a refreshing way. I hear a long, distant whistle. I look down to spot a 100-car freight train passing through.

It takes a lot to build a railway, I'm realizing. Or a Canada.

—**Robert Reid** is a travel writer based in Portland, Oregon, and former editor at large for *National Geographic Traveler*.

Natural Elements

Tierra Patagonia Adventure and Spa Hotel, Torres del Paine, Chile

Designed by Chilean architect Cazú Zegers—whose approach is inspired by Chilean landscapes, weather, and traditions—Tierra Patagonia appears shaped by the notoriously strong Patagonian winds. Reinforcing the natural sense of place is the washed *lenga*, or fireland cherry wood, exterior, which gives the low-slung lodge a weather-worn look. Expansive windows bring in jaw-dropping views of Lake Sarmiento and the snowcapped peaks, surrounding grasslands, and other edge-of-the-world landscapes in Torres del Paine National Park, a UNESCO Biosphere Reserve.

All-inclusive packages cover lodging in one of the 40 rooms and suites; all meals and house drinks; airport transfers; use of the Uma Spa outdoor hot tub and glass-encased heated indoor pool; and two half-day excursions or one full-day excursion, such as horseback riding with a Patagonian *baqueano* (cowboy) guide or kayaking through ice floes on Lake Grey. Tierra Patagonia is closed June to September, winter in Chilean Patagonia.

> "TIERRA PATAGONIA APPEARS SHAPED BY THE NOTORIOUSLY STRONG PATAGONIAN WINDS."

HUB | *Santiago, Chile; Buenos Aires, Argentina*

Nature is brought indoors at the Tierra Patagonia Adventure and Spa Hotel.

Stroll the vines along the Applegate Valley Wine Trail, which includes 19 wineries in southern Oregon.

Wine Country U.S.A.

Jacksonville, Oregon, U.S.

Gateway to southwestern Oregon's Applegate Valley Wine Trail, historic Jacksonville is a foothills community with front-row views of the Siskiyou Mountains. Founded as a gold rush settlement, most of the community is a national historic landmark district due to its 688 historic buildings, the oldest dating back to the 1850s.

Several of the structures are occupied by independent retailers, locally owned restaurants, and charming B&Bs, such as the Jacksonville Inn, housed in a brick building constructed in 1861. The Visitor Information Center offers four history-themed walking tours, available as guide-led excursions or as a downloadable audio narration and map for self-guided touring. Outside town, follow the meandering path of the Applegate River past fields of lavender on a wine-tasting tour of the Applegate Valley, home to 18 artisanal wineries. Combine walking and wine by visiting Jacksonville's three in-town tasting rooms.

Taste local Willamette wines in the Quady North tasting room.

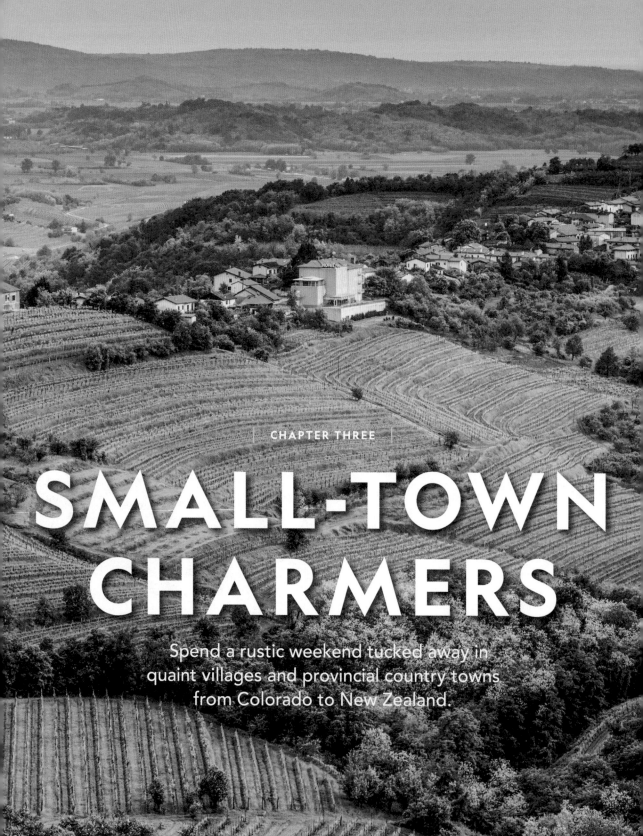

CHAPTER THREE

SMALL-TOWN CHARMERS

Spend a rustic weekend tucked away in
quaint villages and provincial country towns
from Colorado to New Zealand.

Vineyards abound in the Goriska Brda countryside of Slovenia (p. 98).

Fourteenth-Century Chic

Velo Grablje, Croatia

Part of the Dalmatian Islands and a short drive away from the more cosmopolitan Hvar, Velo Grablje is a tiny 14th-century hamlet (permanent population: 11) set among terraced lavender fields. The town is bleached by sun and time—red roofs paled to pink, white stones softened to dun, a small collection of buildings set among rolling rock and green hills overlooking the bright Adriatic Sea.

There isn't much to do here, but you won't be bored. There are new friends to be made, walking and cycle tracks to explore, and siestas to be had during the hard afternoon sun. If you want to soak in the sea air and simply slow down, this is the place to do it.

And should you fancy a day in town, Hvar township is 6.2 miles (10 km) away. The ancient walled city offers wide plazas, stone steps leading to narrow alleyways to explore, artisan shops, and shaded cafés.

"THE TOWN IS BLEACHED BY SUN AND TIME—RED ROOFS PALED TO PINK, WHITE STONES SOFTENED TO DUN, A SMALL COLLECTION OF BUILDINGS OVERLOOKING THE BRIGHT ADRIATIC SEA."

HUB | *Dubrovnik, Croatia*

Traditional stone houses add to Velo Grablje's charm.

Houses and bridges span the banks along the canals of Giethoorn.

A Romantic Hamlet

Giethoorn, the Netherlands

Although Giethoorn is only a 90-minute drive from Amsterdam, it feels a world away, a step back in time. This Dutch hamlet of thatched houses is built on a collection of small peat islands, connected by more than 170 wooden bridges. Known as the "Dutch Venice," the 2,600 people in car-free Giethoorn get around by waterway or walking and biking, and visitors are invited to do the same. (Even the postman delivers the mail by boat.)

Fifty-five miles (88.5 km) of canoe trails and canals link homes, accommodations, restaurants, canal-side cafés, and museums (like Het Olde Maat Uus, a typical Giethoorn farmhouse from a century ago). Visitors can book a canal cruise for a guided excursion or rent their own small electric boat to explore the narrow canals and avenues.

On higher ground, explore by the Giethoorn walking and biking route (2.7 miles/4.3 km) using bridges to cross the canals.

HUB | *Amsterdam, the Netherlands; Major Western European Cities*

Ply through the canals on a guided boat tour.

"A PICTURESQUE REGION OF STONE HOUSES AND ROLLING GREEN HILLS"

A Countryside Cruise

Cotswolds, England

When English country weekends spring to mind, there is nothing more quintessential than the Cotswolds, a picturesque region of honey-colored stone houses and rolling green hills that seems to encapsulate rural England.

A triangle of the M4, M5, and M40 highways surrounds this storybook area famed for its beauty and classically British names—Moreton-in-Marsh, Stow-on-the-Wold, and Bourton-on-the-Water, for example. Equally British is the Cotswolds' official designation as an Area of Natural Beauty (AONB)—and it's the largest AONB in England, covering 790 square miles (2,038 sq km) and stretching 80 miles (128.7 km) from Chipping Campden to Bath. A driving tour is the best way to explore this area, especially if you stick to the byways.

There are any number of sites to see, with something for everyone. Stop by the 56-acre (22.7 ha) Batsford Arboretum and Garden Centre in Moreton-in-March, with its wildflower meadows, Japanese ornamental cherries, and magnolias.

The Cogges Manor Farm in Oxfordshire, a 13th-century manor house with walled garden, orchard, and farm buildings, has been featured in the television series *Downton Abbey*. Children can don historical costumes and enjoy meeting the Shetland ponies, pygmy goats, and Cotswold sheep on its grounds.

For more of an adults-only feeling, the Lygon Arms Spa in Worcestershire is a sanctuary featuring an elegant 42.7-foot (13 m) indoor swimming pool with a retractable roof, a eucalyptus-scented steam room, and beauty treatments, all set on a three-acre (1.21 ha) private garden.

Broadway Tower, also in Worcestershire, is something wilder: The Cotswolds' highest castle is perched in a green field, now housing a museum, café, and rooftop viewing platform that overlooks 16 counties.

Along the drive, there are endless cafés and restaurants. The Priory Inn in Gloucestershire prides itself on serving locally sourced food, while the Noel Arms Hotel features a log fire and flagstone floors befitting of its historical location.

HUB | *London, England; Major Western European Cities*

Broadway Tower sits
on Broadway Hill in
Worcestershire.

Caribbean Country

Saint-Pierre, Martinique

Saint-Pierre was known as the "Paris of the Caribbean," a colonial capital wealthy from trade and resplendent with tropical beauty. In 1902, that came to a rapid, tragic end as Mount Pelée erupted, wiping the town off the map and killing 30,000 people in less than 15 minutes. (Don't pass up the opportunity to see the solitary prison cell that saved Ludger Sylbaris's life, one of only a handful of survivors.)

Now, this tranquil area on Martinique's northwest coast is a soft country Caribbean town that slows visitors down with its charm. Stroll cobblestone streets framed by houses with French-style wrought-iron balconies. Enjoy shopping in the city center, or venture down to the gray sand coastline to laze on the beach, swim, or sail.

Saint-Pierre is bordered by the steamy green rainforest at its back, and weekenders with excess energy can take to the trails surrounding the now dormant Mount Pelée.

HUB | *East Coast United States*

> "THIS TRANQUIL, SOFT COUNTRY CARIBBEAN TOWN SLOWS VISITORS DOWN WITH ITS CHARM."

Sailboats anchor in a cove off Saint-Pierre's coastline.

A river cruise ship plies through the Moselle valley in Cochem.

Castles & Wine
Cochem, Germany

Nestled on a bend of the winding Moselle River, Cochem is a traditional German town surrounded by green hills topped with ancient castles and wineries.

The Reichsburg castle, which dominates the landscape, offers daily tours of its impressive restored, fairy-tale interior and hosts medieval dinners on Friday and Saturday nights. The town itself shares this storybook character, with narrow streets, half-timbered houses with slate roofs, and ancient town gates.

Cochem is surrounded by steep rows of grapes and wineries that produce dry Rieslings renowned throughout the world. Visitors can sample wines at vineyards, cellar doors, and the multitude of cafés and restaurants in town.

Take the opportunity to get on the Moselle River, if even for a day. Watch the landscape slide by—a nonstop succession of castles and vineyards—as you sail a path that centuries of people have plied before you.

HUB | *Frankfurt, Germany*

Take a bike ride with stops at top tasting rooms and vineyards.

The Church of All Saints
in the market town
of Helmsley has stood
since 1086.

PERSPECTIVE

Unfettered Yorkshire

Part Serene Dream, Part Gothic Scream

Just about 15 minutes west of York, at the start of my drive across Yorkshire, I realize I have entered deep English country. The hints are hard to miss. There is the billboard advertising the local chimney sweep. There is the lamb, the sheep, and eventually the whole flock wandering across the road. And then there are the signs I pass for Gordale Scar ravine and Stump Cross Caverns, brooding place-names that seem to telegraph an ominous world ahead.

In fact, that is exactly what I am hoping for. Yorkshire played haunted muse to the Brontë sisters and Bram Stoker, whose 19th-century gothic fiction remains fixed in our collective imagination. So I have come to England to drive from the Yorkshire Dales, through the North York Moors, and on to the east coast for the pure fun of scaring myself a little. I'm also here to understand why some of our deepest nightmares took hold in this homey shire of tearooms and follies.

My first stop is Haworth, 50 miles (80.5 km) west of York. Here in the first half of the 19th century, the three Brontë sisters imagined a world of demonic villains, madwomen in the attic, and disposed spirits in such novels as *Jane Eyre* and *Wuthering Heights*.

The Brontë family parsonage sits at the top of the hilly town. Once I park my rental car and climb the stony spine of Haworth's main street, what immediately strikes me is how swallowed up the home appears. Photos show the house framed by a few small graves. But in reality, the cemetery swamps the parsonage, the high jagged tombstones lined up in wildly slanting rows that record the town's body county.

Clearly, the Brontë sisters were sketching from life when they wrote about death. Maybe they glimpsed their own fate, too. Emily Brontë would be laid to rest beneath the bleak town church at the age of 30.

The home, now owned by the Brontë Society, doesn't offer much relief. As I trail through the dim rooms, I can't help but feel a little claustrophobic, especially in the tiny dining room where the three sisters wrote, sharing space at a small central table.

It isn't until I step outside, into the ocean of wild grass, that I breathe freely again. It's easy to channel Emily's ecstasy, embodied by the unfettered passion of her characters Heathcliff and Catherine, when she broke loose on these moors.

By dusk the town shuts down, so I escape 11 miles (17.7 km) north to the Devonshire Arms Country House Hotel & Spa, a coaching inn at Bolton Abbey that dates to the early 17th century. Everything here is British comedy in comparison: my guest room anchored by a canopy bed; my late afternoon tea complete with scones; and the dog lounge, an ode to the English love of all things canine.

Guide Alan Rowley picks me up for a marathon tour of Yorkshire. We drive 28 miles (45.1 km) east past the whimsical follies and water garden of Fountains Abbey, where a phantom choir of monks is said to chant at night. Forty miles (64.4 km) farther east we pass Castle Howard. Finally arriving at the North York Moors National Park, we circle a squat block of stone in Danby High Moor that appears to have a head.

"That's Fat Betty," Rowley says. "She dates back centuries and is said to be a farmer's wife who got lost on the foggy moor and turned to stone."

I had delayed my visit to Whitby—aka Dracula's home—in order to finish my trip on a high note of macabre melodrama. Perched on the edge of the craggy Yorkshire coastline, the horseshoe town of Whitby rises in stony layers to the cemetery of St. Mary's Church and the arched ruins of the seventh-century Whitby Abbey. Bram Stoker chose this as his setting for *Dracula* while summering in a guesthouse across the harbor from the abbey in August 1890.

I walk up all 199 wide stone steps, panting, weak-kneed, to the church. Then I walk back down into the lap of town, which makes a thriving living off its Dracula pedigree. Boutique shoppers are snapping up chocolate coffins and skull bracelets.

Climbing the steps to the church one last time at dusk, I end up back in a cemetery, a fitting bookend to my trip's first graveyard, at Haworth. It occurs to me that maybe the high gothic tales, dense with all those vampires and ghosts, let us fantasize in an age when so many of our stories, blog posts, and tweets have become prosaic. Or maybe it's because the best horror stories capture something profound: the bogeyman under the bed, our unnamed fears, an elegiac sense of inevitable loss.

—**Raphael Kadushin** is a Wisconsin-based award-winning travel and food writer.

A diver watches a sea dragon swim above sea grass.

Wide Open Spaces
Flinders, Australia

Melbourne's Mornington Peninsula, which nearly encircles Port Phillip Bay, is a deep breath of eucalyptus-scented fresh air, a place of wide spaces, kangaroo-studded fields, and rugged coastlines that are a world apart from the bustling city (population 4.9 million). The tiny coastal community of Flinders (population 905), located in the southeast corner of the peninsula, is a charming village surrounded by windswept coastal walking tracks.

Enjoy a wander through the historic town center, stopping off at the Aboriginal art gallery EVERYWHEN Artspace or pausing to indulge your sweet tooth at Mornington Peninsula Chocolaterie & Ice Creamery. The sweetshop also offers chocolate-making classes.

Take a stroll down the 820-foot-long (250 m) pier that stretches into the sapphire waters where the Western Port meets the Bass Strait, or slip into the sea at the Mushroom Reef Marine Sanctuary for a dive or a snorkel.

HUB | *Melbourne, Australia*

Picturesque Dobrovo sits on a hilltop.

Tuscany of Slovenia
Dobrovo, Slovenia

The hidden gem of Dobrovo (population 400) is hemmed in by mountains in the west of Slovenia, bumping elbows with the border of Italy. It has gained a reputation as the "Tuscany of Slovenia," thanks to picturesque red-and-white buildings settled in an impossibly green landscape, with terraced rows of vines spilling down hillsides and lush orchards.

There is a Renaissance-style castle dating from around 1600 to explore, as well as plenty of walking and cycling on offer. But the main thing to do in and around Dobrovo is wine tasting. There are more than 50 family-run wineries in the area, with a few cellar-door-style cooperatives that offer a variety of tastings. Vinska Klet Goriška Brda has a sommelier tasting of six wines, including a visit to what is rumored to be the largest wine cellar in Slovenia. Vinoteka Brda, located in Smartno, has more than 300 wines from 40 winemakers to try, served with nibbles sourced from the surrounding hillsides.

HUB | *Zagreb, Croatia*

Coober Pedy's opal fields spread out like a lunar landscape.

Mad Max in the Eclectic Outback

Coober Pedy, Australia

D ead-center South Australia, 500 miles (804.7 km) from the nearest city, is the colorful community of Coober Pedy, also known as the Opal Capital. The arid landscape—113°F (45°C) in the shade, a blast of oranges, reds, and white tailings that look like termite mounds of spilled salt— served as the set for the postapocalyptic movie *Mad Max: Beyond Thunderdome.*

More than half of its residents live underground (naturally insulated against the wilting heat and desert cold), and visitors can choose to do the same, staying in subterranean accommodations that range from four-star hotels to underground camping sites. There are even underground bars, restaurants, opal shops, and galleries.

Venture aboveground to "noodle" for an opal of your own or to join the Outback Mail Run, traveling in an air-conditioned, *Mad Max*-esque four-wheel-drive vehicle with an Australian postie, delivering mail to historic outback towns like Oodnadatta and Anna Creek Station, the largest cattle station in the world (slightly smaller than New Hampshire).

HUB | *Adelaide, Australia*

A shopper talks with a pottery vendor at the Oedo Antiques Market in Tokyo.

Must-Stop Antiquing Spots

Discover treasures untold from the antique capital of the world in Pennsylvania to the Edo-era swords in Tokyo, Japan.

1. FES, MOROCCO

Believed to be the largest functioning medieval city, the Fes medina is an emporium of, well, everything. And while there are antiques scattered throughout, the Derb Sidi Moussa area is a particular hot spot for vintage Moroccan treasures.

2. ADAMSTOWN, PENNSYLVANIA, U.S.

This bucolic corner of Pennsylvania Dutch country is also known as Antiques Capital, USA—a fair tip-off to the thousands of dealers who operate out of the local antiques malls, open-air markets, and individual shops.

3. L'ISLE-SUR-LA-SORGUE, FRANCE

Another widely beloved "Capital City of Antiques," this centuries-old Provençal river town boasts one of the world's highest densities of antiques dealers, plus weekend antiques markets and major antiques fairs.

4. ROUND TOP, TEXAS, U.S.

When this 90-person town hosts its thrice-annual antiques fairs, hotels from Austin to Houston (73 and 95 miles/117.5 and 152.9 km away, respectively) fill up. Collectors from everywhere come for this massive—porter- and shipper-equipped—blend of American and European antiques.

5. MARKET AT GRAND SABLON, BRUSSELS, BELGIUM

The local weekend antiques market is one of the continent's most bustling, spilling out from the historic Place du Grand Sablon into the surrounding streets. Hunters of art deco and art nouveau tend to fare particularly well here.

6. TOKYO, JAPAN

The Oedo Antiques Market, the largest one held outdoors in Japan, generally takes place on the first and third Sundays of every month at the Tokyo International Forum. There are 250 dealers at the market, where you'll find everything from antique ceramics to an Edo-era sword.

7. CHARLESTON, SOUTH CAROLINA, U.S.

Between the historic King Street Antique District—home to all manner of silver, china, and furniture—and the annual springtime Charleston Antiques Show, this southern belle draws vintage pilgrims from across the globe.

8. LONDON, ENGLAND

The stretch of Notting Hill's Portobello Road that's dedicated to all things vintage is often dubbed the world's largest antiques market, where the goods may be decades old, centuries old—or, in rare cases, millennia old.

9. PORTSMOUTH TO CONCORD, NEW HAMPSHIRE, U.S.

To turn your treasure hunt into a weekend road trip, hit New Hampshire's Antique Alley. The 51-mile (82.1 km) stretch of Route 4 between Portsmouth and Concord is lined with more than 500 dealers selling everything from antique garden accessories, architectural salvage, early country store items, and more.

10. THE GRAND BAZAAR, ISTANBUL, TURKEY

The Grand Bazaar, one of the oldest and largest covered markets in the world—it stretches across 60 streets and alleys and includes 4,000 shops—is the sort of place where you can find anything if you know where to look, including regional antiques from hookahs to calligraphy. Mind your timing: The Bazaar is closed on Sundays and Turkish holidays.

Make your camp on Moon Island in Squam Lake.

Lakeside Relaxation

Squam Lake, New Hampshire, U.S.

The filming location for *On Golden Pond* is as beautiful to the eye as it is on the silver screen, a foliage-fringed lake bordered by small towns and dotted with more than 30 islands. Located approximately 65 miles (104.6 km) north of Manchester, on the edge of the White Mountain National Forest, Squam Lake is a place to relax, reconnect with nature, and do little of anything else.

The lake itself is the center of this community: Friends boat to each other's houses for a barbecue, families meet on beaches. Take part by renting a canoe or kayak, or by joining a boat tour offered by the Squam Lakes Natural Science Center, which is also worth a day visit. Boardwalks connect forests, marshes, and meadows that are home to some of the area's local wildlife, like bobcats and river otters.

Book a campsite on one of Squam Lake's islands. Spend the evenings listening to the lake lapping at the shoreline and the eerie call of loons, and watching the night brighten with stars.

HUB | *Northeastern United States*

Southern Hospitality

Bluffton, South Carolina, U.S.

Bluffton is Lowcountry, a traditional coastal community that retains its slow southern charm, oblivious to the hustle and bustle of nearby Hilton Head or Savannah.

Slow doesn't mean sleepy. Bluffton is a surprisingly young community of folks attracted to the beaches, small-town way of life, and historical culture that also make it popular with weekenders.

Take to the meandering May River, steeped in the smell of tidal marshes, by kayak, ecoboat tour, or stand-up paddleboard. Keep your eyes peeled for seabirds and bottlenose dolphins.

Stroll through town streets bordered by oak trees bearded with silver-green Spanish moss. Stop in quaint shops, art galleries, and mom-and-pop bakeries. There's also plenty of history to provide a sense of place. Join a walking tour (or guide yourself) through the town's historic landmarks and museums, like the timber-framed Heyward House, built in 1840 and one of eight antebellum homes in Old Town.

HUB | *Southeastern United States*

Bluffton offers plenty of family-friendly outdoor fun.

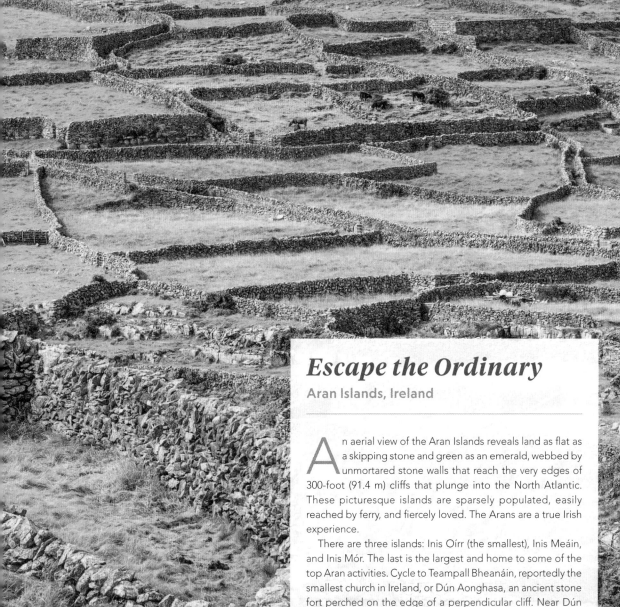

Ancient stone walls create a
grid in the hills of Inis Oírr.

Escape the Ordinary

Aran Islands, Ireland

An aerial view of the Aran Islands reveals land as flat as a skipping stone and green as an emerald, webbed by unmortared stone walls that reach the very edges of 300-foot (91.4 m) cliffs that plunge into the North Atlantic. These picturesque islands are sparsely populated, easily reached by ferry, and fiercely loved. The Arans are a true Irish experience.

There are three islands: Inis Oírr (the smallest), Inis Meáin, and Inis Mór. The last is the largest and home to some of the top Aran activities. Cycle to Teampall Bheanáin, reportedly the smallest church in Ireland, or Dún Aonghasa, an ancient stone fort perched on the edge of a perpendicular cliff. Near Dún Aonghasa is the Worm Hole, a natural rectangular sea pool at the base of the cliffs that was once used in a Red Bull Cliff Diving competition. Don't miss the seal colony, located across the neck of Inis Mór from Dún Aonghasa, near Kilmurvey Beach.

HUB | *Galway City or Dublin, Ireland*

> ## "THERE ARE NO SHORTAGES OF DISCOVERIES TO BE MADE."

Find Your Muse

Cortona, Italy

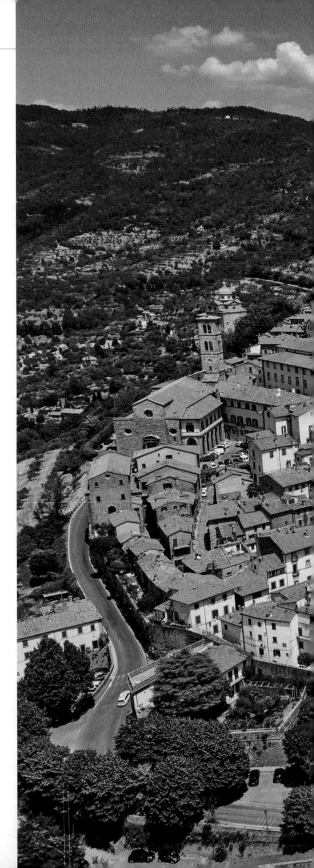

Most familiar as the setting of *Under the Tuscan Sun,* Cortona is small and full of character, the quintessential destination for a small-town Tuscan experience.

This sun-drenched, red-roofed town spills down a hillside, overlooking Lake Trasimeno and the Val di Chiana valley. An ancient wall built by the Etruscans encircles the city, while steep, narrow lanes open up into wide piazzas like the Piazza della Repubblica, with its clock tower and a wide staircase made for people-watching.

Fans of the movie *Under the Tuscan Sun* can take a walking tour of filming locations, including the villa Bramasole, built in 1504.

Interested in tapping into the Cortona muse? Writing and photography workshops are often held in Cortona, ranging from a weekend to a week's duration, and are the perfect opportunity to capture Cortona's vivacious atmosphere and dappled, patient beauty.

Cooking classes abound. Some include a visit to the marketplace to shop for fresh produce and ingredients, some involve a wine tour, and all invite visitors into the most sacred room in the Italian home—the kitchen—to laugh, taste, sample, converse, and create.

Walking is a great way to experience the city, and there are no shortages of discoveries to be made, from the wooden-beamed medieval houses on Via Iannelli to the views from the Basilica of Santa Margherita.

History lovers will delight in the Museo dell'Accademia Etrusca, one of Italy's most important museums (which is saying something). It houses a collection of pottery, jewelry, artifacts, and even a hanging lamp from the Etruscan occupation of the area (eighth century B.C.). Or visit the monastery where St. Francis of Assisi spent time. The peaceful Celle Hermitage is a short walk (1.86 miles/3 km) from Cortona.

HUB | *Florence or Rome, Italy*

Tightly clustered red-roofed buildings make up the town of Cortona, Italy.

A musician carries a double bass down the streets of Havana.

Music Towns

Whether you're looking for Delta blues or a world-renowned symphony, these cities can be considered the music capitals of the world.

1. MEMPHIS, TENNESSEE, U.S.

Considered by many to be the home of soul and rock-and-roll, Memphis has been the birthplace of music legends including Elvis Presley, Johnny Cash, Otis Redding, and Muddy Waters. Don't miss a stop at the legendary Sun Studios, where many American legends recorded their hit albums.

2. NASHVILLE, TENNESSEE, U.S.

Home of the Grand Ol' Opry, the Bluebird Café, and the Country Music Hall of Fame, Nashville brings us more country stars than any other place in the world. Catch a live show at the historic Ryman Auditorium (built in 1892 and designated a national historic landmark) or stop in at the Station Inn to gander at posters signed by the famous singers—Bill Monroe and Alison Krauss, for example—who have performed there.

3. LONDON, ENGLAND

The Beatles. The Clash. The Stones. The Kinks. Modern music history was made in the pubs and dens of London, where an eclectic mix of venues still offer performances by music legends. Visit some of the best, including 02 Academy (opened in 1929 originally as a movie theater) and Ronnie Scott's, a basement-level jazz club.

4. VIENNA, AUSTRIA

The European capital of classical music, Vienna is the creative home of Mozart, Beethoven, Haydn, Schubert, Mahler, and Brahms. You can enjoy regular recitals at classic venues including the Theater an der Wien.

5. LEIPZIG, GERMANY

Johann Sebastian Bach served as music director for the St. Thomas Church in Leipzig from 1723 until his death in 1750. Still a major center for classical music, Leipzig hosts the International Bach Competition Festival, the Leipzig Gewandhaus Orchestra, and the University of Music and Theatre.

6. HAVANA, CUBA

This capital of Cuba offers a hugely diverse music scene that blends African rhythms and percussion, Spanish guitars and mambo, and Cuban jazz. Explore the best beats and dance the night away in the Old Town of Havana.

7. NEW ORLEANS, LOUISIANA, U.S.

New Orleans is the birthplace of jazz, and Bourbon Street has a number of renowned music clubs, lively street musicians, festivals, and parades. Mardi Gras, anyone?

8. AUSTIN, TEXAS, U.S.

"The Live Music Capital of the World" has more music venues per person than anywhere else in the United States. It's also home to two of the biggest music festivals in the country: South by Southwest (typically held in March) and Austin City Limits (held every October). But you don't have to come for the music festivals: Plenty of local artists perform nightly at venues up and down the Sixth Street District.

9. CALI, COLOMBIA

Colombia's "salsa capital" is meant for dancers looking for a long night—there are hundreds of clubs throughout the southern city. For classic salsa, head to Zaperoco, and for the full experience, stop in at Siboney and La Topa Tolondra. Cali also hosts the annual Petronio Alvarez Festival of Pacific Music every August, where you'll find rhythms like the marimba and chirimia to dance to.

10. JOHANNESBURG, SOUTH AFRICA

There's a surprisingly huge range of live music in Johannesburg—everything from jazz to house music, and hip-hop to traditional African music styles. But it's house music that has put this South African city on the musical map.

Bison roam throughout the Tallgrass Prairie Preserve.

PERSPECTIVE

Prairie Home

Discover a Classic American Landscape in Northeastern Oklahoma

Before there were amber waves of grain, there were tall-grass prairies. At least 142 million acres (57.4 million ha) of grass covered the territory from Ohio to Kansas, southern Texas to Canada—nearly a third of what became the United States. Today, most of it is gone, which is why this sight, on the Nature Conservancy's Joseph H. Williams Tallgrass Prairie Preserve in northeastern Oklahoma, is such a treasure. Here, a nearly pristine remnant remains, thanks to a convergence of circumstances that resulted in the initial ownership of 39,650 acres (16,045.8 ha) of protected prairie.

I meet my guide, Harvey Payne, a rancher-attorney-environmentalist, in downtown Pawhuska, population about 3,500, the gateway town to the preserve. Cooking show celebrity Ree "The Pioneer Woman" Drummond has opened the Pioneer Woman Mercantile in one of Pawhuska's historic brick buildings, and the once sleepy town now regularly sees lines of fans stretching around the block, eager to chow down in her eatery or shop for kitchen implements and tchotchkes. A ripple effect has brought new galleries, boutiques, restaurants, and lodgings to downtown Pawhuska. For many visitors, the prairie preserve is serendipity rather than the reason to visit this corner of the state.

As we continue into the preserve, it is obvious just how abundant a tallgrass prairie is. It's early September, when warm-season grasses are at their tallest, but we're not just talking about horizon-to-horizon big bluestem, which reaches up to 10 feet (3 m) this time of year. We also see shorter Indian grass, with its feathery seed heads, and little bluestem, and some truly astounding displays of wildflowers. We pull to the edge of the road beside acres of Leavenworth's eryngo and a herd of bison indifferently munching around the fringe of the field.

Bison tend to be scene stealers wherever they choose to graze, and that's only right. They're irresistible to watch. Signs warn to keep one's distance from the massive wild beasts, but I'll admit to cheating a bit. Not that I'm posing for selfies with them, but I just like to stand nearby, watch, and anthropomorphize—this one's grumpy, this one's looking for affection, how cute is that calf, that guy . . . he's *huge*.

When I visited 20-some years ago, the preserve had around 300 bison. Today, some 2,700 of them are scattered in groups like this, freely grazing 25,000 acres (10,117 ha) in the preserve. A nearly 10-mile (16 km) circular driving route in the western part of the preserve, the Bison Loop, passes through prime bison pasture.

The prairie preserve isn't like a national park, laced with hiking trails and scenic viewpoints overlooking major landmarks. It has a pair of hiking trails that form a 2.5-mile (4 km) figure-eight loop, and scattered turnouts beside 20 miles (32 km) of graded gravel roads. It's possible to drive through, tour the visitor center, and drive back to Pawhuska in a couple of hours. But I spend most of the next three days heeding Payne's advice. Up early. Out late. Stop constantly.

First light is amazing, not for any particular dazzle on the horizon, but for the soothing calm and quiet. When I cut my engine, sometimes I hear absolutely nothing. Then maybe a few early birds. Amazingly, given this is flyover country, I never once hear an airplane above. Sometimes I hear bison grunting, coyotes howling, wild turkeys rummaging.

Last light is a living elegy. The prairie feels like a long-gone relative come to life, and in the fading light, a strong sense of nostalgia comes over me. There was a time when this quality of peace, this quiet abundance, was the norm. Now it's a glaring exception. It's easy to feel sad for what we've lost. But then maybe a white-tailed deer bounds through a field of Maximilian sunflowers, or a Swainson's hawk soars by. I feel settled, and grateful to have this opportunity.

We've saved the hiking loop for last. The trail starts in a remarkable stand of big bluestem, at least 8 feet (2.4 m) tall. The way is marked by a mown strip—we're walking entirely on cropped grass—then circles through deep woods beside Sand Creek.

As we leave the creek and woods and ascend a hillside, we reach a different world. Trees small, grasses tall—a sure sign of fire-managed terrain. Some of the big bluestem, silhouetted against a gauzy sky, are fully 10 feet (3 m) tall. Payne notices my gawking and adds a slightly mind-blowing tidbit: The root systems of prairie grasses extend the same distance as or more than the height of the plant.

I think about that as we reach the apex of the trail, and the views over the hills to the west seem to extend forever. The sky appears infinite. The tallest grasses in the world wave in the breeze, yet half their growth is underground. Life runs deep on the prairie.

—**Robert Earle Howells** is a California-based writer whose passion is public lands that preserve disappearing landscapes.

The Gaucho Life

Buenos Aires, Argentina

Take part in Argentina's rural ranching tradition by spending a weekend at one of the *estancias* (large cattle ranches) scattered across the wide, rolling countryside surrounding the vibrant city of Buenos Aires.

The day usually begins with a country breakfast (garden veggies, freshly laid eggs, and honey from the beehives) fortified by coffee before joining the *gauchos* (horsemen akin to the cowboys of the American West) on a horseback ride around the ranch. Trot along verdant fields and revel in the solitude and freedom that exploring by horseback lends. Lunch (traditionally a barbecue) is waiting when you return to the ranch, followed by an afternoon of leisure—nature walks, hammock siestas, or reading on the porch. Before you know it, the stars will begin to appear, a night made for music and Malbec.

Each of these rural estates has its own feel. Some are more touristy (complete with cowboy demonstrations), others are opulent mansions, and yet others are cozy, six-bedroomed, wood-floored ranch houses on working cattle stations.

> "TROT ALONG VERDANT FIELDS AND REVEL IN THE SOLITUDE AND FREEDOM EXPLORING BY HORSEBACK LENDS."

HUB | *Major South American Cities*

Horses gallop outside Hacienda El Ombú de Areco.

Cool down in the water of the Rio Caldera, which flows through Volcán Barú National Park.

Retire from the Hubbub

Boquete, Panama

Nestled into the Chiriquí Highlands, Boquete is a peaceful village surrounded by mountains, bursts of bougainvillea, and coffee plantations. Once a secret expat retirement hot spot (giving it a more Southern California feel than Central American), Boquete is filled with things to do, from white-water rafting to wildlife-watching.

Bird-watching is one of the most popular activities in Boquete: There are more than 400 species to spot during the dry season (January to April), including the resplendent quetzal. Pack a pair of binoculars and pick a trail, or join a guided expedition into the cloud forest or the area surrounding the Baru volcano.

Coffee tours are also popular. The hills surrounding Boquete are populated with coffee plantations that thrive on the microclimate and the rich volcanic soil. Several operators offer plantation tours that include visits to the coffee *finca* (farm), as well as a tasting of the dark, sweet brew the region is known for.

HUB | *Panama City, Panama*

Coffee beans grow on a branch.

"A TEXTBOOK EXAMPLE OF A TRADITIONAL PORTUGUESE TOWN"

An Ancient Beauty
Óbidos, Portugal

The walled town of Óbidos is a textbook example of a traditional Portuguese town, with painted houses, cobblestoned streets, and even a hilltop castle. From 1214 until the 19th century, Óbidos was presented to the reigning queen of Portugal on her wedding day, a tradition that infused Óbidos with an elegance and pride that is palpable today.

Don a good pair of walking shoes because there's plenty to see. The Muro de Óbidos, the fully intact Moorish wall that surrounds the center of town, can be walked on, offering fantastic views of the town and surrounding countryside. It can be accessed by four staircases, reaching a height of 42.6 feet (13 m) in certain sections.

The medieval Castelo de Óbidos is another popular attraction, now a luxury hotel (or *pousada*). The town's noble-looking main church, Igreja de Santa Maria, contains a Renaissance tomb and 17th-century paintings and is famed for its painted interior.

Stop by Óbidos' main gate, the Porta da Vila, a blue-and-white-tiled beauty featuring an ancient inscription and leading directly onto the main street, Rua Direita. For a more comprehensive tour of the city's history, visit the Museu Municipal, housed in an 18th-century manor house. This museum contains paintings and other artifacts of the area.

All that walking is bound to work up a healthy appetite, and Óbidos is more than happy to help, serving up the cuisine that Portugal is famous for. Try the white-tiled Senhor da Pedra for classic Portuguese cuisine at reasonable prices. Alcaide, reported to be Óbidos' first restaurant, is a venue with a view, with windows overlooking town.

For something special, try a swig of Ginjinha d'Óbidos, a sweet liquor often served in a chocolate cup, or visit the Livraria de Santiago, a bookstore housed in an 18th-century church.

HUB | *Lisbon, Portugal; Major Western European Cities*

Dusk settles over Costa de Prata in Óbidos, illuminating a 14th-century castle.

White
Blue
Brown
Yellow

Try your hand at various
crafts at The Makerie, a
three-day art workshop.

Creative Escapes

Find artistic inspiration in forested Plymouth, Massachusetts; beachy Key West, Florida; and beyond.

1. PINEWOODS, PLYMOUTH, MASSACHUSETTS, U.S.

Tucked into a forested swath of Plymouth, Massachusetts, this summer music and dance camp hosts weekend sessions—mostly for adults, but occasionally for families—that cover everything from Hungarian folk dance to English Scottish contra.

2. THE BELIEVER FESTIVAL, LAS VEGAS, NEVADA, U.S.

For the improbability factor alone—Vegas, baby!—this springtime celebration of writing, music, and art is worth attending. Granted, you'll need a long weekend, but you won't regret spending it with this mix of luminaries and talented emerging artists.

3. KAUAI WRITERS CONFERENCE, HAWAII, U.S.

If you're a writer who can spare a long weekend in November, do. This three-day Hawaiian gathering attracts an all-star cast of authors, editors, and agents for a succession of readings, pitch sessions, workshops—and cocktails.

4. KEY WEST LITERARY SEMINAR, FLORIDA, U.S.

Another literary world legend worth spending a long weekend on, this January seminar in Ernest Hemingway's old stomping grounds will have you in lectures, panel discussions, and parties with an astonishing array of authors and scholars.

5. DIRTY DANCING, MOUNTAIN LAKE LODGE, PEMBROKE, VIRGINIA, U.S.

Step into Johnny and Baby's shoes at the filming location of *Dirty Dancing*. The movie-themed weekend package includes dance lessons, themed camp activities, a barn dance party, and meals.

6. THE IMPROV RETREAT, WISCONSIN, U.S.

At the wooded Perlman Retreat Center outside Milwaukee, improv fans of all experience levels spend a long summer weekend under the guidance of numerous Second City veterans, and other industry pros.

7. CAMP IMPROV UTOPIA, VARIOUS LOCATIONS

If you need to be a bit farther from civilization to lose any improv inhibitions you may have, these adult long weekend retreats, which take place everywhere from Yosemite to the Irish countryside, might be the ticket.

8. MUSIC FOR PEOPLE, VARIOUS NORTH AMERICAN AND EUROPEAN LOCATIONS

Founded on three core beliefs—music is for everyone; any combination of people can make improvised music together; and listening is the most important musical skill—this organization runs short, sweet workshops in North America and Europe.

9. THE MAKERIE, VARIOUS LOCATIONS

Batik, needlework, jewelry making—whatever your craft of choice, odds are the Makerie has—or will—run a related workshop in the United States or abroad. Generally, but not always, you need a three-day weekend to spare to attend one of these sessions.

10. ROCK 'N ROLL FANTASY CAMP, VARIOUS LOCATIONS

For rock fans, this roving camp is the bucket list experience. Over the course of a long weekend (four days), you can jam, write, and record with, say, members of the Rolling Stones, Aerosmith, or Deep Purple. Camp "counselors" have included Slash (Guns N' Roses), Rudy Sarzo (Quiet Riot), and Dave Navarro (Red Hot Chili Peppers).

A church spire in downtown Český Krumlov

Bohemian Rhapsody
Český Krumlov, Czech Republic

Founded by the Lords of Krumlov around 1253, Český Krumlov is far enough from Prague—approximately two and a half hours by car, train, or bus—to make for a wonder-filled weekend. This UNESCO World Heritage site is a Bohemian beauty, a compact collection of quaint red-roofed buildings crowded around the winding Vltava River, with a car-free old town (featuring more than 300 medieval buildings) that can be walked from one cobblestoned end to the other in 20 minutes.

The castle complex, one of the largest in Europe, is the centerpiece. It is made of more than 40 buildings filled with period furnishings. Climb the stairs of the 180-foot-tall (54.9 m) tower for sweeping views of the town below.

Outside town, the landscape widens at your feet. Nearby Šumava National Park offers skiing in winter and hiking and horseback riding in summer. Or take to the Vltava river in a kayak, canoe, or old-fashioned wooden raft.

HUB | *Prague, Czech Republic; Munich, Germany; Vienna, Austria*

Old School Stroll
Colonia del Sacramento, Uruguay

Colonia del Sacramento, a UNESCO World Heritage site, is one of the oldest and most picturesque cities in South America. It was founded by the Portuguese in 1680 and is located on a small peninsula on the Rio de la Plata, a fast ferry ride from Buenos Aires, Argentina.

This is the kind of place where drivers of vintage cars pause to let visitors cross the sycamore-lined stone streets. A drawbridge leads into the walled district of the old city, complete with a lighthouse and an abandoned bullring. Several museums are located within walking distance of each other, including the Indigenous Museum, which displays cultural artifacts from 10,000 years before European conquerors arrived, and the Tile Museum, with displays of Portuguese, Spanish, and French tiles from the 17th and 18th centuries.

It's an old Uruguayan custom to applaud the setting sun: Visit the waterfront to join in celebrating the spectacular sunsets.

Cobblestone streets run through the town's historic square.

HUB | *Buenos Aires, Argentina; Montevideo, Uruguay*

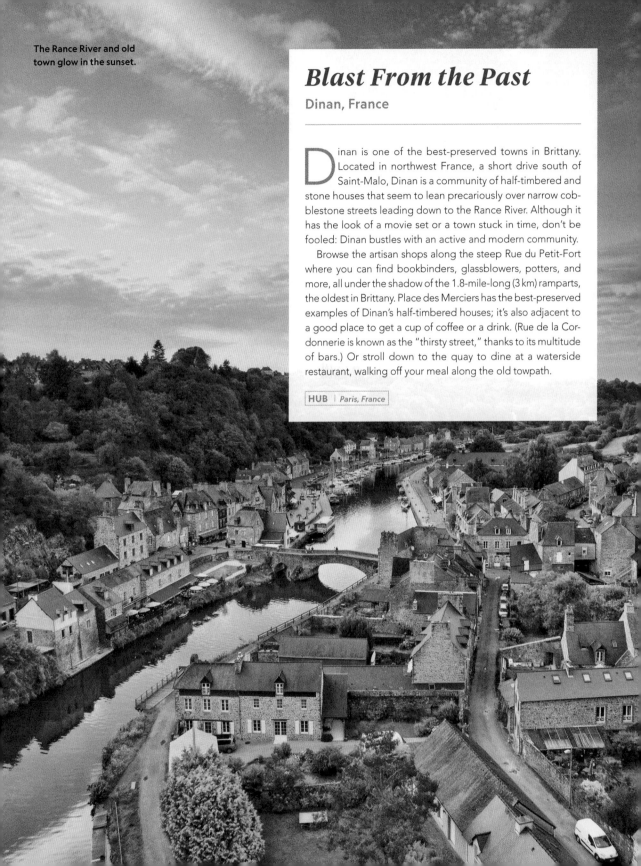

The Rance River and old town glow in the sunset.

Blast From the Past

Dinan, France

Dinan is one of the best-preserved towns in Brittany. Located in northwest France, a short drive south of Saint-Malo, Dinan is a community of half-timbered and stone houses that seem to lean precariously over narrow cobblestone streets leading down to the Rance River. Although it has the look of a movie set or a town stuck in time, don't be fooled: Dinan bustles with an active and modern community.

Browse the artisan shops along the steep Rue du Petit-Fort where you can find bookbinders, glassblowers, potters, and more, all under the shadow of the 1.8-mile-long (3 km) ramparts, the oldest in Brittany. Place des Merciers has the best-preserved examples of Dinan's half-timbered houses; it's also adjacent to a good place to get a cup of coffee or a drink. (Rue de la Cordonnerie is known as the "thirsty street," thanks to its multitude of bars.) Or stroll down to the quay to dine at a waterside restaurant, walking off your meal along the old towpath.

HUB | *Paris, France*

Traditional blue fishing
boats are moored at
the port in Essaouira.

Small Towns

These tiny towns around the world will delight with their charms and plentiful options for exploration, delicious food scenes, and more.

1. COLMAR, FRANCE

Technicolor-timbered medieval buildings, cobblestone streets, and local vineyards decorate this northeastern French town, located on the Alsace Wine Route. Don't miss the town's Petite Venise (Little Venice), a canal that cuts through a stretch of 400-year-old sherbert-colored homes.

2. HALLSTATT, AUSTRIA

Thought to be the oldest continuously inhabited village in Europe, Hallstatt (population: 779) is a narrow Alpine town tucked in the Dachstein Mountains. The lakeside town was named a UNESCO World Heritage site in 1997.

3. ESSAOUIRA, MOROCCO

Step away from the hustle and bustle of Marrakech for this seaside town peppered with blue boats, winding streets, and the freshest seafood eateries. Head here from April to November to watch windsurfers take to the waters.

4. PORT DOUGLAS, AUSTRALIA

Easily mistaken for the Caribbean, this mainland port city offers lush mountain views and beautiful blue water, a worthwhile stop on the way to dive the Great Barrier Reef.

5. POSITANO, ITALY

Though well known to weathered travelers, the Amalfi Coast's Positano retains its charm with stony, flower-lined streets and Mediterranean architecture. The Tyrrhenian Sea views don't hurt, either. Spend a day on the beach—either Spiaggia Grande or the smaller Spiaggia del Fornillo to sunbathe and watch local artists paint the stunning scenery from beachside easels.

6. JINHAE, SOUTH KOREA

Come to this quiet naval town during the annual Cherry Blossom Festival, when this tiny suburb outside Changwon City blossoms with pink flowers, performers, and light shows. There are more than 300,000 cherry trees throughout the city, attracting more than one million tourists every year. Make the trip easier by snagging a day trip ticket to the festival, with transportation to and from Seoul.

7. JIM THORPE, PENNSYLVANIA, U.S.

Also known as the "Switzerland of America," this cozy town's winding streets and Victorian architecture sit at the foot of the Pocono Mountains, with Lehigh Gorge State Park nearby. This is an outdoor enthusiast's dream, with access to more than 20 trailheads from town.

8. RINCÓN, PUERTO RICO

A great spot for whale watching, Rincón, Puerto Rico—a three-hour drive from San Juan—is a beloved, laid-back surfing town with a population of just 15,000 or so permanent residents. Made famous to waveriders after the 1968 World Surfing Championship, the mellow beach town also offers sea cliffs, prime scuba diving sites, and deep-sea fishing charters.

9. FRANSCHHOEK, SOUTH AFRICA

Circled by the Drakenstein and Wemmershoek Mountains, this South African hamlet offers stunning scenery and some of the Cape region's best wines. The estates of Franschhoek, one of the oldest towns in South Africa, also include art galleries and museums focused on the region's Cape Dutch heritage.

10. CARMEL-BY-THE-SEA, CALIFORNIA, U.S.

This under-the-radar California town skips the glitz and glam of the state's better-known destinations like Los Angeles and San Francisco. There are no parking meters, chain restaurants, or high heels without a permit. Instead, you'll find rose-draped cottages, art galleries, and the San Carlos Borromeo de Carmelo Mission.

"THIS IS THE PLACE TO DO SOME SERIOUS SPECTATING."

Immerse Yourself in Horse Country

Middleburg, Virginia, U.S.

Only an hour's drive from Washington, D.C., a picturesque, colonial town of black-board fences, old stone walls, and elegant architecture still lives, breathes, and revolves around horses, as it has done for several centuries. Middleburg was established in 1787 by a Revolutionary War lieutenant colonel who purchased the property from George Washington's cousin. It saw two Civil War skirmishes in 1863 (part of the Gettysburg Campaign) before emerging as the nation's horse and hunt capital.

Horsey activities have to be at the top of any visitor's list, and there are plenty to choose from. The self-guided Hunt Country Stable Tour (established 1959) usually takes place on Memorial Day and is a great opportunity to see how red Middleburg's equestrian blood runs. Opulent and gabled stables, open and airy, are surrounded by undulating grass paddocks and large training rings, grand structures that would put most homes to shame. You can see up to 10 facilities on the self-drive tour, including the 340-acre (137.6 ha) luxury Salamander Resort & Spa, with its world-class equestrian center.

Even if horses aren't in your blood, this is the place to do some serious spectating. From spring through autumn, the calendar is populated with races, point-to-points, three-day events, Polo Under the Lights, and the crème de la crème—the June Upperville Colt & Horse Show, which is the oldest horse show in the United States, first held in 1853.

For an experience of another kind, wander down Main Street. With more than 160 buildings on the National Register of Historic Places, there is plenty to see. The National Sporting Library & Museum (founded 1954) is worth a visit, while the Upper Crust Bakery is where booted riders grab a cup of coffee and a famous cow puddle cookie around midmorning. Dinner at the Red Fox Inn & Tavern is a must. This historic fieldstone inn was built in 1728 and has served centuries of hearty meals.

HUB | *Washington, D.C., U.S.; Mid-Atlantic United States*

A horse pokes his head out of his stall at Middleburg's Salamander Resort & Spa.

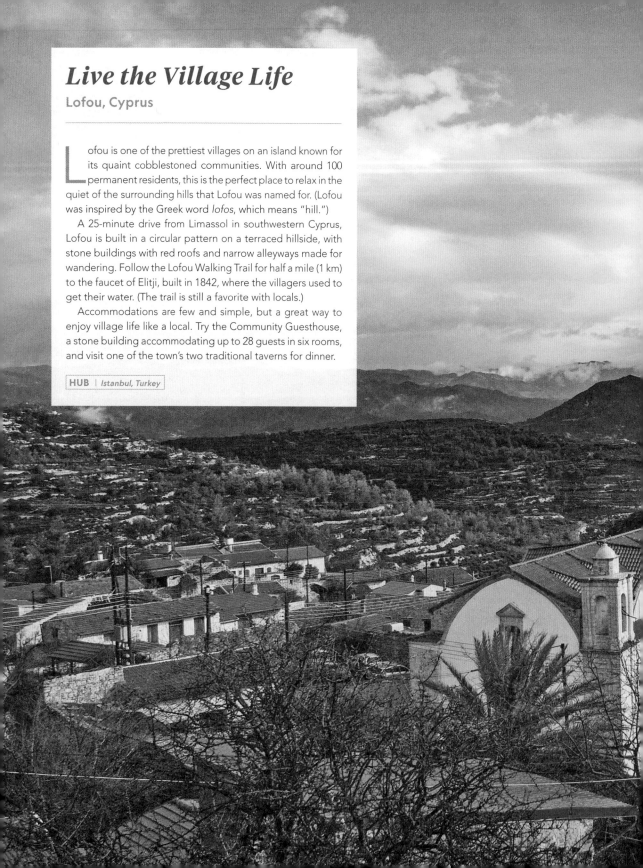

Live the Village Life
Lofou, Cyprus

Lofou is one of the prettiest villages on an island known for its quaint cobblestoned communities. With around 100 permanent residents, this is the perfect place to relax in the quiet of the surrounding hills that Lofou was named for. (Lofou was inspired by the Greek word *lofos*, which means "hill.")

A 25-minute drive from Limassol in southwestern Cyprus, Lofou is built in a circular pattern on a terraced hillside, with stone buildings with red roofs and narrow alleyways made for wandering. Follow the Lofou Walking Trail for half a mile (1 km) to the faucet of Elitji, built in 1842, where the villagers used to get their water. (The trail is still a favorite with locals.)

Accommodations are few and simple, but a great way to enjoy village life like a local. Try the Community Guesthouse, a stone building accommodating up to 28 guests in six rooms, and visit one of the town's two traditional taverns for dinner.

HUB | *Istanbul, Turkey*

Take in the beauty of Lofou in one perfect weekend.

The Château de Castlenaud overlooks the Dordogne River.

Dordogne: Beauty Defined

Romancing the Words, Ways, and Wonder of Southwestern France

Love was born in the Dordogne. Perhaps not really, but there is some literal truth to this. The French word *amour* comes from the word *ameur* in Occitan, an ancient Romance language that was once the pervasive patois of the region. Maybe I shouldn't have been surprised when I fell hard for this region of southwest France. I am hopelessly, crazily in love with everything about it: the prehistoric caves, the fairytale castles, and the resilient locals, who still call the region Périgord, its moniker before the country's historic provinces were renamed during the French Revolution.

Though it is heavenly, you can't exactly say Dordogne is off the tourist map. Just try to find parking in Sarlat or rent a kayak on the Dordogne River on a summer day. And it's hardly unsophisticated. There are nine Michelin-starred restaurants, a smattering of upscale hotels and golf courses, and 15 UNESCO World Heritage sites. But considering that France received 87 million visitors in 2017, the relative emptiness is by far the Dordogne's most luxurious asset.

It is festival day. Beneath a sapphire sky and rows of hanging paper-flower garlands, schoolchildren fidget before the cameras of their doting parents. The heat is relentless, and the sun beats on white bonnets and crimson bandanna-like scarves, emblazoned with a yellow heraldic cross and one word: "Périgord." A group of women in long skirts, lace-collared blouses, and bonnets hook arms and circle, square-dance style, with men dressed head to toe in black, including hats that could be distant cousins of the Stetson.

Over the years, I'd heard about La Félibrée, seen the floral remnants of this annual fete dangling over villages, but never attended. Now I'm seeing what I've been missing all this time.

Le Félibrée (pronounced Fay-lee-bray) first unfurled in 1903 in the village of Mareuil, and 98 times since, this convivial ode to the Occitan language and heritage has moved its pomp and flourish to a different village of Périgord on the first Sunday in July (it ceased for six years during WWII). Marked by events that include the mayor's handing over of the keys to the organizing association, a Mass, a parade, and a familial sit-down feast, called *la taulada*, La Félibrée is a collective remembrance and a renaissance of a long backstory. In 2019 the town of Périgueux organized the hundredth edition.

Throughout the day I hear *bonjorn* for hello, *benvenguda* for welcome, and *encantat* for nice to meet you. In addition to amour, I learn that other commonly used French words can thank Occitan for their existence: bouillabaisse from *bolhir* (to boil) and *abaissar* (to simmer); and aioli, from *alh* (garlic) and *òli* (oil).

The deeper we go into the village, the thicker the flower garlands and the accents. The schoolchildren have dispersed with their families to watch lacemakers ply their wooden bobbins and webs of thread. Hundreds of thousands of vibrant plastic and paper flowers, more than 35 miles (56.3 km) in total, flap overhead, strung between honey-hued stone buildings, dangling from geranium-stuffed flower boxes, and winding around ornate lampposts. These floral festoons are the festival's visual hallmark.

I follow a parade of costumed musicians under a tunnel of wisteria-like flowers. They pound drums, collapse accordions, and squeeze *cabrettes*, a common bagpipe-like instrument. Slowly we make our way to La Félibrée's pièce de résistance, the midday taulada served in St.-Cyprien's former tobacco-drying house. Hundreds of people wedge along communal tables, surrounded by frescoed walls. At least a hundred more overflow outside under a tent. No one is turned away.

Eventually we're served the Périgord menu mainstays of *confit de canard* (duck leg) and *enchaud* (a regional pork specialty), goat cheese with walnuts, and, despite the sweltering temperatures, a bowl of white garlic soup called *tourin blanchi*.

I understand the need for La Félibrée more than ever. In an increasingly small world where more travelers spin the globe in search of what's genuine and where residents of such places grow increasingly resentful as they watch their homes slowly succumb to souvenir shops and selfie sticks, Périgord is decidedly and willfully not that place.

On the contrary, I am invited to a large Périgourdine party decorated with colorful streamers and asked to sit at the family table, where the fun uncle lets me drink wine from a bowl. I've never felt more at home—or more love for the Dordogne.

For days after I leave, I'm still thinking of the word *félibrée*, and I finally find a definition that satisfies. *Félibré* (one e) means a pupil and a follower, a new troubadour, a writer in the Oc language, and a member of the Félibrige.

For one day in July, I became all of these. In my heart. In my mind. In my words.

—**Kimberley Lovato** is a freelance journalist, author, Francophile, and author of *Walnut Wine & Truffle Groves*.

Cycle, Walk & Wine

Martinborough, New Zealand

Martinborough is nestled in the boutique, wine-growing Wairarapa region, about an hour from Wellington, New Zealand's character-filled capital. Martinborough is a square town set around a town square: a sensible grid of delectable eateries (think flaky-crust pies, sweet potato salads, and super-fruit smoothies) and historic homes surrounded by a patchwork quilt of vineyards, pastures, and olive groves.

Weekend outings can include walks, guided excursions, or self-guided bike tours of the wineries that populate the perimeter of town. There are more than 20 to choose from, many of them family owned and all of them friendly, serving up unexpectedly earthy Pinot Noirs and fruity whites.

The area is also known for its abundance of accommodation options, from self-contained heritage cottages to farm-stays to country estates. If you can, visit during Toast Martinborough in November, a local wine and food festival that is one of New Zealand's most popular. (Book early!)

HUB | *Wellington, New Zealand*

> "WEEKEND OUTINGS CAN INCLUDE WALKS, GUIDED EXCURSIONS, OR SELF-GUIDED BIKE TOURS OF THE WINERIES."

Taste from the vines at Cambridge Road Winery, one of Martinborough's well-known spots for a sip.

Saint George island (Ostrvo Sveti Djordje) sits in the Bay of Kotor.

Part of the Past

Perast, Montenegro

The handsome white-stone, red-roofed seaside village of Perast is nestled on the Adriatic blue of the Bay of Kotor, a collection of fjord-like channels and a UNESCO World Heritage site. The town is the result of Byzantine, Venetian, Austria-Hungarian, and French rule, and its picturesque streets are heavy with memories that you can see in the noble architecture, wide plazas, tall watchtowers, and 16 churches that make up this community, once a favorite with the golden goddesses of Hollywood: Marilyn Monroe, Elizabeth Taylor, and Sophia Loren.

Hop on a boat to explore Perast's two most famous landmarks: offshore islands holding the cypress tree–encircled 12th-century Benedictine abbey of Sveti Djordje and the 15th-century Our Lady of the Rocks church. Stroll along seaside promenades, past 17th-century churches, pausing in shops, museums, and at terrace cafés, soaking in the atmosphere of this picturesque place.

HUB | *Major Western European Cities*

Take in the bay from waterfront cafés.

A bull moose walks into a kettle pond in Denali National Park (p. 146).

CHAPTER FOUR

NATURE PARKS

Discover Mother Nature's bounty from the wilds
of Denali National Park in Alaska to the Big Five
on a safari in Botswana.

A double rainbow arches over the Columbia River Gorge.

Escape the City
Columbia River Gorge, Oregon, U.S.

Just one hour from Portland and four hours from Seattle stretches an 85-mile (136.8 km) corridor and four-season wilderness delight. The 292,000-acre (118,168.2 ha) Columbia River Gorge, smack in Lewis and Clark territory, was created in 1984 as a recreational retreat and a clever way of combating urban sprawl. It's the largest National Scenic Area in America: Dozens of waterfalls rush down basalt cliffs, and mysteriously moody forest trails flank the wide Columbia River.

Many Portland and Seattle residents have their favorite getaways within the gorge, from the 627-foot (191.1 m) double cascade of Multnomah Falls, to the outdoorsy hamlet of Hood River (don't miss the Fruit Loop, a collection of orchards and vineyards), to the Bonneville Lock and Dam, a hydroelectric station and salmon hatchery. Pay homage to Herman the Sturgeon, a 10+-foot (3.1+ m), 450-pound (204.1 kg) behemoth who is more than 80 years old and attracts more than 500,000 visitors a year.

HUB | *Pacific Northwest United States*

Manawaiopuna Falls is famed for its appearance in *Jurassic Park*.

Explosion of Color
Nāpali Coast State Park, Kauai, Hawaii, U.S.

Hawaii's wildest coastline is an explosion in color: fluted green peaks rising 3,000 feet (914.4 m) above red cliffs plunging into a sapphire sea. Nāpali (which translates to "the cliffs") is a linked chain of state parks, forest reserves, and conservation areas stretched across more than 6,175 acres (2,498.9 ha) on the north side of the island of Kauai.

The area is best explored by helicopter (take the tour to Manawaiopuna Falls, that stunning ribbon of white that appears at the beginning of *Jurassic Park*), by boat (inflatable boats or kayaks ferry visitors to secluded, remote beaches like Nu'alolo Kai), or on foot.

For ambitious weekenders (and experienced hikers), the Kalalau Trail, a 22-mile (35.4 km) return path crossing five valleys, is an adventure to remember. Originally built in the late 1800s as a foot trail, this undulating track winds above fluted sea cliffs and verdant valleys, dropping to sea level at the beaches of Hanāka pi'ai and Kalalau.

HUB | *Honolulu, Hawaii, U.S.; West Coast United States*

A mountain goat makes a rocky climb up the Needles.

Wild West Journey

Black Hills National Forest, South Dakota, U.S.

The Black Hills National Forest resembles one of those 12-foot (3.7 m) landscape paintings found in prominent U.S. government buildings: a wistful scene of grassland seas and roaming bison. Bordering western South Dakota and northeastern Wyoming, the Black Hills is a collection of 1.2 million acres (485,622.8 ha) of ponderosa pine forests, swaying grass, and craggy rock formations, including the highest U.S. mountain east of the Rockies, the 7,242-foot (2,207.4 m) Black Elk Peak.

Sacred to the Lakota Sioux and once the stomping ground of George Custer, Wild Bill Hickok, and Calamity Jane (Wild Bill and Calamity Jane are buried in nearby Mount Moriah Cemetery), a lot of history has ridden through this area.

Nowadays, the Black Hills is known for outdoor recreation: hiking (353 miles/568.1 km of trails), fishing (1,300 miles/2,092.2 km of streams), camping (more than 30 campgrounds), cave visits (the Jewel Cave National Monument has more than 180 miles/289.7 km of underground passages), rock climbing, and more, not to mention the iconic Mount Rushmore.

HUB | *Rapid City, South Dakota, U.S.; Mountain West United States*

Historic architecture surrounds Lily Pond in Balboa Park.

A *Walk in the Park*

Follow the Glow to Grand, Graceful Balboa Park, San Diego's Remarkable Culture Heart

Balboa Park, named for Spanish explorer and conquistador Vasco Núñez de Balboa, is stepping out of the shadow cast by such celebrated greenswards as San Francisco's Presidio and Boston's (considerably smaller) Common. Climb the seven stories of the Museum of Man's California Tower—which doubled as Xanadu in the 1941 film *Citizen Kane*—and you will gaze out over some 1,200 acres (485.6 ha) spread across three parallel mesas. Bikers, joggers, and downward-doggers crowd the landscape. Look for the century-old Moreton Bay fig tree (trunk girth more than 490 feet/149.4 m), then swivel to take in the San Diego Zoo, home to clouded leopards and other vulnerable species. Walk Balboa Park's paths, and you'll encounter the bronzed statue of Castilian nobleman El Cid, south of the San Diego Museum of Art. The museum is one of 17 cultural institutions here, many housed in Spanish-colonial palaces built in 1915 and 1916, when Balboa Park hosted the epic Panama-California Exposition, drawing more than two million to celebrate what became a coming-out party for the park and the growing city of 50,000. Other, more recent museums include the San Diego Automotive Museum, and the forthcoming Comic-Con Museum (Hello, Spidey! Leia! Mr. Spock!).

I've come to find out how Wonder Woman will fit into what serves as the West Coast's Central Park. Entering the premises by Cabrillo Bridge feels like stepping back in time to Seville, Spain. Ornamented towers and mosaic domes bask in sunshine; arched walkways lead to hidden Moorish gardens. Stucco reliefs of famed Spaniards line the walls of El Prado, a promenade of more than a dozen buildings erected for the 1915 exposition, some of which weren't intended to be permanent. Lobbying by locals, however, has encouraged the city to invest millions to preserve them.

The El Prado complex is a top attraction, along with the San Diego Zoo, acclaimed for its pioneering conservation programs. But as I explore the farther reaches of this expanse of steep mesa valleys, hiking trails, gardens, and dog parks, I discover plants and trees—orchids, palms, bonsai, cacti—from six continents, organic remnants of century-old bravado that demonstrates how pretty much anything can grow in San Diego.

I gravitate to the intricate facade of the San Diego Museum of Art, established in 1925. This evening the action is in its courtyard restaurant, Panama 66. I join the patrons sipping craft beer and eating grilled panini as a quintet of teens plays Freddie Hubbard songs from the early 1960s. The music is good—like, really good.

The next morning, I spring for a multiday Explorer Pass to pop into as many of the park's museums as I can. At the Automotive Museum I see a motorcycle that stuntman Evel Knievel revved up in the 1977 film *Viva Knievel!* I browse little magazines filled with quirky 1950s art at the San Diego History Center. And in the Museum of Us, I read placeholders explaining that missing baskets and pots have been "decolonized" to San Diego's original inhabitants, the Kumeyaay.

My favorite is the San Diego Natural History Museum, which won the museum world's equivalent of an Oscar in 2016. I see why at the "Coast to Cactus in Southern California" exhibit, where I pause on a bench near a tent. Within minutes the silhouettes of two children appear, projected on the tent. As wildlife images and sounds scroll past, one of the silhouettes asks "What was that?" The second answers *"Silencio!"* Here, near the border with Mexico, no translations are offered, nor needed.

Ambling beyond El Prado, I check out cacti, ocotillo, and agave plants at the Desert Garden, then arrive at a barrel-shaped former water tower. Converted in 1996 into the World-Beat Cultural Center, it shouts its existence with colorful murals that represent indigenous figures around the world.

The following day takes me to sloping Florida Canyon, between the park's central and east mesas. I walk a mile (1.6 km), pausing at cactus blooms and to let a lizard pass, before arriving at the Spanish Village Art Center, a 1930s collection of stucco cottages near El Prado. Organized around a courtyard made of tiles painted salmon pink to mint green, the cottages house 37 art studios and galleries. Purple blooms pop from jacaranda trees; eucalyptus trees peek over the arched entryway.

I head to the Prado at Balboa Park restaurant where I order Kobe beef sushi. I'm fueling up to meet park ranger and San Diego native Kim Duclo, who gives tours on Sundays.

What does Duclo think about Balboa Park going superhero with Comic-Con? He says it's only natural. "Balboa Park has always been a window and a mirror," Duclo observes. Changing with the changing times is in the park's DNA. As I look around the landscape, I see that this ethos is engaging a new generation with African drum music, comic book heroes—and at least one very busy fog machine.

—**Robert Reid** is a travel writer based in Portland, Oregon, and former editor-at-large for *National Geographic Traveler*.

Hang With the Herd

Assateague Island National Seashore,
Virginia and Maryland, U.S.

The Assateague Island National Seashore, a 37-mile (59.5 km) barrier island shared by Maryland and Virginia, is one of the few places in the United States where you can still see wild horses. The area was made famous by the 1947 Marguerite Henry children's book *Misty of Chincoteague*, which featured the annual Chincoteague Pony Swim, a tradition that has continued every July for more than 94 years.

These tough little horses live in two main herds: one on the Maryland side and one on the Virginia side—also the two entrance points for Assateague: 8 miles (12.9 km) from Ocean City, Maryland, and 2 miles (3.2 km) from Chincoteague, Virginia.

Visitors can access some of the island by paved road, but the rest requires a sand-driving permit or walking or cycling through the sand dunes and unspoiled beaches, alongside marshes and maritime forests. On offer here are kayak tours, bird-watching outings, and camping, always sharing the area with plucky ponies.

It goes without saying that the ponies should be left alone. Their wildness is what makes them—and this place—special. Give them space.

HUB | *Washington, D.C., U.S.; Mid-Atlantic United States*

"WALK OR CYCLE THROUGH THE SAND DUNES, UNSPOILED BEACHES, ALONGSIDE MARSHES, AND MARITIME FORESTS."

A wild horse walks through the grass on the Maryland side of the island.

Boldt Castle sits on Heart Island in Alexandria Bay.

Island Hop

Thousand Islands National Park, Ontario, Canada

Around 10,000 years ago, retreating glaciers carved up the landscape between Ontario and New York, leaving behind a collection of 24 islands and eight tracts of land in the St. Lawrence River. Located approximately halfway between Ottawa and Syracuse, New York, in one of Canada's smallest parks (5,931 acres/2,400.2 ha), this waterway is packed with charming island cottages, historic lighthouses, eclectic dwellings (including two castles), and forested tracks.

Hop on a sightseeing cruise or rent a boat or kayak to self-explore the waterways, either camping in one of the 68 campsites that dot the islands or returning to one of the main towns on either side of the river to tuck up in a B&B or hotel.

For landlubbers, the Jones Creek Trail System features nearly 10 miles (16.1 km) of pathways, while the Mallorytown Landing Visitor Center features information on the park's history.

HUB | *Montréal, Canada; Northeastern United States*

The lighthouse on Rock Island glows pink at dawn.

Spectacular views await on a hike through Tiger Leaping Gorge in Yunnan, China.

Hiking Trails

Hit the trail for offshore views along the Amalfi coast,
history among ruins in Bolivia, canyon wonderlands in China, and much more.

1. MOUNT OLYMPUS, GREECE

You can hike the Greek gods' old stomping grounds on the nation's tallest mountain (now a UNESCO Biosphere Reserve) if you've got a couple of days. But no matter how well you remember your Greek mythology, be sure to book a knowledgeable guide.

2. PATH OF THE GODS, AMALFI, ITALY

Of course, Greek mythology would be rather dull if the gods had stuck to Mount Olympus. To retrace their Amalfi-based mission to save Ulysses from the offshore Sirens, do this stunning day hike along the coast and down to Positano. The point-to-point trail takes about two hours to finish, one way, but factor in time to take in the breathtaking scenery and snap a few pictures.

3. RIO CELESTE, COSTA RICA

For another variation on the divine, take a jungle-shrouded trail through the Tenorio Volcano National Park to this cascading river of surreal blue. According to local lore, God used the same paintbrush for the heavens and the water here. Make note: For conservation reasons, swimming inside the park is strictly prohibited.

4. ICO ISLAND, AZORES, PORTUGAL

Of the countless trails that lace this stunning Portuguese island group, the most epic snakes up the nation's tallest mountain: Mount Pico. Allot a full day, and bring a camera with an empty memory card. The views, which include other islands, are unreal.

5. LAUTERBRUNNEN, SWITZERLAND

There's almost no bad hiking in the Swiss Alps. But the largest glacial valley, ringed by 72 waterfalls, dazzles even by local standards. To see for yourself in a day, trek from Lauterbrunnen to Mürren.

6. TIGER LEAPING GORGE, CHINA

This famously deep and dreamy river canyon starts outside Lijiang and is one of China's best treks. You could finish in one (long) day, but given the guesthouses along the trail, the two-day version is worthwhile.

7. BOILING LAKE, DOMINICA

Volcanic, lush, and crisscrossed by trails, Dominica is hiking heaven. The signature day trek, and one of the island's toughest, cuts through the jungle to this bubbling, steaming, and utterly surreal lake (actually a flooded fumarole). The hike takes three to four hours, one way.

8. ISLA DEL SOL, BOLIVIA

The mythic birthplace of the Inca—and home to the sun god Inti—this island in Lake Titicaca is dotted with ruins. So the hiking isn't just breathtaking (though at 13,000 feet/3,962 m, it is that) but also totally fascinating.

9. SPRINGER MOUNTAIN, GEORGIA, U.S.

Part of the Blue Ridge Mountains, this peak near the famed Amicalola Falls marks the beginning (or end) of the Appalachian Trail. After a weekend of hiking here, don't be surprised if you want to complete the trail's full 2,190-mile (3,524.5 km) thru-hike.

10. VOLCANOES NATIONAL PARK, RWANDA

A doable weekend trip from Kigali, these lush mountains are home to the nation's biggest tourism draw: mountain gorillas. Booking a guided trek is required to hike into the gorilla territory. On your visit, you can also participate in golden monkey tracking and visit primatologist Dian Fossey's tomb.

"A SCALLOPED COASTLINE OF ORANGE-SAND BEACHES"

Cruise the Coastline
Abel Tasman National Park, New Zealand

New Zealand's smallest national park (87 square miles/225.3 sq km) is its most popular for two reasons. The first is convenience: Located 40 miles (64.4 km) from the town of Nelson (by flight or ferry) on the northwestern tip of the South Island, Abel Tasman is easy to get to and easy to explore.

The second reason is more compelling: You'd be hard-pressed to find a more colorful and charismatic corner of the planet. Abel Tasman is a scalloped coastline of orange-sand beaches washed with the jade green Tasman Sea. Strange granite formations like Split Apple Rock (a granite boulder resembling a cleanly cleaved apple) rise up along the coastline, which is fringed by black beech forests that ring with the metallic birdsong of local species like tui and bellbirds.

For more than 500 years, Māori made their home in this area before Dutch explorer Abel Tasman, the park's namesake, put the park on the map. Now Abel Tasman National Park welcomes visitors to explore on foot or by water.

Kayaking is one of the best ways to nose around the coves and secluded beaches that stud the coastline. Rent a kayak or join a tour (half-day up to three days) to learn more about the history and heartbeat of the park.

Walkers can choose to hike all or sections of the 32-mile (51.5 km) Abel Tasman Coastal Track, one of New Zealand's Great Walks. If you have more than a weekend (three to five days) at your disposal, the track is a one-way, undulating ribbon that follows the coastline, passing remote lodges, huts, and campsites. (Book well in advance, especially in summer.) Or take a water taxi to a drop-off point and hike a section of this coastal paradise for shorter trips.

By land or sea, this New Zealand gem is a weekend away to remember.

HUB | *Wellington or Nelson, New Zealand*

Hikers make their way along Waiharakeke Beach.

A red squirrel finds food in Cairngorms National Park.

Go Absolutely Wild
Cairngorms National Park, Scotland

Windswept and russet, untouched and untamed, the Scottish Highlands are a place of mysterious melancholy and beauty fit to burst. Cairngorms National Park, the largest protected area in the British Isles (1,748 square miles/4,572.3 sq km), is the heart of the highlands, located a few hours' drive from the urban centers of Edinburgh and Glasgow and easily accessible by road and rail.

This is a place of paths. From the 10th to the 18th century, the Scottish clan system dominated this area, and remnants of forts, castles, and historic pathways remain. Many people come here to "bag a Munro," hiking a Scottish mountain at least 3,000 feet (914.4 m) high.

If highland hiking isn't your pace, there are plenty of other activities to choose from: cycling, distillery tours, the Highland Folk Museum (setting for many of the scenes from the *Outlander* TV series), and Balmoral Castle, which is open to the public except when Her Majesty is in residence.

HUB | *Edinburgh or Glasgow, Scotland*

Find mountain bike paths on Longside Edge in the park.

Step Into a Painting
Lake District National Park, England

The picture-postcard beauty of England's Lake District National Park has been shared and enjoyed by visitors since this area was first settled at least 5,000 years ago. The Lake District is easily accessible from London (or Glasgow) by car, train, or bus. Walkers and cyclists enjoy more than 2,175 miles (3,500 km) of public right-of-way, like the Haystacks high fell walk through the area of Buttermere. Follow a footpath past two tarns to a view overlooking Herdwick sheep–grazed slopes that are carpeted with bluebells in the spring. Or try the Bowness walk in Windermere, which is suitable for families, leading to the summit of Brantfell. The adventurous can tackle Scafell Pike, England's highest mountain (3,208.7 feet/978 m), and one of the more than 150 "peaks" in the area.

Don't miss a visit to the Wordsworth Museum and Dove Cottage, the former storybook home of writer William Wordsworth, who published *Guide to the Lakes* in 1810, one of many creatives who have found inspiration here.

HUB | *London, England; Glasgow, Scotland*

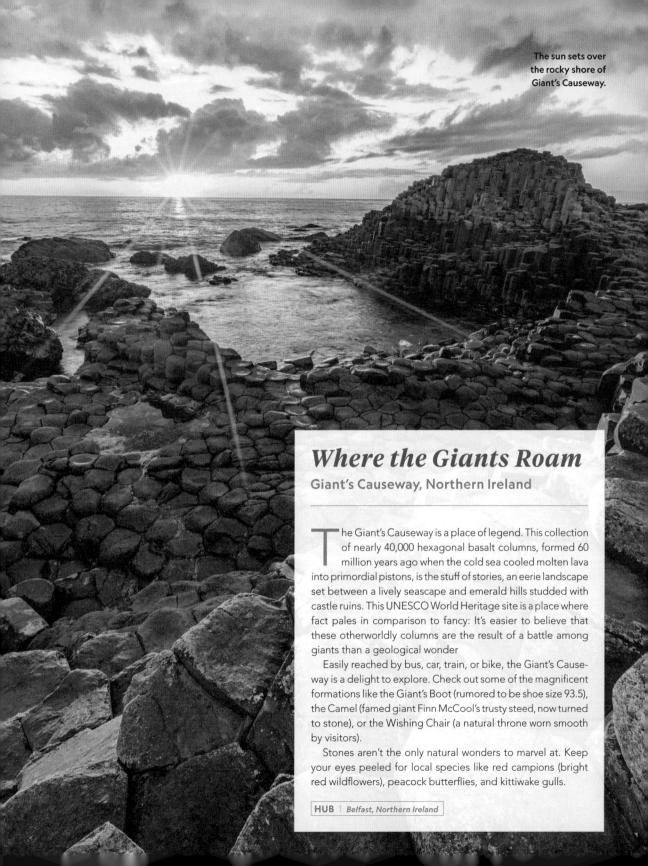

The sun sets over the rocky shore of Giant's Causeway.

Where the Giants Roam

Giant's Causeway, Northern Ireland

The Giant's Causeway is a place of legend. This collection of nearly 40,000 hexagonal basalt columns, formed 60 million years ago when the cold sea cooled molten lava into primordial pistons, is the stuff of stories, an eerie landscape set between a lively seascape and emerald hills studded with castle ruins. This UNESCO World Heritage site is a place where fact pales in comparison to fancy: It's easier to believe that these otherworldly columns are the result of a battle among giants than a geological wonder

Easily reached by bus, car, train, or bike, the Giant's Causeway is a delight to explore. Check out some of the magnificent formations like the Giant's Boot (rumored to be shoe size 93.5), the Camel (famed giant Finn McCool's trusty steed, now turned to stone), or the Wishing Chair (a natural throne worn smooth by visitors).

Stones aren't the only natural wonders to marvel at. Keep your eyes peeled for local species like red campions (bright red wildflowers), peacock butterflies, and kittiwake gulls.

HUB | *Belfast, Northern Ireland*

Unique rock formations are found throughout Theodore Roosevelt National Park.

At Home on the Range

Find Your Corner of Wild in North Dakota's Theodore Roosevelt National Park

I'm drawn to U.S. national parks for many reasons, none unusual, all deeply meaningful. In a world where wildlife is disappearing, where open space is scarce, where noise is ubiquitous and natural beauty and tranquility are hard to come by, places like Theodore Roosevelt National Park represent respite and refuge, a balm for modern life.

For me the vastness of the Dakota horizons, the green of the grass in June, the emptiness of the landscape are utterly thrilling, heart-expanding. Driving scenic byways in the park's two big sections, the South and North Units, hiking their trails, gazing out at smooth prairies yielding to barren escarpments and striking sandstone formations, I exult in the park's grandeur.

It's possible to make the 36-mile (58 km) Scenic Loop Drive through the South Unit of Theodore Roosevelt National Park in less than a couple of hours, take in the views, and move on. But the route, the land, the views, all beg for a slow pace, akin to that of the languidly flowing Little Missouri River, which meanders through the park and its small gateway town of Medora.

My first morning stop: the South Unit Visitor Center. Right behind the visitors center I find Roosevelt's cabin, called the Maltese Cross Cabin, relocated from its original site south of here. I'm moved when I see the small writing desk where Roosevelt wrote several of his books during his Dakota time and a trunk marked with his intials, "T.R."

I motor through Cottonwood Campground, a space shaded by cottonwood trees bordering the Little Missouri River, known hereabouts as the Little Mo. I pause at Scoria Point Overlook to observe some literally scorched earth. Scoria is a red-rock striation that occurs when coal beds in the badlands are torched by a lightning strike, causing them to burn, often for years; the sediment that tops the coal turns red from oxidation of iron. Farther along, I set off on the Boicourt Overlook Trail and soon reach a promontory that casts out over the park's rolling-hills-and-badlands terrain before quickly narrowing to a ridge, then to a skinny path that drops steeply down three sides. I continue my exploration along the Jones Creek Trail. Like me, this trail has no particular destination; it will be as much meditation as hike. Meadowlarks flit around me, frogs blurt from still pools in the creek, and dark-eyed juncos trill from clusters of junipers—perfect examples of the rewards of whimsical travel.

Next stop is the trailhead for a half-mile (0.8 km) hike to the Old East Entrance Station, a small stone hut built by Civilian Conservation Corps (CCC) workers in the mid-1930s. Structures commissioned under this jobs program created by President Franklin Roosevelt dot the national parks. Here its work shows in superb stone craftsmanship, with huge sandstone blocks, quarried by CCC men, neatly fitted into walls.

Back on the road, I come upon my first bison. Several hundred roam the open range in both the South and North Units of the park, showing up where they please and holding up traffic at will. I think I ultimately encounter all of them. More than half a million bison (including a number that reflect crossbreeding with cattle) now live on North American ranges, thanks in large measure to the early conservation efforts of bison hunter Teddy Roosevelt.

One morning, I join ranger Erik Jensen and a group of about 20 visitors for a hike through what is believed to be the third largest aggregation of petrified wood in the United States. A visitor in our group, Marlene Young, of Minneapolis, is such a parks fan that she hosted a viewing party the night Ken Burns's *National Parks* documentary series debuted. "I know this is the same sky as other places, but it's just so big here. That's what I love. That's what I came for," she says.

The petrified forest—really the fossilized remains of fallen tree trunks—lies in rugged badlands in the western part of the South Unit. Accessible by dirt road, the petrified forest itself is roadless. At one point, ranger Jensen invites us to sit and listen. To nothing. A breeze, a swish of prairie grasses, our heartbeats.

When the long summer day finally yields to a moonless night, I join another group of campers and telescope-toting docents for a ranger-guided, no-flashlights-allowed walk to "see the sky as Theodore Roosevelt saw it." Forks of lightning stab the horizon, but overhead the sky remains jet-black clear. We watch the Milky Way appear, and gaze through the park telescopes at a showy Saturn, a half Venus (it has phases), and distant nebulae.

In Theodore Roosevelt National Park I still can draw inspiration from its boundless spaces, stare into its starry skies, sit for hours, and hear only the rustle of its prairie grasses. May this park inspire all of us to appreciate what we have, and motivate us to do what we must do: love our parks, fund them, and preserve them forever.

—**Robert Earle Howells** is a contributing writer to National Geographic's *Guide to the National Parks.*

Where Wild Things Are

Chobe National Park, Botswana

A short flight into Kasane, a tiny town tucked in between the borders of Namibia, Zambia, and Zimbabwe, lands you at the doorstep of Chobe National Park in northern Botswana, one of the most convenient bases for safaris (and an easy day trip to Victoria Falls, page 606). Once here and settled in your accommodation, you can participate in sunrise or afternoon game drives, sunset river cruises, and any number of wildlife-watching activities.

Located on wildlife-attracting Chobe River, which is bordered by forests of mahogany and teak as well as grassy floodplains, Chobe National Park is home to one of the largest herds of free-roaming elephants in Africa, as well as Cape buffalo, giraffes, hippos, and lions. More than 15 species of antelope can be found here, including rare semi-aquatic species like red lechwe and puku, as well as 440 species of bird, including Egyptian geese, sacred ibis, and carmine bee-eaters.

> "CHOBE NATIONAL PARK IS HOME TO ONE OF THE LARGEST HERDS OF FREE-ROAMING ELEPHANTS IN AFRICA, AS WELL AS CAPE BUFFALO, GIRAFFES, HIPPOS, AND LIONS."

HUB | *Gaborone, Botswana; Harare, Zimbabwe*

An African bullfrog surfaces in a lake in Chobe National Park.

Chitwan, a former royal hunting ground, became Nepal's first national park.

The Animal Kingdom

Chitwan National Park, Nepal

Only a stone's throw (44 miles/70.8 km) from the vibrant crowds of Kathmandu, Chitwan National Park is a world apart, a lush jungle surrounded by farms, cut through with a lazy river that shimmers under foggy sunrises and pink sunsets. This UNESCO World Heritage site was formerly the private hunting grounds of the Nepalese royal family and is now one of the most successful wildlife sanctuaries in the world, home to a steadily growing population of Bengal tigers and one-horned rhinoceroses.

Lodges like Barahi Jungle Lodge make visiting the park easy, organizing airport transfers, as well as wildlife game drives, nature walks, and river excursions, all of which are good ways to spot the 68 species of mammals (including sloth bears and leopards), 56 species of reptiles and amphibians, and the more than 544 species of birds. Don't pass up a cultural performance of the local Tharu people.

HUB | *Kathmandu, Nepal*

A great hornbill takes flight in the park.

"ALL TRAFFIC CENTERS
AROUND DENALI'S
ONE ROAD."

The Roof of America

Denali National Park & Preserve, Alaska, U.S.

D enali National Park is 6 million acres (2.43 million ha)—larger than the state of New Jersey and crowned by the roof of North America, the 20,310-foot (6,190.5 m) Denali. A lonely ribbon of road is the only permanent built structure in an undomesticated expanse of taiga forest, tundra, and glaciers (which cover 1 million acres/404,685.6 ha of the park). This is the place to remember what the wild is, why it's important, and how it makes us feel.

Denali was created precisely because of these feelings. Naturalist Charles Sheldon, moved by Denali's beauty and repelled at how the land was being treated by miners and hunters, pushed to preserve the area as a national park in 1917. As time and progress started knocking on Denali's doors, the National Park Service devised an ingenious strategy to manage visitors, including closing all but the first 15 miles (24.1 km) of the park's 92-mile (148.1 km) road to private vehicles. The result is terrain that remains largely untouched since Sheldon's first admirations.

Getting to Denali takes time, but—once there—it's easier to explore than most other national parks. Located halfway between Anchorage and Fairbanks, Denali can be reached by a scenic train or car. Visitors can choose to stay at one of the handful of campsites or private lodges in the Kantishna area, Denali's first permanent settlement and a former gold-rush town, but most stay outside the park in the nearby communities of Healy or Cantwell.

All traffic centers around Denali's one road. Anyone can drive the first 15 miles (24.1 km) of the road, and the rest is open to cyclists, hikers, and guided bus tours, a popular excursion for people wanting information about the park, as well as an unimpeded chance to spot wildlife, the drawing card for this awe-inspiring area: moose, brown bears, caribou, lynx, and Dall sheep, not to mention 130 species of birds, including the golden eagle.

HUB | *Pacific Northwest United States; Western Canada*

Just off Denali's main road lie adventurous hikes with views of Polychrome Pass.

Revel in the Countryside

Snowdonia National Park, Wales

Snowdonia National Park spans 823 square miles (2,131.6 sq km) in northern Wales, encompassing three estuaries and an undulating landscape of mountains and valleys, topped by the 3,560-foot (1,085.1 m) Mount Snowdon (Yr Wyddfa in Welsh), the highest point in Wales and England. Known as an adventure hot spot, Snowdonia is home to more than 26,000 people living in picturesque villages like Beddgelert and Betws y Coed. It's also home to history, with a cluster of medieval castles (four of which—Beaumaris, Conwy, Caernarfon, and Harlech— form a UNESCO World Heritage site) built by Edward I. (The legend of King Arthur is also woven throughout this area.)

Located closer to Liverpool than Cardiff, Snowdonia is easy to reach and easy to get around, thanks to rail lines and bus services. Whether you're looking to summit Mount Snowdon (on foot or via the popular Snowdon Mountain Railway), hop on the Bala Lake Railway around Bala Lake, hike, or surf (Adventure Parc Snowdonia features an inland surf lagoon), Snowdonia has just what you're looking for.

HUB | *London, England; Dublin, Ireland*

> "SNOWDONIA IS HOME TO MORE THAN 26,000 PEOPLE LIVING IN PICTURESQUE VILLAGES LIKE BEDDGELERT AND BETWS Y COED."

The sun sets over Llanddwyn Island with Snowdonia's mountains in the distance.

Original barn structures sit near Jack London's cottage in the park.

The Call of the Wild

Jack London State Historic Park, California, U.S.

Tucked away in the Sonoma Valley, 90 minutes north of San Francisco, is Jack London State Historic Park, once the home of one of America's celebrated authors.

Beginning in 1905, Jack London began acquiring ranches in and around Glen Ellen, financing his parcel of serenity and solitude with proceeds from his best sellers like *Call of the Wild* and *White Fang*. After his death, the property was gifted to California and later declared a state and national historic landmark.

A weekend escape to London's oasis allows visitors to inhale deeply from wildflower meadows and rolling hills, cut through with more than 26 miles (41.8 km) of trails.

The park's main attractions are the historic buildings that dot the landscape, including London's gravesite, The Cottage (London's principal home and workplace), and the ruins of Wolf House, London's dream house, which burned down just before he and his wife were due to move in.

HUB | *San Francisco, California, U.S.; Western United States*

Red Indian paintbrush flowers bloom among green ferns.

The Milky Way shines above Cathedral Rock in Sedona, Arizona.

Ways to See the Stars

Look to the stars at these astrologically minded destinations
where the Big Dipper is just a taste of celestial delights.

1. MAUNA KEA, HAWAII, U.S.

This dormant volcano regularly receives snowfall due to its high elevation—to get here you'll drive from sea level to 14,000 feet (4,267.2 m) above in just two hours—be mindful of altitude sickness. But it's worth bundling up to take in the stars with the help of the resident astronomical research station. The summit area is open from a half-hour before sunrise to a half-hour after sunset.

2. NATURAL BRIDGES NATIONAL MONUMENT, UTAH, U.S.

The first International Dark Sky Park and Utah's first National Monument, Natural Bridges prides itself on skies free of light pollution, offering unobstructed views of the Milky Way. It's possible to see up to 15,000 stars throughout the night in some areas of the monument (by comparison, most urban areas see only 500 stars at night).

3. RHÖN BIOSPHERE RESERVE, GERMANY

The UNESCO-established Biosphere Reserve's residents use sustainable outdoor lighting to keep their view of the Milky Way and the Andromeda galaxy pristine. A Dark Sky Reserve, it is nicknamed the "land of endless horizons."

4. CHERRY SPRINGS STATE PARK, PENNSYLVANIA, U.S.

Though it's named for its black cherry trees, this park is actually best known for its star parties, where astronomers from around the world gather for a meteor shower every August.

5. MONT-MÉGANTIC, CANADA

The world's first International Dark Sky Reserve offers public access to its ASTROlab observatory and hosts astronomy nights for visitors. Don't miss the annual Astronomy Festival , held every summer.

6. ZSELIC NATIONAL LANDSCAPE PROTECTION AREA, HUNGARY

At the Zselic Starry Sky Park, you can get naked-eye views of the Triangulum Galaxy on clear nights. The park also offers full-dome movies in the planetarium and nightly guided tours.

7. PIC DU MIDI DE BIGORRE, FRANCE

NASA scientists studied the moonscape from Pic du Midi, where a cable car takes you to a mountaintop observatory that offers stargazing with astronomers and overnight stays.

8. SEDONA, ARIZONA, U.S.

The red-rock landscape of this desert town has earned the International Dark-Sky Association's Dark Sky Community label for low light pollution. Gaze upon the stars from a night hike or spot the Whirlpool galaxy through a telescope. Take an "Evening Sky Tour" for a guide to stars, led by professional astronomers using state-of-the-art telescopes.

9. AORAKI MACKENZIE INTERNATIONAL DARK SKY RESERVE, NEW ZEALAND

This glacier-studded park is home to Sir Edmund Hillary Alpine Centre and Planetarium, which offers tours that include views of the Milky Way, the Southern Cross, and Alpha Centauri from its telescopes. The reserve honors the land's Māori ancestry, integrating modern astronomy with the culture's traditional star lore.

10. DEATH VALLEY NATIONAL PARK, CALIFORNIA, U.S.

Just two hours from Las Vegas's neon lights, Death Valley is one of the world's largest International Dark Sky Parks. Visit during the twice-a-month astronomy events or the annual Dark Sky Festival.

Find Solitude & Fossils

Yoho National Park, British Columbia, Canada

Yoho is roughly one-fifth the size of neighboring Banff National Park (which is only an hour's drive over Kicking Horse Pass) with a fraction of the crowds. However, Yoho packs the same breathtaking punch: With more than 25 peaks towering above 10,000 feet (3,048 m), turquoise glacial lakes hemmed in by pine trees, and thundering waterfalls, it's easy to understand how Yoho—a Cree word for "awe"—got its name.

Although the 250 miles (402.3 km) of trails attract plenty of hikers and outdoor enthusiasts (including snowshoers and skiers in the winter), the Burgess Shale fossil bed is the park's real draw. Take a guided hike to this UNESCO World Heritage site, a record of one of the earliest marine ecosystems and a window into life 500 million years ago. There are different hiking options—from challenging with steep elevation gains to more family oriented—that lead to the remnants of an ancient sea. Standing on a hillside overlooking turquoise lakes and stands of pines, you can pick up and study a rock embedded with not only the bones but the innards of ocean creatures.

HUB | *Western Canada; Pacific Northwest United States*

"YOHO PACKS A BREATHTAKING PUNCH WITH MORE THAN 25 TOWERING PEAKS, TURQUOISE GLACIAL LAKES HEMMED IN BY PINE TREES, AND THUNDERING WATERFALLS."

Paddling excursions await visitors to Yoho National Park.

A kayaker passes floating icebergs in Torres del Paine's Lake Gray.

Lean Into the Wind

Torres del Paine National Park, Chile

Torres del Paine is one of the world's wonders: Granite teeth of mountains spike vertically above tourmaline-colored glacial lakes, while Andean condors sweep across steppes. This is wilderness undisputed, a UNESCO Biosphere Reserve containing four unique ecosystems.

It used to be a trek-and-a-half to reach Torres del Paine, but now ambitious travelers can spend a weekend. Take a day hiking to the Base of the Towers, one of the most popular treks in the area, part of the famous W circuit, with a steady ascent leading to views of massive granite mountains piercing the clouds.

Or take a boat tour of the iceberg-studded Grey Lake, which allows you to see gigantic ice formations up close. The adventurous can choose to kayak the ice-strewn lake, a special and unparalleled experience.

Whatever you choose, end the day with a pisco sour in Puerto Natales, the nearest town to the park.

HUB | *Santiago, Chile; Buenos Aires, Argentina*

An Andean condor flies over Torres del Paine.

The Eluanbi Lighthouse on the southernmost point of Taiwan

Hike, Surf & Scuba
Kenting National Park, Taiwan

Located on the southern tip of Taiwan, Kenting National Park is a surprise collection of landscapes: deep cuts of gorges, windy cliff-top walks, butterfly-laden forested areas, coral gardens, and some of the prettiest beaches in the world, all bordered by a popular resort village.

This upthrusted coral reef is now green terraces, rugged cliffs, and the occasional tooth of a mountain, bordered on three sides by a turquoise sea. It's no wonder the area is beloved by hikers, cyclists, scuba divers, surfers, and bird-watchers.

Three of the most popular areas to visit are the Kenting Forest Recreation area (a collection of caves and canyons topped by forests), the Eluanbi Lighthouse (built in the 1880s, it's the area's best-known landmark; the adjacent park with hiking trails and lookout points), and Sheding Nature Reserve (a peaceful area of grasslands and bamboo groves that is home to many species of butterflies and birds).

HUB | *Major Asian Cities*

The Three Sisters and rocky cliff formations stand tall in the park.

Step Out of Sydney
Blue Mountains National Park, Australia

A 90-minute drive from bustling Sydney transports travelers into an entirely different Australia.

Named for the blue horizon cast by forests of eucalyptus trees, the Blue Mountains National Park is a collection of native bushland and impressive rock formations, including the iconic Three Sisters. It is rich in biodiversity and wildlife, with more than 400 animal species and 1,500 plant species, many of them rare and threatened.

The park is a favorite weekend getaway destination for Australians, who make the most out of their unique outdoor backyard. Options here range from picnicking to camping and hiking (87 miles/140 km of trails) to rock climbing. You can also see the sights via mountain bike, cable car, or on the world's steepest passenger railway.

For something truly special, take a guided walk to see Aboriginal rock art or learn more about Aboriginal heritage from one of the cultural centers in the area.

HUB | *Sydney, Australia*

Explore algae-covered rocks through caves within the park.

Deep Underground

Phong Nha-Ke Bang National Park, Vietnam

South of Hanoi and north of Da Nang lies an otherworldly, underworld kingdom: Phong Nha-Ke Bang, a UNESCO World Heritage site in Quang Binh Province. The park is home to one of the most expansive cave systems in the world and contains three of the world's four largest caves, a subterranean ribbon of limestone formations, chambers, and rivers.

In this lush, misted jungle landscape with its bullet-shaped rock formations, you can explore Hang Son Doong, a 2.5-mile (4 km) cave that can reach dimensions of 300 feet (91.4 m) wide and 600 feet (182.9 m) long, large enough to fit a Boeing 747. Or tour caves that were once used by North Vietnamese soldiers to hide from U.S. air strikes during the Vietnam War. (A few bomb craters in the region have been converted to peaceful fishponds.)

Local residents run most of the modest businesses in the area—including guesthouses—which is still wonderfully undiscovered despite its impressive nature.

HUB | *Ho Chi Minh City or Da Nang, Vietnam; Bangkok, Thailand*

"SCUBA DIVERS
WILL FEEL RIGHT
AT HOME."

Underwater Garden

Bonaire National Marine Park, Bonaire

Nature parks exist underwater as well as above. The Bonaire National Marine Park is one of the oldest in the world (established 1979), known for its active management of the island's marine resources. It encompasses more than 6,700 acres (2,711.4 ha) of reefs, mangroves, and seagrass beds, making it a top weekend hop for ocean lovers, especially snorkelers and divers.

Located north of Venezuela and west of Curaçao, the tiny Caribbean island of Bonaire is a hot spot of biodiversity, with more than 340 fish species (including the wondrous frogfish), hard and soft coral (such as delicate stag and elkhorn), and turtles (hawksbill, green, and loggerhead).

Scuba divers will feel right at home. Bonaire's license plates say it all—"Diver's Paradise"—and with more than 100 dive sites to choose from (many of them shore dives), divers won't have any difficulty filling their time on the island. Factor in the one-time entrance fee and required orientation dive, both of which are necessary for the protection of the marine park, and slip into a bathwater-warm (80°F/27°C) paradise.

For nondivers, Bonaire is a snorkeling wonderland, with plenty of sheltered spots to choose from, no matter what the weather is doing and excellent visibility to spot what lies below the waves. Sailing and kayaking are also popular water activities.

Visitors to Bonaire might be surprised to learn that the lushness of Bonaire's garden is underwater rather than above. The island is an arid desert, with wild goats and donkeys roaming through cacti and scrub, while flamingos pause in shimmering pools. Flamingo watching, hiking, or visiting the butterfly farm (which houses insects native to the region) are great ways to spend an above-water afternoon.

Another surprise to visitors might be how easy it is to visit Bonaire: Its Flamingo International Airport receives daily direct flights from around the world.

| HUB | *East Coast or Southern United States; Caribbean islands; Amsterdam, the Netherlands* |

Angelfish swim
past a rope sponge
and diver.

The ruins of Terme di Caracalla
showcase the ornate Roman
spa complex.

Urban Oases

Flora and fauna abound just steps outside (or inside)
the world's most famous concrete jungles.

1. TIVOLI GARDENS, COPENHAGEN

Between its old-timey rides and Romantic-era landscaping, this historic retreat feels as much like time travel as a mid-city break. Go for the nostalgia, and stay for the food courtesy of some of Copenhagen's best restaurants.

2. GARDENS BY THE BAY, SINGAPORE

If Tivoli is a trip to the 19th century, this Singaporean spread is all modern, complete with solar energy–harvesting "Supertrees," self-filtering water features, and an all-important cameo in *Crazy Rich Asians*.

3. BROOKLYN BOTANIC GARDEN, NEW YORK CITY, U.S.

Though a worthy destination year-round, this Brooklyn retreat really brings out the charm during cherry blossom season thanks to the pond-side weeping Higans, the Cherry Walk's frilly Kanzans, and the Cherry Esplanade's dual allées.

4. BARBICAN CONSERVATORY, LONDON, ENGLAND

Better known as the home of the London Symphony Orchestra and the BBC Symphony Orchestra, the Barbican Centre also houses one of the city's largest conservatories. Stop at this tower-top hideaway for a spot of the tropics and afternoon tea.

5. AGRIPOLIS FARM AT PARIS EXPO PORTE DE VERSAILLES, PARIS, FRANCE

At more than 150,000 square feet (13,935.5 sq m) this spread atop a reimagined Parisian cultural center is poised to become the world's largest rooftop farm. Naturally, the on-site restaurant is roof-to-table—each dish paired with dreamy cityscapes.

6. BOSQUE EL OLIVAR, LIMA, PERU

Born of a few 16th-century olive saplings from Spain, this now-sprawling grove and national monument in the middle of Lima's San Isidro district has become a refuge for birds and serenity seekers alike.

7. TABLE MOUNTAIN, CAPE TOWN, SOUTH AFRICA

Getting from Cape Town to the top of this UNESCO World Heritage site takes a few minutes on the aerial cableway or a couple of hours on a somewhat challenging trail. But the otherworldly flora, fauna, and vistas that await will make you feel like you've traveled light-years.

8. TERME DI CARACALLA, ITALY

Some of the best preserved proof that the ancients also needed their urban oases, this third-century Roman spa complex still lets you soak in serenity, even if you can no longer take the waters amid the tree-shrouded ruins.

9. JARDIN MAJORELLE, MARRAKECH, MOROCCO

Created by the painter Jacques Majorelle—and rescued from demolition by Yves Saint Laurent and Pierre Bergé—this Technicolor dreamscape of lily ponds and sky-scraping palms is the ultimate breather from the buzz of Marrakech.

10. ACROS FUKUOKA PREFECTURAL INTERNATIONAL HALL, JAPAN

Take a Maya pyramid, drop it in the middle of Kyushu's largest city, then carpet the entire 15-story south side with lush gardens and reflecting pools, and you'll start to get an idea of this beloved urban oasis. Inside find an atrium and the Fukuoka Symphony Hall.

A yawning hippo breaks the surface in the Saint Lucia Estuary.

PERSPECTIVE

Durban

Into the Zulu Kingdom

"Ready for complete sensory overload?" asks Dane For-man, a surf-nut videographer with a hipster moustache. He walks me through Warwick Junction, the hectic hub of Durban's market district and what he calls the "buzzing center of South Africa." Roosters on the loose, potatoes by the ton, township music blasting from overloaded lorries, beaded Zulu *isicholo* hats, and nearby, at the Victoria Street Market, Indian spices like "Atom Bomb" make up this multiblock, multiracial mash-up in South Africa's third largest city.

Durbanites don't mind that their sun-drenched coast is overshadowed by Johannesburg to the northwest or Cape Town to the southwest. "We're culturally richer and a bit more out there," says architect Nokuthula Msomi. "You can't just live in your own bubble when cultures as different as the Zulu and Indian are overlapping all around you." Creative social enter-prise is helping to redefine the city in the post-apartheid era. Cargo-container cafés, craft beers, and pop-up green markets have turned "Durbs" into a city on the verge. And in the wilds beyond, "We've got the bush, the 'Berg, and the braai," says blogger Nicola Ashe. Grab your beads and go.

"Rhino on the road!" Four words every safarigoer dreams of that—as poachers mercilessly advance—are becoming as rare as rhinos themselves. Today, however, all that separates us from our endangered object of obsession is 30 feet (9.1 m) of gravel and a sense of awe.

Leopards, with their rosettes, are only occasionally easier to spot than rambling rhinos. The uMkhuze Game Reserve is a vast veld beloved by birders and populated by pachyderms, giraffes, wild dogs, lions, zebras, and busy little dung beetles.

uMkhuze is part of iSimangaliso Wetland Park, South Africa's first World Heritage site, which stretches from the Indian Ocean to interior grasslands. Its name means "miracle and wonder," and it's easy to see why on a sunrise kayak paddle in Lake St. Lucia, Africa's largest estuary. After nearly capsizing in croc-infested waters, I sensed wonder at the miracle of my own survival.

A guided afternoon boat cruise provides safe distance from the hungry hippos. We see giant kingfishers, herons, yellow weavers, and pods of slumbering hippos—dozens of them rest-ing up for nocturnal adventures that keep locals on their toes. "At night we sometimes have hippos walking the streets," says Stacey Venue, our boat captain and guide. "We call them the 'townies'—they're looking for grass to eat."

It takes three hours to drive from Durban to the Drakens-berg, a misty, mountainous region so epic that your mind turns to Middle-earth. Native South African J.R.R. Tolkien was so taken by the cliffs and kopjes (hills) of the range that they inspired his imagined realm. It's easy to see why. At sunrise, rising fog makes "Dragon Mountains," as the Afrikaners called it, resemble a mythical beast rousing from slumber.

Its Zulu name is equally evocative: uKhahlamba, "barrier of up-pointed spears." Southern Berg, the region around the vertiginous Sani Pass, contains a rich repository of rock paintings by the San hunter-gatherers. In the Central Berg, hikers head to Giant's Castle for more than 25 trails. And in Northern Berg, the 3-mile-wide (4.8 km), 3,280-foot-high (1,000 m) Amphitheatre is a supreme rock star. It's so monumental that it nearly conceals another superlative: Tugela Falls, the world's second highest waterfall, a silvery ribbon cascading from the cliff face.

Beach-bound Durban is considered one of the world's art deco capitals, but locals are more likely to see their city as an urban jumble than an architectural gem. The buildings don't end at the beach; they just take a sandier shape. Seaside Michelan-gelos sculpt sports cars, crocodiles, and Nelson Mandelas in the sand along the Golden Mile, a 4-mile-long (6.4 km) promenade that runs south from the Umgeni River to Durban Harbour. Revitalizing this strand democratizes the city's shoreline from dawn (when the surfers arrive) to dusk (when families stroll).

"The river is our laundromat, old men have three wives, and there are chickens in the yard. You can see all this yourself—it's what I mean by living villages," says Thabo Mokgope, a guide who specializes in cultural tours to the tribal lands around Durban. The Zulu are South Africa's largest ethnic group and their com-munities, ranging from farm settlements to dense townships, are scattered throughout KwaZulu-Natal's Valley of 1,000 Hills.

From a car window, you see rolling green hills and dusty red roads, children in uniforms marching home from school, and beehive huts called iQhugwane—traditional homes that often sit beside brick houses. But walking through a Zulu settlement is an immersion that bridges experiential and cultural divides. Mokgope points out the hues of the homes. "Color is how we express ourselves," he says.

—**George Stone** is the executive editor of travel for National Geographic.

The aurora borealis dances above an Abisko campsite.

Above the Arctic Circle
Abisko National Park, Sweden

Abisko National Park is north of the Arctic Circle, about an hour's drive from Kiruna (Sweden's northernmost town and the gateway hub and airport). This permafrost landscape is one of the most northern national parks in the world, known for three things: the northern lights, outdoor adventure, and ice.

One of the epicenters for aurora borealis watching, Abisko trades its 24 hours of summer sunlight (late June to mid-July) for a darkened sky alive with electric greens, purples, and pinks from November through March.

Whether it's under the midnight sun or northern lights, adventure abounds, from dog-sledding and cross-country skiing, to hiking, biking, and camping.

Nearby is the popular ICEHOTEL, a hotel and art exhibition of ice and snow, re-created anew every year, where guests can take guided tours, dine, or even stay in a room of ice, only a 3.5-hour flight from Heathrow Airport during certain months.

HUB | *Stockholm, Sweden; Major Western European Cities*

Palm trees and rocks cover Wadi Ghuweir.

Dash Away to the Desert
Dana Biosphere Reserve, Jordan

Jordan's largest nature reserve is a collection of fantastic rock formations encircled with hearty green shrubs and spectacular sand dunes. Far from being lifeless, Dana is a melting pot of species from the continents of Asia, Europe, and Africa, including the Syrian wolf and the elusive sand cat.

Equally impressive is Dana's cultural heritage. This area has been occupied since roughly 4,000 B.C., and offers enjoyable village stays and cultural experiences unique to this rich area.

The main draw, however, is hiking. The area abounds with trails (both guided and self-guided options), from the circular 0.3-mile (0.5 km) Rummana Campsite Trail, which is ideal for bird-watching, to the 5-mile (8 km) White Dome Trail, which passes through the Wadi Dana's impressive escarpments.

Located in western Jordan, an easy drive from multiple major townships and populated by lodges and guesthouses, the blooming desert of Dana makes for an exciting and unusual weekend getaway.

HUB | *Major Middle Eastern Cities*

The Temple of Athena Pronaia at the ancient site of Delphi

Commune With the Gods

Mount Parnassos National Park, Greece

Parnassos National Park, one of the oldest in Greece (established 1938), is a treasure trove of nature, a place of rocky peaks and windswept forests of fir, blackthorn, and cedar. Located a short drive north of Athens, Parnassos is enjoyed year-round, from its wildflower-filled spring to its skiing and snowboarding adventures in the winter.

Visitors come to Parnassos for the flora and fauna (eagles, foxes, peonies, jasmine, and more), the activity (hiking, rock climbing, cycling), and its cultural-historical significance. Mount Parnassos was considered sacred to the gods Dionysos and Apollo, and the Sanctuary of Apollo and Oracle of Delphi—an amphitheater and temple dating back to 1400 B.C.—are located nearby in ancient mountains housed with picturesque villages like Eptalofos and Arachova.

This is a place of time well spent, from the surrounding weathered rocks and trees, to monuments that have stood through the ages.

HUB | Athens, Greece

CHAPTER FIVE

ROAD TRIPS

It's pedal to the metal on these drives through breathtaking landscapes and quintessential cities.

A road cuts through the hills near Loch Ness, Scotland (p. 180).

The stunning Cliffs of Moher edge County Clare.

Ireland's Wild West
Cliffs of Moher to Knock, Ireland

Shannon Airport near Limerick makes an ideal jumping-off spot for a weekend cruise along Ireland's rugged western shoreline. Just an hour away, the Cliffs of Moher offer a jaw-dropping first stop—a 700-foot-high (314 m) scarp that plunges straight down into the turbulent Atlantic. At nearby Doolin, hop a fast ferry (15 minutes) to Inis Oírr, the closest of the Aran Islands, and explore the romantic windswept landscape by horse and cart. Back on the mainland, head across a glaciated karst plateau called the Burren on your way to a first night in Galway. Catch breakfast in Galway's cobblestone Latin Quarter before driving out to Connemara National Park and its 4,900 acres (2,000 ha) of pristine coastal mountains, bogs, grasslands, and forest. Stroll the Victorian garden at Kylemore Abbey, visit a working sheep farm, or take a guided horseback ride on a casual afternoon drive to Ireland West Airport in Knock and your flight home.

HUB | *Limerick or Galway City, Ireland*

Into the Clouds
Round-Trip From San José, Costa Rica

Lush tropical forest, a massive lake, and a moody volcano are the focus of a round-trip drive that starts and ends in San José. Costa Rica's Highway 27 drops quickly to the coast and a run along the Pan American Highway through Guanacaste cowboy country. Twisting Route 606 takes the road trip back into the highlands and the Monteverde Cloud Forest Biological Reserve. Inside the reserve, trails and boardwalks take visitors through an incredibly biodiverse park that harbors more than 400 bird species, including the legendary quetzal. From Monteverde, rural Routes 606 and 145 lead to Tilarán and Lake Arenal. Linger along the shore for swimming, fishing, and boating, or cruise the lake's north-shore highway to Arenal Volcano National Park. The mountain last blew its top in 1998, and the summit is closed to visitors, but there are hiking trails across the lava fields, hot springs stoked by underground magma, and white-water rafting on local rivers. Return to San José via route 4 or 702.

A resplendent quetzal perches on a tropical tree.

HUB | *San José, Costa Rica*

Epic Wonders

The Golden Circle, Iceland

Iceland's capital city, Reykjavik, is the launchpad for a weekend jaunt through the country's epic natural and human wonders. The trip kicks off with a one-hour drive along national highways 1 and 35 to the Kerid Crater and its stunning aquamarine lake. Route 35 continues to thunderous Gullfoss (golden falls), which tumbles 105 feet (32 m) into a narrow chasm, almost as if it's being swallowed by the Earth. Round off day one at the Haukadalur geothermal field with its array of mud pots, hot springs, steam vents, and gushers, including the Strokkur Geyser that explodes every 10 to 15 minutes.

After a night in a nearby town like Geysir or Laugarvatn, spend the second day exploring Þingvellir National Park. Located at the fault-line juncture of the North American and Eurasian tectonic plates, the park offers incredible geology (and a chance to scuba dive between two continental plates). But it also preserves the location where the Althingi (Iceland's parliament) convened during Viking times through 1800. Complete the circle with a one-hour drive back to Reykjavik.

HUB | *Reykjavik, Iceland*

Find the Oxarafoss waterfall in Þingvellir National Park.

"THE CAVE ROOF GLITTERING WITH MILLIONS OF GLOWWORMS"

Close Encounters of the Kiwi Kind

North Island, New Zealand

From heli-skiing to bungee jumping, New Zealand's South Island is renowned for outdoor adventure. But the North Island also packs quite a punch, with much of the adrenaline-pumping activities the country is known for located within an easy two- or three-day drive from Auckland.

Literally dive into the weekend by bungee jumping off the Auckland Harbour Bridge from a platform poised 130 feet (40 m) above the surface. Stretch your arms and touch the salty ocean water before bouncing up and down beneath the colossal span.

Change into dry clothes (temporarily) and drive three hours south to Waitomo and its flooded caverns. Disappearing through a narrow slit in the surface, you hike a narrow passage in chest-high water to an underground beach where you slip onto inner tubes and float down a subterranean river, the cave roof glittering with millions of glowworms.

It'll be dark by the time you reach your lodging at Lake Rotorua. Get a good night's sleep because there's plenty to raise your heartbeat on day two: rolling down a mountain in a "zorb" (a giant translucent ball), racing an aerodynamic "shweeb" (single-person monorail pods) at Velocity Valley, or jet-boating on the Waikato River.

It's not all fast and furious. Rotorua is also a great place to learn about Māori culture and view a *haka* war dance performed on a traditional rugby field. Visitors can soak their weary muscles in thermal pools, learn how to shear a sheep at the Agrodome, or view one of those strange-looking kiwi birds at the National Kiwi Hatchery.

Those who stretch the weekend into three days might consider a white-water rafting trip down the Kaituna River—including the world's highest commercially rafted waterfall (23 feet/7 m)—mountain biking the old-growth Whakarewarewa Forest (aka the Redwoods), or climbing Mount Tarawera, an active volcano that last erupted in 1886.

HUB | *Sydney, Australia; Auckland, New Zealand*

Glowworms light
the ceiling of
Waipu cave.

A stainless steel sculpture
by Jaume Plensa
at the 2015 Biennale

Music, Movie & Art Festivals

From the star-studded red carpet of Cannes to laid-back listening at Splashy Fen, these festivals earn five stars.

1. CANNES FILM FESTIVAL, CANNES, FRANCE

Every May, A-list movie stars and filmmakers gather to celebrate the finest art house films. Enthusiasts can watch the opening ceremony live in French theaters or attend screenings of The Directors' Fortnight, which runs parallel with Cannes.

2. SPLASHY FEN, UNDERBERG, SOUTH AFRICA

South Africa's oldest and longest running music festival, Splashy Fen has been dubbed the country's friendliest fete. Set in the foothills of the Drakensberg Mountains, the festivities span four days over Easter weekend in March or April and feature more than 300 local and international artists.

3. AUSTIN CITY LIMITS, AUSTIN, TEXAS, U.S.

Every October more than 130 artists and 225,000 festivalgoers flood Zilker Park in south Austin. Acts ranging from Guns N' Roses to Kacey Musgraves to Billie Eilish take to eight stages.

4. JAZZ FEST, NEW ORLEANS, LOUISIANA, U.S.

This freewheeling festival has grown to welcome more than 400,000 visitors annually. Spanning 10 days in late April and early May, it boasts 12 music stages hosting unforgettable performances ranging from jazz and Cajun to funk and Caribbean.

5. SUNDANCE FILM FESTIVAL, PARK CITY, UTAH, U.S.

Since it launched in 1978, the Sundance Film Festival has provided a platform to showcase risk taking in American film. Pick a weekend during the fest's 10-day run every January and February to view panel discussions along with original features and documentaries.

6. DALHALLA AMPHITHEATRE, RÄTTVIK, SWEDEN

The Dalhalla amphitheater, which opened in 1995, was built in an abandoned limestone quarry outside the ski resort town of Rättvik. The 4,000-seat arena is renowned for its extraordinary acoustics, and some two dozen open-air concerts are held every summer from June to September.

7. GREAT NORTHERN ARTS FESTIVAL, INUVIK, CANADA

Every July, First Nations artists travel to Inuvik, located two degrees above the Arctic Circle, to celebrate the artistic expressions of their cultures. During a weekend segment of the 10-day festival, there are ample opportunities to meet landscape painters, glassblowers, woodcarvers, and beadworkers.

8. VENICE ART BIENNALE, VENICE, ITALY

The arts take center stage at Biennale, dubbed the Olympics of the Art World. Held every two years, it runs for several months from May to November, giving you your choice of weekends to visit 29 pavilions where foreign nations can showcase the works of their artists.

9. HARBIN ICE AND SNOW FESTIVAL, HARBIN, CHINA

Residents brighten frigid winter days by throwing the world's largest ice festival: It spans nearly 6.5 million square feet (600,000 sq m) with immense ice-and-snow sculptures that have included fully scaled replicas of famous landmarks like the Forbidden City.

10. TELLURIDE FILM FESTIVAL, TELLURIDE, COLORADO, U.S.

With no prizes or red carpets, the cozy fest held every Labor Day weekend is a pure celebration of cinema. Festivalgoers come for the excitement of being a movie's first audience. Classics such as *Brokeback Mountain* and *Moonlight* have debuted at Telluride.

A classic car parks outside the Caliente Tropics Resort in Palm Springs.

California Quest for Quiet

The Search for Nature's Hush on a Southern California Road Trip

'm sitting at an amoeba-shaped resort pool in Palm Springs, and a DJ is blasting Drake to a puddle of swimmers doing more soaking than splashing. I measure 84 decibels. My thoughts are screaming for attention they will not get because I'm buffeted by beats, deafened by the din, drowning in a sea of sound in this hip-hop hot tub. I'm longing for an island of silence. I know I'm not alone.

Sometimes I worry that I've forgotten how to listen—how to explore the audible dimensions around me. How much of my life am I missing when I'm not listening?

So I set out on a sound quest that took me from the drumbeat of civilization to nearly noiseless realms. I did not turn on the radio, though occasionally I sang a song that came to mind. I barely spoke; instead I tried to hear whatever came my way. As a traveler, I know there is beauty in stillness and harmony in silence. My path started with a plane (120 dB) smacking down on a runway in Southern California. Which is where my journey begins . . .

Suspicious minds are wondering what I'm up to, holding a microphone to the house where Elvis and his bride, Priscilla, retreated following their 1967 nuptials. A self-guided drive to celebrity homes has led me to the King's banana-colored boomerang-hooded manor.

Palm Springs is a playground of shape and color, a mid-century marvel of manicured lawns, modernist homes, and poolside saturnalia set within an arid ecosystem that can seem like the surface of Mars. The combination of desert minimalism and architectural daring ushered in an era of domestic idealism.

With design in mind I putter around town, ogling the estates of stars from another era: Marilyn Monroe, Liberace, Frank Sinatra. I wind up at the former estate of singer and talk show host Dinah Shore. At 12:26 p.m. it is only slightly louder than Elvis's house—47 dB, about as loud as a babbling brook. A crow caws and flies buzz as gardeners tend to the grass, perhaps in anticipation of the return of current owner Leonardo DiCaprio.

I head 20 minutes south to Indian Canyons, the ancestral home of the Agua Caliente Band of Cahuilla Indians. I park and hike into Palm Canyon, a shaded oasis with a creek that weaves around boulders and rushes over stones. Kneeling beside the water, I measure 65 dB (a working air conditioner). The sun is bright, and the air is dry. As I step away from the creek, I hear my footsteps on gravel and the occasional flitting of a grasshopper.

Date shakes are to this stretch of desert what egg creams are to Brooklyn or key lime pie is to the Florida Keys—indulgent necessities open to infinite interpretation. Only a cold-hearted road tripper heading southeast toward Indio on I-10 would pass Shields Date Garden without tasting the granddaddy of all date shakes. The site is significant in California agricultural history and a relic from an era when roadside attractions were famous for being famous and worthy of seeing just to say you saw them.

In the garden's café, blenders whir quietly behind a screen (no more than 55 dB) as they whip up vanilla ice cream and crystallized dried date flakes into a concoction that is way too sweet but superdelicious.

I need the sugar for the 45-minute drive past Coachella, Thermal, Mecca, Mortmar, and finally to California's largest lake, the Salton Sea, a saline lake in the Sonoran Desert that formed in 1905 when the Colorado River breached its silt-clogged levees and, over nearly two years, flooded a basin along the San Andreas Fault.

I head toward the largest field of aeolian sand deposits in the Mojave Desert. My route from Landers to Kelso Dunes takes me past Joshua Tree National Park. I turn down a potholed road and stop near the base of a sand colossus that looms like a sleeping camel. There are only about 30 aeolian dunes in the world—mountains that "boom" when sheets of consistently sized grains of sand cascade down a steep surface and rub against stationary sand below. Many factors determine whether a dune will sing: the degree of incline, shape of sand, humidity, wind direction.

I feel a breeze whoosh across the sand and imagine tiny grains of silica dancing. Something starts to resonate. I inhale deeply and feel calm, quieted, happy to be in the middle of nowhere, alone and untethered yet connected to the universe.

My journey began in the desert and ends at the sea, to the music of waves crashing on barnacle-covered boulders, children outrunning the tide, seagulls calling, and my bare feet slapping the sand. I decide to drive a few miles along the Pacific Coast Highway to Newport Beach to return to life.

I thought my sonic quest was about silence, but it's not. It's about remembering how to hear harmonious notes in the world.

—**George Stone** is the executive editor of travel for National Geographic.

Relax on beach hammocks at Key West's Reach Resort.

Key to Key
Overseas Highway, Florida, U.S.

Who needs a boat to explore the world's third longest barrier reef when you can drive much of its length on Florida's Overseas Highway. Spanning 113 miles (182 km) between Florida City and Key West, this southernmost stretch of U.S. Highway One is a popular weekend escape from the metropolitan Miami area.

The action starts in Key Largo, where John Pennekamp Coral Reef State Park offers snorkeling and diving among myriad tropical fish and pristine coral gardens. Islamorada provides a base for visiting historic Indian Key and the botanical wonders of Lignumvitae Key. Spend a couple of hours kayaking the mangroves of Long Key and Curry Hammock before cruising into Key West at the end of the road. Closer to Havana than Miami, Key West feels (and often acts) like a Caribbean island, a vibrant blend of bars, restaurants, shops, and historic sites in a city where offbeat or alternative lifestyles are fully celebrated.

HUB | *Miami, Florida*

The floating Melaka Straits Mosque is illuminated over the sea.

Super Highway
North-South Expressway, Malaysia

Southeast Asia's first superhighway makes it easy to stage a three-day weekend road trip between Singapore and Kuala Lumpur. Completed in 1994, the four-lane toll road starts in Johor Bahru, just across the causeway from Singapore's north shore. From there it's a 205-mile (330 km) cruise (and ca U.S. $10 toll) to Kuala Lumpur through the lush Malaysian countryside. While the old Dutch and British colonial city of Malacca is without doubt the major attraction along the way, the North-South offers plenty of other distractions—premium outlet malls, tasty Malaysian food stalls at the Pagoh Rest Stop, the giant golden Fortune Dragon statue at Yong Peng (exit 242), and the jungle trails of Gunung Ledang Johor National Park (exit 236). Right beside the highway on the southern outskirts of Kuala Lumpur are the new Malaysian Chinese Museum and Mine Wonderland—an amusement park, shopping mall, and health spa fashioned around the flooded crater of what was once the world's largest open-pit tin mine.

HUB | *Kuala Lumpur, Malaysia; Singapore*

Look out to the Pacific from Point Reyes National Seashore.

Bridges, Bays & Bluffs

Highway One, California, U.S.

Big Sur gets all the love, but the stretch of Highway One north of San Francisco is just as awesome, starting with the drive across the Golden Gate Bridge to Marin County. With its art galleries and gourmet eateries, funky little Point Reyes Station is the place for breakfast or lunch before heading off into the wilds of the adjacent national seashore or kayaking Tomales Bay (a sunken part of the San Andreas Fault). Hitchcock fans flock to *The Birds* sites around Bodega Bay before continuing to Jenner at the mouth of the Russian River for wineries and rafting and the old Russian fur trading post at Fort Ross. Arriving in Mendocino, browse the art galleries, hike the bluffs, sample the seafood, and sip some local wine before heading to bed. Explore Fort Bragg the following morning before returning to San Francisco via the redwood groves of Jackson State Forest and U.S. Highway 101.

HUB | *San Francisco, California, U.S.*

> ## "THE EASTERNMOST STRETCH OF THE DRIVE IS BY FAR THE WILDEST."

Coast to Coast Charm
The Garden Route, South Africa

They call it the Garden Route because of the lush vegetation, the native fynbos plants that color so much of South Africa's gorgeous cape region. But this 125-mile (200 km) coastal drive is so much more—an alluring blend of small-town charm and adventure sports, golden beaches and gnarly rainforest trails that makes it an ideal weekend escape from Cape Town or Port Elizabeth.

Mossel Bay anchors the route's western end with shark cage diving, whale-watching cruises, and a legendary Post Office Tree where travelers have been leaving messages for more than 500 years. From there, the Garden Route curls around the coast to George, an old timber town more renowned now for its locally produced wines and craft beers. The route hits the shore again at aptly named Wilderness, with its broad beach, lofty viewpoints, and canoeing on the Touw River through Wilderness National Park.

Farther east are the super-secluded beaches of Goukamma Nature Reserve and Protected Marine Area and funky Knysna, celebrated for its art galleries, craft shops, and seafood eateries (try the oysters at 34 South). Knysna Head bluffs on either side of the harbor entrance make for a short but spectacular coastal hike before heading farther up the coast to Plettenberg Bay and its sandy beaches.

The easternmost stretch of the drive is by far the wildest, a journey through the thick coastal forest of Tsitsikamma National Park with a chance to hit the beach at pristine Nature's Valley or walk a portion of the shoreline's Otter Trail. The highway continues across Bloukrans Bridge and its harrowing bungee jump (709 feet/216 m) to Storms River, where the Garden Route ends. But not without a bang—a side road leads down to the Mouth Trail and a suspension bridge over the churning confluence of river and ocean.

HUB | *Cape Town, South Africa*

Visitors cross a suspended
bridge in Tsitsikamma
National Park.

Fall puts on a full show in Japan's Nara public park.

Autumn Spectacles

Visit these fall fantasy locations to take in the brisk weather and changing colorful leaves in spectacular fashion.

1. PARIS, FRANCE

To see the Palais Royal Garden or Versailles surrounded by leafy extravaganzas of orange and red is to see Paris anew—plus you'll have fewer crowds and cheaper prices. Plan your trip for October or November to catch the city at its most dazzling.

2. U.S. ROUTE 550, COLORADO, U.S.

There's a reason Colorado's Route 550 is called the Million Dollar Highway—the road's tree-lined views, turned fiery orange, red, and yellow come fall, are worth, well, a million bucks. Colorado's fall foliage depends greatly on temperatures, but you can typically time your visit between mid-September and mid-October to catch the leaves at their peak colors.

3. NARA, JAPAN

Japan gets a lot of attention for cherry blossoms in spring, but in autumn, the ancient capital of Nara, just a short train ride from Kyoto, truly blossoms in fall's most beautiful colors. Enjoy the leaf show as you walk the city's plentiful parks, temples, shrines, and gardens. Don't miss the Tanzan-jinja Shrine in the Nara Prefecture. Peak fall colors arrive mid-November, and last until mid-December.

4. FOREST OF DEAN, ENGLAND

Once used as a royal hunting ground, these woodlands—a mix of oak, beech, and chestnut—are worth a hike or bike ride to admire their fall beauty. There are more than 20 million trees across the forest and Wye Valley, so this is a leaf-peeping hot spot.

5. BUDAPEST, HUNGARY

Not only will you find stunning fall scenery in Hungary's most walkable city, you can enjoy the colors in the comfort of mild temperatures above 70°F (21°C) during the day through October. Spot the leaves in the city's beloved parks, including Varosliget, which stretches from Heroes' Square to the Vajdahunyad Castle.

6. GREEN MOUNTAIN NATIONAL PARK, VERMONT, U.S.

It's no secret that Vermont is a leaf-peepers' heaven, but if you're looking for the best immersion into the state's bountiful beauty, head to the Green Mountains for meandering trails. Vermont's trees start to turn in mid-September and last through mid-October, but peak season changes year to year, so be flexible in planning, if you can.

7. JIUZHAI VALLEY NATIONAL PARK, CHINA

At this UNESCO World Heritage site—it's home to nine Tibetan villages—you may just spot Sichuan golden monkeys and giant pandas among the autumn-hued trees.

8. NIAGARA FALLS, NEW YORK, U.S.

The falls are awe-inspiring no matter what time you visit, but set against a world of orange and red trees, the flow will really take your breath away. Peak colors tend to arrive mid- to late October.

9. ZEPHYR COVE, LAKE TAHOE, CALIFORNIA, U.S.

Watch the colors turn from green to amber against Lake Tahoe's striking blue water. For peace and serenity, take in the views of the changing aspen trees from Zephyr Cove, a more secluded spot on the lake.

10. CASENTINESI FOREST NATIONAL PARK, AREZZO, ITALY

One of the largest national forests in Europe, it contains beech trees, oak trees, and hornbeams, the leaves of which begin changing in mid-October. Don't miss the view near "Dante's Comedy" waterfall.

Make a stop at the Leaning Tower of Pisa.

Driving La Dolce Vita
Florence to Pisa's Chocolate Valley, Italy

Life doesn't get any sweeter than Italy's "Chocolate Valley," a region between Florence and Pisa renowned for gourmet chocolate and other artful confections. This drive is a yummy interlude between the world-class art and architecture at either end of the route.

The indulgent weekend starts at Prato's Pasticceria Mannori—renowned for its pralines, brioche, and Seven Veils cake—and continues on to the handmade chocolates of Roberto Catinari in nearby Agliana. Grab lunch in Montecatini Terme (try the fresh pasta or beef dishes at Trattoria da Gina) before diving into the heavenly ice cream at Gelateria Di Serio Filippo and a wellness treatment at one of the city's famous spas. From there, it's just an hour to Pisa. Catch the Leaning Tower at first light before hitting the road again—this time bound for Pontedera and its famed Amedei chocolate factory. Pop into a couple of the local wineries before heading up the Arno Valley to Florence's renowned art museums

HUB | *Florence, Italy*

Highland Highways
Glasgow to Inverness, Scotland

High roads and low roads make up this romp through northern Scotland. Starting out from Glasgow, Highway A82 skirts the western edge of serene Loch Lomond on its way to Glencoe, where the highlands tumble down to the sea. Glencoe National Nature Reserve offers short hikes, historic sites, and landscapes where movies including *Braveheart* and *Rob Roy* were filmed. Ben Nevis—the highest mountain in the British Isles—towers over nearby Fort William. From there, the A82 heads straight up lake-filled Great Glen to Fort Augustus (and its cozy hotels) at the southern end of Loch Ness.

Spend day two combing the water for Nessy (there are plenty of boat tours to join) or dive into shoreline attractions like medieval Urquhart Castle and hiking trails through the ancient Caledonian pines of Glen Affric. In the afternoon, continue along A82 to historic Inverness, where Fort George and Culloden Battlefield (1745) resonate with stories of the final conflict between the English invaders and the Scottish clans.

Urquhart Castle stands guard on the shores of Loch Ness.

HUB | *Glasgow, Scotland; London, England*

From various viewpoints you can take in Norway's stunning fjords.

Fjords & Ferries

Bergen to Trondheim, Norway

Highway E39 between Bergen and Trondheim is considered Norway's most spectacular drive. Best done as a three-day weekend, the route includes abundant bridge and ferry crossings over waterways once ruled by Viking longships. North of Bergen, the route rambles through a landscape spangled with fjords, waterfalls, and glaciers to an overnight stay in Ålesund. With its distinctive Jugendstil (art nouveau) architecture, Ålesund begs a morning stroll before resuming the drive. If you're stretching this into a three-day trip, consider a detour to Geiranger Fjord, a UNESCO World Heritage site. Then catch the ferry across Molde Fjord and a stretch along the incredible Atlantic Ocean Road (Route 64) through a tiny archipelago to Kristiansund and another architectural smorgasbord. The undersea Freifjord Tunnel (3.15 miles/5.1 km) takes the route back to E39 on the mainland. From there, it's about a three-hour drive (including one last ferry) to the international airport in Trondheim.

HUB | *Bergen, Norway*

Enjoy waterfall views at
Watkins Glen State Park.

"WALKWAYS, TUNNELS, AND STAIRCASES CARVED INTO THE GORGE'S SHALE AND SANDSTONE WALLS ENTICE US TO VENTURE UNDER VEILS OF FALLING WATER AND THROUGH DARK CAVES WITH DRIPPING SPRINGS"

PERSPECTIVE

Waterfalls & Wineries

The Finger Lakes in Upstate New York Offers Surprises—From Cascades to Tasting Tours

Adventure comes in every variety in the Finger Lakes region of upstate New York. Home to 11 lakes, 15 state parks, and more than 10,000 acres (4,046.9 ha) of vineyards, it invites weekend wanderers to discover their perfect pairing.

My husband and I find ours at Seneca Lake, the largest and deepest of the Finger Lakes, located in the center of the region. Our weekend begins at Watkins Glen State Park, south of the lake, on the Gorge Trail—a stunning juxtaposition of natural beauty and human ingenuity. Walkways, tunnels, and staircases carved into the gorge's shale and sandstone walls entice us to venture under veils of falling water and through dark caves with dripping springs. Arched stone bridges span Glen Creek as it pours over rocky ledges and plunges into pools, offering views of hidden cascades. This out-and-back trail is only 2.1 miles (3.4 km), but it delivers 19 waterfalls, countless photo ops, and a chance to stand on an ancient sea bottom.

The gorge's otherworldly beauty is balanced by the pastoral panorama of sprawling vineyards and farms along the Seneca Lake Wine Trail—a collection of more than 30 wineries, breweries, distilleries, and meaderies surrounding the lake. Traveling north along the western shore, we discover classics like Glenora Wine Cellars, the first winery to open on Seneca Lake. We sample a flight of award-winning vintages and purchase a glass of Riesling to enjoy on the patio overlooking the crush pad, where the winemaking process begins.

Farther north, Earle Estates Meadery puts a modern spin on mead, aka "honey wine," the world's oldest fermented beverage. The estate pairs its brew with a fascinating view inside the industrious world of an active honeybee hive. At the northwestern end of the lake, Belhurst Castle & Winery, once a speakeasy and casino, blends history and mystery with every sip. Whispered tales of romance and tragedy roam the halls like its resident ghost, Isabella, the opera singer who perished in the secret tunnel beneath the castle that collapsed as she and her lover fled authorities.

For a palate-cleansing change of scenery, we stop at Seneca Lake State Park on the northern shore and picnic beneath the willow trees, watching the stir of activity on the water. Known as the lake trout capital of the world, Seneca lures anglers from miles away. Its expansive surface area is a siren call for boaters of all stripes. And its depths—at points more than 600 feet (182.9 m)—beckon scuba divers to hunt for shipwrecks and sunken barges.

Continuing south along the eastern shore, we arrive at Ventosa Vineyards, home to Italian varietals and spectacular views. Here, a sweeping terrace overlooks rows of grapevines and offers vistas of a sparkling stretch of lake, transporting us to Tuscany. If wine doesn't tickle your tastebuds, travel farther south to Two Goats Brewing, which combines simple brewing techniques, sustainable energy, and sunset views for a beer-tasting experience steeped in a hip atmosphere. A mile (1.6 km) beyond that, Finger Lakes Distilling, the region's first standalone distillery, transforms locally grown grapes, berries, rye, and corn into hand-crafted spirits.

We're almost back to Watkins Glen when a giant staircase of tumbling water, known as Hector Falls, appears out of nowhere on the side of the road and is gone in a blink, like a scenic chaser ending our weekend of waterfalls and wineries with a final splash of splendor.

—**Erika Liodice** is a Sarasota-based writer and author of the novel *Empty Arms* and children's series High Flyers.

Visitors watch the sunset
behind the Twelve Apostles.

Ocean, Country & Soul
The Great Ocean Road, Australia

Australia's coolest coastal drive follows the shoreline of Victoria state on a 150-mile (243 km) wander called the Great Ocean Road, which was built by Australian and New Zealand Army Corps (ANZAC) vets returning from World War I. Around 80 minutes from downtown Melbourne, Torquay anchors the road's eastern end with the Australian National Surfing Museum, plentiful surfboard and beach clothing boutiques, and the legendary break at Bells Beach. At the road's southern extreme, Cape Otway nurtures a wildlife-rich national park, marsupial rescue center, and a historic lighthouse. Farther along are the Twelve Apostles—huge, rocky sea stacks rising from the waves. Study them from beach level, bluff-top trails, or scenic helicopter flights. At the Bay of Islands, the road turns inland for a sprint across the Victoria countryside to Warrnambool, where Flagstaff Hill Maritime Village honors the era when this turbulent shore was called the Shipwreck Coast. It's about three hours back to Melbourne via Camperdown and Geelong.

HUB | *Sydney or Melbourne, Australia*

Reutlingen, Germany, boasts the narrowest street in the world.

Record Breakers

Shortest, tallest, longest, widest—from natural wonders to man-made icons, these record holders should be checked off your bucket list.

1. WORLD'S HIGHEST TIDES, BAY OF FUNDY, CANADA

Canada's Bay of Fundy claims the honor of "world's highest tide" with almost 50 feet (15.2 m) of water separating high tide from low. Both times of day are worth experiencing—especially if you time your visit to a Dining on the Ocean Floor event.

2. WORLD'S SMALLEST PARK, PORTLAND, OREGON, U.S.

Occupying a 2-foot-wide (0.6 m) section of median in Portland, Oregon—where a light pole was supposed to go but never materialized—Mill Ends has been the world's smallest park since the site's official dedication in 1976. The park consists of one tree and is located on the SW Naito Parkway.

3. WORLD'S SHORTEST STREET, WICK, SCOTLAND

A part of Scotland once known as Europe's largest herring port is now home to the world's shortest street. Barely long enough to accommodate the average NBA player (sideways), the 6-foot, 9-inch (1.8 m, 22.9 cm) Ebenezer Place is reason enough to visit Wick. The street has only one address, to the entrance of No. 1 Bistro.

4. WORLD'S NARROWEST STREET, REUTLINGEN, GERMANY

Only 12.2 inches (31 cm) across at its narrowest—and not quite 20 inches (53.3 cm) at its widest—Spreuerhofstrasse is the kind of place you shimmy into for photos on arrival in Reutlingen.

5. WORLD'S STEEPEST STREET, WALES

To anyone who's not Welsh, the world's steepest street is also the likeliest spelling bee disqualifier: Ffordd Pen Llech, which winds through the historic town of Harlech at a 37.45 percent incline.

6. WORLD'S LARGEST GOLD TUB, NAGASAKI, JAPAN

Set in the sort of place that curiosity seekers would visit regardless—a Dutch-themed amusement park in Nagasaki—Huis Ten Bosch's 18-karat basin is an unquestionably dazzling spot for a hot spring soak.

7. WORLD'S LARGEST PIZZA, DALLAS, TEXAS, U.S.

If you—and ideally some friends—want to fuel up for a weekend road trip from Dallas, visit nearby Burleson for the world's largest commercially available pizza: Moontower Pizza Bar's "the Bus," which is 8 feet long and 32 inches wide (2.4 m x 81.3 cm).

8. WORLD'S LARGEST PREDATORY BIRDS, COLCA CANYON, PERU

One of the deepest and prettiest gorges in existence is also home to the world's largest predatory birds: male Andean condors, known to ride the thermal updrafts in Peru's Colca Canyon.

9. WORLD'S LONGEST CONTINUOUS OVERWATER BRIDGE, NEW ORLEANS, LOUISIANA, U.S.

Spanning almost 24 miles (38.6 km), the Lake Pontchartrain Causeway connects the famed NOLA suburb of Metairie to Mandeville, the oldest inhabited spot in St. Tammany Parish.

10. WORLD'S LONGEST OPERATING MOVIE HOUSE, WASHINGTON, IOWA, U.S.

When the State Theatre opened in Washington, Iowa, in 1897, the price of admission started at 15 cents. Things here have changed a bit since then, but amazingly, never the redbrick building's role as a movie theater.

Lake Louise reflects the snowcapped Canadian Rockies.

Rocky Mountain High

Banff to Jasper, Alberta, Canada

Two of North America's premier national parks—Banff and Jasper—are the cornerstones of a scenic drive through the snow- and glacier-topped mountains of Alberta Province. Jump-start the weekend by making the 90-minute drive from Calgary to Banff village. Pamper yourself with a hot springs soak, spa treatment, or gourmet meal before bunking down in one of the town's mountain lodges. Saturday is all about cruising the famed Icefields Parkway, a 144-mile (232 km) drive through the heart of the Canadian Rockies. Savor breakfast at the historic Chateau Lake Louise, before a snow-coach tour to Columbia Glacier and gazing down on the frozen giant from the glass-floored Glacier Skywalk. Then make your way down the Sunwapta River Valley to Jasper Village for a second overnight. From summer hiking and horseback riding to winter skiing and snowshoeing, there's plenty to do around Jasper. End your trip here, backtrack to Calgary (five hours), or cruise Highway 16 to Edmonton (four hours).

HUB | *Western Canada; Mountain West United States*

The Green Coast

Costa Verde, Brazil

South of Rio de Janiero and its celebrated beaches lies an even more spectacular stretch of the Brazilian shore: the Costa Verde (Green Coast). Named for its lush tropical Atlantic forest, the coast flits back and forth between party beaches and popular resort towns, secluded strands and uninhabited islands. The journey along Rodovia 101 between Rio and Santos spans 330 miles (530 km), with plenty of spots along the way to sample the region's boundless sun, sea, and sand. Southbound from Rio, the drive highlights include the sheer granite peaks of the Serra do Mar mountains, the Ilha Grande and other tropical islands, and the lush forest of Serra da Bocaina National Park. With its numerous resorts and seafood restaurants, Angra dos Reis is an excellent place to lay your head—or stretch the road trip into three days with a second night in Ubatuba.

Costa Verde boasts a rainforest beach and small fishing villages.

HUB | *Rio de Janeiro, Brazil*

African Sand Safari

Namib Desert, Namibia

With a modern highway system, scant traffic, and plenty of rental options, Namibia is far and away Africa's best road trip nation. And one of its easiest drives is a weekend road trip to Sossusvlei and the ginger-colored giant dunes of the Namib Desert. Setting out from Windhoek, the trip starts with a cruise down Highway B1 to Rehoboth and a right turn into the unrelenting desert. Just below the Tropic of Capricorn, the Solitaire roadhouse (opened in 1949) makes a great stop for gas and lunch or ice cream before continuing to Sesriem and the entrance to Namib-Naukluft National Park. The main park road meanders through the biggest of the desert's sandhills, including 1,256-foot (383 m) Dune 7, which is as tall as the Empire State Building. Off-roading is verboten, but visitors are free to tackle the dunes on foot. Hot-air balloon safaris provide a bird's-eye view of the remarkable landscape, while desert camps like Little Kulala provide posh overnights.

HUB | *Windhoek, Namibia; Cape Town, South Africa*

A gemsbok antelope climbs the sand dunes.

"THE ROAD LOOPS AROUND THE ENTIRE ISLAND."

American Treasures

Big Island Belt Road, Hawaii, U.S.

Given its insular geography, Hawaii doesn't seem like the most obvious place for a substantial road trip. But there's at least one long-distance highway: the 260-mile (420 km) Belt Road that wraps around the Island of Hawaii (aka the Big Island).

Comprising three state highways (11, 19, and 190), the road loops around the entire island from the Kona Coast on the western shore to Hawai'i Volcanoes National Park and Hilo on the east coast, and then to the north via the old highland town of Waimea.

Start the weekend with a bang by checking into an ocean-front hotel and then taking an after-dark snorkel with the plethora of manta rays that gather in Keauhou Bay each night to feed on plankton.

Rise bright and early the next morning for a guided kayak and snorkel trip beneath the 500-foot (150 meter) cliffs of Kealakekua Bay, where native Hawaiian warriors killed Captain James Cook during a 1779 battle, which is marked by a memorial white obelisk.

The Belt Road continues past coffee and macadamia nut plantations through the Kua region at the island's southern extreme before running up the east coast to Punalu'u Black Sand Beach and an overnight stay in Volcano Village. Devote most of the following morning to Hawai'i Volcanoes National Park, driving through the twisted lava along Chain of Craters Road to constantly simmering Kīlauea Volcano and the picturesque Hōlei Sea Arch.

About an hour up the coast, Hilo offers a vintage art deco downtown and an interesting tsunami museum before the road turns inland through the *paniolo* (Hawaiian cowboy) country that dominates this part of the Big Island. Grab some eats in Waimea (it boasts some of the island's best restaurants, including Merriman's and Fish & the Hog) and gallop the grassy highlands on a guided horseback trip before the downhill drive back to Kona.

HUB | *Honolulu, Hawaii, U.S.; West Coast United States*

Coconut trees thrive
on the black sand beach
in Punalu'u.

Restaurants draw diners to Cimadevilla Street at night.

PERSPECTIVE

Asturias, Spain

With Snowy Summits and Iberian Tradition This Is a Province to Savor

This is a meal I could eat nowhere else, it occurs to me around the seventh course. I'm in the mountains of Asturias, and I've been served a dish of sea urchin and ham that unites the coast and peaks of this northern Spanish province in a single bite.

We're dining at Casa Marcial. Housed in an old mansion, or *casona*, decorated with window boxes and topped by a barrel-tiled roof, the restaurant sits at the top of a winding road in La Salgar, a mountain village that smells of pine. The coast is 6 miles (9.7 km) to the north, as the Asturian wood pigeon flies. But La Salgar remains so deeply embedded in the hilly, heavily forested interior of the region that, I'm told, many of its residents spend their entire childhoods without ever seeing the water.

Most visitors come upon Oviedo—the capital, a compact city of roughly 220,000 residents separated from the slightly larger Gijón by rapidly encroaching suburbs—first. They seek out some of the best pre-Romanesque architecture in the world, 14 preserved buildings, including the tall, narrow, ninth-century palace-church complex of Santa María del Naranco. I make a pilgrimage there as soon as I arrive.

Asturias's two largest cities are polar opposites. Oviedo, like many inland cities, tends to be insular, conservative, overtly polite, and socially inaccessible. Gijón is a port town, working-class, and occasionally profane, but open to the sea and new ideas. Oviedo has an opera house and a full program to fill it. Gijón prefers its series of avant-garde festivals.

The following morning I visit the Museum of the Asturian People, which sits just east of downtown Gijón. It sounds like a Cold War tourist attraction in an Eastern-bloc capital, but actually it's a re-creation of a traditional Asturian village. The grounds include a 17th-century peasant house, a covered alley where the recreational bowling game called *cuatreada* is played, a bagpipe museum (bagpipes are a common musical instrument in Asturias and Galicia), and several of the granaries—called *hórreos*—that are ubiquitous in the area.

Like San Francisco and Scotland, bad weather suits Asturias. I leave Gijón and head east along the coast under a steady drizzle. In August, Ribadesella attracts Spaniards who are desperate for a respite from oppressive heat. In November,

with rain misting a cool morning, it becomes a particularly lovely local fishing village.

Not far away is the Tito Bustillo Cave, site of one of the more remarkable discoveries of the last century. In 1968 a group of amateur spelunkers realized that falling rocks many centuries before had sealed an opening of a cave. They returned with full gear and managed to make their way inside. When they did, they were surprised to discover that one cave opened onto another, and then another. On the walls, they found a magnificent series of Cro-Magnon cave drawings, dating back more than 10,000 years. Another mysterious drawing was made some 30,000 years ago, according to carbon dating.

I stop in the hill town of Cangas de Onís, where a much photographed Roman bridge spans an unhurried stream. From there the next morning, it's a short trip to Covadonga, one of the most historic spots in Spain. You could make the argument that modern Spain began when the advance of the Moors was halted here by the Visigoth nobleman Pelagius, the founder of the Kingdom of Asturias, in 718.

I've visited before, but hadn't taken the time to drive to the lakes above Covadonga in the Picos de Europa (Peaks of Europe) National Park. Now up another winding road I go, bound for those lakes. Trees fall away, and the view opens to a wide sky of cotton ball clouds.

Then I hear bells. They start softly, but soon their metallic jangle has drowned out the car radio. I round a bend and see sheep, what looks like several hundred of them, painstakingly crossing the road in front of a line of stopped cars.

I park and walk into the nearby brush, inhaling air so fresh that it sends a jolt of sharpness into my chest. The spiky peaks of the mountains silently surround me from a distance; all I hear is the din of the sheep bells, sounding like church bells ringing at high noon. Eventually the stragglers get across. I see the cars start to move, but I can't walk back just yet.

I've never been anywhere like this. I don't want to leave.

—**Bruce Schoenfeld** is a travel and food writer whose work has appeared in various publications including *Travel + Leisure, National Geographic Traveler,* and *Food & Wine.*

A kangaroo grazes in Kings Canyon.

The Red Center
Alice Springs to Kings Canyon, Australia

Over a long weekend it's possible to visit two of Australia's most spectacular national parks on a road trip through the Red Center. Starting from the oasis city of Alice Springs, drive the Stuart Highway (B7) and Lasseter Highway (4) to Uluru-Kata Tjuta National Park. Previously called Ayers Rock, the sandstone monolith is sacred to Aboriginal peoples. Climbing was officially banned in 2019, but there are plenty of other ways to explore the park, including hiking and biking tours and ranger-guided activities. After an overnight in Yulara village, backtrack 86 miles (138 km) along the Lasseter to a turnoff (Highway 3) for Watarrka National Park. The park centers on Kings Canyon and its imposing 300-foot (100 m) red-rock walls. Trails lead to the lush Garden of Eden, a secluded swimming hole deep in the canyon. After an overnight at Kings Canyon, head back to Alice Springs on Larapinta Drive (Route 6).

HUB | *Sydney or Melbourne, Australia*

The Land of Fire
Tierra del Fuego, Chile and Argentina

Despite being one of the world's most remote places, the legendary "Land of Fire" at the bottom of South America is easily tackled as a two-day drive. Starting from Punta Arenas, Chile, the journey begins with a ferry across the Strait of Magellan (watch for Commerson's dolphins) and rambles across the pampas to the king penguin colony at Parque Pingüino Rey. The route crosses the Chile-Argentina border at Paso San Sebastián and continues to the city of Río Grande.

The second day unfolds as a gradual transition from coastal grasslands into the forest and snowy peaks around Lago Fagnano. Lunch at one of the bakeries in Tolhuin village before threading Garibaldi Pass and coasting down the gorgeous Valle de Lobos (Valley of Wolves) to Ushuaia. Among the adventures available in the world's southernmost city are glacier walks and forest hikes, wildlife cruises on the Beagle Channel (named for Charles Darwin's ship), and a scenic railroad once used for convict transport.

Find opportunity to explore the massive Martial Glacier.

HUB | *Santiago, Chile; Buenos Aires, Argentina*

Hudson Valley Hooky

Hudson Valley, New York, U.S.

Escape the Big Apple by absconding to the Hudson Valley, a 300-mile (480 km) round-trip with an overnight in Albany. Cross George Washington Bridge and head for Bear Mountain State Park with its panoramic river views. Nearby West Point offers military history, while Storm King Art Center boasts the nation's most impressive array of contemporary outdoor sculptures. Farther up the west bank, old colonial towns like Newburgh and Kingston blend vintage buildings, art galleries, antique ships, and narrated river cruises. Explore Albany on Sunday morning—the 19th-century capitol building is a national historic landmark—before heading back to New York City. Famous names spangle the return journey along the valley's eastern side: Martin Van Buren's home near Kinderhook, Washington Irving and the Poets' Walk, Franklin Roosevelt's Hyde Park hideaway, and the fabulous Vanderbilt Mansion. From Poughkeepsie, it's about a two-hour drive back to the big city on the Taconic State Parkway.

HUB | *New York City, U.S.*

Autumn leaves surround Hessian Lake in Bear Mountain State Park.

Find everything from art to ceramics on sale in Madrid's El Rastro flea market.

Flea Markets

Score thrifty finds working your way through markets from Paris to Madrid, California to Alabama.

1. ROSE BOWL FLEA MARKET, PASADENA, CALIFORNIA, U.S.

An event so popular that people pay for a VIP preview admission (entry time: 5 a.m.), this monthly gathering in Pasadena's national historic landmark stadium has been dubbed the greatest flea market on Earth.

2. MARCHÉ AUX PUCES DE SAINT-OUEN, PARIS, FRANCE

Better known as Les Puces (the fleas)—and having been featured everywhere, from *Vogue* to *Midnight in Paris*—this Parisian staple since the 19th century reportedly houses 1,700 dealers across 750,000 square feet (69,677.3 sq m).

3. CHOR BAZAAR, MUMBAI, INDIA

The scene of many Bollywood productions, Mumbai's famous thieves' market dates back more than 150 years and offers merchandise that dates back even further (along with modern electronics, clothing, and knickknacks).

4. FERIA DE SAN TELMO, BUENOS AIRES, ARGENTINA

In the already bustling San Telmo neighborhood—cobbled and colorful—the Sunday market takes liveliness to the next level as shoppers hunt for vintage treasures among street tango performers and food vendors.

5. SHUK HAPISHPISHIM, JAFFA, ISRAEL

This Shuk HaPishpishim (Hebrew for "flea market") neighbors Jaffa's iconic old city and clock tower. Amid a warren of centuries-old alleys, you'll find everything from antiques to kitsch (and plenty of treats to sustain you through a day of bargaining).

6. GRAN BALON, TURIN, ITALY

Reportedly Europe's largest open-air market, this Turin icon is named for a hot-air balloon that may or may not have taken flight here in the 18th century. You can still balloon over the area (Alps included).

7. THE 127 YARD SALE, ALABAMA TO MICHIGAN, U.S.

All the world may not be a flea market, but most of Highway 127 is. Spanning 690 miles (1,110.5 km) and six states for a weekend every August, "the World's Longest Yard Sale" is a road-tripping thrift seeker's dream.

8. EL RASTRO FLEA MARKET, MADRID, SPAIN

Used books, trading cards, vintage clothes, and all manner of treasured castoffs fill this sprawling, centuries-old open-air flea market, a Sunday must in the historic center of Madrid. If you need to refuel, stop in for a beer and tapas in nearby La Latina, one of the oldest neighborhoods in the city.

9. CHATUCHAK WEEKEND MARKET, BANGKOK, THAILAND

Arm yourself with a coconut shell full of local ice cream and accept that you'll get lost in Asia's largest market—a Bangkok icon—and embrace the dizzying glory. Then bargain to your heart's content for everything from clothing to art made by local painters. Don't miss the food stalls, selling seafoods to sweets—everything you need to energize your bargain hunting.

10. MILNERTON FLEA MARKET, CAPE TOWN, SOUTH AFRICA

This Cape Town favorite is a must for its ocean-side setting and Table Mountain views alone—but the endless local and European vintage finds, plus knickknacks of all kinds, make treasure hunters giddy too.

"ONE OF THOSE RARE
GLOBAL ICONS THAT LIVES
UP TO ALL THE HYPE"

Taj, Tigers & Temples
Agra to Jaipur, India

Many of the ingredients that make India such a fascinating place to travel can be sampled during a 260-mile (400 km) road trip between the fabled cities of Agra and Jaipur. Whether you pilot yourself or hire a private driver, the route provides a kaleidoscopic view of the Rajasthan countryside and several of India's iconic attractions.

One of those rare global icons that lives up to all the hype, the Taj Mahal is best seen (and photographed) in the soft, dreamy light of dusk or dawn before hitting the road—in this case, India National Highway 21 running west from Agra. The first stop is less than an hour away: the phantom city of Fatehpur Sikri. Erected by Akbar the Great in the late 16th century, the red sandstone city was mysteriously abandoned just 40 years after it was built, but most of the magnificent palaces and mosques survive.

Just up the road is Keoladeo National Park, a former royal hunting preserve that's now one of India's best bird-watching spots (364 species) as a stop on the migration route between northern Asia and the subcontinent.

In nearby Bharatpur, hang a left onto Rajasthan Highway One and a four-hour drive through rustic India to Sawai Madhopur, the gateway to Ranthambore National Park. Deemed one of the best places to see Bengal tigers in the wild, the park harbors a wide variety of other Indian wildlife, including leopards, antelope, deer, monkeys, sloth bears, and striped hyenas.

Spend the night at one of the many hotels in Sawai Madhopur and take a safari drive through the national park at first light (the best time to spot the elusive tigers) before the 90-mile (150 km) drive to Jaipur. Build in time to explore "Pink City" landmarks like the Hawa Mahal (Palace of the Wind) and Jantar Mantar observatory there before your departure.

HUB | *Mumbai or Delhi, India; Bangkok, Thailand*

The Taj Mahal is one of the New Seven Wonders of the World.

Croatia Z to A

Zagreb to Split, Croatia

Zagreb and the Adriatic Sea are the alpha and omega of a drive across northern Croatia, a white-line odyssey that blends medieval towns and Roman ruins, a gorgeous lake-filled national park, and marvelous beach resorts.

Spend the first day exploring Zagreb's museums, as well as neighborhoods like Gornji Grad and Kaptol that hark back to medieval times. About a two-hour drive south of Zagreb are the Plitvice Lakes, a wonderland of cascades, karst topography, and 16 lakes. Spend the night near the park and get an early start the following morning to the Island of Pag, home to some of the best beaches along the entire Croatian coast.

The oldest town in Croatia, Zadar offers Roman ruins and an old town that feels like a mini-Venice (but without the crowds). The vibe continues farther down the coast, with historic burgs like Šibenik with its exquisite 15th-century cathedral and the UNESCO World Heritage old town in Trogir. Split punctuates the road trip in spectacular fashion with the mountaintop Klis Fortress of *Game of Thrones* fame.

> "A BLEND OF MEDIEVAL TOWNS AND ROMAN RUINS, A GORGEOUS LAKE-FILLED NATIONAL PARK AND MARVELOUS BEACH RESORTS"

HUB | *Zagreb or Dubrovnik, Croatia*

Dubrovnik is famed for coastal treasures and its iconic red roofs.

The Penn Center's Grant Cottage sits on St. Helena Island—Rev. Martin Luther King, Jr., penned "I Have a Dream" here.

Lowcountry Odyssey

Savannah, Georgia, to Charleston,
South Carolina, U.S.

This 100-mile (160 km) drive through the coastal Lowcountry between Savannah, Georgia, and Charleston, South Carolina, features two legendary southern cities. The meandering route features excellent regional cooking and places where road trippers can ponder American history. Exiting Charleston on the old Ashley River Drawbridge, Highway 17 rolls into the ACE Basin, a triple-river watershed with plenty of scope for boating, wildlife-watching, and beach play at Edisto Island. With its boutique hotels and trendy waterfront eateries, Beaufort makes a great overnight stop as well as a base for discovering Gullah culture on nearby St. Helena Island. Over on the south side of the Broad River, Hilton Head Island brandishes golf courses, fancy seafood restaurants, and upscale beach resorts. Another hour and you're breezing into Savannah with its spooky history, striking architecture, and nouvelle southern cuisine.

The Bonaventure Cemetery is an iconic stop in Savannah.

HUB | *Southeastern United States*

CHAPTER SIX

CITY TOURS

Whether on the hunt for good eats, family fun,
or world-class museums, you can find it all
in these metropolises.

A canal borders the
Old Warehouse District in
Hamburg, Germany (p. 211).

Buddhist monks rest outside Rinpung Dzong.

Himalayan Hideaway
Paro, Bhutan

Most people think of Bhutan as a far-off Shangri-La, but Paro is only a short flight (two to four hours) from several major Asian cities, including New Delhi and Bangkok. Besides the romance of a weekend in the Himalaya, Paro offers a glimpse of a highly unique culture. The city's top attraction is Paro Taktsang, the famous "Tiger's Nest" monastery that clings to a 3,000-foot (900 m) cliff. The round-trip hike to and from the monastery takes four to five hours—unless you opt for the express method: 90 minutes on horseback. Spend the evenings discovering Bhutanese cuisine, which includes pork and chicken *momos* (dumplings) and *hentshey datse* (spinach and cheese). Early on day two, arrange a lift to Chele La Pass (13,000 feet/3,900 m) to watch the sun rise over the Himalaya. From there, get dropped off at the Paro Weekend Market, see if anything is flying at the nearby National Archery Ground, and browse the National Museum before departing.

HUB | *Bangkok, Thailand; Mumbai or Delhi, India*

The Jacques Cartier Bridge crosses the St. Lawrence River.

Diversity at Its Finest
Montréal, Québec, Canada

Although it's indisputably a French Canadian city, Montréal is also a global metropolis, home to more than 200 ethnic groups that have stitched their own patches into the urban quilt. Base your weekend at one of the boutique hotels in revitalized Old Montréal beside the St. Lawrence River, and spread out from there to the various ethnic enclaves. St. Laurent Boulevard leads from the old town through the Historic Jewish Quarter (check out Schwartz's Deli) and Mile End with its Greek eateries, art galleries, and renown as the place where William Shatner (aka Captain Kirk) was born and raised. Farther along the boulevard is Little Italy, home to the flavorsome Jean Talon gourmet food market and a growing Latin American influence that has generated Salvadorian, Peruvian, and Mexican restaurants. Located on the south side of Mont Royal, Côte-des-Neiges offers an exotic blend of Asian, Haitian, and Middle Eastern culture, while Little Burgundy is the city's historically black neighborhood.

HUB | *Toronto, Canada; Northeastern United States*

Once Upon a Time

Oaxaca City, Mexico

Tucked high in the mountains of southern Mexico, Oaxaca City offers a heady blend of history, gastronomy, and indigenous Indian culture. Flanked by the ruins of Monte Albán and celebrated craft villages, Oaxaca also hosts the world's most extravagant Día de los Muertos (Day of the Dead) festival in late October. With its buskers and outdoor cafés, the Zócalo offers a good starting point for exploring the city center. Stretching north from the plaza, Calle Macedonio Alcalá provides a vehicle-free path to Santo Domingo de Guzmán monastery, where the Museum of Oaxacan Cultures safeguards the treasures of Monte Albán and other archaeological sites. Soak up more local culture during Sunday morning mass at the Oaxaca Cathedral (built 1535–1733) or the 16th-century Jesuit Church before heading to Monte Albán, the impressive hilltop city founded by the Zapotec around 500 B.C. In the afternoon, look for ceramics, textiles, and other keepsakes in artisanal towns like Atzompa, Teotitlán del Valle, or Coyotepec.

HUB | *Mexico City, Mexico*

Find hidden nature retreats, like a garden of giant cacti, in Oaxaca City.

> ## "A HEADY BLEND OF OLD AND NEW THAT BOTH DELIGHTS AND ASSAULTS ALL OF OUR SENSES"

Cairo Quartet

Cairo, Egypt

Visiting in the early 1600s, English writer and traveler William Lithgow called Cairo the "Microcosmus of the greater world . . . the greatest city seen upon the Earth." To a large extent, the largest city of Africa and the Middle East (population: 20 million) still feels that way—a heady blend of old and new that both delights and assaults all of our senses. Despite its grand size, Cairo is manageable as a weekend getaway because its main sights are clustered in four concentrated areas.

While the Giza pyramids and that inscrutable Sphinx remain the city's top attractions—and rightly so, given their age and exalted place in history—the helter-skelter Egyptian capital offers much more. Take, for instance, the new Grand Egyptian Museum. Rising near the pyramids, it's the world's largest museum dedicated to a single civilization and will eventually house all of the most prized artifacts from the old Museum of Egyptian Antiquities, including the entire King Tut collection.

Islamic Cairo reaches an artistic apex within the walls of the medieval Saladin Citadel, which contains the imposing, silver-domed Mosque of Muhammad Ali and the Al-Gawhara Palace museum. The citadel overlooks Old Cairo and its legendary Khan el-Khalili bazaar. The sprawling market is at its best after dark—and especially along El Moez Street with its architectural wonders—when the locals throng the shops and outdoor cafés.

Cairo also has its Christian side, the thriving Coptic population and more than 400 Coptic churches, including the fourth-century St. Sergius (the city's oldest church), the famous Hanging Church (with its suspended nave), and the incredible Cave Church of St. Simon.

Then there's the modern Cairo, where you'll find chic shopping along Road 9 in the Maadi district, live music joints in the hip Talaat Harb area, and cocktails-with-a-view at the Crimson and other riverside bars.

HUB | *Luxor, Egypt; Jerusalem, Israel*

The Mosque-Madrassa of Sultan Hassan is the center of the city's skyline.

Shanghai, China, is a city of towering glass and chrome high rises.

Skylines

Behold iconic skyscrapers and legendary feats of architecture from New York to Dubai.

1. CHICAGO, ILLINOIS, U.S.

Widely considered the birthplace of the skyscraper, where early versions topped out at around 10 stories, Chicago still harbors a number of 19th-century holdovers (not least, the Manhattan Building) among the legendarily modern behemoths. Its tallest building is the 110-story Willis Tower (formerly the Sears Tower), which was completed in 1974.

2. DUBAI, UNITED ARAB EMIRATES

If Dubai's skyline wasn't etched into the collective consciousness after the legendary helipad tennis match or after Burj Khalifa's debut as the world's tallest building—the new (and *even taller*) Dubai Creek Tower seals the deal. Scheduled to be completed by 2022, the observation tower will be at least 2,717 feet (828 m) tall.

3. MANHATTAN, NEW YORK, U.S.

No two New Yorkers agree on the best skyline-gazing spot, but you can't go wrong with a classic: the views of the Empire State, Chrysler, and Met Life buildings (just for starters) from the Brooklyn Bridge. Don't forget a visit to the city's tallest skyscraper: One World Trade Center, completed in 2014.

4. SHANGHAI, CHINA

Though it's become a globally recognized icon, with its orb-accented Oriental Pearl Radio & Television Tower (1,535 feet/467.9 m tall) at one end and the vertiginous Shanghai Tower (2,073 feet/632 m tall) at the other, the Pudong skyline is still best seen in person from the colonial-era Bund.

5. EDINBURGH, SCOTLAND

This historic skyline is iconic and well preserved and is cited among the reasons Edinburgh was granted World Heritage status in 1996. One quick scan from the Balmoral Hotel clock tower (built in 1902) to the Edinburgh Castle—one of the oldest fortified places in Europe—and you'll see UNESCO's point.

6. SEATTLE, WASHINGTON, U.S.

The Columbia Center may be the tallest building west of the Mississippi, but the Space Needle is the undisputed star of the show—at least architecturally. Built for the 1962 World's Fair, the Space Needle stands at 605 feet (184.4 m) tall and offers 360-degree views of the city from its observatory. As impressive as that may be, plenty of locals and visitors alike would argue that beautiful Mount Rainier is the skyline's true star.

7. CAPE TOWN, SOUTH AFRICA

Table Mountain has made the Cape Town skyline an internationally renowned beauty. But certain architectural elements are equally memorable: City Hall was seen around the world when Nelson Mandela first spoke from its balcony.

8. SINGAPORE

Gazing upon the Singaporean skyline is unforgettable, and immersing yourself in it even more so. The triple-towered Marina Bay Sands is home to the world's largest infinity pool at 656 feet (200 m) in the air.

9. BUDAPEST, HUNGARY

All spires and domes and flying buttresses, the architecture alone would make for a stunning skyline. But the fact that Budapest is bisected by the Danube and connected by several iconic bridges takes this cityscape over the top.

10. CUENCA, ECUADOR

Another wonderland of domes—many painted an ethereal blue—colonial Cuenca is a frequent contender for most beautiful skyline in South America. Of course, having the Ecuadorian Andes for a backdrop doesn't hurt either.

Pavilions and lotus fields zigzag above West Lake.

China's Liquid City

Hangzhou, China

Although it's the linchpin of China's fourth largest urban area (population: 22 million), Hangzhou feels almost rural at times thanks to its many parks and water features. Like a Chinese watercolor come to life, West Lake and its medley of pagodas, temples, gardens, and bridges is worthy of a whole day on its own. The UNESCO World Heritage site is surrounded by wooded highlands with trails to scenic spots like Lingyin Temple, Nine Creeks in Misty Forest, and the Dragon Well tea fields. Boats also cruise the historic Grand Canal, passing the massive new Zhejiang Science & Technology Museum and the Hangzhou Arts and Crafts Museum with its antique swords, fans, and umbrellas. Come evening, you can catch the extravagant Zuiyi Hangzhou water show on West Lake, hit one of the city's jazz clubs, or dig into typical Hangzhou dishes like beggar's chicken, *dong po* pork, and sweet and sour West Lake fish.

HUB | *Shanghai or Beijing, China; Hong Kong; Tokyo, Japan*

Along the Silk Road

Samarkand, Uzbekistan

A crossroads of culture for nearly 3,000 years, Samarkand has attracted many celebrated visitors. Some came to conquer (Alexander the Great, Genghis Khan, and Tamerlane) while others just passed through (writers Ibn Battuta and Colin Thubron). Despite its location in remote central Asia, the Uzbekistan city is a realistic weekend escape thanks to four-hour flights from Moscow or Istanbul. Samarkand offers some of the world's finest Islamic architecture, in particular the blue domes, flamboyant archways, soaring minarets, and intricate mosaic decorations of the Registan madrassas and Shah-i-Zinda mausoleums. Tamerlane's Tomb and Ulugbek's Observatory, both dating to the 15th century, are two other must-see structures. But it's not all brick and mortar. The Silk Road city also tenders exotic central Asian cuisine (similar to Persian cooking) and wineries that produce dessert libations made from locally grown grapes, as well as art galleries and an El Merosi cultural show that showcases traditional Uzbeki music and fashion.

Take a walk through the Shah-i-Zinda necropolis in Samarkand.

HUB | *Istanbul, Turkey; Moscow, Russia*

Hamburg's
Philharmonic Hall is
the city's showpiece.

Brahms & Bach

Hamburg, Germany

Although it's still a hardworking seaport, Hamburg has transformed into a modern cultural capital, architectural treasure, and entertainment hub. Snatch a lofty view from the steeple of baroque St. Michael's Church, where Brahms was baptized and the Bach family honed their organ-playing skills. Among the old town's other landmarks are the neo-Renaissance Rathaus (City Hall), the exquisite Mellin-Passage shopping arcade, and the Hamburger Kunsthalle art museum with its old masters. Saturday night offers two vastly different entertainment options: a classical concert at the futuristic Elbe Philharmonic in harborside HafenCity or a sing-along Beatles tour of the once notorious Reeperbahn. Make like a local and relish Sunday morning brunch at the cavernous Altonaer Fischauktionshalle and then browse the sprawling riverside market. While away the afternoon exploring the city's harbor and canals by bike or boat before ending the day with a stein of local *weizenbier* (wheat beer) on the roof terrace at riverside Blockbräu brewery in St. Pauli.

HUB | *Berlin, Germany*

Even pups will enjoy the views of Porto, its famous suspension bridge, and the Douro River.

Portugal's North Star

Porto, Portugal

The question is not whether you should spend a weekend in Porto, the grand dame of northern Portugal. It's what to obsess about when you get there: the region's iconic port wine, the *bacalhau* and other seafood specialties served at riverside and beachfront eateries, or the mélange of Gothic, baroque, and Renaissance architecture that earned the city UNESCO World Heritage status. Flush with bars, restaurants, and pastel-colored houses, the old Ribeira district scales a hillside on the north bank of the Douro River. Historic spans like the Ponte de Dom Luis I leap the celebrated waterway to the Vila Nova de Gaia, the site of many of the port wine lodges. Watch sunset over the Atlantic during a walk along the Foz do Douro coast and catch a musical performance at Porto Calem, Café Guarany, Mal Cozinhado, or another atmospheric *casa de fado* (a fado music venue) before retiring to your boutique hotel in the Ribeira.

HUB | *Lisbon, Portugal*

Find walkways of blooms at the International Rose Test Garden.

Oregon's Hip Hub
Portland, Oregon, U.S.

Portland is renowned as a hipster haven and craft brew hub. But the "Rose City" at the confluence of the Columbia and Willamette Rivers is also a great base for outdoor adventure. Start the weekend with flowers and forest at the International Rose Test Garden and Crystal Springs Rhododendron Garden, the Lan Su Chinese Garden and the Portland Japanese Garden, or the Hoyt Arboretum and rambling Forest Park (one of the nation's largest urban woodlands). All that walking works up quite a thirst, best quenched at microbreweries in the revamped Pearl District. Get out of town on Sunday with a drive up the gorgeous Columbia Gorge to perpetually snowcapped Mount Hood, or through the Willamette Valley wine country south and west of Portland. Alternatively, you can linger in the city, biking or hiking more than 100 miles (160 km) of urban trails, or cruise the rivers on a guided boat tour.

HUB | *Pacific Northwest United States; Vancouver, Canada*

The Kinkaku-ji Temple's top two floors are covered in gold leaf.

Geishas & Temples
Kyoto, Japan

Kyoto channels ancient Japan like no other city, especially if you're spending the weekend at a traditional *ryokan* inn with tatami mats, futon bed, and private *onsen* (hot spring) bath. The city boasts an astounding 17 UNESCO World Heritage sites, including the glimmering Kinkaku-ji (Golden Pavilion), the Ryoan-ji with its famous Zen garden, and the hilltop Kiyomizu-dera with its awe-inspiring views. You can spot geishas coming and going to work at traditional *ochaya* teahouses in the Gion district and watch a kabuki dance-drama unfold at the historic Minami-za Theatre. Kyoto also earns kudos for its cuisine, especially its traditional 14-course feast, *kaiseke*, with seafood, meat, and vegetable dishes arranged so artistically it's almost a shame to eat them. And Kyoto is probably the best city to buy traditional Japanese arts and crafts in tiny specialty shops offering kimonos, lacquerware, tea serving sets, and hand-carved *noh* masks. After dark, Kyoto's sake bars can be explored solo or via guided tours.

HUB | *Tokyo, Japan*

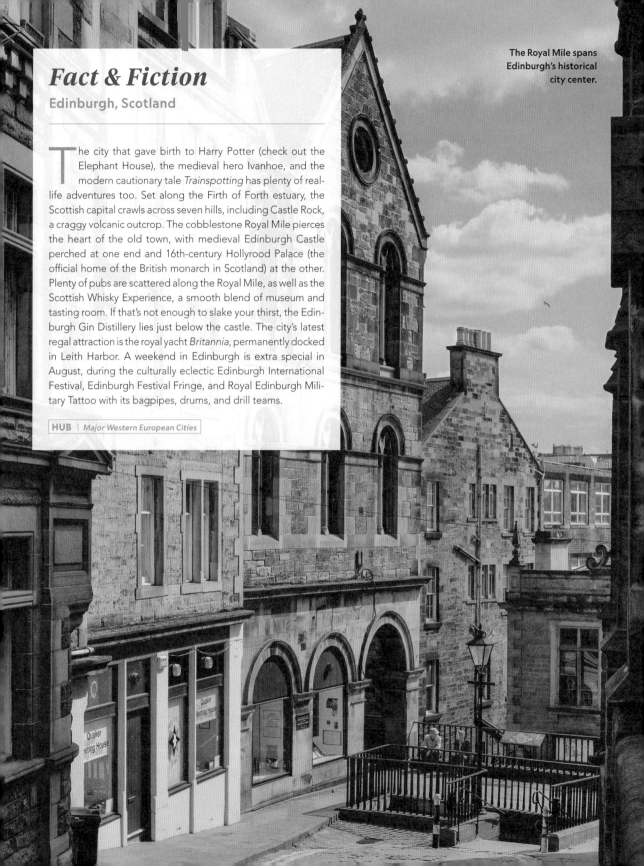

Fact & Fiction

Edinburgh, Scotland

The city that gave birth to Harry Potter (check out the Elephant House), the medieval hero Ivanhoe, and the modern cautionary tale *Trainspotting* has plenty of real-life adventures too. Set along the Firth of Forth estuary, the Scottish capital crawls across seven hills, including Castle Rock, a craggy volcanic outcrop. The cobblestone Royal Mile pierces the heart of the old town, with medieval Edinburgh Castle perched at one end and 16th-century Hollyrood Palace (the official home of the British monarch in Scotland) at the other. Plenty of pubs are scattered along the Royal Mile, as well as the Scottish Whisky Experience, a smooth blend of museum and tasting room. If that's not enough to slake your thirst, the Edinburgh Gin Distillery lies just below the castle. The city's latest regal attraction is the royal yacht *Britannia*, permanently docked in Leith Harbor. A weekend in Edinburgh is extra special in August, during the culturally eclectic Edinburgh International Festival, Edinburgh Festival Fringe, and Royal Edinburgh Military Tattoo with its bagpipes, drums, and drill teams.

HUB | *Major Western European Cities*

The Royal Mile spans Edinburgh's historical city center.

The Süleymaniye
Mosque sits on a hill
overlooking Istanbul.

Imperfectly Perfect Istanbul

A Ferry Ride and a Love Letter to an Unforgettable City

A few months ago I came across an online study that compared the places a city's visitors photographed to places its residents photographed. In some cities, like London and New York, visitors and residents took pictures in notably different places. In Venice and Rome, tourists took many more pictures than locals. In some cities—I won't name them, so as not to hurt anyone's feelings—travelers couldn't find much to photograph at all.

And then there was Istanbul. The study seemed to indicate that Istanbul's longtime residents took at least as many pictures as its first-time visitors, in the same spots—especially on the water, on the routes of the ferries that constantly shuttle between the two continents that the city straddles.

Yes, there's a lot to love about Istanbul. As the capital of the Byzantine and Ottoman Empires (and even of the Roman Empire just before its collapse), it has a rich history to offer. As a commercial and political center—and the largest city on Earth for a very long time—it attracted many ethnic groups, all of whom left their marks. At its height, it was even called "the city of the world's desire," and for good reason.

The desire is still here—for both visitors and locals. One day, I board one of the city's beloved ferries on the European side. I stand on the open deck at the stern. As we depart, the city's modern silhouette emerges beyond the waters of the Bosporus. The air smells of spring and sea. As the sun disappears behind Süleymaniye Mosque, considered by many to be the finest in Istanbul, the sky to the west glows orange, then purple. I think this is going to be the sort of evening when the sunset has a different kind of beauty to it.

One of the most famous poems about the city has the memorable line: "I listen to Istanbul, my eyes closed." But this ferry ride is turning out to be the exact opposite. I see every element that should make a sound: minarets, the Spice Bazaar, long lines of cars on bridges, crowded seafronts, seagulls—but none of the sounds reach me. I am left alone with the magnificent view.

Or not so alone. I look at the people on the ferry. Some are enjoying the view with headphones on. Some, probably regular commuters, are more used to the view and are reading their books. And there are a number of people leaning against the rails and taking pictures.

It is nearly impossible not to, no matter how many times we see that view. Especially if it is spring and the sun is setting. From the ferry, from a terrace, from the Galata Bridge, or from the window of their own homes, thousands of strangers looking at the same sight share a connection. All of them are reminded that they are looking at a special city.

Istanbul rises above mortal cities formed of buildings, roads, and parks. Istanbul is a city of exceptions, everyone knows that. Cities don't sit on two continents; Istanbul does. Mosques don't have mosaics of Jesus; in Istanbul they do. There is no such thing as seeing dolphins during your morning commute to work; in Istanbul there is. It doesn't snow much on palm trees; in Istanbul it does. In Turkish, the letter *n* is never followed by *b*; in Istanbul it is.

Istanbul's unique beauty comes from its inability to stay the same and its irrepressibility as well. Throughout history, whoever ruled Istanbul was able to shape it only to a degree; in the end Istanbul does what it pleases.

As my ferry passes cargo ships and the Historic Peninsula's historic minarets, I sense all those old Istanbuls. I don't see them from my boat; I don't hear them. But I feel them. And I can't help but think: If Istanbul were the kind of city where the four minarets of Hagia Sophia were identical, as is almost always the case with mosques, perhaps it would not be loved as much.

Istanbul will continue to change, and we'll continue to look at its old photographs with envy. But the day will come when the Istanbuls we have not yet built will take their place in somebody's memories. Maybe in the future, commuter ferries will only be running for nostalgia's sake. Maybe one day, there will be a drone congestion in the old bazaar instead of a human one.

Regardless, when that day comes, someone will turn to a sun setting over the town to snap a picture of it or will use the appropriate emotion-recording technology of the day. And we will keep loving it, not in the usual way of loving a city but like loving a character, a real person made of flesh and bone—and soul.

—**Onur Uygun** is the managing editor of *National Geographic Traveler Turkey*. Based in Istanbul, he loves coming home as much as he loves traveling.

"THE NATIONAL CAPITAL IS AN ALL-STAR CITY WHEN IT COMES TO ITS PARKS."

Bipartisan D.C.

Washington, D.C., U.S.

Beyond the iconic museums, monuments, and political landmarks is an entirely different side of Washington, D.C.—a city of flora and fauna rather than filibustering. The national capital is an all-star city when it comes to its parks.

A stroll along the National Mall—even if you're not popping into one of the adjacent Smithsonian museums or ascending the Washington Monument (reopened in the summer of 2019)—is obligatory for just about any weekend in the U.S. capital. But the popular green space also has its quiet side, like the flower-filled United States Botanic Garden below the Capitol building or the cherry-tree-lined walkways around the Tidal Basin.

Named for the president who started the federal conservation effort, Theodore Roosevelt Island floats in the Potomac River just upstream from the Lincoln Memorial. You've got to think that T.R. would have loved this tiny slice of wilderness in the middle of a great metropolitan area—a park that features woodland, swamp, and upland trails and shelters deer, fox, and 200 bird species.

Rock Creek Park, the district's largest green space at 1,754 acres (709 ha), is also the most diverse in terms of outdoor activities. In addition to the Smithsonian National Zoo and copious hiking and biking routes, the park offers a tennis center, 18-hole golf course, guided horseback treks and riding lessons, outdoor concerts, and ranger programs.

Over on the east side of town, the massive United States National Arboretum harbors plants from around the globe that can be discovered along almost 10 miles (16 km) of walking routes. The leafy collections range from the National Grove of State Trees to historic rose gardens and a bonsai museum.

Those craving a longer hike or bike ride should make a beeline for the Chesapeake & Ohio Canal National Historical Park. The "Grand Old Ditch"—the brainchild of George Washington—stretches 184.5 miles (297 km) along the Potomac River between Georgetown and Cumberland, Maryland, and offers various routes from easy strolling along the canal to rock scrambling on the beloved Billy Goat Trail.

Walk through columns that were once part of the Capitol in the National Arboretum.

Frida Kahlo's sculptures
are displayed on a wall
in her garden.

Museums

Take in world-renowned statues in Paris, ancient artifacts in London, and art in Washington, D.C.

1. THE LOUVRE, PARIS, FRANCE

The "Mona Lisa" accounts for untold numbers of visitors here. But remember that everyone from the "Venus de Milo" to "Winged Victory" lives at the world's largest art museum too.

2. STATE HERMITAGE MUSEUM, ST. PETERSBURG, RUSSIA

Second only to the Louvre among the world's largest museums, the Hermitage houses millions of works, perhaps most famously Rembrandt's "Return of the Prodigal Son," Titian's "Danaë," Matisse's "Dance," and da Vinci's "Madonna Litta."

3. THE BRITISH MUSEUM, LONDON, ENGLAND

In a city full of bucket list museums, don't miss the original: The British Museum (1759) is said to be the first public national museum in the world. Another claim to fame? The Rosetta Stone is here.

4. THE FRIDA KAHLO MUSEUM, COYOACÁN, MEXICO

While Mexico City is no stranger to monumental museums, the intimately scaled Blue House—Frida Kahlo's former home in the colorful Coyoacán district—rivals any of the big boys with an astonishing array of art and artifacts.

5. YAYOI KUSAMA MUSEUM, TOKYO, JAPAN

Tokyo recently opened its own ode to an iconic female artist, Yayoi Kusama, whose traveling exhibits have become the hottest tickets in town all over the globe. This master of mirrors, lights, and patterns now has her own homeland museum.

6. THE ACCADEMIA GALLERY, FLORENCE, ITALY

You'd be forgiven for overlooking the supporting characters in a place where Michelangelo's "David" takes center stage. But you should still try not to miss them, as they include everyone from Botticelli to Uccello.

7. THE NATIONAL PORTRAIT GALLERY, WASHINGTON, D.C., U.S.

From Michelle Obama's portrait that made a spellbound little girl go viral to the super-cazh rendering of George W. Bush, much of this collection shows America's upper crust through a powerfully humanizing lens.

8. MUSEO NACIONAL DEL PRADO, MADRID, SPAIN

Home to many Spanish masterpieces—among them, Velázquez's "Las Meninas" and Goya's "Majas"—this global icon is also a must for "The Garden of Earthly Delights" by Hieronymus Bosch. After all, there's a reason the museum is oft described as the museum of painters, not a museum of paintings.

9. ZEITZ MOCAA, CAPE TOWN, SOUTH AFRICA

This relative newcomer to the Victoria & Alfred Waterfront is not only the world's largest collection of contemporary African art (headliners include Njideka Akunyili Crosby and Kehinde Wiley) but also the only museum topped off by an award-winning design hotel, the Silo.

10. THE METROPOLITAN MUSEUM OF ART, NEW YORK CITY, NEW YORK, U.S.

A monumental museum full of must-sees may be the last place you'd expect to find zen, but the park-adjacent (and millennia-old) Temple of Dendur inside the Met makes for a magical city break—as does the vista-blessed members' restaurant (actually no longer members only).

Stop for dinner and café theater at Bewley's Oriental Café.

A Literary Masterpiece
Dublin, Ireland

Few other cities can match the Irish metropolis when it comes to words. Dublin has a literary heritage that embraces many maestros—from James Joyce (*Ulysses*) and Oscar Wilde (*The Picture of Dorian Gray*) to Jonathan Swift (*Gulliver's Travels*) and Bram Stoker (*Dracula*). With its personal mementoes, precious first editions, and well-stocked bookshop, the Dublin Writers Museum offers an ideal opening chapter to the wordsmith weekend. Join a guided walking tour of Joycean Dublin at the nearby James Joyce Centre and cross the River Liffey to Mulligan's Pub, a longtime literary hangout (established 1782) renowned for its draft Guinness. After dark, catch a play at the Abbey Theatre (founded by W. B. Yeats and other poets). Day two entails a pilgrimage across Dublin to George Bernard Shaw's birthplace, Jonathan Swift's grave, and Oscar Wilde's house. Round off the weekend with dinner and café theater at bard-friendly Bewley's Grafton Street.

HUB | *Major Western European Cities*

Above & Below
Kraków, Poland

In the wake of Solidarity, this alluring city in southern Poland has resumed its role as a cultural hub of global significance. Any weekend in Kraków should start in the Old Town and the sprawling Rynek Główny, the largest town square in Europe. Arrayed around the plaza are St. Mary's Basilica, the Town Hall Tower (with its lofty viewing deck), and a majestic Renaissance-era trade emporium, the Sukiennice (Cloth Hall), while underneath is a warren of passages where local history is illuminated via artifacts, holograms, and videos. Wawel Castle on the Vistula River has morphed from the seat of the Polish monarchy into the nation's foremost fine art museum. Kraków's role in Jewish history and the Holocaust is highlighted by sights like old Kazimierz Jewish Quarter, Ghetto Heroes Square, and Oscar Schindler's Factory. Farther out of town, Wieliczka Salt Mine offers regular guided tours and an immersive experience that emulates the life of an underground salt miner.

HUB | *Warsaw, Poland*

Fourteenth-century St. Mary's Basilica sits in the Market Square.

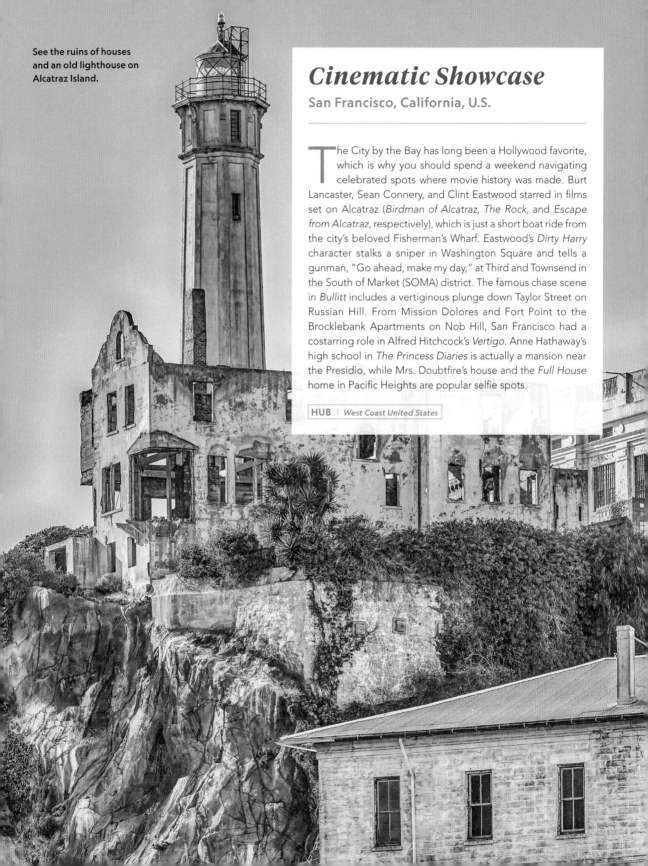

See the ruins of houses and an old lighthouse on Alcatraz Island.

Cinematic Showcase

San Francisco, California, U.S.

The City by the Bay has long been a Hollywood favorite, which is why you should spend a weekend navigating celebrated spots where movie history was made. Burt Lancaster, Sean Connery, and Clint Eastwood starred in films set on Alcatraz (*Birdman of Alcatraz*, *The Rock*, and *Escape from Alcatraz*, respectively), which is just a short boat ride from the city's beloved Fisherman's Wharf. Eastwood's *Dirty Harry* character stalks a sniper in Washington Square and tells a gunman, "Go ahead, make my day," at Third and Townsend in the South of Market (SOMA) district. The famous chase scene in *Bullitt* includes a vertiginous plunge down Taylor Street on Russian Hill. From Mission Dolores and Fort Point to the Brocklebank Apartments on Nob Hill, San Francisco had a costarring role in Alfred Hitchcock's *Vertigo*. Anne Hathaway's high school in *The Princess Diaries* is actually a mansion near the Presidio, while Mrs. Doubtfire's house and the *Full House* home in Pacific Heights are popular selfie spots.

HUB | *West Coast United States*

> "THE METROPOLIS BOASTS
> SEVEN OF THE WORLD'S
> BEST ART MUSEUMS."

Artful L.A.
Los Angeles, California, U.S.

The City of the Angels may wallow in pop culture—Hollywood, Disneyland, and the Beach Boys—but the Southern California metropolis also boasts seven of the world's best art museums. These unique collections form the core of a weekend far removed from Mickey Mouse and the Sunset Strip.

A progeny of the robber barons who built the transcontinental railroads, the Huntington is the oldest of L.A.'s iconic museums. Established in 1919, the San Marino complex features an expansive botanical garden, a rare-books library, and an art collection that includes 18th-century English portraits of "The Blue Boy" and "Pinkie."

The Huntington is easily combined with the Norton Simon Museum in Pasadena, celebrated for its Asian art and sculpture garden. Finish the day with eats and drinks along Pasadena's lively Colorado Boulevard for the annual New Year's Day Tournament of Roses Parade.

The art action shifts to downtown and the Broad (pronounced *brode*) museum with its honeycombed facade that became an instant landmark when it was unveiled in 2015. The museum showcases leading contemporary artists like Jean-Michel Basquiat, Jeff Koons, and Takashi Murakami. Grab lunch in Little Tokyo on the 20-minute walk to the Geffen Contemporary at MOCA, located inside an old hardware factory reworked by local architect Frank Gehry. And then explore the nearby Arts District, a revamped industrial area invaded by galleries, trendy bars and cafés, and amazing graffiti.

Start your last day at the L.A. County Museum of Art, an eclectic array of artwork from every epoch and major civilization. After lunch at The Original Farmers Market, head for the west side. Take a monorail up to the Getty Center and gaze down on La La Land from the artfully arranged garden. Crowning the western end of the Angelino art trail is the Getty Villa in Malibu with its priceless collection of Greek and Roman statues and mosaics. Round off the weekend watching nature's canvas: the sunset over the Pacific from Malibu Beach.

The J. Paul Getty Museum
overlooks downtown
Los Angeles.

St. Basil's Cathedral stands out in Moscow's Red Square.

PERSPECTIVE

Moscow Now

An Ex-Pat Reflects on What Makes Russia's Capital City Feel Like Home

Seeing the Kremlin at night always enthralls me, even after my 22 years in Moscow. The vista of brick towers and crenellated ramparts, so magnificent as to appear unreal, calls to mind an illuminated print from an old book of fairy tales.

My sighting of Russia's most famous (or infamous) fortress comes as my cab trundles over the Bolshoy Kamenny Bridge, through air shimmering with a fierce frost. Gusts of wind stir snowdrifts along the banks of the Moskva River below us. No less the seat of power now, during the era of Vladimir Putin, than it was in Ivan the Terrible's day (or Stalin's), the Kremlin evokes, for me, a mix of dread and majesty—the emotions I experienced as a child of the Cold War when I both feared Russia (I lived in Washington, D.C., aka ground zero) and marveled at it. My fascination led to graduate studies in Russian and East European history, to my first visit in 1985, and to a move here for good in the summer of 1993. In 1999 I married a Russian. Moscow is the city I call home.

The Kremlin, a walled citadel with five palaces and five churches, looms on my right as we shoot past vast Red Square, presided over by St. Basil's Cathedral, with its candy cane cupolas. We drive by the State Duma (parliament), faceless and modern (and totally subservient to President Putin). Then comes Lubyanka Square and another bunker of a building, today housing the KGB's successor, the FSB. Here one August night in 1991, crowds of Russians cheered as cranes dismantled the statue of Felix Dzerzhinsky, the blood-soaked founder of the Soviet secret police.

Those were promising days, when real democratic change in Russia seemed possible. These days, Western sanctions threaten the highest living standard Russians have ever known. For all but dollar- and euro-bearing travelers (feeling blessed by the ruble's devaluation), now should be a cheerless time in Moscow. But it's not.

My cab leaves me at a restaurant near Lubyanka, Ekspeditsiya ("expedition"). It's crowded, loud with folk songs sung by a group of musicians and customers clinking glasses and toasting. I have come for lively conversation and traditional Russian cuisine; since the fall of the Soviet Union more than two decades ago, Russian cooking has become something of a rarity in Moscow, at least outside people's homes. (Most top restaurants are international.)

I'm joined by Irina, a Muscovite friend who staunchly defends Putin. The evening promises to be interesting. Over drinks and cedar nuts, Irina enlightens me.

"Russians," she says, "have always been conquering wild country. We are always ready to light out for the wilderness, even in subzero frosts. We need difficulties to thrive. That is just who we are."

Settling wilderness also meant eating unpalatable things, including some "delicacies" on our menus—marinated moose with cabbage, grilled reindeer tongue with cowberry sauce. I choose a safe favorite, *pelmeni* (dumplings), specifically Siberian pelmeni stuffed with deer meat and smothered in delicious *smetana*, or sour cream. We wash the meal down with a half liter of vodka, which we drink straight, the Russian way.

The next time we meet, it is at Club Mayak, a now closed restaurant in the middle of "Old Moscow," a web of lanes winding between low stucco houses dating from a century or two ago. Once the dining area of the Mayakovsky Theater, next door, Club Mayak now serves as a low-key gathering place for some of Moscow's best known actors, writers, and journalists. With a red-walled interior, careworn furniture, and sepia-tinted lighting, there are no pretensions here.

Over some wine and a plate of European cheeses, served despite an official ban on such goods, I ask Irina what the future holds.

"We went through World War II and we won," she replies. "I am not worried."

I'm feeling a bit less sanguine. But I do know this: Whatever happens in Russia, its fate will be decided, one way or another, here in Moscow—a fact that continues to fuel this city's indomitable spirit.

—**Jeffrey Tayler** is a contributing editor at the *Atlantic* magazine and has written several books on Russia.

The Stanley Hotel inspired Stephen King's *The Shining*.

Movie Sets

Take a tour through cinematic history from Guatemala (*Star Wars*)
to Colorado (*The Shining*).

1. *STAR WARS: EPISODE IV— A NEW HOPE*, GUATEMALA

The Massassi rebel base on the fourth moon of Yavin is not actually out of this world, but in the vistor-friendly Maya temple ruins of Guatemala's Tikal National Park. For the ultimate vantage point, climb Temple IV, where you'll look out to the familiar Temples I, II, and III seen in the film.

2. *THE SHINING*, ESTES PARK, COLORADO, U.S.

The movie was actually filmed on a set, but *The Shining*'s haunts were inspired by the 142-room Stanley Hotel in Estes Park, Colorado, where Stephen King and his wife had stayed in the hotel's room 217. Its haunted history led the horror author to pen the beloved novel, turned movie.

3. *BLACK PANTHER*, SOUTH KOREA

You may not be able to visit Wakanda, but you can find your way to Busan, South Korea, where many of the *Black Panther* characters were filmed walking the streets, passing through food markets, and, most memorably, speeding away in an epic car chase. Stop in nearby Seoul to visit *Avengers: Age of Ultron* filming locations.

4. *DJANGO UNCHAINED*, LOUISIANA, U.S.

Quentin Tarantino chose to film *Django Unchained* on the 250-year-old Evergreen Plantation. Once home to more than 103 slaves, the plantation offers regular tours of its grounds and 22 original slave cabins. The plantation has also served as the setting for *Free State of Jones* and *Roots*.

5. *ESCAPE FROM ALCATRAZ*, CALIFORNIA, U.S.

It's easy to make your way to the film set of this prison drama. Alcatraz, which no longer operates as a prison, sits just offshore of San Francisco. It operates regular tours of the facility.

6. *HARRY POTTER*, OXFORD, ENGLAND

If you're still waiting for your acceptance letter to Hogwarts, consider a trip to Oxford Christ Church Cathedral instead. Its exterior was used as the basis of the magical school in all eight films.

7. *X-MEN 2*, COLWOOD, CANADA

You don't have to be a mutant to attend Xavier's School for Gifted Youngsters. Just make your way to Hatley Castle, which is also the set for *Smallville*, *Arrow*, and *Mac-Gyver*, among other films and television shows.

8. *GHOSTBUSTERS*, NEW YORK, U.S.

Hook & Ladder Company 8, used as the Ghostbusters' headquarters in the 1984 film, is an operating firehouse in Manhattan's Tribeca area. Newly remodeled, it may not look the same as it did on screen, but it certainly highlights the movie's spirit.

9. *THE TALENTED MR. RIPLEY*, ISCHIA, ITALY

Filmed up and down Italy's coastline, most of the *The Talented Mr. Ripley*'s beach scenes were made on the white-sand shores of Ischia. Neighboring real-life town Procida served as Mongibello in the film.

10. *THE BEACH*, KO PHI PHI LEH, THAILAND

The beautiful setting behind *The Beach* is not as much of a secret as it appears to be on the big screen. The uninhabited island of Ko Phi Phi Leh is just a boat ride from Krabi. What's true to the movie? The island's stunning vertical, greenery-draped cliffs and white-sand beaches.

The Majorelle Garden is an artists' landscape inside the city.

North African Magic
Marrakech, Morocco

With its snake charmers and monkey handlers, magicians and acrobats, red-clad water bearers and Chleuh dancers—as well as all of those handicraft stalls and romantic rooftop cafés—Jemaa el-Fna square is reason enough to spend a weekend in Marrakech. But the Moroccan city is so much more. Marjorelle Garden offers a magical mix of small museums in electric-blue buildings surrounded by artistic fountains, flora, and even fauna (the resident cats). The meticulously restored Medersa Ben Youssef, Bahia Palace, Saadian Tombs, and Dar Menebhi Museum—each of them an architectural gem—render glimpses of the city's illustrious past. You could spend your entire weekend—and then some—wandering the walled Medina quarter, a warren of tiny shops selling carpets, jewelry, spices, leatherwork, kaftans, and *babouche* slippers. Round off the day with a soak at Le Bains de Marrakech or another hammam (steam bath), a fabulous Moroccan meal, and tuneful cocktails at a *Casablanca*-inspired piano bar.

HUB | *Paris, France; London, England; Madrid, Spain*

Tour the Hermitage, a UNESCO World Heritage site.

Venice of the North
St. Petersburg, Russia

Peter the Great created St. Petersburg in 1703 as his royal capital and Russia's window to the West. More than 300 years later—having survived the Revolution and World War II—the city glimmers again as one of the globe's cultural treasures. The czars are a distant memory, but their former palaces form the nucleus of a St. Petersburg weekend flush with extraordinary museums, gardens, and performing arts. With 120 rooms of priceless art and antiquities, the Hermitage Museum (Peter's Winter Palace) could occupy an entire weekend all on its own. But there's also the Fabergé Museum in the old Shuvalov Palace (including nine Imperial Easter Eggs), the Catherine Palace with its celebrated Amber Room and sprawling gardens, and the house where Dostoyevsky wrote *The Brothers Karamazov*. After dark, catch ballet, opera, or symphony at the historic Mariinsky Theatre (opened 1860), and then wander the city's many bridges and canals in the lingering summer light.

HUB | *Moscow, Russia*

If You Like Piña Coladas

San Juan, Puerto Rico

Puerto Rico's capital city offers an exotic blend of beaches and rainforest, salsa and reggaeton, Spanish and American history, an emerging culinary scene and tropical drinks (the piña colada was invented here). Kick off the weekend in historic Old San Juan, founded by the Spanish in 1509 as one of the first European settlements in the New World. Grab a lofty view of the city and port from El Morro fortress and stroll cobblestone streets flush with museums, souvenir shops, and locally flavored restaurants. After lunch head for the shore. Find sun and sand at Condado or Isla Verde beach. Be sure to stick around after dark for the beachside eats and bars. On Sunday morning, head into the hills for a hike in El Yunque, the only tropical rainforest in the entire U.S. National Forest system. Return to San Juan via Loíza or Piñones for one last dip in the deep-blue sea.

HUB | *Houston, Texas, U.S.; Southeastern United States*

Relax on the wide open
Condado Beach in San Juan,
Puerto Rico.

"A SHOWPLACE FOR ARTISTS, CRAFTSMEN, AND FASHION DESIGNERS"

Market Forces

London, England

Between Harrods, Oxford Street, and the King's Road, England's capital has always been a great place to shop. But more than anything else, London is a city of markets. All told, the city boasts 20 major markets and more than 80 smaller neighborhood markets, many of them open for business only on weekends.

Start where retail London was born 2,000 years ago, Leadenhall Market, which sits atop the remains of an ancient Roman forum. Located in the heart of the financial district, the ornate Victorian structure doubled as Diagon Alley in the *Harry Potter* films. Grab a bite at Leadenhall's gourmet food outlets (Cheese and Chamberlain's are must-tries) or an early pint at historic Lamb Tavern (opened 1780).

Set off on foot to Old Spitalfields Market, a 15-minute walk from Leadenhall, past the futuristic bullet-shaped "Gherkin" building. Established by Charles I in 1638, Spitalfields has morphed from a wholesale produce market into a showplace for small, independent artists, craftsmen, and fashion designers, with craft workshops and Sunday morning yoga sessions in the mix.

Market mania extends across London in every direction. For those who want to be entertained, there's nothing quite like Covent Garden with its sundry street performers, Royal Opera House, and West End theater scene.

Portobello Road, the world's largest antiques market, boasts around 1,000 vendors. It's also famed for its cinematic and literary history—a medley of pop culture that ranges from *Paddington Bear* to the bookshop where Hugh Grant courted Julia Roberts in *Notting Hill*.

In north London, Camden Lock is a chaotic sprawl of new and used fashion, jewelry, and accessories, as well as vintage curiosities that attract a quarter-million people on weekends. Keep an eye out for hipster gin distillery Half Hitch and the statue of singer Amy Winehouse, who lived in Camden until her death in 2011.

Take a stroll under
Leadenhall Market's
roofed arcades.

Vertical forests climb the residential towers of the Porta Nuova business district.

> " 'MILAN HAS BEEN STUCK
> FOR SOME YEARS,
> AND NOW THERE'S
> A NEW WAVE OF ENERGY.' "

Fashionably Forward Milan

Italy's Finance and Fashion Capital Looks Toward a Creative and Green Future

Several hundred years ago, some genius decided to put a doorway directly under Leonardo da Vinci's masterpiece "The Last Supper"—chopping off Jesus' feet in the process. Planners in Milan today wouldn't commit that mistake. The fashion and finance capital is obsessed with making shoes as visible as possible. And we're not just talking Ermenegildo Zegna loafers. Pedestrian-friendly projects are all the rage across the northern Italian city, which is deploying design elements to combat a skyline that had become known as smoggy and stale.

The showstopper is Porta Nuova, a formerly dead zone located between the central train station and Milan's top tourist attractions (including its original grand shopping arcade, the Galleria Vittorio Emanuele II). Over the past five years, Porta Nuova has become the place to geek out over architecture. Stand in the elevated Piazza Gae Aulenti, with its LED-enhanced fountains, while gazing up at the steel spire atop the UniCredit Tower—the tallest building in Italy. Just beyond a mod botanic garden is the ultimate tree house: two residential high-rises covered in leafy vegetation and named Bosco Verticale (Vertical Forest). The whole development has become a magnet for coffee drinkers, cocktail sippers, and, of course, shoppers. International brands abound, but the main fashionista focus is just a short stroll to the south. Behind an understated entrance draped with vines, 10 Corso Como combines art gallery, restaurant, bookshop, and clothing store.

It's easy to imagine a similar scene emerging soon on the opposite side of Milan at CityLife, a mixed-use project that's one of the largest car-free zones in Europe. A trio of big-name architects—Zaha Hadid, Arata Isozaki, and Daniel Libeskind—are the creative talent behind what is currently a ridiculously pleasant construction site with cranes soaring beside gleaming skyscrapers, and kids and dogs frolicking in the park below.

Expo 2015, the world's fair that brought global attention to the city, jump-started many of these changes. It forced Milan to move forward, says Marco Tabasso, co-curator and press officer for Galleria Rossana Orlandi, which features quirky, independent designers. He's gradually seen local tastes evolve from traditional to open-minded.

"Let's say Milan has been stuck for some years, and now there's a new wave of energy," says Francesca Picciocchi, a native Milanese who works for an Italian menswear brand. For instance, there wasn't much reason to visit the industrial Porta Romana area until it recently welcomed Fondazione Prada, a contemporary art complex with a retro-inspired bar designed by director Wes Anderson. A revitalization of the Darsena, the city's dock, has made it even more appealing to wander through the Navigli neighborhood, where Picciocchi hunts down vintage goods. Even trendy Zona Tortona, the center of design in the city, is buzzing more than ever with new businesses and museums (including one from Giorgio Armani).

The only downside to exploring all of these offerings? The potential for blisters.

—**Vicky Hallett** is a freelance writer and editor based in Florence, Italy.

Oahu's Valley of the Temples was featured as a wedding backdrop in *Lost*.

Television Locations

From *Game of Thrones* to *Outlander*, walk in the footsteps of your favorite stars on a weekend getaway.

1. *GAME OF THRONES*, NORTHERN IRELAND

HBO's all-time greatest hit was shot across six countries, but its spiritual home was Northern Ireland. Hit Belfast's Kelly's Cellars before exploring the Kingsroad (Bregagh Road) and Winterfell's backyard (Tollymore Forest).

2. *LOST*, OAHU, HAWAII, U.S.

Oahu remains a hot spot for the fans of this hit series. From Papailoa Beach (the main camp) to the Valley of the Temples (a wedding backdrop), locations abound and dazzle.

3. *THE CROWN*, ENGLAND

The Netflix juggernaut that's given new meaning to royals-watching is filmed throughout the United Kingdom, with enough London locations to make for several city tours. Particularly popular are day trips to Hatfield House (a sub for Marlborough House).

4. *NORTHERN EXPOSURE*, ROSLYN, WASHINGTON, U.S.

Fans of this 1990s cult favorite still visit Roslyn to experience the real-life "Cicely, AK," where the Roslyn's Café mural lives on—among other hallowed sites.

5. *BIG LITTLE LIES*, MONTEREY, CALIFORNIA, U.S.

Playing its gorgeous self on this HBO hit, Monterey, California, has become a pilgrimage site for fans. Must-dos include the iconic Monterey Bay Aquarium (bonus if you're with someone you can kiss by the bubble curtain) and Old Fisherman's Wharf. Don't forget a drive across Bixby Bridge—the stunning arched overpass along the coast featured in the show's opening credits.

6. *NARCOS*, MEDELLÍN, COLOMBIA

For travelers exploring the much heralded reemergence of Medellín's art, culture, and food scenes, *Narcos* has added a fascinating layer to the visit, as you'll find on the local Escobar-themed tours. Don't miss the drug lord's crazy suburban estate, Hacienda Napoles, now a theme park.

7. *BREAKING BAD*, ALBUQUERQUE, NEW MEXICO, U.S.

Bryan Cranston (aka the fabled Walter White) noted that "Albuquerque itself has become a character in our show." If a lap around the filming locations leaves your car dusty, visit Mister Car Wash—the real-life A-1.

8. *THE SOPRANOS*, BLOOMFIELD, NEW JERSEY, U.S.

While this HBO hit ended in 2007, the real-life diner from the infamous series finale, Holsten's Brookdale Confectionery Ice Cream Parlor, offers seats at the iconic table where the famous family sat. It remains reserved on Saturdays in honor of the late James Gandolfini.

9. *OUTLANDER*, SCOTLAND

Though this Starz hit has filmed internationally, its roots—and most stunning locations—are in Scotland, from Culross (Geillis's village) to Doune Castle (a stand-in for *Outlander*'s Castle Leoch and, at one point, for *Game of Thrones*' Winterfell). Don't forget a stop at Linlithgow Palace (Wentworth Prison), originally a 12th-century royal manor, rebuilt into a grand residence by King James I after a fire destroyed the town in 1424.

10. *LAW AND ORDER: SVU*, NEW YORK CITY, U.S.

The longest running live-action prime-time series in U.S. history, *Law and Order: SVU* has used countless locations around New York. But if you visit only one, make it the iconic staircase outside the New York courthouse at 60 Centre Street, part of the real-life New York Supreme Court.

A novice monk prays at Wat Phra That.

Northern Soul
Chiang Mai, Thailand

Despite its name, Chiang Mai (New City) is actually very old. The walled city was founded in the 13th century as the capital of a long-lost kingdom. The oldest temples, Wat Chiang Man and Wat Chedi Luang, recall those ancient days. There are plenty of other Buddhist shrines, including the golden Wat Phra That Doi Suthep with its hilltop views across Chiang Mai. But the city is most renowned for night markets that mingle local handicrafts and tasty Thai cuisine. Seek out local specialties like *sai oua* sausages, *khao soi* (egg noodle curry), *kâab moo* (pork rinds), and various sticky rice concoctions. Fill the rest of your time with excursions just outside the city center, including seeing rescued giants at the Elephant Nature Park, day-trekking the surrounding hill tribe country, or watching professional kickboxing matches. Chiang Mai also offers offbeat museums, including the Museum of World Insects and Natural Wonders and mind-bending 3-D visuals at Art in Paradise Chiang Mai.

HUB | *Bangkok, Thailand; Singapore*

Abu Dhabi is home to its own ornate Louvre Museum.

Arabian Days & Nights
Abu Dhabi, United Arab Emirates

Although often overshadowed by that other emirate city (Dubai), Abu Dhabi has slowly grown into one of the most intriguing urban areas in the Middle East, and it may actually boast more world-class attractions than its sister city. Unveiled in 2017, the new Louvre Abu Dhabi, the largest museum on the Arabian Peninsula, is noteworthy for both its artwork (borrowed from top French museums) and its spectacular design. The city's other architectural treasure is Sheikh Zayed Grand Mosque, an exquisite example of modern Islamic design that offers free guided tours to all visitors. Action is the theme of day two in Abu Dhabi. Adrenaline rides—including the world's fastest roller coaster—are on offer at Ferrari World theme park. Or try a dune-bashing desert safari, camel rides, or sandboarding in the Arabian Desert around Al Ain Oasis. Then there's speed boating or Jet Skiing in the gulf. Punctuate your Abu Dhabi weekend with a sunset walk along the Corniche waterfront.

HUB | *Dubai, United Arab Emirates*

Footloose & Fancy Free

Montevideo, Uruguay

Just two hours by high-speed ferry from Buenos Aires, Uruguay's compact capital is like a trip back in time to a slower and more gentle age when people had time to linger in bars and sidewalk cafés and tango until dawn. Stretching across a peninsula between Montevideo Harbor and the Río de la Plata, the Ciudad Vieja (Old City) revolves around plazas connected by the Peatonal Sarandi pedestrian street. Plaza Constitución is flanked by the Spanish-colonial cathedral and a museum dedicated to the Uruguay rugby players—those who survived and those who died—in the 1972 Andes plane crash. The outlandish Palacio Salvo (a 1920s skyscraper that blends Gothic and art deco architecture), a tango museum, and the elegant Teatro Solís surround Plaza Independencia. Solís is the best place in Montevideo to catch opera, symphony, and ballet on Saturday night—if you haven't already scored tickets to see soccer (football) at Estadio Centenario, home of the first World Cup (1930).

HUB | *Buenos Aires, Argentina; Rio de Janeiro, Brazil*

The sun sets over the Plaza Independencia.

With an easy train ride,
you can see Machu Picchu
in a weekend (p. 255).

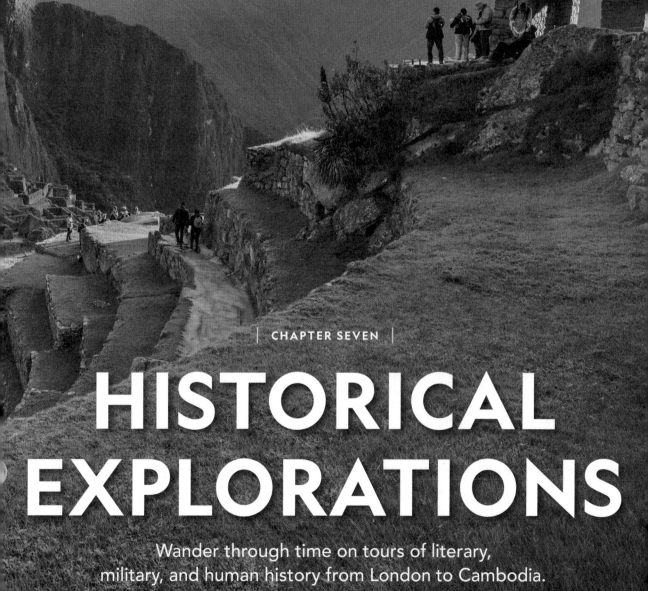

CHAPTER SEVEN

HISTORICAL EXPLORATIONS

Wander through time on tours of literary,
military, and human history from London to Cambodia.

See live jazz shows at Preservation Hall in New Orleans.

Delta Blues Highway

Memphis, Tennessee, to New Orleans, Louisiana, U.S.

A string of cities and towns along U.S. Highway 61 in the Deep South is renowned as the primary birthplace of blues, jazz, soul, and even rock-and-roll. Graceland and Beale Street are obligatory stops in Memphis before the weekend rolls down the Mississippi River to the Devil's Crossroads in Clarksdale, where blues legend Robert Johnson allegedly sold his soul to Satan in the 1930s. Browse the interactive GRAMMY Museum Mississippi before bunking down for the night in Cleveland. Catch a live jam session the following day at Dockery Farm and learn more about the cultural and social impact of the region's music at the B.B. King Museum and Delta Interpretive Center in Indianola. From there it's a straight shot down to New Orleans for an afternoon gig at Preservation Hall, live tunes at the New Orleans Jazz Museum (in the Old U.S. Mint), or an evening savoring the music joints along Frenchmen Street.

HUB | *Southeastern United States*

Arizona Desert Days

Tucson, Arizona, U.S.

Tucson provides a sophisticated urban base for a weekend that covers more than 300 years of Arizona history. The I-19 corridor between Tucson and the Mexican border offers plenty of fodder for day one, starting with San Xavier del Bac, an 18th-century mission and masterpiece of Spanish colonial architecture that's now the parish church for the Tohono O'odham Nation San Xavier Indian Reservation. The nearby Titan Missile Museum has tours of a supersecret Cold War military bunker, while Tubac Presidio State Historic Park and Tumacácori National Historical Park preserve more Spanish colonial relics. Wild West is the theme of day two's drive across the Sonoran Desert that includes Tombstone and its infamous O.K. Corral, the Amerind Museum in Dragoon, and the old U.S. Cavalry outpost and Butterfield mail stagecoach station in Fort Bowie. On the way back to Tucson, fast-forward into the 20th century at the Pima Air & Space Museum and its "Boneyard" of 4,400 vintage military aircraft.

Jet sculptures soar at the Pima Air & Space Museum.

HUB | *Phoenix, Arizona, U.S.; Southwestern United States*

A statue of George Washington in Boston's Public Garden

Patriots & Pilgrims

Boston, Massachusetts, U.S.

The United States and many of its ideals were largely born along the shore of eastern Massachusetts and the age-old cities that crown its coast today. Base yourself in downtown Boston, within walking distance of Boston Common, Faneuil Hall, and the Freedom Trail, as well as the bridge that leaps across the Charles River to the USS *Constitution* and Bunker Hill.

History buffs have three choices on day two. One is to follow a trail of pilgrims and presidents to the JFK Library at Columbia Point, Adams National Historical Park in Quincy, that famous rock in Plymouth, and all the way out to the Kennedy family sights in Hyannis Port. Or you can head inland for tales of Concord and Lexington at Minute Man National Historical Park, and environmental history at Walden Pond. Option three is exploring old seaports along the North Shore like sinister Salem (famed for more than just witchcraft) and gorgeous Gloucester.

HUB | *Northeastern United States*

This ancient village, in ruins from the Spanish Civil War, is memorialized in Belchite, Spain.

Battlefields

Walk hallowed ground where the greatest battles in history took place—
from the Battle of Culloden to World War II.

1. CULLODEN, SCOTLAND

The 1746 Battle of Culloden, the conflict that ended the Jacobite uprising, has been depicted everywhere from the BBC's *Culloden* to Starz's *Outlander*. The real-world site is well marked and—because it's in the Scottish Highlands—eerily beautiful. Guided tours take you through key areas of action on Culloden Moor, as well as a memorial cairn, around which lie the graves of nearly 1,500 Jacobites.

2. YORKTOWN BATTLEFIELD, VIRGINIA, U.S.

Even if you'd forgotten that the 1781 Battle of Yorktown was the last major conflict of the Revolutionary War, *Hamilton* has surely reminded you. The megahit Broadway show has also spurred a renewed interest in Yorktown battlefield tours through Virginia's Colonial National Historical Park. Ranger-guided tours and non-firing demonstrations are also on offer at the park.

3. PAMPA DE LA QUINUA, PERU

Also known as the Pampas de Ayacucho Historic Sanctuary, this obelisk-punctuated field near the eastern slopes of the Andes is where the 1824 battle secured not only Peru's independence from Spain, but eventually that of most of the continent.

4. FORT SUMTER, CHARLESTON, SOUTH CAROLINA, U.S.

In April 1861, the Civil War began when Confederate forces fired on the U.S. garrison at this Charleston Harbor sea fort. Now the island is in the hands of National Park Service rangers, who offer multiple daily guided tours.

5. ISANDLWANA, SOUTH AFRICA

South Africa's KwaZulu-Natal has seen so many skirmishes that an entire region is called Battlefields. Perhaps the most famous site is Isandlwana, where traditonal Zulu warriors bested British forces in 1879 during the first major battle of the Anglo-Zulu War.

6. BEAUMONT-HAMEL, FRANCE

This battlefield in northern France is among the best preserved of World War I. Around the Beaumont-Hamel Newfoundland Monument to the Canadian soldiers who fought here during the 1916 Battle of the Somme, you can still see trenches and craters.

7. BELCHITE, SPAIN

Reportedly one of Hemingway's stops during his war correspondent days, this ancient village on the frontlines of the Spanish Civil War has sat in ruins as one of the nation's most stirring memorials since the 1937 Battle of Belchite.

8. EL-ALAMEIN, EGYPT

World War II brought repeated action to this site outside Cairo, but the second Battle of El-Alamein in 1942 proved the turning point: The Allied victory led to the end of the North African campaign, as you'll learn at the on-site museum.

9. THE BEACHES OF NORMANDY, FRANCE

Scene of the largest amphibious invasion in history and a pivotal Allied victory, the Normandy coastline saw more than 150,000 troops land on June 6, 1944. Now, the area's museums, memorials, and tours make for a stirring introduction to D-Day.

10. HIROSHIMA PEACE MEMORIAL PARK

The haunting A-Bomb Dome—one of the only buildings to withstand "Little Boy" on August 6, 1945—is now a UNESCO World Heritage site and the heart of this deeply affecting park, where the Children's Peace Monument—dedicated to the thousands of children who were victims of the bombings—is another must.

Canterbury Tales

London to Hastings, England

Although it was largely a social commentary on 14th-century English society, Geoffrey Chaucer's magnum opus was also one of the world's first travel books. And like the pilgrims of his epic tale, this weekend journey starts in London with a drive down the A2 along the route of an ancient Celtic track and Roman road. With its falconry and jousting demonstrations, Leeds Castle gets you in a medieval mood before rambling across Kent Downs to Canterbury Cathedral. The A2 continues down to Dover and its fabled White Cliffs. Spend Saturday night in a cozy B&B beside the coast before resuming your history quest the following morning with a drive along A259 to Hastings. The town's True Crime and Shipwreck museums are worth a look before heading inland to Battle, where the fate of England was decided in the year 1066. From there it's just two hours back to London via roads through the High Weald countryside.

HUB | *London, England*

"THIS WEEKEND JOURNEY STARTS IN LONDON WITH A DRIVE DOWN THE A2 ALONG THE ROUTE OF AN ANCIENT CELTIC TRACK AND ROMAN ROAD."

There are more than 900 years of history within the walls of Leeds Castle in Kent.

Cherry blossom trees frame the U.S. Capitol in spring.

American History 101

Philadelphia, Pennsylvania, to Washington, D.C., U.S.

How much American history can you cram into 240 miles (390 km)? Turns out quite a bit if that distance stretches between Philadelphia and Washington, D.C. Independence Hall marks not just the start of the United States as a nation, but also the start of this weekend. Pick up a Philly cheesesteak to eat on the drive out to Valley Forge, where George Washington and his troops barely survived the frigid winter of 1777–78. Then it's on to Gettysburg. If the South had won the 1863 battle, the country most likely would have split in two. Just down the pike is Baltimore, where the national anthem was born at Fort McHenry during the War of 1812. The grand finale is the District of Columbia, home to the White House, the U.S. Capitol, 11 memorials along the Mall, and the Smithsonian Museum of American History.

The Liberty Bell and Independence Hall

HUB | *Mid-Atlantic United States*

The Abbey Library of St. Gall dates to medieval Switzerland.

Turn Up the Volumes

In a Digital Age, Travelers Find Novel Appeal in the Splendor and Secrets of Grand Libraries

I knew I had a library problem the first time I stood under the Pantheon-scale dome of the State Library Victoria in Melbourne, Australia. In that impossibly grand temple of books, my heart thumped with a sudden realization: Libraries can capture and hold history in a spectacular way. Ever since that moment, I've been a full-blown library lover.

In 2012 my daughter, Thea, was born. By the age of five, she already knew her quartos from her octavos, her Penguins from her Puffins. I wanted, though, to turbocharge her love of libraries. Around the dinner table, my wife, Fiona, and I planned a family trip: a world tour of great collections.

We reeled off our must-sees. The evocative medievalism of the Bodleian, in Oxford, England; the jewel box perfection of New York's Morgan; the cozy idiosyncrasy of the Folger Shakespeare and the stunning grandeur of the Library of Congress, both in Washington, D.C.

"But we have to go to the British Museum too," Thea countered, "to see the mummies from ancient Egypt."

The British Museum, in London, has only a modest collection of books, and its famous reading room is closed indefinitely as the museum considers how best to use it. But the museum had a right to be on our list, and it was a walkable distance from its uber-bookish sister institution, the British Library. Plus, Thea's interest in mummies gave me an idea.

"Let's make a deal," I said. "If the British Museum is your favorite, we also have to go to my favorite."

We shook hands and added two destinations to our list: the British Museum and the Swiss valley where an old monastery houses what I think is the most beautiful library in the world, the Abbey Library of St. Gall.

That library's history began in the Dark Ages when a party of Irish monks traveled deep into Europe. In mountainous country near Lake Constance, one of the monks tripped. Taking this as a sign, he set up a hermit cell. The hermitage soon grew into a monastery where scribes painstakingly copied and illuminated manuscripts, decorating them with gold and silver and lapis lazuli.

In the 10th century, the library survived a Hungarian invasion and a fire. In subsequent centuries the books suffered neglect; visitors reported seeing them in dusty and moldy condition. In the 1700s, however, St. Gall entered a second golden era. Master craftsmen built an exquisite library hall with elaborate fittings and a trompe l'oeil ceiling that created the illusion of bookcases extending into the heavens.

About an hour's train ride from Zurich, St. Gallen today is a city of around 70,000 people. We arrived on a sunny day. Snow had fallen the night before, and there were piles of it in the street.

After Thea made and threw her first snowball, we walked through the twisting cobblestone streets of the old town, famous for its half-timbered buildings and their carved wooden figures. Reaching the clearing that surrounds the abbey, we were struck by the building's scale and its pristine state of preservation. Upstairs in the library wing we donned the felt slippers that visitors must wear over their shoes to protect the patterned pinewood floor. The Greek inscription over the library entrance echoes that from the Great Library of Alexandria: "Sanatorium for the soul." When we entered the library hall, it was bathed in golden light. Thousands of books in their original bindings stood spine-outward behind protective wire lattice. Pyramid-shaped cases held the principal treasures, such as the oldest known German book in the world and an illustrated "pauper's bible."

The hall also has its secrets. Extending along either side are hinged wooden pillars that, when opened, reveal an ingenious catalog system of cards and pins. A hidden staircase leads to a room that houses even more of the library's rare manuscripts.

Their majestic utility aside, the world's libraries are under threat. New forms of media are supplanting the physical book, and libraries are being closed, as in Britain, or looted and destroyed, as in Baghdad and Timbuktu. But places like St. Gall show that libraries have always been at risk and that people have always been willing to step forward to protect them.

Near the end of our visit to St. Gall, I led Thea to the surprise I'd been planning for her from the beginning when we'd made our deal. It was also one of the library's greatest treasures: the mummy Schepenese, a young Egyptian woman from Thebes, beautifully preserved with her ebony skin and immaculate teeth. After that thrilling encounter, I could see that Thea had joined the ranks of bibliophiles for whom libraries shelter much more than books.

—**Stuart Kells** is a Melbourne, Australia–based writer and the author of *The Library: A Catalogue of Wonders.*

Katz Castle looks downstream from the riverside at St. Goar.

Bold Castles & Wild Rocks
Frankfurt to Cologne, Germany

Germany's River Rhine became a tourist lure in the early 19th century thanks to writers like Lord Byron and Mary Shelley, who idealized the region's "bold castles on wild rocks." Two hundred years later, the storied waterway continues to channel that romantic aura. Jump-start the weekend by hopping a train from Frankfurt Airport to Bingen and boarding an early morning KD Rhine riverboat. The 11-hour downstream journey features dozens of medieval bastions (like Burg Katz and Burg Maus—"Cat" and "Mouse" castles), as well as villages, vineyards, and fabled Lorelei Rock, a 433-foot (132 m) cliff that looms above a bend in the Rhine. Spend the night in Koblenz with its mighty hilltop fortress, historic old town, and *neue Deutsche küche* (new German cuisine). After a morning exploring Koblenz, continue to Cologne by riverboat or train with a stop along the way in Bonn to see the house where Beethoven was born and the excellent Haus der Geschichte der Bundesrepublik Deutschland, which traces Germany's post–World War II history.

HUB | *Frankfurt, Germany*

A statue of Horus guards the entrance to the Temple of Horus.

Gifts of the Nile
Luxor to Aswan, Egypt

Luxor and Aswan are renowned for their ancient Egyptian landmarks. But several lesser known towns along the Upper Nile boast impressive pharaonic treasures of their own. About 30 miles (50 km) downstream from Aswan, the riverside Temple of Kom Ombo is dedicated to Sobek, a crocodile-headed god closely associated with the Nile. The site museum displays hundreds of mummified crocodiles uncovered around the temple. The falcon-headed god of ancient Egypt is master of the Temple of Horus, a towering shrine in Edfu that ranks among the largest and best preserved temples in all of Egypt. Reaching Esna, the river gets funneled through Victorian-era canal locks (great for boat watching) near the Temple of Khnum, another impressive shrine, this one dedicated to a ram-headed deity. From Esna it's another 43 miles (70 km) downstream to Luxor. This weekend-long journey can be undertaken by private car, luxury riverboat, or even on the deck of a felucca.

HUB | *Cairo, Egypt*

Antiquities & Arts

The Rhône Delta, France

Born of an Alpine glacier, the Rhône River makes its way to the Mediterranean via an expansive delta region that reveals three different eras of French history and some of its most astonishing landscapes. Less than three hours from Paris on the TGV high-speed train, Avignon renders a perfect start to the weekend with medieval monuments like the ruined but romantic Pont Saint-Bénézet bridge, a 12th-century Romanesque cathedral, and the Gothic Palais des Papes (Palace of Popes). Farther downstream, Arles cranks the clock back another thousand years with Roman ruins that include an almost perfectly preserved arena (host to summer concerts and theater), public baths, an aqueduct, and a sizeable necropolis. Arles is also well endowed with tributes to Vincent van Gogh, who painted more than 300 scenes in and around the city. Round out the weekend in Aix-en-Provence, birthplace and longtime home of Impressionist maestro Paul Cézanne and the last resting place of Pablo Picasso.

HUB | *Paris, France; Rome, Italy*

Lavender and sunflower fields bloom in Provence's countryside.

"A HERITAGE RIPE FOR EXPLORING OVER A TWO- OR THREE-DAY WEEKEND"

Mexico City Mosaic

Mexico City, Mexico

Rather than the often crowded and chaotic metropolis of global repute, think of Mexico City as a vast archaeological dig—layer upon layer of history piled atop one another by the various civilizations that have ruled this valley over the past 2,000 years. It's a heritage ripe for exploring over a two- or three-day weekend.

Perched on the city's northern edge, Teotihuacan flourished as a religious and government center around the same time as the Roman Empire. This still-mysterious culture built huge palaces and pyramids along the Avenue of the Dead. Sunrise flights in hot-air balloons provide an incredible bird's-eye view of the ancient architecture.

A thousand years later, the Aztec created the city of Tenochtitlan on an island in the middle of a vast lake that once covered much of the valley. The ruined Templo Mayor in downtown Mexico City is the outstanding relic of that age, a UNESCO World Heritage site with an on-site museum that displays many archaeological treasures.

Hernán Cortés vanquished the Aztec in the 1520s and set about replacing Tenochtitlan with a Spanish city that revolved around the Metropolitan Cathedral and its lurid blend of baroque, neoclassical, and homegrown churrigueresque decorations. A weekly historical musical, "Voces de Catedral," is one of many performances staged inside Latin America's largest church.

The only royal castle in the Americas, Chapultepec Castle was home to the 19th-century monarchy that ruled independent Mexico. It also played a role in the Mexican War as the "Halls of Montezuma" stormed by U.S. Marines in 1847.

Rounding out the Mexico City time trip, Coyoacán district was home to some of the country's most memorable characters. Frida Kahlo's colorful Casa Azul is now a museum, as are the Casa Estudio she shared with artist husband, Diego Rivera, and the bright-red home where exiled Russian revolutionary Leon Trotsky was assassinated with an ice pick in 1940.

HUB | *Buenavista, Mexico; Houston or El Paso, Texas, U.S.*

Chapultepec Castle on the eponymous hill was built in 1725.

The *Jacobite* steam train is better known as the *Hogwarts Express*.

Train Rides

All aboard! Capture the best the world has to offer
on a steam engine expedition.

1. *VENICE SIMPLON-ORIENT-EXPRESS*

True icons, Belmond's dazzlingly restored vintage carriages take you to not only the grandes dames of European cities (weekend itineraries include Venice to Paris and Verona to London) but also the golden age of train travel. The train's cabins will also whisk you back in time, with elegant wood paneling and luxury touches.

2. THE *BLUE TRAIN*

If the *Orient-Express* is Europe's bucket list train, the *Blue Train* is Africa's. While the luxuries may be similar—from gourmet feasts to elegant lounges to cushy sleeper cars—the scenery between Cape Town and Pretoria is a bit different. Think a "rail safari" that may include wildlife spotting of flamingos, animals roaming savannah grasslands, and Africa's Big Five, for starters.

3. THE *GLACIER EXPRESS*

If the name strikes you as something out of a kids' Christmas movie, your expectations won't be too far off. Few rides are more magical in winter, or any other time, than this eight-hour expedition through the Swiss Alps. The journey takes you to two of Switzerland's major mountain resorts: St. Moritz and Zermatt.

4. THE *NAPA VALLEY WINE TRAIN*

Its own kind of magic, this restored collection of vintage first-class cars offers everything from two-hour dinner outings to day-long winery tours. Or go full Agatha Christie and join one of the Prohibition-era Murder Mystery rides.

5. THE *HIRAM BINGHAM*

You *could* drink wine aboard this retro luxe Andean train—the bar is impeccably stocked—but don't do so to the exclusion of pisco sours, which pair perfectly with the dreamy, riverside ride to Machu Picchu.

6. *CUMBRES & TOLTEC SCENIC RAILROAD*

Travel the 64 miles (103 km) between Chama, New Mexico, and Antonito, Colorado, on this national historic landmark train, and you'll experience the highest rail-accessible mountain pass in the United States, among other stretches of gorgeously secluded—truly wild—West.

7. THE *JACOBITE*

Odds are you know this Scottish steam train by another name: the *Hogwarts Express.* Harry Potter fan or not, you can't but help love the 84-mile (135.2 km) ride through the Highlands, from Fort William to Mallaig and back—and across their trademark viaduct.

8. *AMTRAK CASCADES*

The greatest hits of the Pacific Northwest are all rolled into a 10.5-hour ride on a route through Vancouver, Canada, Seattle, Washington, and Portland and Eugene, Oregon—with unreal views of the Columbia River Gorge and Mount St. Helens along the way.

9. *SEVEN STARS*

If it's a Japanese volcano you'd prefer, try for seats aboard *Seven Stars* (such hot tickets, there have been lotteries). Reportedly the world's most luxurious train, it comes with painstakingly handcrafted interiors that rival Kyushu's legendary landscapes. The lounge car is considered a "saloon on wheels" and offers a bar, sofas, and live piano performances, and the guest compartments are spacious suites.

10. *TRANZALPINE*

Running between Christchurch and Greymouth, this nine-hour round-trip route through New Zealand's Southern Alps offers mountain views as the train races along the Waimakariri River.

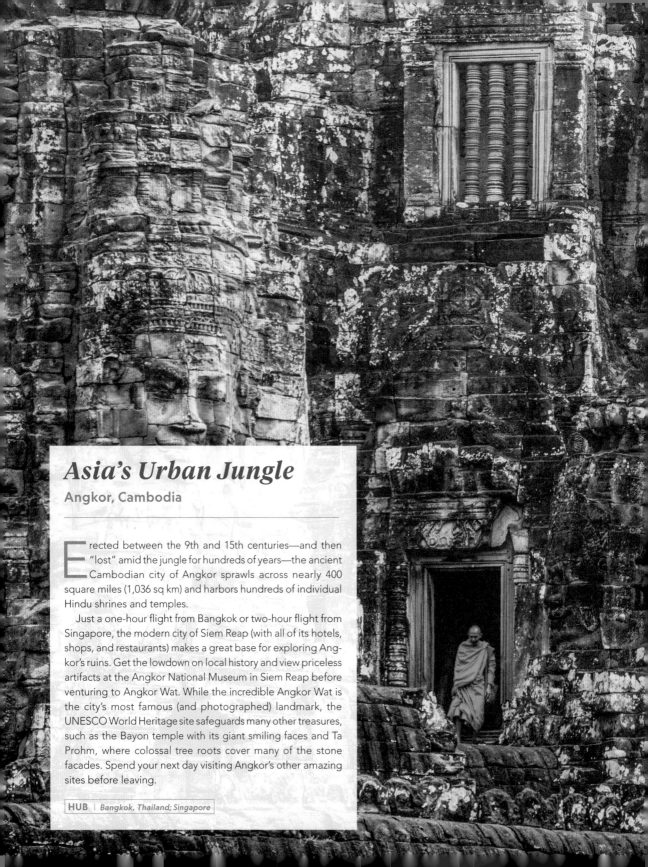

Asia's Urban Jungle

Angkor, Cambodia

Erected between the 9th and 15th centuries—and then "lost" amid the jungle for hundreds of years—the ancient Cambodian city of Angkor sprawls across nearly 400 square miles (1,036 sq km) and harbors hundreds of individual Hindu shrines and temples.

Just a one-hour flight from Bangkok or two-hour flight from Singapore, the modern city of Siem Reap (with all of its hotels, shops, and restaurants) makes a great base for exploring Angkor's ruins. Get the lowdown on local history and view priceless artifacts at the Angkor National Museum in Siem Reap before venturing to Angkor Wat. While the incredible Angkor Wat is the city's most famous (and photographed) landmark, the UNESCO World Heritage site safeguards many other treasures, such as the Bayon temple with its giant smiling faces and Ta Prohm, where colossal tree roots cover many of the stone facades. Spend your next day visiting Angkor's other amazing sites before leaving.

HUB | *Bangkok, Thailand; Singapore*

A monk emerges
from Bayon temple
in Angkor.

The Beasley Building Mural was painted by Michael Webb.

The City of Brotherly Love

An American Classic Returns With a Creative Splash

Philadelphia wears history like an embroidered cloak. It settles on the city's shoulders at legendary squares like Rittenhouse, with its towering shade trees and gurgling fountain.

But scratch the surface and you might find what Albanian-born fashion designer Bela Shehu describes as "fancy hooligans squatting in a space." This is how she characterizes the pop-up design consortia called Private Schools that she organizes. "Doing something different has always been a thing here," she says from her Rittenhouse Square atelier NinoBrand, where she makes chic clothing with cutting-edge silhouettes and urban energy.

If Shehu's work is artful, peppering Philadelphia with signature style, then Isaiah Zagar's is kaleidoscopic. For more than five decades, Zagar has been installing mosaics—made of everything from mirrors and Mexican crockery to old wine bottles and ceramic baby dolls—that glint and catch the sun along South Philly's side streets. At his Magic Gardens, Zagar's masterworks jam-pack the three-story-tall outdoor space, transporting the visitor to a place not entirely earthly.

Murals have become Philly's calling card—a clue and possibly a catalyst to the city's inventive revival. Thirty-five years ago, Philadelphia Mural Arts founder Jane Golden started as a city servant on an anti-graffiti gig, repurposing graffiti artists as public art purveyors, putting color on canvases several stories high. "It's the story of us, and it's a story that's unfolding," says Golden. To date, there are more than 4,000 murals splashed and dabbed, pasted and wrapped around the city's architecture, each composed with input from the neighborhood where it resides so that it reflects the community where it blooms.

To turn any corner in Philly is to catch sight of Golden's army's handiwork. And sometimes of actual hands at work. Some murals are colossal, including a September 2019 scene rising 18 stories high over the Schuylkill, calling to mind the chutzpah of artists and volunteers willing to balance on a scaffold all those floors up, paint can in one hand, brush in another. Other times, they pop up in the warren of streets surrounding Walnut and Locust in the center of town, lanes so narrow they make passing buildings feel like the gentle brush of shoulders. It's an intimate scale to take in street art.

The orange-flamed neon sign at cheesesteak baron Geno's is still lit, but food in America's first capital city is being reinvented at a radical clip. Philly-born-and-bred owner Nicole Marquis of vegan Charlie Was a Sinner serves up meatless meatballs, and Grindcore House takes vegan coffee and pastries to another level, backgrounding them with blistering heavy metal music. At the other end of the volume meter, soft-pink rose petals levitate on chai foam at Suraya, a vegetarian-friendly Lebanese café and restaurant with an expansive patio that feels like it might have been plucked from a way station on the Silk Road and gently laid down in the heart of hip Fishtown.

Indonesian hole-in-the-wall Hardena has some locals pondering leaving cheesesteaks behind forever. At the tiny South Philly restaurant—a 2019 James Beard Award upstart—lines weave out of the bright blue building, with diners waiting patiently for brilliantly colored curries, rich beef *rendang*, spicy peanut salads, and spongy yellow eggs sidling up to pillows of golden tofu delivered on polystyrene plates from an indoor food cart.

"What do you love about Philly?" I ask my taxi driver as we turn one of the corners of City Hall. Philadelphia's heart and hub, City Hall radiates arteries to every quadrant of the city. His Philly elongations in full flare, the cabbie answers matter-of-factly, "I've lived here my whole life." It seems like a nonanswer at first.

But having recently decamped from Brooklyn for a pilgrimage around America, I know that home needs no explanation.

A stroll down Passyunk (pronounced Pash-unk) Avenue—passing shops and restaurants and something called the Singing Fountain, which was once said to produce musical notes—is a lesson in Eclectic Philly 101. Like the Mad Hatter's top hat, Philly Typewriter crowns East Passyunk. It's the kind of anachronistic shop that makes you do a double take.

As I walk the aisles, I'm charmed both by the machines—I'm a writer, after all—and the sweet jottings they've inspired. "Olivia was here," one claims. "I am having so much fun," reads another. Ditto.

I'm tempted to type a paean to the charms of Philly, but I'm reminded of something said to me the day before: "I wouldn't call it charming. It's just trying to be itself." Perhaps now that the city's been liberated from the pressure to make what the world needs, Philadelphia has reignited its revolutionary spirit to make what Philly wants. And the world is watching.

—**Johnna Rizzo** is a former staff writer for *National Geographic* magazine. She is writing a series of nonfiction graphic novels with the U.S. National Park Service.

Monks walk through Borobodur, a ninth-century Buddhist temple.

A Regal Relic
Yogyakarta, Indonesia

Whether you take the express train from Jakarta or wing in from Singapore or Kuala Lumpur, Yogyakarta offers an array of sites to behold on a weekend, plus sounds and even smells covering the three great epochs of Indonesian history—Buddhist, Hindu, and Muslim. Located on the south side of Java island, the city harbors the archipelago's only remaining monarchy. In addition to hosting the current sultan, the capacious Kraton Ngayogyakarta Hadiningrat palace offers free weekend royal dance troupe and gamelan orchestra performances. The chaotic neighborhood around the palace is crowded with restaurants, batik shops, art galleries, and handicraft stores, especially along busy Jalan Malioboro. Perched on the city's northern edge, the ninth-century Borobodur stupa is the largest stone monument of any kind in the Southern Hemisphere and still a place of Buddhist pilgrimage. The Hindu sites at Prambanan Temple are even older, as well as a venue for spectacular outdoor performances of the Ramayana epic.

HUB | *Jakarta, Indonesia; Singapore*

Explore the Monastery of San Juan de los Reyes in Toledo.

Castilian Odyssey
Madrid to Toledo, Spain

Madrid is surrounded by a trio of historic cities that rose to prominence during the Middle Ages, when the Kingdom of Castile spearheaded the reconquest and Spain's quest for a global empire. Start the weekend with a one-hour drive across the Sierra de Guadarrama mountains to Segovia, its old town dominated by the Alcázar (a perfectly proportioned medieval castle) and the last Gothic cathedral constructed in Spain. It's another hour to Ávila, the red-roofed old town completely enclosed by fortified walls featuring 88 towers and nine gates. With the ramparts romantically lit at night—and a range of accommodations—Ávila makes a great place to stay overnight. Toledo beckons the following day, about a two-hour drive via the scenic Rio Alberche Valley. One of Spain's oldest cities offers a beguiling blend of Moorish, Gothic, and Renaissance architecture, as well as a museum dedicated to the artist El Greco, who produced many of his greatest works in Toledo.

HUB | *Madrid, Spain*

El Santuario de Chimayó is a designated national historic landmark.

In Old New Mexico

Santa Fe to Los Alamos, New Mexico, U.S.

Northern New Mexico paints a colorful canvas of American history, from ancient pueblos and the Wild West to artistic superstars and the Manhattan Project. With its Spanish colonial architecture and world-class museums, Santa Fe renders a brilliant starting point for a weekend suffused with tales from the past. The old High Road to Taos (Route 76) blends aspects of Native American and Spanish colonial heritage into a unique hybrid New Mexican culture reflected in the plazas, churches, and cuisine of mountain towns like Chimayó and Trampas. Taos Pueblo is a living anachronism (and UNESCO World Heritage site), while the "new" town of Taos offers Kit Carson's House and other frontier relics. On the other side of the Rio Grande Valley, artist Georgia O'Keeffe's home and studio in Abiquiú is now a museum, while Los Alamos is the place where the bomb that changed the world was engineered during World War II.

HUB | *Southwestern United States*

The Pyramid of the Sun
is the largest structure
in Teotihuacan.

Historic Monuments

From the Great Pyramids to the Great Wall of China,
pay homage to our human history.

1. THE GREAT PYRAMID OF GIZA, EGYPT

The only surviving member of the original Seven Wonders of the World, this Cairo-area icon is pushing 5,000 years. Amazingly, the pharaonic burial pyramid used to be even bigger, standing as the world's tallest built structure until Gustave Eiffel's day.

2. MACHU PICCHU, PERU

Though its exact function remains a matter of some debate, this mist-shrouded Inca citadel in the Peruvian Andes—one of the New Seven Wonders of the World—is indisputably among the most beautiful and bucket-listy places on Earth. For an informational spot away from the crowds, head to the Museo de Sitio Manuel Chavez Ballon, tucked at the end of a long dirt road at the base of the more visited ruins.

3. PETRA, JORDAN

Another one of the New Seven Wonders of the World (as are the next two spots on our list), this more or less 2,000-year-old city is carved directly into the pinkish-red sandstone cliffs of the Jordanian desert. Don't miss a chance to visit Petra at night, where you'll take a two-hour walk of the full canyon to the Treasury, lit by more than 1,000 candles—a magical experience.

4. THE GREAT WALL OF CHINA, CHINA

This isn't, in fact, a single wall, but rather a series of bulwarks built by various dynasties over the centuries. The aggregate effect is amazing—as is the accessibility of several sections, Mutianyu being a Bejing-area favorite.

5. THE COLOSSEUM, ITALY

At nearly two millennia old, the most iconic Roman amphitheater is still going strong. Even without gladiator fights and executions, it draws about 7 million people annually—thus, its recent designation as the world's most visited tourist attraction.

6. LALIBELA, ETHIOPIA

The cave churches of Lalibela are unquestionably ancient, having been carved from northern Ethiopia's volcanic rock in the 12th century. They still feel very much alive, drawing daily worshippers to this UNESCO World Heritage site.

7. CAPPADOCIA, TURKEY

Another UNESCO-designated architectural site, this stunning central Turkish town has harbored subterranean homes, storehouses, and chapels for more than 1,500 years. See it all by hot-air balloon.

8. TEOTIHUACAN, MEXICO

This World Heritage site, whose name means "the place where the gods were created," stands in serene contrast to nearby Mexico City—even if you don't feel the reported energy at the 1,800-year-old Pyramid of the Sun. The Meso-american settlement was once the most powerful and influential city in the area and named by the Aztec who found it in 1400.

9. POMPEII, ITALY

Nearly 2,000 years ago, Mount Vesuvius unleashed a torrent of volcanic debris that destroyed (and ironically preserved) this once thriving Roman town (population estimates run between 10,000 and 20,000 inhabitants at the time of the eruption). Now a popular excursion from Naples, the World Heritage site is equal parts horrifying and fascinating.

10. THE ACROPOLIS OF ATHENS, GREECE

"The greatest architectural and artistic complex bequeathed by Greek Antiquity to the world," in UNESCO's estimation, this hilltop icon boasts not only the Parthenon, the Odeon, the temple of Athena Nike, and all manner of Greek temples but also some of the best views of Athens.

"STILL, HERE AND THERE THE COLD WAR LINGERS."

In From the Cold

Berlin, Germany

In the decades since its infamous wall came down, Berlin has morphed from an economic backwater and political hot potato into Germany's cutting-edge capital and one of the world's most socially progressive cities, an urban area where food, fashion, nightlife, and even the German language are in constant flux.

Still, here and there, the Cold War lingers—in memorials, museums, monumental boulevards, and the few remnants of the Berlin Wall left standing.

Rising right behind the wall for 30 years, an old Prussian monument called the Brandenburg Gate symbolizes the plight of East Germans who couldn't escape. A broad boulevard, the Unter den Linden, leads into the heart of old East Berlin, across Museum Island to the Alexanderplatz, where a million protesters gathered in November 1989 demanding that the wall be pulled down.

Snatch a bird's-eye view of Berlin during lunch in the revolving restaurant atop the Berliner Fernsehturm (1,207.4 feet/368 m tall) before joining a Trabi-Safari for a self-drive caravan tour of East Berlin with commentary about many of the Communist-era sights around the city like Karl-Marx-Allee with its colossal Stalinist structures. Also see the Cold War Stasi Prison, where as many as 11,000 political dissidents and others deemed troublemakers were interned at any one time.

Three sections of the Berlin Wall endure, including a portion along Niederkirchnerstrasse near Check Point Charlie and the Berlin Wall Museum. The Berlin Wall Memorial is set inside a modern tower with views over the longest-remaining stretch of wall. Yet the most evocative display is a graffiti-covered 4,318 feet (1,316 m) of the wall memorialized in the open-air East Side Gallery along the River Spree. Then there's the eerie Tränenpalast (Palace of Tears), a border crossing where families were once split apart. Captured secret agents were exchanged on the Bridge of Spies in suburban Potsdam, not far from the former KGB headquarters and prison (now a museum) on Leistikowstrasse.

HUB | *Major Western European Cities*

Berlin's city center lights up at dusk.

The statue of Johann Strauss in Austrian Music Municipal Park

Classical Gas
Vienna, Austria

Rock like Amadeus during a melodious weekend in Vienna and Salzburg, the Austrian cities where classical music was largely born in the 18th and 19th centuries. Kick things off with a tour of the Vienna homes where Beethoven, Mozart, Schubert, and Strauss once lived; then visit their graves at the Vienna Central Cemetery (Zentralfriedhof). After dark, catch a performance at the Vienna State Opera or the Vienna Mozart Orchestra at the Wiener Musikverein. The following morning, explore the wonderful Haus der Musik (House of Music), an interactive museum that covers the development of sound from prehistoric through modern times. Then hop a train to Salzburg, about an hour and a half west of Vienna. Pay homage to the great one at Mozart's birthplace and the home on Makartplatz where he spent his adolescence. Catch an afternoon gig at one of the city's churches or historic halls, and then create a rousing coda for the weekend with a grand concert at Grosses Festspielhaus.

HUB | *Major Western European Cities*

Lounge Around
Luang Prabang, Laos

An Asian version of old Havana, more than half a century of conflict and isolation from the outside world has preserved Luang Prabang as an almost perfect portrait of a different age. A mosaic of French colonial villas, Buddhist monasteries, and royal compounds crowds onto a thumb-shaped peninsula on the Mekong River in central Laos. Toss in lively street markets (night and day), excellent French-influenced Asian cooking (you'll love the smell of fresh baguettes in the morning), a range of boutique hotels, and plenty of ice-cold Lao lager, and you've got all the fixings for a perfect weekend getaway from the big cities of Southeast Asia. Climb Mount Phousi for an overall view of the town and the Mekong River Valley, and explore the palace that hosted the Laotian royal family until 1975 when they were ousted by the communist Pathet Lao. Then contemplate Wat Xieng Thong and other monasteries filled with saffron-clad monks who also march through the town early each morning asking for alms.

HUB | *Bangkok, Thailand; Singapore*

Night market stalls are set up below Haw Pha Bang temple.

The King's Highway

Jerash to Wadi Rum, Jordan

One of the historical hubs of the Middle East, Jordan is just the right size for a weekend look into the past. Take in the lofty Amman Citadel and Roman ruins in Jerash before striking off down King's Highway. Celebrated as the spot where Moses first viewed the Promised Land, Mount Nebo offers fabulous mosaics and views of far-off Jerusalem. In nearby Madaba, St. George's Church safeguards a Byzantine mosaic map (the Madaba Map) of the Holy Land. Two hours farther south lies Kerak Castle, an imposing 12th-century crusader bastion and active military base until 1917 when the Ottoman Turks were dislodged. Another crusader castle hovers above Shoubak (try the local apples) before the route reaches the fabled red-rock city of Petra. King's Highway continues to coastal Aqaba, with a side road leading into the desert wilderness of Wadi Rum, where *Lawrence of Arabia*, *The Martian*, and many other movies were filmed.

HUB | *Amman, Jordan; Jerusalem, Israel*

Climb desert sand dunes through Wadi Rum.

The Guggenheim Museum Bilbao, designed by Frank Gehry, stands on the bank of the Nervión River.

Architectural Feats

From the Taj Mahal to the Eiffel Tower,
these wonders are worth a visit.

1. LA SAGRADA FAMÍLIA, BARCELONA, SPAIN

For sheer persistence, you can't beat the still-in-progress masterpiece of Catalonia's favorite architectural son, Antoni Gaudí. Projected to be completed in 2026—100 years after his death—the fantastical basilica has long stood as a symbol of Barcelona.

2. FALLINGWATER, PENNSYLVANIA, U.S.

Among all Frank Lloyd Wright's iconic creations, only this Pennsylvania home has opened for tours with its furnishings, art, and setting intact. It has graced the cover of *Time* magazine and occupied an actual waterfall.

3. THE GUGGENHEIM MUSEUM BILBAO, SPAIN

Asked to name the most important building of the past few decades, many leading architects, architecture critics, and scholars have picked this swirling titanium wonder by Frank Gehry—in and of itself, worth a trip to northern Spain.

4. HEYDAR ALIYEV CENTER, AZERBAIJAN

The first woman to win the coveted Pritzker Architecture Prize, Zaha Hadid left behind a striking global legacy. But this preternaturally flowy cultural center—a hallmark of Baku's redevelopment—is perhaps her most beautiful creation.

5. THE EIFFEL TOWER, PARIS, FRANCE

Though its 41-year reign as the world's tallest structure ended in 1930 (welcome, Chrysler Tower), Gustave Eiffel's wrought-iron icon still looms large in the collective consciousness, where little else is as symbolic of Paris.

6. THE TAJ MAHAL, AGRA, INDIA

Upon the death of his favorite wife, a 17th-century Mughal emperor commissioned Agra's vision in white—now a UNESCO World Heritage site, one of the New Seven Wonders of the World, and perhaps the most romantic mausoleum on Earth.

7. NATIONAL STADIUM, BEIJING, CHINA

A singular collaboration among heavyweights—from architects Jacques Herzog and Pierre de Meuron to artist Ai Weiwei—the aptly nicknamed Bird's Nest has become a famous draw since its debut at the 2008 Beijing Olympics.

8. TWA HOTEL, NEW YORK, U.S.

After a meticulous restoration, the onetime TWA Flight Center at New York's JFK Airport was recently reborn as a hotel. Check in at Eero Saarinen's curvaceous neofuturist masterpiece or have an atmospheric meal there between flights.

9. SYDNEY OPERA HOUSE, AUSTRALIA

The world has Saarinen to thank for this nautical-inspired stunner too—at least indirectly. He was one of the judges who selected Jørn Utzon from 233 candidates to design a national opera house for Sydney's waterfront (Utzon won £5,000 for his design). The iconic building on Bennelong Point took 14 years to complete and cost $102 million to build—largely paid for by a state lottery.

10. LEANING TOWER OF PISA, ITALY

Though its notorious tilt was reduced at the turn of the 21st century from a perilous 5.5 degrees to less than 4, this medieval icon has continued to inspire some of the most creative architectural poses. After grabbing your shot, head to a few of the other tilting towers in Pisa, including the bell tower at the church of St. Michele dei Scalzi.

A priest reads his Bible in the quiet of Abuna Gebre Mikael church.

If These Walls Could Talk

Legends and Rumors Trail the Elusive Queen of Sheba

I'm standing by the remains of a stone palace in Aksum, the onetime capital of the ancient Aksumite kingdom and now a World Heritage site. Many believe it also was once the home of the Queen of Sheba. The day is slipping toward dusk here in northern Ethiopia. From darkening hillsides comes the soft tinkle of sheep bells.

Inside I explore a long passageway where, once upon a time, royal guards might have seized me as an intruder. Making my way through a labyrinth of ruined rooms and passages, I arrive in a large central hall, a throne room. Atop a keystone, a tuft-eared eagle owl turns its head to peer at me with orange eyes. Then it opens wide angel wings and flies off, leaving me alone with the biblical world.

The Queen of Sheba is the Greta Garbo of antiquity. A glamorous, mysterious figure immortalized in the Bible and the Quran, celebrated in an oratorio by Handel, an opera by Charles Gounod, a ballet by Ottorino Respighi, and depicted in paintings by Raphael, Tintoretto, and Claude Lorrain, she remains tantalizingly elusive to the inquiries of historians. Across swaths of modern-day North Africa her legend lives on, despite—or perhaps because of—the fact that no one knows for sure if she existed, or if she did, where she lived.

No one, that is, but the Ethiopians, to whom this queen is very real. They consider her the mother of the nation, the founder of the Solomonic dynasty that would last three millennia until its last ruling descendant, Haile Selassie, died in 1975. It was from this palace, they believe (and archaeologists dispute), that their Queen of Sheba set out for Jerusalem around 1000 B.C.

Ethiopia strains credulity. It could belong to an atlas of the imagination. The presence of the Ten Commandments offers just a hint of what this world of cloud-high plateaus and plunging gorges, of Middle-earth peaks and blistering deserts of salt, of monasteries forged by serpents and castles fashioned for a tropical Camelot will reveal to me. To ancient Egyptians, Ethiopia was the Land of Punt, an exotic world where the Nile River flowed from fountains. Medieval Europeans believed it was a place inhabited by unicorns and flying dragons, birthplace of Prester John, keeper of the Fountain of Youth, protector of the Holy Grail, and a supposed descendant of one of the Three Magi.

Its isolation bred mythologies: Ethiopians today admit they have two histories, the one that historians work with and the one that the people believe.

The ruggedly mountainous, ravine-riven northern province of Tigray is considered the cradle of Ethiopian civilization. This is the land Ethiopians believe constituted the original home of Sheba, a land that now has me walking its trails. Here, the queen remains a persistent rumor, woven into village tales and depicted in frescoes on the walls of remote rock-cut churches—more than 120—that honeycomb Tigray's mountainsides and remained virtually unknown to the outside world until 50 years ago.

Daily life here has changed little over millennia. I see farmers plowing and harvesting fields of sorghum and barley by hand. With no motorized vehicles in sight, getting around means astride a donkey or on foot.

I meet up with two Tesfa Tours guides and head into the Tigrayan highlands. Entering Erar Valley, we are silenced by its beauty. Orchards stand under lattices of sun and shade. Mingling aromas of wood smoke, harvested hay, and spring flowers scent the morning. Beyond the valley, beyond the enclosing mesas and escarpments, mountains edge the horizon, their sawtooth peaks wreathed with cloud.

We keep to the flat valley for much of the day's walk, our bags carried by a stout-bellied donkey. In the late afternoon, our intrepid donkey leads us upward, raising a thin haze of dust. Eventually we reach the top of the mesa as the late afternoon sun rakes through expanses of dry grasses. Ahead, a troop of brown-furred gelada monkeys lope across our path, led by a shaggy-maned male.

My Tigray trek takes me to one of 123 rock-cut churches, Maryam Korkor, thought to be well over a thousand years old and marked by a simple wooden door in a cliff face.

Twilight is gathering, and I have yet to see the Queen of Sheba's palace. I hurry to the site west of town and find myself clambering over the back wall to wander alone through the haunted ruins. But haunted by what?

I still have no idea how the queen acquired her haughty reputation, but her descendants in modern-day Ethiopia have all shown me warmth and hospitality and the kind of old-fashioned courtesies my mother would have admired. Perhaps their fabled queen is alive after all, in her people's dignified manner and in the collective memory of the proud land she once ruled.

—**Stanley Stewart** is the author of the award-winning book *In the Empire of Genghis Khan.*

The Church of Bouvines' stained glass depicts battle scenes from 1214.

Paths of Glory
Brussels, Belgium, to Dunkirk, France

Four of Europe's iconic battles are the focus of a weekend in Belgium and northern France that begins with Waterloo. Thirty minutes south of Brussels, Napoleon's final defeat is marked by the famous Lion Mound, the Wellington Museum, and a colossal panoramic painting. Across the border in France, the Somme is where the largest battle of the Western Front unfolded during World War I. A 57-mile (92 km) Remembrance Trail from Péronne to Albert features museums, cemeteries, and battlefield remnants. Occupied by Germany during both world wars, Lille is the perfect spot to break for the night. Day two starts with a visit to Bouvines, where one of the key battles in medieval Europe played out in 1214. The French victory is memorialized by the marvelous stained-glass windows of Saint-Pierre de Bouvines church. Dunkirk, where the British made their miraculous 1940 escape from Hitler's army, lies an hour to the west on the English Channel.

HUB | *Brussels, Belgium*

Find your way to Galicia's Santiago de Compostela on the Camino de Santiago in Spain.

Religious Pilgrimages

Connect with the faithful—and find your own divine light—
on these excursions to holy grounds.

1. CAMINO DE SANTIAGO, SPAIN

However famous this pilgrimage, few people realize that walking all 499.5 miles (804 km) isn't a prerequisite for the coveted certificate: You earn one just by doing the last 62 miles (100 km), a manageable distance walked over the course of a three-day weekend, to Galicia's Santiago de Compostela.

2. VIA FRANCIGENA, ITALY

Similarly, there's no need to complete the full journey from France to Rome and Apulia, which fully covers more than 1,242.7 miles (2,000 km). If you walk the last 62 miles (100 km) of this ancient pilgrims' path—the lush, hilly stretch between Viterbo and Rome—you're entitled to the Francigena Testimonium, a certificate of pilgrimage completion.

3. ST. OLAV'S WAY, NORWAY

A third variation on the theme, this ancient pilgrims' path to the sainted King Olav's tomb in Norway will grant you the coveted Olav's Letter. To earn yours, you just need to walk a short segment—the last 62 miles (100 km) to Trondheim's Nidaros Cathedral. You can always make a return trip to complete all 1,860 miles (2,993.4 km).

4. CANTERBURY CATHEDRAL, ENGLAND

Bikers do especially well on the route to Thomas Becket's shrine. There's a gorgeous Pilgrim's Cycle Trail between Rochester and Canterbury that experienced cyclists can handle in a day or two.

5. THE GALILEE, ISRAEL

For Christian pilgrims, Jerusalem and Bethlehem go without saying, but a weekend in the north takes you everywhere from the Church of the Beatitudes (presumed site of the Sermon on the Mount) to Yardenit, the reported scene of Jesus's baptism.

6. ESSAOUIRA, MOROCCO

This Moroccan town once housed a large Jewish community, and while most have left, many return for a few days in September to pray at the famed Rabbi Pinto's gravesite in a surreal seaside cemetery.

7. THE SHIKOKU PILGRIMAGE, JAPAN

Impossible to complete at once unless you have 40 spare days, this celebrated Japanese trek is often broken into segments. To get a sense of it in a weekend, walk to the first nine of the circuit's 88 Buddhist temples.

8. SKELLIG MICHAEL, COUNTY KERRY, IRELAND

This small island off the west coast of Ireland is home to beautifully preserved, centuries-old monks' cells, and a supercompact pilgrims' path: the 670 steps that take you from the boat landing to the monastery at the top.

9. ADAM'S PEAK, SRI LANKA

The sacred footprint that brings pilgrims of various faiths is said to belong to Buddha, Shiva, or Adam, depending on the religion you follow. Regardless of your beliefs, catching sunrise from the summit is worth starting the 5,500-step climb. Be prepared: The trek up the crumbling steps can take two to four hours, depending on your fitness level, and the return trip will take about another two hours.

10. THE BASILICA OF OUR LADY OF GUADALUPE, MEXICO

The world's most visited Catholic pilgrimage site (dating to 1536)—receiving so many faithful it even has conveyor-belt flooring—is home to an iconic image of the beloved Virgin of Guadalupe, official patroness of the Americas since 1946 and the patron saint of Mexico City since 1737.

"ANY VISIT SHOULD START WITH A STROLL ALONG THE LOFTY RAMPARTS."

Ambling Old Québec

Québec City, Québec, Canada

N o other urban area comes as close to the pivotal role that Québec City has played in Canadian history. It was the first French settlement in North America (1608), the battlegrounds that established British rule over Canada (1759), and ground zero for the clash that kept Québec Province from becoming part of the newborn United States in 1775.

Any visit to Québec City should start with a stroll along the lofty ramparts that surrounded the Haute Ville (Upper Town). In addition to wide-ranging views of the St. Lawrence River, the wall-top Dufferin Terrace features an underground archaeological crypt with remnants of 17th-century Château Saint-Louis.

Exit the old town via the medieval-looking Porte Saint-Louis onto the Plains of Abraham, where the battles that decided the fate of Canada played out during the French and Indian War and War of 1812. Study the conflicts at the Plains of Abraham Museum and snatch an overall view of the battlefield from the 31st-floor observatory atop the Édifice Marie-Guyart.

Round out day one with dinner in one of the outdoor cafés along the Grand Allée and a stroll through the romantically illuminated Haute Ville.

You could easily spend a day delving into various aspects of Québec's city walls. Still an active Canadian Armed Forces base, the star-shaped Citadelle de Québec offers guided tours, historical exhibits, and a flamboyant changing of the guard ceremony in summer. The Fortifications of Québec National Historic Site of Canada along the western side of the old town offers living history programs in a restored French redoubt, British officers' quarters, and arsenal.

A historic funicular (opened in 1879) descends to the Basse-Ville (Lower Town) and the 17th-century Place-Royale, a cobblestone square surrounded by some of the oldest buildings in North America, including Notre-Dame-des-Victoires church (built in 1688). And be sure to see the five-story historical "Fresque des Québécois" mural on nearby Rue Notre-Dame.

HUB | *Montréal or Toronto, Canada; Northeastern United States*

Frontenac Castle, now a hotel, towers over the city and waterfront.

The historic Prague astronomical clock is still a wonder to behold.

When the Planets Aligned

An Astronomy Geek Explores the Czech Capital

Around 10 p.m. on a clear night in early June, I'm staring down the end of a Zamboni-size reflector telescope. I'm in the eastern dome of the Stefánik Observatory, in the hills above Prague's Malá Strana neighborhood. Unlike unruly Old Town, things are quiet here.

Overhead, the entire hemisphere of the roof swivels. I can hear the groan of cogs turning like spokes on a giant bicycle wheel.

In the facility's western and even larger dome, we finally catch Jupiter, rising between the same two trees. Climbing to the top of the ladder, I peer through the lens, and witness, to my shock, the sharpest rendering of the planet I've ever seen. It looks like a pastel orange gumball floating in the pure black of space. The image is so crisp that I can even discern two bands of cloud on its smooth surface. Three moons—Callisto, Io, and Europa—punctuate the scene.

Looking around me at the four or five other figures gathered in the dark, I am perplexed: How are there not more people up here, seeing this? Then I remember: It's Saturday night, and pilsner, not planets, is what's on most visitors' minds.

Prague isn't necessarily known for stargazing, but its history with astronomy and astrology goes back to the 17th century, a time when the two disciplines often blurred together. Under Emperor Rudolf II, a patron of the arts and sciences, Prague became a beacon for astronomers, alchemists, and philosophers.

One of them, Johannes Kepler, was a talented math teacher who was banished in 1600 from Austria for his non-Catholic beliefs. Kepler's seminal text, *Harmonices Mundi*, is an expansion of his studies on planetary motion, in which he proved the planets move in an ellipse—not a circle—around the sun.

For me, the text holds a deeper meaning: It develops the idea of the "music of the spheres," or the harmonic theory of planetary motion. It is the basis of my work as a sound therapist, where I apply a tool known as a planetary tuning fork to acupuncture points on the body. When I learned that Kepler spent the bulk of his time in Prague refining the theories that went into *Harmonices Mundi*, I knew I had to go.

At first, I had a hard time squaring the raucous beer halls of today's Prague with its radical beginnings. My guide, Lenka, who leads custom city tours through a company called JayWay, explained: "Prague is in the center of Europe, and there is an extreme amount of energy here. People who are sensitive, they feel it." In other words, the same force that inspired all those philosophers back then is what lures travelers today, even if they don't know it.

Clues to Prague's cosmic side are scattered throughout the city. Some are hiding in plain sight, such as Old Town Square's giant astronomical clock, which draws a crowd of photo-snapping tourists every hour when it strikes. Gazing up at its cryptic overlay of rotating disks, medieval numerals, and heavenly symbols, I struggle to read the actual time. But that's because its function is more astrolabe than clock. The front-facing hands trace the movements of the sun and moon across the zodiac—useful for townspeople who wanted to learn the correct day to receive medical treatment or buy a new house.

I spend an afternoon at the Astronomical Tower inside the Klementinum, an old, sprawling Jesuit university in the center of the city. Filled with astronomy tools from the 17th and 18th centuries, it is in many ways the last intact monument to starry Prague. The tower's first floor opens into the National Library of the Czech Republic, with its spiraling wood columns and collection of celestial globes, a hall little changed since 1722.

On the floor above, in the boxlike Meridian Hall—an active meteorological station—we stand where Kepler's contemporaries once measured the positions of planets with sextants the size of hockey goal posts. Another 50-some nearly vertical steps, and we find ourselves at the top of the tower. On four sides, all of Prague, with its red pointed roofs and saint-bedecked spires, is bathed in golden light.

It is an unforgettable panorama, and one I never would have found had I not let my inner astronomy nerd lead the way. Lesser known than Prague Castle and St. Nicholas Church, this watchtower is a more gratifying visit, as it affords unbroken views of all those other sites, minus the long queues.

Esoteric Prague is still here, a quiet contrast to the city's "beer bike" tours. If you hunt for it, a sharper image of choreographed skies and thrilling stellar discoveries comes into view, harking back to a time when humans were just waking up to the mysteries of our solar system.

—**Alex Schechter** lives in Los Angeles, where he works as a freelance writer and sound therapist.

Istanbul's Green Mosque is ornate inside and out.

To the Dardanelles
Istanbul, Turkey

From Hagia Sofia to Topkapi Palace, Istanbul boasts enough historic sites to fill an entire week, let alone a single weekend. But the waterways that connect the Turkish metropolis with the Aegean Sea tell their own stories. A drive along the Sea of Marmara's north shore leads to Gallipoli, where British Empire and Ottoman troops waged one of the bloodiest battles of World War I. A vehicle ferry crosses the Dardanelles strait to Çanakkale and ancient Troy. The Trojan Horse is long gone, but archaeological digs have revealed some of the Greek city-state's walls and foundations. Highway E90 along the Sea of Marmara's south shore leads to Bursa, one of the crown jewels of the Ottoman Empire. Among its many relics are the Ulu Cami (Grand Mosque), Koza Han (a silk bazaar), and the historic Irgandı Bridge. From Bursa, it's an easy two-hour drive back to Istanbul via the Avrasya (Eurasia) Tunnel.

HUB | *Eastern Europe*

A llama stands atop the hills of Machu Picchu.

Adventures in the Andes
Cusco and Machu Picchu, Peru

The capital of the Inca Empire and a Spanish colonial outpost, modern Cusco has morphed into the staging point for visiting Machu Picchu, the "lost city" rediscovered by Hiram Bingham in 1911. Most of Cusco's historic landmarks are within a short walk from the Plaza de Armas, including the 16th-century Cusco Cathedral, the incredible Inca stonework along Calle Hatun Rumiyoc, and the artistic Barrio de San Blas. But the city's most impressive monument—the ancient Inca shrine at Sacsayhuaman—lies in the nearby Sacred Valley. Although you can spend a week trekking the mountainous trails leading to Machu Picchu, it's possible to visit the lofty Inca ruins on a long day trip from Cusco. Three train companies offer the journey (3.5 hours each way). Alternatively, you can spend the night in the village of Aguas Calientes below Machu Picchu and make your way up the mountain by bus or foot the following morning.

HUB | *Lima, Peru*

Tunisian Time Trip

Tunis, Tunisia

N orth Africa's smallest nation draws applause for its beaches and desert escapades. But with a history stretching back to the 12th century B.C. (when the coast was settled by Phoenicians), Tunisia offers plenty of ancient tales. Orient yourself with a first-day visit to the Bardo National Museum in Tunis, where three millennia of local history are illuminated through Greek shipwreck treasures, Roman mosaics, historic Korans, and other artifacts. The ruins of ancient Carthage (Hannibal's hometown) are scattered across a coastal site on the eastern edge of Tunis. The nearby North Africa American Cemetery and Memorial honors more than 6,500 GIs who were killed in action or went missing during the Tunisia campaign of World War II. Rising early on the second day, venture two hours west of the city to hilltop Dougga, considered "the best-preserved example of an Africo-Roman town in North Africa" by UNESCO. Round off the weekend by meandering the medina of Tunis, where some 700 medieval structures endure.

HUB | *Major Western European Cities*

The Medina of Tunis has some 700 monuments, including mosques and madrassas.

CHAPTER EIGHT

FAMILY-FRIENDLY VACATIONS

Whether you're heading for Mexico's sandy shores or New York's towering skyscrapers, everyone can come along on these weekend getaways.

Acacia trees are silhouetted against the sun in Meru National Park, Kenya (p. 298).

Gaudí's "La Sagrada Família" will be completed in 2026.

Barcelona con Niños
Barcelona, Spain

As if La Sagrada Família and the other works by eccentric architect Antoni Gaudí aren't enough to stimulate a child's imagination, the colorful Catalan city of Barcelona boasts plenty of other weekend wonders. The grown-ups might cherish a casual stroll, gourmet meal, and sip of wine along Las Ramblas, the boulevard that graces central Barcelona. But youngsters are more likely to savor a couple of hours exploring the CosmoCaixa science museum with its many hands-on exhibits, the football (soccer) tour at legendary Camp Nou Stadium, or the Museo de la Xocolata where kids can taste, smell, and paint with liquid chocolate. A giant golden fish sculpture hovers above Barcelona's downtown beaches, while Las Golondrinas offers harbor tours and day trips on the Mediterranean. Ride the Telefèric cable car between the port and the star-shaped castle on Montjuic or catch the funicular railway to mountaintop Tibidabo amusement park where the Muntanya Russa roller coaster plunges 101 feet (31 m) in a single drop.

HUB | *Major Western European Cities*

Wild Singapore
Singapore

Despite its sleek high-rise facade, the tiny Southeast Asian nation offers a surprising amount of nature, both modern and built, as well as relics of the time when the island was covered in rainforest and mangroves. Start at Singapore Zoo, which is especially strong on tropical animals, including rarely seen creatures such as the cat-like fossa, the cotton-top tamarin monkey, and the electric blue gecko. The neighboring Night Safari takes visitors on an after-dark journey. At botanically infused Gardens by the Bay, kids can cool themselves in the mist from the world's tallest indoor waterfall (100 feet/30 m) that tumbles from the heights of an indoor cloud forest, or scramble through a canopy of colorfully lit and musical "SuperTrees" inspired by the movie *Avatar*. Singapore's heartland is still flush with some of its original jungle, bisected by wilderness walks like the MacRitchie Rainforest Trail and its bouncy TreeTop Walk suspension bridge. Along the shore, Sentosa Island offers a Mega Adventure Park with a zip line and treetop obstacle course.

Sea otters play above Singapore Zoo visitors on the River Safari.

HUB | *Bangkok, Thailand; Hong Kong*

Rock iguanas take over the beaches on Leaf Kay in the Exumas.

Before the Mast
Exuma Islands, the Bahamas

Although it's a lesser known part of the Bahamas, the Exuma islands offer ideal sea and weather conditions for a weekend sailboat adventure. The 130-mile (209 km) archipelago harbors more than 360 islands—many of them uninhabited and little more than sand spits—surrounded by warm tropical waters. With myriad bays, coves, and reef-protected lagoons, the Exumas are blessed with plenty of safe places to swim, snorkel, and anchor overnight. Great Exuma, the largest island, was once a real-life pirate haunt, while scenes from *Pirates of the Caribbean: Deadman's Chest* were filmed on location at Sandy Cay. Snap a selfie astride the Tropic of Cancer at Pelican Beach on Little Exuma Island or swim with saltwater-loving swine at Pig Beach on Big Major Cay. Most boat charters depart from Nassau, which lies around 35 nautical miles (65 km) from the northernmost Exumas. You can also join long day sails to the archipelago.

HUB | *East Coast United States*

"KIDS GET CLOSE-UP VIEWS
OF MANATEES, SLOTHS,
AND MACAWS."

Into the Jungle

Amazon River, Peru

Bugs and snakes, hot and humid weather, vast distances to cover and not a lot of great places to stay overnight. Visiting the Amazon rainforest can be trying even at the best of times. But one place makes it easier than others: the city of Iquitos in northern Peru, which serves as home base for riverboats that help families visit the vast emerald forest.

Just a two-hour flight from Lima or Cusco, Iquitos lies right beside the Amazon River, and watching life unfold in the stilted homes and houseboats along the waterfront is fascinating. Just outside the city, the amazing Amazon Rescue Center (run by Dallas World Aquarium and local conservation groups) lets kids get close-up views of manatees, sloths, macaws, and other creatures that are normally hard to see in the wild. Among the other highlights of Iquitos are a living butterfly farm, the Museum of Indigenous Amazon Cultures, and Casa de Fierro—a quirky prefabricated iron house created in France by the same man who designed the Eiffel Tower in Paris.

Riverboats depart from Nauta, near the spot where the Marañon and Ucayali Rivers flow into the Amazon River. Wedged between the three great waterways is Pacaya-Samiria National Reserve, one of the biggest and best nature parks in the entire Amazon. Sprawling across an area larger than Yellowstone, Yosemite, and the Grand Canyon combined, the park harbors more than 2,000 plant and animal species, including iconic animals like the jaguar, giant river otter, anaconda, and pink dolphin.

In addition to comfy cabins and good food, family-oriented riverboats like *La Perla* (operated by Jungle Experiences) offer short rainforest treks, piranha fishing, after-dark excursions in search of nocturnal creatures, and even a chance to swim in an Amazonian river. There's also cultural contact: shore landings at Amerindian villages on the outskirts of the park, where passengers can visit a school, purchase locally made handicrafts, and participate in a sacred shaman ceremony.

HUB | *Lima or Cusco, Peru*

Take in the sights on a river cruise through the Peruvian Amazon.

Wet & Wild

The Galápagos Islands, Ecuador

Renowned for their wildlife, water sports, and wilderness landscapes, the Galápagos Islands are close enough to mainland South America for a long weekend exploring one of the globe's greatest natural wonderlands. Santa Cruz Island—about a two-hour nonstop flight from Quito—makes an ideal base for a family adventure that combines day trips by land and sea. The most incredible thing about the Ecuadorian archipelago is the fact that after 60 years of protection, many of the animals have lost their fear of people. You can literally walk among the sea lions, shorebirds, and iguanas without them so much as flinching. Darwin Research Station provides a great orientation to Galápagos human and natural history, as well as your first glimpse of giant tortoises, some of them more than 100 years old. Be sure to schedule a snorkeling trip to nearby Bartolomé Island, a hike to wildlife-rich Tortuga Bay, and a walk through the island's creepy lava tubes.

"AFTER 60 YEARS OF PROTECTION, MANY OF THE ANIMALS HAVE LOST THEIR FEAR OF PEOPLE."

HUB | *Quito, Ecuador*

A Galápagos sea lion swims by snorkelers at Champion Islet near Floreana Island.

Prinsengracht canal is the outermost waterway in Amsterdam.

Going Dutch

Amsterdam, the Netherlands

The Netherlands boasts more than 4,000 miles (6,437 km) of canals, including 165 artificial waterways just in Amsterdam. By winter, the many frozen-over canals transform into impromptu outdoor ice-skating rinks. By summer, they offer countless places to swim, fish, or undertake a weekend canal boat adventure. In addition to the novelty of sleeping on a boat, Dutch float trips often feature landlubber experiences like cycling, jaunts through tulip fields, windmill tours, and visits to art museums. Pick-up points are scattered around the countryside within easy reach of Amsterdam in towns like Loosdrecht, Woubrugge, and Broek op Langedijk situated in the heart of the canal country. Boaters can cook meals onboard, dive into tasty canal-side eateries, or plan a picnic with provisions from the Edam Cheese Market. Those who feel like staying in one place can choose from scores of rental houseboats moored along the canals of Amsterdam.

Keukenhof Gardens are open just 51 days of the year.

Ride stomach-flipping
turns in LEGOLAND
Billund's Polar Land.

Theme Parks

Find amusement, thrill rides, and plenty of entertainment at parks from Copenhagen to Connecticut.

1. BAKKEN, DENMARK

Outside Copenhagen you'll find the world's oldest continually operating amusement park. Bakken (officially Dyrehavsbakken) opened in 1583 and now features everything from a 19th-century carousel to the 2020 Supernova swing, which sends riders soaring 68.9 feet (21 m) above ground.

2. LEGOLAND BILLUND, DENMARK

Almost four centuries after Bakken opened, Denmark debuted another historic first: the original Legoland, which opened in 1968 next to the toy's birth factory and has since drawn tens of millions of fans. In 2020, the park opened the Lego Movie universe featuring rides and attractions inspired by both blockbuster hits.

3. LAKE COMPOUNCE, CONNECTICUT, U.S.

The longest-running amusement park in the United States opened near Hartford, Connecticut, in 1846 and remains a beloved family escape, complete with a beach and New England's oldest roller coaster. Along with high-speed thrills and water rides, the park offers atypical theme park food, with options that include a Bavarian nut cart, a lakefront restaraunt, and Doc Popcorn.

4. DISNEY'S ANIMAL KINGDOM, FLORIDA, U.S.

The largest theme park in the world at 580 acres (237.7 ha), this zoological-focused Orlando destination includes an *Avatar* world, great bird adventure, and safari experience with giraffes, elephants, lions, and more.

5. PACIFIC PARK, SANTA MONICA PIER, CALIFORNIA, U.S.

Where else would you expect to find the world's first solar-powered Ferris wheel? But more than the photovoltaic panels, of course, it's the quintessential Southern California beach vibe that draws visitors to this iconic park on a pier.

6. LOTTE WORLD, SOUTH KOREA

Seoul's indoor and outdoor amusement park offers an artificial island and lake, monorail, shopping malls, and a Korean folk museum, among many other features.

7. ALTON TOWERS, ENGLAND

Built around an aristocratic estate, the United Kingdom's largest theme park resides in Staffordshire and boasts Oblivion, the world's first vertical-drop coaster.

8. LA RONDE, CANADA

Just outside the old port of Montréal, La Ronde sits on the tip of St. Helen's Island. The family-friendly park offers 40 rides and attractions, including 10 thrilling coasters. New to the park in 2020 is Canada's first ever free-fly roller coaster: Riders on The Vipere will sit extended from the track on a free-falling and tumbling ride.

9. WARNER BROS. WORLD ABU DHABI, UNITED ARAB EMIRATES

Meet an indoor theme park record breaker. This one's the world's largest and the first to be branded by Warner Bros. with the Jetsons Cosmic Orbiter, the Batman Knight Flight, and countless cartoon-based thrills in between.

10. DISNEYLAND PARIS, FRANCE

A short trip east of the Parisian city center, Disneyland Paris—formerly called Euro Disney Resort—offers two parks, seven Disney hotels, a golf course, Disney village, and plenty of magic. Stars Wars fans in particular will love this spot, where out of this world attractions are split between the two parks, including live-action shows and the Star Wars Hyperspace Mountain roller coaster.

"ENOUGH FAMILY-FRIENDLY SIDESHOWS TO FILL A DOZEN WEEKENDS"

Tokyo for the Ages
Tokyo, Japan

While Japan's colorful pop culture seems fresh, original, and sometimes outlandish to the rest of the world, many of these quirky modern customs trace their roots to medieval Japan, a blend of old and new that visitors can sample during a pop culture weekend in the world's largest city.

The mega-popular cartoon character Hello Kitty—the mascot of Tokyo's Sanrio Puroland theme park—was born in the 1970s. But her inspiration was the *maneki-neko*, or "beckoning cat," of the Japanese Middle Ages, with its one paw perpetually waving to invite customers into a shop or tavern. Take the kids to Sanrio's flagship store in the neon-studded Ginza district for Hello Kitty merchandise or to the seven blocks of traditional handicraft shops along Nakamsie Street in the Asakusa district for more authentic maneki-neko.

The bustling Akihabara neighborhood is ground zero for manga and anime, with dozens of shops selling comic books, videos, and action figures. But the classic *ukiyo-e* (woodblock prints) and illustrated books at the Ota Museum in Harajuku district show how the tradition got started more than 400 years ago when artists of the Edo period were depicting samurai, geisha, and kabuki actors in ways similar to modern comics or cartoons.

Kiddy Land, one of the world's largest toy stores, is also located in Harajuku. And while you're in the neighborhood, keep an eye out for Harajuku Girls, whose fashion flair blends goth, steam punk, rococo, Lolita, and other sartorial subcultures. Second-hand clothing stores and colorful dessert outlets like Totti (jumbo-size cotton candy) and Rainbow Sweets (rolled ice cream and cheese sand) also flavor the neighborhood.

From professional baseball games at the Tokyo Dome and sumo wrestling tournaments at Ryōgoku Kokugikan arena to the Samurai Museum in Shinjuku and the National Museum of Emerging Science and Innovation on an artificial island in Tokyo Bay, the Japanese metropolis offers enough family-friendly sideshows to fill a dozen weekends.

HUB | *Kyoto, Japan; Hong Kong*

Shoppers make their way through the modern Harajuku district.

Tradition and relaxation mix on the beaches of Bali.

Beaches & Barong
Bali, Indonesia

Between Sanur, Kuta, and Nusa Dua, Bali boasts some of the most popular beaches in Southeast Asia. While families can easily plan an entire weekend around sun, sea, and sand, the exotic Indonesian isle offers plenty of other ways to keep kids amused: white-water rafting on the Telaga Waja or Ayung Rivers through jungle valleys, biking the emerald green rice terrace region near Ubud, and trekking to the summit of Mount Batur volcano to catch the sunrise over its crater lake. There is tons of culture too: traditional *wayang* shadow puppet theater, dazzling stage shows starring a mythical lion-like creature called the Barong, and performances of the mesmerizing Kecak fire and trance dance. When all else fails, the island also has theme parks: Bali Wake Park where kids can learn how to water-ski or wakeboard, or scramble across large inflatable water structures; and the huge waterslides and lazy river at Waterbom Bali.

HUB | *Jakarta, Indonesia; Singapore*

Control, Alt, Delight
Silicon Valley, California, U.S.

The internet and cyberspace, smartphones and personal computers, Facebook and Google—the modern age was largely born and raised in California's Silicon Valley. Located between San Francisco and San Jose, the high-tech hub is a paradise for kids with a keen interest in science and technology.

Kick off the weekend at the excellent, interactive Computer History Museum in Mountain View, which harbors robots, autonomous vehicles, historic video games (like the first Pong prototype), and early Apple computers. Then take a stroll through the nearby Googleplex with its giant Android lawn statues and snap a selfie in front of the famous Facebook sign before heading for the NASA Ames Exploration Center to see moon rocks, Mars rover footage, and a vintage Mercury space capsule. But it's not all circuit boards and bots. Silicon Valley also features the Winchester Mystery House (California's "most haunted" building), Godzilla-size trees at Big Basin Redwoods, and mummies at the Rosicrucian Egyptian Museum.

Tour Google headquarters and its Android lawn statues.

HUB | *Los Angeles or San Francisco, California, U.S.*

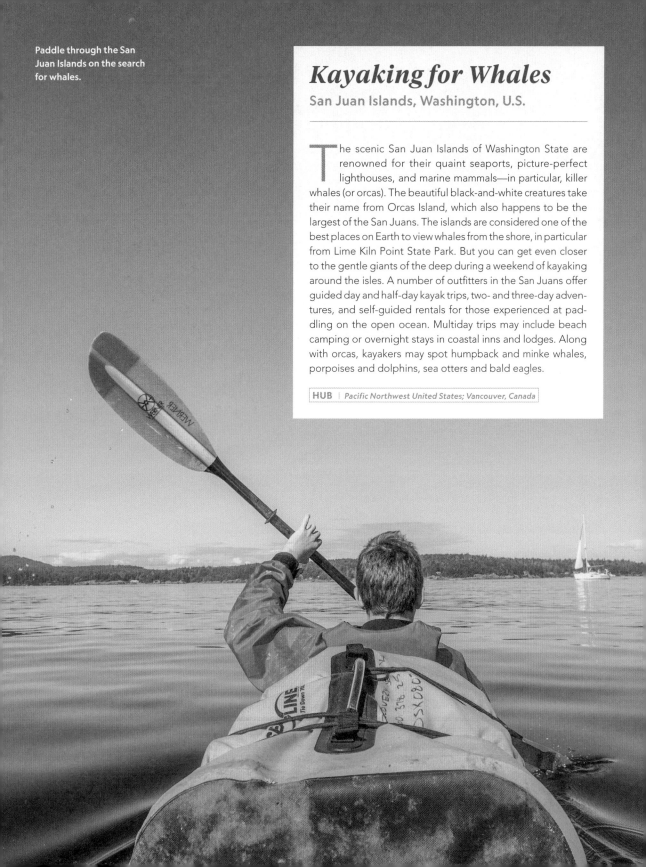

Paddle through the San Juan Islands on the search for whales.

Kayaking for Whales
San Juan Islands, Washington, U.S.

The scenic San Juan Islands of Washington State are renowned for their quaint seaports, picture-perfect lighthouses, and marine mammals—in particular, killer whales (or orcas). The beautiful black-and-white creatures take their name from Orcas Island, which also happens to be the largest of the San Juans. The islands are considered one of the best places on Earth to view whales from the shore, in particular from Lime Kiln Point State Park. But you can get even closer to the gentle giants of the deep during a weekend of kayaking around the isles. A number of outfitters in the San Juans offer guided day and half-day kayak trips, two- and three-day adventures, and self-guided rentals for those experienced at paddling on the open ocean. Multiday trips may include beach camping or overnight stays in coastal inns and lodges. Along with orcas, kayakers may spot humpback and minke whales, porpoises and dolphins, sea otters and bald eagles.

HUB | *Pacific Northwest United States; Vancouver, Canada*

A flag-bearing cowgirl opens the Cody Night Rodeo.

A Wild Ride

Cowboys and Cowgirls Wrangle the Old West at Wyoming's Classic Rodeo

My eight-year-old daughter flew off the back of the mechanical bull and landed in a heap of curly hair and denim. Grinning, Ivy picked herself up off the padded surface and set her black cowboy hat back in place. She begged for just one more go.

But the sun was setting over Cody, Wyoming, and it was almost time for the Nite Rodeo to start. Here, outside the arena on the edge of town, the rodeo clowns had finished painting kids' faces and the cowboys were coiling their ropes, lasso lessons over. Everyone was heading toward the stands to find a seat. "Tomorrow, sweetie," I said, steering her into the crowd.

Cody has been holding an annual July 4th rodeo, called the Stampede, since 1919, and a nightly rodeo most summer evenings since 1938, making the Cody Nite Rodeo the longest running event of its kind. The town's location 52 miles (83.7 km) east of Yellowstone National Park helps ensure a steady stream of tourists, but the rodeo is a community event as well. It's geared to families and first-timers, or folks who are both, like us.

We found a spot in the front row of the elevated grandstand. People called out to friends in the stands and in the contestants' area below. We could hear snippets of French and Japanese and smell farm dirt and fried food.

We had arrived the day before from our home in Portland, Oregon. Our visit to Cody would be Ivy's first real exposure to this red-blooded streak of American culture, and our first daddy-daughter overnight trip. I wanted everything to be perfect—as long as she didn't come home begging for a horse.

The Cowgirl Up Rodeo Drill Team rode out and galloped in complex formations as the announcer read off the names of local sponsors. Ivy's eyes were bright, and she clutched my arm in excitement. It was time for the first event: bareback bronc riding. Below us, a knot of cowboys surrounded a horse and rider in a gated chute. They held the animal still as the young rider grabbed the leather and rawhide "rigging" handhold with his left hand and took a deep breath. There was a moment of stillness, the rider nodded, and the gate flew open.

The pair exploded outward in a blur of kicking, plunging, and spinning. The three-dimensional thrashing flung the man almost horizontal along the horse's back. Within seconds he was airborne and in the dirt.

A ride has to last eight seconds to earn a score from the judges, which is based equally on the performances of rider and horse. The rider must have one arm free at all times and it must not touch any part of the animal or the equipment; doing so means disqualification.

Tonight only a few rides lasted the full eight. I cringed as each successive contestant hit the ground. But Ivy was transfixed. Two "pickup men" on horseback waited nearby to make sure things ended safely for everyone if the rider managed to stay on: One pulled him to safety on his own horse, and the other ushered the barebacked animal out of the arena.

My own daughter apparently wasn't fazed a bit at seeing grown men tossed around like crash test dummies. Granted, Ivy has an indoor trapeze and once managed to overturn a trampoline in our dining room. But I wondered what she would think of the next event.

A calf bolted from a gate, followed seconds later by a galloping rider swinging a lasso in wide circles. A quick toss settled the loop around the animal's neck and the horse stopped on a dime. The rope pulled taut and jerked the calf off its feet. The cowboy sprang down with a short "piggin' string" in his teeth. He quickly looped it around three of the calf's feet and leaped back, hands in the air. The time counted only if the knot held for six seconds.

After a few early winces, we saw how the lassos missed more often than not, and how the calves who were caught always scrambled up and trotted off, indignant but unhurt. By the end we were cheering as much for the animals zigzagging across the dirt as the riders trying to catch them.

In between events, a rodeo clown kept the crowd entertained with corny jokes and banter. At the halfway point of the evening, he called all the kids in the crowd down from the stands. Ivy rushed to join them. Everyone lined up at one end of the field and a pair of calves with red flags tied to their tails were let loose at the other end. Anyone who grabbed a flag won a gift certificate to the local Dairy Queen.

It was madness: children howling, dirt clods flying, calves trotting bemusedly away along the fence line. Two local kids, clearly benefiting from experience, ended up with the prizes. Ivy limped back to her seat, grimy but glowing. "I don't think I should have worn my new boots," she said sheepishly. I bought her some kettle corn as a consolation prize.

—**Julian Smith** is writing a book about rodeo history, even though the fastest he's ever ridden is a brisk trot.

"A WIDE VARIETY
OF AFRICAN
LANDSCAPES"

Miniature Safari
Nairobi to Loisaba, Kenya

A safari doesn't have to be a long, drawn-out affair. Using Nairobi as a jumping-off point, a family can easily undertake a weekend of classic African wildlife viewing at various spots around Kenya, including the Masai Mara, Tsavo National Park, the lakes of the Great Rift Valley, or East Africa's newest safari hot spot—the region around snowcapped Mount Kenya just north of the capital.

From Nairobi it's about a three-hour drive or 35-minute flight to Nanyuki, the gateway to the Mount Kenya region. On the western edge of town, Ol Pejeta Conservancy safeguards the world's last two northern white rhinos and the Sweetwaters Chimpanzee Sanctuary, created with help from Jane Goodall. The nearby Mount Kenya Safari Club offers horseback riding around the base of Mount Kenya and an animal orphanage where kids can interact with cheetahs, monkeys, ostrich, and other wild creatures saved from harrowing circumstances.

About an hour's drive north of Nanyuki, Lewa Wildlife Conservancy is another superstar of wildlife conservation, known for its efforts to save the endangered black rhino, Grevy's zebra, swamp-dwelling sitatunga antelope, and reticulated giraffe. All of the Big Five wander the park: lions, leopards, elephants, buffalos, and rhinos. From woodlands and wetlands to savanna and grassy prairie, Lewa also boasts a wide variety of African landscapes.

Reaching wilder, more remote places like Meru and Loisaba is best accomplished by direct flights from Nairobi's Wilson Airport to dirt airstrips in the park. Meru National Park is famous as the setting of the beloved book and movie *Born Free*. There are still plenty of lions about and herds of elephant that run 100 strong. Perched on the lofty Laikipia Plateau, Loisaba Wildlife Conservancy offers local Samburu guides, walking safaris, posh camps, and the possibility of sleeping under the stars.

HUB | *Nairobi, Kenya*

A herd of Grevy's zebras gather in the Lewa Wildlife Conservancy.

Take in ancient ruins at the Roman Forum.

Rome Giovanile

Rome, Italy

What's the best way to see the Italian capital with kids? Start with allotting three days for a long weekend packed with art, history, and pasta. Hit the three big landmarks—the Colosseum, Forum, and Vatican City—on day one. And consider skipping the almost always crowded Sistine Chapel in favor of the gardens. With the icons under your belt, you'll have two full days for offbeat Rome. The sprawling Villa Borghese, the city's biggest green space, offers boating, biking, and a modern (largely cageless) reincarnation of the municipal zoo, the Bioparco di Roma. The nearby Explora is a fully fledged children's museum for kids aged three to 11. If your kids are into slightly creepy stuff, descend into the skeleton-filled catacombs beneath Santa Maria della Concezione dei Cappuccini church. Several Roman restaurants—like Enoteca Ferrara and Rec23—offer weekend brunch with storytelling, science workshops, cooking classes, and other kids' activities to complement their spaghetti and ravioli.

HUB | *Major Western European Cities*

One Small Step

Ulaanbaatar, Mongolia

For a family vacation that's completely different, make your way to Ulaanbaatar, just two hours from Beijing, four hours from Seoul, or six hours from Tokyo. Why on earth would you schlep the kids to the steppes of Central Asia? Maybe for the fact that it's got one of the world's greatest bone collections at the Central Museum of Mongolian Dinosaurs and the planet's largest equestrian figure, a Godzilla-size, stainless steel statue of Genghis Khan on horseback that you access via a walkway through the horse's torso to a viewing deck on the animal's head. Families can bunk in a modern hotel or the contemporary version of the *gers* (yurts) used by Mongol hordes when they conquered most of Eurasia 1,000 years ago. Don't expect Mongolian barbecue (which was actually invented in Taiwan) for lunch or dinner. But the local dining scene has gone fully international in recent years, with burger, pizza, and salad options to satisfy all taste buds.

HUB | *Tokyo, Japan; Beijing, China; Seoul, South Korea*

Stay in a traditional *ger* at the Three Camel Lodge.

Four Seasons Vacation

Lake Tahoe, California, and Nevada, U.S.

Floating in the Sierra Nevada mountains along the California-Nevada border, "Big Blue" is one of the world's deepest, purest, and most picture-perfect lakes. It's also one of the most diverse when it comes to recreation, a lake for all seasons and many different reasons to explore the great outdoors. Half a dozen snow resorts—including Squaw Valley, where the 1960 Winter Olympics were staged—expedite downhill and cross-country skiing, snowboarding, tobogganing, and sleigh rides in winter. As soon as the snow melts, the resorts morph into hiking and mountain biking mode, with dozens of trails through woodlands and meadows and along the pristine lakeshore. By summer, the lake is warm enough for swimming, boating, water-skiing, wakeboarding, and other aquatic activities. A weekend in Tahoe wouldn't be complete without a meal at one of the region's gourmet restaurants (try the Lone Eagle Grille in Incline Village or Six Peaks Grille in Olympic Valley). And if you're there in July or August, catch an alfresco performance at the Lake Tahoe Shakespeare Festival on the Nevada side.

HUB | *Los Angeles or San Francisco, California, U.S.*

Along with its famed Maya ruins, Tulum offers clear waters and sandy shores.

Maya Riviera

Yucatán Peninsula, Mexico

It's not easy to find a place that combines sun and fun on a tropical beach with rich history and cultural activities. But Mexico's Yucatán Peninsula ticks off all those boxes. South of Cancún, the Maya Riviera boasts scores of beach resorts, many of them with water parks, game arcades, kid or teen clubs, and other family-friendly amenities. About halfway down the coast is Excaret, a unique theme park that blends waterslides and speedboat rides with cultural shows, archaeological sites, and a reproduction ancient Maya village. Among the offshore excursions are snorkeling the world's third largest barrier reef and swimming with whale sharks, those gentle giants of the deep (May to September). Away from the coast, families can swim or snorkel underground cenotes—dazzling limestone caverns partially filled with freshwater. If it's a three-day weekend, take a day trip to Chichén Itzá, the well-preserved ruins of a pre-Columbian Maya metropolis once "lost" amid the Yucatán jungle.

HUB | *Cancún or Mexico City, Mexico; Miami, Florida, U.S.; Houston, Texas, U.S.*

Surf Pacific waves on Santa Teresa's beach.

"WE WILL LOSE TRACK OF TIME, FORGET WHAT DAY OF THE WEEK IT IS."

La Vida Local

A Family Escapes Manhattan for Costa Rica's Mellow Coast

My husband, our three kids, and I are 45 minutes into a bumpy ride along a dusty, winding road on the Nicoya Peninsula of Costa Rica when I flash back four months. Sitting pretty on a groomed beach on Long Island, my husband, Manny, and I were talking about—well, what does anyone talk about at the end of one vacation but the planning for the next? Tired of spending a fortune on the same conventional family trips everyone else we knew was taking, Manny vowed the next one would be different. We would travel to an unfamiliar place to live like locals, or as close to locals as we could get. Which is how we find ourselves en route to the small seaside settlement called Mal Pais—"bad country," a name derived from the area's steep, rugged terrain, not suitable for farming.

To get to Playa Hermosa, we first must drive through Santa Teresa, a small, hectic town that is crammed with surfboard and sunglasses shops in a swirling cloud of dust. People buzz around on mopeds and ATVs, nearly all wearing bandannas over their faces. We drive by a French bakery and an open-air chicken restaurant, where we see whole chickens being cooked on a grill on the ground only a few feet from our passing tires.

The Shaka Surf School is just off the road, but we miss it because it looks like little more than an encampment. Pulling up to it, I find myself wondering about the safety protocols of this "school." But before I can mortify Manny by questioning a staff member, he quickly, perhaps preemptively, hires Brent Newell, a 23-year-old blond transplant from Cocoa Beach, Florida, to coach him and our oldest son.

Before he begins his lesson, Brent steers me and my two younger children to a through-the-jungle shortcut that he assures us will lead to the beach. Or not.

The pathway turns into a river of mud, and I'm left to slip-slide along with one child hiked up on each hip. Together the three of us pass under a canopy of giant trees bedecked with dozens of mud clumps: termite colonies, a fact I keep to myself. Little brown spider monkeys up in the branches rain nuts down to the ground. Then we see it, a beach even bigger, more wild, and more beautiful than the one we visited yesterday, the only commerce on it two men selling coconut water out of the husk.

Later, hungry from all the beach time, we descend on Koji's in Santa Teresa, in our beach cover-ups and flip-flops. The sushi is incredibly fresh and the crowd casual, in a St. Barth's-beautiful-people sort of way. Still, the vibe is decidedly Tico, with friendly dogs roaming between the tables.

And so begins the routine of our vacation, although really it will be the opposite of routine. We will lose track of time, forget what day of the week it is, and, near the end of our stay, discover a beach with tidal pools where hundreds of snails cling to the primordial rock. Our children will play for hours, splashing among the hermit crabs, starfish, and other sea creatures.

"It's like SeaWorld," I tell them.

"No," my 11-year-old will correct me, "it's the real one."

—**Johanna Berkman**'s writing has appeared in the *Washington Post*, the *New York Times Magazine*, and *Harvard Review*.

"IT MIGHT BE HARD TO KNOW WHERE TO START."

A Bite of the Big Apple

New York City, New York, U.S.

New York City may not seem like the most obvious place for a weekend with kids. But think about everything the Big Apple has to offer: famous sports teams and Broadway musicals, sky-high views and underground trains, carnival rides and hot dogs, famous parks and multiple zoos. In fact, there are so many things to do and see that it might be hard to know where to start.

Maybe they can't spend the night in a museum like the popular movies, but they can spend hours exploring the Metropolitan Museum of Art or the American Museum of Natural History ("Dum Dum"—the *Night at the Museum*'s famed Easter Island head—and the movie's monkey both live on the third floor).

The 102-story Empire State Building offers the city's most iconic view. But the Top of the Rock at 30 Rockefeller Plaza and the observatory at the top of One World Trade Center are also worthy—and sometimes less crowded. So are the views while walking or cycling across the Brooklyn Bridge, trekking the 1.4-mile (2 km) High Line elevated park, or taking a Circle Line sightseeing cruise around Manhattan.

Boats are also the way to visit the State of Liberty and Ellis Island (where families can trace their genealogy), while the free-of-charge Staten Island Ferry offers an excellent way to voyage across America's most celebrated harbor.

The Lion King, Frozen, Beetlejuice, Wicked, Aladdin, and *Harry Potter and the Cursed Child* are just a few of the family-friendly plays that have appeared on Broadway in recent years (if you didn't get tickets in advance, last-minute options are available at the TKTS booth in Times Square). Watching a baseball game in Yankee Stadium is the ultimate Big Apple sports experience. But you can also see the Knicks or Rangers at Madison Square Garden, or the Giants and Jets just a short train ride away in the Meadowlands of New Jersey.

Round off the weekend with a trek out to Coney Island for a Nathan's hot dog, a spin on the Cyclone roller coaster, and even a dip in the Atlantic come warmer months.

HUB | *East Coast United States*

Head to the Statue of Liberty for iconic skyline views.

Innsbruck's funicular brings visitors into Austria's Alps.

Alpine Antics
Innsbruck, Austria

One of the oldest cities in the Alps (founded as a fourth-century Roman army outpost), Innsbruck is also one of the region's most diverse when it comes to family fun weekends. While it's world-renowned for snow sports—the Winter Olympics were staged there in 1964 and 1976—the Austrian metropolis might be even better during the warmer months when the city's outdoor cafés spring to life, and hiking and biking overtake skiing as the favorite outdoor activities. Innsbruck's Altstadt (Old City) flaunts historic castles, palaces, and churches, as well as a colorful Christmas Market. In addition to the Bergisel Ski Jump, Olympia World offers guests bobsled rides. On the eastern outskirts of town, Swarovski Crystal World revolves around a museum of art and curiosities entered through a giant, leaf-covered head. But the ultimate Innsbruck adventure is riding the funicular to the lofty Alpenzoo and continuing upward to a station at 7,444 feet (2,269 m) above sea level.

HUB | *Vienna, Austria; Munich, Germany*

Interpreters reconstruct Viking life at the Ribe Viking Center.

Valhalla Rising
Copenhagen, Denmark

Let your kids get in touch with their inner Viking on a weekend jaunt across Denmark that features longboats, castles, and living history. From Copenhagen's Kastrup Airport, it's around a half-hour drive to Roskilde, where the Viking Ship Museum preserves five 11th-century Norse watercraft and a shipbuilding yard where reproduction Viking vessels are created by modern craftsmen. On the outskirts of Roskilde, Lejre Land of Legends is an open-air archaeological park with reconstructed Iron Age homes, workshops, a marketplace, and a sacrificial bog. Hopping over to Denmark's west coast on the North Sea, Ribe Viking Center offers "warrior training" for children aged seven to 13 under the tutelage of historical actors, as well as Viking crafts and cuisine (pancakes, sausages, salmon, and mead for those of age). On the drive back to Copenhagen, pay a visit to Trelleborg, where the remains of an ancient Viking ringed fortress are complemented by a museum and living history presentations.

HUB | *Major Western European Cities*

Catch the sunset over Hout Bay.

As Good as It Gets

Cape of Good Hope, South Africa

Contrary to popular belief, the Cape of Good Hope is *not* Africa's southernmost point (that's Cape Agulhas). But the rugged, hook-shaped peninsula south of Cape Town is far more fabled and much more amenable to a short family break in South Africa. The weekend should start with a flight on the Table Mountain Aerial Cableway. The flat-topped summit (3,558 feet/1,084 m) offers awesome views and wilderness hiking trails. Clifton, Camps Bay, and other beaches along the cape's western edge render excellent swimming and surfing conditions. The actual Cape of Good Hope lies inside a national park with zebra, antelope, ostrich, baboons, and other African wildlife. But the best place to view the cape's famous penguins is along the boulder-strewn beaches of Simon's Town on the east coast. The seafaring burg is also home to the South African Naval Museum, as well as sea kayaking, whale watching, and scuba diving outfitters.

HUB | *Cape Town, South Africa*

Book a visit to Aruba's Flamingo Beach on Renaissance Island to see the pink birds in action.

LGBTQ Family Destinations

While many LGBTQ travelers can face unique challenges,
these inclusive destinations are worth the trip.

1. AMALFI COAST, ITALY

In a culture that reveres children and families, LGBTQ families are treated no differently from others. Visit the less expensive Praiano, which is perfect for families. Hop on the convenient local buses to sightsee, let the kids scramble over the rocks at sandless Marina di Praia beach, and explore the vast and ancient grounds of nearby Pompeii.

2. ARUBA

Aruba is one of the only islands in the Caribbean that is expressly welcoming of LGBTQ travelers and attracts a gay-friendly crowd. With a progressive mind-set that makes it safe for all travelers, Aruba offers blinding white-sand beaches and crystal clear waters, as well as superb snorkeling and diving, the Aruba Butterfly Farm, and catamaran tours.

3. PUERTO VALLARTA, MEXICO

Even outside of its world-renowned Pride celebrations, Puerto Vallarta is one of Mexico's most LGBTQ-friendly destinations. Enjoy a quieter beachfront scene at Marina Vallarta and Nuevo Vallarta. For a family outing, try a Vallarta Adventures tour of Yelapa or Islas Marietas.

4. BARCELONA, SPAIN

Spain was one of the first countries to legalize same-sex marriage, and Barcelona's established LGBTQ community—plus its historic legacy of art, literature, and music—makes it well worth a trip. Plan a visit to some of the city's more than 55 museums and explore iconic architecture by Antoni Gaudí.

5. PLAYA DEL CARMEN, MEXICO

High-service, waterfront resorts along the Riviera Maya offer enticing family packages. This place is known for Caribbean beauty without Caribbean crowds, boasting some of Mexico's best-preserved Maya ruins.

6. LONDON, UNITED KINGDOM

There's always something new to do in the United Kingdom's queer-friendly capital. Stay in tony Mayfair or Knightsbridge for views of Hyde Park and a short walk to Buckingham Palace. If your kids are Harry Potter fans, don't miss a stop at the King's Cross tube station for a priceless photo op at Platform 9¾.

7. HONOLULU, HAWAII

Hawaii is among the U.S. states with the highest percentage of LGBTQ adults, and Honolulu has long been a favorite destination for LGBTQ travelers. For families with older kids, the Pedego Waikiki electric bike tours are a great way to whiz down the beach front and watch surfers.

8. CORK, IRELAND

In 2015, Ireland became the first country in the world to legalize same-sex marriage by popular vote, and though Dublin might have a livelier gay community, Cork offers a mix of contemporary and traditional at a slower pace.

9. SIEM REAP, CAMBODIA

Though it doesn't rival the lively scene in neighboring Thailand, Cambodia is accommodating to LGBTQ visitors—the official tourism board once even sponsored a campaign welcoming gay tourists—particularly in Phnom Penh and Siem Riep.

10. AMSTERDAM, THE NETHERLANDS

The queen of gay-friendly cities, Amsterdam is the colorful, walkable capital of a country with a long history of legal protections for LGBTQ people. Don't bother with a car—bike tours are a great way to tour the city's bridges and canals.

> "PACK A GOOD PAIR OF
> SHOES AND BE PREPARED
> TO WALK."

Paris Plus Jeune

Paris, France

Paris is the capital of romance. It's certainly a dreamy destination for honeymoons and anniversary trips, but it's also a pretty good place for a weekend with the kids. Pack a good pair of shoes and be prepared to walk—through museums and parks, along the grand boulevards, and along the River Seine—because Paris is one of those cities that begs you to explore on foot.

Start at the Trocodéro, the fountain-splashed plaza across the river from the Eiffel Tower, with its awesome selfie ops and jaw-dropping views of the cast-iron giant. The tower beckons with an elevator ride to one of the globe's most iconic viewpoints. From there it's just a 30-minute walk or short Metro ride to the Arc de Triomphe, another of the French capital's enduring landmarks, and then down the Avenue des Champs-Élysées. Grab lunch in a sidewalk café or buy the fixings for a picnic in the Tuileries Gardens, where a summer fun fair features bumper cars, a merry-go-round, and other carnival rides. Spend the rest of the afternoon exploring the Louvre, the world's greatest art museum, before a sunset stroll along the Seine.

Day two commences in the Île de la Cité, the ancient island where so much Parisian history unfolded. Following the tragic fire of 2019, Notre-Dame Cathedral is closed for renovation until further notice, but you can still admire its elaborate facade and bell towers from outside. Guillotine blades and other gruesome relics are on display at the island's La Conciergerie prison. Hop across the river to the Pompidou Center and its insane outdoor sculpture garden and indoor Galerie des Enfants with art exhibits and creative activities especially designed for kids.

Rest your tired feet on a Bateau Mouche scenic boat tour along the Seine, descend into the creepy Catacombs, and then while away the rest of the afternoon in the Luxembourg Gardens, attending a puppet show at the marionette theater or renting a toy boat to sail on the garden pond.

HUB | *Major Western European Cities*

Splash fountains below the Eiffel Tower make for family fun with epic views.

Fog from Lake Michigan covers Chicago's skyline.

Windy City Escapade
Chicago, Illinois, U.S.

Big buildings, awesome museums, famous sports teams: Chicago is a natural when it comes to kids, especially during the warmer months when families can take full advantage of the city's parks and beaches. Depending on what your kids are into, you can eyeball ancient beasts (like "Sue," the ferocious *Tyrannosaurus rex*) at the Field Museum of Natural History or an incredible variety of living animals at the free-of-charge Lincoln Park Zoo. View famous works by Van Gogh, Picasso, and Andy Warhol at the Art Institute of Chicago or a celestial canvas of planets, galaxies, and nebulae at Alder Planetarium. Snatch a lofty look at Chicago through the translucent SkyDeck at the top of the 110-story Willis Tower or a bird's-eye view of Lake Michigan while riding the Centennial Wheel on Navy Pier. Root for the home team at Wrigley Field or watch the Bulls or Blackhawks at United Center.

HUB | *Midwestern United States*

Look out over panoramic views from the top of Cabo Girão.

Magma-nificent
Madeira, Portugal

The Portuguese island may be famed for wine, but it's also a pretty cool place for a family weekend blending culture, nature, and aquatic activities. Hop over on a 90-minute flight from Lisbon or four-hour flight from London or Paris. Then start the weekend with a guided tour of historic Funchal town in a "Tukxi" (a three-wheeled Vespa) and snatch a bird's-eye view of the island from the amazing, see-through skywalk at Cabo Girão. Hop aboard a whale- and dolphin-watching cruise through the deep-blue Atlantic that surrounds the island or catch a 4x4 tour into Madeira's rugged volcanic heartland. The volcanic vibe continues in the lava tubes of São Vicente and the natural rock swimming holes at Porto Moniz. If your kids play soccer, be sure to include a visit to the CR7 Museum—dedicated to superstar Portuguese footballer Cristiano Ronaldo No. 7, who was born, raised, and kicked his first ball on Madeira.

HUB | *Lisbon, Portugal; Marrakech, Morocco*

Where America Was Born
Southeast Virginia, U.S.

Home to the first permanent English settlement in the Western Hemisphere, the Hampton Roads area of southeast Virginia has evolved from a tiny colony that barely survived into a modern metropolitan area with nearly two million people and an amazing array of weekend getaways. Kids can immerse themselves in American history at the Jamestown settlement, Colonial Williamsburg, Yorktown Battlefield, and the Battleship *Wisconsin* at the Nauticus maritime museum in Norfolk. Nearby Virginia Beach is all about sun, sea, and sand along a wide, 3-mile (4.8 km) boardwalk with street performers, live music, huge outdoor sculptures, alfresco dining options, and rental bikes. More into nature? Explore the Great Dismal Swamp or First Landing State Park by foot, bike, or boat. Or splurge on two-day tickets to the local theme parks: Williamsburg's Busch Gardens with its hair-raising coasters and thrill rides and the adjacent Water Country USA with its giant slides and lazy rivers.

HUB | *Washington, D.C.; Mid-Atlantic United States*

Find a re-created Powhatan Indian Village in Jamestown.

> "NIGHT PARADES FEATURE MASSIVE LIT-UP FLOATS AND DOGSLEDS."

Icescapades

Québec Winter Carnival, Québec City, Québec, Canada

Québec City, the capital of Canada's Québec Province, knows all about winter: It's the world's fifth snowiest city, receiving an annual average snowfall of 124 inches (315 cm), and temperatures can drop to nearly 40 below zero. Residents embrace the cold, throwing a spirited winter carnival over 10 days in February. Take a weekend to bundle up and take part in a wide variety of outdoor activities for people of all ages.

With origins dating back to 1894, the first modern version of the Québec Winter Carnival took place in 1955 and quickly became the highlight of the season for Québécois. Join locals cheering on the canoe races in the frigid waters of the St. Lawrence River, where teams have to paddle around chunks of ice and at times push their canoes across the frozen surface. Night parades feature massive lit-up floats, and dogsleds carry visitors through the snowy Plains of Abraham parkland. There's more: A recently added EDM night creates a thumping electronic music party outside, and a visit to Bonhomme's Ice Palace, made of 300 tons (272 tonnes) of ice, is a must. The bravest souls can join in the annual snow bath, where skimpily dressed cold-weather enthusiasts cavort in the snow.

The official icon of the carnival is Bonhomme, a cheerful snowman sporting a red toque and colorful arrow sash. A blend of Native American and French-Canadian weaving, the sash, with its unique pattern of arrowheads and zigzagging lightning bolts, was worn by French settlers and fur traders in the 19th century to tighten coats against the winter chill. The sashes were on the verge of being lost to history until the Winter Carnival revived the art. Now arrow sashes can be purchased in shops around Québec City, the ultimate accessory for the carnival.

HUB | *Montréal or Toronto, Canada; Northeastern United States*

Part of Québec's winter festivities, a castle and slide are built from carved ice blocks.

Among other treats, traditional cotton candy is for sale at the fair.

Longhorn Celebration
Texas State Fair, Dallas, Texas, U.S.

Everything's bigger and better in Texas—including its state fair, one of the largest in the United States. The fairgrounds cover 277 acres (112 ha) and host more than two million people every year over 24 days in October. A 55-foot (17 m) talking cowboy called Big Tex welcomes all visitors.

Since its founding in 1886, the fair has celebrated Lone Star heritage and agriculture, along with providing a wide array of entertainment. If you love college football, come during the weekend of the AT&T Red River Showdown between the Texas Longhorns and the Oklahoma Sooners. An iconic staple of the fair, the game has been played in the historic Cotton Bowl Stadium since 1929. The next day, go wild among the midway's 70-plus rides, including the Top o' Texas Tower and the 1914 Dentzel carousel. After dark, the nightly Starlight Parade features dazzling floats and music, followed by a water and light show punctuated by fireworks and liquid-fire fountains. Watch the sparkling display from the top of the Texas Star Ferris wheel.

HUB | *South Central United States*

Take to the Skies
International Balloon Fiesta, Albuquerque, New Mexico, U.S.

Albuquerque proudly claims the title of "hot-air ballooning capital of the world," and for good reason: For more than 40 years, it has hosted the International Balloon Fiesta. With more than 500 hot-air balloons that take flight every October, it's the largest ballooning event on Earth.

At the 365-acre (148 hectare), custom-designed Balloon Fiesta Park, visitors join in the action. You can wander directly among the balloons on the launch field, watching them slowly fill for takeoff, or blaze with color during the "glows" after dark. You'll have a lot to see no matter what portion of the nine-day festival you attend. There are contests where professional pilots test their flying accuracy as well as events that delight in sheer wonder. A fan favorite is the Special Shape Rodeo, with 100 whimsically shaped balloons that range from a rocketship to a stagecoach to a giant Yoda head. The showstoppers are the mass ascensions, when all 500-plus festival balloons lift off to silently drift through the clear blue skies over the Rio Grande Valley.

Colorful hot-air balloons soar above the Sandia Mountains and Rio Grande.

HUB | *Southwestern United States*

The fair's Strates Midway rides seem even more magical at night.

Rides & Games

Erie County Fair, Hamburg, New York, U.S.

Held annually since 1841 (but with origins dating as far back as 1820), the Erie County Fair is the oldest fair in the United States. Located just 20 minutes from downtown Buffalo, the 275-acre (111 ha) fairgrounds host 12 days of events every August. During your weekend, pack your schedule with interactive agriculture education exhibits and performances by country stars and comedy acts, and enjoy some 70 rides and 100 games on the Strates Midway, produced by the last remaining railroad carnival in North America.

It's not a fair without outrageous eats, of course. Snack your way through 125 food stands that have introduced such novelties as flaming hot Cheetos fries, pierogi poutine, and possibly even the modern hamburger. Legend has it that a pair of inventive brothers created the ground beef sandwich at the 1885 fair and christened it the "hamburger" after the Erie County Fair's hometown of Hamburg, New York. After all the indulgence, cap off your visit with a view of natural splendor: The fairgrounds are located only 45 minutes from Niagara Falls.

HUB | *East Coast United States*

"THE FAIR FEATURES
NEARLY 70 UNUSUALLY
SKEWERED BITES."

Everything on a Stick

Iowa State Fair, Des Moines, Iowa, U.S.

As the growing season draws to a close, more than a million people come to revel in Iowa's agricultural heritage in late August. Farmers show off their biggest accomplishments—from pigs to produce—while industry exhibitions demonstrate the latest technology in harvesting and husbandry. The fair is a superb blend of tradition and innovation, offering up what's new while also featuring games and competitions that have been a staple since the first fair in 1854, like hog calling and tallest corn.

The fair spans 11 days, but you can enjoy it in a weekend. Buy your tickets in advance: There's usually a 30 percent discount before the fair, along with deals on ride wristbands and food stands. You're going to be sampling a lot of food, most of it likely on a stick. The fair features nearly 70 unusually skewered bites, from apple pie and pork chops to peanut butter and jelly and deep-fried Twinkies.

The chainsaw carvers, Budweiser Clydesdale horses, and the acrobatics of the Red Trouser Show are perennial favorites with fairgoers. But the Butter Cow is the star attraction. A staple of the fair since 1911, the cow is sculpted anew every year from 600 pounds (272 kg) of pure cream Iowa butter. And don't skip the competitions. Friendly rivalry epitomizes the spirit of the fair, and contests go beyond weighing the heftiest hog or beefiest tomato—there are photography, quilt, and cooking competitions, considered some of the largest in the world. You can enter, even if you're not a master farmer or quiltmaker—there are on-site bouts for all skill sets, from fiddling to spelling to yo-yoing.

The "Swifty Swine" miniature pot-bellied pig race is one of many draws to the state fair.

Rulantica, Germany, boasts a mega-water park with an indoor water world.

Water Parks

Splish, splash, and slide in the world's greatest water parks,
from Germany to Brazil.

1. GREAT WOLF LODGE, WISCONSIN DELLS, WISCONSIN, U.S.

Great Wolf's original outpost in Wisconsin Dells—the spiritual birthplace of the American waterpark craze—is a perennial favorite, whether you like racing your pack members face-first down a four-story drop or kicking back in the family warming pool.

2. KALAHARI, POCONO MOUNTAINS, PENNSYLVANIA, U.S.

Another Dells favorite that's expanded across the United States, Kalahari runs the (for now) nation's largest contiguous indoor water park: a 220,000-square-foot (20,438.7 sq m) spread in Pennsylvania's Pocono Mountains, where the can't-misses include the Flowrider and the underwater virtual reality experience.

3. WORLD WATERPARK, WEST EDMONTON MALL, CANADA

Topping Kalahari's largest outpost by about 5,000 square feet (464.5 sq m), this Canadian giant is the continent's largest water park. The thrill menu is accordingly extensive, from beginner to extreme (if you're the latter, don't miss the trapdoor-equipped Sky Screamer).

4. TROPICAL ISLANDS, BERLIN, GERMANY

The world's largest water park—more than triple the size of North America's largest—occupies a one-time zeppelin hangar south of Berlin, where you'll find not just the expected but also scuba diving courses, a palm-fringed beach, and a spa.

5. RULANTICA, GERMANY

Not to be outdone, southwestern Germany recently debuted its own mega–water park, where fresh ideas (from the Nordic fantasy theme to the sustainability measures) are making as many waves as the resident Surf Fjørd.

6. THE WATER CUBE, BEIJING, CHINA

For an Olympic-grade experience, visit the Beijing National Aquatics Center. Better known as the Water Cube, it was built for the 2008 Summer Olympics swim competitions and now houses a massive water park, complete with the Crazy Tsunami pool.

7. BEACH PARK, FORTALEZA, BRAZIL

The rare beachfront water park, this family favorite on Brazil's northeastern coast offers amazing views of the Atlantic—nowhere more so than the start of the Insane (the ride's actual name) free fall—14 stories up.

8. HAPPY ISLAND WATERWORLD, JOHANNESBURG, SOUTH AFRICA

This newcomer to the Johannesburg area is Africa's largest water park, where crowd favorites range from the exciting Typhoon (a slide that sucks you through a funnel) to the continent's most expansive wave pools.

9. AQUAVENTURE AT ATLANTIS DUBAI, UNITED ARAB EMIRATES

Its location alone—a palm-shaped island in the Persian Gulf—makes this water park unique, but so do the rides. Consider the Leap of Faith, a dramatic plunge into a sharky lagoon (don't panic; you're inside a clear tube).

10. SCHLITTERBAHN NEW BRAUNFELS, TEXAS, U.S.

If you do nothing else at this sprawling Texas Hill Country icon, hit the Raging River. Estimated to be the world's longest tube shoot, it's certainly the only one fed by—and overlooking—the New Braunfels' Comal River.

Village Vibe

Busch Gardens Williamsburg, Williamsburg, Virginia, U.S.

Virginia's branch of Busch Gardens has serious thrill rides. Among the 134-acre (54 ha) park's more than 50 attractions are one of the world's tallest dive coasters, Griffon, which plunges 205 feet (62 m) at 75 miles an hour (121 km/h), and North America's fastest multilaunch coaster, the 72-mile-an-hour (116 km/h) Pantheon, launched in 2020. In addition to high marks for its collection of coasters, Busch Gardens Williamsburg also wins praise for its lushly landscaped, European village setting.

Named World's Most Beautiful Amusement Park every year since 1990 by the National Amusement Park Historical Association, Busch Gardens Williamsburg is an appealing place to visit, even if you skip the rides. The all-ages entertainment destination offers live stage shows, shopping, dining, gardens, and wildlife exhibits. Meandering walkways connect nine villages, each featuring cuisine and attractions (such as Germany's autobahn-themed Verbolten roller coaster) inspired by its "home" country.

HUB | *Washington, D.C.; Mid-Atlantic United States*

"NAMED WORLD'S MOST BEAUTIFUL AMUSEMENT PARK . . . BUSCH GARDENS WILLIAMS-BURG IS AN APPEALING PLACE TO VISIT."

Take your pick of coasters at Busch Gardens, including the Griffon, Alpengeist, and Loch Ness Monster.

The 12-story Wildfire coaster includes five stomach-turning loops.

Digging It

Silver Dollar City, Branson, Missouri, U.S.

B uilt in 1960 atop the Ozarks' original tourist attraction, Marvel Cave (opened for tours in 1894), Silver Dollar City put Branson, Missouri, on the map as a family entertainment destination. The cave, and the early explorers who ventured inside, inspired the Silver Dollar City 1880s-style theme. Several of the more than 40 rides—from the old-school Fire in the Hole indoor roller coaster to the new Mystic River Falls, a raft ride with a 45-foot (14 m) drop that debuted in 2020—evoke the Wild West spirit of life on the Ozark frontier.

Celebrating Ozark heritage arts are the park's 100 resident craftspeople. Visit the blacksmith, glassblower, and other studios to see demonstrations and buy souvenirs. The culinary arts masters teach cooking classes, where you can learn to whip up dishes like homestyle Ozark chicken croquettes with sweet pepper sauce. Buy tickets in advance for the daily Marvel Mine lantern-light tour, led by guides in period costumes.

Drop 50 feet (15.2 m) for a splash on the American Plunge.

Mickey and Minnie Mouse wave during a parade at DisneySea.

Land & Sea
Tokyo Disneyland and Tokyo DisneySea, Tokyo, Japan

Only a five-minute walk from Japan Railways' Maihama Station, the two-for-one Tokyo Disneyland and Tokyo DisneySea resort is at once comfortably familiar and completely different for fans of the House of Mouse theme parks. The Disneyland portion, opened in 1983, was the first international version of the original Disneyland in California and features iconic attractions like Cinderella's Castle and It's a Small World.

Opened in 2001, DisneySea is one of a kind. As the name implies, a water theme flows through the park, which is brimming with cascades, ponds, fountains, bays, and other man-made water features. Rides and attractions are arranged by ports, such as Mermaid Lagoon, American Waterfront, and Mediterranean Harbor, where gondolas glide through canals. A new port, Fantasy Springs—based on the animated Disney films *Frozen*, *Peter Pan*, and *Tangled*—is slated to open in 2023. Buy a Two-Day Passport to spend a full day in each park.

HUB | *Japan*

Make your own candy bar at the park's Chocolate World.

Sweet Rides
Hersheypark, Hershey, Pennsylvania, U.S.

Hersheypark is a pretty sweet paradise for chocolate lovers and thrill seekers. Although the Coal Cracker flume ride is fueled by flowing water, not liquid chocolate like the river in *Willie Wonka and the Chocolate Factory*, park guests do enjoy free admission and a chocolate factory tour at the adjacent Hershey's Chocolate World. For an extra fee, you can even play chocolatier by choosing ingredients and designing a wrapper for your own custom chocolate bar. The mouthwatering aroma of chocolate wafting from the Hershey's Kitchens Food Hall is free; however, the double chocolate s'mores are worth the calorie-and-cash splurge.

While candy is the raison d'être for Hersheypark, which originated as a recreation area for chocolate factory employees, this is also a seriously fun theme park featuring more than 70 rides. The impressive roster includes 14 roller coasters, the wildest of which—the gravity-defying SooperDooperLooper—should be attempted only on an empty stomach.

HUB | *Mid-Atlantic United States*

Scream Machines

Cedar Point, Sandusky, Ohio, U.S.

The Wicked Twister drops you, nearly vertically, from 206 feet (62.8 m) high.

Celebrating 150 years in 2020, Cedar Point—named for its Lake Erie peninsula location—only gets better with age. Historic attractions, such as the steam-powered Cedar Point & Lake Erie Railroad train and the 1905 Hotel Breakers, evoke memories of simpler days when the fastest park ride hit speeds of up to 10 miles an hour (16.1 km/h). The ever growing collection of thrill rides, like Steel Vengeance—the current world-record-breaking and world's first hyper-hybrid coaster—perennially earn the park rave reviews from fans of big and fast scream machines.

There are 18 world-class coasters among the park's 70 rides. Summer visitors can also splash in Cedar Point Shores Waterpark, chill out on mile-long (1.6 km) Cedar Point Beach, and play in and on Lake Erie. Buy a Rock & Ride combo ticket for discounted admission to Cedar Point, the Rock & Roll Hall of Fame and Museum (an hour east of the park), and the Pro Football Hall of Fame (two hours southeast).

HUB | *Midwestern United States*

The *World of Color* show in Disneyland sets the park in magnificent, lit-up hues.

"WALT DISNEY'S VISION FOR HIS PARK LIVES ON."

The Original

Disneyland Resort, Anaheim, California, U.S.

Disneyland started it all. Opened in 1955 on the site of former orange groves, Walt Disney's first theme park revolutionized the theme park industry and launched the Disney vacation empire. Today, the original park is known as Disneyland Park and is part of the much larger Disneyland Resort, which also includes Disney California Adventure Park and three hotels: Disney's Grand Californian Hotel & Spa, Disneyland Hotel, and Disney's Paradise Pier Hotel.

Although a lot has changed since the 1950s, the resort retains original Disneyland essential elements, such as the Main Street U.S.A. gateway; Sleeping Beauty's Castle; the four original Adventureland, Fantasyland, Frontierland, and Tomorrowland themed areas; and tried-and-true rides, including Dumbo the Flying Elephant. Walt Disney's vision for his park lives on too. As he famously said, "Disneyland will never be completed. It will continue to grow as long as there is imagination left in the world."

Imagination, technology, and a slew of movies created under the Disney umbrella (including those from Pixar, Walt Disney Animation, and Marvel) continually inspire new rides and attractions at Disneyland Resort. When Star Wars: Galaxy's Edge opened in 2019, it became the eighth land in Disneyland Park, along with Critter Country, New Orleans Square, and Mickey's Toontown.

The adjacent Disney California Adventure Park, opened in 2001, features attractions straight off the big screen or native to the Golden State. The Buena Vista Street entrance plaza is styled after 1920s Los Angeles, and the themed areas are Hollywood Land, the Pixar-inspired Cars Land and Pixar Pier, Pacific Wharf, Grizzly Peak, and Paradise Gardens Park.

Both parks feature Broadway-worthy live entertainment; after-dark pyrotechnic and special-effects shows (*Fantasmic!* at Disneyland Park and *World of Color* at California Adventure); and indispensable mobile apps for necessities like buying tickets, tracking wait times, and navigating your way through all the lands and attractions.

Shinta Mani Wild is the epitome
of remote luxury (p. 337).

CHAPTER NINE

ULTIMATE RETREATS

Find luxury, rest, and relaxation among desert oases, mountain peaks, and sandy shores.

Conservationist Charm

Woodstock Inn & Resort, Woodstock, Vermont, U.S.

What started as a tavern more than 200 years ago is today an elegant, garden-encircled 142-room hotel thanks to conservationists and former owners Mary and Laurance Rockefeller. A luxurious and cozy retreat in central Vermont's Green Mountains—a region blanketed with maple forests, covered bridges, and charming clapboard towns—Woodstock Inn & Resort is a quick stroll to local artisan shops and independent bookstores, as well as surrounding nature. The forested trails of Marsh-Billings-Rockefeller National Historical Park are less than a mile away. Visit the 3-acre (1.2 ha) Kelly Way Gardens, where more than 200 varieties of vegetables and 75 varieties of berries and fruit trees provide the base for the inn's two main restaurants. Or cast flies in the Barnard Brook or the larger Ottauquechee River on a quest for trout. On the property, sip tea in the conservatory or relax in the LEED-certified spa's Scandinavian saunas. The inn is great any time of year, but autumn is particularly spectacular.

> "A LUXURIOUS AND COZY RETREAT IN CENTRAL VERMONT'S GREEN MOUNTAINS—A REGION BLANKETED WITH MAPLE FORESTS, COVERED BRIDGES, AND CHARMING CLAPBOARD TOWNS"

HUB | *Burlington, Vermont, U.S.; Northeastern United States*

Flowers adorn the lush grounds of the inn every spring.

An oasis of calm, Mii Amo Resort sits below Sedona's famous red rocks.

Red Rock State of Mind

Mii Amo Resort, Sedona, Arizona, U.S.

The mystical red-rock stacks in Sedona's Boynton Canyon, an area long associated with healing and wellness, is a fine setting for an immersive spa experience. Check in at the adobe-clad Mii Amo boutique spa resort for a three-night weekend to rest and recharge. Restorative options abound. Try guided meditation, canyon bathing (the local take on Japanese forest bathing), or visiting the calming Crystal Grotto, a circular room inspired by Native American kiva buildings traditionally used for religious rituals or spiritual ceremonies. Daily spa treatments—from massages to facials—use desert botanicals such as piñon and prickly pear to connect you to the landscape. When you're ready to stretch your body and mind, try activities including watercolor painting, vision board collage making, mountain biking, wine and food tastings, stargazing, and red-rock photography. Cool off with a dip in the pool during the day; on chilly desert nights cozy up by your private casita's beehive fireplace.

HUB | *Phoenix, Arizona, U.S.; Southwestern United States*

The Crystal Grotto focuses the sun's rays into the sacred space.

> "ITS VERDANT LANDSCAPE IS A ROMANTIC SETTING KNOWN FOR ITS RUINS."

Relax Among Ruins

Tivoli, Italy

A retreat from the bustle of Rome since at least the second century, Tivoli's verdant landscape is a romantic setting known for its historic ruins. The area's top attractions, Villa Adriana and Villa d'Este (both UNESCO World Heritage sites), are not only wonderlands for history buffs but also ethereal sanctuaries where spindly pines back crumbling archways and gorgeous gardens with fountains make for a weekend of quiet reflection.

The town entrance, via the canyon-spanning Ponte Gregoriano bridge, sets the tone as it arcs over the River Aniene. The hilltop city is ringed by remnants of its former fortification, constructed in the fourth century B.C. Wander through the red-roofed town past historic churches; then relax with a cappuccino in an outdoor café overlooking the Piazza Giusseppe Garibaldi and adjacent Rocca Pia, a 15th-century castle turned prison. Nearby is Villa d'Este, one of the first *giardini delle meraviglie* (gardens of wonders), where immaculately manicured landscapes abut elaborate hillside waterfalls and multitiered ponds with fountains lined with ornate statues made from travertine marble mined close by. The 16th-century garden is Renaissance refinement at its finest and was an early model for many other European gardens. End your day with a plate of comforting ravioli or fresh seafood from Ristorante Sibella, where tables are set atop waterfalls and a cave at the base of two ruined Roman temples.

Spend the next day exploring the sprawling Hadrian's Villa (Villa Adriana), an archaeological complex and ideal city crafted by second-century Roman emperor Hadrian. The ruins are made up of around 30 buildings—temples, residences, theaters, libraries, and public baths—as well as gardens and reflecting pools spread over nearly 300 acres (120 ha). Then take a picnic lunch into the surrounding Monti Tiburtini hills where hikes into the valley below Tivoli follow the river as it disappears underground. If there's time afterward, soothe aching muscles in warm thermal waters at Bagni di Tivoli.

HUB | *Rome, Italy; Major Western European Cities*

Hadrian's villa was
constructed between
A.D. 118 and A.D. 134.

Practice yoga and mindfulness on an Ayurvedic retreat.

Yoga & Meditation
The Raj, Fairfield, Iowa, U.S.

Five hours west of downtown Chicago, southeastern Iowa's rural patchwork of farmland is an unlikely outpost for a center of authentic Ayurvedic medicine. Yet the Raj, founded in 1993 and set atop 100 rolling acres (40 ha) of gardens, forest, and ponds, is one of the most expansive Ayurvedic retreats in the United States. Based on a system of traditional medicine that dates back more than 3,000 years in India, Ayurveda uses a vegetarian diet, yoga, silent meditation, and spa-like treatments—including herbal steam baths and oil massages—to detoxify and treat imbalances in the body and mind. Book into these luxury villa accommodations for a long weekend (a three-day session is the shortest allowable length of stay) for basic rejuvenation or to target what ails you; an initial consultation will help reveal your treatment plan if you're unsure. The center accepts just 15 patients at a time and offers tips and tools to continue with your transformation after you've returned home from the heartland.

HUB | *Midwestern United States*

A weaver threads together a silk cloth.

World Heritage Retreat
Luang Prabang, Laos

The World Heritage city of Luang Prabang sits where sleepy stretches of the Mekong and Nam Khan Rivers collide. Spend a peaceful weekend learning and soaking in its ebbs and flows. Start before dawn on the main street to observe Sai Bat: residents quietly dispensing rice alms to more than 200 Buddhist monks in a tradition that dates back to the 14th century. After a breakfast of *Khao piak sen* (noodle soup) in a French-style café–a fusion from the country's colonial era—head to Ock Pop Tok where weaving classes teach the art atop traditional looms. The fair-trade enterprise employs 50 local weavers who impart wisdom about local plants used for dyes, prepare and set looms, and assist guests through the meditative practice of moving the shuttle back and forth. Later, retire to the luxurious Rosewood Luang Prabang, and heal tired hands with a spa treatment in an above-river tent. The Hmong Experience uses traditional healing knowledge and Laotian remedies made from herbs gathered in the spa's garden and surrounding native forest.

HUB | *Bangkok, Thailand; Southeast Asia*

Remote Luxury

Shinta Mani Wild, Cambodia

The epitome of remote luxury is Shinta Mani Wild, a series of 15 teak-lined open-air tents in a private wildlife corridor of a rainforested river valley in southern Cambodia. It's a three-hour drive (plus a 20-minute 4x4 ride) from Phnom Penh. Behind the camp to the west, the uninhabited and little-touristed Cardamom Mountains sprawl for miles.

Shinta Mani's accommodations are exquisite. Old steamer trunks, rich leathers, and whimsical art collide with the rocks and trees outside. A National Geographic–themed tent has vintage magazines and a waterfall view—some months you can even shower beneath the cascade.

While the resort makes it easy to while away a weekend soaking in a riverside outdoor tub to the sounds of pileated gibbons and kingfishers, its six adventure butlers will ensure you're never bored. These hosts also arrange activities such as bird-watching hikes to find colorful species; adventurous kayaking excursions; river stone foot massages, swims, and locally foraged picnics at the base of waterfalls; guided hikes with a butterfly expert; and antique Jeep safaris that stop in a meadow to watch for wild elephants with sundowners.

HUB | Bangkok, Thailand; Southeast Asia

Guests enjoy riverside foot massages and a bonfire at the resort.

Outdoor wading pools are just one of the luxe amenities in Ananda in the Himalaya.

Spas

Get a massage on the banks of the Zambezi, take a wellness retreat in Saint Lucia's rainforest, or soak in California's hot springs—R&R awaits.

1. ANANDA IN THE HIMALAYA, INDIA

As befits a spa whose reception area occupies a one-time maharaja's palace, this northern India retreat has welcomed everyone from Prince Charles to Oprah. Must-do's include a four-handed Ayurvedic massage and an aarti ceremony by the Ganges.

2. BODYHOLIDAY SAINT LUCIA, SAINT LUCIA

Set amid an epic jungle gym—on Saint Lucia's rainforested, trail-laced slopes—BodyHoliday has an extensive fitness menu year-round, to say nothing of the months when you can train with Olympic swimmers or champion sailors.

3. TWO BUNCH PALMS, DESERT HOT SPRINGS, CALIFORNIA, U.S.

This desert oasis offers all kinds of immersive treatments, from ancient hot springs to new sound baths. The famed Capone Suites are a nod to Al, who reportedly hid out here well before digital detoxers ever did.

4. LEFAY RESORT & SPA LAGO DI GARDA, ITALY

Achieving peak wellness here requires little more than one look at Lake Garda from the infinity pool's edge. This northern Italian refuge employs experts in osteopathy, physiotherapy, and natural medicine, among other disciplines.

5. COMO SHAMBHALA ESTATE, BALI, INDONESIA

Surrounded by mist-shrouded jungle and transected by a sacred river, this Balinese hideaway *feels* like a retreat, whether you're here for a structured wellness program or going à la carte. Either way, don't miss the Javanese Royal Lulur Bath.

6. RANCHO LA PUERTA, TECATE, MEXICO

Tecate may be best known for beer, but in spa circles, this Baja town is synonymous with "the Ranch," an 80-year-old bastion of clean eating and holistic fitness. For weekend wellness seekers, there's a Saturday at the Ranch option.

7. LAKE AUSTIN SPA RESORT, AUSTIN, TEXAS, U.S.

Giving new meaning to the ancient wellness practice of taking the waters, this Texas Hill Country icon offers paddleboard yoga, floating meditation, aquatic massage, and sundown wine cruises.

8. SCHLOSS ELMAU, KRÜN, GERMANY

If the heads of state looked particularly well at the 2015 G7 Summit, consider their accommodations: This regal Bavarian retreat comes with six spa outposts, two gyms, one yoga pavilion, and limitless Alpine views.

9. AMANGIRI, CANYON POINT, UTAH, U.S.

After exploring the surrounding national parks—Grand Canyon, Bryce, and Zion—you'll find a place to relax at this desert spa featuring terraces overlooking red mesas and dunes. Its 25,000-square-foot (2,322.6 sq m) Aman Spa follows Navajo traditions, and it offers outdoor treatment terraces, and even a floating, private pavilion for relaxation. The hotel also offers guided excursions to the parks.

10. THE ROYAL LIVINGSTONE VICTORIA FALLS ZAMBIA HOTEL BY ANANTARA, ZAMBIA

The award-winning treatment menu here includes the best of the African spa world: a massage on the banks of the Zambezi (the river that becomes Victoria Falls). Try the Pinda version with local pink-pepper-spiked oil and warm compresses.

"IT'S A CHOOSE-YOUR-OWN-ADVENTURE NOVEL IN HOTEL FORM."

A True Southern Belle

Greenbrier Resort, White Sulfur Springs, West Virginia, U.S.

On the outskirts of the George Washington and Jefferson National Forests and amid the undulating landscape of the Allegheny Mountains, the Greenbrier Resort is a centuries-old retreat. Just under 250 miles (400 km) from Washington, D.C., and 200 miles (320 km) from Richmond, Virginia, the hotel counts 27 U.S. presidents among its notable guests. In fact, this national historic landmark has a huge underground bunker beneath its West Virginia Wing, a (formerly) top-secret Cold War bomb shelter ready to house all of Congress in an emergency.

But don't expect a quaint historic boutique: The monstrous white, neoclassical column-fronted property boasts 710 rooms across its sprawling 11,000-acre (4,500 ha) estate. The resort includes 10 lobbies, a basement casino, a bowling alley, tennis courts, and enough boutique shops to fill a small shopping mall. It's easy to get lost, but that's all part of the charm—it's a choose-your-own-adventure novel in hotel form. Feeling fancy? Stroll through tulip gardens, take a carriage ride through the grounds, and then hit the spa. The area's sulfur-rich mineral waters were what drew outsiders here in the first place. Feeling outdoorsy? Try white-water rafting, horseback riding, clay pigeon shooting, the on-site ropes course, or stand-up paddleboarding on nearby Lake Moomba. Hungry? Watch a culinary demonstration, choose from 18 dining and bar options, or pay a visit to the on-site candy maker. You can also play golf, fly falcons, watch a tennis match, take a glassblowing lesson, or go for a dip in the indoor or the outdoor pool.

This ostentatious southern belle is loud and proud—eccentric floral patterns line hallways, showy wallpaper and floral drapery blanket almost every surface, and vibrant color abounds. Still, it's hardly hodgepodge. The design forms a unified elegance, and much of the existing decor dates back to the influence of famed interior designer Dorothy Draper.

A clamshell fountain adorns one of the Greenbrier's lobbies.

Take trail rides through Montana's picturesque backcountry.

How the West Was Fun
Broken Arrow Lodge, Alder, Montana, U.S.

Backed by a fir- and pine-forested ridge in southern Montana's upper Ruby River valley, Broken Arrow Lodge is a traditional Western-style retreat that promises to connect you with your inner outdoorsman. Eschewing the traditional week-long stay requirement of most dude ranch adventures, you can get down and dirty in Big Sky Country here for as few as three nights. The small, family-owned, lodge-style ranch can accommodate just 12 guests, so the experience is intimate and the meals are home-cooked.

Start at dawn with a hearty breakfast before mounting one of the property's more than 20 horses for a guided ride along scenic trails. In the afternoon, you can wander the riverside grounds or nearby hilltops for panoramic views of the surrounding mountains. If you're feeling lucky, head down to the riverbank to pan for gold, dig for garnets, or try fly-fishing for trout. There are also plenty of chores on this working ranch, so pitching in is always welcome (but not required).

HUB | *Bozeman, Montana, U.S.; Mountain West United States*

Tribeca is one of Manhattan's most expensive neighborhoods.

City Indulgences
Tribeca, New York, U.S.

Not all retreats are to wild, natural places; it's just as possible to escape by walking through a forest of cast-iron buildings and the cacophony of taxi horns—you just have to know where to go. And Tribeca, the triangular slice of urban jungle in southern Manhattan below Canal Street, could be just the ticket for respite in the city.

One of the most expensive neighborhoods in already expensive Manhattan, Tribeca is a place to splurge and indulge. Stay at a five-star hotel such as the Greenwich with its 250-year-old imported Japanese farmhouse at the center of its Sibiu Spa; the Roxy with its cinema featuring a rotating roster of indie films; or the Frederick, a retro-meets-modern hotel with minimalist rooms and a color-block bar.

The ultimate Tribeca indulgence may be in the 1883 textile factory that is now an underground spa, AIRE Ancient Baths New York. Amid moody chandeliers and original brick walls lie a series of pools and tubs with the aura of a Roman bathhouse.

HUB | *East Coast United States*

Sixth Sense
Six Senses Kaplankaya, Turkey

Amid whitewashed towns, cypress forest, tangerine and olive groves, and sleepy fishing coves, the Six Senses Kaplankaya offers dueling opportunities to stay put and relax or take leisurely Aegean cruises to ancient ruins on offshore Greek isles. Start at the spa's alchemy bar, where you can experience the textures and smells of local botanicals (chamomile, cloves, rosemary, rose petals) to create a personalized scrub used in your treatment. Targeted multi-day spa programs focus on what ails you—from sleep issues to aging and mental wellness—and recommend a regimen for your stay, managed in part by a global team of visiting practitioners. In between yoga sessions and massages, take a dip in the Aegean (the resort has three private beaches) or float in one of three sparkling pools. For an afternoon of archaeological history, take the Didyma-Miletus-Priene excursion to visit the ruined Temple of Apollo, a fourth-century B.C. theater, and an ancient Ionian city. Or book a private yacht to explore the isles of Patmos, Léros, Lipsí, Kos, and Kálymnos.

HUB | *Istanbul, Turkey; Major Western European Cities; Middle East*

The Anhinga deck at
Six Senses overlooks
the Aegean Sea.

Botticelli's "Birth of Venus" is on display in Florence's Uffizi.

"FLORENCE IS THE BIRTHPLACE OF THE RENAISSANCE, THE CULTURAL SHIFT THAT INTRODUCED DIPLOMACY TO POLITICS, OBSERVATION TO SCIENCE, AND PERSPECTIVE TO ART."

PERSPECTIVE

Chasing Venus

The Trail of Botticelli's Goddess of Love in Tuscany

For the past five years, a poster of Sandro Botticelli's "Birth of Venus" on my office wall has intrigued me. I stare at the Venus on the Half-Shell and sense that she wants to tell me something. But what? Does she have a secret? Some ancient wisdom to soothe my 21st-century, working-mother soul? I imagine what the goddess of love might say if we met at the corner coffee shop. Pulling myself back to reality, I add viewing the Renaissance painting to my bucket list.

One day while walking in downtown D.C., I spot something shiny on the ground. Never one to overlook a free dime or single earring, I stoop to pick it up. It's a small silver charm with a figure I can't make out on one side and, on the other, a large M with "Italy" stamped beneath it. A Google search reveals that I've found a Miraculous Medal. Since 1832, Catholics have been wearing them, believing in Mary's promise that all who do "will receive great graces."

It's a sign. I'm going to Italy.

Florence is the birthplace of the Renaissance, the cultural shift that introduced diplomacy to politics, observation to science, and perspective to art. Perspective is exactly what I've come to seek.

One of the oldest museums in the world, the Uffizi displays works by Leonardo da Vinci, Michelangelo, and Caravaggio. But I go straight to Botticelli's "Birth of Venus."

Reaching this moment has taken me five years, four airplanes, and the synchronization of a yoga retreat. I sit on a bench directly in front of the enormous painting, and my field of vision is filled with . . . buttocks. Tourist buttocks of all shapes and sizes.

I catch glimpses of the seafaring, voluptuous goddess with alabaster skin and Rapunzel hair. Art critics have deemed Venus's elongated proportions "anatomically improbable" and her pose "impossible," as she would certainly tip over her shell and face-plant into the sea. It's also true that her dark outline and lack of shadows render her flat, like a sticker you can peel. Everything in the painting is moving, fluttering. Yet Venus herself looks as calm as the clamshell she rode in on.

Note to self: *Be calm.*

Next, I notice her gaze. She is looking toward us, but her eyes indicate that her thoughts are far, far away.

Go inward, I think.

How to decipher her expression? A slight smile plays upon her lips, but her eyes look wistful. Is she happy? Sad? Homesick? Tender is the best I can surmise.

Be tender.

Shocking display of white skin, belly gently rounded.

Be authentic, vulnerable, and brave.

Eventually I rise to leave. No dramatic "aha" moment, but one can't argue with the subtle wisdom. I make my way through the throngs for a close-up goodbye. As soon as I draw near the canvas, my head fills with one word. It's as if the volume of my female intuition turned to its highest setting. *"Love!"*

I want to smack the painting. Venus drags me all the way to Florence to tell me the secret to life is love? Doesn't everyone know that? Can she be a bit more specific? No. Venus sticks to her monosyllabic script. "Love, love, love, love, love."

As I leave the Uffizi, it hits me. Venus didn't let me down at all. She simply finished my soul's incomplete question: Can you receive . . . *love?*

—**Melina Bellows** is the chief education officer of the Sustainable Forestry Initiative, Inc., and an internationally published author.

Luxury resorts offer plunge pools with views throughout Big Sur.

Coastal Hideaway
Ventana Big Sur, California, U.S.

A forested hideaway on the gorgeous central California coast, Ventana Big Sur has been a popular retreat for urbanites from both San Francisco and L.A. (it's roughly equidistant from both cities) since 1975. Stay in a cozy high-ceilinged, wood-walled room with a fireplace, chunky cable-knit throws, and artisan-curated minibar, or get closer to the landscape in a glamping tent amid California redwoods—you can still smell the salty air filter through the forest while bathing in teak-enclosed showers. The property makes the perfect jumping-off point for coastal exploration. It's just over 3 miles (6.1 km) north on Highway 1 to Pfeiffer Big Sur State Park where you can walk among redwoods. Another 24 miles (40 km) north is the kelp forest playground of harbor seals and sea otters at Point Lobos State Reserve. Or head south to see the cascade of McWay Falls rain down onto a secluded beach.

HUB | *Los Angeles or San Francisco, California, U.S.*

Boat trips guide you to icebergs surrounding Fogo Island.

The Edge of the World
Fogo Island Inn, Newfoundland, Canada

It's hard to find refined luxury as remote—and still as accessible—as the Fogo Island Inn. This breathtaking retreat is perched on the eastern seaboard's last holdout before the wild, broad Atlantic. Settling into your slice of the 29-room stilted architectural marvel made, in part, by traditional wooden shipbuilders, you'll be immersed in rugged Newfoundland. Floor-to-ceiling windows overlook Iceberg Alley, an offshore current corridor that ferries Greenland's icy glacier castoffs south like cars on a highway. Activities get you out in the landscape: Wander through a field picking wild blueberries, look for seals in rocky tide pools, take a guided geology hike, go ice skating on the harbor with locals, watch for the caribou herds, and make friends with members of this closely knit local community at the edge of the world. The inn has all of the necessary creature comforts as well as a few extras: the town's only cinema and arts theater, top-floor saunas and hot tubs, and in-room wood-burning fireplaces.

HUB | *Eastern Canada; Northeastern United States*

Ethereal Entertainment
Blue Lagoon, Iceland

Many of Iceland's visitors journey to the Blue Lagoon to bathe in the otherwordly geothermal waters on the eastern Reykjanes Peninsula—but most stay for only an hour or two before moving on. Opt to spend a full weekend for a truly luxurious treat with overnights in one of the two minimalist modern on-site hotels. Not only will you have more time to see the sky blue water—many rooms have pool views—but you'll also be able to immerse yourself in the bleak steam-filled snow-capped lava rock landscape beyond. Book into the chef's table experience at the Michelin-recommended Moss restaurant with a seven-course, locally sourced feast. And don't skip a visit to the Retreat Spa, which boasts private lava rock grottoes, a sub-terranean earthen steam cave, and massages and treatments incorporating localized components of geothermal seawater like algae and silica. Even better? Visit this popular resort in the late autumn low season (with smaller crowds) and opt for entry times after dark for the chance to float in the warm pools beneath the shimmering aurora borealis.

HUB | *Reykjavik, Iceland*

Find restoration by floating in the Blue Lagoon's geothermal seawater.

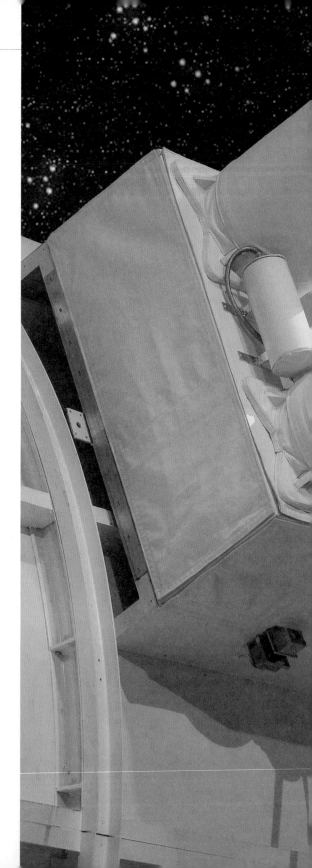

"AND THEN THERE'S THE CHANCE TO EXPERIENCE WEIGHTLESSNESS."

Adult Space Camp
Huntsville, Alabama, U.S.

If your idea of a retreat is less spa and more out-of-the-box mental stimulation, Huntsville, Alabama (aka "Rocket City"), has just the ticket: Adult Space Academy. NASA's Marshall Space Flight Center hosts adults-only programs year-round.

Over the course of the three-day, two-night adventure, you'll exercise creative problem-solving skills while performing an ongoing simulated space mission with fellow participants. Previous camp missions have included safely executing a simulated crew swap at the International Space Station (ISS), as well as Mars and lunar missions. You'll also construct and launch your own rocket, learn team building on a ropes course, engineer (and test) a mini protective heat shield out of an ad hoc assortment of items such as foil and pasta, and learn about the history of the U.S. Space and Rocket Center over breakfast with emeritus docents—military retirees and former NASA Marshall Space Flight staff. The setting is inspiring, and the experience is immersive. This is the site of space history. The Saturn V Moon Rocket is housed here, other rockets developed here put men on the moon, and ISS modules were built on-site. You'll sleep in dorm-style "habitats" and dine in a galley abutting aeroponic gardens where crops are grown with technology being tested for future space flights.

And then there's the chance to experience weightlessness. Harnessed in a seat, two metal rings of a multi-axis trainer spin every which way to simulate in-flight inertia; early astronauts trained the same way.

The weekend is guaranteed to fly by, and you never know what could come of it. Ten past Space Camp graduates have gone on to become professional astronauts.

Experience weightlessness on a simulated mission in space.

Porto's Livraria Lello is said to have inspired J. K. Rowling's Hogwarts.

Bookstores

Bookworms will devour the page-turners found
in these literary pilgrimage sites.

1. SHAKESPEARE AND COMPANY, PARIS, FRANCE

Originally run by the first publisher of James Joyce's *Ulysses,* this legendary site is as much a clubhouse as a place of business. In fact, writers and book lovers have long been allowed to spend the night.

2. LIVRARIA LELLO, PORTO, PORTUGAL

This neo-Gothic beauty dazzles everyone, but Potter fans more than most others. The swirling central staircase—which J. K. Rowling climbed routinely during her Porto years—is said to have inspired one of Hogwarts' signature features.

3. COLLECTORS TREASURY, JOHANNESBURG, SOUTH AFRICA

More than a million volumes strong, this is the largest used and rare bookseller in Africa, if not the whole Southern Hemisphere. Leave yourself ample browsing time; there are maps, prints, and vinyl, too.

4. SINGBAL'S BOOK HOUSE, PANAJI, INDIA

American moviegoers may not have recognized this shop when Matt Damon walked by it in *The Bourne Supremacy,* but bibliophiles have long revered the cornflower blue Goa icon, home to endless travel books and international publications.

5. CITY LIGHTS, SAN FRANCISCO, CALIFORNIA, U.S.

Owned by San Francisco's first poet laureate, Lawrence Ferlinghetti, this beat generation legend remains a vital part of the city's cultural life, decades after Jack Kerouac, Allen Ginsberg, and Lenny Bruce were regulars.

6. GROLIER POETRY BOOK SHOP, CAMBRIDGE, MASSACHUSETTS, U.S.

When the revered late philosophy professor Ifeanyi Menkiti bought this ailing Harvard Square mainstay in 2006, some dubbed him the man who saved poetry. Grolier remains the oldest continually operating poetry bookstore in the United States.

7. LIBRERIA AQUA ALTA, VENICE, ITALY

Equal parts beauty and quirk, this canal-side legend, just a short walk from St. Mark's Square, uses everything from a gondola to vintage tubs to keep books safe from the inevitable high water, which is also the translation of the store's name.

8. THREE LIVES & COMPANY, NEW YORK CITY, U.S.

In a city of epic bookstores, this fan favorite occupies just 600 square feet (55.7 sq m). Staffed by voracious readers whose recommendations are bibliophile gold, Three Lives & Company is so beloved among booklovers, one Pulitzer Prize–winning patron has said he'd like to be buried here.

9. ACADEMIC BOOKSTORE, HELSINKI, FINLAND

Even if the name doesn't scream bucket list, the architecture does. Designed in the 1960s by Finnish modernist giant Alvar Aalto, the copper-clad facade and gleaming, light-filled interiors make for happy browsing—and the book selection goes well beyond the academia its name implies.

10. EL ATENEO GRAND SPLENDID, BUENOS AIRES, ARGENTINA

Though the shop itself is just 20 years old, it's housed in a 1919 theater that hasn't changed much since Argentina's earliest talkies debuted here. We're talking beautiful rounded balconies, red stage curtains, and golden details throughout. What was once its stage is now a café—a great spot to crack open your selection.

The northern lights shine bright above the base camp.

Under a Winter Sky
Borealis Basecamp, Alaska, U.S.

Fully embrace the cold silence of winter from a domed habitat in black spruce and birch forest north of Fairbanks. Though just under 30 miles (48.3 km) from the state's third largest population center, this remote outpost eschews TVs and puts the focus on the surroundings—there's not much to do here but get cozy and explore. The main event requires little more than curling up under the covers; the heated fiberglass habitats feature 16-foot-long (5 m) curved viewing ceilings so you can sink into dreamland watching stars in the clear sky and the nearly nightly northern lights show. By day, venture out for hearty meals in the camp yurt, or head farther afield to the nearby White Mountains or Wickersham Dome on snowshoes or a snowmobile. Dog mushing sessions impart lessons of life in the snow, and aurora photography sessions help capture the moment so you can take it home.

HUB | *Fairbanks, Alaska, U.S.; Western Canada*

Seaside Gardens
Oyster Box, Durban, South Africa

Tack on a weekend seaside getaway at the Oyster Box, a historic luxury property, to your next South African safari. The site, right on Durban's Umhlanga beachfront surrounded by monkey-filled tropical gardens, has been a hotel and operational lighthouse since the 1950s. There's an airy central courtyard, piano-accompanied high tea in the leafy Palm Court, and red-and-white striped pool loungers that match the red-topped lighthouse. Rent a poolside cabana for a day, or catch a charter and head offshore to find whales or the winter (July) sardine run when millions of fish (and ensuing predators) congregate in a fascinating annual spectacle. Stretch your legs along the Golden Mile of beaches and visit the nearby Botanic Gardens, home to pink pelicans and ancient cycad trees thought to predate the dinosaurs. Then, slip into the Oyster Box's marble spa for a stint in the hammam or a massage utilizing a *rungu*—a wooden club with East African tribal significance—before retiring to your four-poster bed.

The Oyster Box looks out over Durban's iconic lighthouse.

HUB | *Johannesburg, South Africa*

Watch the sun set over
Dubai's impressive skyline
from the hotel's pool.

Arabian Luxury

The Retreat Palm Dubai, Dubai, United Arab Emirates

On the arching circle surrounding the faux island of the Palm Jumeirah, the Retreat Palm Dubai, the Middle East's first holistic well-being resort, offers views across the Arabian Gulf to the skyscrapers of the desert metropolis. Focus on health with a multiday wellness retreat featuring spa and fitness sessions as well as nutritionist-designed meals and juices. Or find a slower pace of being with a hotel stay (rooms were designed according to the principles of feng shui), dips in the infinity pool, and visits to the spa, with a traditional Moroccan hammam, oxygen-infused relaxation rooms, a cryotherapy room, and wellness activities like laughter yoga. Try the 1,001 Arabian Nights treatment, which includes a massage, desert botanical scrub, and camel milk facial. If the thrum of the city still feels too close, the hotel can arrange an overnight at a Bedouin outpost where you'll learn about desert wildlife, eat a meal under the stars, and enjoy a spa treatment atop the shifting sands.

HUB | *Middle East*

"THE CASTLE'S OFFERINGS
ARE DECIDEDLY REGAL."

A Royal Fantasy

Ashford Castle, County Mayo, Ireland

Indulge in royal fantasies with a luxurious weekend at an 800-year-old Celtic castle. Restored and renovated into a private residence in the late 1800s by the family behind Guinness beer, the 83-room castle was converted into a luxury hotel in 1939 and has been named one of the world's best hotels year-after-year. The interior is awash with sumptuous, dark fabrics and dim light from elaborate chandeliers, while the outside has gardens, tennis courts, and woodland hunting grounds.

Spend the day in the spa wrapped in warmed Atlantic seaweed in a bespoke body treatment or in the sunny mosaic-tiled room that houses the blue-green plunge pool and views of Lough Corrib, Ireland's largest lake. Lounge in the library with floor-to-ceiling bookshelves—borrow a book and curl up by the peat-burning fireplace on chilly days. There's an on-site movie theater, a nine-hole golf course, and a 20-mile (32 km) trail that meanders through surrounding forest, prime turf for biking.

Other offerings are decidedly regal. Try your hand at falconry with one of the manor's Harris hawks or fly-fish on local streams, learn archery, or join a horseback fox hunt with a pack of hounds. A sumptuous afternoon tea with scones and sandwiches is served overlooking the estate's 350 acres (142 ha) of private grounds. When dinner rolls around, choose between service in the Dungeon—a banner-draped and suit-of-armor-guarded lower level room serving bistro fare—or the regal, blue George V Dining room, built in 1905 in honor of a visit by the king himself, which serves a luxury tasting menu featuring such delicacies as oysters and caviar, locally harvested morels, smoked eel, and duck.

In the evening, explore the ancient stone cellars with the on-site sommelier for a wine tasting, or sip whiskey in the billiards room. Each room is uniquely outfitted—many have a color theme, four-poster beds, ceiling drapes, and lake views. For a real retreat, opt for the Hideaway Cottage, a restored boathouse removed from the main estate that sits directly on the lake.

HUB | *Galway City, Ireland*

Get the royal treatment in Ashford Castle's Stateroom.

All-Local Eco-Escape

Jicaro Island Lodge, Nicaragua

Jicaro Island Lodge sits on a forested private island in a secluded cove on Lake Nicaragua, a short boat ride from the city of Grenada. This conservation-minded resort maintains strong ties with the local community; the lodge and its nine private casitas were built with the help of local workers and continues to employ an all-local staff. The ecolodge even helped area residents start a chicken co-op, pig farm, and edible gardens that underpin the on-site restaurant's Nicaraguan cuisine. Start your day with yoga and meditation on the floating dock as local children row themselves to school; then breakfast on fresh fruit along the waterfront amid tropical butterflies. With the cloud forest–topped Mombacho Volcano in the distance, spend a quiet day watching for green parrots and Montezuma oropendolas, and hunting kingfishers around the lakeshore. After a stand-up paddleboard outing, unwind with a massage in the lakeside spa.

HUB | *Managua, Nicaragua*

Dine outside with epic views
at Jicaro Island Lodge.

> "PADDLE A CANOE, TIE-DYE
> A T-SHIRT, THEN ROAST
> S'MORES UNDER THE STARS."

Summer Camp Do-Over

Camp Halcyon, Wautoma, Wisconsin, U.S.

Imagine you could have a summer camp do-over. A chance to stay overnight in an electricity-free cabin in the great outdoors, paddle a canoe, tie-dye a T-shirt, then roast s'mores under the stars—and wake up and do it all again the next day. Well, you're in luck. Camp Halcyon is just that idyllic blast from the past: a summer camp for anyone over the age of 21. It's offered over just three long weekends each summer because, unlike other outposts tackling this burgeoning trend, this experience is held at a decades-old purpose-built and still operational lakeside camp for children when the kids aren't around.

Campers claim cots and bunk up four people per cabin (couples' units are available). Daily activities are structured just like you remember—in rotating hour- or hour-and-a-half-long slots; there's even glorious after-lunch naptime. Fun-loving artists and business owners from the local community sub in for camp counselors. Play paintball or beach volleyball, try archery, or choose from an expanded activities roster of more adult offerings such as wine and painting, searching for a hidden speakeasy school bus in the woods, beer making, and cigar and scotch tasting. The all-you-can-drink bar opens at 3 p.m.

The food's nothing to sneeze at. Breakfast includes rotating daily offerings as well as a six-variety bacon bar, locally made muffins, multiple coffee roasts, and breakfast cocktails. Throughout the weekend, you'll also experience a build-your-own-burger bar, "Sausage Fest" with five fire-smoked varieties, and a Friday night fish fry with representatives (and beer) from a local brewery. Vegetarian selections are available. Late-night cravings? There's no need to hoard candies from the canteen; a food bar is open and available 24-hours.

Each day is capped with an all-hands-on-deck activity such as bingo or team trivia, then concludes around the campfire with Milky Way views, sounds of the barred owl, and music—"Kumbaya" optional.

| HUB | *Green Bay or Madison, Wisconsin, U.S.; Midwestern United States; Ontario, Canada* |

Freshly tie-dyed
shirts hang to dry.

Lounge on private pink beaches outside the Aman Sveti Stefan hotel in Montenegro.

Hotels of a Lifetime

From a palace in India to a farm in Vermont, these stunning retreats offer a memorable weekend stay.

1. INKATERRA LA CASONA, CUSCO, PERU

No less than Simón Bolívar has stayed in this stunning 16th-century manor house—among other notable celebrities—on one of Cusco's loveliest cobbled squares. And though the place has since become a boutique hotel, he'd likely still recognize everything from the original murals to the colonial furniture.

2. ARISTI MOUNTAIN RESORT AND VILLA, GREECE

Set high in the Pindus Mountains amid leafy green forests, this one-of-a-kind resort sits perched above the stone-and-slate town of Zagori with spectacular views of Vikos Gorge. Adventures await just beyond its cliff face, but inside you will find a restaurant serving fresh, local Greek fare and a luxurious spa for a day of relaxation.

3. KASBAH DU TOUBKAL IMIL, MOROCCO

Though just more than an hour from the Marrakech airport, this High Atlas hideaway places you in another dimension: one where your porters are mules, your neighbors are sheep, and your constant companion is utter calm.

4. &BEYOND NGORONGORO CRATER LODGE, TANZANIA

Perched on the rim of the world's largest intact caldera, this unforgettable and luxurious lodge—outfitted with banana-leaf ceilings and thatched-palm roofs—offers sweeping views of the grazing grounds for elephants, zebras, rare black rhinos, and seas of pink flamingos.

5. POST RANCH INN, CALIFORNIA, U.S.

Stay in the Platonic ideal of a treehouse. Or feel like your cliffside pool is one with the ocean. Or lounge on a floating mountain-view deck. If there's a magical way to soak in Big Sur's vibes, the inn has clearly thought of it.

6. BORGO EGNAZIA, ITALY

Justin Timberlake and Jessica Biel got hitched here. Madonna celebrated her 59th birthday party here. This is a go-big kind of place. More village than hotel, Borgo's bougainvillea-draped alleys, villas, and rustic *casettas* are peak Puglia.

7. AMAN SVETI STEFAN, MONTENEGRO

If you'd like to stay in an actual village, this one's hard to beat. Set mostly on an island, the estate blends pink beaches, turquoise waters, forested cliffs, and the occasional secret cove.

8. BELMOND REID'S PALACE, PORTUGAL

The Garden Island or the Island of Eternal Spring? Whichever Madeira nickname you choose, it's beautifully borne out at this oceanside spread, whose lush landscaping and year-round alfresco offerings are unrivaled.

9. TWIN FARMS, VERMONT, U.S.

Set on 300 acres (121.4 ha) of forests, meadows, and ponds, this Relais & Chateaux hideaway is Vermont imago. There's everything on the property from canoeing, cycling, and fly-fishing to skiing, sledding, and ice skating. You can also tour the property's beehives or indulge in a chef-catered picnic.

10. TAJ LAKE PALACE, INDIA

That this 18th-century pleasure palace sits in the middle of a lake is generally all people need to know to book a stay. But the views to the City Palace of Udaipur and the Aravalli and Machla Magra Hills certainly don't hurt.

Ancient Wisdom

Kumarakom Lake Resort, Kerala, India

In the steamy jungles of Kerala, where a series of mangroves and sleepy inland canals line the Malabar coast, reconstructed 16th-century *manas* (the traditional noble homesteads) serve as modern luxury accommodations. All have traditional wood detailing, local art, and Jacuzzi tubs, and some have private infinity pools. Set on the state's largest lake and the country's largest wetland system, it's the ultimate retreat, one fit for royalty. Indeed, the huge restaurant Ettukettu is a reconstructed former mansion originally commissioned by King Marthanda Varna as a gift to his favorite martial arts tutor; Prince Charles and Camilla have celebrated birthdays on the property. Take a meandering boat tour of the backwaters to see village life. Or hole up and enjoy the secluded privacy while sampling relaxing and therapeutic Ayurvedic treatments like warm oil forehead drips and massages with milk and medicated rice bundles—the ancient healing tradition is thought to have originated in Kerala.

HUB | *Southern India*

"SET ON THE STATE'S LARGEST LAKE AND THE COUNTRY'S LARGEST WETLAND SYSTEM, IT'S THE ULTIMATE RETREAT, ONE FIT FOR ROYALTY."

Stay in a reconstructed traditional, yet luxe, *mana* on the resort's jungle property.

Frank Lloyd Wright's Fallingwater is considered one of his architectural masterpieces.

Architectural Wonderland

Laurel Highlands, Pennsylvania, U.S.

F rank Lloyd Wright's organic architecture creatively integrates built structures with the natural environment. Spend a luxurious weekend immersing in southwestern Pennsylvania's Laurel Highlands region, an undulating hillscape of rocky forests and waterfall-laced rivers and home to three of the famed architect's tourable masterpieces. Start at Polymath Park in Acme, site of the relocated Duncan House, and opt to stay; it's one of just seven global Wright properties receiving overnight guests. Or head south, where you can stand atop the 30-foot (9 m) cascade at Wright's 1935 masterwork, Fallingwater, inscribed in 2019 as part of a UNESCO World Heritage site. Seven miles (11 km) farther, take a woodland walk at Kentuck Knob; the house itself is snuggled into a hillside overlooking Youghiogheny River Gorge. The high-end, butler-appointed rooms at Falling Rock boutique hotel round out a great Wright-themed escape.

Take on the rapids of the Youghiogheny River during your stay.

HUB | *Mid-Atlantic United States*

CHAPTER TEN

OFF-THE-GRID

Unplug, recharge, and escape in these remote
and often tech-free destinations.

Praia do Beliche is a swimmer-friendly beach backed by high cliffs near Cabo de São Vicente, Portugal (p. 366).

End of the World

Cabo de São Vicente, Portugal

As the farthest southwest location in Europe, Cabo de São Vicente is nicknamed the "End of the World." For centuries, this was the literal jumping-off point for off-the-map adventures. Get wind-whipped at the precipice of the great beyond while looking out from 250-foot-high (76 m) sea cliffs above the churning Atlantic. Then spend your weekend in the village of Sagres 4 miles (6 km) from the cape, where you'll find relatively small crowds, a 15th-century wall built to deter marauding pirates, and top-notch lounging and surfing beaches. Or spend your weekend on foot. Two long-distance hiking trails terminate at the End of the World. Follow the Via Algarviana inland through white-washed villages, fruit orchards, and the Algarve countryside, or the coastal Rota Vicentina atop majestic cliffs and through forests and wildflower fields, as far as your legs will carry you. Both signed paths terminate more than 100 miles outside Cabo de São Vicente, 206 miles (333 km) from Lisbon and 191 miles (308 km) from Seville, Spain.

HUB | *Lisbon, Portugal; Seville, Spain*

"YOU'LL FIND RELATIVELY SMALL CROWDS, A 15TH-CENTURY WALL BUILT TO DETER MARAUDING PIRATES, AND TOP-NOTCH LOUNGING AND SURFING BEACHES."

View the historic Alcoutim village from the castle walls in Algarve.

A rainbow shines above Sani Pass at the South Africa and Lesotho border.

Kingdom Come

Maloti-Drakensberg Park, South Africa

High basaltic and sandstone escarpments ring the eastern half of the Kingdom of Lesotho and rise from the plains of South Africa's KwaZulu Natal and Free State. These are the ancient Drakensberg Mountains, and this is southern Africa's big sky country. The green cliffs, high-altitude wetlands, deep caves, and montane forests are protected in the Maloti-Drakensberg Park. While you can grab a pint in Africa's highest pub and drive the winding clifftop Sani Pass to the Lesotho border, it's relatively desolate terrain. Yet the region has supported life for eons. In 1973 researchers uncovered the first cluster of fossilized dinosaur eggs in the northerly Golden Gate Highlands Park. More than 600 unique rock art sites are sprinkled across the landscape. Together they feature some 35,000 individual images of animals, humans, and plants that tell stories of San bushman life and spirituality millennia ago; it's the largest and most concentrated collection of rock art in southern Africa.

HUB | *Durban or Johannesburg, South Africa*

Ancient rock art is visible in the Game Pass Shelter.

The *ksar*, earthen buildings, at Ait-Ben-Haddou

Peak Experience
Atlas Mountains, Morocco

Just beyond the bustling souks and spice markets of Marrakech, the rocky peaks of the vast High Atlas cut across central Morocco and tumble down into ochre dunes, the pre-Sahara in Morocco's south. With uninterrupted miles between remote valley villages, it's easy to get away from it all. Hire a guide to climb toward tall, snowy peaks. Or navigate rocky terrain to mountain villages and share tea with the Amazigh ancestors of traditional nomad traders, far beyond the reach of cell signals and Wi-Fi. If settling in isn't your thing, head south to spot Draa Valley oases, stopping along the way at Ait-Ben-Haddou in Ouarzazate Province, a village of rectangular red earthen dwellings along a traditional caravan route. From here, the end of the road and desert sands beckon. Take a camel ride to a billowing desert tent to dine on a tangy tagine at sunset; then, lulled by the strum of an *oud* (a traditional string instrument), sleep under the stars.

HUB | *Marrakech, Morocco; Southern Europe*

Night settles over Great Basin National Park.

Best of the Backcountry
Great Basin National Park, Nevada, U.S.

It's a dusty desert drive from glitzy Las Vegas to the upland pine forests of northern Nevada, but virtually-to-yourself vistas await in remote Great Basin National Park. The park sees three times fewer annual visitors than nearby Zion National Park in its busiest month. And with a vertical mile (1.6 km) of elevation difference between the lowest and highest hiking trails, visual variety abounds. Tour Lehman Cave to spy some of Great Basin's 10 species of bats; hike to a valley cirque enclosing one of the southernmost glaciers in the United States; or spend the whole weekend trekking a backcountry loop through sagebrush and birch forest to Baker and Johnson Lakes in barren mountain nooks. There's also a mysterious stand-alone six-story limestone arch, creeks with native Bonneville cutthroat trout, archaeological sites, and a grove of 4,000-year-old bristlecone pine trees. The nights here promise magic: five planets, the Andromeda galaxy, and the Milky Way are all visible to the naked eye.

HUB | *Las Vegas, Nevada, U.S.; Western United States*

Remote Nordic Beauty

Faroe Islands, Denmark

These 18 misty isles in the North Atlantic are wild, wind-swept, remote—and yet just a direct flight away from Copenhagen, Reykjavik, and Edinburgh. Don't forget your wide-angle lens: It's virtually impossible to capture the scale of lighthouses and quaint grass-topped cottages against the dramatic and expansive sea cliffs without it. Grab a cozy Faroese wool sweater, and spend your weekend rosy-cheeked and sauntering through Nordic villages and across sheep-dotted hills. See waterfalls or a lake hovering over a sea cliff precipice on Vágar; peer into the soulful eyes of nesting puffins at Mykines; and kayak over seaweed forests to a fjord or grass-capped sea stacks off Tjørnuvík. Even the islands' best dining option, KOKS, is off the grid: A hike is required to reach the tiny lakeside cottage, the only structure in sight, where you'll dine on a 17-course salted, smoked, dried, fermented, and Michelin-starred feast with wine pairings.

HUB | *Copenhagen, Denmark; Reykjavík, Iceland; Edinburgh, Scotland*

Two sea stacks—known as Drangarnir—sit between Tindhólmur and Vágar island.

"CELL SIGNALS ARE EXPRESSLY FORBIDDEN."

Into the Quiet Zone

Green Bank, West Virginia, U.S.

Some of the most connected U.S. cities—New York, Philadelphia, Boston—lie along its eastern seaboard, so it might be surprising to learn that just 200 miles (322 km) inland from Washington, D.C., there's a place that not only doesn't get cell phone service, but cell signals are expressly forbidden. The United States National Radio Quiet Zone is a 13,000-square-mile (33,670 sq km) region in the Allegheny Mountains centered in Green Bank, West Virginia, where sensitive government equipment, including the world's largest steerable telescope, operates.

Enter the Quiet Zone for your own forced unplug. Start the weekend at the Green Bank Science Center, which has interactive exhibits and runs regular tours of its facilities. Not only will you arrive without cell phone bars (there are no nearby cell towers to provide you with a network), but also you'll have to put your phone in airplane mode, just in case. Unlike optical telescopes that use light to see objects in space, the Robert C. Byrd Green Bank Telescope operated by the National Radio Astronomy Observatory listens for energy waves from outer space, which requires electromagnetic silence. One of the center's most popular tours focuses on the Search for Extraterrestrial Intelligence (SETI) program, which listens for potential signals of life emanating from other planets. Scoping stars and planets with very little light pollution might be the only late-night activity in this sleepy town, so time your visit with one of the center's monthly dark-sky–viewing parties. The following day, hike a nearby section of the Greenbrier Trail, a 78-mile (126 km) former railroad line and one of the 50 Millennium Legacy Trails in the United States. Parts are within the Radio Quiet Zone, so cell phones won't work. If you still have time and are visiting in winter, check out the nearby Snowshoe Mountain Resort for skiing without interference (the property also has hiking, a spa, and a concert venue for summer trips). To stay disconnected there, stay outside; through a special partnership with the telescope, the resort has recently introduced select cell service and Wi-Fi in many of its buildings.

HUB | *Washington, D.C.; Mid-Atlantic United States*

The Robert C. Byrd Green Bank
Telescope at the National Radio
Astronomy Observatory

Find serenity on a walking
path through birch trees in
Acadia National Park.

A Walk in the Woods

Reconnect With Nature Through the Japanese Art of Forest Bathing

I rub the pine needles between my thumb and forefinger. "Really get in there," Josh Heath says, grabbing fistfuls of needles, crushing them between his bearlike palms and inhaling deeply. I follow his lead and roll the prickly red-spruce needles between my hands, bring my palms to my face, and breathe in the citrus scent.

After I do, Heath shows me how to do a fox walk, placing my foot down in a semicircular fashion so I strike the ground with my heel, then my big toe, followed by my little toe. We creep down the path, and he asks me to notice what is moving. I feel more like Elmer Fudd than an observant fox, and I have to quiet my skeptical inner monologue and concentrate on my surroundings. When I do, I notice the ferns bowing and waving. I spot a chipmunk skittering across the path. As we approach the lake, I watch a damselfly skim along the dock.

By the time we reach the dock, I realize that having something specific to look for helps me focus and stay present. The sun warms my face as we watch a few kayakers paddle along the small inland lake in Pennsylvania's Poconos where I've come for a forest-bathing lesson.

The Japanese practice of *shinrin-yoku* works to soak up nature with all the senses. Guided forest-bathing sessions typically include deep-breathing exercises, suggestions for aspects of nature to focus on, and invitations to share what you've noticed.

This mindful approach to nature has interesting health benefits. Research studies in Japan and Italy have shown forest bathing lowers blood pressure, heart rate, and concentrations of the stress hormone cortisol. It increases sleep duration and boosts the number of natural killer cells, a type of white blood cell that fights infected or tumor cells. There are theories as to why it works, but science has yet to prove them.

In 2012 wilderness guide Amos Clifford founded the California-based Association of Nature and Forest Therapy, which certifies programs and trains guides. I called Clifford to ask how he discovered forest bathing and, most important, why I need a guide to go play in the great outdoors. He explained that you can do it all on your own, but a guide slows you down and deepens the discipline. Several resorts offer forest bathing, and I traveled to Pennsylvania's Lodge at Woodloch, one of the first resorts in the United States to have gone through Clifford's certification.

I fight my cynicism and try to approach it with an open mind. That Heath, my guide, isn't straight out of central casting for this role helps. Tall with spiky blond hair that looks like he's growing out a boot-camp buzz, the former park ranger admits he didn't think much of forest bathing at first, but he realized that whenever something was gnawing at him, he would go fishing or head out into the woods. He found that forest bathing essentially took that instinct one step further and encouraged more mindfulness. On a small campfire, he heats up a thermos of tea made from local herbs and pours us both a cup. Heath, who used to run a skills-building program for middle school kids, says children ask "Why?" all the time. Adults don't do that as easily, but nature encourages us to do so, even subtly.

I wonder if he realizes he's touching on an idea known as attention restoration theory, which is one of the arguments for why nature is so healing. At its simplest, the theory says our urban environments are draining because they bombard us with a level of stimulation that requires constant, directed attention (responding to emails, navigating traffic). Nature, however, engages our attention in a much more effortless way, and this allows us to restore and reset.

While forest bathing is having a moment, many cultures believe being outside is a balm for mind, body, and spirit. I suspect it's why so many Swiss skip church and head to the mountains on Sundays. It's the idea behind the Norwegian word *friluftsliv,* which means "free air life" but really defies translation, as it's a deeply rooted philosophy that embodies a profound appreciation for nature and a way of living in and with the world—or part of what the Germans mean with the word *waldeinsamkeit,* which is a feeling of solitude when you're alone in the woods.

The next day I attempt forest bathing on my own. I nestle into the hammock, set the timer on my phone for 15 minutes, and try to settle in. The muscles in my back are tight. I feel like I should be doing something. I close my eyes and watch the intensity of the sunlight shift behind them and listen to the birds chattering above me. Despite my initial resistance, when the timer goes off, I'm relaxed.

—**Kelly DiNardo** is the author of several books, including *Living the Sutras: A Guide to Yoga Wisdom Beyond the Mat.*

> "THEIR CULTURES ARE ONE OF THE TOP REASONS TO MAKE THE JOURNEY."

A Tribal Home

Nagaland, India

Nagaland begins where the paved road ends. This is the land of Assamese tea estates. The mountainous frontier state in India's northeast stretches all the way to the border with Myanmar and Arunachal Pradesh, dotted along the way with thatch-roofed homes and cinderblock villages. It's a place with a feel all its own, palpable as soon as you cross the threshold. There are few crowds and almost no saris here. Some 16 different Tibeto-Burmese tribal groups call the region home, each with a distinct dialect and traditions. Their cultures are one of the top reasons to make the journey.

With a base in the hill station of Mon, take the bumpy road to explore Longwa and the surrounding villages on the Myanmar border to learn about the local Konyak tribe. Like many other Naga communities, the Konyak had a long tradition of head-hunting to settle skirmishes. After missionaries successfully converted huge swaths of the population to Christianity, the practice was outlawed; the last reported instance was recorded in 1963. Sip tea with a translator to talk with tribal elders adorned with blue face tattoos, wearing tiger tooth necklaces and hornbill headdresses as they recall the practice with a tinge of nostalgia. Next, tour the smoky interiors of longhouses in Mon, many of them ornamented with the horns of gaur and antelope, wooden statues, and skeleton-esque masks used in ceremonies. Each village has at least one morung, a clubhouse used for training young warriors and home to the intricately carved village war drums.

Because distances can be deceptive and tourism infrastructure limited, the best way to get a sense of Nagaland is to go slow and soak it in. If possible, time a visit to the Hornbill Festival in Kohima at the start of December when representatives from all 16 tribes gather to showcase their traditions.

Naga tribesmen from Yimchunger gather at the Hornbill festival in Kohima.

Find a true wilderness experience hiking in Torngat Mountains National Park.

"ALWAYS CURIOUS, THE BEARS STOP,
LOOK US UP AND DOWN, TRY TO
FIGURE OUT IF WE ARE FOE OR
POTENTIAL FOR THEIR NEXT MEAL."

PERSPECTIVE

Remote & Unplugged
Embark on the Ultimate Secluded Adventure

There's rhythm in the wilderness. My boat makes a *slap slap slap* sound as it tugs through the silky black water of Saglek Bay. A polar bear huffs while swimming in the scattered islets off the coast in search of her next meal. The wind sighs, a feathery touch on my cheek.

I've ditched the daily tapping of my computer and the confines of my windowless office to travel to one of Canada's wildest places, Torngat Mountains National Park, at the northern tip of Labrador. Just north of the Arctic tree line, the 3,700-square-mile (9,583 sq km) park is an ancestral home of the Inuit, whose word *tongait* means "place of spirits." Their seminomadic ancestors held a deep connection with the environment, and this land whispers of generations past, thousands of years reflected in the ebb and flow of migration.

Inuit cultural guides share stories from their childhood—of caribou hunts, polar bear encounters, and dogsledding across open snow-covered land.

The clouds hang low, heavy with rain. As we zip through the water on Zodiac boats, I spot a glimmer of white in the distance that flashes like a tooth jutting out of the sea. The iceberg was calved long ago from western Greenland or the Canadian Arctic and traveled down the coast to dwindle in the summer sun.

We unload the boat on Saglek Bay's sandy North Arm beach and build a fire as a soft rain falls. We learn that this beach has been used for millennia as a summer retreat, a place for Inuit to commune with family and friends, a place to hunt and fish and gather food for the cold winter to come.

After a short hike to view archaeological sites, some of us set about casting lines at the mouth of the river that empties into the Arm, where Arctic char amass, for an afternoon feast. Our efforts bring in large, silvery char, a member of the salmon family. We pull out our knives and savor deep-red sashimi right there on the rocks, the freshest dining experience I've had in years.

The next morning, after an aerial tour of the park and its majestic fjords, our helicopter returns to Saglek Bay and lands on Sallikuluk (Rose Island). The island is quiet, but the past echoes loudly here.

Archaeological sites on the island stretch back 5,000 years. Lying scattered about are whale bones and shards of Ramah chert, a fine-grained, glasslike stone found only in this region and used by the Inuit for tool-making.

We continue on until we reach a mound of large rough rocks, carefully heaped over a sacred burial ground. Underneath lie the bones of more than a hundred people; all had been removed from Sallikuluk at one point. Their remains have now been returned and their spirits remembered in words and song by a new generation.

I feel like an astronaut. Decked out in orange safety suits that will keep us warm and buoyant in the event of falling overboard, we cruise from island to island off the coast to catch a glimpse of polar bears. Always curious, the bears stop, look us up and down, try to figure out if we are foe or potential for their next meal. Then they go about their business. They dot the landscape of one islet, making it look like a polar bear lounge. Most of them spend their afternoon dozing in the sun.

In the middle of summer, the warm sun makes us sweat, but nights are cold, compelling us to don layers of clothing and inch closer to the campfire. The sky sinks from blue to black as we gravitate to the mess hall. Coffee and brownies are plentiful. We while away the evening, swapping stories, encircled by the camp's electrified fence that keeps us safe from bears. If we're lucky, the northern lights will dance across the sky and remind us of the spirits that travel these mountains.

—**Anne Farrar** is the director of photography for National Geographic Travel.

Huge trees stand tall in the Sierra Gorda Biosphere Reserve.

Ancient History
Reserva de la Biosfera Sierra Gorda, Mexico

With a reputation for being hard to reach, this massive protected area in northeast Querétaro houses little-visited historic sites, authentic villages, clear rivers with waterfalls, and all six of Mexico's wild cat species. Rent a car and get off the beaten track. From Jalpan, spend a day visiting elaborate 18th-century Franciscan mission churches (five of them make up a UNESCO World Heritage site), and the dozens of third- to 10th-century mounds and structures in Tancama Valley. Overnight in cabins outside Santa Maria Cocos so you can begin a 5 a.m. trek to the rim of Sótano del Barro, a collapsed pit cave 1,350 feet (410 m) deep and the nesting site for one of the last wild populations of rainbow-hued military macaws; early morning is the best time to spot them. Afterward, stop by the shaded pool beneath the 100-foot (30 m) Chuvejé waterfall en route to Cuatro Palos for ridge hiking and sweeping scenery where semidesert and gnarled oak forest meet.

HUB | *Mexico City, Mexico*

Freedom Cove's gardens help maintain the island's sustainability.

Lost to Nature
Tofino and Freedom Cove, British Columbia, Canada

The vibrant arts and surf town of Tofino is certainly remote—it exists on a tiny peninsula jutting into the Pacific-fronting Clayoquot Sound. Inland, misty old-growth rainforest is the domain of towering cedar trees, salmon, black bears, and bald eagles. In the waters beyond offshore islands speckle the Sound. But one island is more unusual than most.

Freedom Cove is a man-made, entirely self-sustainable floating island. The brainchild of two prolific artists (the island's only permanent residents), it is tucked into a tiny inlet a 30-minute boat ride from town. Crafted in the early 1990s, Freedom Cove features multiple colorfully painted and constantly evolving structures including a living room with a fish-viewing portal, a shower disguised as a lighthouse, a faux beach, sculptures, and even a dance floor. Elaborate organic gardens and greenhouses grow fresh produce year-round. Visit Freedom Cove on a guided tour, usually offered June to October.

HUB | *Vancouver, Canada; Pacific Northwest United States*

Water Labyrinth

Everglades National Park, Florida, U.S.

Disconnect by slipping into the 1.5-million-acre (607,000 ha) south Florida wildlands of Everglades National Park. Entering via the Flamingo Visitor Center will not only ensure you'll begin from the park's most remote entry point, but the 90-minute drive south from Miami snakes through varied park scenery. From here you can canoe or kayak the Marjory Stoneman Douglas Wilderness Waterway, a 99-mile (159 km) liquid trail that cuts a clearly marked path through the labyrinthine mangrove-lined creeks and open water passages just inland from the coast. Hire a permitted outfitter, or go it alone. With good weather and just one night, the backcountry camps at Hell's or Pearl Bay, 11.5 and 13.5 miles (18.5 and 22 km) in, respectively, are attainable. Requisite permits ensure you'll secure a chickee—an overwater, roofed platform that serves as a private island campsite and encourages airflow to funnel away the swamp's notorious bugs—all to yourself.

HUB | *Miami, Florida, U.S.; Southeastern United States*

On a paddle trip through the Everglades, camp on backcountry chickees.

> "THE ISLAND HAS NO CHAIN RESTAURANTS OR STORES, AND ITS LARGEST TOWN IS THREE BLOCKS LONG."

Cast Away

Molokai, Hawaii, U.S.

The sleepy isle of Molokai is off most Hawaii tourists' radar, but for an offline getaway, it should be on yours. Unlike urban Oahu less than 50 miles (80 km) away, the 38-mile-long (61 km) and 10-mile-wide (16 km) island has no chain restaurants or stores, and its largest town is three blocks long. Get even farther off the grid—and take a journey back in time—by venturing beyond the island's paved roads to explore its natural and cultural beauty.

It's worth timing a visit to the guided, once-a-month hikes through Mo'omomi Preserve. The remote dune ecosystem stretches along the northeastern part of the island and is home to nesting green sea turtles, a colony of wedge-tailed shearwaters, *pueo* (Hawaiian owl), and more native grasses, shrubs, and rare coastal species than any other place in the state. Managed by the Nature Conservancy and fenced off to protect the site, it's open to the public only during these monthly guided hikes. Afterward, consider a one-hour guided tour of the 55-acre (22 ha) Keawanui Fishpond on the other side of town. It's the largest enclosed and fully operational *loko i'a* (traditional fishpond) in Hawaii and dates back some 800 years. Meticulously restored over the last 25 years, it's a living laboratory for native Hawaiians to explore their cultural history and learn traditional aquaculture practices.

The following day, journey to Kalaupapa, a flat peninsula walled off by some of the world's tallest sea cliffs. It's a place so isolated it served as a leper colony for many decades in the late 19th and early 20th centuries. Today, the area is a National Historical Park, and the only way in is by air, foot, or mule if the steep trail isn't washed out. Tours of the buildings and cemeteries (more than 8,000 of the banished died here) are given by former resident patients who explore the complicated and emotional history of living in isolation.

HUB | *Honolulu, Hawaii, U.S.; West Coast United States*

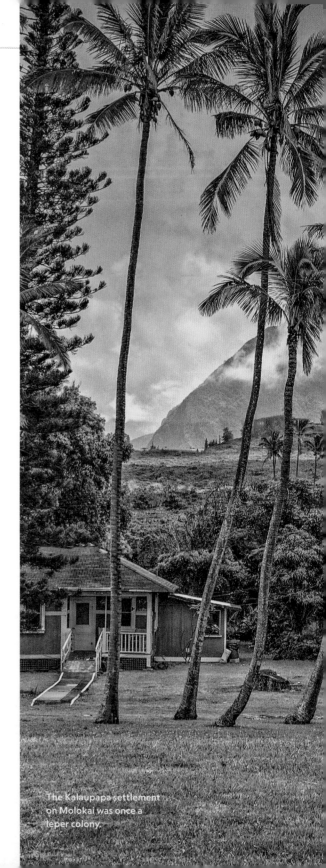

The Kalaupapa settlement on Molokai was once a leper colony.

Campgrounds on Isle Royale offer expansive views.

Rugged & Wild
Isle Royale, Michigan, U.S.

The rugged and wild island of Isle Royale (and hundreds of smaller offshore islands) sits 56 miles (90.1 km) offshore of Michigan's mainland in inky black, icy cold, and shipwreck-filled Lake Superior. A two- to six-hour ferry ride from Michigan Copper Country or northern Minnesota is required to reach it. The large (132,018-acre/53,426 ha) and isolated outpost supports populations of moose and wolves that have long served as subjects in predator/prey dynamic studies. There's no public Wi-Fi or cell signal and it's the only U.S. National Park that fully closes in the off-season (November through mid-April). A long weekend is essential to fully immerse yourself here. Unless you've booked into the single rustic lodge, all accommodations in this national park are backcountry campsites available on a first-come, first-served basis. You'll have to tromp through forests of spruce, fir, and paper birch, wildflower and blueberry meadows, inland peat bogs, and marshes to find the next place to rest your head.

HUB | *Detroit, Michigan, U.S.; Midwestern United States*

Harbor Hopping
Kampot & Kep, Cambodia

Head first to coastal Kep, fronting the Bay of Kampot on the Gulf of Thailand. A giant crab statue protrudes from an ocean platform proudly announcing the local delicacy: fresh cracked crab covered in a gravy of fried peppercorns. Kep was a seaside retreat for early 19th-century French colonialists, and some of the original architecture remains. Nearby White Elephant Cave, named for its interior formation, is 6 miles (10 km) from the beach. Nine miles (14 km) beyond is Phnom Chinork, where you can climb through skylit caverns to view sixth-century bricks of pre-Angkorian ruins.

You'll want to be back in Kampot town well before sunset to dine aboard a moored boat or take a sunset cruise through the estuary to see wetland birds, stars, and fireflies. The following day, visit a peppercorn farm and learn about the processes used to make the area's namesake product: Kampot pepper. Follow the road outside of town to see Bokor Hill Station, a former French hotel turned Khmer outpost, now in ruins.

A giant crab statue symbolizes culinary tradition.

HUB | *Southeast Asia*

The Heart of the Canyon
Havasu Falls, Grand Canyon National Park, Arizona, U.S.

Waterfalls rain into bright blue pools in red-rock desert canyons on the eastern edge of the Grand Canyon, but you'll have to work for these dramatic views. It's 10 miles (16 km) one-way from the hilltop trailhead on the Havasupi Indian Reservation to the first of five stunning falls and the overnight campsite (17miles/27 km if you opt to follow the water down Sinyella Mesa to its intersection with the Colorado River). The vibrant hue of the waters here is evidence of its long, underground history dissolving light-refracting minerals—some say they haven't seen the sun for 30,000 years—and intricate travertine deposits drip down around the falls like open-air stalagmites. Though Havasu is definitely off the grid, its beauty is no secret. Still, these views are only for a treasured few. Permits are required and getting one can feel like the backcountry equivalent to unwrapping Willy Wonka's golden ticket. An entire year of permits almost always sells out the day that permitting opens.

HUB | *Las Vegas, Nevada, U.S.; Southwestern United States*

Havasu Falls spills from the red-rock canyon into a turquoise pool.

Half a million North Atlantic puffins use the Witless Bay Ecological Reserve as breeding grounds.

"HOME TO MILLIONS OF
SEABIRDS—MANY TIMES
THE HUMAN POPULATION"

Seabird Paradise
Witless Bay, Newfoundland, Canada

The Witless Bay Ecological Reserve on Newfoundland's central Atlantic coast is home to millions of seabirds—many times the entire human population of the province—that fill the cliffs and sky come spring and summer. The bay and its four offshore islands support the world's second largest colony of storm petrels (620,000 breeding pairs), the largest breeding colony of puffins in North America (250,000 pairs), and numerous other seafaring flappers, including fulmars, kittiwake, guillemot, razorbill, gulls, and murre.

Sightseeing inflatable boats and catamarans are some of the best ways to get up close to the shrieking, swirling clouds. Boats depart for the reserve from the tiny fishing community at Bay Bulls, a half an hour drive from the city of St. John's. Opt for a tour that offers the full Newfoundlander experience: crews that sing sea shanties and offer "screech-ins" (a welcoming ceremony that includes kissing a cod) to their guests. If you visit in early to mid-June, when ocean nutrients fuel shoals of capelin, you'll have the best chance of seeing what else these waters can drum up, including migrating humpback whales, dolphins, orcas, and even icebergs. The bluish masses haunt the coast, lending the nickname "Iceberg Alley." Melting in the sun and sculpted by wind and waves, many have traveled up to four years since calving from Greenland and will continue south to melt in the Gulf Stream. Mid-June is the tail end of their season here.

On the second day, get out on the land via Mickeleens Path, a 4.5-mile (7.2 km) coastal trail connecting Bay Bulls to Witless Bay. Hurricane Igor exposed new ocean views from the forest-topped cliffs along the trail when it barreled through in 2010. Stop for a picnic at Chest Cove, look for bald eagles, and check out the still-functional 1909 lighthouse at Bull Head. The trail is part of the larger, continuous East Coast Trail that rims the Avalon Peninsula's Atlantic seaboard, crossing 30 coastal fishing villages and spanning nearly 210 miles (336 km) of wild coastal scenery.

HUB | *Eastern Canada; Northeastern United States*

Luxury safari-style tents are just one camping option at El Cosmico in the high desert of Marfa, Texas.

Sites to Camp & Glamp

Pitch a tent in a high desert or spot the Big Five
from luxury safari digs at these one-of-a-kind outdoor hot spots.

1. THE RESORT AT PAWS UP, MONTANA, U.S.

Sit under the stars in Big Sky Country before retiring to your butler-attended tent. Other popular activities at Paws Up include fly-fishing, horseback riding, and, naturally, wine tasting.

2. WALDSEILGARTEN HÖLLSCHLUCHT, GERMANY

For a more literal take on over-the-top camping, try sleeping as you dangle off a cliff (or tree) in the German Alps, where Waldseilgarten Höllschlucht uses custom portaledges to create extreme camping heaven on (not quite) Earth.

3. THANDA SAFARI TENTED CAMP, SOUTH AFRICA

Canvas walls and an elevated private deck are all that separate you from the surrounding KwaZulu-Natal bushland and the Big Five that call it home. The best après-game drive? The tented spa.

4. VENTANA BIG SUR, CALIFORNIA, U.S.

Some of the glampsites (picture bespoke mattresses in safari-style tents) here are drive-in, but if you crave serious seclusion, book a hike-in spot. Either way, you'll achieve peak California dreaming—with far more redwoods than humans for neighbors.

5. COLLECTIVE GOVERNORS ISLAND, NEW YORK, U.S.

If you think metropolitan glamping is an urban myth, you'll be proven wrong in New York City, where Lady Liberty's torch doubles as your nightlight (or at least one of them, with a skyline full of light in sight) at the Collective Governors Island tents.

6. NAYARA TENTED CAMP, COSTA RICA

Though the tents in this rainforest retreat are gorgeously situated and lavishly appointed, complete with volcano views and spring-fed private plunge pools, here's what beats all: You're staying in a sloth sanctuary.

7. EL COSMICO, MARFA, TEXAS, U.S.

Whatever your ideal camping structure—teepee, yurt, safari tent, trailer—you'll find it at this Instagram darling of the West Texas high desert, where you might also find concerts, screenings, and art workshops.

8. WASDALE, ENGLAND

See where Wordsworth "wander'd lonely as a cloud" and camp in England's Lake District. Wasdale, home to the area's highest mountain and deepest lake, pairs stunning views with cute sleeping pods.

9. CLAYOQUOT WILDERNESS RESORT, VANCOUVER ISLAND, CANADA

This Vancouver Island rainforest retreat requires a long weekend (there's a three-night minimum), but you'll thank yourself for making the time: Your antique-filled, stove-warmed prospector-style tent is the cushiest possible home base for exploring the UNESCO-designated Clayoquot Sound Biosphere Reserve.

10. UNDER CANVAS, U.S.

With glampsites in some of the most naturally endowed swaths of the United States—from the Grand Canyon to the Great Smoky Mountains—Under Canvas can be addictive. Thus the passports: Collect four stamps, and the fifth camp is free. Don't believe it's worthwhile? The camping includes healthy café-style dining and luxurious safari-style canvas tents outfitted with king-size beds, en suite bathrooms, and wood-burning stoves.

Steamed blue crabs are a must-try on a visit to Smith Island.

Wetland Oasis
Smith Island, Maryland, U.S.

On the watery boundary of Maryland and Virginia in the Chesapeake Bay, waterlogged and low-lying Smith Island is a world apart. Separated from Crisfield, Maryland, by 12 miles (19 km) of rich blue crab and oyster habitat, this is Maryland's last inhabited island, reachable only by boat. Just 200 people live here year-round, most of whom descend from 17th-century Welsh and English settlers and speak in a unique dialect and cadence cultivated by their isolation. Learn about the island's long human history—evidence of Native American habitation stretches back 12,000 years—in the Smith Island Cultural Center and Museum in Ewell, one of three island villages. Then spend time casting for rockfish along the coast or kayaking the thousands of acres of inland eel grass marsh abutting the protected and off-limits Glenn Martin Wildlife Refuge. Before departing, sink your teeth into a slice of Maryland's official state dessert: the 10-layer Smith Island cake.

HUB | *Mid-Atlantic United States*

Adventure in the Jungle
Semuc Champey, Guatemala

Semuc Champey is an adventurer's jungle oasis. From the town of Lanquín, ride or walk the 7-mile (11 km) road to the main event—a series of six stunning blue-green natural karst pools etched into a nearly 1,000-foot (300 m) stretch of the Río Cahúbon. Take a rewarding short hike to a nearby hilltop for a bird's-eye view; then soak it all in with a refreshing swim in the cool water. The following day, dig further into the limestone landscape with a swimsuited, barefoot, hour-long wet cave tour. Posada Las Marias, a local inn, organizes tours into the cave's interior. A river carves through Las Cuevas de K'an Ba, leaving passages both narrow and as wide as 35 feet (10 m) across; you'll use nothing but a wax candle to light your way. Top it all off by scaling a small waterfall and, if you dare, swinging or cliff jumping from points around the river. Plan ahead: Twice-daily shuttle service to remote Lanquín from Antigua takes eight hours, so make this a long weekend excursion.

HUB | *Guatemala City, Guatemala*

Small waterfalls cascade down green rocks in Semuc Champey.

Explore Beach & Rainforest

Olympic Peninsula, Washington, U.S.

Tiny towns, wild windswept beaches, and misty, mossy rainforests await just across the Puget Sound from Seattle on the Olympic Peninsula. The region contains some of the last pristine stretches of temperate rainforest in the United States, filled with 500-year-old Sitka spruce trees. Steeped in myth and legend, these verdant forests were unexplored by Westerners until the 1890s. Now it's your turn to enter. From the gateway at Bainbridge Island, wind north to check out the offshore 6.8-mile-long (11 km) Dungeness sand spit—the longest such formation in the United States—jutting out in the Strait of Juan de Fuca. From there, head into Olympic National Park and journey through mountain scenery to the impossibly green Hoh Rain Forest. Visit the Elwha River where the largest rewilding dam-removal project in the country took place in 2011; the area now supports eagles, otters, and spawning wild salmon. Don't miss the pebble- and driftwood-coated Ruby Beach with its offshore spires and sea stacks. Wind down with a dip in the Sol Duc volcanic hot springs.

HUB | *Pacific Northwest United States; Vancouver, Canada*

Take a hike through the brilliantly green Hoh Rain Forest Hall of Mosses.

A tori shrine gate marks
the entrance to Oyunohara
on the Kumano Kodo trail.

Mountain Pilgrimage

Kumano Kodo Trail, Japan

Escape Japan's big cities with a long weekend on an ancient forest path. The traditional Kumano Kodo pilgrimage trail has been followed by devout and intrepid commoners, emperors, and samurai since at least the 12th century. Less a regimented linear walk and more a series of connected thoroughfares through sacred forests, the Kumano Kodo's seven sections wind over mountains in the remote Kii Peninsula south of Osaka, past streams and giant cedar and camphor trees and up mossy steps to temples and waterfalls. While the trails do connect significant Shinto shrines, the experience is as much about being present as it is about getting anywhere. More than 100 small *oji* (subsidiary shrines) along the route enshrine animist deities, encourage rest, and are thought to have been built by ancient ascetics. Turn your phone off, and send your luggage forward with prearranged transport. Then bathe in the forest and soak in *onsen* hot springs along the way. At night, stay in *shukubo* (Buddhist temples) or *ryokan* (traditional guesthouses) for the full experience.

HUB | *Kyoto or Osaka, Japan*

The deserted Houtouwan fishing village in China has been abandoned since the early 1990s.

Ghost Towns

From abandoned villages to haunted mining towns,
these desolate spots around the world will give you plenty of spooks.

1. AIT BENHADDOU, MOROCCO

One of the most Instagrammed *Game of Thrones* locations (better known to fans as Yunkai), this UNESCO World Heritage–designated 17th-century town is mostly abandoned, though a few families still live among the striking earthen dwellings.

2. HOUTOUWAN, CHINA

What happens when a deserted fishing village is devoured by greenery and then goes viral? So many weekenders arrive from Shanghai that authorities had to add infrastructure. Go now, and you'll find everything from a viewing platform to B&Bs.

3. AL MADAM, UNITED ARAB EMIRATES

Sand dunes rival plants in a stunning display of village-consuming natural forces. See for yourself just outside Dubai, where this deserted 20th-century settlement is shrouded in as much mystery as sand. Some say *jinns* (aka genies) caused the abandonment.

4. JEROME, ARIZONA, U.S.

Once home to the world's richest individually owned mine, "the wickedest city in the West" had a mere handful of residents by the 1950s, after the mine closed. Revived by creatives and wine-makers, Jerome now pairs ghost and winery tours.

5. HUMBERSTONE AND SANTA LAURA, CHILE

The Great Depression was the nail in the coffin of Chile's nitrate boom, but these neighboring ghost towns from the saltpeter heyday have since become UNESCO World Heritage sites and popular stops along the Atacama tourist trail. The desert conditions have kept the towns well preserved, and you can still see the old company store where miners bought provisions.

6. CRACO, ITALY

A medieval Italian hill town that had survived quakes, marauders, and the black plague, Craco finally gave up the ghost after a 1991 landslide. Still, several religious festivals reanimate this abandoned corner of Matera between May and October. Attend one and you'll take in a striking castle built in 1300, a church housing a statue of the Virgin Mary, and plenty of uninhabited cliffside dwellings.

7. RHYOLITE, NEVADA, U.S.

A famous stop on Nevada's Free-Range Art Highway, this ruined mining town—where everything from an opera house to a stock exchange once stood—neighbors the equally eerie Goldwell Open Air Museum (see *The Ghost Rider*).

8. BODIE, CALIFORNIA, U.S.

This California gold mining town that is now a historic park is preserved in a state of "arrested decay," with period-appropriate provisions inside the remaining wooden structures. Check the Bodie Foundation's website for rare evening ghost walks.

9. VAL-JALBERT, QUÉBEC, CANADA

A once flourishing mill town, Val-Jalbert collapsed in 1927. But this lovely hamlet, whose falls are taller than Niagara's, was eventually awarded development funds, so you can now tour (and stay in) its restored homes.

10. DUNTON HOT SPRINGS, COLORADO

For the poshest possible ghost town stay, head to this 19th-century mining outpost in an alpine valley near Telluride, where the lovingly restored miners' cabins, saloon, dance hall, and bathhouse are now a rustic-chic resort and spa.

Pitch your tent on the rocky shore of Småskär island.

A Taste of the North
Östergötland Archipelago, Sweden

Imagine the traditional Swedish landscapes of pine forests and quaint seaside towns complete with matching red houses and fishing shanties; then imagine that landscape fractured into a zillion tiny pieces with seawater seeped in between. That's the St. Anna, Gryt, and Arkösund archipelagos (together they compose the larger Östergötland archipelago), 140 miles (227 km) south of Stockholm: quite literally thousands of islands—nearly all of them uninhabited—in a wild, kayakable offshore maze. Rent your gear, and get an orientation from a local outfitter before setting off on a choose-your-own adventure. No island is off-limits for backcountry camping. See gray seals and shorebirds, stop into long-abandoned fishing camps, and on larger islands, hike to lookouts, old kettle holes, and even a ruined castle. Some companies offer guided options. Do the North has a culinary kayak where participants forage for shoots, berries, mushrooms, roots, and nuts before creating an inventive meal with the help of a paddling chef.

HUB | *Stockholm, Sweden*

Squirrel monkeys peek from the trees inside the park.

Amazonion Wonders
Parque Nacional Yasuní, Coca, Ecuador

If you're able to swallow a fear of insects, head into Yasuní where you can actually *swallow* insects—citrus-flavored "lemon ants" are a local favorite. With traditional cultures—including two uncontacted tribes—and forests literally buzzing with life, this is the wild Ecuadorian Amazon. Three daily hour-long flights connect Coca to Quito, and from there you'll travel by longboat to a rustic camp. The rest of your time will be spent in the forest or on the river. Learn about plants that indigenous people use, and visit a village to see what life is like beyond the reach of power lines. Travel to a riverside salt lick—watching out for swimming anacondas—where brightly colored parrots, peccaries, and monkeys congregate. In the late afternoon, cruise a sleepy, tanin-stained stretch of the Amazon to listen for the breaths of *boto*, or pink river dolphins. Then catch and release piranhas using chunks of beef. At night, use a headlamp to catch dart frogs, caiman eyes, tarantulas, and centipedes in your beam.

HUB | *Quito, Ecuador*

A Biotecture house, built from recycled bottles, tires, and concrete

Community Living
Earthship Biotecture, Taos, New Mexico, U.S.

Considering switching to an off-the-grid lifestyle? Try it out for a night or two outside Taos, one of the few places on the planet to hobnob with homesteaders and test-drive a truly autonomous way of life. Earthship Biotecture, a community of around 70 independent and complimentary homes fronting the Sangre de Christo mountains, has everything needed to be self-sustaining. Each bungalow is fashioned using old car tires, straw, adobe, and other natural and upcycled materials into a design that helps keep interior temperatures comfortable year-round. There's no need to veer too far from modern creature comforts: Solar power fuels TVs and computers, and wastewater is continually recycled through systems used to grow wildflowers and edible plants in attached greenhouses; some have tilapia ponds and chicken coops out back. The community maintains a visitor center and runs internships on Earthship building. Rental units are a staple later sold to full-time converts/residents.

HUB | *Southwestern United States*

CHAPTER ELEVEN

CAMPING SPOTS

Explore the great outdoors at these nature-forward camping destinations around the globe.

Spend a night in the trees at Green EcoCamp in Nuuksio National Park, Finland (p. 418).

Spot American bison grazing in the fields of Antelope Island.

Where the Antelope Play

Antelope Island State Park, Utah, U.S.

E xtending 15 miles long (24.1 km) and about 5 miles wide (8 km), Antelope Island State Park, an International Dark Sky Park, is the largest island in Utah's Great Salt Lake. Although a causeway connects Antelope to the mainland, the park—with its free-roaming bison, namesake pronghorn antelope, and rugged rangelands—seems a world away from Salt Lake City, about 40 miles (64.3 km) to the south. The park has two drive-in campgrounds (Bridger Bay and White Rock Bay); one group campsite; and the hike-in, tent-only Ladyfinger campground. From the Bridger Bay campground, it's only 1 mile (1.6 km) to Bridger Bay Beach, where you can float in the Western Hemisphere's largest inland saltwater lake.

Hike backcountry trails to spot wildlife like mule deer, bighorn sheep, and bison, as well as multitudes of birds assembled on the shores. To see more of the park, rent an electric bike or take a guided tour with Antelope E-Bike Company.

HUB | *Salt Lake City, Utah, U.S.*

Southern Living

Charit Creek Lodge, Big South Fork National River and Recreation Area, Tennessee, U.S.

S traddling the Kentucky-Tennessee border, Big South Fork National River and Recreation Area encompasses 125,000 acres (50,586 ha) of the Cumberland Plateau. The area's namesake fork of the Cumberland River flows freely through the rugged landscape, rich in spectacular gorges, cliffs, and natural rock arches.

Staying at the backcountry Charit Creek Lodge ensures you'll see the Twin Arches, the most dramatic arch formations in Big South Fork and, arguably, in the eastern United States. While Charit Creek isn't a campsite, the rustic wilderness lodge has no electricity and is heated by a wood-burning stove. Also, getting there requires hiking, biking, or horseback riding more than 1 mile (1.6 km) from the nearest parking lot. Once you're there, it's a short hike up to the Twin Arches: The 60-foot-high (18.3 m) North arch spans 93 feet (28.3 m) and the 103-foot-high (31.4 m) South arch stretches 135 feet (41.1 m).

HUB | *Southeastern United States*

Take in the natural beauty of Big South Fork.

A wooden bridge crosses a river canyon in the park.

Simply Gorge-ous
Tallulah Gorge State Park, Tallulah Falls, Georgia, U.S.

Camping on the rim of 1,000-foot-deep (304.8 m) Tallulah Gorge improves your chances of scoring the northeast Georgia state park's golden ticket: a gorge floor permit. Only 100 are issued each day (except during water releases and bad weather), beginning at 8 a.m. On summer weekends, the permit line often hits 100 people before dawn, giving early-rising campers an edge.

With permit, picnic, and at least 32 ounces (1 L) of water in your pack, channel your inner mountain goat on a strenuous, 1.25-mile (2 km) scramble down to Sliding Rock, a natural waterslide fed by Bridal Veil Falls. Schedule four hours for the excursion: The round-trip trek will take about three hours, including two passes over an 80-foot-high (24 m) swinging bridge, and you'll want at least an hour to spend repeatedly sliding into an ice-cube-cold swimming hole. The next day, hike the North Rim Trail to stand where high-wire artist Karl Wallenda began his death-defying walk over the gorge in 1970.

HUB | *Southeastern United States*

"SUGAR-SAND BEACHES, SURREAL ROCK FORMATIONS, AND AZURE WATERS"

Aussies' Wild West
Coral Coast, Australia

The wild Coral Coast of Western Australia (WA) is an edge-of-the-world adventure hub located within easy driving distance of Perth, the WA capital and its largest city. The coast boasts sugar-sand beaches, surreal rock formations, and the azure waters of the Indian Ocean, along with wildflowers (September to October) and wildlife such as kangaroos, emus, sea lions, and whales.

Covering the entire coast—about 1,750 miles (2,816 km) round-trip—isn't possible over a weekend, but there's plenty to see and do over two to three days if you camp in Cervantes, a rock lobster fishing village and Coral Coast gateway about two hours north of Perth. The renovated RAC Cervantes Holiday Park is an ideal base camp for a surf-and-sand adventure weekend. Located close to the beach, the park has sites for tents and camper vans (available for rent at the Perth airport) and stylish, new modular villas (think sleek mobile homes). Amenities like a heated pool, beachfront café, grills, and a playground make it possible to spend the whole weekend at the park, but you'll want to take short day trips to explore.

Devote a full day to playing on the water in Geraldton, 140 miles (225.3 km) north of Cervantes. The foreshore area of the port city is a big-thrill, big-splash playground offering activities such as wakeboarding, flyboards, and water-powered jet packs.

About 12 miles (19.3 km) south of Cervantes, hike among some of the thousands of limestone pillars in Pinnacles Desert, located within Nambung National Park. Follow the one-way Pinnacles Desert drive through the rock forest and periodically pull off for a closer look and photos. Farther south—about 50 more miles (80.5 km)—experience the adrenaline rush of surfing down the Lancelin dunes, a natural sandbox covering about 500 acres (202.3 ha). Rental boards sell out quickly on weekends, so reserve one online before you arrive. Plan to board midmorning when the wind is typically light and the sand isn't scorching hot.

Visit Pinnacles Desert in Western Australia's Nambung National Park.

Grey Towers was home to Gifford Pinchot, the first U.S. chief forester.

"WAKE WITH THE RISING SUN
AND ROAST MARSHMALLOWS
BENEATH THE STARS."

Forest Fun

Explore the Home of America's Great Conservation Movement

Tucked along the western bank of the Delaware River, 70 miles (112.7 km) northwest of New York City, Milford is a small town with big appeal for outdoor enthusiasts. Bikers can pedal the McDade Recreational Trail, following the Delaware River south for 31 miles (49.9 km) to the Delaware Water Gap, passing through forests, farms, and historic landmarks along the way. Boaters can launch kayaks and canoes at Milford Beach and paddle downstream to Minisink Island for a chance sighting of a bald eagle. For hikers, there's a network of wooded paths to explore, like the Milford Knob Trail, which rewards the steep climb with a scenic view overlooking the Historic District's postcard charm.

My husband and I come to Milford to camp beside the river. To wake with the rising sun and roast marshmallows beneath the stars. To disconnect and escape among the trees.

We arrive on a Friday afternoon and set up camp at River Beach, an 18-acre (7.3 ha) wooded campsite located 3 miles (4.8 km) northeast of town. We stake our claim to a riverfront tent site that has a big boulder to lean against while we fish and small rapids to lull us to sleep at night. In the mornings we drive to town for coffee and egg sandwiches from the Naked Bagel Company on Broad Street and wander through the ARTery Gallery, admiring how local artists have captured the area's natural beauty in oil and ink.

We spend Saturday afternoon trying to coordinate our paddles as our canoe zigzags down the Delaware. We find our rhythm by Sunday but abandon the canoe to make the climb up to Raymondskill Falls—a three-tier waterfall billed as the tallest in the state.

To have an adventure in the forest is to experience Milford the way former resident Gifford Pinchot, father of the American conservation movement, intended. Though to see this wooded wonderland through his eyes, you'd have to step back in time to the turn of the 20th century, where you'd find a very different landscape—one stripped almost entirely of its trees.

In Pinchot's day, unregulated logging practices had laid waste to two-thirds of Pennsylvania's 29 million acres (11.7 million ha) of forestland, leaving charred earth and jagged tree stumps in their place. Though many considered the country's timber supply inexhaustible, Pinchot saw the forest for the trees, so to speak, and foresaw the bleak legacy deforestation would leave for future generations. He became the first American to pursue a formal education in forestry, which led to his appointment as the first chief of the U.S. Forest Service and a career dedicated to conservation awareness and sustainable forest management.

A century of new growth, propagated by Pinchot's principles and policies, has done wonders to restore the nation's forests, including Milford and the surrounding Pocono Mountains. Considering this history, a visit to Milford isn't complete without a trip to Grey Towers, Pinchot's ancestral home. Perched on a hilltop 1 mile (1.6 km) northwest of town, the 20,000-square-foot (1,858.1 sq m) blue stone mansion with its three turreted towers and moat sits watchful over the land below. It's here, in the leafy green panorama that stretches to the horizon, that Pinchot's vision comes to life.

A weekend in Milford and its abundant forests is a gift from the past. And whatever adventure you seek, you'll find it beneath the trees.

—**Erika Liodice** is a Sarasota-based writer and author of the novel *Empty Arms* and the children's series High Flyers.

Kiwi Escape

Bay of Islands, New Zealand

Bay of Islands more than lives up to the name bestowed on it by Captain Cook in 1769. Some 144 islands dot the sheltered waters of the bay, located on North Island's northeastern coast. Home to early Māori settlers and site of the 1890 Treaty of Waitangi, which made New Zealand a British colony, the idyllic bay boasts calm, warm waters; secluded, sandy beaches; and impossibly blue skies.

Wake up to views of the water and surrounding forest-cloaked islands at the Urupukapuka Bay Campsite. Located on the Urupukapuka Island Recreation Reserve, it's the Bay of Islands' largest island at 514 acres (208 ha). The campground has 60 tent sites facing the beach. From your tent, follow trails to scenic overlooks and some of Urupukapuka's more than 65 archaeological spots, most from the pre-European Māori settlement that flourished here. Seasonal ferries and year-round water taxis take campers from Paihia (a 45-minute flight from Auckland) to Urupukapuka.

HUB | *North Island, New Zealand*

"WAKE UP TO VIEWS OF THE WATER AND SURROUNDING FOREST-CLOAKED ISLANDS AT THE URUPUKAPUKA BAY CAMPSITE."

Take a hike on Urupukapuka Island for panoramic vistas.

Take the 2.6-mile (4.2 km) hiking trail around Lost Lake in Buena Vista.

Pony Up

Buena Vista, Colorado, U.S.

Spend one night camping out near Buena Vista, and you'll realize that the "beautiful view" the central Colorado town was named for is above your head. Whether moonlit or filled with stars, the skies over the town and surrounding Collegiate Peaks Wilderness area mesmerize after dark. The daylight vistas aren't too shabby either. The town is situated 8,200 feet (2,499 m) above sea level, ideal for viewing multiple mountain peaks, the pristine San Isabel National Forest, and the churning white water of the Arkansas River.

There are mountain and valley campsites, some along the river and others on the Collegiate Peaks Scenic Byway, which follows an 1800s Pony Express route. In addition to tent and RV sites, yurts, and rustic and deluxe cabins, Arrowpoint Campground and Cabins (open April 15 to October 15) on the byway is home to an original Pony Express and stagecoach stop, complete with the historic bunkhouse, stable, and tack room.

HUB | *Mountain West United States*

Hike the rocky paths along Missouri Mountain.

Giraffes gather at a watering hole in Namibia's Etosha National Park.

National Parks

Explore everything Mother Nature has to offer—from red-rock canyons to majestic waterfalls—in these protected places.

1. GRAND CANYON NATIONAL PARK, ARIZONA, U.S.

A quintessential American national park for good reason, the Grand Canyon never disappoints—offering panoramic views of striated rock canyon and plenty of hiking options for day or weekend visitors. Plan accordingly: The South Rim of the park is open all year, but the North Rim closes for the winter.

2. ARENAL VOLCANO NATIONAL PARK, COSTA RICA

Though its volcano no longer puts on its nightly lava show, Arenal park still delights with its natural hot springs, emerald green rainforest, and hidden waterfalls. The full park spans 29,692 acres (12,016 ha), and protects a second volcano—the smaller Chato Volcano, which has been inactive for nearly 3,500 years and has a collapsed crater with a beautiful blue lagoon.

3. IGUAZU NATIONAL PARK, ARGENTINA & BRAZIL

On the border of Argentina and Brazil, Iguazu has been drawing visitors to its mist, not just for its epic waterfall but for more than 2,000 plant species and a plethora of wildlife living nearby.

4. ETOSHA NATIONAL PARK, NAMIBIA

History (2,000 ancient rock paintings) and wildlife combine in this unique African park, where giraffes, zebras, and leopards regularly stop for a drink at the park's watering holes.

5. NATIONAL PARKS OF SVALBARD, NORWAY

The Svalbard islands, tucked between the North Pole and mainland Norway, offer a chance to spot Arctic wildlife, such as polar bears, walruses, and harbor seals during endless daylight in the summer.

6. ZION NATIONAL PARK, UTAH, U.S.

Utah's first national park never ceases to wow visitors with its impressive canyon. Skip the popular Angels Landing hike for the less populated Watchman or Babylon Arch trails. Or make quick work of the park using its shuttle system.

7. KRKA NATIONAL PARK, CROATIA

You can take a swim in the turquoise waters of Skradinski Buk falls at Krka National Park—or go for a tour of a different kind through the park's 15th-century monasteries.

8. TULUM NATIONAL PARK, MEXICO

Ancient Maya ruins take over Tulum's beaches and surrounding land, where your tour may include walking by nesting turtles or exploring the mangroves of nearby Sian Ka'an Biosphere Reserve. As for the ruins themselves, you'll find archaeological sites dating back more than 1,000 years and once home to nearly 1,600 inhabitants.

9. GÖREME NATIONAL PARK, TURKEY

A park of a different sort, Göreme protects one of the world's oldest remains of human civilization, including Byzantine cave drawings and subterranean cities. Named a UNESCO World Heritage site in 1985, the park's underground dwellings are thought to date back to the Bronze Age.

10. SEQUOIA NATIONAL PARK, CALIFORNIA, U.S.

Stand among giants—hundred-year-old massive sequoias, the largest trees in the world—especially in the Giant Forest Grove of this beloved park nestled below the Sierra Nevada mountains. Don't miss day hiking in Grant Grove—the Grant Tree Trail leads to the General Grant Tree, the second-largest tree in the world.

Dine outside your private hut beneath the stars.

Hut, Sweet Hut

Huttopia White Mountains, Albany, New Hampshire, U.S.

First-time campers and families will appreciate the camping-light approach of Huttopia. Founded in France, Huttopia brings some comforts of home—like mattresses, mini-fridges, and stylish wood platform tents—to a summer camp setting. Rough it (relatively) in a Bonaventure tent for two or a two-bedroom Canadienne tent. Or glamp in a family-size Trappeur tent or wood chalet, both with indoor bathrooms.

The New Hampshire Huttopia village (one of only three in North America) is tucked on a wooded, lakeside site near the Kancamagus Scenic Byway, the east-west artery running through the heart of White Mountain National Forest. When you're not off exploring, play in the pool, paddle on the lake, and join in group activities like outdoor movies. And if your only camp recipe is s'mores, relax. The on-site pizza-grill Airstream serves cheesy pies and fresh salads. Huttopia White Mountains is open mid-May to mid-October.

HUB | *Northeastern United States*

Bison & Buttes

Badlands National Park, Interior, South Dakota, U.S.

Badlands National Park is best known for its rugged buttes, canyons, and geologic formations open to climb on (with care) all year. Yet rocky formations account for only about half of the 379-square-mile (982 sq km) park. The rest is mixed-grass prairie, which supports the park's abundant—and frequently spotted—wildlife, such as bison, Rocky Mountain bighorn sheep, pronghorn, and prairie dogs.

It's possible to see all of the above by driving the 38-mile (61.2 km) Badlands Loop Road (SD 240). But to witness how nature changes the look of the Badlands over the course of an entire day, you need to camp in the park. There are two campgrounds, and backcountry camping is permitted at least a half-mile (0.8 km) off any road or trail. Cedar Pass, the bigger of the two campgrounds, has 96 sites (reserve online), is open April to mid-October, and faces the stunning rock formations. The primitive Sage Creek Campground is open year-round and free.

HUB | *Mountain West United States*

Look out over the park's layered rock formations and canyons.

Rock On

Red Rock Canyon National Conservation Area, Nevada, U.S.

Red Rock is close enough to Las Vegas (about a 20-minute drive) to catch a nightly show at Planet Hollywood, yet far enough to sleep under real stars instead of bright lights. Located only 17 miles (27.4 km) west of the world-famous Strip, Red Rock Canyon Campground has 53 drive-in camper/tent sites, 14 walk-in sites, six RV sites, and seven group sites nestled in a sandstone and scrub brush bowl. There's no shade, so be sure to reserve a site with a covered picnic shelter.

The rainbow-striped rock backdrop makes it seem as if you've wandered onto an old Western movie set. Embrace the vibe by taking a guided horseback ride. At night, hike to the Cottonwood Valley and Late Night trailheads, located in the darkest part of the park, for expansive views of a full moon, meteor shower, or planets and stars. Due to the extreme heat, the campground is closed June 2 to August 31.

HUB | *Las Vegas, Nevada, U.S.; Western United States*

There is a 13-mile (20.9 km) Scenic Drive around Red Rock Canyon's main sites.

"THE UNDISPUTED JEWELS OF THIS COLLECTION ARE TWO SHIMMERING LAKES."

Paddle & Pedal

Parc National d'Opémican, Témiscamingue Region, Québec, Canada

Officially opened in June 2019, Parc National d'Opémican, in far southwestern Québec, is a stunning, new Sépaq (the Québec governmental agency that manages provincial parks and wildlife reserves) park preserving an 1880s timber-rafting relay station and 97 square miles (251 sq km) of pristine hardwood and boreal forest. Thundering whitewater rapids, rocky cliffs, and towering red and white pine trees—some reaching heights of 130 feet (39.6 m) or more—are among the park's myriad natural treasures. The undisputed jewels of this collection, however, are two shimmering lakes: Témiscamingue on the Ontario-Québec border and deepwater Kipawa, with its countless islands, shoals, and bays.

Named Opémican, derived from the Algonquin Anishinaabe word *opemikon*, meaning "along the path followed by the Amerindians," the park features canoe trails (some with portage connections between the two lakes) first followed by indigenous peoples more than 6,000 years ago. Backcountry campers can trace the same water routes as part of an epic canoe-bike circuit offered by the park. Combining canoeing about 7 miles (11.3 km), biking 6 miles (9.7 km), and spending two nights at one of the wilderness campsites on an island within the Strawberry Island area of Kipawa Lake, the adventure can be self-guided or booked as a package (including food, guide, transportation, and equipment) with Exode bâtisseur d'aventures.

The route features canoe and bike rental depots, so you can paddle to the island, return to shore at a different point, and swap out the canoe for a bike to complete the circuit at the end of your stay. Depending on your paddling experience and water conditions, rangers may suggest an alternate bike-canoe route, since the initial canoe trail can be challenging.

For a less strenuous adventure, stay in one of the park's ready-to-camp units, available from late June to October. The units are canvas-sealed wood cubes equipped with comforts of home: beds, heat, lights, cookware, and a covered porch.

HUB | *Eastern Canada; Midwestern United States*

Fishing and other recreational
water sports are on offer
in the park's lakes.

The Colchester Causeway bike and walking trail stretches across Lake Champlain.

"WE BEGIN OUR DAYS WITH
A SERENE BIKE RIDE ACROSS THE LAKE,
THE MIDMORNING SUN DANCING
ON ITS SURFACE."

PERSPECTIVE

The Cause(way) Effect

Just Outside Burlington, Vermont, Lies an Island of Natural Exploration

The first time I laid eyes on Vermont's Colchester Causeway, it was through the aerial lens of Google Maps. I zoomed in on the thread-thin line, certain that my eyes—or the map—were betraying me. It appeared to be a bike path right in the middle of Lake Champlain. Considering there are few things my husband and I enjoy more than a waterfront bike ride, we had to see it for ourselves.

The Causeway was built in 1899 as part of the Rutland Railroad's Island Line, connecting Vermont's mainland to the Champlain islands. Today, it has been given new life as a recreational trail that cuts through the lake's cobalt waters, offering views of New York's Adirondack Mountains to the west and Vermont's Green Mountains to the east. It's 3 miles (4.8 km) of paradise and a conduit to countless weekend adventures.

We set up our base camp at Grand Isle State Park on the eastern shore of Grand Isle, the largest of Lake Champlain's 80 islands. It's a prime spot for launching a kayak to explore the lake's northern islands, casting a line to see what's biting among its 90 species of fish, or searching for Champ, the legendary lake monster.

The Causeway's northern trailhead is 9 miles (14.5 km) south of the campground on Martin Road in South Hero. We begin our days with a serene bike ride across the lake, the midmorning sun dancing on its surface as gentle waves lap against the giant marble slabs that flank the trail. Midway across we reach "The Cut," a 200-foot (61 m) gap where a swing bridge once stood, allowing boats to pass between train traffic. A seasonal bike ferry, which runs daily 10 a.m. to 6 p.m. June through September, shuttles us across the divide.

The Causeway ends in Colchester, on the western shore of Vermont, but the Island Line trail continues south along the lake, passing through Delta Park, which the National Audubon Society has designated an Important Bird and Biodiversity Area (IBA) for over 23 species of both waterfowl and shorebirds, including the endangered common tern. The trail crosses a pedestrian bridge that spans the mouth of the Winooski River, where anglers fish for trout, bass, and landlocked salmon. We stop at Waterfront Park in Burlington and lock our bikes while we enjoy coffee and crepes at the Skinny Pancake. Afterward, we walk up the hill to Pine Street, where local vendors assemble on Saturday mornings for the weekly farmers market, offering vibrant displays of fresh flowers, organic vegetables, and homemade soaps that infuse the air with lavender. By afternoon, the Church Street Marketplace comes alive with food carts and street performers, and a line begins to form at Ben & Jerry's, a stone's throw from the chain's original location on the corner of St. Paul and College Streets.

The Island Line Trail ends in Oakledge Park in Burlington's south end. Here you can delight your inner child with a visit to the Forever Young Treehouse, relax on the sandy beach, or stand in the center of the Earth Clock, a sundial made of 14 granite stones that uses your shadow to mark time.

Our weekend at Lake Champlain ends in the same place it began—on the Causeway. We park our bikes on the side of the trail and climb down the marble boulders on its western bank, where we watch the sun set over the lake. As the last rays disappear beyond the mountains, it sets the indigo water ablaze in an orange glow, a perfect end to a perfect weekend.

—**Erika Liodice** is a Sarasota-based writer and author of the novel *Empty Arms* and the children's series High Flyers.

A lighthouse watches over Lake Huron from Manitoulin.

Unhurried Huron
Manitoulin Island, Ontario, Canada

At close to 1,100 square miles (2,800 sq km), northern Ontario's Manitoulin Island is nearly the size of Rhode Island. Sitting at the northern end of Lake Huron, Manitoulin is the world's largest freshwater island and an extraordinary place to camp. In addition to Lake Huron coastal campgrounds, there's camping near many of the island's more than 100 inland lakes and some sites on islands within the lakes.

The main island is sparsely populated, with full-time residents spread between six Anishinaabe First Nation reserves, two towns, and eight smaller communities. Most campgrounds and visitor services, such as restaurants and the all-important ice cream shops, operate from May to early October. Among the camping options are teepee glamping at Spirit Island Adventures and wilderness camping at Gordon's Park Eco Resort, the world's first privately owned Dark Sky Reserve. May to early October, the MS *Chi-Cheemaun* ferry runs from Tobermory to Manitoulin.

HUB | *Toronto, Canada; Midwestern United States*

Angel Island offers views of San Francisco and Alcatraz.

Stay in the Bay
Angel Island State Park, San Francisco, California, U.S.

Wake up to views of the Golden Gate Bridge and Alcatraz on the largest island in San Francisco Bay. Accessible by ferry from San Francisco and Tiburon, Angel Island State Park is the most affordable place to stay (under $20 per night plus ferry fee) in the famously expensive City by the Bay. Most visitors only spend the day hiking or biking, particularly to the Angel Island Immigration Station museum and grounds (open Wednesday to Sunday), where millions of mainly Asian immigrants were ferried for quarantine and processing between 1910 and 1940.

To be among the lucky ones to camp overnight at one of the island's 11 tent sites, make reservations up to six months in advance and consider a midweek stay. Arrive prepared for backcountry camping, including hiking up to 2 miles (3.2 km) to your site and hauling all your gear: food, water, tent, and, if you want to cook, a camp stove or charcoal.

HUB | *West Coast United States*

A sandy beach path leads to the Gulf of Mexico.

Beach Camp

Fort Pickens Area, Gulf Islands National Seashore, Florida, U.S.

The largest national seashore in the United States, Gulf Islands runs 160 miles (258 km) along the northern Gulf of Mexico coast from Mississippi east to Florida. Protected and pristine, the Fort Pickens Area of the seashore in Florida offers the increasingly rare opportunity to camp close to a beach.

The campground at Fort Pickens (named for an 1834 brick fort that's still standing and open to walk through) sits on Santa Rosa Island between the Gulf and Pensacola Bay. All of the more than 180 campsites (arranged in four loops) are a short walk away from sugar-sand Gulf and Bay beaches. Try to book a Loop A site since most are shaded by live oaks. There are beach access points from all the loops, and the 6.9-mile (11.1 km) Florida Trail leads through the campground and along the beach and a coastal marsh. From March 15 to October 31, a ferry runs between Fort Pickens, Pensacola Beach, and downtown Pensacola.

HUB | *Southeastern United States*

"THE DRIVE IS UNDENIABLY
ONE OF THE MOST SCENIC
ON THE EAST COAST."

Skyline Living

Shenandoah National Park, Virginia, U.S.

The closest national park to Washington, D.C., Shenandoah is a linear area spanning 300 square miles (777 sq km) of ridgeline. For many people, visiting Shenandoah is a drive-through experience. Skyline Drive, a 105-mile-long (169 km) scenic parkway, runs north to south along the spine of the park from Front Royal, Virginia (US 340), to Rockfish Gap (I-64), where the road connects to the Blue Ridge Parkway. From the 75 Skyline Drive overlooks, you can see sky-high views of the Appalachian Piedmont to the east and the Shenandoah Valley to the west.

The drive is undeniably one of the most scenic on the East Coast; however, there's much more to see and do in Shenandoah National Park than what's visible from the main road. Only by hiking and camping in the park can you reach secluded waterfalls and swimming holes, and visit the backcountry cabins and cemeteries of the homesteading families that first settled the mountains in the 1750s.

There are more than 500 miles (804.7 km) of trails in the park and five campgrounds along Skyline Drive: Matthews Arm (at mile 22.2), Big Meadows (mile 51.2), Lewis Mountain (mile 57.5), Loft Mountain (mile 79.5), and a group camping site, Dundo (mile 83.7). All are open May to October, and Big Meadows and Lewis Mountain open in late March.

To hike to waterfalls and watch for white-tailed deer and black bear, camp at Big Meadows, the park's largest open vista. In early morning and just before sunset, in particular, you're likely to spot wildlife feeding on the berry bushes and native grasses in the rolling meadowlands. The campground is first-come, first-served early in the season and by reservation and first-come, first-served from May until the closing date. October weekends are busiest. The rest of the year, if you don't have a weekend reservation, arrive on Thursday to increase the odds of getting a site.

Hiking trails lead to overlooks of the stunning Shenandoah Valley.

The Tahquamenon Falls spill into the eponymous river below.

Chasing Waterfalls
Tahquamenon Falls State Park, Michigan, U.S.

Tahquamenon Falls State Park's location is close to the community of Paradise, which doubles as a fitting description of the Eastern Upper Peninsula park. Six cascading waterfalls, known as the Lower Falls, encircle an island near the Hemlock and Portage campgrounds. Rent a boat at the park to row to the island, where a quarter-mile (0.4 km) hiking trail along the shoreline brings you close enough to feel the spray from the falls. The trek is particularly stunning in fall when fiery red and orange foliage cloaks the surrounding woodlands.

From the Lower Falls, it's a 4-mile (6.4 km) hike to the park's more famous Upper Falls. Spanning more than 200 feet (70 m) across and with a nearly 50-foot (15 m) drop, the waterfall is one of the largest in the eastern half of the United States. In addition to the falls, the 48,000-acre (19,425 ha) park features 13 inland lakes and 24 miles (38.6 km) of the Tahquamenon River. Track chairs (electric off-road wheelchairs) are available to help people with physical limitations explore the park.

HUB | *Midwestern United States*

A suspended tent is your home for a weekend in Nuuksio.

On the Treetop
Nuuksio National Park, Finland

Take camping to the next level at the world's first Tentsile Experience EcoCamp, launched in 2016 in Finland's Nuuksio National Park. Campers sleep about 7 feet (2 m) above the ground in three-person, tented hammocks pre-hung between two trees. Beneath each tree tent is a mesh hammock, anchored 3 to 4 feet (1 m) above the ground. The bottom hammock serves as a step for climbing into and out of the tree tent, storage space, and a place to hang out or accommodate more campers. Rates include the use of sleeping bags and linens; drinking water; and a common area with firepit and firewood, tables, benches, and dishware.

Elevating the experience even higher are glamping amenities like breakfast and admission to the nearby Haltia Finnish Nature Centre, use of an indoor toilet and shower, and a headlamp. The site is located 22 miles (35.4 km) northwest of Helsinki and can be reached using public transportation.

HUB | *Helsinki, Finland*

Stairway to Heaven

HOSHINOYA Fuji, Japan

Part of the Hoshino Resorts group, HOSHINOYA Fuji puts a Japanese spin on luxury glamping. The 15-acre (6.1 ha) resort is arranged stairstep style on a forested mountainside overlooking Lake Kawaguchi in the Fuji Five Lakes region about two hours west of Tokyo. Guests stay at the lowest level in minimalist wood-and-glass cabins. Floor-to-ceiling windows and balconies (outfitted with a fireplace and comfy futon) face majestic Mount Fuji, which towers over the lake.

Glamping amenities include such essentials as a backpack, binoculars, and a headlamp to use during your stay. Breakfast boxes, packed with goodies like granola, sausage, and yogurt, can be delivered daily for an extra fee. From the cabins, it's a steep hike up a series of stairs to the resort's dining hall (wild game is a house specialty) and Cloud Terrace, a series of platforms with a small library and café and outdoor areas where guests gather around a firepit after dark.

HUB | *Central Japan*

See snowcapped Mount Fuji from your cabin's terrace.

A fishing boat ties up on the shores of Lough Currane, Ireland, a popular spot to catch salmon.

Fishing Holes

Anglers can reel in the big one in these celebrated fishing spots from Montana to Brazil.

1. ARMSTRONG'S SPRING CREEK, MONTANA, U.S.

Legendary for fly-fishing, the faster water in this spring-fed creek—filled with more than 1.5 miles (2.4 km) of fishable riffles, pockets, and runs—gives the local trout less time to inspect your flies, promising a nice catch. Reservations are required—book early for this popular spot—and fees range from $40 to $120 per day, depending on the time of year.

2. KEY WEST, FLORIDA, U.S.

The home of Ernest Hemingway, Key West was built for fishing, with charter boats aplenty to take you out any time of year to reel in everything from snapper to grouper—and onshore restaurants to cook your catch. To try your hand at the large migratory tarpon the Keys are known for, book your trip sometime between late March and early June, when water temperatures are steadily warmer.

3. CAIRNS, AUSTRALIA

The black marlin—one of the most coveted catches—here can weigh up to 1,653 pounds (750 kg) and swim up to 80.8 miles an hour (130 km/h), challenging even the most seasoned anglers. If you don't catch a marlin, you may reel in a baracuda or wahoo.

4. AMAZON BASIN, BRAZIL

Tours throughout Manaus offer the chance to hook piranha by the dozen. Be warned: Their razor sharp teeth can cut though both steel hooks and fingers.

5. BRAINERD, MINNESOTA, U.S.

If you don't mind the cold weather, try your hand at ice fishing during the annual Brainerd Jaycees Ice Fishing Extravaganza, when more than 12,000 fishermen try their chance in 20,000 predrilled holes. More than $200,000 in prizes is given away to festival anglers.

6. AZORES, PORTUGAL

At least 22 world fishing records are held in the Azores for largest game fish. Try to add your name to the record holder list surrounded by volcanic scenery; you may also spot mako sharks and whales.

7. MARTHA'S VINEYARD, MASSACHUSETTS, U.S.

If you're not on the hunt for giants, head to Martha's Vineyard, where the fishing is easy: Large striped bass pass through regularly on a migratory route and require nothing more than natural bait and a spinning reel.

8. EAST CAPE, BAJA, MEXICO

From May through November, your chances of catching a blue or striped marlin (and we're talking big) increase with the warmer weather and more abundant fishing grounds. Cast your line into the Sea of Cortez, which is also known for world-class dorado, yellowfin, sailfish, and bonito.

9. PI-AS BAY, PANAMA

Inshore, you'll find plenty of small game fish to keep you occupied on a short winter trip. For larger catches, charter a boat out to sea, where blue marlin and sailfish are plentiful from December to March and July to September. For sailfish, plan your trip for April to June.

10. LOUGH CURRANE, COUNTY KERRY, IRELAND

Try your hand at salmon fishing at this spot on Ireland's west coast. The picturesque setting, just east of the village of Waterville, comes alive with salmon at the beginning of every spring. Currane is also known for quality sea trout fishing, which typically is best from April to September, with the largest fish being caught between April and June. Popular fishing spots on the lake include Black Point, Church Island, Reenaskinna Rock, and Rough Island.

Stay in one of the camp's turf-roof huts.

Double Dutch
D'Olde Kamp, Ansen, the Netherlands

Experience traditional Dutch village life at d'Olde Kamp, a pastoral campground 90 minutes northeast of Amsterdam. Ideal for family camping, d'Olde Kamp has 40 grassy and shaded sites open to tents, camper-vans, and motorhomes. For the village vibe without actually camping, stay in one of the six Hobbit-style turf-roof huts, equipped with electricity and Wi-Fi.

The campground is dog friendly, and there also are resident goats, chickens, donkeys, and rabbits that kids can help feed (and earn a "farmer's diploma" for a job well done). The campground's backyard is neighboring Dwingelderveld National Park, which protects more than 9,100 acres (3,700 ha) of cool and damp bog, forest, and meadowlands. Rent a bike from d'Olde Kamp to pedal around the park, or explore on foot via the more than 35 miles (60 km) of trails. After biking or hiking, chow down on piping-hot, homemade pizza fresh from the d'Olde Kamp outdoor oven.

HUB | *Amsterdam, the Netherlands*

Take a break from hiking on the banks of Lake Seeleinsee.

Best of Bavaria
Berchtesgadener Land Biosphere Reserve, Bavaria, Germany

Camp in the shadows of the snow-capped Berchtesgaden Alps in Germany's only Alpine Biosphere Reserve. Encompassing the forested, southeasternmost tip of Germany and surrounded on three sides by Austria, rural Berchtesgadener Land is home to Berchtesgaden National Park—with its emerald green mountain lake, Königssee—and the atmospheric Bavarian towns of Bad Reichenhall and Freilassing.

At the family-owned Camping-Resort Allweglehen, bordering the national park, there are tent-camping, trailer, and camper-van sites, as well as three-person wooden huts and six-person chalets for rent. The on-site restaurant, with an adjoining beer garden, serves a number of local specialties, including fried *leberkäse* (liver cheese), a SPAM-like, Bavarian sausage meatloaf served with a fried egg and fried potatoes. There's also a heated outdoor pool, indoor sauna, and rental e-bikes and e-cars for rides into the national park.

HUB | *Munich, Germany; Salzburg, Austria*

A rustic village separates Isthmus Cove from Catalina Harbor.

Made for the Movies

Santa Catalina Island, California, U.S.

During Hollywood's golden age, car-free Catalina Island gained fame as a glamorous playground for the likes of John Wayne and Humphrey Bogart. Located 30 miles (48 km) southwest of Long Beach, the 22-mile-long (35.4 km) island still attracts its share of yachting glitterati and is steeped in movie history (1935's *Mutiny on the Bounty*, starring Clark Gable, is among the more than 500 productions shot here).

Experience a slice of Hollywood history by camping on the island's secluded west end at Two Harbors, once dubbed the Isthmus Movie Colony. The hilltop Two Harbors Campground overlooks the Pacific (and the boats bobbing in the harbor) and has tent and tent-cabin sites. From here, hike to a restaurant, store, and water sports rental shop in the village of Two Harbors. Most high-speed ferries to Catalina arrive on the southeast end of the island at Avalon; only the Catalina Express from San Pedro goes directly to Two Harbors.

HUB | *West Coast United States*

> "A SMALL BEACH, VIEWS
> ACROSS THE LOCH, AND
> WOODLAND HIKING TRAILS"

Bonnie Banks

Loch Lomond & the Trossachs National Park, Scotland

In addition to being lyrics etched into our collective memory by the melancholy Scottish anthem, the "bonnie, bonnie banks o' Loch Lomond" are an actual place you can camp in Scotland's first national park. Opened in 2002 and spanning about 720 square miles (1,865 sq km), Loch Lomond and the Trossachs National Park protects a wealth of water features, including 24-mile-long (38.6 km) Loch Lomond, Britain's largest inland body of water. Balloch, the park's gateway at the southern end of Loch Lomond, is located 50 minutes north of Glasgow by train or 35 minutes by car.

March to September, a reservation or permit is required to camp at most sites along a loch shore or river. The 30-site Sallochy Bay campground, on the eastern shores of Loch Lomond near Rowardennan, has 10 lakeside tent sites. Bare-bones amenities (there are composting toilets and drinking water but no showers) give Sallochy a wilderness feel befitting its rugged backdrop. It offers a small beach, views across the loch of the Arrochar Alps, and woodland hiking trails. Scotland's most popular long-distance trail, the 96-mile (154.5 km) West Highland Way, also runs right through the campground in case you'd like to strike out on a longer trek.

For an even wilder Loch Lomond camping experience, pitch a tent on Inchcailloch ("island of the old women"), the most accessible island in the park. Up to 12 people can camp per night (for up to two nights) at the small, rustic campsite on the island's southern tip. The island, which is part of the Loch Lomond Nature Reserve, is accessible year-round via ferry or waterbus, but camping is permitted only March to September.

The "Trossachs" area of the park is the Great Trossachs Forest, one of the largest National Nature Reserves in the United Kingdom. Covering 62 square miles (161 sq km), the forest is a native woodland restoration project begun in 2009 and slated to run for 200 years.

HUB | *Glasgow, Scotland*

Even the little ones will enjoy the misty Loch Lomond.

Life's a Beach

Brittany, France

Jutting into the Atlantic on the northwestern edge of France, the coast of Brittany is wild, windswept, and one of the best places in Europe for beach camping. Rustic campgrounds and more elaborate holiday parks (with amenities like water parks and ready-to-glamp mobile homes and chalets) fringe sandy beaches, dramatic cliffs, and historic fishing ports along the province's 1,740-mile (2,800 km) coast.

Some of the most secluded campsites and sparsely populated beaches are found on the rugged and remote Crozon Peninsula. Boasting offshore sea caves, sheer cliffs, white-sand beaches, and Caribbean-like turquoise waters, wildly scenic Crozon has a low-key, edge-of-the-world vibe. April to September, pitch a tent or rent a minimalist mobile home at a campground near the seaside village of Morgat so you can both walk to the beach and feast on fresh shellfish and quintessential Breton *galettes de blé noir,* savory crêpes made from buckwheat flour.

HUB | *Paris, France*

> "BOASTING OFFSHORE SEA CAVES, SHEER CLIFFS, WHITE-SAND BEACHES, AND CARIBBEAN-LIKE TURQUOISE WATERS, WILDLY SCENIC CROZON HAS A LOW-KEY, EDGE-OF-THE-WORLD VIBE."

From campsites on the beaches of Brittany, watch the sun set below the horizon.

The park offers ready-to-camp canvas shelters, so you can sleep under the stars.

Star Struck

Mont-Mégantic National Park, Québec, Canada

Fall asleep under a blanket of stars in the world's first International Dark Sky Reserve, at Mont-Mégantic National Park. The Sépaq park is part of a 3,300-square-mile (8,547 sq km) area where the night skies are so dark it's nearly impossible to see a hand directly in front of your face.

At the foot of Mont-Mégantic is the ASTROLab (open to the public during the day), featuring exhibitions and multimedia presentations. Positioned at the summit is a scientific observatory housing Québec's most powerful telescope. Campsites in the park run the gamut from rustic shelters to cabins. To sleep indoors with a clear view of the night sky, reserve an EXP. Cabin. With walls built with more windows than wood and skylights over the sleeping quarters, you can watch the elusive Milky Way before dawn, and night sky wonders like planets, stars, and, on occasion, the northern lights.

HUB | *Québec City, Canada; Northeastern United States*

The Milky Way shines above Mont-Mégantic National Park.

FOOD & WINE

Culinary delights abound—from Michelin-starred restaurants to market street stalls—in every corner of the globe.

A dish of pig cheeks with potato cakes and beet glaze epitomizes New Nordic cuisine (p. 432).

A local woman eats a typical meal of regional foods.

Novo-Andean Food
Sacred Valley, Peru

In Peru, you can still eat like the Inca. The mighty Andean empire feasted on hearty foods such as quinoa, maize, and endless types of multicolored potatoes. The starchy vegetable originated near the shores of Lake Titicaca, and more than 3,000 potato varietals have been recorded in Peru.

Star chefs such as Gastón Acurio led the charge in adding modern flair to these base ingredients. Take a weekend journey to one of the best places to eat novo-Andean cuisine: the Inca heartland itself, the Sacred Valley running from Cusco to Machu Picchu. In Cusco, pop into Chicha por Gastón Acurio for alpaca carpaccio and *lomo saltado* (stir-fried steak). Then head deep into the valley, cruising among snowcapped peaks and centuries-old irrigation canals and circular agricultural terraces left by the Inca. Stop for lunch at Mil; the restaurant's eight-course menus are a sampler of Andean diversity and flavors, from duck in black quinoa to chips made from potatoes freeze-dried in the cold mountain air.

HUB | *Lima or Cusco, Peru*

Indulge in pies from the birthplace of pizza.

The O.G. Pizza Pie
Naples, Italy

Pizza is beloved the world over. Where better to spend a weekend indulging than Naples, the birthplace of the modern dish? The city in southern Italy's Campania region boasts more than 800 pizzerias, nearly 100 of them officially certified by the Associazione Verace Pizza Napoletana (AVPN), which ensures that the ingredients and cooking methods follow Neapolitan traditions. Look for the Pizza Vera signs granted by the AVPN above restaurant doors for the mark of a top-rate pizzeria. But the surest sign of quality? A line out the door.

The wait at Sorbillo, in the Centro Storico, can take up to an hour and a half as hungry Neapolitans gather for huge pizzas made with organic Campania produce. Pizzeria Gorizia 1916, in the Vomero neighborhood, and Pizzeria da Attilio, in Monte-santo, also draw ardent fans. Just be sure to order a margherita pizza. Said to have been named for Italy's Queen Margherita in the late 19th century, the simple blend of tomato sauce, buffalo mozzarella, and basil is the quintessential Italian combination.

HUB | *Major Western European Cities*

Wine O'Clock

Mendoza, Argentina

I n Argentina's western Mendoza Province, rows of grapevines unfurl for miles backed by the spectacular Andes mountains. Abundant sunshine, a dry climate, and the high altitude (nearly 4,000 feet/1,200 m at some vineyards) combine to form one of the world's leading wine regions, where the purple-black Malbec grape is king.

The three main winemaking hubs of the province—Maipú, Lujan de Cuyo, and Uco Valley—are all within easy reach of Mendoza city along Ruta 40, making for a leisurely weekend getaway. Vineyards line the route on both sides, and during the harvest season from December to March, green leaves and deep purple grapes shine vividly against the snowy peaks of the Andes in the distance. Stop in at top wineries such as family-owned Mendel and art-adorned Bodegas Salentein, where you can taste the region's award-winning Malbec and other elegant varietals, including Torrontés, Cabernet Sauvignon, and Merlot, paired with a typical Argentine *asado* (grilled meat) cookout among the grapevines.

HUB | *Buenos Aires, Argentina; Santiago, Chile*

Vines are carefully cared for in the vineyards of Uco Valley, Mendoza's wine region.

Chef René Redzepi (center) put the innovative Noma restaurant on the map.

"AWARD-WINNING EATERIES THROUGHOUT THE SMALL NATION"

The New Nordic Cuisine
Copenhagen, Denmark

Traditional Danish food emphasizes the sturdy fare found and harvested locally during Denmark's short summers: herring, rye bread, and vegetables like cabbages and beets. These ingredients come together in the ubiquitous national dish *smørrebrød*, which are open-faced sandwiches that layer endless combinations—most commonly pickled fish, eggs, or shrimp—atop slices of rye bread. Over the past couple of decades, Danish chefs have reinvented old recipes, using seasonal ingredients in unexpected ways. The result, dubbed New Nordic cuisine, has led to a wave of award-winning eateries throughout the small nation. As of 2019, Danish restaurants hold 35 Michelin stars, more than any other Nordic country.

In Copenhagen, the temple of gastronomy, Noma, spearheaded the New Nordic trend, with head chef René Redzepi's seasonal tasting menus that pair unusual proteins like musk ox with wild herbs grown in Scandinavia. Reopened in 2018 as part of an urban farm on the waterfront, Noma has a reservations waiting list that can be months long, so book well in advance. Even if you can't get in, there's no end of other choices. Geranium, with views over the Fælledparken (Common Gardens) in the center of Copenhagen, and AOC, located in the cellar of a 17th-century building, boast two Michelin stars each.

The Danish capital isn't the only hot spot for New Nordic cuisine, however. Make it a long weekend to afford yourself a night at Henne Kirkeby Kro, situated on the wild moor of Denmark's western Jutland. Chef Paul Cunningham transformed a nearly 230-year-old property into a charmingly rustic 36-seat restaurant and inn. The restaurant was awarded its second Michelin star in 2017 for Cunningham's local dishes, such as Limfjord oysters and Varde Ådal lamb, which he seasons with ingredients from his immense kitchen garden.

Food market vendors offer bites of traditional Laotian vegetable and noodle dishes.

PERSPECTIVE

An Appetite for Laos

The Complexity, Grace, and Taste of Luang Prabang

Raise a spoonful of *tom kha kai*, a traditional Laotian coconut chicken soup, to your lips, and a tantalizing perfume of lemongrass, lime, and galangal wafts upward. Its scent is sublime and earthy, hot and sour. The fragrant plume comes with a peppery kick. The sensation is vivid, somehow poignant, and utterly transporting.

I've come for a taste of the real thing. Upon leaving the Luang Prabang airport, my first views of Laos are the Phou Thao and Phou Nang mountain ranges, which surround the ancient royal city of Luang Prabang like an embrace. The slopes are lush with trees that comb and catch the low-lying clouds. As I enter the city, a cluster of motorbikes overtake my taxi, trailing fumes and impatience.

Built on a peninsula formed by the confluence of the Nam Khan and Mekong Rivers, the city was once an important Buddhist religious center and seat of empire. Eventually, Laos fell into European possession following the creation of the French protectorate in 1893. The French recognized Luang Prabang as the Laotian royal seat once more. Beside the ancient temples, a new Parisian-designed palace and French administrative buildings filled the historic core, now a UNESCO World Heritage site.

The next day, my friend Van invites me for breakfast in the heart of the historic district on Sakkaline Road. We sit down at a family-run, open-air restaurant across from a gilded temple where monks clad in marigold orange robes whitewash the walls. An iron pot full of a tangle of rice noodles bubbles away, heated by a wood fire. The owner welcomes us with big broth-filled bowls and piles of fresh mint, basil, and lettuce leaves in a dozen shades of green. We spoon in *jeow bong* sauce—orange and scarlet and sweet and sour. Additional plates of sticky rice, bean sprouts, limes, and long beans, as well as small bowls of fish sauce and fermented shrimp paste, crowd the table. All is simple, yet with complexity of flavor.

"Identity is in the very food you eat here," Van says. "It's profoundly important to Luang Prabang. Our cuisine is central to how we understand ourselves. Our sense of place and relationship to the sacred are found in the ingredients we harvest along the river and the food we cook at home."

What happens when you can no longer experience the food that so defines you, I wonder, knowing that with suitcases and ambitions each wave of newcomers to U.S. shores brings memories and yearnings for a taste of home. According to a study by the National Restaurant Association, the top three global cuisines eaten in America—Chinese, Mexican, and Italian—are scarcely considered foreign anymore, and nine out of 10 Americans eat them. But only 20 percent of Americans have sampled cuisines such as Korean, Ethiopian, and Brazilian. Laotian food is so uncommon it didn't even make the list, but for Van and his sister Vanvisa, it became their meal ticket. "How you tend your land is how you honor your family," Van says, who made the difficult choice to sell a piece of ancestral land to finance their restaurant in Raleigh, North Carolina.

In 2012 he and his sister opened Bida Manda (Sanskrit for "father mother") in a revitalized neighborhood around the corner from the city's bus station. The mix of Laos and Dixie created a sensation. With co-owner and brewer Patrick Woodson, the siblings opened Bhavana, a craft brewery and community café that introduced Raleigh's techies and Tar Heels to the piquancy of the Laotian delicacies like *mok pa*—aromatic steamed fish in a banana-leaf wrap, spiced with coconut curry and served with sticky rice—and handcrafted ales brewed with mangoes and peppercorns. Purple hydrangeas from the house flower shop and art books from the house bookstore grace its interior, which fills out a light-washed warehouse-size space. As his grandmother said, it was all in the details. "A showstopper," proclaimed *Bon Appétit*. Soon after, Bhavana was nominated for a James Beard award, the Oscar of edibles.

—**Andrew Nelson** is an award-winning writer based in Washington, D.C.

Mugaritz has been named one of the world's best restaurants.

Michelin Mecca
San Sebastián, Spain

E picureans are spoiled for choice in San Sebastián. The seaside city of fewer than 200,000 people in northern Spain's Basque region has among the highest number of Michelin stars per capita in the world, providing a weekend of unparalleled fine dining. The area's restaurants boast a combined 18 Michelin stars within a 15-mile (25 km) radius, and of Spain's 11 three-starred restaurants—the highest Michelin achievement—three are in San Sebastián.

Founded in 1897, three-starred Arzak has ranked among the 10 best restaurants in the world for more than a decade. Now run by the fourth generation of the family, Elena Arzak (named the world's best female chef in 2012 by the World's 50 Best Restaurant Awards), the elegant taverna focuses on traditional Basque cuisine with a modern twist, such as pigeon with hibiscus flowers or a *huitlacoche* mushroom puff with foie gras mousse. Other dining standouts are Akelare, Martín Berasategui, and Mugaritz, but don't miss newly starred up-and-comers Kokotxa and Amelia.

HUB | *Madrid, Spain*

Palate Pleasures
Shanghai, China

I n Shanghai, foodies will find flavors from every corner of the globe and an ever expanding roster of restaurants serving regional cuisine. There's something magical about *xiao long bao*, soup dumplings made with delicate dough filled with steaming broth. Arrive early in the day to snag the specialty at local institution Jia Jia Tang Bao or try them at Nanxiang Mantou restaurant. Hairy crab is the delicacy of choice for locals (named for the "hairy" substance on the claws) from late October through early December. The crab's sweet meat is served with golden roe at one of Shanghai's oldest eateries, Wang Bao He, which plucks its crab from Yangcheng Lake.

Harking back to the era of art deco decadence, speakeasies are shaking up the city's cocktail culture. To access the four-story Speak Low, hopeful sippers must visit a bar-supply shop, then open a hidden door.

Hairy crab is in season from October to early December.

HUB | *Hong Kong; Eastern China; South Korea*

Chestnut Madness
Marunada Festival, Lovran, Croatia

Croatians love *maruni*—the sweet species of chestnut that grows on the Opatija Riviera at the foot of Mount Učka in northern Croatia. The area's mild yet invigorating Mediterranean climate produces large, pale chestnuts that are easy to peel, and they've been a major export of the region since the 17th century.

Mid-October brings the fall harvest and the annual Marunada Festival, considered to be among the best European gastronomy events. You can choose from among three weekends. The nutty goodness begins in Lovran, a historic coastal resort with sweeping views of the Adriatic Sea, before neighboring villages Liganj and Dobreć take up the mantle. During the first weekend, feast on every type of chestnut-infused dish, from pancakes to pie to goulash to ice cream, while the Lovran Brass Band plays in the town square. Wash it all down with *medica*, Croatia's beloved honey brandy, and burn off the calories by joining the locals in bocce and biking tournaments.

HUB | *Zagreb, Croatia*

Grilled chestnuts are just one of the nutty offerings at the festival.

MANCHEGO 34 €/KG

BERGER DOUREY 37 €/KG.

Brebis FENUGREC 37 €/Kg. CROTONESE 33 €/KG

SPENWOOD 52 €/KG

FILETTA 5 €80 Le demi

Fiore di Muntagna 22, €/KG

FIORE Di MONTAGNA BREBIS CORSE 42 €/KG

LOU CLAOUSOU 6 € le demi

Le Claousou du Causse Méjean

LOU BREN 32 €/KG

BRIN D'AMOUR 42 €/KG
PÉCURA 44 €/KG

French and Italian cheeses are displayed for sale at the Aligre Market in Paris.

Food Markets

From ramen burgers in New York to fried crickets on a stick in Thailand, these food markets will keep your taste buds excited.

1. SMORGASBURG, NEW YORK, U.S.

The largest weekly open-air food market in America, this Brooklyn hot spot offers bites from 100 local vendors, including treats like lobster sticky rice, icing-coated soufflé pancakes, and ramen-bun hamburgers. If you can't make it to the Big Apple, Smorgasburg has expanded to other cities including Los Angeles, California, and Washington, D.C.

2. WEST SIDE MARKET, CLEVELAND, OHIO, U.S.

At Cleveland's oldest public market, held within a historic brick hall, you'll find 100 vendors and plenty of meat counters selling sausages, bratwursts, and kielbasa, alongside sellers offering fresh fruit, seafood, vegetables, and pastries.

3. TORVEHALLERNE MARKET, COPENHAGEN, DENMARK

With more than 60 vendors, it's no wonder you'll find such diverse options—from sushi to tapas to Danish rice porridge—in this beloved market. The buzzing food hall is easy to access—it's right in the middle of Copenhagen's city center—so there are no excuses not to stop in when it's running all day Friday through Monday.

4. SUNDAY WALKING MARKET, CHIANG MAI, THAILAND

Cutting through the heart of Chiang Mai, you'll find handicrafts and souvenirs sold alongside food vendors offering everything from fried rice to fried crickets.

5. JEMAA EL-FNA, MARRAKECH, MOROCCO

The souks of Jemaa el-Fna are legendary for good reason—and not just for the snake charmers. Vendors with colorful piles of spices sell next to vendors offering dishes like *méchoui*—a local lamb dish— and mint tea.

6. TOYOSU FISH MARKET, TOKYO, JAPAN

No visit to Tokyo is complete without a stop at this iconic fish market, where before dawn, you can watch the ancient tuna auction while you sip hot tea and eat the freshest sushi in the world.

7. ST. LAWRENCE MARKET, TORONTO, CANADA

This 200-year-old market (open every day) serves up Montréal-style bagels, fresh produce, and meats. It also features antiques. Saturdays bring a farmers market and Sundays an antiques market.

8. MAHANE YEHUDA, JERUSALEM, ISRAEL

Winding through the maze of alleys and stalls, Mahane Yehuda is a feast for the senses. You'll find everything from nuts, seeds, and fruits to olives, falafel, and shawarma. Many local outfitters offer guided tours of the market, highlighting top vendors and including multiple tasting opportunities.

9. MERCADO DE LA MERCED, MEXICO CITY, MEXICO

At the largest market in Mexico City—and the city's hub since the 17th century—you'll taste from an impressive selection of more than 300 permanent vendors, each hawking delights like cacti, avocados, homemade tortillas, and fresh fruit. Pro tip: It's easy to get lost in the market, so a Spanish-speaking tour guide may be worth booking if you are unfamiliar with the market and nearby areas.

10. MARCHÉ D'ALIGRE, PARIS, FRANCE

Stop here to gather everything you need for a Parisian picnic: right-out-of-the-oven baguettes, fresh berries, gourmet local cheeses, and more. The market is held six days a week and includes a covered section spanning three halls.

Münsterland's beloved white asparagus is the focus of most dishes when in season.

For the Love of White Gold

Stalking Germany's Trusty Asparagus in Münsterland

I'm scouring the flat upper surface of the knee-high, gray-brown mound of soil for the tiny undulations that might indicate a spear of white asparagus trying to break through.

Standing next to me, Lukasz Dominikowski, armed with his asparagus cutter (a long, flat tool with a sharp, forked blade), has detected a ripple. He plunges two thickly gloved fingers into the soil, pushes it away to expose a single cream-colored spear, then slides his asparagus cutter down alongside it, perfectly parallel, and breaks it away from its root. Picking up a flat trowel, he smoothes over evidence of his operation.

It's all over in less than 30 seconds, and I'm left trying to work out how he knew anything was there.

It's hardly surprising Dominikowski has an eye for spotting white asparagus: The 33-year-old has traveled to Hof Grothues-Potthoff, a farm estate with a bakery, farm shop, and hotel, in Senden, Germany—about 10 miles (16 km) southwest of Münster—for the past eight years to help harvest and sort up to 100 tons (90.7 tonnes) of Germany's white gold. Every April, he leaves his wife and job in Poznań, Poland, to work 10 hours a day, six days a week, until the official end of the season on June 24, the Feast Day of St. John the Baptist. It looks like backbreaking work, but Dominikowski thoroughly enjoys it.

White asparagus season is celebrated with a passion in Germany, and I've come to the flat, castle-filled region of Münsterland, with its maritime climate and sandy soil prime for the spring vegetable's production, to find out why. Elmar Grothues, who with his siblings oversees a 14-generation-old family farm, takes me to a newly planted field. Pulling a bundle of roots from the soil—a cluster of earthy rats' tails attached to a feathery green shoot—he explains the labor-intensive white-asparagus-growing process. It requires precision planting and constant monitoring of the soil that's heaped over the spears to prevent them being exposed to sunlight: If it's too hot, too cold, too wet, dry, or hard, the growth of the spears is affected.

The day before, in the lively student city of Münster, I'd seen signs of the city's culinary history everywhere, from plaques among cobblestones marking the old salt trading route, to white asparagus carved into the stone facade of a private mansion. Münster's old town, almost completely destroyed in World War II, was rebuilt in its prewar style, and the buildings along the Prinzipalmarkt—tall, pale, and narrow with acutely angled roofs—look not unlike a row of white asparagus tips themselves.

The city's weekly market, a maze of trucks and stands shaded by colorful awnings, takes place in a large, leafy square by the cathedral. The fresh produce stands are currently dominated by baskets of jewel-red strawberries and stacks of bright white asparagus. The annual harvest is a source of great local pride.

It's a short walk from the marketplace to Altes Gasthaus Leve, a traditional German restaurant that's been in the same family for three generations. Some of its customers have been eating at Leve for more than 50 years. Nothing here goes to waste. Peelings are used to make a delicate creamy soup; broken spears are added to stews. And they've been buying their asparagus from the same farm for more than 20 years.

With a backdrop of wood-paneled walls and hand-painted tiles; a tall, flickering candle; and a glass of honey-colored Mosel Riesling, my lunch could be a Dutch Golden Age painting. The raft of white asparagus—straight and meticulously aligned—shares the plate with waxy, yellow new potatoes and a crumpled heap of wafer-thin, dark pink Westphalian ham.

This is the best of the best local produce, prepared and cooked very simply, and I suddenly feel terribly spoiled. The waitress puts down two stainless steel sauce boats next to my plate. One is filled with a bright yellow hollandaise so thick it wobbles, the other with a pool of glossy melted butter.

Over the course of my three days here, I try white asparagus several ways. There's the soup, garnished with chives. I eat it grilled, served with poached quails' eggs and dots of bright green moss mayonnaise. But it's the potatoes and ham that I keep thinking about: It's an old-fashioned dish, yet it doesn't feel outdated.

White asparagus, I've learned, represents what's important to many people in Münsterland—a deep pride in their regional produce and respect for hard work, a love of quality ingredients prepared simply and without waste, and an appreciation for tradition. Isn't it lucky, I think, that it tastes so good.

—**Christie Dietz** is a food and travel writer who has lived in Wiesbaden, Germany.

On-the-Street Eats

Manila, Philippines

Manila, the capital of the Philippines, is the most densely populated city on Earth, with more than 100,000 people jostling for space in each square mile. In this bustling metropolis, residents on the go need access to quick and easy meals—and street food fits the bill. Spend a weekend devouring a dazzling array of varieties that satisfies every craving, from hot to cold and savory to sweet.

The crowded alleys around Quiapo Market in Manila's old downtown are street food central. Start with *taho*, the blend of silky tofu, caramelized sugar syrup, and sago balls that is a common Filipino breakfast. Then dig into the wealth of *tusok-tusok*, deep-fried skewered meats that range from pork belly to chicken intestine, the local favorite. Munch on *kwek-kwek*, deep-fried quail eggs, and finish with a refreshing dragon fruit smoothie. Feeling bold? Dare to try *balut*, a fertilized duck egg that Filipinos down with salt and vinegar—feathers, beak, and all.

HUB | *Southeast Asia*

Taste the best of Manila's culinary traditions at the city's night markets.

Snails in garlic butter are on the menu at the Wildfoods Festival.

Not for the Squeamish
Wildfoods Festival, Hokitika, New Zealand

Located on the rugged West Coast region of the South Island, one of the most remote and sparsely populated areas of New Zealand, the small town of Hokitika packs a big punch: Every March it challenges adventurous eaters to test their taste buds. The Wildfoods Festival celebrates all that's wonderful and weird and (mostly) edible.

Some 50 stalls offer items to tempt every palate, from West Coast delicacies like whitebait and venison to the festival's more iconic daunting foods. With worm truffles, possum pie, lamb testicles, and live huhu grubs on the menu, this eating experience isn't for the squeamish. The thick, white huhu grubs are the larval form of New Zealand's endemic longhorn huhu beetle. They may wriggle going down, but don't fret: They taste like chicken. Long snacked on by Māori, the grubs reportedly have a flavor of buttery chicken or peanut butter. Walk off any indigestion the next day with a hike along the Hokitika Gorge Track that traverses pools of milky blue.

HUB | *New Zealand*

What the Shell
International Shellfish Festival, Prince Edward Island, Canada

Prince Edward Island may be Canada's smallest province, but it hosts one of the country's biggest festivals. Surrounded by the Gulf of St. Lawrence, the maritime province is renowned for its seafood, and every September the International Shellfish Festival puts on a massive feast starring the island's lobsters, mussels, and Malpeque oysters.

Backed by traditional Irish-Scottish Canadian Maritimes music, the four-day weekend bonanza features culinary demonstrations, fierce cook-offs, and visiting celebrity chefs—plus the world's largest oyster bar. Stop by the Shellfish Pavilion to sample inventive takes like lobster grilled cheese and popcorn mussels. Above all, don't miss the oyster-shucking competitions. "The excitement is intense as the shuckers pry open a dozen oysters in about a minute," says Carol Horne, the festival's sponsorship manager. "If you've ever tried to release an oyster from its gnarly shell, you know that isn't easy!"

There are plenty of variations of potato chowder to sample.

HUB | *Eastern Canada; Northeastern United States*

Spice shops in the bazaar offer pyramids of colorful aromatics.

SUMAC
ΣΟΥΝΑΚ
ΓΙΑ ΣΑΛΑΤΑ
● SUMAK

CURRY
ΚΑΡΗ

CORIANDER
ΚΟΡΥΑΝΤΡΟ

X SPICE
ΚΕΦΤΕΔΕΣ
TE
BAHARI

GARAMMASALA
ΓΙΑ ΚΟΤΟΠΟΥΛΟ
TAVUK BAHARI

PAPRICA
POWDER

MIX PEPPER
ΠΟΠΕΡΙ
ANAM
KARIŞIC

STAR
ANIS

WHITE PE
ΑΣΠΡΟ ΠΙΠ
Beyaz Biber

APPLE TEA
MHA. TEAY

Spice Bazaar
Istanbul, Turkey

Straddling Europe and Asia, Istanbul was once the capital of three great empires—Roman, Byzantine, and Ottoman—and its cuisine reflects its international character. Turkish dishes are a blend of Arabic and Middle Eastern flavors, heavily emphasizing tomatoes, olives, lamb, and spices—a lot of spices.

During a weekend spent exploring the awe-inspiring sites of Istanbul's Old City, including the Hagia Sophia and Blue Mosque, get lost in the city's centuries-old Spice Bazaar, located at the foot of Galata Bridge on the shore of the Golden Horn. Also known as the Egyptian Bazaar (Mısır Çarşısı in Turkish), the market's vaulted lanes are filled with spices heaped into brilliantly colored fragrant domes that you can sniff and even taste. Saffron, curry, and paprika are in abundance here, but don't overlook the essential Turkish seasonings: burgundy-colored sumac, made from the berries of the wild *Rhus coriaria* bush; the smoky red pepper flakes of *pul biber*; and *çörek otu*, black cumin seeds sprinkled atop breads. Satisfy your sweet tooth with the bazaar's mounds of baklava and Turkish delight.

HUB | *Eastern Europe*

Kids collect coffee beans at the Kona Coffee Cultural Festival.

Feel the Buzz

Kona Coffee Cultural Festival, Hawaii Island, Hawaii, U.S.

I n Hawaii, "November is coffee time," says Malia Bolton, co-owner of the Kona Coffee and Tea company. For nearly two centuries, farmers of native Hawaiian and Japanese descent have grown the pungent crop in the Big Island's rich, volcanic soil, and the Kona Coffee Cultural Festival toasts this history of cultivation every year during the harvest season.

Choose your weekend from among 10 days of events. Coffee farms on the island's west coast open their gates so visitors can get a firsthand look at where the beloved morning beverage comes from—even trying their hand at picking their own beans. Sip various blends of Kona coffee, known for its mild flavor profile enlivened by citrus and berry notes, during the Coffee and Art Stroll in the village of Holualoa. While you're enjoying your cup, the farmers will educate you on what makes it so special.

HUB | *Honolulu, Hawaii, U.S.; West Coast United States*

A chef prepares shrimp and grits at Charleston's Husk.

Southern Comfort

Charleston, South Carolina, U.S.

G enteel Charleston knows how to eat well, especially when it comes to soul food. Over two days, dive into area chefs' new takes on iconic southern dishes that are rooted in the city's African-American heritage.

Start with a steaming bowl of shrimp and grits, a local breakfast favorite. Frequently made from heirloom corn, grits come in a rainbow of hues and flavors, from nutty to sweet. In Charleston's historic district, restaurant Millers All Day combines Guinea Flint grits (a once lost strain rediscovered in Africa) with fresh shrimp, country ham, and red-eye gravy. Then chow down at Rodney Scott's Whole Hog BBQ in the North Central neighborhood. Order a platter of spareribs slathered in Scott's special sauce, with potato bread and collard greens on the side. The next day, don't miss *perloo*, a flavorful rice pilaf dish. At the Grocery in Midtown, chef Kevin Johnson mixes Lowcountry seafood into his perloo made with Charleston Gold, a locally grown heritage rice.

HUB | *Southeastern United States*

Ecuadorian Pacari Chocolate produces native flavors that have won international awards.

Chocolate Cravings
Quito, Ecuador

Farmers in Ecuador proudly say they produce "black gold"—not oil, but cacao beans. The small South American country is the world's largest producer of gourmet beans used to make fine chocolate. The confection may even have originated here. Recent archaeological finds have unearthed ceramic pottery dating to 3300 B.C. that contains trace amounts of cocoa, suggesting that cacao beans were being harvested in Ecuador more than 5,000 years ago.

The nation's equatorial location and sharply varying terrain produces beans of intensely different flavors, some more nutty, others with a floral profile of black currants and spice. The recently rediscovered Nacional variety—the oldest and rarest in the world, long thought extinct—is considered to be the finest expression of cacao. Spend a weekend sampling it and other bean varietals during the Salón de Chocolate, which hosts tastings and workshops on Latin American chocolate every June in Quito. Then stock up on organic bars produced by homegrown Ecuadorian brands Pacari and Kallari to take home.

HUB | *Guayaquil, Ecuador; Cali, Colombia*

Montréal-style bagels are one of the "big three" on Spade & Palacio's tours of the city.

Food Tours

A weekend may not feel like enough time to capture the taste of a place, but on these tours, you'll be able to sample from the best eateries in town.

1. BREW-ED CRAFT BEER TOUR, ASHEVILLE, NORTH CAROLINA, U.S.

There are more than 25 breweries in this small mountain town, so sip only at the best on a walking tour guided by Certified Cicerones (internationally recognized beer experts) to the city's small-batch brewers. Tastings along the tour include everything from IPAs to barrel-aged sours.

2. VANCOUVER FOODIE TOURS, VANCOUVER, CANADA

Choose between a tour of Vancouver's historic restaurant district (the Gastronomic Gastown Tour), the city's famous public market (Granville Island Market Tour), or an insider's guide to world-class Chinese cuisine (the Authentic Asian Eats Tour) through this foodie-centric outfitter founded in 2010. Tastings along each tour are included in the ticket price.

3. CULINARY BACKSTREETS, LISBON, PORTUGAL

Founded by American expats, the Song of the Sea walking tour offers a taste of the city's best seafood—found outside the usual tourist spots and far from the city's center. Tours include a visit to the historic port district and city markets.

4. XO TOURS, SAIGON, VIETNAM

Get introduced to the best street food in Vietnam on the back of a motorbike. The first all-female motorbike company in Vietman, XO Tours has been voted one of the top food tours in the world by Forbes. On your tasting adventure, a local guide will zip you through city streets to vendors that usually cater to locals.

5. BERLIN FOOD STORIES, BERLIN, GERMANY

Tour the culinary side of Germany's capital on a half-day adventure that includes doner kebabs from Berlin's thriving Turkish community, as well as staples such as *eisbein* (pickled ham hock) and veal meatballs in cream sauce. You can join one of the monthly open tours (up to 12 people maximum) or book a private, custom tour for the ultimate foodie adventure.

6. A DAY COOKING WITH THE DUCHESS, PALERMO, ITALY

Dive into the unique blend of cultures in Palermo's cuisine—Arab, Jewish, Greek, and Italian—on a tour of Palermo's Mercado del Capo, where you'll find fishmongers, fruit and vegetable traders, and stalls with fresh pasta.

7. UNTOUR, SHANGHAI, CHINA

On this three-hour tour, you'll start with a breakfast of Shanghai's "four heavenly kings" and end with pork-filled soup dumplings and a brownie.

8. OISHII TOKYO FOOD TOURS, TOKYO, JAPAN

There are five stops at sit-down restaurants and almost-full meals at each one on this four-hour tour, which features a hidden food alley called Ebisu Yokocho. Tasty treats include yakitori, sushi, udon noodles, and Japanese ice cream.

9. EATING PRAGUE TOURS, CZECH REPUBLIC

Taste your way through Prague's Old and New Towns on a tour that includes both the traditional (braised beef dumplings in cream) and new (an open-faced sandwich with beetroot and goat cheese) cuisines of this capital city.

10. SPADE & PALACIO TOURS, MONTRÉAL, CANADA

Montréal is a food mecca, and there's no better way to explore it than on a tour of the "big three": poutine, Montréal-style bagels, and smoked meats.

> "YOU COULD SPEND A
> LIFETIME SAMPLING
> MEXICO CITY'S ENDLESS
> ARRAY OF FOOD."

Market Fare

Mexico City, Mexico

There's a common saying in Mexico: *sin maíz, no hay país*—without corn there is no country. Corn was first domesticated in Mexico roughly 10,000 years ago, and there's evidence that people were making tortillas out of corn as early as A.D. 500. The grain is an integral part of the nation's cuisine, along with other ancient ingredients including chili peppers, tomatoes, and beans.

You could spend a lifetime sampling Mexico City's endless array of restaurants, markets, and street stands, but a weekend is the perfect entry point to exploring the central neighborhoods. Start with a street food tour through Cuauhtémoc with Eat Mexico, which hits the best stalls for authentic eats. As always, corn takes a starring role, whether in sweet or savory tamales, freshly steamed in banana leaves; *tlacoyos*, griddled corn patties stuffed with beans or cheese; or the ever present tortillas. Thousands of small family-run *tortillerías* pepper the streets of Mexico City, and you can get a sizzling half-dozen for about 25 cents. In the Colonia Roma neighborhood, organic tortillería Cintli offers a more gourmet version made with heirloom corn.

Try your hand at crafting these flavors yourself with a Casa Jacaranda cooking class. Chefs Beto Estúa and Jorge Fitz begin with a tour of Mercado Medellín, one of the city's most important markets in Colonia Roma. Among its 500 stalls, you can chat with vendors and sample fresh coffee, cheeses, and chilies while gathering ingredients for the cooking lesson at colorful Casa Jacaranda. Underneath the central skylight, grind spices in traditional *molcajetes*, shape and wrap tamales, season tender pork *cochinita pibil*, and roll out your own tortillas to be topped with crumbly cotija cheese, chorizo, and handmade green salsa. The result: a feast to enjoy on the rooftop in the shade of the home's namesake jacaranda tree.

HUB | *Buenavista, Mexico; Houston or El Paso, Texas, U.S.*

LONGANIZA $28 KILO

L-ONG DE LA 3

ilharra DE Prime 42

MANTECA BLANCA $15 KILO

Pressed mince and sausage
are on offer at a stall in
the Merced Market.

Mil restaurant offers contemporary twists on traditional Peruvian ingredients.

Peruvian Palate

Culinary Pioneers Are Perfecting the Flavors of the Sacred Valleys

Generations of travelers have come to Peru's Sacred Valley, which stretches from Cusco northwest to Machu Picchu, to see the intricate stonework the Inca left behind. In their wake fast-food joints and restaurants catering to a Western palate have sprung up. Peruvian farmers have taken to planting white spuds instead of the heirloom potatoes in a rainbow of colors that their ancestors cultivated.

Fried chicken and fries may be delicious, but so is guinea pig. This is what I learned from my first trip to Peru in 2018. Everything I ate in each dirt-floored Quechua kitchen was memorable, from fire-seared duck to heirloom potatoes roasted in a sod *huatia* oven to simple barley soups spiced with ají chilis. Now I was back in the Sacred Valley to get a fuller taste of the Inca's living culinary heritage.

I didn't have to go far for my first stop. The only place in Cusco pinned on my map was Three Monkeys. Plenty of hipster cafés in Cusco can pour a solid shot of pure Peruvian espresso, but I found Three Monkeys closer to the center of town, down the narrow cobblestoned Calley Arequipa.

Three Monkeys sources beans from farmers in the region, one of whom, Dwight Aguilar Masías, won the top two spots in Peru's national Cup of Excellence competition in 2018. A sign on the counter told me that the coffee I was drinking was grown and washed in the nearby mountains by Julian Huamon Turpo.

The Inca were deeply invested in eating well. I realized this while driving past steep, terraced fields on the way to Chinchero. In some places, water still runs through their elaborate, centuries-old irrigation canals and pipes.

Mil is perched on the other side of Moray and surrounded by farms. At Virgilio Martínez's first restaurant, Central, the chef collected ingredients from around Peru and arranged them into courses by elevation. At Mil, Martínez seems to invite guests to travel dusty roads and go into the field with him to explore food, from the Urubamba market, through Maras, and up to the restaurant and beyond.

In the rustic-chic dining room, I sat at a polished table made of variously colored types of wood. Each of the eight courses on the menu transported me from one part of the Andes to another via ingredient-forward dishes. Duck in black quinoa served with blue-green algae and kale chips took me to a high-altitude lake. Frozen granules flavored with *kjolle* brought me to the foot of the glacier where that herb grows. A hot stone, partially hollowed out and packed with clay and topped with four kinds of potatoes, called up the smoky, earthen huatia ovens that Quechua families build for parties.

The menu has real implications for those who live in the area, with the potential to renew market value for traditional crops as well as to introduce new food varieties.

As the final plates were cleared away, I looked out the window toward Moray, marveling at the range of flavors that generations of people had squeezed from the harsh mountain environment.

At the northwestern end of the Sacred Valley, the town of Ollantaytambo juts out over the Urubamba River. My goal: El Albergue Ollantaytambo, the town's oldest hotel, which also houses, in a barn out back, Destilería Andina.

Inside the distillery, the atmosphere was pure experimentation. Honeyed light played off of two small stills and countless bottles, filled with alcohol and herbs, that lined every shelf and packed every corner. Andina produces *cañazo*, a traditional Peruvian *rhum agricole*, a rum made from sugarcane juice rather than molasses. It is rapidly disappearing from home stills in the mountains as international spirits flood the market.

That night, I stopped at Chuncho on Ollantaytambo's main square. The server brought out a tray with finger foods that looked like the snacks farmers eat in the fields around town: massive boiled corn kernels, fava beans, salty cheese, alpaca *charky* (jerky). Next to arrive was a hearty but complex pumpkin soup with spicy *rocoto* peppers.

Chuncho means "native" or "wild" in Quechua, and the restaurant aims to serve purely traditional dishes. Chef Josefina Rimach, who grew up in a subsistence farming village a short hike from Ollantaytambo, came out of the kitchen smiling, with a platter of small dishes including roast lamb and guinea pig.

Virgilio Martínez's restaurant may be the best known for leading the charge of novo-Andean cuisine in the valley, but I realized that Chuncho is the next wave. The recipes haven't been honed in Michelin-starred kitchens, but passed down through generations and plated simply and beautifully—uniquely Peruvian food made by locals meant for their neighbors, but enjoyed by their visitors as well.

—**Alec Jacobson** is a National Geographic Explorer and photojournalist based in Colorado.

Champagne bottles are stored in an underground cellar.

The One & Only
Champagne, France

In any other place, it's called sparkling wine, but the tiny bubbles that stream up from stemmed glasses in this northeastern French province are the real deal. Just an hour and 45 minutes by train from Paris, Champagne warrants at least a weekend to wander through the region's hillsides, houses, and cellars, collectively named a UNESCO World Heritage site in 2015. Though not all of the 260 houses can be toured, you'll find enough to keep your cheeks rosy by basing yourself in Reims. The impressive cellars and production lines at outfits such as Maison de Champagne Taittinger, Maison de Champagne Charles Mignon, and Veuve Clicquot offer tours and tastings. That's not all: The region's history is as effervescent as its wine. Some of the houses' subterranean cellars are reformatted chalk quarries (*crayères*) that were dug during the Roman era and served as impromptu bomb shelters during World War I.

HUB | *Paris, France*

The stained-glass ceiling at Pottsville Breweries is historic.

A Classic Lager
Pottsville, Pennsylvania, U.S.

Some 82 craft breweries in and around the Philadelphia area make it the perfect city to grab a pint. Innovation here is high and competition is fierce. But true American beer aficionados' bucket lists aren't complete without a pilgrimage to the working-class town of Pottsville, some 95 miles (153 km) to the northwest—home to America's oldest brewery. Six generations of the family-owned company have been crafting no-frills lagers and seasonal specialties since its German immigrant namesake, David G. Yuengling, settled in the coal mining town in 1829. Yuengling & Son moved into its current redbrick brewery in 1831, weathering Prohibition by brewing low-alcohol near beer and opening an adjacent dairy creamery. Free tours explore chilly subterranean tunnels, hand dug by workers to cool casks before the advent of commercial refrigeration in the mid- to late 1800s. Don't forget to look up: The colorful stained-glass ceiling is as remarkable as this beer's story.

HUB | *Mid-Atlantic United States*

In Périgord, find opportunity to hunt for—and taste—the town's beloved truffles.

On the Hunt

Périgord, France

It's the ultimate treasure hunt: searching for the elusive, deeply aromatic, and highly valuable black truffle. The subterranean fungi grow at the base of oak and hazelnut trees in the Périgord region, an hour's drive from Bordeaux in southwest France. Overlying the Dordogne Valley, the region is renowned for its gastronomy, producing sumptuous foie gras, Bergerac and Monbazillac wines, and origin-protected walnuts, along with the black truffles.

The truffles mature and are ready for harvest from December to February (with the peak in January), so you have an ample choice of weekends to join in the hunt yourself. Truffle experts from farms guide expeditions that are open to visitors. Tramp alongside *les trufficulteurs* (truffle farmers) through misty forests as specially trained dogs and pigs sniff out the delectable mushrooms. Their pungent, earthy aroma is the sign of an exceptional truffle. In Sorges, you can also walk the nearly 2-mile (3 km) Sentier des Truffières (Truffle Discovery Trail) that winds through several truffle farms, some of them more than 100 years old.

HUB | *Toulouse, France*

"VISIT MAJOR TEQUILA
DISTILLERIES AND SMALLER
RAICILLA OUTFITS."

Traditional Libation

Jalisco, Mexico

I t's no surprise which alcoholic beverage dominates the tiny Mexican town of Tequila—it gave the world-renowned spirit its name. What is surprising? The same region boasts another libation, more internationally obscure—also made from agave—that may actually be older and more traditionally beloved: raicilla.

In order to evade Spanish colonial taxes when fees were levied against agave spirits to buoy imported liquor sales in the 1700s, raicilla went underground. It remained there even after *mezcal de tequila* emerged from the shadows to become a billion-dollar global industry. Nicknamed "Mexican moonshine" and "Mexico's native gin," and cousin of Oaxaca's roasted agave mezcal, raicilla has for centuries been made in secretive bootleg-style *tabernas* using closely guarded family recipes. It recently garnered international attention only when the first bottles legally imported to the United States arrived in 2014.

A long weekend visit to the area around the legendary Jalisco town of Tequila is enough time—if you're temperate with your tastings—to couple visits to major tequila distilleries and smaller raicilla outfits. In Tequila, hire a guide or take an on-site tour—like those at La Rojeña Distillery, founded in 1758 and makers of the Jose Cuervo brand, or the newer family-run La Alteña—to learn about the tequila production process, as well as how to taste subtle notes across varietals. Casa Sauza, another major distillery, offers the chance to plant your own spiky blue agave plant and taste spirits right from the barrel.

Raicilla is king in the Sierra Madre towns between Tequila and the coastal resort town of Puerto Vallarta. A two-hour drive inland from Puerto Vallarta, charming Mascota makes a good headquarters. It is home to master *tabernero* Don Ruben Peña, maker of Raicilla Sierra for La Venenosa, as well as the Estancia Distillery, a raicilla exporter. If you can, plan your visit for early December when the Raicilla Festival hosts cocktail contests, tastings, folk dancing, and more.

A *jimador* (agave worker) cuts the leaves off the heart of a blue agave plant.

Weekend Wine Down
Stellenbosch, South Africa

If a luxurious weekend biking past historic manor houses and sipping on fine wine in idyllic, sun-drenched vineyards sounds up your alley, Stellenbosch has you covered. This mountain-backed wine region less than an hour from Cape Town has been perfecting its trade since it was settled by French Huguenots in the 1600s. Luxury tour operator &Beyond will navigate you through the history and the region's gorgeous scenery via its full-day 12-mile (20 km) cycling tour. Savor a four-course lunch and wine pairing in the jaw-dropping Clos Malverne dining room, and swirl countless glasses of Chenin Blanc and the uniquely South African Pinotage. Overnight in the Lanzerac Wine Estate's regal rooms (some with private pools and gardens), and don't forget to take in the included cellar tour and wine tasting or the spa's vineyard views. Meet up with a local Cape Wine Master in the morning for a day of selective tastings and industry insights.

HUB | *Cape Town, South Africa*

Look out over the Stellenbosch mountains from the Tokara Wine Estate.

Cheers at the Oregon Brewers Festival

Center of the Crafts
Portland, Oregon, U.S.

One of America's great beer cities, the wider Portland area is home to 84 craft breweries—enough to try one each week for a year and a half with zero repeats. Rather than rush around the blocks between East Portland and Vernon to compare tasting notes, roll up to the Tom McCall Waterfront Park in late July for Beervana—better known as the Oregon Brewers Festival, one of the longest running craft beer festivals in the United States. Virtually the entire state is on tap here with some 100 breweries represented. Pay for tasting tokens, get a pint glass, then roam about filling it with classic Oregon creativity. Past samples have included guava-infused pale ale, Color Me Kush made from noncannabis flavor sources, a marionberry lavender sour ale, guacamole-inspired lager, a malted milkshake IPA, and a Raspberry Radler whose label reads: "Feel the audible texture of ukuleles playing in the pine forest." No one ever said Portland wasn't weird.

HUB | *Pacific Northwest United States*

Wine on the Water
Traverse City, Michigan, U.S.

The sparkling blue waters and golden sandy shores of Lake Michigan appear almost tropical along this charming lakeside town. Yet cool-climate Traverse City, five hours northwest of Detroit and six hours northeast of Chicago, sits almost exactly halfway between the North Pole and the Equator, a similar latitude to Piedmont and Bordeaux. This up-and-coming midwestern wine region boasts more than 40 wineries and vineyards spread across the Old Mission and Leelanau Peninsulas, where expansive lake and farmland views mingle from modern tasting rooms. Long summer days, a relatively short growing season, lake breezes, and mineral-rich glacial till soils make an interesting terroir for white wine such as Riesling, Chardonnay, and German Gewürztraminer, as well as lighter bodied reds. Area orchards offer inspiration for fruit-flavored wines and ciders, such as Chateau Grand Traverse's cherry wine. Some outlets—like Black Star Farms and Chateau Chantal—offer ice wine, a northerly treat fashioned from grapes harvested after the first freeze.

HUB | *Detroit, Michigan, U.S.; Chicago, Illinois, U.S.*

Grapes are ready for the picking at a vineyard.

The Temple Bar, founded in 1880, is an excellent spot to start a Dublin bar crawl.

Pub Crawl
Dublin, Ireland

World renowned for its drinking scene, rowdy Dublin has perfected the recipe of the pub. While beverage diversity may be limited—the city of Portland boasts more breweries than the entire country of Ireland, and Murphy's Guinness and Harp are omnipresent—drinking establishments are not. Local surveys indicate the city is home to some 750 pubs, which is plenty to fill a weekend. Take in a themed handful on a pub tour. The Dublin Literary Pub Crawl, which starts at Trinity College, includes recitations of Irish writers—James Joyce, Seamus Heaney, and Oscar Wilde among them—while visiting their haunts and discussing the importance of the pub to literature. Musical Pub Crawls, guided by local musicians, combine brew tastings in a harmonious melody with fiddles and traditional Irish folk music. And haunted tours hop pub to pub with chilling tales told while wandering the Medieval Quarter around Dublin Castle and St. Patrick's Cathedral. By day, seek out establishments you may have missed on tour: Brazen Head, built in 1198, and Dawson's Lounge, the self-proclaimed world's smallest pub.

HUB | *Major Western European Cities*

"TO MAKE THE MOST OF
YOUR WEEKEND, LET SOME-
ONE ELSE DO THE DRIVING."

Napa Without Crowds

Paso Robles, California, U.S.

Virtually equidistant from San Francisco and Los Angeles and just inland from the Central Coast, Paso Robles is an easy three-hour drive from either major city. This lesser visited viticultural region has everything you'd want out of a wine-fueled weekend: scenic vineyards, great shopping and local restaurants, delicious wines, and more than 200 wineries— all without the crowds of more popular Napa and Sonoma. *Wine Folly* has called Paso Robles (Paso, for short) "the Wild West of California wine," not only for its origins as a former outpost town founded by Jesse James's uncle, but also for its innovative and boundary-pushing mishmash of varietals. Surrounded by dry uplands and bathed in cool ocean breezes, the region sports some 45 different soil types great for growing grapes such as Zinfandel, Cabernet, and Nebbiolo. And greater San Luis Obispo County boasts nine small-batch distilleries proffering brandy, grappa, gin, vodka, vermouth, and more.

Wineries run the gamut from smaller family affairs like Whalebone Vineyard—named for fossils found in its fields—to J. Lohr, which produces more than a million cases of wine a year.

To make the most of your weekend (and to be safe), let someone else do the driving. The Wine Line, a hop-on, hop-off luxury bus, lets you customize your itinerary from 70 wineries, though you're limited to just one region a day. Choose between the easterly stretch around Highway 46, which has many heavy hitters including Eberle, Le Vigne, and Barr Estate, or take a western route featuring a higher concentration of boutique outfits such as Hope Family Wines, Dark Star Cellars, and the Barton Family Grey Wolf Cellars.

The 16-room equestrian-themed Hotel Cheval, right off the tree-and boutique-lined plaza in downtown Paso, is a fine place to hang your hat. Walk to art galleries and restaurants, then recline in the lush leather library or sit by the outdoor firepit while the s'mores butler whips you up a nostalgic treat.

HUB | *Los Angeles, California, U.S.; San Francisco, California, U.S.*

A chapel stands above vineyards along Highway 46 east of Paso Robles.

Absinthe ingredients like dried wormwood are displayed at La Valote Martin distillery.

MENTHE
piperita

CORIANDRE
Coriandrum sativum

OPE
fficinalis

GRANDE ABSINTHE
Artemisia absinthium

PETITE ABSINTHE
Artemisia Pontica

A Spirited Return

Absinthe Is Being Poured With Panache

As I take a sip, I can't help but think the setting is a little incongruous. I'm not perching on a barstool but standing in a sun-dappled forest at Fontaine à Louis, a spring-fed woodland fountain in the region where absinthe originated, the Swiss Jura. Yann Klauser, head of the local absinthe museum, Maison de l'Absinthe, is adding water from the spring to his own shot. It was at tree-shrouded springs like this, he tells me, that absinthe was covertly sipped during the century-long ban.

I almost expect the police to jump out and arrest us for illicit drinking, but as of 2008 in Switzerland (2011 in France), this is all aboveboard. Nevertheless, absinthe is still a drink that strikes fear into the heart of some spirit lovers. During the heady days of the belle epoque, La Fée Verte (the Green Fairy) acquired a reputation as the mind-bending tipple of choice for van Gogh, Zola, Rimbaud, Toulouse-Lautrec, and a host of other bohemian artists and writers active in Paris. Even in places where it wasn't banned, absinthe has always been something of a daring novelty—an edgy ingredient in cocktails like the Sazerac and Corpse Reviver No. 2 or a flaming shot knocked back by fearless hell-raisers.

But this trip to absinthe's heartland on the French-Swiss border has convinced me that the drink's notoriety is undeserved. Here you find the good stuff: a refreshing spirit distilled with up to 10 botanicals—including aniseed, mint, and lemon balm—to disguise the bitter taste of the key ingredient, wormwood.

With an alcohol content typically ranging from 50 to 60 percent, absinthe isn't for the fainthearted, but in moderation it can be enjoyed just like any other spirit. Traditionally, it's served *à la Parisienne*—an elaborate ritual centered around an absinthe fountain (a large, ornate jar with spigots, resting on a stand). From this, ice-cold water is dripped through a sugar lump perched on a slotted spoon lying on the rim of a glass of absinthe. The moment the water is added, the spirit turns cloudy, like pastis.

My journey begins in Pontarlier, a laid-back town at the foot of the Jura Mountains in eastern France. Its ties with absinthe are strong, and by all accounts the town was once awash with the stuff. By the end of the 19th century, there were 25 distilleries in and around Pontarlier producing absinthe and providing a living for some 3,000 of the town's 8,000-odd inhabitants. Today, at the Pontarlier Museum, a whole floor is given over to the drink.

Over lunch with Fabrice Hérard, who heads up the French part of the Route de l'Absinthe (a Franco-Swiss absinthe tourist route), we tuck into a steak flambéed in the spirit and served in a deliciously aromatic absinthe sauce. As we chat about the approaches of distillers on either side of the border, Hérard says he finds it interesting that the French, for all their reputed rebelliousness, simply accepted the ban, whereas the Swiss—often typecast as rule driven—carried on in secret in Val de Travers. If they hadn't, the recipes and production methods could easily have been lost.

It's too early for a drink, so Klauser shows me around Maison de l'Absinthe. The museum, set in a former judge's office, tells how absinthe never really went away. Its exhibits explore the ingenious methods used to hide the distillation process and the various ways the finished product was concealed.

Back in the museum's bar area, I admire the 28 different brands made by 17 different Swiss distillers—all with labels beautifully adorned with fairies, art nouveau curves, or scenes from historic posters. While most distilleries here create a clear spirit, there are a few brands of green absinthe. "The green color comes from chlorophyll in the nettle or mint, or hyssop, or even spinach, but it's very difficult to get the balance and the color right," explains Klauser.

In the next village, Boveresse, Philippe Martin runs his family's once clandestine distillery and grew up with absinthe ever present. Martin's distillery, La Valote Martin, is one of very few that oversees the whole process, from growing the plants to drying them to using them in the spirit. Set in a large chalet building, his copper stills take pride of place in one of the huge fireplaces. In the walled garden, the gray-flowered wormwood plants grow alongside the other vital herbs and flowers.

We finish with a tasting in the small bar area. As I'm driving, I take only a sip, but the flavor is refreshing, the tartness of the aniseed softened by a gentle blend of other botanicals.

Later, I meet Klauser back at Maison de l'Absinthe and we drive to a trail in the woods that leads to one of the town's former illicit drinking dens. Fifteen minutes later, we arrive at the spring, top up our glasses of absinthe, and raise a toast. *"Santé!"* we say—good health. After this foray into the Green Fairy's heartland, I know both my santé, and sanity, are safe.

—**Carolyn Boyd** is a travel writer, journalist, and editor who often writes about French fare.

A worker moves a barrel of rum at Mount Gay Distilleries.

A Historic Rum(ble)

Barbados

The tropical base for mojitos and mai tais has dreamy origins—the breezy sugar plantations of the Caribbean. Though rum's history is complicated, the small island nation of Barbados harbors a long legacy with the drink as well as three tourable distilleries and a working sugar plantation. Wander through the production process of the world's oldest rum maker, Mount Gay Distilleries (est. 1703), to see its stills, molasses house, fermentation house, and more, before sipping samples of the same amber product that buoyed sailors across the seven seas. At St. Nicholas Abbey in the northern parish of St. Peter, visitors can see two of just three remaining original Jacobean mansions in the Caribbean, which lord over tropical gardens and a sugar plantation. The on-site distillery employs bourbon oak casks to infuse a signature spicy flavor. The smaller Foursquare Rum Distillery allows visitors to overlook its modern fermentation room, built inside an old sugar factory; the industrial, beachside West Indies Rum Distillery also runs tours.

HUB | *Southeastern United States*

Walk through the ornate entrance to the Orval Abbey ruins.

Belgian Beer Route

Le Roeulx to Mariembourg, Belgium

Taste coveted Belgian sour ales right from the source on a tour through Belgium's forested Ardennes region near the country's border with France. Here, six serene countryside Trappist monasteries, which have been brewing beer for centuries, mingle short distances from modern gastropubs and historic family breweries. In Le Roeulx, the fifth-generation family-owned St. Feuillien microbrewery churns out tripels, saison, brown ales, and more. Farther south, the Silenrieux Brewery has white and blonde ales, as well as a buckwheat-based brew. Stop by Scourmont Abbey for authentic Trappist ales and cheeses in Chimay; there's a seven-room inn nearby for overnights. Though you cannot tour the brewery, you can walk through other parts of the abbey and purchase the monks' handiwork on site. Just outside the medieval fortified town of Mariembourg, Brasserie des Fagnes, a modern gastropub, runs tours of its productions, which include blonde and brown ales, as well as sour ales made with local woodland berries.

HUB | *Brussels, Belgium*

The Land of Pisco

Lima, Peru

Peru's national drink is pisco, and Lima is awash in it. First fashioned here in the 1600s, the brandy-like wine distillate—which some say has bright or citrus undertones—was enjoyed for centuries, lost for decades, and only recently restored to star status. Since 1999, the first Saturday in February is National Pisco Day. To dive in, start at the Museo del Pisco, an educational cocktail bar founded by three *pisqueros* (pisco fanatics). Choose a tasting flight, buy a bottle, or learn pisco sour mixology—try it infused with passion fruit, chili, or *muña* (a local mint-like herb). Then head to the 1924 Gran Hotel Bolivar, off the Plaza San Martín, to try its famous pisco sours once sipped by Hemingway and Faulkner. Farther afield in Mira Flores, sample chilcano cocktails at late-night hot spot Mayata. Round out your weekend with a day trip to learn about the pisco-making process at a Mala Valley vineyard and distillery.

HUB | *Cusco, Peru*

The pisco sour is the traditional drink of Lima.

"PUNCHY, BOLD REDS AND THE REVIVAL OF CARMÉNÈRE GRAPES"

Grape Stars

Colchagua Valley Wineries, Chile

Just two hours south of Santiago, the Colchagua Valley has been making wine since Jesuit missionaries planted vines in the mid-1500s. With the town of Santa Cruz as a base, while away hours with vineyard picnics, sleepy countryside drives, and, of course, winery tours where you can learn about the time-tested and innovative techniques that have made this region renowned.

Colchagua is known for its punchy, bold reds—think hints of tobacco and cherry—and for the revival of Carménère grapes, all but extinct in their native Bordeaux. Some of the deepest and darkest red wine grapes, Carménère was used in blends for centuries before disease killed off most French vines in the mid-1800s. It wasn't until 1994 that DNA testing of Chilean Merlot vines proved the varietal had been thriving in Chile all along. Here, the grape is a star.

Be sure to try Viña Lapostolle's version in its underground tasting room, which plunges six stories via a spiral ramp—a massive central pendulum draws circles in a patch of sand below—and keeps wines chilled naturally. The winery was founded by the great-granddaughter of the maker of Grand Marnier, and unique bottles of the liquor are sold in the gift shop. Santa Cruz Winery features a cable car to the top of Chamán hill for vineyard views. Things get even more interesting at Montes, where, since 2004, its Purple Angel Carménère has received heavenly treatment: The harmonies of chanting monks are played on loop to aging barrels. The music is said to imbue the wines with a unique flavor thanks to the constant micro-ripples created by sound waves. For great wine without theatrics, don't miss the Cabernet Franc and Petit Verdot blends at Laura Hartwig, a smaller boutique winery.

Rental cars or hired drivers are recommended for visiting wineries, which can be some distance apart. Many of the wineries require advance bookings, and organized tours streamline this process. Luxury outfitter UPSCAPE organizes bespoke experiences like bike rides through vineyards and the chance to blend your own wine.

HUB | *Santiago, Chile*

A cable car hovers above the Colchagua Valley vineyards.

Vineyards surround
the village of Epesses,
overlooking Lake Geneva.

Vineyards & Wineries

Cheers to the best whites, reds, rosés, and bubblies to be found
in the world's most beautiful vineyards and wineries.

1. LAVAUX VINEYARDS, SWITZERLAND

This UNESCO World Heritage site sits along the shores of Lake Geneva and can be traced back to the 11th century. Its terraced vineyards can be accessed by ferry, car, or hiking trail—a 20-mile (32 km) footpath takes you from Lausanne-Ouchy to Chillon Castle, with information panels on the local viticulture along the route.

2. BODEGA GARZÓN, URUGUAY

Just north of Punta del Este, this relative newcomer features a luxury hotel along with state-of-the-art wine. Named the 2018 New World Winery of the Year by *Wine Enthusiast*, this spot has plenty to offer oenophiles, including cooking classes—with wine pairings, of course.

3. CLOS APALTA WINERY, CHILE

Home to one of the world's most iconic red wines, this stunning six-level family-owned winery in a century-old vineyard produces the delicious Carménère/Cabernet Sauvignon–based blend. Stay at the private residence—an elegant complex with modern details and views of the Apalta vineyards—for the ultimate experience.

4. CHÂTEAU MARGAUX, FRANCE

Found in the Bordeaux region of France, this is one of the oldest châteaus in the Médoc, tracing its roots to the 16th century. A bottle of its wine from Thomas Jefferson's private cellar, a 1787 vintage, is valued at $500,000.

5. SCHLOSS JOHANNIS-BERG, GERMANY

This winery was the first estate to produce the sweet Rieslings that have become coveted around the world today. The winery has a remarkable 1,000-year-history—and is the birthplace of late-harvest wine—but continues to modernize its winemaking.

6. KIR-YIANNI, GREECE

There's a 200-year-old Ottoman watchtower on the property, but this vineyard can also boast some of Greece's best "noble" red, Xinomavro.

7. CREATION WINES, SOUTH AFRICA

Serving top-notch South African Pinot Noir and Chardonnay, this waterfront estate also offers a seven-course food menu with wine pairings at its popular on-site restaurant.

8. MISSION HILL FAMILY ESTATE, CANADA

Overlooking Lake Okanagan, this British Columbia spot features mission-style architecture, an artwork-adorned wine cellar, and the lakeside Terrace restaurant. Named "Winery of the Year" at the 2019 WineAlign National Wine Awards of Canada, this estate also offers tours and wine tastings.

9. CHATEAU MONTELENA, CALIFORNIA, U.S.

One of Napa Valley's finest, Chateau Montelena is one of the oldest wineries in the valley. It offers regular tours, tastings, and cellar door sales in its Gothic-style castle. The views are just as delicious as the wine, overlooking a Chinese garden, lakes, and the estate's vineyards that stretch out to Mount Saint Helena. Walk-ins are welcome at the bar for tastings, but reservations are required for groups of eight or more.

10. CHARD FARM WINERY, NEW ZEALAND

New Zealand is a mecca for wine, and this picturesque winery fits in for good reason. The family-run estate allows experimentation and interesting blends into its tasting room, and it doesn't enter any of its bottles into competitions.

"SELF-GUIDED BEER TOURS
ALLOW YOU TO LINGER IN
POPULAR SPOTS."

Traditional Brews

Bamberg, Bavaria, Germany

Beyond the beer houses of Munich sits the Bavarian town of Bamberg. A UNESCO World Heritage site settled since the 10th century makes a historic base for exploring the region's long-standing brewing tradition.

Bamberg boasts 11 breweries and more than 50 styles of beer within its 21-square-mile (55 sq km) city limits (more than 60 other breweries inhabit the immediate countryside).

Many of the venerable establishments—some dating as far back as the 1500s and others opened in the past 15 years—offer outdoor beer gardens atop their subterranean cellars.

If you prefer some guidance in navigating the robust offerings, the BierSchmecker Tour sold through Bamberg Tourism can recommend eight breweries and includes vouchers to try half-liter specialties at four of them. The tour also gets you a commemorative stein and brochure listing all area breweries, so you can continue tasting.

True zythophiles shouldn't miss the Franconian Brewers Museum on the city's west side. Exhibition space carved from a former 11th-century Benedictine monastery brewery explains various aspects of the beer-making process, and an on-site education center offers tasting lessons and seminars.

Once you have your bearings, self-guided beer tours allow you to linger in popular spots like Schlenkerla (sample its Hefeweizen or try the city's renowned smoky Rauchbier here) and lively Mahrs Bräu with its award-winning Heller Bock. In others, you may opt to stop in the *schwemm*—a corridor where you can grab a quick taste without waiting for a seat or buy beer to go. The best part? As you wander, you'll experience the riverside city's well-preserved medieval layout and take in baroque buildings, half-timbered houses, and the impressive, skyline-dominating four-spired Roman Catholic imperial cathedral.

HUB | *Munich or Frankfurt, Germany*

Beer tasters look into their glasses to discern the subtle differences in their brews.

Diners sit in the lemon tree garden of a local restaurant.

"IF YOU CAN SEIZE JUST ONE
TRUE CAPRESE MOMENT,
TASTE CAPRI YOURSELF WITH
A SIP OF ISLAND-MADE
LIMONCELLO."

PERSPECTIVE

Divine Drinks Capri

Lemon-Infused Spirits Are the Life Force of This Island's Glamour

On the Italian island of Capri, lemons pendulous with juice dangle from white-painted garden pergolas. Here the air tastes of salt from the Tyrrhenian Sea, and the softball-size fruit, thick-skinned and nubbly, emits an intoxicating perfume. Glimmering in the sun, the Sorrento lemons (specific to the southwestern region of Italy) infuse Capri, a longtime jet-setters' retreat, with an organic glamour. From these lemons, islanders concoct their famous *limoncello*—a more-potent-than-it-tastes, sweet-as-honey liqueur savored in the evening after a meal or tippled at dusk in the swank, alfresco cafés that line Capri Town's piazza.

Not everybody visits Capri in Gucci shoes. A trio of sneaker-wearing, khaki-clad hikers come across a gardener, who holds out slices of a lemon from his tree. Also underdressed by island standards, the gardener has cut a lemon, sliced it into pinwheels, and offers each trekker a piece to try.

When they hesitate, he grabs a section and pops it into his own mouth—skin and all. They follow his lead, as he nods approvingly. Below them, down a 90-degree precipice, a sapphire sea swirls like a van Gogh night sky.

"You have just tasted Capri," he says, before presenting each walker with a neon yellow fruit.

Sharing Protected Geographical Indication status with the Sorrentine Peninsula for its lemons, Capri, located a 30-minute ferry ride off the Amalfi coast, figures prominently in the legendary provenance of limoncello.

Some say shepherds first nipped the lemon-infused spirit to ward off illness. And at some point, locals began making their own lemony libation, each according to closely guarded family recipes. Today, in shops across the island, bottles of the digestif are sold as a veritable elixir of Amalfi sunshine.

Former home to shepherds, Greek gadabouts, Roman emperors, Russian émigrés, and 20th-century artists, Capri has also been the playground of untold numbers of celebrities, from Elton John to Sophia Loren to Giorgio Armani. But it's more than fast boats and flutes of prosecco.

Anyone can explore the island's intensely blue lagoons, caves full of lore, and grand villas. Olives and grapes grow beside lemons, as do herbs, such as rosemary and basil. In early summer, butter-colored broom gives the terrain a glow, and lavender-hued bougainvillea punctuates the isle's uncanny rose-colored light.

On a seaworthy day, cruise over to the Blue Grotto in an azure-painted *gozzo*, a traditional wooden fisherman's boat. Watch as the water transforms from cobalt to tinsel-silvery.

But if you can seize just one true Caprese moment, taste Capri yourself with a sip of island-made limoncello. You can learn to make the spirit with local outfitters who specialize in culinary tours, such as Capri Time.

After all, when Capri offers you lemons, shouldn't you make limoncello?

—**Becca Hensley** is an award-winning travel and lifestyle writer, poet, and essayist based in Austin, Texas.

Sake bottles from Homare Sake Brewery Company

Sake to Me

Fukushima, Tohoku Region, Japan

Head off the beaten path to northeast Japan's Tohoku region in search of the perfect sake. Breweries in this temperate landscape of beech forest, marshlands, and mountain-backed lakes craft some of the country's winningest rice wine. Its cold winter weather is key; that's when sake is brewed to ensure slower fermentation. Base your weekend in the mountainous area of Fukushima Prefecture, with its prized sake rice farms and dozens of area breweries. Start at the Daishichi Sake Brewery, where tours in English outline its traditional kimoto rice sorting and fermenting techniques said to enhance the flavor profile and eschewed by other breweries in favor of more modern processes. Don't miss the eight-generation family-owned Suehiro Sake Brewery, one of the largest in the region. Try their award-winning sake in the on-site tasting room; the brewery is the official supplier for an important shrine, as well as several sumo and kabuki events. It's all just over an hour from Tokyo by bullet train.

HUB | *Tokyo, Japan*

Local Brews

Hanoi, Vietnam

Wash down pungent local cuisine on steamy days with *bia hoi*, some of the world's cheapest draft beer. Bia hoi, or "fresh beer," is a pilsner-style ale made without additives or preservatives. Said to have been a gift from Czech brewers, the local brew is crafted daily by hundreds of small-batch brewers around Hanoi.

Though you'll find beer corners throughout Hanoi, both the Old Quarter intersection of Ta Hien and Luong Ngoc Quyen Streets nicknamed "beer junction" and the crossing of Nha Hoa and Duong Thanh in the west Old Quarter are among the more popular places to post up for the evening. As the sun sets, stools and matching polypropylene tables emerge from ramshackle restaurants to encroach on the pavement. Nab your perch and take turns foraging for street food such as *bánh cam* (mung bean–filled fried sesame balls), roast duck, and dried squid sold from passing mobile carts. As the evening progresses, a bona fide block party sprawls into the streets blocking the passage of traffic.

Dine on street food and *bia hoi* in the Old Quarter "beer junction."

HUB | *Southeast Asia*

The terraced vineyards of the Douro Valley are breathtaking to behold.

Port of Ports

Douro Valley, Portugal

The picturesque seaside city of Porto is the gateway to the Douro Valley, the UNESCO-listed region that brought the world rich, fortified port wine. With a weekend, follow the Douro River inland through a landscape of steep terraced vineyards—river cruises and trains traverse the route regularly—making Peso da Régua your home base. Get your bearings in the modern Douro Museum with its on-site wine bar and exhibits detailing regional wine culture. On the opposite bank of the river, Quinta da Pacheca pours tastings of its tawny, ruby, white, and pink ports and affords the opportunity to truly immerse yourself in the spirit of port by overnighting in a massive decked-out wine barrel. The next day rise and wander to several area vineyards—such as Quinta da Roeda, known for wood-aged reserves and tawnies; Quinta do Crasto with gorgeous riverside views; and Quinta do Seixo offering vineyard picnics.

HUB | *Lisbon, Portugal; Madrid, Spain*

Select a craft cocktail in the hip Sovereign Remedies bar.

Happily Ever Asheville

Artists, Musicians, and Makers Brew Up Urban Magic

A witch, an herbalist, and a ghostbuster walk into a bar The sentence could jump-start a joke anywhere in the United States. In Asheville, North Carolina, it's just another happy hour. I'm at Sovereign Remedies, an elegantly high-windowed lounge on North Market Street, where I find myself in a conversation with witch Byron Ballard, herbalist Maia Toll, and haunted-tours guide Joshua P. Warren, who are downing cocktails mixed with sarsaparilla, milk thistle, and evening primrose.

Drive-by magic, I soon learn, is a thing in Asheville. Blithe spirits (drinkable and thinkable) thrive in this nontraditional city of 88,512 that spoons with the southern Appalachian Mountains in ancient Cherokee lands drained by the French Broad River. Asheville already is high on the list of smart cities, with walkable neighborhoods, business start-ups, and a welcoming, friendly vibe that on Fridays at dusk is audible to all: Downtown reverberates with the drumming of its citizenry who gather at Pritchard Park to welcome the weekend with a rhythmic pound and stomp.

The drums herald a city that is melding new energies with hallowed traditions. Asheville embraces solar power and potter's wheels, new age crystals and Roycroft rocking chairs, zip-lining and contra dancing. The air is scented with hops, roasting coffee, barbecued pork, and ambition, depending on what artisans are firing up along the South Slope, a reviving neighborhood of old brick warehouses. Asheville supports an equally spirited music scene, pumping out tunes by funk practitioners, bluegrass fiddlers, and Moog synthesizers.

I stand on the downtown sidewalk staring up at what looks to be a Jazz Age Hogwarts: the 13-story Jackson Building, built in 1924 and topped with decorative gargoyles. It is just one of the architectural pearls I'm discovering on a walking tour with Asheville historian Kevan Frazier as we work off the biscuits with bacon gravy we devoured at Early Girl, a local restaurant.

Asheville was always a town of dreamers, builders, and doers. Still is.

"Something's going on here seven days a week," Scott Woody asserts while touring me through the Isis Music Hall, a former movie theater built in the 1930s on Hayword Street in West Asheville and named for the Egyptian goddess. Other Asheville performance venues such as the Orange Peel and the Grey Eagle are equally popular with patrons.

Asheville's cultural energy now is extending to the visual and material arts. Sometimes dubbed "Santa Fe East," the town teems with painters, ceramists, textile artists, jewelers, and graphic designers. Work by that last group is on display at the Center for Craft, and at Horse + Hero, where posters by local artists hang for sale.

The afternoon I visit the River Arts District, its studios, kilns, and forges are busy. Everyone looks like an artist, but the tourists are the ones with shopping bags. There's not a chain store to be seen. Asheville wouldn't have it any other way.

Local also is the clarion call for Asheville's foodies. The city prizes both southern comfort—OWL Bakery's cardamom buns with lemon glaze, Buxton Hall Barbecue's buttermilk fried chicken sandwiches—and international flair: "salt & pepper" tofu at Gan Shan West, Bollywoody tandoori dishes at the exuberant Indian restaurant Chai Pani. It also likes foods found in the wild. My dinner at Nightbell (now closed, but you can visit sister restaurant Curate), four-star chef Katie Button's restaurant, is a realm of the senses all its own and a world away from Asheville's shamanic men's circles, golf resorts, and yoga studios.

One morning I hike up a mountain trail just 30 minutes from downtown via the Blue Ridge Parkway, fingering the waxy, jade-hued leaves of rhododendrons as they flap against my hands. Soon I am drawn to the murmur-roar of a coursing stream swollen with recent rain. When I reach it, I can taste the cold tang of the waterfall's spray as it shoots over the smooth rocks into crystalline pools.

It's a transcendent moment. And that may be Asheville's entire point. Witches and herbalists can concoct all they want, but spirits here don't need conjuring. They've already materialized. Creative, natural, or communal, Asheville's energy is as present as the white water rushing below my feet.

—**Andrew Nelson** is an award-winning writer based in Washington, D.C.

"TAKE SOME TIME TO FIND
YOUR FAVORITE ALONG
THE OFFICIAL KENTUCKY
BOURBON TRAIL."

The Bourbon Trail

Louisville to Lebanon, Kentucky, U.S.

This ain't no moonshine. Fine Kentucky bourbon has been a point of national and international pride since the late 1780s when a Baptist minister reportedly (and ironically) transformed the local corn-based hooch by aging it in a charred oak barrel. Take some time to find your favorite along part of the Kentucky Distillers Association's official Kentucky Bourbon Trail, which charts an epic road trip course through Bluegrass Country between Owensboro and Lexington.

American whiskey, or bourbon, has a few tweaks to its European counterpart. It's made by fermenting a mix of grist that is at least 51 percent corn—a grain endemic to the Americas—and its fermenting barrels must be oak, new, and charred to lend characteristic smokiness. Further, all Kentucky bourbon is stored for at least four years in U.S.-bonded warehouses before it can be released, to guarantee its authenticity.

Given the long driving distances, it would take a week-plus to complete the 36-stop, state-spanning dueling signature bourbon and craft distillery trails. But you can fill a solid weekend running just the 65-mile (105 km) stretch between Louisville and the Limestone Branch Distillery outside Lebanon, where you'll still have your pick from a diverse assortment of 15 stops.

Choose from six urban distilleries along a short stretch of the Ohio River in downtown Louisville, including Old Forester, bourbon of choice for the Churchill Downs mint julep, whose tours navigate their production process and include tastings. From there, check out Peerless Distillery's rye whiskey or head south to Jim Beam's American Stillhouse in Clermont, where the on-site Fred's Smokehouse is a great BBQ lunch stop. It's a short detour to craft distillery Boundary Oak in Radcliff before an overnight in Elizabethtown. Get up, and do it all again, choosing from Bardstown's three traditional and two craft distilleries, before heading 25 miles (41 km) south to Maker's Mark and Limestone Branch and completing your loop back to Louisville.

HUB | *Southeastern or Midwestern United States*

A Maker's Mark tasting is ready at the distillery.

Gin Crazy

London, England

London's "gin craze" in the early 18th century made production of the juniper berry distillation boom. Today, it's experiencing a second wind as modern mixologists shake countless locally made cocktails using gin from the city's 24 distilleries. To immerse yourself in the full gin experience, stay in one of three on-site rooms at The Distillery. The building's 400-liter copper pot still is fully functioning and produces its branded Portobello Road Gin. There is also an on-site gin bar with 100 options (and many mixers) and a "Ginstitute," where "Ginstructors" help you navigate your favorite botanical flavors to create your own bespoke bottle of blended gin. If you still aren't sated, tour the iconic Beefeater Distillery across the Thames in Kennington. Or head west to Chiswick for a taste of the lauded 10-botanical artisinal small-batch gin at relative newcomer Sipsmith (opened in 2009, it was the first new copper pot distillery to open in 200 years). You can also try the distillery's canned gin and tonics.

> "TODAY, IT'S EXPERIENCING A SECOND WIND AS MODERN MIXOLOGISTS SHAKE COUNTLESS LOCALLY MADE COCKTAILS USING GIN FROM THE CITY'S 24 DISTILLERIES."

HUB | *Major Western European Cities*

Grab a gin-focused cocktail at The Distillery, the U.K.'s first gin-themed boutique hotel and distillery.

There are plenty of fine wines to sample from the magnificent vineyards in McLaren Vale township.

Coming of Age
Southeastern South Australia, Australia

Head down under to the South Australian city of Adelaide, whose outskirts are home to 18 distinctive wine regions, including some of the best in the country. From this urban base, you'll have access to both city wine culture and some 200 cellar doors (local lingo for tasting rooms) less than an hour's drive into popular wine regions like Adelaide Hills and Eden Valley. In the city, take a master class at the National Wine Center of Australia, sip some of Cantina Social's straight-from-the-barrel selections, and grab a bottle and some grub from the Adelaide Central Market—one of the largest produce markets in the Southern Hemisphere. In the countryside beyond, tour small, family-owned Kellermeister Wines in the Barossa Valley, whose punchy Australian Syrah (Shiraz) has won gold medals in international tasting competitions. Or spend time sampling wines in the five-story geometric d'Arenberg Cube in McLaren Vale overlooking Mourvèdre vines.

HUB | *Adelaide, Australia*

Visit the d'Arenberg Cube, a five-story tasting room.

CHAPTER THIRTEEN

ENABLED ADVENTURES

From wheelchair-accessible beaches and hikes
to sensory-aware museums and hotels, there's a weekend
for everyone and every body.

The iconic "Surfhenge" art installation decorates the entrance to San Diego's Imperial Beach (p. 510).

Freta Street offers views of the Church of the Holy Spirit.

A City Breaking Barriers
Warsaw, Poland

Winner of the European Commission's 2020 Access City Award, Poland's capital city is breaking down barriers to improve accessibility for all. All Warsaw metro stations, trains, and buses are accessible. Ongoing renovations—such as Braille elevator panels, wider doors, and wheelchair lifts—are increasing accessibility to museums, hotels, and historic sites. And new sidewalks and infrastructure projects are required to meet accessibility standards.

Warsaw is also using leading-edge tech tools to build accessibility solutions. A network of sensors equipped with next-generation Bluetooth is being installed across the city to expand "Virtual Warsaw," a micro-navigation system that people with visual impairments can access on smartphones. To stay close to public transportation and Warsaw Old Town, consider the Crowne Plaza Warsaw—The HUB. Opened in late 2020, the stylish hotel offers accessible guest rooms and features, such as assistive listening devices and Braille restaurant menus.

HUB | *Major Western European Cities*

"Taking Flight" by artist Doug Roper stands in the park.

A Theme Park for Everyone
Morgan's Wonderland, San Antonio, Texas, U.S.

Built in 2010 by the parents of a child with cognitive and physical challenges, Morgan's Wonderland is the world's first theme park designed to ensure "100 percent enjoyment by everyone." The 25-acre (10.1 ha) park is completely inclusive and wheelchair-accessible, meaning all children and their families can fully experience the more than 25 attractions, such as a Ferris wheel, carousel, and stocked lake for fishing.

Plan to visit June to mid-August so you can split your weekend between Morgan's Wonderland and neighboring Morgan's Inspiration Island, the world's first ultra-accessible splash park. Opened in 2017, the barrier-free water park has five splash pads, a leisurely boat ride, and helpful amenities like the free use of waterproof wheelchairs and waterproof bags for ventilators and O_2 water-collar covers for tracheostomies. Admission to both parks is free for guests with disabilities, and the nearby La Quinta Alamo City (which has six accessible rooms) offers discounted rates to Morgan's Wonderland guests.

HUB | *South Central United States*

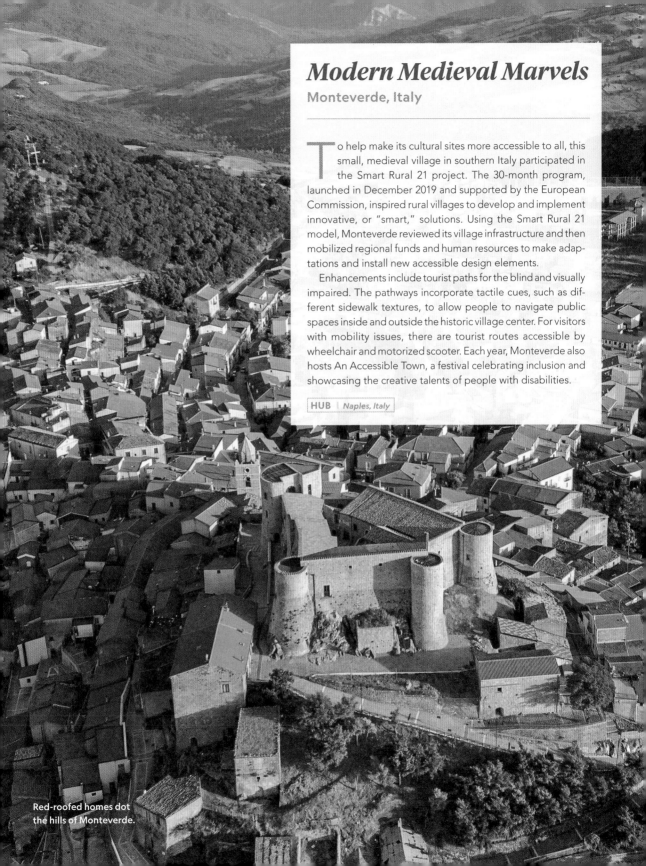

Modern Medieval Marvels

Monteverde, Italy

To help make its cultural sites more accessible to all, this small, medieval village in southern Italy participated in the Smart Rural 21 project. The 30-month program, launched in December 2019 and supported by the European Commission, inspired rural villages to develop and implement innovative, or "smart," solutions. Using the Smart Rural 21 model, Monteverde reviewed its village infrastructure and then mobilized regional funds and human resources to make adaptations and install new accessible design elements.

Enhancements include tourist paths for the blind and visually impaired. The pathways incorporate tactile cues, such as different sidewalk textures, to allow people to navigate public spaces inside and outside the historic village center. For visitors with mobility issues, there are tourist routes accessible by wheelchair and motorized scooter. Each year, Monteverde also hosts An Accessible Town, a festival celebrating inclusion and showcasing the creative talents of people with disabilities.

HUB | *Naples, Italy*

Red-roofed homes dot the hills of Monteverde.

A Refuge of Calm

Hotel Port aux Basques, Newfoundland,
Canada

For most guests, location—close to the dock where the ferry departs for Sydney, Nova Scotia—is likely the biggest draw of this basic, affordable hotel. But, for families who have children with autism spectrum disorder (ASD), Hotel Port aux Basques can be a refuge. Billed as North America's first autism-friendly hotel, the property offers a variety of amenities to help kids with ASD and their families feel more comfortable and at home.

The hotel workout room was converted into a sensory room, providing a safe, calm, and quiet environment for young guests who may have issues processing sensory information effectively. The room's relaxing elements include a padded hammock, climbing wall, inflatable chair, carpeted flooring, and dimmed lighting. In addition, hotel staff are required to complete ASD training, and there's a familiarization slideshow to help kids with ASD prepare for their visit.

> "BILLED AS NORTH AMERICA'S FIRST AUTISM-FRIENDLY HOTEL, THE PROPERTY OFFERS A VARIETY OF AMENITIES."

HUB | *Eastern Canada; Northeastern United States*

The Rose Blanche Lighthouse stands over Channel-Port aux Basques in Newfoundland.

Small falls trickle past Reagan Mill along the Roaring Fork Motor Nature Trail in Great Smoky Mountains National Park.

Roll With a View

Great Smoky Mountains National Park, Tennessee, U.S.

The nation's most visited national park is one of the most accessible thanks, in part, to two trails: a scenic driving loop and a paved, wheelchair-accessible path. Both are located near the Gatlinburg, Tennessee, entrance to Great Smoky Mountains National Park, which covers 800 square miles (2,072 sq km) along the North Carolina-Tennessee border.

To take a rolling hike in your car follow the Roaring Fork Motor Nature Trail. The 5.5-mile-long (8.8 km), one-way, loop road snakes past mountain streams, historic log cabins and grist mills, and through dense, old-growth forest. About six miles (9.7 km) away is the Sugarlands Valley Nature Trail. The paved, wheelchair-accessible path is only a half mile long (0.8 km) yet ticks several Great Smoky Mountains boxes: serene forest setting, remnants of settler homesteads, and the rushing waters of the West Prong of the Little Pigeon River.

HUB | *Southeastern United States*

A hickory tree stands in the mist at Cades Cove.

"IMPROVING ACCESS FOR
THE BLIND . . . HAS BEEN
A TOP PRIORITY."

All Access Pass

Stockholm, Sweden

Built on 14 islands, Stockholm is one of the most strikingly impressive capital cities in Europe and one of the most accessible. The city's public transportation system, Storstockholms Lokaltrafik AB, or SL, has an accessibility guarantee, ensuring that all travelers with disabilities can reach their destinations via stations, lines, and routes designated as accessible. If an escalator is out of service, SL staff will help you complete your trip via an alternative route.

Stockholm-based OURWAY Tours also offers private driving excursions that include door-to-door transportation in an accessible van, scenic city views, and a guided tour through one of the city's many accessible museums. In the wheelchair-accessible ABBA: The Museum, iPads and other interactive smart tools give all guests the opportunity to embrace their inner 70s pop star. Available virtual experiences include trying on costumes, mixing music, and belting out "Dancing Queen" or another ABBA blockbuster on stage as a fifth member of the band. The museum's Curator's Guide (available in English and Swedish) provides audio descriptions of the memorabilia and other exhibits, which is particularly helpful for visitors who are blind or have low vision.

Throughout Stockholm, improving access for the blind and people with visual impairments has been a top priority since the 1990s. The city's e-Adept mobile phone–based tool combines real-time data and digital maps to give users step-by-step audio directions to any local destination. There's also a share-your-location and camera option that allows a family member, friend, or caregiver to monitor your travels and locate you quickly in case of emergency.

For easy access to public transportation and views of the city's ubiquitous waterways, consider staying at the Radisson Blu Waterfront Hotel on Riddarfjärden Bay. The modern hotel has a limited number of wheelchair-accessible rooms with roll-in showers and is conveniently located near the fully accessible Stockholm Central Station, Sweden's largest.

Take in costumes, album covers, and more at the ABBA museum.

Find a poker room in the lodge at Stagecoach Trails Guest Ranch.

Live the Dude Ranch Life

Stagecoach Trails Guest Ranch, Yucca, Arizona, U.S.

Channel your inner cowpoke at Stagecoach Trails, a fully accessible dude ranch designed to look like an Old West town. No matter the disability, everyone can ride. The ranch has accessible riding equipment available for trail rides, as well as safe, supervised rides in an enclosed area for people who aren't able to hit the trail but who want to experience real horseback riding.

The founder's oldest daughter uses a wheelchair to get around, which is why Stagecoach Trails was built barrier free from the ground up. Although the ranch is located in the northwestern Arizona desert, the nearest major airport is two hours north in Las Vegas, Nevada. Rent a car to make the drive to the ranch. Once there, there's no reason to leave, since daily rates include three meals, two horseback rides, unlimited stargazing and wildlife viewing, and other complimentary guest activities, such as nighttime campfires and, with a three-night stay, an authentic stagecoach ride.

HUB | *Southwestern United States*

A masked folkloric dancer walks in the Virgin of Candelaria procession in Puno, Peru.

Holiday Celebrations

Celebrate Diwali, Hanukkah, Easter, Ramadan, and more in the grandest of fashions around the world.

1. CANDELARIA, PUNO, PERU

During the first two weeks of February, thousands of folkloric dancers, procession goers, and onlookers flock to the shores of Lake Titicaca for this UNESCO-designated festival, a dazzling ode to the Virgin of Candelaria, the local patron saint.

2. PARO TSHECHU, BHUTAN

Paramount among Bhutanese Buddhist festivals, this springtime lineup of devotional dances—all performed in eye-popping costumes—is pegged to the lunar calendar, so the Gregorian dates change. But at five days total, the festival tends to include weekends.

3. SEMANA SANTA, SEVILLE, SPAIN

Holy Week is particularly epic in Seville, where dozens of church brotherhoods carry centuries-old images of Jesus and Mary through packed streets, with brass bands and point-hatted pentitents marching along for the hours-long processions.

4. GOOD FRIDAY, ROME, ITALY

A Friday night like no other, this one sees the pope at the head of a torch-lit procession from the Roman Colosseum to Palatine Hill, with thousands of the faithful behind to pray at the stations of the cross.

5. EASTER SEASON, ANTIGUA, GUATEMALA

Between Palm Sunday and Easter Sunday, this little colonial Guatemalan town fills with visitors, all here for the famously colorful festivities—from the kaleidoscopic sawdust "carpets" along the cobblestone streets to the legions of locals in amethyst robes.

6. RAMADAN, CAIRO, EGYPT

An especially vibrant spot to experience the Muslim holy month of Ramadan, Cairo comes to life at night with endless decorative lights and lanterns and open-air gatherings filled with revelers breaking the day's fast.

7. NAVRATRI, VARANASI, INDIA

A 10-day Hindu fall festival, Navratri is particularly grand in Varanasi, where the local version of the Ramlila (a UNESCO-designated dance-drama about the life of Lord Rama) captures the collective imagination.

8. DIWALI, TRINIDAD & TOBAGO

So many locals are ethnically East Indian, Diwali is a national holiday in this corner of the Caribbean, where the lamp-lit festivities last at least a week and the world's first Diwali Nagar (essentially, a Diwali theme park) always dazzles.

9. HANUKKAH, JERUSALEM, ISRAEL

A special time throughout Israel, the eight nights of Hanukkah are extra magical in Jerusalem's Old City, where retro, oil-lit menorahs illuminate countless windows and the scents of holiday treats (think potato latkes and jelly-filled doughnuts) fill the narrow streets. The holiday is so transformative, many local outfitters offer guided "Hanukkah Strolls" through the city and family activities are held throughout the week.

10. LAS POSADAS, SAN MIGUEL DE ALLENDE, MEXICO

The nine-night Advent tradition of Las Posadas is famous in this part of Mexico, where a string of events held throughout December, including processions of children in search of "room at the inn" (as Mary and Joseph did), are set against a gorgeous colonial backdrop.

> "LIFE IN SYDNEY REVOLVES
> AROUND ITS WORLD-
> FAMOUS HARBOR."

Aussie Accessibility

Sydney, Australia

Sydney, capital of the state of New South Wales (NSW), is Australia's largest city. It's also one of the easiest to navigate for people with mobility disabilities since NSW is committed to making public transportation accessible to all. The majority of NSW public buses, ferries, metro and light rail cars, and trains are designed so that anyone—no matter their disability—can board, travel, and disembark safely.

Use the real-time Transport for NSW trip planner to plot an accessible public transportation route to most of the city's major attractions. The city of Sydney also has an online accessibility map highlighting accessible parking spaces and public toilets, and potential barriers—such as stairs and inclines.

Life in Sydney revolves around its world-famous harbor and its iconic landmarks, like the Sydney Opera House and Sydney Harbour Bridge. For Instagram-worthy views of all three, take a sightseeing cruise on the Captain Cook *MV Sydney 2000*. There's ramped access to the ship's Show Deck—however, when the tide is low, the ramp can be steep. When making reservations, ask for the most accessible sailing time based on the tides.

After the cruise, get up-close views of the Sydney Opera House on the daily access tour. Advance reservations are required for this guided "look" (specifically designed for the blind and for people with low vision or mobility issues) at the facilities and history of the world-famous Opera House. Live audio descriptions of select performances are also available for guests who are blind or have low vision.

From the Opera House forecourt, there are two accessible entrance gates into the Royal Botanic Garden Sydney, a 74-acre (29.9 ha) urban oasis. Take a free, wheelchair-accessible guided tour to learn about the site's Aboriginal history and extensive collection of plants, such as the rare and threatened palms, ferns, and orchids seen in the Australian Rainforest Garden.

The iconic Sydney Opera House stands out on the harbor at night.

White Sands offers wheelchair-accessible boardwalks.

Dunes & Desert Days
White Sands National Park, New Mexico, U.S.

Named a national park in December 2019, White Sands looks like it belongs on another planet. The white dunes covering the park's 275 square miles (712.2 sq km) of desert contain gypsum, a mineral that makes the sand shimmer and shine. The world's largest gypsum field, it sits at the northern edge of the Chihuahuan Desert, North America's largest desert.

People with limited mobility can meander through the otherworldly landscape on the eight-mile (12.9 km) one-way Dunes Drive. Wheelchair-accessible picnic tables are located along the drive, as is the quarter-mile (0.4 km) Interdune Boardwalk, a wheelchair-accessible trail with handrails. Walk or roll along the boardwalk to the top of a dune for a closer look at the glimmering gypsum. Additional accessibility features include Braille and large-print versions of the park brochure in both English and Spanish and assistive listening devices (reserve at least two weeks in advance) for ranger programs.

HUB | *Southwestern United States*

A tricolored heron lands on water at Myakka River State Park.

It's a Wild Life
Myakka River State Park, Sarasota, Florida, U.S.

Observing wildlife in the actual wild is an activity that's often off limits to people with disabilities. That's not the case, however, at Myakka River State Park. Located about 30 miles (48.3 km) east of Sarasota, the 38,000-acre (15,378.1 ha) state park—one of Florida's largest, oldest, and most biodiverse—levels the wildlife-viewing field with a boardwalk extending into Upper Myakka Lake, wheelchair-accessible tram and flat-bottom boat tours, and four concrete, ADA-compliant campsites in Palmetto Ridge campground.

And, thanks to the Myakka, Florida's only state-designated wild and scenic river, there's a wealth of wildlife to see. The river provides and nourishes essential habitat, including pinelands, wetlands, and wildflower prairies to support iconic Florida creatures, such as the American alligator and the pale-pink roseate spoonbill. You're also likely to spot a few unlikely creatures such as armadillos, bald eagles, and wild boars.

HUB | *Southeastern United States*

Access Granted

Berlin, Germany

A vigorous Barrier-Free Berlin program is transforming Germany's capital city into a European leader in accessible venues, routes, and transportation for people with mobility, vision, and hearing issues. Download the free accessBerlin smartphone app for information on all things accessibility, such as accessible hotels, public restrooms, restaurants, and out-of-service reports for elevators at Berlin U-Bahn metro stations. Recent app updates include more extensive information and directions for people with visual impairments.

Use accessBerlin for inside tips on visiting iconic attractions, including the Reichstag parliament building and glass dome. There's a separate entrance to the dome for people with disabilities, and with advance notice, special tours can be arranged for visitors with low vision or blindness. At the accessible Botanic Garden and Botanical Museum, the Fragrance and Touch Garden was designed for people with visual impairments. The garden's aromatic plants and herbs were planted in raised beds, making it easier for visitors to touch and smell the flora.

HUB | *Major Western European Cities*

The Berlin television tower stands above Nikolai Quarter in Berlin.

Beaches along the Gulf of Mexico offer wheelchairs designed for rolling over sand.

"BUT CHANGE IS UNDER WAY, AND COASTAL ESCAPES IN BOTH TROPICAL AND COOLER CLIMATES ARE INVESTING IN . . . TECHNOLOGY TO MAKE SURE THAT THEIR SANDY STRETCHES ARE PLAYGROUNDS FOR ALL."

PERSPECTIVE

Wheelchair-Friendly Beaches in the U.S.

Five Coastal Areas in America Have Made Accessibility a Top Priority

Beaches aren't always the first destinations that wheelchair users consider for holidays. Navigating soft sandy approaches to the shore can be a serious challenge for people with limited mobility.

In a Centers for Disease Control and Prevention study, roughly 13.7 percent of adults in the United States report a mobility disability, defined as serious difficulty walking or climbing stairs. This functional disability can make vacation planning a challenge and can put some destinations off limits. But change is under way, and coastal escapes in both tropical and cooler climates are investing in beach access mats, wheelchairs designed specifically for easier rolling in the sand, and other technology to make sure that their sandy stretches are playgrounds for all.

San Diego, California, tops the charts as one of the most accommodating beach cities on the West Coast. Nine beaches in the city offer free manual or powered beach wheelchairs. To discover which beach has the best options for you, contact the city's beach wheelchair line (*coastal.ca.gov*) prior to visiting. San Diego's North County Coastal region stretches for miles and includes other beach towns, such as Encinitas. For people who love to soak and swim, manually powered floating beach wheelchairs are available at Moonlight Beach in Encinitas.

Located on Alabama's coast, Gulf Shores and its neighboring city, Orange Beach, share 32 miles (51.5 km) of coastline. In addition to family-friendly attractions and restaurants, Gulf Shores offers both manual beach wheelchairs and motorized beach chairs, available to rent from Beach Power Rentals. The joystick-operated motorized chairs have large inflatable tires that can roll across sand. Or stick with your standard chair and reach the beach by access mats, which stretch toward the water on west and east ends of Gulf Place Public Beach.

The coastal city of Wilmington, North Carolina, has plenty of attractions for wheelchair users and three accessible beaches. Head to Carolina Beach, Kure Beach, or Wrightsville Beach, where manual beach wheelchairs are available for free and can be reserved for up to a week at a time. At Kure Beach, the chairs are available from the local fire department; at Carolina Beach and Wrightsville Beach, contact the local parks and recreation department. Beach access mats for wheelchair users are available near Carolina Beach's Boardwalk. Multiple hotels are within rolling distance, making this an ideal place to stay.

With one of the longest coastlines in the United States, Michigan has several accessible beach options. Muskegon's shores stand out thanks to the Action Trackchair—an off-road wheelchair that can roll in the sand, dirt, and mud and even go over rocks. It also has recline and tilt capabilities for a more comfortable ride. To reserve it, contact Muskegon State Park. If the Action Trackchair isn't available for your travel dates, manual beach chairs are available.

Averaging 220 sunny days per year—and with one of the longest piers in the Gulf of Mexico—Pensacola Beach in Florida is a prime place for accessible coastal relaxation thanks to Access Mobility of Pensacola's motorized beach chairs. Sid and Lynn Hargis, owners of the small company, saw a need for greater independence on sand and offer motorized wheelchairs for rent. If you're traveling with a companion, Scooter Hut Rentals and The Fun Store rent manual beach wheelchairs. Rolling through Pensacola's Gulf Islands National Seashore? Be sure to seek out the accessible nature trails in Perdido Key, Naval Live Oaks, and Davis Bayou areas.

—**Cory Lee Woodard** is a wheelchair user and travel writer. He is the author of the award-winning travel blog Curb Free With Cory Lee.

"PARTICIPATE . . . IN ADAPTIVE
EXPERIENCES DESIGNED
WITH INCLUSION IN MIND."

Designed for Inclusion
National Ability Center, Park City, Utah, U.S.

The Utah-based National Ability Center (NAC) makes recreation and outdoor adventures accessible to people of all abilities. At NAC's Park City Ranch headquarters (there are smaller NAC basecamps in Moab and Salt Lake City), children and adults with disabilities can participate year-round in adaptive experiences designed with inclusion in mind. Based on the season, activity options could include Alpine and Nordic skiing, horseback riding, mountain biking, rafting, or snowshoeing.

NAC has the specialized equipment and expertise to accommodate people with any disability. Past participants in NAC lessons, camps, and other programs have included, among others, adults with Alzheimer's disease, teens with autism spectrum disorder, children with cystic fibrosis, and burn and brain injury survivors. On Monday evenings and Saturdays free military family programs—in sports, such as archery, cycling, and indoor climbing—are available to active-duty service members, veterans, and their family members.

For a weekend getaway, the best option is booking a private, overnight NAC experience, available to families and other small groups traveling with one or more members who have a disability. When you make your reservation, NAC staff will work with you to design a weekend itinerary matching your group's varied ages, abilities, and interests. Depending on your specific requirements, the weekend could include opportunities to recreate together as a group and also participate in individual lessons or adventures.

To maximize the time spent skiing, pedaling, paddling, and enjoying other indoor and outdoor activities, stay at the NAC Park City Ranch in the affordable Lodge. All 25 rooms in the lodge are accessible (five have roll-in showers), and rates include a daily continental breakfast. Park City is within a day's drive of most major cities in the western United States, and the closest airport, Salt Lake City International, is only 35 minutes away.

A National Ability Center cyclist rides a recumbent hand cycle on Park City's Silver Quinn Trail.

Adaptive Snow Play

Telluride Ski Resort, Colorado, U.S.

Tucked nearly 1,000 feet (304.8 m) above the historic mining town of Telluride, elevation 8,750 feet (2,667 m), Telluride Ski Resort offers sky-high San Juan Mountain views, more than 2,000 skiable acres (809.4 ha), and a welcoming environment in which to try adaptive skiing or snowboarding. Accessible cars are available on the free, pedestrian gondola, or "G," linking the town to the resort's Mountain Village. Stay in either location and ride the "G" to get around. From the gondola you can experience the freedom of gliding above mesas, mountains, and waterfalls.

At the resort, the nonprofit Telluride Adaptive Sports Program offers a wide variety of winter sports programs, such as adaptive ski and snowboard lessons, ski-buddy services for independent skiers, and guiding services for hearing- or visually impaired skiers. Book programs at least a month in advance. Some activities—including fat-tire biking and backcountry snowmobiling—can be adapted to fit families and small groups whose members include someone with a disability.

> "TELLURIDE SKI RESORT OFFERS . . . A WELCOMING ENVIRONMENT IN WHICH TO TRY ADAPTIVE SKIING OR SNOWBOARDING."

HUB | *Mountain West United States*

Telluride Ski Resort offers 2,000 skiable acres (809.4 ha) with adaptive experiences for adults and children.

Shoppers make their way through Grote Markt Square in Breda, the Netherlands.

Mobility in the City

Breda, the Netherlands

Led by the local Breda-Gelijk! (Equal Breda!) foundation, this regal, medieval charmer near the Belgian border has become one of Europe's most accessible cities. The city removed, sliced, and reinstalled the historic cobblestones surrounding Grote Markt and Grote Kerk marketplace and church, creating a flat surface for people who use wheelchairs and other mobility devices. And Breda's Valkenberg Park and southern forest, Mastbos—one of the oldest pine forests in the Netherlands—are both wheelchair accessible.

Portable ramps are becoming ubiquitous at entryways to shops and restaurants as more businesses join the effort to make Breda barrier free. The city has also updated its websites to make navigation and content user friendly for people with sensory impairments. Future plans include installing a tactile-navigation line to help people with visual impairments travel safely from Breda's main train station to the city center.

HUB | *Amsterdam, the Netherlands*

A statue stands in front of cafés in Breda.

Cruise with waterslides
and Disney characters
on board.

Spots for Family Fun

Bring the whole family along to the kid- and adult-friendly destinations, designed with inclusivity in mind.

1. SUNDANCE TRAIL GUEST RANCH, COLORADO, U.S.

The ranch is built to be wheelchair accessible, including mobility-friendly cabins, and wheelchair-accessible docks and forest trails. The lodge, Jacuzzi, and other facilities are barrier free, and there is assistive technology for other mobility impairments.

2. DOLLYWOOD, PIGEON FORGE, TENNESSEE, U.S.

Dollywood has a Ride Accessibility Center to tailor your visit to your family's needs. In 2016, the park added a sensory room for children with autism, and in 2017 a calming corner at its water park.

3. SMUGGLERS' NOTCH, VERMONT, U.S.

The Smugglers' Notch Adaptive Program offers 10 adaptive camp activities including guided hiking and horseback riding, swimming and watersliding, and mini golf and kayaking. The campground also offers inclusion programs for group activities.

4. TRADEWINDS ISLAND RESORT, ST. PETE BEACH, FLORIDA, U.S.

Tradewinds is certified as a Center for Autism and Related Disabilities (CARD), so all staff is trained to assist families with special needs. Tradewinds also offers mobility access throughout the property and free beach wheelchairs.

5. DISNEY FANTASY CRUISE, VARIOUS LOCATIONS

The mobility-friendly cruise ship includes 25 accessible rooms and an onboard mini golf course that is wheelchair accessible. Youth counselors on the ship are specially trained in special needs, and Disney's private island, Castaway Cay, has paved pathways for easy access to restaurants and shops.

6. SHARED ADVENTURES, SANTA CRUZ, CALIFORNIA

This nonprofit offers adaptive experiences year-round. But most famously, its "Day on the Beach" event, held every July, offers plywood paths along the beach for wheelchair access, as well as adaptive kayaking and scuba diving with trained guides.

7. SESAME PLACE, LANGHORNE, PENNSYLVANIA, U.S.

Sesame Place is the world's first theme park designated as a Certified Autism Center. The park offers an IBCCES Sensory Guide with insight on sensory processing for each ride and an accessibility program to pair park attractions to your family's needs.

8. SPLORE, MOAB, UTAH, U.S.

This nonprofit outdoor destination is an affordable option for adaptive rock climbing, hiking, riverboating, horseback riding, mountain biking, and four-wheeling. The resort also has fully accessible rooms, including wheelchair-friendly lodging.

9. ASPEN SNOWMASS, COLORADO, U.S.

All four Aspen Snowmass mountains participate in Challenge Aspen, a program designed for children four and older with physical and cognitive disabilities. Adaptive activities are offered year-round, including skiing and snowboarding, hiking, and fishing.

10. HOLIDAY WORLD, SANTA CLAUS, INDIANA, U.S.

This family-friendly theme park is built around accessibility. A Calming Room at the park gives children a sensory break with beanbag chairs, a tent, couch, and adjustable lighting.

> ## "ITS HISTORIC CAPITAL CITY OFFERS AN ABUNDANCE OF ACCESSIBLE OPTIONS."

Meeting Family Needs

Boston, Massachusetts, U.S.

Massachusetts perennially ranks among the top states in the United States for living with a disability, so it's no wonder that its historic capital city offers an abundance of accessible options—particularly for families. In Boston proper, parents and kids can take a spin together on New England's most ADA-compliant merry-go-round, the Greenway Carousel at the Tiffany & Co. Foundation Grove. Open mid-April to mid-October, the 36-seat Greenway Carousel features 14 different hand-carved characters designed with features to accommodate wheelchairs and people with physical, sensory, and cognitive disabilities.

Being a place "where everyone can participate equally in the excitement of science and technology learning" is the vision of Boston's Museum of Science, one of the world's largest science centers. For help planning a visit to meet your family's specific accessibility needs, contact the museum's dedicated Accessibility Coordinator. Quieter weekend times to visit the museum tend to be Saturday and Sunday mornings before 11 a.m.

Plan ahead to ride an amphibious Boston Duck Tours landing vehicle from the museum, along the Charles River, through the city, and back again. With advance reservations, tours can accommodate two wheelchairs on the back deck. The land-and-water excursion employs some of the same vehicles used to carry members of the New England Patriots and other championship-winning Boston sports teams.

Although not inside the city of Boston, the accessible Discovery Museum and Discovery Woods is well worth the 25-mile (40.2 km) drive west to suburban Acton. Designed to ensure all kids can play and discover, the sensory-friendly and ADA-compliant attraction regularly offers free events for families with children who are on the autism spectrum, who are deaf or hard of hearing, or who are blind or experience low vision. The centerpiece of Discovery Woods is a fully accessible, 550-square-foot (51.1 sq m) tree house. Elevated boardwalks and ramps provide barrier-free access to the tree house and through surrounding, parklike landscape.

Accessible tours and experiences are offered at the Museum of Science in Boston.

Moonlight is known for sandy beaches with accessible options.

A Beach Within Reach
San Diego County, California, U.S.

San Diego County puts the beach within easier reach of people with physical disabilities. At least nine beaches in the county, which boasts 70 miles (112.7 km) of coastline, offer free use of manual or powered beach chairs. Multiple beaches—such as Cardiff State Beach, Coronado, Imperial Beach, and Moonlight State Beach in Encinitas—have mobility mats leading over the sand, creating a firmer, flatter surface for anyone with mobility issues.

Moonlight Beach also earns bonus accessibility points for three helpful amenities: two floating beach chairs reserved for people with disabilities, a lifeguard stand that's staffed year-round, and a large, free parking area—saving the hassle of searching for a spot close to the beach. For a beachfront stay, consider booking an accessible oceanfront or ocean-view suite with balcony at the Pier South Resort in Imperial Beach. The all-suite resort has an ADA-compliant pool and fitness center, and convenient front-row access to the sand and surf.

HUB | *West Coast United States*

Enjoy waterslides at the resort's pool areas.

Stay & Play
Beaches Resort Ocho Rios, Jamaica

Beaches was the first resort company in the world to complete International Board of Credentialing and Continuing Education Standards training and Autism Certification. This means the all-inclusive Beaches resorts offer families with children who have ASD (autism spectrum disorder) helpful amenities such as custom dietary options for kids with food allergies and those who eat a limited variety of foods, sensory-friendly spaces, and age-specific Kids Camp programs led by staff with autism certification.

The family-focused Ocho Rios location, designated as an Advanced Certified Autism Center, is particularly attractive for a weekend stay because it's only a 90-minute direct flight from Miami to Ocho Rios. There are rooms (including generously sized doubles and two-level suites) to accommodate families of all sizes, and the property includes a water park and private beach. Parents also can request an autism-certified, one-on-one Beach Buddy to accompany their child during the stay.

HUB | *Caribbean; Southeastern United States*

Enjoy the Pier

Navy Pier, Chicago, Illinois, U.S.

A Lake Michigan landmark since 1916, 3,040-foot-long (926.6 m) Navy Pier is the longest public pier in the world. And, thanks to the multiyear reimagining launched in 2011, the iconic pier has become a more inclusive destination for dining, shopping, and recreation. Recent improvements include elevator access to all levels of the pier and enclosed, wheelchair-accessible gondolas on the 196-foot-high (59.7 m) Centennial Wheel, opened in 2016.

The new Sensory Friendly Navy Pier app helps kids with disabilities—especially those with autism spectrum disorder—and their families prepare for a day at the Pier. The app includes a sensory-friendly map highlighting quiet zones, places with limited lighting, and other helpful information. From the pier, you can also board wheelchair-accessible architecture boat tours or dinner cruises.

HUB | *Midwestern United States*

Historic buildings line Navy Pier along Lake Michigan.

Take to the skies in a
hot-air balloon over
the Pyrenees mountains.

> "THERE ARE SOME AWESOME ADVENTURES TO BE HAD—FROM RIDING A CAMEL IN THE SAHARA TO SOARING HIGH IN A HOT-AIR BALLOON."

PERSPECTIVE

Adrenaline-Pumping Adventures

These Five Wheelchair-Accessible Thrills Are for Everyone

Adventure and sporting opportunities are increasing for people with physical disabilities, thanks to organizations such as Adaptive Adventures. But for more than three million Americans relying on a wheelchair daily, finding these activities and verifying that they have proper equipment can still be a challenge.

There are some awesome adventures to be had—from riding a camel in the Sahara to soaring high in a hot-air balloon. Here are a few of our favorite wheelchair-accessible experiences around the world.

Less than a two-hour drive from Barcelona, Catalonia's Garrotxa Volcanic Zone Natural Park features lush greenery, Roman-era landmarks, and accessible hiking trails. Make the day more scenic with Vol de Coloms, a hot-air balloon company that takes high fliers over dormant volcanoes and provides remote-controlled seats for wheelchair users. On a clear day, you can see as far as the Mediterranean Sea and Pyrenees mountains. (On U.S. soil, see Las Vegas from above with Love Is in the Air Ballooning, which provides easy ramp access and permits wheelchair users to stay in their chair.)

After getting lost in the souks of Marrakech, take the nine-hour drive to Merzouga for the ultimate bucket-list experience. Morocco Accessible Travel Consultants offers travelers with limited mobility an adaptive camel saddle with a backrest and headrest to provide comfortable support while trekking through the Erg Chebbi sand dunes, the largest in Morocco. You can spot regional birds including Kittllitz's plovers, ruddy shelducks, and Egyptian nightjars year-round, but in spring, flocks of pink flamingos steal the show.

Sheboygan, Wisconsin, a city about 50 miles (80.5 km) north of Milwaukee, is a terrific spot for travelers interested in trying adaptive sailing. The Sailing Education Association of Sheboygan (SEAS), a nonprofit sailing program, has a mechanism to lift wheelchair users aboard its custom-designed Sonar boats for a sail around Lake Michigan. For sailors whose upper body mobility is limited, bite switches are available for hands-free sailing. Sailors can work up a hunger! Once ashore, it's easy to fuel up with a grilled brat piled high with sauerkraut and Bavarian mustard in Sheboygan, the "Bratwurst Capital of the World."

Take in one of Costa Rica's most spectacular sights by soaring over Arenal Volcano National Park. Go with outfitter Il Viaggio Travel, whose experts will help seat visitors in an upright sling before zipping them down seven adrenaline-pumping lines. Travelers feel as if they are flying while catching glimpses of the forest below and the smoke clouding the volcano's rim. Seek rainforest views from below in Mistico Hanging Bridges Park, located in La Fortuna—the gateway city to Arenal Volcano. Several paths are accessible and offer glimpses of frogs, birds, and bats.

Beeline to Chattanooga, Tennessee, to feel the brisk water of the Tennessee River splashing in your face via adaptive waterskiing. Sports, Arts & Recreation of Chattanooga (SPARC)—a local chapter of Disabled Sports USA—takes adventurers with limited mobility down the river with the support of seated skis. Check the calendar for events, then buckle in tight and hold on for a wild ride.

—**Cory Lee Woodard** is a wheelchair user and travel writer. He is the author of the award-winning travel blog Curb Free With Cory Lee.

> "LOCATIONS IN CLONAKILTY ARE CONTINUALLY WORKING TO REMOVE THE MAIN ASD BARRIERS TO INCLUSION."

Autism-Friendly Town

Clonakilty, County Cork, Ireland

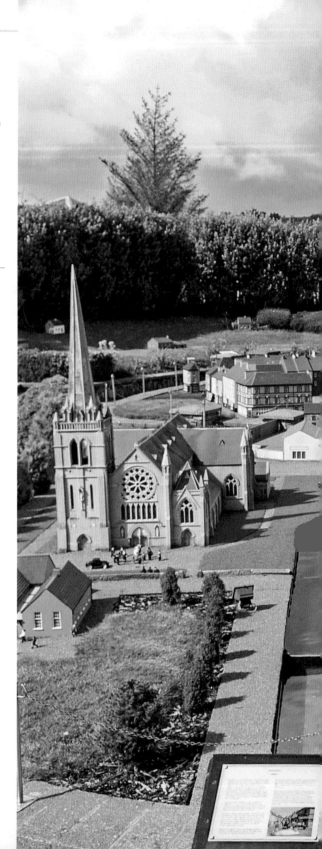

Perched near the southernmost tip of Ireland in West Cork, Clonakilty, known locally as Clon, is a picturesque stop on Ireland's scenic Wild Atlantic Way touring route. More important to people with autism spectrum disorder (ASD) and their families, Clon is also recognized as Ireland's first autism-friendly town. Under the direction of AsIAm (Ireland's largest ASD charitable organization), public spaces, residents, retailers, restaurants, and other organizations and locations in Clonakilty are continually working to remove the main ASD barriers to inclusion: communication, predictability and control, sensory processing, and judgment and attitudes.

There are some 200 Clonakilty "Autism Friendly Champions," with more working toward accreditation. Becoming a Champion requires meeting AsIAm criteria, such as conducting ASD-friendly staff training and creating printed, video, and digital orientation materials to help people with ASD prepare for their visit. Clonakilty Champions can easily be identified by the Autism Friendly Champion and Service Dog Friendly stickers posted on their front window or entrance door. Call ahead to learn about each location's ASD-friendly amenities, such as special quiet hours or a dedicated quiet space.

The Champions list includes numerous places to stay, including the family-friendly Clonakilty Park Hotel. Before checking in, download the hotel's sensory map to locate high-intensity, low-intensity, and quiet areas. At the Fernhill House Hotel, a captioned, visual guide prepared especially for people with ASD introduces guests to the property's interior and exterior spaces. Guests can also find quiet spaces in the hotel's gardens and pathways.

Among the local ASD-friendly attractions are Clonakilty's secluded beaches and the West Cork Model Railway Village, a handmade, miniature model of Clonakilty in the 1940s, complete with working G scale trains. The village also features an outdoor play area where children with ASD can release restless energy and where families can picnic together.

HUB | *Dublin or Galway City, Ireland*

Visit the West Cork Model Railway Village in Clonakilty.

An Update to History

Évreux, France

Situated halfway between Paris and the coast of Normandy, Évreux is best known for its imposing Romanesque and Gothic cathedral, Notre Dame de Evreux. Built between 1194 and 1198 (and heavily damaged during World War II), the cathedral is the city's most recognizable landmark. Less obvious are the improvements historic Évreux has been making to better meet the needs of people with hidden, or invisible, disabilities, such as sensory or cognitive disorders that aren't readily apparent to others.

Among the ongoing enhancements are new panels, directions, and visitor guides written in easy-to-read French, making essential information accessible to people of all abilities, including those with low literacy skills. Évreux is also building an outdoor play area designed with input from an association for children with autism spectrum disorder, and is installing new pedestrian guide rails, audible and tactile warnings, contrasting step edges, and audible signals at traffic lights throughout the city.

HUB | *Paris, France*

> "ÉVREUX IS . . . BUILDING AN OUTDOOR PLAY AREA DESIGNED WITH INPUT FROM AN ASSOCIATION FOR CHILDREN WITH AUTISM SPECTRUM DISORDER."

Canals in Évreux offer a picturesque French setting.

Instantly feel welcomed at the Main Gate to the Richard & Helen DeVos Japanese Garden in the Frederik Meijer Gardens & Sculpture Park.

A Hidden Gem for All

Grand Rapids, Michigan, U.S.

Located close to 20 Lake Michigan beaches, Grand Rapids is a bit of a hidden gem for travelers with disabilities. In addition to the close proximity to major Midwest metropolitan areas, this low-key college town (home to, among others, Western Michigan University) has made being barrier free a priority. To quickly locate accessible hotels, restaurants, and attractions, visit the Experience Grand Rapids website and download the Accessibility Guide.

Several city museums, including the Gerald R. Ford Presidential Museum, are ADA compliant. Grand Rapids is also home to one the most accessible places in the nation to enjoy indoor and outdoor sculptures: the Frederik Meijer Gardens & Sculpture Park. The 30-acre (12.1 ha) park's 200 permanent works are viewable via ramps and paved pathways. Free wheelchair rentals are available, and trained service animals (dogs and miniature horses only) are permitted.

See the "I, you, she or he" statues in Meijer Gardens.

HUB | *Midwestern United States*

Capital Resources

London, England

England's capital city is home to world-class museums, and many are among London's most accessible visitor attractions. The Tate Modern, which holds the national collection of British art, has free wheelchairs, walkers, and mobility scooters available for use with advance reservations. Large-print guides for the visually impaired are available for all exhibitions, and visitors with dyslexia can request colored overlays and magnifying glasses at exhibition entrances.

At the Science Museum, multiple galleries feature elements—such as touchable objects, large-print and Braille labels, and tactile cane detector markers highlighting potential hazards—designed to enhance the experience for people who are blind or partially sighted. The free Audio Eyes app for iOS also provides audio-only descriptions of more than 60 exhibits.

Visit the British Museum, whose collection covers two million years of history, in the morning, when there are typically fewer visitors. Admission is free, and special morning tours are regularly available for visitors with disabilities

> "THE TATE MODERN . . . HAS FREE WHEEL-CHAIRS, WALKERS, AND MOBILITY SCOOTERS AVAILABLE FOR USE."

HUB | *Major Western European Cities*

Bruce Nauman's neon installation "One Hundred Live and Die" is featured at the Tate Modern.

Six Peaks Grille offers five-star cuisine with gorgeous views from panoramic windows overlooking Squaw Valley.

Alpine Glory

Resort at Squaw Creek, Lake Tahoe, California, U.S.

With a dedicated disability ambassador and a wheelchair-accessible fitness center, the Resort at Squaw Creek is particularly well suited for active guests with disabilities. The resort is open year-round; however, winter is the season to experience the thrill of zipping across the snow at nearby Alpine Meadows ski resort in North Lake Tahoe.

Alpine Meadows is home to the Achieve Tahoe Program Center. December to April, Achieve Tahoe offers private adaptive skiing and snowboarding lessons. Classes are custom tailored to fit each participant's accessibility needs and experience level, ensuring anyone with an intellectual, physical, or sensory disability can fully enjoy a day on the slopes. Adaptive equipment options include TetraSki—a seat mounted on two skis that's controlled by a joystick and/or sip-and-puff mechanism—for people with complex mobility impairments.

HUB | *West Coast United States*

The Sierra Nevada peaks tower above the Resort at Squaw Creek.

> ## "AN EASIER WAY FOR TRAVELERS WITH DISABILITIES TO EXPERIENCE THE PARK"

A *Grand Experience*

Grand Canyon Railway & Hotel, Williams, Arizona, U.S.

Making Grand Canyon Railway & Hotel home base for a Grand Canyon National Park adventure makes it easier for travelers with disabilities to experience the park. The 298-room hotel, built in 1995 next door to the historic Williams Depot has accessible rooms and easy access to the Grand Canyon Railway.

Accessible, restored coaches are available on specific train tours, which depart daily from Williams and arrive 2 hours and 15 minutes later at the South Rim of Grand Canyon National Park. From here, board a wheelchair-accessible motor coach for a driving tour (advance reservations required) along the South Rim or ride the wheelchair-accessible National Park shuttle to accessible overlooks and trails.

Disembark at Verkamp's Visitor Center to explore the relatively flat Trail of Time, a 2.83-mile (4.56 km) wheelchair-accessible path leading to the Yavapai Geology Museum. The short Trail of Time covers Grand Canyon's long geologic history. Brass markers placed at three-foot (1 m) intervals represent one million years of time, and interpretive exhibits, such as viewing tubes and touchable rock samples, give people with disabilities access to experiences commonly reserved for those able to hike the park's steep, rocky trails. The Science on the Sphere video display inside the Grand Canyon Visitor Center also has touchable exhibits, all with open captioning for the hearing impaired and with Braille labels for the blind.

To get the most out of your Grand Canyon weekend, take the train (with motor coach or shuttle bus tour) the first day and drive to the park the following day for a self-guided tour. At any entrance station or visitor center, request a Scenic Drive Accessibility Permit. Available to visitors with mobility issues, the permit allows you to drive on Hermit and Yaki Point roads, two scenic routes typically off-limits to private vehicles.

Park visitors look out over
the canyon's South Rim
from Mather Point.

CHAPTER FOURTEEN

ECO-ESCAPES

Think green on these immersive and conservation-focused experiences around the globe.

Conservation-forward bures dot the water at Likuliku Lagoon Resort in Fiji (p. 524).

A snorkeler explores the reef around Likuliku Lagoon.

Marine Sanctuary
Likuliku Lagoon Resort, Malolo Island, Fiji

From Fiji's largest island, Viti Levu, it's only 10 minutes by seaplane or 45 minutes by private water taxi to Malolo Island, home to Likuliku Lagoon Resort. The short hop makes the resort—an adults-only wilderness retreat—a convenient weekend getaway during a longer Fijian vacation.

Staying here supports local environmental protection efforts, such as dry forest restoration; coral, clam, and other marine transplanting; and the natural recovery and restoration of house reefs and marine life. In 2005, the waters and reefs in front of Likuliku Lagoon were declared Na Tabu, or a Marine Protected Area. Restricted areas where an official Na Tabu ceremony was performed are marked by palm frond–topped poles. On land, the resort supports efforts to ensure the survival of the Malolo Island crested iguana, considered extinct until 2010. Learn about the species while touring the resort's iguana sanctuary, breeding cages, and dry forest habitat.

HUB | *Fiji; Brisbane, Australia*

Northern Forests
Trout Point Lodge, Nova Scotia, Canada

Recognized by National Geographic for being among "ten of the most innovative, sustainable travel programs around the world," the remote Trout Point Lodge of Nova Scotia is secluded yet accessible for a weekend from Saint John, New Brunswick, or Bar Harbor, Maine.

The luxurious eco-lodge is hidden on 100 forested acres (40.5 ha) within the UNESCO Southwest Nova Scotia Biosphere Reserve. No cell service means no distractions from the main attractions: guided forest bathing in the Acadian Forest, hiking in the surrounding Tobeatic Wilderness Area, kayaking on the Tusket River, and, on clear nights, guided stargazing with the staff astronomer. Trout Point also led efforts to designate the Tobeatic as the hub of Acadian Skies & Mi'kmaq Lands, North America's first certified Starlight Reserve and Starlight Tourist Destination. Other eco-friendly initiatives include the lodge's Atlantic Acadian cuisine crafted using handpicked and sustainably harvested ingredients.

HUB | *Eastern Canada; Northeastern United States*

Trout Point Lodge is surrounded by forest and river.

Waste Not, Want Not
Kamikatsu, Japan

Rural Kamikatsu is well on the way to becoming a zero-waste town. Some 80 percent of waste is recycled or reused, and there's a palpable passion for avoiding excess packaging. Living waste free isn't easy (recycling bins are divided into 45 different categories), but Kamikatsu's residents are proving it can be done, at least on a small scale.

To experience Kamikatsu-style green living, stay at the new Hotel Why, opened in 2020 as a "zero waste call-to-action hotel." The circular hotel is the "dot" in the Kamikatsu Zero Waste Center, which is shaped like a question mark to inspire people to think about waste. The center also houses a free-for-all thrift store and a craft center featuring artisan products made from upcycled fabrics. Nearby, visit the sustainable RISE & WIN Brewing Co., BBQ, and General Store where everything but the barbecue is sold by weight and customers bring their own containers.

HUB | Japan

Kamikatsu Town is nestled in the lush mountains of Shikoku, Japan.

Sacred Protections

Karitane, New Zealand

For hundreds of years, the Māori have inhabited the area in and around Karitane, a seaside community situated on the spectacularly rugged southeastern coast of New Zealand's South Island. Today, Karitane is the starting point for Māori-led *waka* (canoe) tours on the Waikouaiti River and coastal walks on the Huriawa Peninsula. Most of the rocky and rugged peninsula is protected as the Huriawa Historic Reserve, a New Zealand Historic Trust *wāhi tapu*, or place that is historically significant or sacred to the Māori.

Erosion threatens the stability of the majestic headland, which is flanked by the Waikouaiti and the Pacific. To help stabilize the soil, stop erosion, and create nesting bird habitat, the local Māori *iwi* (people), Kati Huirapa ki Puketeraki, are involved in ecological restoration efforts, such as planting *harakeke* (flax), an ancient plant species endemic to New Zealand. Help plant harakeke, learn about Māori culture, hike ancient coastal trails, and take walking excursions with Māori-owned Karitane Maori Tours.

HUB | *South Island, New Zealand*

The yellow-eyed penguin is endemic to New Zealand and found on the Otago Peninsula.

Fireworks explode during the Yamayaki Festival at Wakakusa.

Cultural Celebrations

Take part in local festivals, religious holidays, and beloved traditions during these spectacular celebrations.

1. HOLI, UTTAR PRADESH, INDIA

Much of India bursts into color every year during Holi, the Hindu festival that celebrates new beginnings and the coming of spring. The two-day holiday sees millions toss water and brightly colored powder on each other in a glorious storm of pigment.

2. DIA DE LOS MUERTOS, SAN MIGUEL DE ALLENDE, MEXICO

The colonial city of San Miguel de Allende throws a fiesta over a long weekend spanning the end of October to the beginning of November. La Calaca—the Skull Festival—delights in death with parades, art installations, public altars, and all-night parties.

3. NOTTING HILL CARNIVAL, LONDON, ENGLAND

With more than two million people attending, the Notting Hill Carnival has become the largest carnival in the world after Rio. Spend a weekend listening to the music of steel pan drums and watch dozens of exuberant performances.

4. SONGKRAN, CHIANG MAI, THAILAND

Songkran rings in the Thai New Year with exuberant mass drenchings from bowls, buckets, water pistols, and water cannons. The Thai people believe water washes away bad luck from the previous year.

5. MARDI GRAS, NEW ORLEANS, LOUISIANA, U.S.

Mardi Gras has enraptured New Orleans since the 1730s, a legacy of the city's original French settlers. The merriment has grown to include lavish masked balls and raucous nighttime processions that run for more than a month between January and February.

6. FIESTA DE LA TIRANA, LA TIRANA, CHILE

Every July, more than 200,000 people gather in the tiny town of La Tirana to revel in Chile's most popular festival, a mix of indigenous culture and Catholic veneration. Dancing takes the spotlight at this fest in the arid Atacama Desert, accompanied by music of the Altiplano peoples.

7. KING'S DAY, AMSTERDAM, THE NETHERLANDS

Every April 27, the entire Kingdom of the Netherlands throws a birthday party for the monarch. Join orange-clad revelers at the open-air party in the old center of the city, where bands play and pleasure boats fill the canals.

8. WAKAKUSA YAMAYAKI, NARA, JAPAN

For some 350 years, Buddhist monks have set fire to the treeless hillside of Mount Wakakusa. Held on the fourth Saturday of January, the festival features a procession up Mount Wakakusa, where monks ignite a massive bonfire, then set the grassy slopes alight.

9. HOGMANAY, EDINBURGH, SCOTLAND

Edinburgh's Hogmanay is one of the world's leading New Year's festivals. The three-day event begins on December 30, when you can march with thousands of people carrying flaming torches through the streets of the city, and culminates in the Loony Dook, a plunge into icy waters.

10. VENICE CARNIVAL, VENICE, ITALY

The Venice Carnival is a celebration of make-believe, with sumptuous balls and masks that allow revelers to take on new identities. Join the frivolity by donning a period costume and wandering through landmarks throughout the city.

"THE REGION RESPECTS LAND, SEA, AND ALL THINGS HAWAIIAN."

Living Pono

North Shore, Oahu, Hawaii, U.S.

Escape the hubbub of touristy Waikiki Beach by driving an hour north to Oahu's laid-back North Shore. Legendary for its monster surf breaks, the North Shore is a rural refuge where multi-generation family farms cultivate homegrown crops and maintain cultural traditions. The region's respect for the land, sea, and all things Hawaiian also makes the North Shore one of the best places in Oahu to experience living *pono*, a native Hawaiian concept that generally means "to do what is right" for yourself, for others, and for the environment.

To help visitors travel pono, the Sustainable Tourism Association of Hawaii (STAH) maintains an online database of STAH-certified activities, locations, and operators. There's also a planning tool so you can customize a North Shore ecotourism weekend based on your interests, such as mountain biking on a wooded, purpose-built trail system with Bike Hawaii Tours and purchasing locally grown produce at the Old Waialua Sugar Mill Saturday farmers market. Among the market's regular vendors is Mohala Farms, a six-acre (2.4 ha) organic farm and nonprofit organization founded on a village model of mutual cooperation and local self-sufficiency. Buying organic fruits and vegetables from Mohala helps support the farm's efforts to revitalize the soil and to foster a healthier North Shore through sustainable agriculture.

At fourth-generation Kahuku Farms, you can learn about North Shore agriculture on a tractor-pulled wagon tour through the commercial fields. After the tour, sample the fruits of the farm—such as hydroponic lettuce, tangerine, and *liliko'i* (passion fruit)—at the Farm Café. While in Kahuku, visit nearby Gunstock Ranch to join in the effort to reforest rangelands that were clear-cut for grazing more than a century ago. The ranch has partnered with the Hawaii Legacy Reforestation Initiative to create a permanent forest of native monarch milo trees. Guests on Gunstock eco-tours can plant a sapling tagged with a high-tech tracker used to monitor the tree's health and location.

HUB | *Honolulu, Hawaii, U.S.; West Coast United States*

Children cast a line into the fishpond at Kualoa Ranch.

A Green Ski Weekend

Whistler, British Columbia, Canada

Whistler rose to fame as a world-class skiing destination, as showcased in the 2010 Winter Olympics, but it's a focus on environmental protection that beckons travelers who want to leave a light ecological footprint. The all-season resort community, which is working toward becoming carbon neutral by 2030, was recognized by Canada's Partners for Climate Protection as the first Canadian community to complete its five milestones toward reducing greenhouse gas emissions. Hydroelectricity powers the ski resort's snow cannons, ski lifts, restaurants, and hotels, and an off-street trail system, shuttle system, and cross-country mountain biking routes enable car-free travel.

For a car-free weekend, take a shuttle bus or coach from downtown Vancouver or Vancouver International Airport to Whistler Village, located at the base of the Whistler and Blackcomb Mountains. Choose a hotel located along the pedestrian-only Village Stroll to easily walk to shops, restaurants, art galleries, and other attractions, and to rent skis, snowboards, and bikes.

HUB | *Vancouver, Canada; Pacific Northwest United States*

> "WHISTLER IS FOCUSED ON ENVIRONMENTAL PROTECTION THAT BECKONS TRAVELERS WHO WANT TO LEAVE A LIGHT ECOLOGICAL FOOTPRINT."

Skiers ride a hydroelectricity-powered lift to powdery runs on Whistler's peak.

Bird-watchers gather on a boardwalk at Magee Marsh to watch the warbler migration.

Urban Birding

Cleveland, Ohio, U.S.

O f all the reasons Cleveland rocks, bird-watching isn't one that naturally comes to mind. Yet a recent push by the Western Cuyahoga Audubon Society (WCAS) to promote urban birding has made the city a fledgling avi-tourism destination. Visitors can join WCAS field trips and other programs to get the inside scoop on urban birding and on the need to conserve, preserve, and restore wildlife habitats.

Cleveland is located on the southern shores of Lake Erie, which, along with its associated habitats, is among the most bird-rich ecosystems in the United States. Each spring and fall, birders flock here to see millions of migrating winged things. Year-round, all it takes is patience and a pair of binoculars to go bird-watching at sites along the Cleveland Area Loop of the Lake Erie Birding Trail. Other wildlife-rich areas include the forests, meadows, and wetlands of Rocky River Reservation, part of the "Emerald Necklace" of parks ringing the city.

An eastern bluebird is spotted in the winter in Ohio.

Embers at Bushmans Kloof
offers dinner under the stars in
a sandstone amphitheater.

Eco-Escapes

Commune with nature while working toward conservation
at these Earth- and animal-friendly destinations.

1. FINCA ROSA BLANCA, COSTA RICA

Widely considered the spiritual birthplace of ecotourism, Costa Rica is home to every conceivable variation on the theme. One favorite is this sustainable coffee plantation/boutique hotel, near San José. Don't miss the organic coffee tour or the nearby hiking.

2. THE WILLAMETTE VALLEY, OREGON, U.S.

Plot an eco-weekend in Oregon's electric byway–laced wine country, where you can visit the world's first LEED-certified winery (Sokol Blosser) and LEED Gold–certified winery (Stoller), then overnight at the bucolic—and LEED Gold–certified—Allison Inn & Spa.

3. INKATERRA HACIENDA CONCEPCION, PERU

A surprisingly accessible—yet utterly remote-feeling—swath of the Peruvian Amazon, this private and absolutely beautiful reserve places you squarely in monkey and macaw territory, especially on the canopy walkway. Back at ground level, don't miss the local medicinal plant tutorial or a trek to the wildlife-rich lakes near the property.

4. TOPAS ECOLODGE, VIETNAM

This environmentally-friendly lodge is a hilltop hideout in northern Vietnam's Hoang Lien National Park overlooking mountains and rice terraces, both of which make for spectacular hiking and biking, as do the local hill tribe villages.

5. MILIA MOUNTAIN RETREAT, GREECE

A few ecovisionaries with a "lunacy" (as they call it) for land restoration decided to refurbish several 15th-century homes on the island of Crete. The result? This mountain sanctuary and its stellar organic cuisine.

6. MASHPI, ECUADOR

Part high-end ecolodge, part research station, this biologist-staffed complex is hidden away in the Mashpi Reserve outside Quito. At this sustainability-focused lodge, don't miss the Dragonfly ride over the canopy, the Jungle Swing Trail through the forest, or any of the waterfalls.

7. HOTEL CENTRAL PARK, NEW YORK, U.S.

If your idea of an eco-escape doesn't also involve proximity to Broadway shows, this sustainability-minded urban oasis aims to change your mind with everything from shower timers to Central Park ecology tours.

8. BUSHMANS KLOOF WILDERNESS RESERVE, SOUTH AFRICA

This unique lodge on South Africa's Western Cape protects wide-ranging local treasures, from ancient cave art to rare Cape leopards. Humans are exceedingly well cared for too, as you'll find at the spa or any of the gorgeous dining spots.

9. ION ADVENTURE HOTEL, ICELAND

Once the staff dorm of a geothermal plant, this ecohotel near Iceland's Þingvellir National Park is an outsized object lesson in upcycling. The best green feature is the aurora; watch for it from the Northern Lights Bar.

10. SONEVA KIRI, KOH KOOD, THAILAND

Of all the ways this ecoluxe island retreat connects you to the neighboring rainforest, the most memorable may be the Treepod Dining: Local, organic cuisine is delivered via zip-lining servers to your perch in the branches.

> "EXPERIENCE AND LEARN
> ABOUT SARASOTA'S
> NATURAL SIDE."

Nature Made

Sarasota County, Florida, U.S.

Home to idyllic Siesta Beach—regularly ranked among the nation's best—and 80 miles (128.8 km) of freshwater canals open to stand-up paddleboarders, southwest Florida's Sarasota County is nature-made for outdoor recreation. Throughout the Gulf Coast county, eco-conscious travelers can experience and learn about Sarasota's natural side—and lend a hand to help protect it.

Several local hotels and resorts, such as the Hyatt Regency Sarasota and the Resort at Longboat Key Club, appear in the Florida Green Lodging registry, which lists properties committed to recycling, energy efficiency, and water conservation.

Take a deep dive into the undersea world at Mote Marine Laboratory & Aquarium. Showcasing 100 species of marine mammals and research laboratories, Mote is a serious scientific facility that's seriously fun for anyone interested in what lives in the water. Mote's Dolphin and Whale Hospital, Sea Turtle Rehabilitation Hospital, a 135,000-gallon (511,030.6 L) shark habitat, and other facilities and exhibits focus on protecting, understanding, and promoting awareness of marine life.

Plan ahead to get the most out of a Mote visit with the Choose Your Adventure program. The private, behind-the-scenes program includes tours and activities, such as guided coastal walks and sea turtle rehabilitation education sessions for couples, families, and small groups. Visit the Events Calendar on Mote's website to schedule multiple Adventures over a single weekend. Individuals and couples also can join one of Mote's regularly scheduled morning or full-moon, guided kayaking trips to watch for dolphins and manatees in Sarasota Bay.

When you're not participating in a Mote program, explore the downtown Sarasota campus of Selby Gardens, covering 15 tropical acres (6.1 ha) on the bayfront. Selby is the only botanical garden in the world dedicated to the study and conservation of air plants like bromeliads and orchids. Take a docent-led tour to learn more about the living museum's natural collection, which includes more than 6,000 orchids.

HUB | *Miami, Florida, U.S.; Southeastern United States*

Encounter rays at the Ray Touch Pool in the Mote Marine Laboratory & Aquarium.

Tomatoes are freshly picked from the farm's garden.

Home Grown

Eumelia Organic Agrotourism Farm, Laconia, Greece

Experience off-the-grid life in southern Greece at Eumelia (Greek for "harmony"). The sustainable organic farm is nestled in an olive grove in the legendary Peloponnese peninsula, home to the ancient cities of Corinth, Sparta, and Olympia. Rent a car or arrange a private transfer to make the three-and-a-half-hour drive south from Athens to the farm

Once there, settle in for a serene stay in one of five eco-friendly stucco cottages. All are heated and cooled with geothermal power and feature a kitchen, private garden, and veranda. Each is styled inside to reflect an aspect of the surrounding environment—either olive or almond trees, grape vines, sunflowers, or lavender. Plan to visit in August or September to participate in the grape harvest, help press grapes, and learn the art of winemaking. In November or December help pick olives and learn how to make organic extra virgin olive oil.

HUB | *Athens, Greece*

The lighthouse stands over Hunting Island State Park.

Wild Retreat

St. Phillips Island, South Carolina, U.S.

Pristine and protected to stay that way, St. Phillips Island, which lies northeast of Hilton Head in South Carolina's Lowcountry, is the former beach retreat of CNN founder and conservationist Ted Turner. During the nearly 40 years he owned the 4,682-acre (1,894.7 ha) barrier island, Turner restored habitats for numerous species, such as bobcats, loggerhead turtles, and eastern indigo snakes—the longest native snake in the United States at up to 9 feet (2.7 m) long.

Hunting Island State Park acquired St. Phillips in 2017 and launched boat tours to the island in 2019. With its rare ancient dune system, towering Spanish moss–draped live oaks, and abundant wildlife—including alligators and bald eagles—roadless St. Phillips is a powerful reminder that protecting the planet matters. There's no lodging on the island, but you can spend the day hiking the maritime trails and hanging out on the rugged beach. For a wild-island weekend, camp at Hunting Island State Park and take a day trip to St. Phillips.

HUB | *Southeastern United States*

Private villas on Fregate
Island Private overlook the
Seychelles coastline.

An Island Ecosystem

Fregate Island Private, Seychelles

Dubbed a "mini-Galápagos," Fregate is a former colonial plantation that's been reclaimed by nature, thanks
to habitat restoration work by Fregate Island Private.
The exclusive, 500-acre (202.3 ha) island retreat in the middle
of the Indian Ocean has 16 villas, one estate home, and seven
private beaches, including some of the only beaches on Earth
where you can observe sea turtles nesting during the day.
Staying here helps support the lodge's ecosystem regenera-
tion projects, such as the successful effort to save the black-
and-white-winged Seychelles magpie robin from extinction.

Guests are welcome to participate in ongoing conservation
programs like cultivating sea coral, planting endemic tree
saplings, and assisting turtle hatchlings. To see and learn about
the island's many rare, endemic, and endangered species—
including thousands of free-roaming giant Aldabra tortoises
and thousands of different tropical birds—go on guided walks
led by Fregate Island's resident naturalist.

HUB | *Seychelles; Kenya; Tanzania*

Paddle your canoe
through the white water
on the Androscoggin River.

"THE WATERWAYS WERE 'NOT ONLY OUR HIGHWAYS, BUT THE BASIS OF ALL LIFE—AND THEY STILL ARE.'"

PERSPECTIVE

An Epic Canoe Trail

See New England's Vibrant Fall Foliage on a Stretch From New York to Maine

Pines, spruces, and larches stand tall in the 30-million-acre (12.14 million ha) Northern Forest, the largest intact ecosystem east of the Mississippi. But that's not the only draw of this boreal and hardwood forest that stretches across northern Maine, New Hampshire, Québec, Vermont, and New York. The longest inland water trail in the United States winds through these dense woodlands—at their most vibrant with autumn colors. And in these thick forests, Indigenous roots run deep.

The extensive waterway—now designated the Northern Forest Canoe Trail (NFCT), which stretches for 740 miles (1,190.9 km)—was a life-sustaining artery for Native Americans, who traveled back and forth along its length to trade food and supplies.

The waterways were "not only our highways, but the basis of all life—and they still are," says Sherry Gould of the Abenaki Trails Project. Now, the NFCT has become a lifeline for a different constituency, providing open-air recreation and boosting well-being.

Starting in New York State's Adirondack Region and ending in Fort Kent, Maine, the NFCT links 22 rivers and streams, 56 lakes and ponds, and more than a dozen watersheds. The Haudenosaunee (also known as the Iroquois) and Wabanaki peoples navigated much of the current-day route for hunting and gathering and trading goods such as meats, corn, medicines, and herbs.

Then came the European explorers in the early 1500s. They watched Indigenous canoers glide across the waterways with ease and followed suit with their own vessels—spreading disease and disrupting Indigenous hunting patterns along the way. Wars soon followed.

In 1976, outdoorsmen Mike Krepner, Ron Canter, and Randy Mardres of nonprofit Native Trails became fascinated by the forest's epic narratives. They spent a decade studying old maps and blueprints to revitalize the historic water routes, only to later call it off due to the project's overwhelming scope and scale.

In the early 2000s, husband-and-wife duo Rob Center and Kay Henry, the former marketing and management principals of Mad River Canoe in Vermont, picked up where Native Trails left off.

Center and Henry collaborated with local Native communities to ensure infrastructure, including campgrounds, avoided sacred burial sites. All 13 trail-section maps highlight the area's Indigenous roots; trail kiosks do the same.

When the NFCT opened in 2006, the country had few like it. It remains the ultimate prize in long-distance paddling, but it's still an under-the-radar adventure. While a full thru-paddle requires one to two months, paddling individual sections can take between three and five days each—shorter excursions make for the perfect long weekend. Use the NFCT's virtual trip planner before venturing out.

Novice paddlers will appreciate the easier downstream flow while traveling west to east. More experienced oarspeople can find upstream stints and tricky Class IV rapids along the full route. For short trips or long expeditions, NFCT encompasses everything from camping on isolated Saranac Lake islands (trail map 2) to paddling through landscapes made famous in Henry David Thoreau's journals in remote northern Maine (trail maps 11 and 12).

—**Stephanie Vermillion** is a travel and outdoors journalist, filmmaker, and photographer.

> "CONNECT TRAVELERS TO THE
> JORDANIAN WILDERNESS
> WITH MINIMAL IMPACT."

A Community Affair

Feynan Ecolodge, Jordan

A t night, only candlelight illuminates the 26 guest rooms at off-the-grid Feynan Ecolodge. The sustainable stucco lodge does have electricity (fully generated through rooftop solar panels), but it's primarily used to power energy-efficient kitchen appliances and essential lighting. Conserving electricity, water, and other resources is a cornerstone of Feynan's mission: to connect travelers to the Jordanian wilderness with minimal impact on the environment.

Built in 2005 by the nongovernmental Royal Society for the Conservation of Nature (RSCN) and managed by EcoHotels since 2009, Feynan is part of a larger sustainable ecotourism project designed to safeguard the biodiversity and natural environment of the surrounding UNESCO Dana Biosphere Reserve. This astonishingly scenic and wild area encompasses more than 120 square miles (310.8 km), four biogeographical zones (Mediterranean, Irano-Turanian, Saharo-Arabian, and Sudanian), and multiple Bedouin communities and villages.

Everyone on staff at Feynan comes from the immediate area, and most of the food and supplies—such as bread baked by a local Bedouin woman—are locally sourced. In the two on-site workshops, local artisans create the candles and leather furniture used at the lodge. There is also a gift shop where guests can purchase original pieces by artists living in and around Jordan's nine protected areas: Dana, Wadi Mujib, Azraq, Shaumari, Dibeen, Ajloun, Fifa, Yarmouk, and Wadi Rum.

Creating sustainable economic opportunities is key to the RSCN model, which pairs protecting Jordan's wilderness areas with improving quality of life in neighboring rural communities. So when Feynan banned disposable plastic water bottles, for instance, they chose a local alternative: authentic Nabataean clay water jugs crafted by a women's pottery cooperative in Petra. The lodge also employs local Bedouin drivers who, using their own pickup trucks, ferry guests on the bumpy 30-minute ride from the Reception Centre to Feynan.

Stucco walls and chic white decor make up the rooms at Feynan Ecolodge.

China's "rainbow mountains" in Zhangye Danxia National Geological Park are worth hiking through.

Natural Wonders

Waterfalls, glaciers, and auroras—oh my! The world has plenty to offer when it comes to easily accessible wonders of the natural kind.

1. PERITO MORENO GLACIER, ARGENTINA

As most glaciers famously trend in the other direction, Patagonia's Perito Moreno is actually growing. Take in the surreal mass of turquoise and white by boat, on a hike, or from viewing platforms.

2. THE NORTHERN LIGHTS, ICELAND

With vast swaths of dark night sky within easy reach of Reykjavik, Iceland is the ideal stage for the psychedelic light show that powers up when solar winds hit the Earth's magnetosphere.

3. BIOLUMINESCENT BAYS, PUERTO RICO

If you relocated the aurora to the tropics and then submerged it, you'd get something like Puerto Rico's trio of bioluminescent bays—Laguna Grande, La Parquera, and Mosquito Bay—where motion-triggered microorganisms glow greenish blue by night.

4. THE GRUNIONS OF SOUTHERN CALIFORNIA, U.S.

Their name is suggestive of Dr. Seuss characters, but these beach-running fish are a very real Southern California thing—and particularly easy to see on spawning nights between March and September.

5. THE GEYSERS OF EL TATIO, CHILE

The Southern Hemisphere's largest geyser field, El Tatio, is best seen at dawn, when dozens of steaming, spewing holes transform the Atacama Desert into a Vegas-caliber waterworks display. That awe-inspiring show is thanks to more than 60 geysers and hundreds of fumarols stretching across 12 square miles (31.1 sq km) sitting 14,173 feet (4,320 m) above sea level.

6. THE MOONBOWS, ZAMBIA

Granted, Victoria Falls is never *not* amazing. But go the night of a full moon (or the night before or after) and you may experience bonus awe as lunar rainbows tint the legendary mists.

7. RAINBOW RIVER, COLOMBIA

In a land famed for magic realism, a rainbow river should come as no surprise. Still, you can't help but be taken aback by the plant-based reds, yellows, and greens of Caño Cristales (best June to November).

8. RAINBOW MOUNTAINS, CHINA

Prefer your rainbow-colored wonder in solid form? You'll find it in northwestern China's Zhangye Danxia National Geological Park, where the hiking (and even bus touring) is otherworldly. Named a UNESCO World Heritage site in 2009, the mountains get their coloring from various levels of oxidation that has occured on the deep red sandstone.

9. PAMUKKALE, TURKEY

A series of cascading, snow-white travertine terraces, each a self-contained pool of aquamarine water, Pamukkale (translation: "Cotton Castle" in Turkish) would be worth visiting alone. But the neighboring Hierapolis ruins make this UNESCO World Heritage site a must. Both sites receive nearly two million visitors every year, making them Turkey's most visited attractions.

10. GLOWWORM GROTTO, NEW ZEALAND

The North Island's Waitomo Caves turn the thousands of *Arachnocampa luminosa* (glowworms) in these 30-million-year-old grottoes into a dreamy series of subterranean constellations, all best experienced by a guided boat trip through the underground world.

"SAVOR THE QUINTESSEN-
TIALLY SWISS SIGHTS
AND TASTES."

E-Car Road Trip
Switzerland

Go green for a weekend by mapping out a three-day route on the E-Grand Tour of Switzerland, the world's first long-distance road trip for electric vehicles. The entire tour covers more than 1,000 miles (1,600 km) and has more than 300 charging stations at places like hotels, restaurants, and public parking garages. It's possible to zip through the route in a weekend, but you'll want to set a leisurely pace to savor the quintessentially Swiss sights and tastes: Think dramatic alpine passes, glassy lakes, and to-die-for cheeses and chocolates.

For a weekend e-road trip, rent an electric car (options include sporty and family-size Tesla SUVs) and drive about 217 miles (349.2 km) from Geneva to Bern, Switzerland's capital city, and back. Before leaving Geneva, join Geneva Bike Tours' e-bike ride to pedal past iconic Geneva sights, such as St. Peter's Cathedral, built between 1160 and 1260. From the cathedral's North Tower platform you can see sweeping views of the city and its namesake lake.

Drive northeast along Lake Geneva to Lausanne, a compact city easily explored on foot, by bike, and by public transportation, including Switzerland's only metro. Wander the narrow lanes of the old city, centered around Lausanne Cathedral, a Gothic jewel constructed in the 12th and 13th centuries. Just outside the city (six minutes east by train) walk the zigzagging pathways through the steeply terraced vineyards of the Lavaux UNESCO World Heritage site.

From Lausanne, continue north on the e-route to Bern. Stay and charge the car at the classically luxurious Bellevue Palace. Opened in 1865, the grand hotel is named for its "beautiful view" of the Bernese Alps. Soak in Bern's natural and cultural landscapes while strolling the *lauben* (covered walkways) in Bern's Old Town, a UNESCO World Heritage site, and along the banks of the River Aare.

HUB | *Geneva, Switzerland*

Drive an e-car through the winding old road in St. Gotthard Pass.

Minimal Impact

Croan Cottages, County Kilkenny, Ireland

Velvety green fields and hills earned Ireland its Emerald Isle nickname, so it's no wonder the country supports the European Green Deal, a forward-thinking framework for a resilient, carbon-neutral Europe. Visitors can help keep Ireland green—and bring home some simple tips for sustainable living—by staying at Croan Cottages in Kilkenny, two hours south of Dublin airport.

Named for the historic manor house located on the property, the five Croan Cottages are two- and three-bedroom holiday homes designed to make a minimal environmental impact. Electricity is generated using wind and other renewable power sources, and wood ash from the fireplaces is used to fertilize the garden. All kitchen waste is composted, and used cardboard, glass, paper, and plastic products are collected for recycling. Guests share a courtyard and, spring to fall, can register for courses (when available) covering sustainable-living topics such as beekeeping, foraging, and residential cooking.

> "REGISTER FOR COURSES ...COVERING SUSTAINABLE-LIVING TOPICS SUCH AS BEEKEEPING, FORAGING, AND RESIDENTIAL COOKING."

HUB | *Dublin or Limerick, Ireland*

Croan Cottages co-owner Francis Nesbitt feeds some of the animals on the property.

Cyclists pedal through the bike-friendly streets of Copenhagen.

Carbon-Neutral Capital

Copenhagen, Denmark

Green solutions—such as an extremely efficient public transportation network and a web of cycling paths—have put Copenhagen on track to become the world's first carbon-neutral capital by 2025. City leaders see sustainability as good for the planet and for the people, creating an urban area that is more resilient, equitable, and healthy.

CopenHill, the city's waste-to-energy power plant, embodies the city's holistic approach to eco-friendly living. The plant burns 70 tons (63.5 tonnes) of waste per hour and produces clean energy for 60,000 families. Although impressive, it's not the only way CopenHill helps improve quality of life. The plant's multipurpose design includes outdoor recreation spaces on top and on the facade. Spend a day hiking, skiing, and snowboarding on the rooftop and scaling the exterior stacked-block climbing wall. Then, rent an e-bike to experience the city like the locals, more than 60 percent of whom bike to work.

Amager Bakke, a waste-to-power plant, has a ski slope on top.

Relax seaside at Olas in Tulum.

Eco-Chic
Olas, Tulum, Mexico

With only eight suites, oceanfront Olas is considerably smaller than typical Riviera Maya resorts. That tiny footprint, in part, has helped the laid-back hotel capture a highly coveted Platinum LEED certification. Designed to complement, not compromise, the surrounding Yucatán Peninsula nature—including neighboring Sian Ka'an Biosphere Reserve and UNESCO World Heritage site—Olas successfully balances pampering guests and protecting the environment.

The property's planet-friendly practices are a mix of traditional and leading-edge approaches. For instance, a Maya "humidal" system transforms gray water (relatively clean wastewater) into water for plants, while solar panels generate enough clean energy to meet all of Olas's needs. An ingenious gravity-fed system diverts clean water from natural, underground sources directly into each guest suite. Rates include a communal breakfast prepared using ingredients grown on regional family farms or harvested by local fishermen.

HUB | *Cancún, Mexico*

HSBC Rain Vortex is the largest indoor waterfall in the world.

Layovers of the Future
Changi Airport, Singapore

The futuristic Jewel complex at Singapore's Changi Airport brings the outdoors indoors in a spectacular way. Opened in 2019, terrarium-like Jewel makes any long layover in Singapore a reason to celebrate. On a practical level, the 10-story, multi-use restaurant-retail-recreation complex connects three of the airport's four terminals. But, the Jewel's green spaces—landscaped with more than 900 trees and palms and 100,000 shrubs from around the world—boost the glass-and-steel gem's eco-friendly bona fides.

In the four-story Shiseido Forest Valley, feel the rush of the HSBC Rain Vortex, which, at roughly 130-feet-tall (39.6 m) is thought to be the world's tallest indoor waterfall. The cascade is partially powered by collected rainwater, which is also recycled and used to irrigate vegetation in the indoor forest. In the upper-level Canopy Park, stroll along the Topiary Walk, navigate a hedge maze, and wander through themed gardens before walking the Sky Nets suspended under the dome.

HUB | *Southeast Asia*

Jungle Paradise
Isla Palenque Resort, Panama

This jungle island resort delivers on its promise to be a *palenque*, meaning "sanctuary" in the language of Panama's indigenous Ngäbe-Buglé tribes. Located on the Gulf of Chiriquí, off the country's western Pacific coast, the 400-acre (161.9 ha) tropical oasis features eight thatched-roof casitas and a six-room villa sheltered by old-growth forest. To prevent deforestation of this unspoiled wilderness, only sustainably sourced indigenous hardwoods, like plantation teak, and rapidly renewable materials, such as bamboo, were used in building construction. Much of the furniture was also crafted from naturally felled trees.

Guests can participate in Isla Palenque's ongoing reforestation program by transplanting a seedling from the primary rainforest into an area of secondary growth. There's also a behind-the-scenes tour covering the resort's sustainability practices, such as banning single-use plastics and treating wastewater on-site for reuse in irrigating the resort's organic farm. The fruits of the farm and of a "dock-to-dish" sustainable fishing program supply ingredients for the all-organic menu.

HUB | *Panama City, Panama*

Enjoy the view from a beachfront bungalow at Isla Palenque Resort.

A farmer walks through *silleta* flower arrangements at the Parade of the Feria de las Flores in Medellin.

Blooms

For fans of everything botanical, these flower-forward destinations
are worthy of a weekend escape.

1. GREAT SMOKY MOUNTAINS NATIONAL PARK, TENNESSEE, U.S.

Besting all other North American national parks on the floral front, this southern belle is home to more than 1,500 varieties of flowering plants—hence, the nickname "Wildflower National Park"—and April's Springtime Wildflower Pilgrimage.

2. CAPE FLORISTIC REGION, SOUTH AFRICA

So special it's UNESCO protected, this color-saturated swath of South Africa blooms more than once a year. Peg your visit to August's Hopefield Fynbos Show, where you can't miss the king protea, among other endemic beauties.

3. ANZA-BORREGO DESERT STATE PARK, SAN DIEGO, CALIFORNIA, U.S.

To put on their best show—a red, purple, and orange superbloom—the local wildflowers require precise conditions. Start checking the hotline (760-767-4684) in February, and if you're anywhere within driving distance during a promising update, just go.

4. ENNIS, TEXAS, U.S.

The official Bluebonnet City of Texas and home of the Official Texas Bluebonnet Trail, Ennis is the place to be for true fans of the flower—especially in April, when the town's Bluebonnet Trails Festival takes place.

5. HOLLAND, THE NETHERLANDS

Lisse's rainbow-colored fields and Keukenhof Gardens may be the best places to experience April tulip mania, but Holland is small enough that you can squeeze more into a weekend: Amsterdam's Tulip Festival, say, or a drive on the Tulpenroute.

6. PROVENCE, FRANCE

The rare floral event that smells as divine as it looks, the blossoming of the lavender—typically in June and July—has become synonymous with summer in Provence, where you shouldn't miss Notre-Dame de Sénanque or the fields of Valensole.

7. CHERRY BLOSSOMS, JAPAN

Japan's iconic cherry blossoms (*sakura*) and increasingly famous wisteria tunnels could fit into one late April weekend. Start with Ashikaga's wisteria tunnels, then head about three hours north for Sendai's late-blooming sakura.

8. KAZANLUK, BULGARIA

Whether you get here for the official Rose Festival the first weekend of June or any given weekend during the May–June picking season, you'll find Damask rose-themed everything (be sure to try the brandy) in the pink-petaled heart of Bulgaria's Rose Valley. During your visit watch the process of creating rose oil—it takes about 50,000 petals (or 1,500 rose flowers) to produce just one milligram of the essential oil.

9. MEDELLÍN, COLOMBIA

Famously (and infamously) horticulture friendly, Colombia's City of Eternal Spring grows a huge proportion of the nation's flowers and celebrates them with the most important social event of the year: August's Feria de las Flores, complete with eye-popping floral parades.

10. LAKE TEKAPO, NEW ZEALAND

Lupins aren't native to New Zealand's South Island, yet they've thrived so gorgeously since their introduction to these shores—around Lake Tekapo, especially—people now make weekend lupin pilgrimages from Christchurch and beyond in November and December.

"FREIBURG IS ON TRACK TO . . . ACHIEVE CLIMATE NEUTRALITY BY 2050."

Renewable Stars
Freiburg, Germany

Located on the southern edge of the Black Forest near Switzerland and France, Freiburg is known as Germany's ecological capital. Renewable energy, such as solar, biomass, wind, and hydroelectricity powers the city, whose urban district is more than 40 percent woodland. Waste is converted into biomass energy, and city leaders and residents readily embrace the planet-friendly measures—including traffic calming and mixed-use development—put in place to create "a city of short distances."

Walking, biking, and riding public e-buses and trams are the main modes of transportation, and only pedestrians and public transportation are permitted in the city center. Mosaics crafted from colored pebbles and stones carpet this car-free zone, creating an open-air art gallery of sorts on the ground. The mosaics depict various historic, cultural, religious, artistic, and retail symbols, such as geometric designs and a cup and saucer in the entryway of a café.

Due to the community's all-in focus on sustainable living, Freiburg is on track to meet its goals of cutting CO_2 emissions in half or more by 2030 and achieving climate neutrality by 2050. To experience the city at its greenest—and to gather ideas for ways to live more sustainably when you return home—stay in the Quartier Vauban, recognized as one of the world's most sustainable city quarters.

Completed in 2016, Vauban, developed on a reclaimed brownfield site, was built using practices in green infrastructure, such as cooperative housing with rooftop solar panels, urban gardens, and incentives for living car free. Travelers can sample the Vauban lifestyle at the Green City Hotel, conveniently located only 10 minutes by tram from city center Freiburg. The hotel's modern, minimalist design incorporates numerous eco-friendly elements, including highly insulated facades with climbing plants, heating and hot water fueled by solar power, a regional wood chip–burning system, and other renewable energy sources.

HUB | *Munich, Germany; Zurich, Switzerland*

The historic Gothic Münster Cathedral stands among the red roofs of Freiburg.

The central hub of Denver's Union Station dates back to 1914.

Mile High Conservation
Denver, Colorado, U.S.

The Mile-High City is a model for how urban areas can exist in harmony with the natural world. Keeping Denver on track to achieve planet-friendly goals, such as adding 125 miles (201.2 km) of bike lanes by 2023, is the city's Office of Climate Action, Sustainability, and Resiliency. Visitors can plan a planet-friendly weekend by shopping, dining, and staying at some of the nearly 2,000 local businesses participating in the office's Certifiably Green Program. To be Certifiably Green, a business has to commit to using less water and energy, producing less air pollution waste, and reporting verifiable results.

Stay at the city's most historic Certifiably Green property, The Brown Palace Hotel and Spa, open since 1892. Conveniently located close to Denver Union Station (37 minutes by train from the airport), The Brown is an eco-friendly home base for exploring on foot and by public transportation. Among the hotel's buzzy green features: five rooftop bee colonies.

HUB | *Mountain West United States*

Mega Biodiversity
Lapa Rios Lodge, Osa Peninsula, Costa Rica

A conservation easement ensures that the 1,000-acre (404.7 ha) private nature reserve surrounding Lapa Rios Lodge will be protected forever. The reserve, located on Costa Rica's Pacific coast, was established in the 1990s as a protective wildlife corridor for mega-biodiverse Corcovado National Park. Called "one of the most biologically intense areas in the world," Corcovado is home to the world's only remaining primary lowland rainforest.

To maintain a light footprint on this pristine wilderness, the safari-style Lapa Rios Lodge bakes sustainability into all its practices. The main building and private bungalows and villas are fully powered by renewable solar and hydro energy, and guests pay a nominal US$25 Conservation Fee to directly support local conservation efforts, such as hiring more rangers in the national park. Take the behind-the-scenes "Twigs, Pigs, and Garbage" tour to meet the resident pigs, which help reduce kitchen waste and fertilize the gardens.

HUB | *San José, Costa Rica*

Take a hammock break with a view on the lodge balcony.

Alaskan Wilderness

Kenai Fjords Glacier Lodge, Alaska, U.S.

To connect guests with pristine natural environments while maintaining a low impact, Alaska Wildland Adventures built three small wilderness lodges: Kenai Riverside, Kenai Backcountry, and Kenai Fjords Glacier. The off-the-grid seacoast lodge—located within the Native-owned, 1,700-acre (688 ha) Pedersen Lagoon Wildlife Sanctuary—is accessible only by boat. From Seward (about 2.5 hours south of Anchorage), you can watch for humpback whales, nesting puffins, Dall's porpoises, and other marine life as you cruise through Kenai Fjords National Park to the lodge.

Before arriving, all guests are invited to take the 30-minute Travel Better online course sponsored by Sustainable Travel International. At the lodge, sustainability is built into the 16 guest cabins and the communal lodge, all constructed away from the shore to blend into the surrounding nature.

HUB | *Pacific Northwest United States; Western Canada*

Canoers paddle through Alaska's scenic Pedersen Lagoon.

All a Buzz

Bohol Bee Farm Hotel, Bohol, Philippines

Nature faces significant threats from human-driven activities in the Philippines, a biodiversity hot spot that hosts more than two-thirds of the plant and animal species found on Earth. To help stem the tide of habitat loss, pollution, unsustainable harvesting, and illegal wildlife trafficking, the archipelago nation is actively promoting sustainable, community-based ecotourism ventures, such as the Bohol Bee Farm Hotel.

Located on the Bohol Sea in the island-province of Bohol, the rustic farm-stay empowers community members to protect nature. Local farmers tend the farm's beekeeping operation and organic gardens, the fruits of which—including honey, edible flowers, and vegetables—are served in the restaurant and used in products like insect repellent and beeswax lip balm. Along with farming and beekeeping, staff members can develop other marketable skills, such as creating traditional handicrafts. Learn about the farm's eco-friendly practices (and, maybe, incorporate some at home) on the guided tour available to guests.

HUB | *Southeast Asia*

A honeybee gathers pollen on a yellow flower at Bohol Bee Farm.

"THERE'S AN ABUNDANCE
OF WILDLIFE YEAR-ROUND."

The Last Wild Places

Duba Plains Camp, Botswana

Hidden deep in northern Botswana's Okavango Delta, frequently described as "Africa's Garden of Eden," Duba Plains Camp offers a rare glimpse of one of the world's remaining wild places. The intimate lodge (maximum 10 guests) is a "conservation tourism" project of National Geographic filmmakers Dereck and Beverly Joubert, co-founders of Great Plains Conservation, which has conserved nearly a million acres (404,685.6 ha) of land for African wildlife.

Guests at Duba Plains Camp stay in five safari-style tents, perched on platforms made from recycled railroad ties. Guided boating excursions, bush and night walks, and open-vehicle safaris wind through the surrounding 77,000-acre (31,160.8 ha) Duba Plains Reserve, home to all manner of extraordinary wild things. There's an abundance of wildlife year-round, and, depending on the season, the cavalcade of creatures passing by could include elephants, giraffes, hippos, lions, water buffalo, and wildebeests.

This front-row access to where the wild things are isn't cheap. Rates (which include lodging and all meals and activities) range from about US $1,500 to US $3,000 per night. The camp does offer specials—such as four nights for the price of three—throughout the year, which can make the once-in-a-lifetime African wilderness experience somewhat more affordable.

Staying here also supports the long-term survival of Africa's wild places. Through the Conservation and Community Levy added to each stay at Duba Plains Camp, guests directly contribute to local conservation and community development projects, such as the Women's Crafts Groups, where women can earn money by creating traditional basketwork, hand-beaded glass, and other items sold in Great Plains Conservation camps. Guests also can participate in Pack for a Purpose, which encourages travelers to buy and bring supplies needed at their destination. So, for instance, when packing for a long weekend at Duba Plains Camp, leave space in your luggage for crafting essentials like knitting needles, tape measures, and yarn.

HUB | *Gaborone, Botswana; Harare, Zimbabwe*

Take a boat ride to explore the floodplain in the heart of the Okavango Delta.

CHAPTER FIFTEEN

PET-FRIENDLY VACATIONS

Bring Fido and the whole furry gang along on these animal-focused getaways around the globe.

A golden retriever stands in front of "Kissing Camels" at Garden of the Gods park in Colorado (p. 577).

Felines share the space at Mocha Lounge cat café.

Cat Adventures

Tokyo, Japan

Cats hold a place of honor in Japan. where they symbolize protection and good fortune. Feline fanatics will make quick work of a cat-centric weekend itinerary in Tokyo. Start by shopping the multistory Neco Sekai near Kichijoji Station, offering everything from colorful collars and cat hammocks to feline-inspired human gifts, or boutique Neco Action in Yanaka with cat-themed stationery, art, pottery, and jewelry, as well as several takes on *maneki-neko*, the paw-raising "lucky cat." When you're ready to snuggle up to the real thing, start cat café hopping. Since the first felines-included café opened in 2005, dozens of the popular coffee-with-cat creations have clawed out a home in Tokyo. Popular haunts are homey Monta in Asakusa, with nine resident kitties including a Maine Coon and a Norwegian Forest Cat; whimsical Temari no Ouchi in Kichijoji with fairytale-like forest cottage nooks; and chic Mocha Lounge Ikebukuro, where, twice daily, more than two dozen felines feast for an audience in an adorably fluffy row.

HUB | *Kyoto, Japan*

A West Highland white terrier strolls down Sixth Avenue.

Scottish Delight

Tartan Week Parade, New York City, New York, U.S.

If you or your mutt is proudly Scottish, it's time to pay a visit to the Big Apple. Tartan Day celebrates the anniversary of the 1320 signing of the Scottish Declaration of Independence at Arbroath Abbey. Manhattan's Tartan Day parade is the United States' largest annual gathering of Scots, Scottish-Americans, and Scottish enthusiasts—as well as Scottish terriers, West Highland white terriers, Skye terriers, Scottish deerhounds, Shetland sheepdogs, and other breeds. The parade includes Scottish pipers and drummers, as well as societies and clan members, who march up 10 blocks of Sixth Avenue. Register in advance to join in. After the parade, pamper your pooch with a visit to Café Bark and Pet Boutique to peruse bespoke pearl collars and hand-sewn doggie outfits and share a baked treat with your buddy. Book a "pawty package," reserving a designated space for up to 10 dogs and their companions; human treats and a cake for the beasts are included.

HUB | *East Coast United States*

Doggie Field Day

Kauai, Hawaii, U.S.

The state of Hawaii's pet entry policies are notoriously strict, so for vacationers missing dogs at home, the Kauai Humane Society found the perfect win-win: For one afternoon, you can take a shelter dog with you on your Hawaiian adventure. Some field-trippers venture to nearby Kalapaki Bay, a stretch of golden sand with warm, protected waters, stand up paddleboard rentals, and a walk-up lunch spot. Others take the Mahaulepu Coastal Trail, an easy 4-mile (6.4 km) round-trip clifftop hike that takes you to cliff-jumping spot Shipwrecks Beach and sandy Gillin's Beach, and winds past rocky inlets, dunes, and kiawe trees. Forest lovers follow Sleeping Giant Trail, a climb up jungle-covered Nounou Mountain for sweeping ocean views, and finish with a visit to Wailua Shave Ice, where pampered pound pooches—easily identified by their "adopt me" vests—always get a free frozen treat. The popular program, one of the first of its kind in the country, started in 2012 and has fostered many permanent bonds.

HUB | *Honolulu, Hawaii, U.S.; West Coast United States*

One of Kauai Humane Society's shelter dogs hikes on a field trip.

Take your pup on a stroll through downtown Charlottesville.

"THIS VACATION ISN'T ABOUT PLEASING ME. IT'S ABOUT INTRODUCING OUR NEWEST FAMILY MEMBER TO ONE OF OUR FAVORITE PLACES."

The First of Many
One Family Discovers the Joy—and Ease—of Traveling With the Family Pet

The anticipation builds as we approach our destination after a year away. I look for the familiar landmarks: the rolling hills that line Route 29, the bagel shop that has a cult following, the gourmet deli in a gas station. But this vacation isn't about pleasing me. It's about introducing our newest family member to one of our favorite places. Gosh, I hope the puppy likes Charlottesville, Virginia.

It's our first road trip with Sibby, and we're counting on her being as good a traveler as our children. We're visiting the small southern city where my husband Todd and I attended college—a school that welcomes dogs, even maintaining a listserv for sightings. Our weekend stay at the Boar's Head Resort is a stopover on the way to North Carolina's Outer Banks, breaking up the long drive from our home outside Boston.

There's something sweet about returning to the hotel where we spent our wedding night, now with our kids Graham and Elinor, and new pup Sibby, in tow. Admittedly, the location was picked more for its pet-friendly policy than for sentimental reasons. "Bring Fido along," encourages a page on the resort's website, highlighting the "500 green acres" (202.3 ha) and access to nature trails. The waste stations with baggies don't hurt either.

We make use of one after arriving, then drop our duffels in the room, heading to the patio for dinner. The waitress brings Sibby a bowl of water; she's in good company with a dog one table over. Perhaps it's the summer heat, but she seems content in her surroundings. Why not, with a small lake to explore as we wait for our food? When our attention turns to fried green tomatoes and pimento cheese, Sibby settles under my seat.

As Graham and Elinor try the tomatoes and biscuits with pepper jelly, I consider how traveling with a puppy is like traveling with children, an activity we mastered while living abroad in Paris. It doesn't take reading *Bringing Up Bébé* to understand that expectations and exposure are the secrets to smooth sailing. Graham and Elinor will eat and sleep most anywhere, and it appears Sibby will as well. Her foldable playpen helps in that department.

Thanks to a night's rest, our remaining time is as pleasant as that first meal. Sibby sprints off-leash on the farm where a friend grew up and avoids the resident fox who has a taste for hot dogs. She strolls the lawn at the University of Virginia, a destination in its own right. And she sneaks some baguette during a picnic at the vineyard where Todd and I got married. All in all, I'd say she fell in love with "C'ville"—and with road tripping, too.

—**Megan Lisagor Stoessell** is a travel writer who contributes to the *Boston Globe*.

Dachshunds ride a float—satirizing
A Streetcar Named Desire—
through the French Quarter.

"ELABORATE FLOATS TOPPED WITH MASQUERADING MUTTS AND PRIMPED-UP PURE BREEDS"

Carnival for the Dogs

Mardi Gras, New Orleans, Louisiana, U.S.

The wild reverie of Mardi Gras in New Orleans—the weeks-long celebration leading up to Fat Tuesday in February—is world renowned. True participation and entrée to the best parties and parades requires membership, or at least a connection, to a local krewe. Dog owners in the Crescent City can find their clique in the Mystic Krewe of Barkus, the decadent annual festival's only canine-centric club. Since its founding in 1993, positions of honor in the organization—including parade royalty—are held by noteworthy dogs. And through its Mardi Gras activities, including doggie dress-up contests and a royal ball, the outfit raises proceeds for animal welfare organizations in New Orleans and the Gulf Coast region beyond. Its annual pop culture dog-themed parade—Hairy Pawter and the Sorcerer's Bone (2005), Game of Bones: Barkus Marks Its Territory (2018), and Tailtanic: Dogs and Children First (1998), to name a few—includes elaborate floats topped with masquerading mutts and primped-up pure breeds.

To join in on the fun—including "pre-pawty" and "post-pawty" events in Armstrong Park—you'll need to register with the krewe, but revelers and onlookers of both the furry and human kind are welcome on parade day along the 15-block route through the Vieux Carré. Out-of-town visitors wanting to get away from (some of) the revelry can visit the Dog Levee, a grassy berm off-leash dog park along the Mississippi, or stroll along the 25.7-mile (41.4 km) Mississippi River Trail. You'll also want to secure pup-friendly lodging—especially in the highly coveted, centrally located W New Orleans in the French Quarter (small dogs only) and the Old No. 77 Hotel and Chandlery (up to three pets per room, bowls, beds, and ID tags with hotel address included)—as far as a year in advance.

HUB | *Southeastern United States*

STREET DOG
NAME DESIRE
'...BONES'

DESIREE

Stare into the underworld of
a kelp forest at California's
Monterey Bay Aquarium.

Aquariums

Water world magic is on display from whale sharks in Atlanta, Georgia, to Europe's longest underwater tunnel.

1. THE GEORGIA AQUARIUM, ATLANTA, GEORGIA, U.S.

The largest aquarium in the United States harbors hundreds of species, but the unequivocal stars are the whale sharks that you can swim, dive, or even sleep with—overnighting just outside the tank.

2. OREGON COAST AQUARIUM, NEWPORT, OREGON, U.S.

Another surreal spot to dive and sleep with the fish, this aquarium lets you stay overnight in the famed Passages of the Deep tunnels, where you'll be surrounded by some of Oregon's most notable locals (goodnight, broadnose sevengill shark!).

3. TWO OCEANS AQUARIUM, CAPE TOWN, SOUTH AFRICA

Its coordinates alone (at the crosscurrents of the Atlantic and Indian Oceans) make this aptly named spot worth a visit. But then, so do the endemic seahorses, starfish, and, most intriguing, shysharks.

4. THE SHEDD AQUARIUM, CHICAGO, ILLINOIS, U.S.

You need not love fish to love this aquarium. It's housed in a beaux arts masterpiece that thrills aesthetes as much as anyone else. But if the life aquatic *does* appeal, so much the better: 1,500 species cohabitate here, including beluga whales, giant Pacific octopus, penguins, and sea otters.

5. L'OCEANOGRÀFIC, VALENCIA, SPAIN

Another spot that's as much for design lovers as fishophiles, this Jetsons-evoking structure houses—among other things—Europe's longest underwater tunnel, where Elroy might not be psyched about all the sharks.

6. VANCOUVER AQUARIUM, VANCOUVER, BRITISH COLUMBIA, CANADA

Canada's largest aquarium and headquarters for the conservation-focused Ocean Wise organization knows how to make learning fun. Case in point? The Be a Biologist Behind-the-Scenes Encounters, which let kids (and grownups) help out with animal care.

7. MYSTIC AQUARIUM, MYSTIC, CONNECTICUT, U.S.

Two words: *beluga whales*. These comically adorable beasts—whose trademark bulging melons you can pet here—would be reason enough to visit, though peering into the marine animal rescue clinic is a close second.

8. CORAL WORLD, ELIAT, ISRAEL

Not the world's most extensive aquarium or Israel's newest, the beloved Coral World is still nothing if not unique. This offshore tower has an underwater observatory where you feel as if you're diving into the Red Sea in street clothes.

9. MONTEREY BAY AQUARIUM, MONTEREY, CALIFORNIA, U.S.

From its TV and film cameos, this Northern California icon could get by on cultural currency alone but would never have to: The kelp forest, jellyfish gallery, and wave crash tunnel are borderline addictive.

10. CHIMELONG OCEAN KINGDOM, ZHUHAI, CHINA

The Georgia Aquarium had long been the world's largest until this "kingdom" surpassed it in 2014 with almost 13 million gallons (49,210 cubic m) and more than 800 species. The sensory overload pairs perfectly with neighboring Macau, where casino culture blends with Sino-Portuguese relics of the past.

Pup-Friendly Paris

Paris, France

If a weekend in Paris is in the cards, don't leave Fido at home. Though many of Paris's parks are on-leash only and have strict rules for dogs, Parisians welcome well-mannered pooches in spaces reserved for humans only in other parts of the world (on public transport and in many restaurants and shops). No dog-themed cafés necessary—just vacation in style with your best friend! Splurge on the ritzy historic hotel Le Meurice, where pets are welcomed with an engraved collar tag and embroidered carpet featuring their name. First opened in 1835, the property has housed royal overnighters and served as a second home to artist Salvador Dalí. It's adjacent to the bustling 55-acre (22.3 ha) Tuileries Gardens. A pleasant 20-minute stroll through the gardens, past the Louvre, and across the Seine will get you to Petsochic in the sixth arrondissement. There you can purchase high-end leather leashes and their award-winning non-GMO dog kibble. You can also send your pup to the spa, where it will be shampooed, lathered in oils and Italian creams, and receive a haircut, beauty diagnostic, and custom fur regimen.

HUB | *Major Western European Cities*

> "VACATION IN STYLE WITH YOUR BEST FRIEND!"

A pup enjoys the rest while his owner takes a coffee break at a Parisian café.

Paddle board with Fido close to the Austin Boardwalk on Lady Bird Lake.

Take to the Water

Austin, Texas, U.S.

Take to the water to beat the Texas heat. At "Barking Springs," the nickname for a section of Barton Springs just below Zilker Park's 3-acre (1.2 ha) spring-fed Barton Springs Pool, dogs convene and frolic year-round in refreshing 68°F (20°C) water. On the section of the Colorado River known as Lady Bird Lake, Rowing Dock rents pet-friendly kayaks, canoes, and stand-up paddleboards within view of the downtown skyline. When you're ready to dry off, stroll through nearby Zilker Botanical Garden or romp off-leash on Zilker Park's great lawn. Then it's time to grab some grub. With the most pet-friendly restaurants per capita in the United States—there's even a doggie restaurant week featuring feasts for fur babies—options abound. Dogs will appreciate Yard Bar's attached off-leash park or Lustre Pearl East's huge yard with bar games and chilled covered patio; bring your dog to The Cavalier to earn punches on a card redeemable for gratis drinks.

HUB | *South Central United States*

Paddleboard rentals include life jackets for your pet.

Scales & Tails

ReptileFest, Chicago, Illinois, U.S.

Slithering scales and slime—oh my! This annual family-friendly expo put on by the Chicago Herpetological Society at Northeastern Illinois University is the largest educational reptile and amphibian show in the country. Over a full weekend in April, it affords the opportunity for kids to learn about, and become more comfortable with, all kinds of reptiles and amphibians via educational displays and hands-on interaction. In attendance are hundreds of representatives from some 200 species including tree frogs, axolotl, leopard geckos, giant tortoises, alligators, boa constrictors, and chameleons. Though you won't be able to purchase your next pet here (other reptile expos have notorious reputations for selling wild-caught creatures, which puts unnecessary pressure on populations and ecosystems), you will find contact information for sustainable breeders and adoption outlets, as well as tips on how to care for a present or future reptilian or amphibian family member.

HUB | *Midwestern United States*

A green tree snake coils around a branch.

A miniature Doberman cheers on the Padres at Petco Park.

Dog Days
San Diego, California, U.S.

America's Finest City is just as nice for your pooch as it is for their humans. In October, join Hornblower Cruises' two-hour Bow Wow Brunch along Silver Strand State Beach. On the cruise, dogs and their owners will both take part in a buffet feast and city views. Or opt for the shorter Pet Day on the Bay, a narrated animal-friendly tour of more than 50 city landmarks held every April. Both cruises are aboard a multistory dining yacht with an onboard sundeck doggy relief station. If you'd rather take a self-guided cruise, consider paddling offshore on a dog-friendly Hydrobike through the bay. Back on dry land, head to Petco Park, home to the Padres baseball team. Watch a game from the stadium's Barkyard—a series of private, turf-lined viewing boxes in left center field specifically designed for dog owners. Overnight at Hotel Republic, which includes dog amenity packages and a Thursday Yappy Hour, or Hotel Indigo with no pet restrictions or additional fees; both are downtown.

HUB | *West Coast United States*

A Shore Thing
Biloxi, Mississippi, U.S.

For a dog-friendly beach vacation, base yourself in one of the tropically colored private Front Beach Cottages in Ocean Springs, Mississippi. Along with plenty to do with your pooch, the cottages offer free use of beach gear and kayaks throughout the weekend. Paddle out with the pup into Biloxi Bay and visit the offshore islands including 400-acre (161.9 ha) Deer Island Coastal Preserve, home to endangered birds and archaeological sites dating to 8000 B.C. Dine at Shaggy's Biloxi Beach, a seafood joint with a beach bar vibe and dog-friendly scene. The following day board the Biloxi Shrimping Trip's hour-long dog-friendly cruise. The boat drags a net for part of the tour so you can see what it's like to fish for shrimp. If you're in town for baseball season, extend your trip through Monday night for MGM Park's Barks and Brews. Home to the Biloxi Shuckers, the park offers discount beer, a pregame dog parade, and a grassy berm in right field for pups and their owners to watch the action.

HUB | *New Orleans, Louisiana, U.S.; Southeastern United States*

A shrimp boat floats in the Gulf of Mexico near Ocean Springs.

Tour With Your Pup
Colorado Springs, Colorado, U.S.

Ever wished you could spend the day exploring indoor spaces with your furry companion? Colorado Springs has got your back. At the Peterson Air & Space Museum, you and your pet can wander through two hangars and a historic terminal chock-full of U.S. Air Force memorabilia and retired planes while learning about aviation. Visit the Manitou Cliff Dwellings' indoor museum of Native American artifacts with leash in hand, as well as explore a series of 40 700-year-old relocated Anasazi cliff dwelling ruins inside and out. Then share a meal at Pub Dog—the only Colorado restaurant permitted for indoor dining with dogs. Enjoy burgers, salads, sandwiches, and quesadillas while your dog feasts on beef patties, bacon, a "popsicle" made of chicken broth and celery, or their signature "Bark Bowl" with brown rice, sweet potatoes, and meat patty. It'll be hard to tell who's more excited about the outing—you or the pooch.

HUB | *Mountain West United States*

Pets and their humans can enjoy the Colorado snow.

"PAUSE TO LET THE PONIES PERUSE THE RIPENED HEDGEROWS."

Pony Up

Sevenoaks, Kent, England

An hour's drive south of London, and also accessible by commuter line, the British countryside beckons in Kent's Sevenoaks, where animal-loving children and children at heart can live out pony-owning fantasies. Plan a weekend around a visit to the region, home to numerous stables, equestrian centers, and riding schools as well as historic homes, country gardens, and the forested High Weald hills of North Downs.

Outside the town of Knockholt, head into a private pasture near Chevening House, an estate that dates to the 13th century, to meet some adorable attention-seeking ponies. Ponies tend to have thicker hair than standard horses, so spend some time learning grooming techniques and proper care of their hooves, manes, and tails. Then get creative bedazzling their flowing locks, incorporating flowers, ribbons, bows, and clips. Finally, parade your pony to greener pastures for a grassy reward. In the afternoon, take a horse- or pony-riding lesson at one of several area stables before meandering toward your accommodations down a quiet country lane in Chiddingstone Hoath. Overnight in a cozy cottage at Spokeshave, a converted horse stable turned two-story, two-bed, and two-bath contemporary home surrounded by gardens and the start of several trails leading into Puckden Wood.

The following day, join a small group for a pony walk through the idyllic countryside, learning about the area's native and wild-growing plants and shrubs. Along the way, you'll pause to let the ponies peruse the ripened hedgerows. See the ponies' different personalities and give pets and scratches to all. Both pony experiences are bookable through Airbnb. Cap the day with a leisurely late lunch in the Three Horseshoes village pub in Knockholt. And if these experiences stirred, rather than satiated, your pony dreams, visit *preloved.co.uk* for riding loans and shared care of horses and ponies in need of some extra love near you.

HUB | *London, England*

Shetland ponies huddle together to keep warm on a wet day.

A Great Dane cruises along the open road.

Friendly Giants

Great Dane National Specialty Show, Kansas City, Missouri, U.S.

Whether you own a Great Dane or are just a fan, it's hard not to smile when you watch herds of the gentle giants gallop and play together. Get your fix at the Great Dane National Specialty Show, held every six years in October in Kansas City. The event highlights the best of the Great Danes' obedience and agility skills and features some 800 lanky purebreds. Want to expand your experience? The Kansas City Great Dane Meetup organizes breed-specific park gatherings. Previous events have seen congregations of up to 150 frolicking beasts. While in town, check out the towering 217-foot-tall (66.1 m) World War I Memorial, then take a stroll through the larger-than-life shuttlecocks on the pet-friendly lawn of the Nelson-Atkins Museum of Art. Top it off with a visit to the warehouse-style Bar K Dog Bar, a huge restaurant and coffee bar fashioned from recycled shipping containers and connected to a 2-acre (0.8 ha) dog park.

HUB | *Midwestern United States*

Fairgoers visit the animals at the agricultural fair.

Dog Town

Oregon State Fair, Salem, Oregon, U.S.

The sprawling state fairgrounds in north Salem hosts its annual state fair every August to September. Pets are allowed throughout, but the main grounds can be a bit chaotic, so if your pup isn't great with crowds, be cautious. If you don't have your own furry friend to tow along, you can still get your fix: First, check out winning agricultural pets in the historic Poultry Building. Then swing by the petting farm, an enclosure where wallabies, miniature ducks, potbellied pigs, fallow deer, and llamas mingle with fairgoers. Be sure to beeline to DogTown for some truly incredible canine feats. Nimble, agile, and high-flying dogs run courses while catching Frisbees, attempt high jumps, speed swim, and generally defy expectations of just being a "good boy." Plus, you can meet inspirational service dogs and learn tips from professional trainers. The fair's grand finale is the X-Treme Air Dog World Championships, where pooches jump from the end of a dock into a pool; champs have leaped more than 29 feet (8.8 m).

HUB | *Pacific Northwest United States*

Running With Dogs
Various Locations, Northern Ireland

Runners rejoice! Canicross—the sport of running with your dog attached to a bungee around your waist—is an ideal way to exercise and bond with your best friend. Started as a way to exercise sled dogs during snow-free months, the mushing-like sport is gaining popularity worldwide. Learn to match your cadence with your dog's via expert one-on-one sessions at Dog Trails NI in Mid Ulster or Belfast, then join a group run with the local canicross community. Since canicross can be done in any park with well-maintained trails, the scenic region doesn't disappoint; popular paths include those through the moody 12 peaks of Newcastle County Down's Mourne Mountains; Drumnaph, a grassy trailed Woodland Trust forest in Mid Ulster; the cliff-backed sandy crescent of Benone Beach on the North Atlantic Coast; and the pond-dotted boglands of Peatlands Park in County Armagh.

HUB | *Belfast, Northern Ireland*

Practicing Canicross, a runner takes his beagle for a sunny morning run.

Orphaned African elephant Isholta plays in a mud bath at the David Sheldrick Wildlife Trust.

Zoos

These conservation-focused animal kingdoms from San Diego, California, to Sweden offer one-of-a-kind encounters with nature's finest.

1. THE SAN DIEGO ZOO, CALIFORNIA, U.S.

Though its exhibits and experiences (including several behind-the-scenes tours) make this the nation's most visited zoo, it's equally well known for its conservation efforts—a major focus since the first international conference on zoos and conservation took place here in 1966.

2. THE DAVID SHELDRICK WILDLIFE TRUST, NAIROBI

This acclaimed Nairobi National Park sanctuary—which will utterly wow you with cuteness during the single hour a day that it is open to visitors—not only rescues orphaned elephants and rhinos, but also leads antipoaching efforts in the region and beyond.

3. THE BRONX ZOO, NEW YORK, U.S.

The New York home of the Wildlife Conservation Society—whose aim is to preserve the world's largest wild places—this zoo is as much about fieldwork as exhibits. Still, the resident bison, bears, and big cats never fail to dazzle.

4. THE WOODLAND PARK ZOO, WASHINGTON, U.S.

Seattle being Seattle, sustainability reigns supreme here (you can even buy "Zoo Doo" compost for home use). And while every exhibit is mindfully created, the Wildlife Survival Zone—home to red pandas, Asian cranes, and maned wolves—is a must.

5. CHENGDU RESEARCH BASE OF GIANT PANDA BREEDING, CHINA

Given panda habitat loss, this acclaimed rescue aims to create the best possible breeding conditions. Beyond observing the adults in their lush surrounds, you may get to see impossibly adorable babies in incubators.

6. SMITHSONIAN'S NATIONAL ZOO & CONSERVATION BIOLOGY INSTITUTE, WASHINGTON, D.C., U.S.

Its American Trail Exhibit is as good as you'd expect from the official national zoo (do not miss the underwater viewing), but the institution does as much work in research field stations around the world as in D.C.

7. THE AUCKLAND ZOO, NEW ZEALAND

A renowned protector of New Zealand's unique wildlife—and key participant in the Department of Conservation kiwi recovery program—this zoo is home to a huge cast of colorful creatures (see: kakariki), plus photography workshops and behind-the-scenes experiences.

8. THE ARIZONA-SONORA DESERT MUSEUM, TUCSON, ARIZONA, U.S.

Some of the best habitats at this Tucson icon are so sprawling, you're not sure where they end and the desert begins. So even if you have to do some extra scouting for javelinas, you feel good about it.

9. NORDEN'S ARK, SWEDEN

Actively involved in the breeding and reintroduction of endangered species, this acclaimed zoo and wildlife park tells you in advance that you'll need patience (and maybe binoculars) to see certain residents.

10. THE DENVER ZOO, COLORADO, U.S.

This super-fun zoo offers remarkably close encounters (don't miss the giraffe feeding), carousel and train rides, and 4-D theatrical productions. It also manages conservation projects that range from Mongolia to Botswana.

> "CARMEL-BY-THE-SEA
> IS ONE OF THE MOST
> DOG-FRIENDLY TOWNS
> IN THE U.S."

Road Trip Warriors

Pacific Coast Highway, California, U.S.

S ling that doggy hammock across the backseat, choose a pup-friendly playlist, and roll the windows down—some of the best bits of winding coastal Scenic State Highway 1, with plenty of stop-offs for both you and your furry friend, are within a weekend's reach.

Start at San Francisco's Crissy Field, where dogs can romp off leash seaside or tethered on trails with a gorgeous Golden Gate Bridge backdrop. Then, soak in the 170-mile (273.6 km) winding coastal stretch to Big Sur, a manageable turnaround point, stopping at the sites that move you. You'll cross Bixby Bridge, one of the Central Coast's most Instagrammed features; pass Julia Pfeiffer Burns State Park, home to the scenic 80-foot (24.4. m) McWay Falls—for this stop, dogs can't go beyond the day-use parking lot; and inland find Pfeiffer Big Sur State Park with a handful of dog-friendly forest trails. You'll also cruise past Carmel-by-the-Sea, rated one of the most dog-friendly towns in the United States. Take a break here to stroll past shops that provide gratis dog biscuits and doggie water, dine in pet-friendly restaurants, and let your dog enjoy the freedom of an off-leash romp on the white sand of Carmel Beach or through meadows, oak, and Monterey pine forest within the city's 37-acre (15 ha) preserve at Mission Trail Park.

In Big Sur, pop a pup tent and bed down beneath the stars at Kirk Creek Campground. Be sure to arrive in daylight hours: Campsites are on a granite escarpment 100 feet (30.5 m) above the Pacific with sweeping coastline views that you'll want time to enjoy by a campfire before the chilly evening sets in. Sound a bit too rugged? Forest glamping—in an electrified safari tent with separate doggie bed and human mattress featuring luxury linens—is also on offer at nearby Ventana Big Sur. In the morning, take a walk along Sand Dollar Beach or explore one of several trails leading into the surrounding Los Padres National Forest before returning north.

Dogs enjoy a beach walk as the sun sets over the Pacific Ocean.

Part of the Herd

Pioneertown, California, U.S.

Just 20 miles (32.2 km) northwest of Joshua Tree Park lies the opportunity to cuddle and play with floppy-eared Nubian goats. Yogi Goats Farm & Retreat in Pioneertown is a small, off-the-grid working farm that hosts a veggie garden, chickens, turkeys, and peacocks. But most important for your visit: Twenty-two goats live and interact with guests on the property. Learn to milk the goats, and in turn how to turn goat milk into cheese, ice cream, yogurt, or kefir. Outside the goats' pen, you can also practice guided yoga. In the evening, join 15 of the friendliest Nubians—a breed well suited to the vast temperature swings of the high Mojave Desert—on an easy and scenic 3-mile (4.8 km) sunset walk past piñon trees and boulders. One of the farm's co-owners and self-described goat whisperer, Emmanuel, knows how to bring out each of the goats' unique personalities: "Pina and Pipa are the ones to watch during the hikes," he says. Then there's "Boca, named mouth in Spanish, because he loves to kiss people." And "Laluna and her daughter Cielita are the best massage therapists. Everyone loves it!"

HUB | *Western United States*

> "TWENTY-TWO GOATS LIVE AND INTERACT WITH GUESTS ON THE PROPERTY."

From milking goats to cuddling with them, guests can mingle among 22 goats on the property.

Blue skies and clouds are reflected in Chatcolet Lake inside Heyburn State Park.

Stretch Your Legs
Heyburn State Park, Idaho, U.S.

There's nothing like the great outdoors with man's best friend, and northern Idaho's Heyburn State Park offers numerous opportunities to enjoy nature together. Nearly a third of the more than 8,000-acre (3,237.5 ha) park is water—so you can rent a boat, fish, or take a dip with your pup. On land, the Indian Cliff Trail, an under 3-mile (4.8 km) loop past a burbling brook through cedar, hemlock, and Ponderosa pine forest, offers a stunning lookout over Chatcolet Lake, the perfect spot for a rest and water break for both of you. Take a dip with your dog at Plummer Point beach. Then, as the day winds down, pitch a tent in one of three pup-friendly campgrounds or opt to stay in one of the pet-friendly cottages or rustic camper cabins built by the Civilian Conservation Corps in the 1930s. Rise and stretch all six of your legs along part of the paved 72-mile (115.9 km) Trail of the Coeur d'Alenes, which runs through the park and along the lakeshore.

HUB | *Pacific Northwest United States*

Fish off floating docks around Chatcolet Lake.

> "MAKE A LOOP THROUGH THE HEART OF THE STATE WITH A LAZY LONG WEEKEND."

In the Vines

Northern Virginia, U.S.

Rolling vineyards, forested hikes, and history beckon a short drive outside of the nation's capital. Though grape growing here dates to the late 1700s, it wasn't until almost 2010 that the region blossomed into the wine country it is today with more than 300 vineyards and wineries. From Barrel Oak Winery in Delaplane—which goes by its acronym BOW and features dogs on its wine labels—to Chateau Morrisette, which proudly owns the domain name thedogs.com and holds adoption days, Virginia is one of the top states for sipping alongside your furry best friend.

Make a loop through the heart of the state with a lazy long weekend based at the Inn and Tavern at Meander in Locust Dale. The historic property, founded in 1766, has seven contemporary pet-ready cottages and goody bags with homemade dog treats and to-go water bowls. When you're not off exploring, there's outdoor pet-friendly dining and a 1-mile (1.6 km) walking trail on the property.

Set off with a picnic basket and a leash to lively BOW for fireside wine tastings and a hillside lunch overlooking the vines. From there head to the smaller, equally dog-friendly DuCard Vineyards with a Blue Ridge Mountain backdrop. Wrap your day in the quaint town of Culpeper, home to nano-brewery Beer Hound, whose beers are named for movie-famous dogs: Olde Yella (American Pale), Fang (Oatmeal Stout), and Scrappy Doo (Specialty Ale), to name a few.

The next day, experienced hikers can head to White Oak Canyon, a 9.5-mile (15.3 km) out-and-back trail through Shenandoah National Forest (park fees apply). Those looking for more of a stroll will enjoy the 8.5 miles (13.7 km) of trails around James Madison's Montpelier. Dogs are welcome on both but must be leashed. Spend the rest of your time relaxing and hopping between other popular dog-friendly wineries and vineyards including Early Mountain and Three Fox Vineyards— or closer to D.C., have a tasting and an on-leash stroll at the stunning and pup-friendly Stone Tower Winery in Leesburg.

HUB | *Washington, D.C., U.S.; Mid-Atlantic United States*

With your dog on-leash and wine in hand, stroll the beautiful grounds of Stone Tower Winery in Leesburg.

A diver safely watches
a tiger shark swim by
in the Bahamas (p. 597).

CHAPTER SIXTEEN

ADRENALINE RUSHERS

Get your thrills in these adventure capitals, from diving with sharks in the Bahamas to sandboarding in Chile.

Northern Baja is an excellent place to surf.

Surfing Safari
Baja, Mexico

The Baja Peninsula stretches some 747 miles (1,202 km) from Tijuana to Cabo San Lucas. The eastern coast borders the narrow Gulf of California, but the western coast is one long line of Pacific Ocean.

The area has been popular with surfers since the 1940s, famous for right-hand swells, isolated breaks, and beautiful barrels. Although Baja Malibu is 5 miles (8 km) south of the U.S. border, its chilly winds keep the crowds away. This area is known for its summer beach breaks and big barrel surfing during the winter. Party town Rosarito has some good, consistent all-level surf near the pier. For the full immersion, ride the mechanical bull at Papas & Beer, as well as the surf. K-38 is the favorite with dedicated wave riders: In the right conditions, it has a near-perfect swell that can be surfed in any direction.

Beginners or wannabe surfers should head south to Todos Santos, where surf schools take newbies to the easy waves lapping the beach at Los Cerritos.

HUB | *West Coast United States*

A boarder carves into the dunes, sending sand flying.

Carve Up a Desert
San Pedro, Chile

The Atacama Desert is one of the driest places on Earth. At a high altitude of nearly 8,000 feet (2,438.4 m), this remote landscape is home to a uniquely suited adrenaline sport: sandboarding.

The town of San Pedro, located near the corner of where the long sliver of Chile meets Paraguay and Bolivia, is reached by Calama and home to several companies offering guided tours or sandboard rentals. Travelers are either ferried by car or—for the bold brave enough to pedal through sand at altitude—cycle to the base of dunes rising up in relentless red and tan waves.

Riders forge their way through ankle-deep sand to the top of a ridge before stepping onto their boards and blazing a trail down a glittering face of sand. For beginners, progress can be slow, but experts can reach speeds of 51 miles an hour (82 km/h). It's a big day out, with the altitude and heat intense, but it's something deliciously different.

HUB | *Santiago, Chile*

Saddle Up

Nicoya Peninsula, Costa Rica

The rugged Nicoya Peninsula, Costa Rica's largest peninsula, located in Guanacaste Province, is best seen by horseback. There are a number of outfitters and rides to choose from, whether you're after a full day in the saddle or a multiday ride, stringing together stops like Tamarindo, Playa Junquillal, and San Juanillo.

Walk and canter along golden beaches, weaving along a shoreline and swimming the horses across channels as the sun warms your shoulders. It's rumored that the offshore islands that stud the sapphire sea used to be where pirates stashed their treasure, so keep an eye out: You never know what you might find.

Instead you can wander along forested trails, kicking up dust through fishing villages and ranching towns bright with bougainvillea in vibrant purples and pinks. The cowboy country legacy is apparent everywhere, from the wandering Brahman bulls with their long ears, velvet skin, and humped backs, to the spirited horses that visitors come here to ride. By taking to the saddle, you're instantly part of that tradition.

HUB | *San José, Costa Rica*

Riders roam the coast of Playa Conchal on their steeds.

"NO ONE HERE SLOWS DOWN IN WINTER."

No Matter the Weather

Bend, Oregon, U.S.

Bordered by the Cascade Range, cut through by the Deschutes River, and fringed by high desert and Ponderosa pine forests, the town of Bend lives and breathes adventure all year round: Skiing, hiking, kayaking, mountain biking, fat biking, and camping are just some of the activities on offer. And each day brings with it outdoor food truck courts, microbreweries, and coffee carts.

Spring fever hits Bend hard, and everyone takes to the trails, from the popular Deschutes River Trail (a 12-mile/19.3-km track through the heart of Bend that can be hiked in sections or shorter loops), an after-work favorite with locals, to one of the 71 parks in and around Bend, including Smith Rock State Park or Pilot Butte State Park. For something special, check out the lava tubes that tunnel under Bend, including the Lava River Cave, a mile-long (1.6 km) self-guided lava tube hike; dress warmly—the average temperature in the tube is 42°F (5.5°C).

Summer is the time to get on the Deschutes River. Stand-up paddleboarding, kayaking, and canoeing are all popular, with plenty of shops offering rentals or guided excursions. Surfers and white-water kayakers should check out the centrally located Bend Whitewater Park, which has an ideally placed viewing bridge.

Cycling is a way of life in Bend, and autumn is a perfect time to explore the more than 300 miles (482.8 km) of linked trails that circle the city and surrounding area.

No one here slows down in winter, which turns Bend into a wonderland. The mountains surrounding Bend get piles of snow every year, but the town gets only around 30 inches (76.2 cm), making it an easy city to navigate in winter. Mount Bachelor Ski Resort is the place for downhill skiing and snowboarding, while cross-country skiers enjoy more than 44 miles (70 km) of trails around Bend.

At the end of every day, no matter what the season, people gather at hot spots like the Lot (a collection of food trucks serving everything from Thai food to burgers, with heated outdoor seating available) to trade the day's tales and adventures.

The Deschutes River Trail offers water views for runs and walks.

Take your mountain bike on Slickrock Trail in Moab.

Red Rock Playground
Moab, Utah, U.S.

Moab is a rust and rose jungle gym of spires, slabs, and dusty, boulder-strewn trails. This beckoning expanse has a global reputation as the best mountain biking destination in the world. Located in eastern Utah, near the border of Colorado, Moab, surrounded by national parks and forests, struck the geography jackpot.

Mountain bikers started using the area's old mining roads years ago, eventually expanding the trail network to an adrenaline-dripping web of hundreds of miles of single-track trails. There is something for everyone in Moab, from the beginner Brand Trails (15 interconnecting loops that can be connected any way you choose, like different levels of ski runs) to the Moab classic, the Slickrock Trail, a nearly 10-mile expanse (16.1 km) of rock that will redefine your feelings about mountain biking.

This is desert country, and the weather plays a role here, with baking heat to snow to mud. Check in with local outfitters about the best time to visit before your weekend of riding.

HUB | *Mountain West United States*

Paloheinä offers miles of cross-country skiing.

Cross-Country Tracks
Helsinki, Finland

Helsinki, Finland's capital, is a cosmopolitan, compact, seaside city surrounded by nature. Come November to March, the city crystallizes into a winter wonderland. Although Lapland to the north is better known for cross-country skiing—the sport is ingrained in Finnish culture and was once the main means of transport—vibrant Helsinki offers visitors 124 miles (200 km) of groomed trails to swoosh along.

The Paloheinä recreational area has forest trails for all levels, while the Tali neighborhood makes use of snow-covered golf courses, allowing skiers to soak in stunning views from frosted fairways. Herttoniemi, located in east Helsinki, has a connected network of trails that makes it popular with skiers of all levels: families enjoying outdoor time together, serious sportsmen in color-coordinated gear flashing past in a sweat, smiling amateurs finding their feet. And if the weather turns, there's always Kivikko Ski Hall, an indoor cross-country ski track with ever perfect conditions.

HUB | *Major Western European Cities*

Lemon sharks gather around a seabed in crystal clear Bahamian waters.

Shark Attack

Tiger Beach, the Bahamas

Share the ocean with one of the most impressive predators on the planet: tiger sharks. These striped beauties average 12 feet (3.7 m) in length and exude presence. At Tiger Beach, you can have the privilege of seeing them in their natural environment.

Tiger Beach is a shallow bank of sand, sea grass, and coral reef located about 25 miles (40.2 km) north of Grand Bahama Island. Divers descend to the seafloor, getting into position behind the shark feeders, trained divers with crates of fish that they gently, deliberately offer up to the tiger sharks (and lemon, Caribbean reef, and sand tiger sharks) that slowly glide in, ready for a snack. These are wild animals in a wild place, but it's far from a feeding frenzy: Divers get the chance to sit still and marvel at the grace, beauty, strength, and individual personalities of these extraordinary creatures.

Wrap up your sharky adventure with a drink at the Margaritaville Sandbar, a quirky beach shack in Freeport that's a favorite among locals.

HUB | *Grand Bahama, the Bahamas; Miami, Florida, U.S.*

Kayakers paddle under the bridges of Venice's canals.

Paddling Adventures

Ply the waters on a canoe, kayak, or raft from the white waters
of Marrakech to the scenic canals of Venice.

1. THE THOUSAND ISLANDS ARCHIPELAGO, U.S. AND CANADA

Belying its own name, this dreamy stretch of the St. Lawrence River at the New York–Ontario border is home to more than 1,800 islands (some big enough for only a single tree)—and countless kayak and canoe itineraries.

2. BOUNDARY WATERS CANOE AREA WILDERNESS, MINNESOTA, U.S.

It's the lake count that tops 1,000 when you go farther west along the border to Minnesota's Boundary Waters Canoe Area Wilderness. Though you could spend an eternity paddling this serene, wildlife-rich refuge, local outfitters also offer day trips.

3. VENICE, ITALY

Whether you join the thousands who participate in May's fabled Vogalonga noncompetitive race from St. Mark's to Burano (any rowed or paddled vessel is allowed) or calmly kayak through the city's canals, the backdrop can't be beat.

4. NAPALI COAST, HAWAII, U.S.

These soaring, jagged emerald cliffs, which you'll likely recognize from their cameos in *Fantasy Island* and *Jurassic Park*, make a surreal backdrop as you kayak this often challenging 17-mile (27.4 km) stretch on Kauai's North Shore.

5. TENA, ECUADOR

Tucked into the Ecuadorian rainforest, this town is surrounded by so many rivers—a major Amazon tributary among them—that whitewater enthusiasts flock here for the smorgasbord. Options range from gentle floats to Class IV rapids.

6. JOHNSTONE STRAIT, VANCOUVER ISLAND, CANADA

Reportedly the world's largest resident orca pod, the killer whales that call the Johnstone Strait home each summer make Vancouver Island kayaking heaven. (The surrounding temperate rainforest doesn't hurt either.) Organized trips, including weekend options, abound.

7. AHANSAL RIVER, MOROCCO

This rafting hot spot outside Marrakech is equal parts fun (Class III and IV rapids) and awe. Cutting through the Atlas Mountains, the water is often a clear turquoise.

8. DALMATIAN COAST, CROATIA

Transparent blue-green waters, hundreds of islets, stunning beaches, and a litany of UNESCO World Heritage sites—Split, Korčula, Dubrovnik—make for spectacular kayaking along this stretch of coastline. Day trips are offered by local guides.

9. PRINCE WILLIAM SOUND, ALASKA, U.S.

This Alaskan inlet offers countless kayaking opportunities, but the one that arguably packs the most awe into a day trip is Blackstone Bay. After paddling alongside harbor seals through an ice floe, you'll reach an epic glacier-viewing zone. There are in fact seven glaciers in the cliffs bordering Blackstone Bay, but the most impressive is Blackstone glacier, which you can watch calve into the blue waters from a safe distance away.

10. MAE TAENG RIVER, CHIANG MAI, THAILAND

Depending on the section you choose, this Chiang Mai rafting favorite comes with serious rapids (up to Class IV), beautiful scenic views, riverside villages, and the occasional strolling elephant. The one constant? The staggering beauty of the surrounding jungle.

Hike, Ski, Glide & Ride
Interlaken, Switzerland

As the name suggests, Interlaken links two glacier lakes, Thun and Brienz, on a narrow meadow of land, surrounded by the daunting peaks of Eiger, Jungfrau, and Mönch. With a backyard like this, it's no wonder the town has a reputation as a retreat for the adventurous, offering up any number of outdoor experiences.

Hiking, of course, is popular, and there are almost too many routes to choose from, such as Pizol 5-Lake track (a mountain pass that takes you past five crystal lakes) and the easier two-hour circuit of Panoramaweg.

Although Interlaken isn't a ski resort town, it is an excellent base for taking to the nearby slopes of the Jungfrau region and the Beatenberg-Niederhorn area, which is better suited to beginners and families. Heli-skiing is on offer between December and May, serving up pure powder from Lauterbrunnen, just south of Interlaken. For slower tracks, there are plenty of cross-country ski trails, plus a 9.3-mile (15 km) toboggan run from Faulhorn peak to Grindelwald.

For a bird's-eye view of the Swiss Alps, try tandem paragliding. Snow-capped peaks glide past at eye level as you drift over a green landscape populated with quaint cottages.

HUB | *Geneva or Zurich, Switzerland*

Take in all of breathtaking Interlaken from the Harder Kulm observation tower.

See steaming fumaroles on a hike around Boiling Lake.

"WITH MOUNTAINOUS RAINFORESTS, BLACK-SAND BEACHES, AND DRAMATIC UNDERWATER REALMS, THIS ISLAND NATION LOCATED BETWEEN GUADELOUPE AND MARTINIQUE HAS EMERGED AS ONE OF THE WORLD'S PRIME ECOTOURISM DESTINATIONS."

PERSPECTIVE

Great Escapes, Dominica

Big-Time Adventure Awaits on This Unexpected Caribbean Island

Nature dictates the day plan in Dominica—especially for adventure travelers. With mountainous rainforests, black-sand beaches, and dramatic underwater realms, this island nation located between Guadeloupe and Martinique has emerged as one of the world's prime ecotourism destinations.

Don't expect the typical Caribbean tourist scene here, as Dominica has resisted the mass-market glitz that defines its more developed neighbors. Some experiences, such as snorkeling with resident sperm whales, are purposefully low volume. To protect the whales, only a few permits are granted each year.

The island has achieved a remarkable recovery from 2017's Hurricane Maria, making now an excellent time for not-so-everyday excursions, including fishing for an invasive species, trekking to a massive hot spring, and canyoning in deep gorges.

Countless trails crisscross Dominica's mountainous terrain, clinging to cliffs above black-sand beaches or winding through lush jungle. Some routes, like the path to Emerald Pool or the Syndicate Nature Trail, reward almost instantly with cascading falls and parrot sightings, while the 115-mile (185.1 km) Waitukubuli National Trail—the longest in the Caribbean and conquerable in a long weekend—reveals its magic more slowly. But it's the hike to Boiling Lake, a flooded fumarole deep in the rainforest, that is Dominica's most iconic. The six-hour trek (out and back) passes through Morne Trois Pitons National Park into an alien-looking landscape of steaming vents, mud pots, and sulfur springs known as the Valley of Desolation.

Every year Dominica receives more than 300 inches (762 cm) of rain—or liquid sunshine, as the locals call it. Over millennia, deep gorges formed that conceal pristine waterfalls and rushing rivers. Akin to a natural water park, the resulting topography is ideal for canyoning—a thrilling blend of hiking, climbing, rappelling, and swimming. Inside stone chutes, bromeliads and ferns sprout from crevices in moss-covered walls flanking crystalline pools far below. Take the plunge with Extreme Dominica, which offers excursions geared toward novices. After getting your feet wet in smaller canyons, try the 260-foot (79.2 m) rappel down Trafalgar Falls or a night adventure by headlamp.

Native to the Indo-Pacific, lionfish are an invasive species in the Caribbean, where they feed voraciously with no predators—except for hungry humans. On Dominica's southwestern tip, Nature Island Dive's Simon Walsh teaches hunting techniques to skilled scuba buffs before leading lionfish-spearing missions at some of the island's best dive sites, including those within Soufrière–Scott's Head Marine Reserve, a submerged volcanic crater. Coral and rock formations create an underwater zone supporting a proliferation of colorful creatures. Easy access from shore means that snorkelers, too, can take in Soufrière Bay's subaquatic scenery.

—**Gina DeCaprio Vercesi** is a New York–based storyteller, adventurer, and nature girl with a passion for history and conservation.

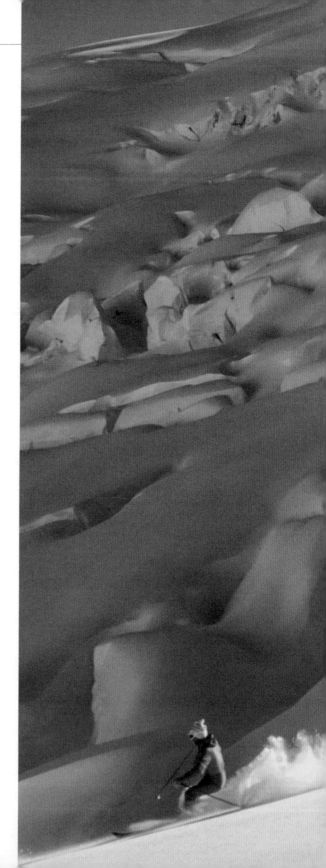

"DELVE INTO THE HEART OF THIS UNTOUCHED LANDSCAPE."

Heli Everything
Wanaka & Queenstown, New Zealand

The alpine towns of Queenstown and Wanaka are located in New Zealand's Southern Alps, a mountainous spine on the western side of the South Island that borders Te Wahipounamu, a UNESCO World Heritage site. Here, rumpled mountains stretch 13,000 feet (3,962.4 m) skyward just 19 miles (30.5 km) from the Tasman Sea.

The Crown Range road, a winding mountain pass, connects the two towns, which are roughly an hour's drive apart; otherwise, roads are few. Helicopters are the quickest, best, and easiest way to delve into the heart of this untouched landscape, and there are plenty of options for a weekend of wonder.

A heli-scenic flight is adventure 101: Soak in 360-degree views soaring over vast lakes, glacially carved valleys, and high alpine landscapes studded with tussocks. Some options included with your flight are a picnic or a visit to one of the filming locations for the Lord of the Rings or Hobbit trilogies.

Heli-hiking is a great way to access a pristine and private wilderness that would normally require days, if not weeks, to trek into. Helicopters offer a mountain drop-off; then follow your guide at an easy pace from cloud level down to beech forests, cut through with glacial streams.

During the summer months, heli-biking is popular, following an itinerary similar to that of heli-hiking, except you're descending swiftly on mountain bikes through private high-country stations, traversing 6,500 feet (1,981.2 m) of dirt tracks and stream crossings.

In winter, heli-ski or heli-board virgin slopes, dodging the resort queues to lay first tracks on a sparkling carpet of white.

There are also several heli-accessible-only accommodations in the area. Minaret Station, a luxury alpine lodge, is a 50,000-acre (20,234 ha) working farm with four luxury chalets, making it one of the most secluded lodges in the world. Whare Kea Chalet is even more remote, perched at 5,700 feet (1,750 m) in the Albert Burn Saddle. You haven't seen stars until you've spent the night here.

Helicopters drop skiers onto Tyndall Glacier for the ride of their lives.

Moonlight guides the way on Maine's Allagash River.

Keep Calm & Paddle On
Allagash River, Maine, U.S.

Take a page out of Henry David Thoreau's book *The Maine Woods*, an account of his 1857 canoeing and hiking trip, and paddle on northern Maine's remote Allagash River. "Here was traveling of the old heroic kind over the unaltered face of nature," he wrote. Today, days still rise and fall with the sparrow's whistle, water lapping against canoe, and the cry of the loon. Canoeing down the 92-mile (148.1 km) national "wild and scenic" river to Canada yields wide lakes, waterfalls, Class I and II rapids, trout-filled streams, and relics from this one-time logging highway.

The classic Allagash canoe trip takes seven days from Chamberlain Lake north to Allagash Village, with 80 rustic campsites along the way. But if you've only got a long weekend to spare, favorite four-day routes include Allagash Lake to Chamberlain Bridge—the waterway's wildest segment, complete with ice caves, a fire tower, and a historic tramway to explore—and Churchill Dam to Allagash Village, with Class II rapids.

HUB | *Northeastern United States*

Take a dip at the lip of Devil's Pool at Victoria Falls.

Take the Plunge
Victoria Falls, Zambia & Zimbabwe

Known by locals as Mosi-oa-Tunya, the "smoke that thunders," Victoria Falls might not be the highest or widest waterfall in the world, but it is the largest: 5,604 feet (1,708 m) wide and 354 feet (108 m) tall, with a plume that can be spotted 12 miles (19 km) away.

Located on the edge of Zambezi National Park and accessible from either Zimbabwe or Zambia, this force of nature is well suited for adventures. Share a bird's-eye view with the falcons and black eagles by taking a helicopter ride over the falls. Feel like flying? Try a bungee jump from the Victoria Falls Bridge, or zip-line across the gorge. Fancy getting wet? Take on the Zambezi River during a white-water rafting trip.

For a unique perspective, try a soak in the Devil's Pool (accessible from the Zambia side during the dry season), a naturally formed basin with an underwater lip near Livingstone Island that allows bathers to peer over the edge of the falls—think infinity pool with a more than 300-foot (91.4 m) drop.

HUB | *Harare, Zimbabwe; Johannesburg, South Africa*

Take to the trails on a run through the mountains of Chamonix.

Hit the Trails

Chamonix, France

The Alpine town of Chamonix, beloved by skiers, has also become a mecca for trail runners seeking to leave crowds and cities behind. Creek-threaded meadows rise up from valley floors into imposing granite peaks, a picture-perfect landscape paired with pure mountain air that provides an instant runner's high to jaded joggers.

Located a stone's throw from both Italy and Switzerland, Chamonix has hundreds of miles of tracks to explore. There are plenty of summer running groups to join (some town shops offer free trail runs with their elite athlete ambassadors) and coaches on hand to coax the best out of your game.

Feeling adventurous? Run (or walk) the 7,000 feet (2,133.6 m) to Refuge du Plan de l'Aiguille, for a well-deserved overnight in its rustic accommodation, to use it as a base for another vertical launch the following day, or to refuel with one of its legendary pies (lemon, cherry, and more) before returning to Chamonix.

HUB | *Geneva, Switzerland; Milan, Italy*

Glowing lanterns carry wishes into the sky during the Pingxi Sky Lantern Festival.

Festivals

From live music performances to artist gatherings, these are the ultimate celebrations of life around the world.

1. INTERNATIONAL SAND SCULPTURE FESTIVAL, PORTUGAL

The largest sand sculpture event in the world, held in Pera, Portugal, since 2003, features more than 50 towering sculptures made with nearly 40,000 tons (36, 287 tonnes) of sand by 60 artists from around the world. The festival chooses a different theme every year; past examples include music, mythology, and lost worlds.

2. PINGXI SKY LANTERN FESTIVAL, TAIWAN

Held on the last day of the lunar New Year, Taiwan decorates the sky with thousands of lanterns and the streets with large lantern installations of everything from dragons to butterflies. Release your own lantern—and an accompanying wish—into the sky in hopes that your ancestors will answer your prayers.

3. BONNAROO MUSIC & ARTS FESTIVAL, TENNESSEE, U.S.

Not as big as Coachella or Lollapalooza, Bonaroo (a three-hour drive from Atlanta) includes more than 150 performances across more than 10 stages of music. Past headliners have included Miley Cyrus, Phish, Billy Joel, Mumford and Sons, Jack White, and Childish Gambino.

4. MONTREUX JAZZ FESTIVAL, SWITZERLAND

One of the oldest music festivals in the world (founded in 1967) this jazz festival is second only to Montréal's. More than two million people attend annually to take in riffs from the shores of Lake Geneva.

5. WAKAKUSA YAMAYAKI, JAPAN

Meaning "The Mountain Roast," this festival held on the fourth Saturday of January each year sets the dead grass on Mount Wakakusa ablaze—after an epic fireworks display.

6. SNOWBOMBING MUSIC FESTIVAL, AUSTRIA

The biggest party on the snow is held in Mayrhofen, Austria, every April. Watch pros take on serious tricks in the park to a soundtrack of eclectic live music acts. Make your own runs during the shows on 404 miles (650 km) of trails.

7. DOWNLOAD, LEICESTERSHIRE, ENGLAND

This three-day festival held in Donington Park since 2003 has featured such legendary bands as KISS. Single-day tickets are available for those who don't want to camp on the grounds.

8. COMIC CON INTERNATIONAL, CALIFORNIA, U.S.

Cosplay is on display at this ode to animation. From comic books to Marvel movies, fantasy novels to video games, meet the superheroes of your favorite franchise in San Diego's Convention Center. Attendance has topped 130,000 guests, so get your tickets early and book accommodations as soon as you can. Space goes fast.

9. EPCOT FOOD & WINE FESTIVAL, FLORIDA, U.S.

If you love food and you love Disney, this is the place for you. The month-long Epcot International Food & Wine Festival showcases food, wine, and beer from Epcot's 11 countries and more spots around the world, with a side dish of your favorite Disney characters and celebrity chefs. Events and seminars include a Junior Chef Kitchen and Sunday Brunch with a Chef.

10. LOY KRATHONG, THAILAND

On the night of the full moon of the twelfth lunar month, Thai people gather around lakes and canals to pay respects to the goddess of water by launching *krathongs*—lotus containers of banana leaves, candles, flowers, and incense—into the water.

"KNOWN FOR ITS
PILES OF SNOW
AND BLUEBIRD DAYS"

Hit the Slopes
Nagano, Japan

Seeking a vibrant winter weekend with a smash of culture? Japan is the place to go. Nagano, home of the 1998 Winter Olympics and an easy 90-minute bullet train ride from Tokyo, is known for its piles of snow and bluebird days. It's flanked by two very different resort areas, both located about an hour's drive (27 miles/44 km) from Nagano City.

The first, Hakuba, is a valley surrounded by rugged peaks over 9,800 feet (3,000 m) high. There are 11 ski resorts linked by a shuttle service, nine of which can be accessed with a shared lift ticket. This place has it all: groomed runs for beginners, off-piste and forested alpine terrain for more advanced skiers and snowboarders, and mogul runs for intermediate riders. (Kids' group lessons and child care are also available.) A vibrant nightlife and restaurant scene round out a weekend in Hakuba.

Nozawa Onsen, on the other side of Nagano, is a world apart. Its fame comes from more than 30 natural hot springs, discovered in the eighth century, which shroud the town—temples, cobblestone streets, *ryokan* inns—in steam. This charming village with its traditional architecture is considered to be the birthplace of skiing in Japan; an Austrian introduced the sport here in 1912. Like Hakuba, it has something for everyone. Its single ski area has 31 miles (50 km) of slope terrain, with trails for beginners, advanced skiers, and snowboarders, as well as a snow play park for kids, in addition to lessons and child care services.

Whichever resort strikes your fancy, don't miss the opportunity to see Japan's famous snow monkeys (Japanese macaques) at the Jigokudani Yaen-koen (Snow Monkey Park), about 21 miles (34 km) from Nagano. Established as a conservation area in 1964, the park preserves the macaques in their natural habitat, allowing visitors the opportunity to observe them in the wild, including as they bathe in *onsens* (natural hot springs).

HUB | *Tokyo, Japan*

Elisabeth Gerritzen participates in the Freeride World Tour skiing competition in Hakuba.

Paragliders soar over the stunning landscapes of Pokhara.

Take to the Skies
Pokhara, Nepal

A 20-minute flight from Kathmandu (approximate population 1.4 million) lands you in smaller Pokhara (approximate population 200,000), a Himalaya-fringed town that is every bit as friendly and mystical as Kathmandu. Pokhara is one of the gateways to the Annapurna circuit—the 100- to 145-mile (160–230 km) trek through the mountain ranges of central Nepal.

For those who aren't trekking, Pokhara is also a mecca for paragliders, thanks to its low-lying valleys and high mountains, which provide consistent rising thermals. There are a variety of operators offering everything from 30-minute tandem flights to weekend-long paragliding courses. For most visitors, the experience begins with a leap of faith: launching from a hill in tandem with your guide until the colorful canopy catches in the wind and pulls you skyward. From there, it's soaring and circling in lazy swirls, taking in views of snowcapped mountains, Phewa Lake, and impossibly green landscapes.

HUB | *Kathmandu, Nepal*

Athletes train in a Muay Thai gym.

The Rules of Fight Club
Koh Samui, Thailand

Eat, breathe, and sleep the sport of Muay Thai at training camps on the island of Koh Samui, cradled in the Gulf of Thailand and an easy one-hour flight from Bangkok.

This ancient combat sport is a world away from the Full Moon Parties that Thailand is known for, requiring sweaty, spartan dedication. Whether training for a fight or brand new to the sport, Muay Thai campers wake up to the ring of a bell to train for two hours in the cool of the morning and again for another two hours in the afternoon. In the heat of the day, rest is advised: Soothe tired muscles in the sea off Koh Samui's white-sand beaches.

In the evenings, head into town to watch Thailand's national sport in action: Live fights are held several nights a week, and it's a cultural spectacle to behold, electric and fierce. The Chaweng Muay Thai Boxing Stadium and Lamai Boxing Ring are both great spots to check out professional boxers in action.

HUB | *Bangkok, Thailand; Singapore*

Yosemite's other trails lead to stunning views of Half Dome.

A One-of-a-Kind Hike

Half Dome, Yosemite, California, U.S.

Half Dome is a Yosemite icon, an 8,800-foot (2,682.2 m) granite monolith rising out of the Yosemite Valley, the stage for some of the greatest sporting achievements the world has ever seen.

For mere mortals up to the challenge, Half Dome can be hiked rather than climbed. This 14- to 16-mile (22.5-25.8 km) round-trip hike gains about 4,800 feet (1,463 m) in elevation during the 10- to 12-hour trek. Hikers begin in the Yosemite Valley, a place of wonder carved by glaciers, before rising past waterfalls to the final push and showstopper: a vertigo-inducing, heart-pounding cable ascent leading to a panoramic view that will never be forgotten.

It's joked that the Half Dome is the hike "you can't die without doing, and the one you're most likely to die while doing." Research the trek thoroughly. This popular hike requires a lottery-distributed permit to climb to the top, and every year several visitors have to be rescued.

HUB | *Western United States*

A kayaker plies the waters around the Scandinavian archipelago.

Adventures in Sweden
Move With Intention and Enjoy the Freedom

Buffering Sweden's capital from the Baltic Sea, the islands of the Stockholm archipelago—called the *skärgården*—are a wonderland of rocks, skerries, and islets with pine forests, fields of wildflowers, and bare granite. The exact number of islands is debatable, but the general consensus is about 30,000.

The archipelago stretches from downtown Stockholm and brings wilderness into the city. Although regular ferry services visit most of the larger islands, I've chosen to experience these glacier-carved isles by kayak.

Exposure to nature is a central part of life in Sweden, where the country's constitution guarantees *allemansrätten* ("everyman's right"), a freedom to roam in natural spaces. The vast archipelago is ideal for exploration by kayak because one can linger among the quiet coves and passages.

Only 40 minutes by ferry from the mainland, Utö provides a quick transition to island time. Once an active mining community with some of the oldest iron mines in the country, the island of about 250 people and only a few cars is known today for its beaches, restaurants, and the famed Utö dark rye bread that tastes of molasses and anise.

The bread makes an appearance nearly everywhere, including at seasonal fish restaurant Båtshaket. Hungry visitors arrive by bike or boat, claim a spot on the deck, and enjoy smoked salmon and shrimp on rye while letting the brief but intoxicating Swedish summer sun soak into their skin. Nobody rushes to leave, and time slows to accommodate even the napping dogs.

Despite having a tent in my pack, I find a cottage at Utö Värdshus with a view of the island's main harbor. At the tail end of summer, families are starting to head home for work and school, but many are enjoying one last summer fling. The next day, called to the sea, I pack my dry bag.

My guide, Mats Andersson, and I launch our kayaks at Södra Fladen, a small south-facing bay halfway down the island's center, Gruvbyn. Mats lives on Utö and has paddled among many of the islands in the archipelago, often kayaking between Utö and Stockholm. For a skilled paddler, it can take eight hours, but for intermediate folk, it's easier as a two-day trip from the Swedish capital.

A watery obstacle course, the bay is scattered with skerries, or rocky isles. After navigating the passage through two small islands, Brunskär and Långskär, we're no longer in the sheltered waters. Far out in the southern part of the archipelago, Utö isn't protected on its south shore, and we encounter choppy seas as we paddle toward the island's northern tip.

The brackish water splashes my arms and face, and I learn to focus exclusively on my body's actions—paddle, breathe, paddle, breathe—like a seafaring meditation. As we pass through the waves, I notice the landscape at Utö's edge. Granite boulders with green-gold lichen curve down to the water. Plants and trees hesitate higher up the incline, as if too shy to dip a toe into the sea.

We break for a picnic on the islands of Mellankobbarna and settle in among the low scrub, ferns, and rosy pink flowers that Mats identifies as *tjärblomster*. Between bites, he schools me on the rights of allemansrätten. Aside from the requirement not to disturb or destroy, people can forage, catch fish, swim in lakes, visit beaches, set up a tent, and access any land as long as they stay out of private gardens and maintain the stipulated 229 feet (70 m) from a dwelling.

I scan the area to see if any boaters are eyeing our private island, but nobody's in sight. Even if there were interlopers, the island is large enough for a few more people. No need to ditch my clothes.

From Mellankobbarna, it's a long, straight shot east to Huvudskär, one of the archipelago's final outposts. The water out here is deep blue, and I pause as the boat drifts, silently bobbing on the surface. It's just us and the sea. In a month or two, the weather won't allow such a far-flung trip.

On Huvudskär, heather, cotton grass, and crowberry grow in rock crevices. A lighthouse rises over small red cottages—all closed up tight against the elements. There have been fishermen and hunters here for more than 700 years, but there are no longer any permanent residents on this remote rock slab.

I watch gulls soar overhead and let my eyes rest on the unbroken horizon. It'll soon be time to return to Utö and, eventually, Stockholm. Until then, the rocky archipelago surrounds me—a shelter but not a fence, where I can roam far and free.

—**Jill K. Robinson** is a writer, adventurer, and traveler whose work has been featured in *The Best Travel Writing* and *The Best Women's Travel Writing* anthologies.

Run With the Dogs

Ely, Minnesota, U.S.

E ly is one of the most remote U.S. outposts, set near the border of Minnesota and Ontario, two hours north of Duluth. The town is surrounded by state forest, at the gateway to the Boundary Waters Canoe Area Wilderness, the largest wilderness preserve east of the Rockies. Once plied by French *voyageur* fur traders, Ely is now enjoyed by canoeists (in summer) and dogsledders (December through March).

Visitors can choose from a variety of dog-sledding expeditions offered by a number of outfitters, including single-day adventures and the more popular multiday trips, which allow more time for the dogs to "train" new drivers (no experience necessary). Try your hand at guiding the team and maneuvering the sled, standing on the back of the runners as the dogs pull you along a snow-covered track under the dark green boughs of a pine forest. Or have a rest in the padded sled enclosure, soaking in the views of frozen lakes, blanketed fields, and spruce bogs. Overnight options vary from cozy lodges to yurt-style tents to camping for those who want the complete winter experience and wilderness solitude.

"TRY YOUR HAND AT GUIDING THE TEAM, STANDING ON THE BACK OF THE RUNNERS AS THE DOGS PULL YOU ALONG A SNOW-COVERED TRACK UNDER THE DARK GREEN BOUGHS OF A PINE FOREST."

HUB | *Midwestern United States*

Dogs pull a sled across a frozen lake in Ely, Minnesota.

The road leading into Grampians National Park offers awe-inducing views.

Get High

Grampians National Park, Australia

Grampians National Park is a series of five sandstone ridges beloved by climbers for steep and craggy slopes, as well as outdoor enthusiasts for forested hiking, panoramic lookouts, and an impressive number of waterfalls.

More than 60 percent of the park is open to climbers (the rest is designated conservation area), and beginners have plenty of guided adventures to choose from. Get a taste of climbing and rappelling during a four- or six-hour outing, or tackle the walk from Mount Stapylton to Hollow Mountain, which requires a harness for the walk's rock climbs and abseils.

Located a three-hour drive west of Melbourne, the Grampians is also popular with hikers (from gentle strolls like the Venus Baths Loop Walk to the multiday Grampians Peaks Trail) and is home to the largest number of rock art sites in Southern Australia, with guided tours available through the area's 22,000-year-old history.

HUB | *Sydney or Melbourne, Australia; New Zealand*

Climbers try their hand at an ascent on the Prow.

> "THERE'S ONLY A SEAT BELT
> TO HOLD YOU IN AS YOU ARC
> OVER THE SLOPE BELOW."

Go for a Swing

Baños, Ecuador

Baños de Agua Santa is a swinging little adventure town, set smack in the middle of Ecuador and bordered by two national parks. There is more to do in this town than there are hours in the day. Perhaps being in the shadows of one of South America's most active volcanoes, Tungurahua, keeps everyone on their toes. Whatever energy is in the air, people are on the move here: hiking, biking, rafting, horseback riding, and getting airborne in any way that they can.

From zip-lining between jungle treetops, to canyoning down waterfalls on the Rio Blanco, Baños offers ample opportunities to get the adrenaline pumping. One of the most popular is *puenting* (roughly translated as "bridging"). Adventure seekers swing on a rope secured to two bridges, a free fall that's similar to bungee jumping, only without the bounce.

The most popular aerial activity by far is the Instagram-darling Swing at the End of the World. The swing became popular in 2014 when a pair of tourists snapped a photo mid-flight with Tungurahua erupting in the background. (The photo was a National Geographic Travel Photo Contest winner.) To get to the swing, hike up to La Casa del Arbol (the Treehouse), which sits 8,530.2 feet (2,600 m) above sea level, and take a turn soaring out over a 98.4-foot (30 m) ledge, with the world below you and Tungurahua looming large in your unobstructed view. There's only a seat belt to hold you in as you arc over the slope below. (There are also zip lines available for those who want another dose of adrenaline.)

Whatever adventure you choose, wrap up the day at the thermal springs that give the town its name. There are a number of hot springs baths to choose from, with pools ranging from barely tolerable (for those who like it hot) to ice cold (for those who don't).

HUB | *Quito, Ecuador*

Swing above the edge of the world at La Casa del Arbol.

Cycle through the historic
streets of Ghent and its
remarkable architecture.

> "GHENT HAS A LONG
> LOVE AFFAIR WITH THE BIKE . . .
> IT IS A CITY TO BE EXPLORED
> WITH LEGS AND STOMACH."

Belgium's Other Side

Your Next Adventure Is Everywhere in Ghent

"I bought a bike and started cycling" was the response veteran Irish traveler Dervla Murphy gave when she was asked how she planned her odyssey across India that would become the beloved travelogue *Full Tilt: Ireland to India With a Bicycle*. It's proof that adventure can start with a simple push of the pedal.

Ghent, in the northern Flemish region of Belgium, may not be India, but it has a long love affair with the bike. The city has the largest pedestrian zone in Europe, with more than 296 acres (120 ha) of car-free space to roam. Sandwiched between the capital, Brussels, and the fairy-tale city of Bruges, Ghent delights in being the underdog, but the city is far from being the ugly duckling of the trio. French novelist Victor Hugo described Ghent as "a kind of Venice of the North," thanks to the pretty, medieval twist of streets that cluster around swan-patrolled canals.

Ghent isn't sleepy in the least, though. For 10 days in July, close to two million people turn up to enjoy a riot of free concerts and street theater known as the Gentse Feesten. And the green credentials extend further, too. Ghent is dubbed a vegetarian capital, and every Thursday is a meat-free day with restaurants and cafés dishing up veggie options for all.

In fact, I find Ghent is a city to be explored with legs and stomach. So after dipping into Sint-Baafskathedraal to see the famous 15th-century polyptych "Adoration of the Mystic Lamb," I bump across the cobblestones and turn down onto Graslei quay. The city's first commercial port, it's lined with ancient guild houses, and I find students cooling their ankles in the water. Then it's on to Groentenmarkt, home to Tierenteyn-Verlent, a 229-year-old delicatessen known for its homemade mustard doled out of wooden barrels, and stalls selling *cuberdons*—local cone-shaped purple candy also known as *neuzekes* (little noses).

I pass Dreupelkot, a slip of a café serving shots of *jenever* (a gin-like liquor made from malt wine) in flavors ranging from garlic to grapefruit, then pedal across the bridge to the medieval maze of Patershol. Once a working-class district home to brothels and dingy drinking dens, it was gentrified in the '80s and now conceals some of the most exciting (and exclusive) restaurants in the city.

For me, biking trumps other modes of transport because you don't just see the city, you feel it. The cobblestones judder your bones, the wind streaks your hair, scents surround you, and then you can park right in front of your destination.

I wend westward away from the crowds. The streets seem to fold in on themselves, as if hiding a secret. I step off and gently roll the bike along Proveniersterstraat. I've entered the Oud Begijnhof of Sint-Elisabeth, a medieval community founded by pious Catholic women who wished to serve God without entering a monastery. Whitewashed cottages frame the dormouse-quiet cobbled street, and time seems to dial back centuries.

I cycle back toward Patershol for a beer at local bar 't Velootje, its wacky decor so crammed with old bikes I can barely get in the door. Bearded owner Lieven de Vos has run this cherished spot for more than a quarter of a century.

Exiting the bar, I find the city has had a costume change, with all its iconic buildings lit from the ground up. Ready for a whole new two-wheeled adventure, I set off into the jaws of the night.

—**Emma Thomson** is a writer for National Geographic Travel and the *Daily Telegraph*.

Take on Class IV rapids on the Gauley and New Rivers.

Top-of-Class White Water
The Gauley, West Virginia, U.S.

In West Virginia, wild and tangled rivers beckon, providing weekenders with the opportunity to tackle some of the best white-water rafting on the planet. The Gauley, one of the most beloved recreational rivers in the United States, plunges more than 668 feet (203.6 m) in 25 miles (40.2 km), throwing up more than five Class V rapids, which are knocking on the upper level of rapids that can safely be guided. Waves curl against river-sculpted sandstone walls, thundering with purpose through a lush gorge filled with trees (oak, beech, dogwood, and poplar), birds, and wildlife.

An easy drive from Washington, D.C., West Virginia water weekends are a favorite with locals and visitors alike. For people wanting to get their feet wet, the upper section of the New River (ironically one of the oldest rivers in the world) and the Narrows section of the Cheat River spike adrenaline without taking it into overdrive, which is ideal for beginners and families with kids.

HUB | *Washington, D.C., U.S.; Mid-Atlantic United States*

Reap the Wind
Tarifa, Spain

Two types of wind blow across Tarifa's golden beaches: the Levante wind (easterly, more powerful, and relentless) and the Poniente wind (westerly and more constant). Both make Tarifa one of the most popular wind- and water-sports destinations in the world, a beloved spot for windsurfers and kitesurfers just 40 minutes from Gibraltar's airport.

Located on the Strait of Gibraltar, where the Mediterranean meets the Atlantic Ocean, a mere 9 miles (14.5 km) from the continent of Africa, Tarifa is an ancient area that has been settled since around 711. Its beaches are backed with a nature reserve hemmed by mountains, so there are ample activities on offer no matter which way the wind is blowing.

Whether you're interested in a lesson or happy to take to the turquoise seas yourself, Tarifa's wide, unspoiled coastline winds for an impressive 6 miles (9.7 km), generously accommodating thrill seekers, wind riders, and families alike. It's also a favorite with bird-watchers.

HUB | *Seville, Spain; Marrakech, Morocco*

Harness the breeze on a windsurfing excursion.

Coastal Bounty

British Columbia, Canada

The fractured coastline of British Columbia, where the Canadian Rockies meet the Pacific Ocean, contains nearly 40,000 islands along 16,000 miles (25,749.5 km) of rugged, remote, and wild coastline. Bald eagles perch in old-growth Sitka spruce that stand tall on rocky cliff faces. Bears patrol the stone coastlines fringed by mossy rainforests. Sea otters, humpback whales, orcas, dolphins, and sea lions cruise the sounds, feeding in the underwater kelp and coral gardens.

Kayaking is the best way to see all of this bounty at eye level. Operators offer a wide variety of tours, from Johnstone Strait (summer camp for orcas), to the Discovery Islands (10 boat-accessible islands tucked between Vancouver Island and the mainland), to Moresby Island and the area around the Haida First Nations ancestral lands.

Trips can range from day tours to multiday excursions, which are better suited to a long weekend due to the remote nature of the landscape.

HUB | *Vancouver, Canada; Pacific Northwest United States*

There's nothing but open water to paddle through on the Johnstone Strait.

CHAPTER SEVENTEEN

WILDLIFE ADVENTURES

From African safaris to spot the Big Five to canopy walks for the world's top bird-watching, these weekends offer a chance to see animals in the wild.

Fireflies streak through the Great Smoky Mountains for Tennessee's greatest light show (p. 636).

Binocular Ready

Casanare, Colombia

Take a South American safari in Colombia's eastern Orinoquía, just three hours (by flight; a two-hour drive) from Bogotá. This rarely visited ecosystem of rolling tropical grasslands abuts the Amazon and is home to pumas, anteaters, and capybaras. Spend days in tree-slung hammocks or atop 4x4s with binoculars at the ready, scouting for the region's 700-plus bird species. Nearly a fifth of the world's bird species call Colombia home, including unusual jabiru storks, scarlet ibis, and the color-blocked chestnut-eared aracari. Or paddle a canoe down sleepy rivers in search of elusive pink river dolphins, scanning the banks for ocelots and howler monkeys. With a base at luxurious Corocora Camp, you can get a feel for the local herding culture. Shadow Colombian cowboys on horseback as they sing to calm their cattle herds. Before retiring to your tented camp's four-poster bed under a blanket of stars, share a meat-heavy fireside *mamona* barbecue with a side of spirited *tres cuerdas* guitar music.

> "NEARLY A FIFTH OF THE WORLD'S BIRD SPECIES CALL COLOMBIA HOME, INCLUDING UNUSUAL JABIRU STORKS, SCARLET IBIS, AND THE COLOR-BLOCKED CHESTNUT-EARED ARACARI."

HUB | *Bogotá or Yopal, Colombia*

The safari-style tents at the Corocora Camp offer stunning views from your private balcony or the comfort of your cozy bed.

A quiver tree stands tall above a rocky landscape at sunrise in Namibia.

Desert Dunes & Wild Cats

Kalahari Red Dunes Lodge, Namibia

Just a two-hour drive south of the Namibian capital and its international airport, the dueling desert landscapes of the Great Karoo and the Kalahari meet in a nearly 10,000-acre (4,050 ha) reserve. The regions are visibly different: The Kalahari here is laced with red dunes and green valleys, while the Karoo has steppes and tree-dotted savanna. The two ecosystems up your chances of spotting diverse wildlife. Stay in luxuriously outfitted yet traditional round mud-and-thatch huts at Kalahari Red Dunes Lodge. Several trails stretch from 3 to 12 miles (5–20 km) beyond your living quarters offering the chance to encounter giraffes, bat-eared foxes, small wildcats, eland, springbok, nyalas, and gnu on foot. Guests can day-hike solo or opt for a three-day, two-night weekend package of guided treks. To cover more ground quickly, game drives in open-topped jeeps depart at dawn and dusk to look for other desert-adapted wildlife like pangolin, warthogs, weaver birds, and zebras.

HUB | *Windhoek, Namibia*

Meerkats peek out from their burrows in the Kalahari.

A tiger walks among the mangroves.

> "FRAIL NETTING PROVIDES THE ONLY BOUNDARY BETWEEN THE VILLAGES AND TIGER TURF."

The God of the Tigers

Sundarbans, India

An immense forest controlled by the ebb and flow of tides, the floor of the Sundarbans is alternately awash and littered with spiky roots. Shared by India and Bangladesh and formed by the deltas of the Ganges, Brahmaputra, and Meghna Rivers as they empty into the Bay of Bengal, it's the world's largest continuous stretch of mangrove habitat. The Sundarbans encompass an area totaling more than 1,600 square miles (4,264 sq km), larger than the entire state of Rhode Island. Muddy islands hump above the brackish water, providing refuges for brightly colored crabs, some 260 species of wetland birds, wild boar, troops of monkeys, and herds of spotted deer. Sea turtles, otters, monitor lizards, and huge crocodiles prowl the waters. Villagers eke out an existence on the swamp's larger islands, but this is one of the few remaining ecosystems on Earth where humans are not the top of the food chain.

Bengal tigers slink through the forests, frail netting providing the only boundary between the villages and tiger turf. Residents never speak their word for the feared and revered tiger, afraid that verbalizing it will summon one. Temples throughout the region feature images of the deity Dakshin Roy, the god of the tigers to which villagers pray before crossing the boundary into tiger territory to fish or forage for honey. Annually, the tigers are blamed for dozens of human deaths. The population of the endangered species here is said to be more aggressive due to its rough-and-tumble existence among the mangroves and shrinking access to traditional prey. Still, the chance to see one is remote. They're aloof and secretive, and their population is low (estimates range from 500 to 2,500). Spend a weekend plying the waters in a traditional tall-hulled wooden boat scanning the mud for prints with one of the village-based ecotourism outfits as home base. The forest begins just over an hour's drive from Kolkata (Calcutta).

HUB | Kolkata, India

All Aflutter

Southern Jutland, Denmark

From mid-September to mid-October and March to mid-April, migratory starlings on their route between Scandinavia and southern Europe rest and feed in the reedy marshes of southern Jutland. Their two-week emergence each evening just before sunset has been called Sort Sol (Black Sun). Like schooling fish in an aerial sea, as many as half a million starlings move together in unity, forming mesmerizing patterns known as murmurations. Their rhythmic motions constantly shift direction—seeming to shimmer like a living black aurora—in an attempt to befuddle predators such as peregrine falcons. Recent computer modeling studies have shown each bird needs to keep track of its seven closest neighbors to maintain its place within the flock. See them on your own or as part of a nature tour in the Tønder Marsh near the border with Germany or in the Wadden Sea marshes outside the town of Ribe.

HUB | *Copenhagen, Denmark*

"THEIR RHYTHMIC MOTIONS CONSTANTLY SHIFT DIRECTION—SEEMING TO SHIMMER LIKE A LIVING BLACK AURORA."

Thousands of starlings come together in what are known as murmurations above the Jutland wetlands.

Mexican free-tailed bats fly from their cave and take to the skies at night.

Absolutely Batty

Mason, Texas, U.S.

On summer days, a sleepy hole in the ground amid dusty shrubland 17 miles (27 km) south of Mason, Texas, appears nondescript. Come late afternoon, the aptly named Bat Cave awakens. The first few creatures flutter outside the cave mouth and begin a shrieking chatter that crescendos through nightfall. By the last twinkle of dusk, the cave has belched its full contents—some four to six million Mexican free-tailed bats take flight in a sky-darkening living tornado. It's one of the largest aggregations of warm-blooded animals on the planet.

In late spring, the roost fills with pregnant females that flap up from Mexico to give birth to a single pup. Between July and August, when pups are ready, mother and baby leave the cave to feast on a nightly buffet of moths, mosquitoes, and other insects. The private Eckert James River Bat Cave Preserve surrounds the cave and opens to the public only during peak bat season.

HUB | *South Central United States*

Spectators await the nightly bat show.

Spot whale sharks—the ocean's giants—from Isla Holbox.

Swim With Giants
Isla Holbox, Quintana Roo, Mexico

You're awash in a sea of blue, paddling your palms through the warm ocean, looking every which way. Then a distant shadow emerges, and in a blur of moving spots, the head of a whale shark comes into focus, its tail still too far distant to see. The world's largest fish sashays toward and underneath you, until you're floating directly above it. Swiveling your head, you can appreciate its full 40-foot (12 m) length.

A magical encounter with a gentle 5-ton (4.5 tonne) wild animal can be a perception-shifting and life-altering experience, and there's perhaps no more reliable place on the planet to have such an encounter than off Isla Holbox, two hours from Cancún. Though whale sharks are mysterious and usually solitary, up to 800 of them congregate here between May and September (peak is July to August) to feed on plankton, krill, and fish eggs. See the area's whale sharks on full-day boat charters that cruise in search of them from Playa de Holbox; then slip in the water in groups of two with a guide.

HUB | *Cancún, Mexico*

Creatures of the Swamp
Okefenokee, Florida & Georgia, U.S.

The headwaters of the Suwannee and St. Mary's Rivers emerge from Okefenokee Swamp, a Wildlife Refuge and Wetland of International Importance spanning nearly half a million acres (177,000 ha) near the Florida/Georgia line. Intrepid explorers can canoe or kayak beneath cypress trees past alligators, anhingas, and otters and then overnight on remote islands, lulled to sleep by a nightly frog chorus. An impressive 60 species of amphibians call the park home. There are more than 120 miles (193 km) of water trails through the shallow peat wetland to explore. Download the mobile app of interactive maps before setting off. Want something tamer? Hop in the car and follow the 7.2-mile (11.6 km) Swamp Island Drive to the historic Chesser Island Homestead and a boardwalk lookout for endangered birds such as wood storks and red-cockaded woodpeckers. You can also visit the Okefenokee Swamp Park in Waycross, Georgia, for guided motorboat tours down traditional Seminole waterways.

HUB | *Southeastern United States*

The Okefenokee Swamp offers canals for paddling.

Hummingbird Madness
Sedona Hummingbird Festival, Sedona, Arizona, U.S.

Arizona hosts more hummingbird species than arguably any other U.S. state; some 15 migratory and resident species flit amid flowers and trees in the land of the red rocks. Around Sedona, where high-elevation forested red rock canyons remain cooler, seven species—including the coveted Rivoli's and calliope hummingbirds—can be spotted in late July and early August with several often appearing in record quantities. To celebrate, the city hosts an annual hummingbird festival the last weekend of July. Visitors meander through a market of hummingbird-themed arts and crafts, assist in banding demonstrations, take garden tours, or sit in on presentations extolling the latest hummingbird science. If you haven't had your fill by the end of the weekend—or if the popular Audubon-led birding treks are full—take a drive three hours south to the Arizona-Sonora Desert Museum, where several species, including green-winged Anna's, purple-topped Costa's, and colorful broad-billed, can easily be spotted in their hummingbird aviary.

HUB | *Southwestern United States*

Hummingbirds migrate to Sedona en masse during the summer.

> "THE BAY IS HOME
> TO THE WORLD'S MOST
> DRAMATIC TIDES."

Whale Tales

Digby, Nova Scotia, Canada

A two-hour drive from Nova Scotia's main airport in Halifax—and connected by regular ferry service to St. John, New Brunswick—the coastal Digby area, "Canada's Natural Aquarium," is an excellent headquarters for Bay of Fundy exploration. The bay is home to the world's most dramatic tides—in some places dropping 40 vertical feet (12 m) in a single day. The constant motion flushes nutrients that support a huge assortment of wildlife, especially during spring and summer. To see a slice of it up close, take a whale-watch charter around Digby Neck and the offshore islands; with the huge cetacean diversity, it's one of the best places in North America to do so. Finback, minke, humpback, pilot, sperm, blue, and the endangered North Atlantic right whale have all been sighted here. You're also likely to see other species, such as harbor porpoises, white-sided and beaked dolphins, fast-moving bluefin tuna, turtles, basking sharks, gannets, and Atlantic puffins. Choose a charter with a hydrophone on board that amplifies whale songs for your listening pleasure.

Back on land, head to the visitor center at the Annapolis Tidal Station and see how humans have harnessed the power of the tides via the only saltwater-powered generator in North America. Pass back through town for a dinner of Digby's renowned sea scallops, collected just offshore. Then, as night falls, head to the area around Clare, an hour south of town and part of the Acadian Skies and Mi'kmaq Lands noted for their exceptional dark sky stargazing.

The following day, explore the exposed seafloor with a tidal zone expert on a guided tour. See billions of barnacles and feeding periwinkles tucked amid the slippery rocks and seaweed. Watch the circle of life play out in tide pool pockets, hunt for anemones and sea slugs, and use a field microscope to enlarge the tiny planktonic creatures that form the base of the Bay of Fundy food chain.

HUB | *Eastern Canada; Northeastern United States*

Northern right whales breach the surface in the Bay of Fundy.

Glow in the Dark

Great Smoky Mountains National Park, Tennessee, U.S.

Each year in late spring or early summer when evening temperatures and soil moisture are just so, one of the 19 species of Great Smoky Mountain fireflies, *Photinus carolinus*, does something remarkable: Tens of thousands of them release luciferin and oxygen simultaneously to blink in synchrony. The effect is mystical. Coordinated blinks come in bursts and move across hillsides like light waves. As moonlight filters through the leafy canopy, it's as though the trees have been outfitted in a living, moving string of twinkling lights, set to flash to the sounds of the forest.

Because the display is nearly impossible to catch on film, and because the exact timing of the natural phenomenon varies from year to year, advance planning is required if you want to witness blinking at its peak. Visitor numbers are limited to around 1,000 lucky lottery winners and are awarded in late April for each evening of peak flashing time—a shifting two-week period in late May to mid-June.

> **"AS MOONLIGHT FILTERS THROUGH THE LEAFY CANOPY, IT'S AS THOUGH THE TREES HAVE BEEN OUTFITTED IN A LIVING, MOVING STRING OF TWINKLING LIGHTS."**

HUB | *Southeastern United States*

Synchronous fireflies light up the forests of the Great Smoky Mountains in a breeding ritual.

Hawaiian monk seals play on the shores of Ka'ena Point State Park.

Whale-Watch
North Shore, Oahu, Hawaii, U.S.

When winter weather whips otherwise calm beaches into towering peaks up to 50 feet (15 m) high between November and March, big-wave surfers aren't the only ones who make the pilgrimage to Oahu's North Shore. The season is also when migratory humpback whales journey from the colder waters off Alaska each year to Hawaii's warm waters—large swaths of which are protected in the Hawaiian Islands Humpback Whale National Marine Sanctuary—to mate and give birth.

Time your weekend with the last Saturday of the month during peak whale season (January–March) and make your whale-watching count. That's when the National Oceanic and Atmospheric Administration (NOAA) hosts morning citizen science counts that help researchers keep tabs on the sanctuary's namesake visitors.

HUB | *Honolulu, Hawaii, U.S.; West Coast United States*

Oahu's North Shore is a surfer's paradise and surreal landscape.

A Guatemalan black howler monkey peers out from a tree in the Community Baboon Sanctuary.

> "YOU'LL UNDOUBTEDLY
> HEAR THE PRIMATES
> BEFORE YOU SEE THEM."

Monkeying Around

Monkey River, Belize

Wild primates are noticeably absent from the United States, but it's all monkey business on a quick weekend to Belize. For the aptly named Monkey River Village in Belize, first fly to the international airport in Belize City; then drive three hours south to catch a boat from the popular resort area of Placencia. The shallow sea journey affords the chance to spot dolphins and, in the mangrove estuary formed from the mouth of the Monkey River, manatees and turtles before heading into the jungle. You'll undoubtedly hear the primates before you see them: The loud whoops of endangered black howler monkeys can reverberate through 3 miles (5 km) of trees. Clinging from branches and swinging through riverside fruit trees, howler monkeys are the largest of all New World monkeys, topping out at around 22 pounds (10 kg), with tails as long as their bodies. The day-long boat tours also point out other wildlife amid the cacophony, including toucans, the Montezuma oropendola, iguanas, crocodiles, and even bats and tarantulas.

The following day, book a tour at the Community Baboon Sanctuary, a half-hour drive from the airport. *Baboon* is the Creole colloquialism for the black howler monkey, and the sanctuary is actually a 20-square-mile (52 sq km) swath of community-driven wildlands with a visitor center and small museum. Howler monkey troops need several acres each to forage and frolic, but hunting and habitat distraction have crunched their range to just a few small pockets in Belize. Some 200 landowners from seven villages have committed to preserve their private lands as "baboon" habitat, now home to about 2,000 howlers. Take a guided hike to see the loud mouth of the jungle as well as other species, including naturally occurring hummingbirds, boa constrictors, armadillos, and hard-to-spot ocelots, jagarundi, and jaguars.

HUB | *Belize City, Belize; Southern United States*

Safarigoers enjoy
sundowners in the
Kapamba River.

Under African Skies

A Wild Adventure, a Spectacular Sense of Place, and a Shocking Discovery

Everything is bigger when you're on the ground. I'm at the confluence of the Luangwa and Kapamba Rivers, and grasses that looked like fronds from afar turn out to be shoulder-high thorn walls. I'm following guide Kelvin Zulu on an afternoon walk beside the river. We're trailed by Zambia Wildlife Authority scout Isiah Mvula. We investigate a towering termite mound and spot a lion's paw print in the sand the circumference of a cabbage. Kelvin is "reading the dirt" when a scampering waterbuck rustles the bushes. I shiver and get goose bumps. Suddenly I feel naked standing on the soil, exposed in my foolish attempts to achieve invisibility by wearing green clothing. The survival tools I've packed—sunblock, hand sanitizer, and a cell phone (there's no cell service here)—reveal me to be a creature of the material world, a person whose inclinations are to subdue, not embrace, the wild. And yet here I am, listening, observing, walking—with each step returning to the land, sensing the space around me, and sending warthogs dashing into the underbrush.

Back in the truck, returning to camp, we spot a leopard in a tree, chomping on a baboon. We drive close and snap pictures. South Luangwa is one of the world's top spots for viewing leopards, and this one knows it. He's unbothered and proud and lazy enough to be falling asleep before our eyes.

As sunset nears, the land exhales with the cough of water buffalo, ticking toads, and an elephant's trumpet in the distance. It's as if all the Earth is slowly venting heat. We return to camp on the trail of a honey badger, and I see that the marsh below is filled with grazing impalas. It occurs to me that not every animal that sees tonight's moon will see tomorrow's sun.

That night a lion walked past my tent. I was awoken by a deep vibrato lament rolling down the river. As the call increased in volume, it was accompanied by the crunch of dry leaves. The lion approached my tent and moaned on the opposite side of a gauzy screen, 10 feet (3 m) from my head. The call grew fainter as the beast crept away. I fell asleep despite the fear of becoming a lion's midnight snack.

A pink sun rises and I find Kelvin beside a campfire as the Kapamba River reemerges from its dark night. I ask about the lion, who turns out to have a colorful history. Cassius and his partner, Brutus, were dominant males who banded together to control their territory and increase and protect their prides.

The lions had been named by the human population and respected for their control of a vast area. But then one day Brutus disappeared, the coalition frayed, and Cassius walked alone. When Brutus reappeared months later, he'd lost his mane, he was gaunt, and his hip seemed to be dislocated. The solitary lions turned to smaller game, even scavenging like hyenas. This downfall set the stage for a new pair of lions to steal their territory, a challenge now under way. When Cassius walked past my tent at night, he was calling out—for Brutus perhaps, or to let the usurpers know that he would not go down without a fight.

On my last morning the sun radiated an angry orange over the Kapamba River. We trailed a pack of African wild dogs crossing the water and found a lioness tearing into a zebra while her two cubs waited their turn and hyenas lurked in the grass. In the distance, a kettle of vultures circled the sky. Kelvin steered the truck over a dry lagoon mottled with hippo prints to get closer. The vultures swooped down to nip and peck at a massive carcass. The air was rank and moist. We studied the mound. We puzzled. And then we realized.

Of all safari sightings, we had tracked down the worst: a poached elephant, eviscerated, butchered of its meat, trunk removed, tusks torn out, exposed rib cage buzzing with insects. Safari is about death as well as life. Animals sometimes eat each other to survive. This is the circle of life. But what I saw that day isn't a necessary part of that pattern, and it will be a long time before I digest it.

A bushcamp tradition awaits: sundowners at the river. Not beside the river or near the river, but *in* the river. Chairs are lined atop a sandbar in the middle of the Kapamba, a card table serves as a makeshift bar, and popcorn explodes from a pan on the fire. To the crocs we probably look like Kardashians. Noisy, possibly tasty, but not worth the effort.

Back at camp, we discover an unexpected visitor. Brutus has returned, limping along the bank. His mane is growing back, and his proximity suggests that he's either wise or desperate, so we keep our distance. That night Brutus sleeps in the camp. Being on safari is a dream, I think, and I fall asleep too.

—**George Stone** is the executive editor of Travel for National Geographic.

A rhinoceros hornbill perches in a riverside tree.

Intimate Encounters
Lower Kinabatangan Sanctuary, Sabah, Borneo, Malaysia

A three-hour flight from the urban chaos of Kuala Lumpur, the sleepy, brown Kinabatangan River snakes nearly 350 miles (560 km) through the backwaters of northeastern Sabah in Malaysian Borneo. Instead of skyscrapers, fig and massive vine-filled trees tower over the shore, their branches dotted with herons, rhinoceros hornbills, kingfishers, and loud troops of potbellied proboscis monkeys. As more and more palm oil plantations fill Borneo's landscape, wild places like these are becoming increasingly rare. The lower Kinabatangan is one of the last forested alluvial floodplains in Asia; its riverbanks are one of the only places to sight Sumatran rhinos, pygmy elephants, orangutans, and the tiny bug-eyed slow loris in the wild. Ecotourism river lodges and tour outfitters are plentiful, but if possible, seek out a homestay. Most locals are knowledgeable about the patterns of surrounding wildlife and own their own boats to conduct intimate tours.

HUB | *Southeast Asia*

Bathing Beauties
Jigokudani Yaen Koen, Yamanouchi, Japan

Few primates tolerate frigid winter temperatures, but in the temperate forests of the Jigokudani Valley north of Nagano, fluffy Japanese macaques reign. In the early 1960s, their populations declined as their traditional forest habitat was cleared to build ski resorts. As they were pushed into the surrounding villages, locals witnessed startling behavior: Japanese macaques mimicked humans and used an *onsen* (hot spring bath) of a local guesthouse. Shortly after, an enterprising individual built the monkeys their own park—luring them back to their traditional habitat in the Jigokudani Snow Monkey Park. Today, a wild troop of more than 150 monkeys socialize, groom, and bathe in their man-made pool of geothermal spring water, their faces bright red and blushing from the heat. The best time to visit is between the snowy months of January and February, when more monkeys frequent the pool. Overnight nearby in historic Shibu Onsen, where you can dip in a traditional onsen of your own; it's an hour's drive from Nagano and 3.5 hours from Tokyo.

Snow monkeys take a dip in the Yamanouchi hot springs.

HUB | *Tokyo, Japan*

Three black bears gaze out at visitors in Yellowstone National Park.

American Icons

Spring Creek Ranch, Jackson, Wyoming, U.S.

Just north of Jackson, Wyoming, sits Spring Creek Ranch, a luxury hotel with a view of the craggy Grand Tetons. The ranch has its own 1,000-acre (405 ha) wildlife refuge, which is home to moose and elk. Take one of the three- or four-day safaris originating at the lodge and guided by staff naturalists through neighboring Grand Teton and Yellowstone National Parks in the spring when the land is verdant and the wildlife active. You might see bald eagles, northern sage grouse, baby mule deer, wolves, and bears all in one go. Already explored the parks? Make a relaxing weekend of guided nature hikes through wildflower meadows, fly-fishing for cutthroat trout on the Snake River, and stargazing with the aid of large telescopes and a visiting astronomer. Don't miss a foraged feast at the property's Granary Restaurant, where grilled quail, elk loins, and smoked trout Caesar salad are all on the menu.

HUB | *Mountain West United States*

Forest Finds

Białowieża Forest, Poland

One of Europe's last stands of primeval woodland is tucked away just three hours from Warsaw within the Białowieża Forest, which stretches for miles along Poland's border with Belarus. The protected old growth is also a UNESCO World Heritage site supporting a full food web—from some 12,000 invertebrates, including the vulnerable and vibrant green *Buprestis splendens* beetle, to larger species like deer, wolves, and lynx. Take an old-world safari, like the long weekend offering by Wild Poland, to scan the dense perimeter for European bison. The bison were hunted to extinction in the wild in the early 1900s, but zoo specimens were reintroduced in the 1950s, the progenitors of all European bison today (including the forest's 900-odd residents, Europe's largest herd). Walk amid spruces and oaks to wet swamp alder forests and shaded meadows to spot pine marten, fox, and otters. Don't forget to look up: More than 250 bird species, including numerous woodpeckers and the Eurasian pygmy owl, live in the canopy.

HUB | *Warsaw, Poland*

"HUNTED TO EXTINCTION IN THE WILD IN THE EARLY 1900S, ZOO SPECIMENS WERE REINTRODUCED IN THE 1950S, THE PROGENITORS OF ALL EUROPEAN BISON TODAY."

A herd of European bison, reintroduced to the area decades ago, walk through the snow.

A snorkeler swims through a school of yellowtail fusilier.

The World's Greatest

Great Barrier Reef, Australia

It's no secret that the Great Barrier Reef is the ultimate sub-surface wildlife adventure—its fringing coral stretches more than 1,250 miles (2,000 km), the only animals visible from space. With climate change threatening to tip the balance, you'll want to visit soon. If a weekend is all you have, opt for full immersion. Reefsleep, an offshore platform 39 nautical miles (72 km) from the Port of Airlie, lets visitors camp out on the reef. The cruise to reach it passes Whitsunday resort islands and tiny coral atolls; it's home to humpbacks (July to September), clownfish, and giant clams. You'll spend two days swimming, snorkeling, and diving from the platform, in an underwater observatory, or on a helicopter tour for a different sense of scale. Regular flights from Brisbane and Cairns service the Whitsunday Airport near the port; cruises depart in the morning and return the following evening.

HUB | *Cairns or Brisbane, Australia*

Grab cocktails to watch the sunset from the Reefsleep deck.

"ORANGE BODIES FLUTTER IN THE SKY AND CLUSTER ON TREES."

Wild Monarchs

Piedra Herrada, Monarch Butterfly Biosphere Reserve, Mexico

Each year, as many as a billion butterflies descend on high-altitude forests in central Mexico. There, 14 colonies arrive from eastern Canada in early November, and eight of them, roughly 70 percent of the overwintering eastern population, are protected within the 217-square-mile (562 square km) Monarch Butterfly Biosphere Reserve, a UNESCO World Heritage site spanning two Mexican states.

Though you can find monarchs in several locations, the best and closest place to Mexico City (a two-hour drive west) is Piedra Herrada. Local guides are required, and you can choose to make the steep mile-long (1.6 km) journey from the parking lot to the oyamel fir forest at 10,000 feet (3,850 m) by horseback or on foot. Along the dusty trail, you'll notice when you're getting close: Orange bodies flutter in the sky and cluster on trees. By the time you've reached the main colony, butterflies consume every square inch of visible tree, bending branches with their sheer volume. The insects will remain in a state of tired hibernation, occasionally fluttering into the skies to shift position or bask in the sun, until March. Round out the weekend with a visit to Bridal Veil waterfall and an overnight in the lakeside town of Valle del Bravo before heading on to one of the three other monarch-viewing sites in Michoacán.

Although the sight is visually stunning, what truly amazes is the mystery of how the butterflies find this forest in the first place. Unlike many migratory bird species that can live for years and follow annual travel patterns, most adult monarchs live about a month. It takes a special "Methuselah" generation, born in Canada at the end of August with a life span of up to nine months, to make the migration. Every four generations, this generation finds their way to fill the trees here and complete the cycle each winter. The individual butterflies in these trees have never been here before and will never return.

HUB | *Mexico City, Mexico*

Monarch butterflies
fly in the oyamel fir
forest of the reserve.

The sun rises over Cadillac
Mountain on Mount Desert
Island in Acadia National Park.

Sunrises & Sunsets

From sweeping views over Arizona's Grand Canyon to the first rays hitting Machu Picchu's spectacular ruins, these sunrises and sunsets will take your breath away.

1. CADILLAC MOUNTAIN, MAINE, U.S.

From early October until early March, Maine's tallest peak is the first spot in the United States to see morning sun. Beyond that claim to fame, sunrise here is spectacular, with hot pink skies illuminating the island-dotted waters below.

2. ULURU, AUSTRALIA

As if to underscore its sacred local status, the majestic centerpiece of the Uluru-Kata Tjuta National Park in Australia's Red Centre takes on an ethereal, otherworldly glow at both sunrise and sunset.

3. SANTORINI, GREECE

Yes, as you've likely heard, there will be crowds (mostly at Oia)—and not for nothing. The backdrop of sea, windmills, and whitewash is sunset perfection. Plus, the collective joy—and final round of applause—heightens the experience.

4. ANGKOR WAT, CAMBODIA

Watching the sun rise over these ancient, UNESCO-designated Cambodian temples is doubly gorgeous. Beyond the early morning pale pinks and fuchsia that surround the site, there's the reflected version of them—and of the iconic towers—in the pond.

5. GRAND CANYON, ARIZONA, U.S.

The sunrises and sunsets here are almost as iconic as the canyon itself, which turns more gradations of red, pink, and purple than you knew existed. Try sunrise from Mather or Yaki Points, and sunset from Hopi Point, which offers a stunning and clear view of the canyon in both directions.

6. MACHU PICCHU, PERU

You never know if the clouds will cooperate at this world-famous sunrise spot. But when they do—and those first rays start bringing the ruins, mountains, and mists to life—you'll see why the Inca considered the sun divine (especially if you are at the Sun Gate).

7. HALEAKALĀ NATIONAL PARK, HAWAII, U.S.

The sunrise in this Maui national park is so renowned, you need reservations to see it. What you can't plan for is the effect of standing atop a dormant volcano as the first rays hit the crater and the clouds below you. Make the trip extra special with a bike ride to the bottom after taking in the scene.

8. MOUNT FUJI, JAPAN

If you'd rather catch the sunrise from an active volcano—and gain a new appreciation for Japan's reputation as the land of the rising sun—summit Japan's highest peak (12,388 feet/3,775.9 m) during the summer climbing season (mountain huts make overnight hiking doable).

9. JEMAA EL-FNA, MOROCCO

To watch the Red City get even redder, head to Marrakech's main square and find an upper-story café balcony, where you'll appreciate sipping on hot mint tea while being bedazzled by both the setting sun *and* the bustling scene below (snake charmers, magicians, and peddlers of everything). After the sun finishes its show, head down to the scene and taste local delicacies served up in the square.

10. THE ZAMBEZI RIVER, ZAMBIA & ZIMBABWE

Victoria Falls may be the best-known natural phenomenon in the neighborhood, but the river that creates it boasts some of the best sunsets (and sunset cruises) on Earth, with elephants and massive hippo heads silhouetted against the blazing sky.

> "TO MAXIMIZE WILDLIFE SIGHTINGS, GO SLOW AND STOP OFTEN."

Weekend Safari
Kruger National Park, South Africa

If you have only one weekend to fit in an African safari, make it Kruger. It's one of the most wild and accessible safari parks on the planet, just a four-hour drive from South Africa's largest city. Some tours will even pick you up and drop you off at the airport in Johannesburg.

The park is vast, covering 7,722 square miles (20,000 square km) of South African lowveld, and its biodiversity is remarkable, with 114 species of reptiles, 507 species of birds, and more than 140 species of mammals, including elephants, hippos, and antelope.

Most quick visits take in the park's popular southern region where wildlife tends to be most concentrated, particularly in the dry winter months (July to October). Following the busy road between Skukuza to Lower Sabie Rest Camp, checklist enthusiasts can make a solid stab at the Big Five (Cape buffalo, leopard, elephant, lion, and rhino), and start searching for the birding Big Six (ground hornbill, kori bustard, lappet-faced vulture, martial eagle, Pel's fishing owl, and saddle-billed stork). These creatures are the most coveted to spot, and you'd have to be very lucky indeed to see them all in one go.

Early mornings and dusk are the best times for game drives; check the sightings maps at park reception areas for the times and locations of recent rare sightings. Don't miss a night drive; it's often the only way to spot Kruger's nocturnal creatures like honey badgers, civets, and big-eyed bush babies. Though you may not cover that much ground, the key to maximizing wildlife sightings any time of day is to go slow and stop often.

Those hoping for the luxurious overnight in a four-poster bed with billowing mosquito nets won't find it inside the park proper, but instead in neighboring private parks. In addition to the comforts these private parks provide, they are also convenient for time-tight visitors, with packages that include meals and game drives.

HUB | *Cape Town or Johannesburg, South Africa*

A mother leopard walks down a dead log in Kruger National Park to her cub.

A wild northern fulmar rests on a rock above the water.

Animals of the Sea
The Hebrides, Scotland

Just a two-and-a-half-hour train ride from the airport at Inverness, bucolic Scottish countryside clashes with the wild North Sea on the Isle of Skye. During the long summer hours—breeding season for dozens of seabirds—head off on a wildlife boat charter to search for the many nonhuman (and nonsheep) residents of the Hebrides. Scan the shoreline through the salty spray for hauled-out seals, and the horizon for spouts of porpoises, the occasional minke whale, and telltale splashes of subsurface basking sharks, the world's second largest fish. Don't forget to pack your binoculars—Arctic-migrating seabirds, black- and red-throated divers, gannets, sea eagles, and even cartoonish puffins tuck their nests into noisy coastal cliffs. Back on land, tromp across boggy moorland to inland lochs to look for stoic deer stags, delicate orchids, and flowering butterwort with birds of prey like falcons and harriers cruising overhead.

HUB | *Glasgow, Scotland*

Elusive Creatures
Transylvanian Carpathians, Romania

Medieval castles, bat caves, and Dracula lore aren't all that's hidden in Transylvanian forests. Join a small group trek led by a local English-speaking researcher into the craggy Carpathian mountains to track enigmatic Eurasian lynx. The medium-size carnivorous cats with tassel-tipped ears are critically endangered in some parts of their range but thrive amid the barren peaks and surrounding valleys. The lynx hunt for deer, fox, and rabbit at dawn and dusk, the same times that you'll be on the lookout. Keep your eyes peeled for tracks and signs of other forest creatures such as Ural owls, marmots, the elusive pine marten, and the occasional brown bear or gray wolf. And don't forget to bundle up! Predawn treks are popular, and the best time to visit is in March when their camel coats pop against a snowy backdrop as they begin an active and vocal spring mating season.

A Eurasian lynx looks out from its snowy forest spot.

HUB | *Eastern Europe*

A plumed basilisk can run short distances across water without sinking.

Biodiversity Blitz
Manuel Antonio National Park, Costa Rica

The tiny Manuel Antonio National Park, Costa Rica's smallest at just 3 square miles (6.83 sq km), packs a lot of punch for its size. A biodiverse forest home to more than 100 mammal species fronts and fills Punta Catedral, a peninsula of white-sand beaches. With a long weekend in front of you, travel the three hours from San José to the town of Quepos, gateway to the park's wildlife. Enlist a guide who knows the cues that signal sightings of sloths, iguanas, and the rare and adorable squirrel monkeys for a half-day forest tour. Afterward, take the 1-mile (1.6 km) loop trail down the peninsula, stopping to spend the afternoon lounging by the sea and peeking below the waves at fan coral and pufferfish. The following day, kayak through the sun-dappled Damas Mangrove searching for tiger herons, mangrove hawks, white-faced monkeys, boa constrictors, and millions of colorful little crabs, before returning to modernity.

HUB | *San José, Costa Rica*

A hiker descends a ridgeline trail down Mount Washington (p. 656).

CHAPTER EIGHTEEN

HAPPY TRAILS

Lace up your hiking boots and explore the great outdoors from New Hampshire to Australia.

Birch trees turn golden yellow during Breckenridge's fall.

Happy Trails to You
Breckenridge, Colorado, U.S.

A t only two hours' west of Denver International Airport, Breckenridge makes it possible to go skiing, hiking, or biking in the heart of the Rocky Mountains all weekend and be back in time for work on Monday morning. The former gold rush–era mining town sits at the base of Breckenridge Ski Resort and its 187 ski trails, 12 of which become mountain biking trails mid-July to early fall and most of which are open to hikers before and after ski season.

From late May to mid-November, mountain bikers can access hundreds of miles of trails in the White River National Forest. In summer, the resort's Colorado SuperChair hauls bikers up to Peak 8 for a wild romp down. Hike the Burro Trail into the forest to connect to an extensive network of backcountry trails. Ski season typically runs from November to May at the resort, and from mid-November to April at the Breckenridge Nordic Center, offering over 18 miles (30 km) of cross-country trails and over 12 miles (20 km) of snowshoeing trails.

HUB | *Mountain West United States*

Cascades are hidden along trails within Bretton Woods.

Into the Woods
Bretton Woods, New Hampshire, U.S.

H ome to the Mount Washington Hotel, a national historic landmark opened in 1902 (and centerpiece of the luxurious Omni Mount Washington Resort), Bretton Woods is designed to be explored outdoors. Miles of hiking, biking, Nordic and alpine skiing, and snowshoeing trails crisscross the village (part of the town of Carroll), which sits in the heart of New Hampshire's White Mountain National Forest.

Relatively close proximity to two transportation hubs—Boston, 160 miles (257.5 km) south, and Portland, Maine, 95 miles (152.9 km) east—makes it possible to spend two days on the trails. To bag one of the White's famous 4,000 footers (1,219 m), hike the 6.2-mile (10 km) out-and-back trail to the summit of Mount Pierce, elevation 4,312 feet (1,314 m). For lake, waterfall, and wildflower views, follow the moderate Zealand Hut Trail. From late May to mid-October, head an hour east to drive the Mount Washington Auto Road to the 6,288-foot (1,917 m) summit, the highest peak in the Northeast.

HUB | *Northeastern United States*

Down East

Acadia National Park, Maine, U.S.

Founded in 1916 as Sieur de Monts National Monument, Acadia was the first national park in the eastern United States. It's also one of the easiest to explore on foot or by bike due to 45 miles (72.4 km) of broken-stone carriage roads, originally built for horse-drawn vehicles by oil tycoon and philanthropist John D. Rockefeller, Jr. There also are 158 miles (254.3 km) of coastal, lake, forest, and summit hiking trails. For breathtaking ocean views, walk the park's Great Head Trail (1.4 miles/2.2 km). To test your breathing on a more challenging trek, clamber up to the summit of Beehive Mountain (520 feet/158 m).

Most of the park is located on 108-square-mile (280 sq km) Mount Desert Island, also home to four classic Maine towns: Bar Harbor, Mount Desert, Southwest Harbor, and Tremont. Stay in Bar Harbor (3 miles/4.8 km south of Acadia's Hulls Cove Visitor Center) or at the park's Blackwoods Campground. Late June to early October, go car free by using the free Island Explorer shuttle to get around.

HUB | *Northeastern United States*

A lighthouse looks out over the Acadia coastline.

> "THE SKI AREA AND THE TOWN HAVE AN UNPRETENTIOUS, FRIENDLY VIBE."

Like a Local
Whitefish, Montana, U.S.

With 700 miles (1,127 km) of trails in nearby Glacier National Park and more than 40 miles (64.4 km) of the Whitefish Trail looping around public and private lands outside downtown, there's no shortage of ways to wander in Whitefish. The northwest Montana ski town sits close to the Canadian border in the Northern Rockies yet is easily accessible via direct flights from several major cities in the West and Midwest to Glacier Park International Airport. Amtrak's long-distance *Empire Builder* line running from Chicago to the Pacific Northwest also stops in Whitefish. The walkable downtown that organically grew around the railroad station has a covered-walkway Main Street. Historic buildings along the primary thoroughfare and adjacent blocks house restaurants, bars, live-music venues, shops, coffeehouses, galleries, and cozy places to stay.

While the biggest outdoor recreation hub in town is named Whitefish Mountain Resort, it's disingenuous to label low-key Whitefish a resort. Community members built the ski area and the town, both of which have an unpretentious, friendly vibe. To experience Whitefish like a local, bunk close to town at a charming bed and breakfast like the Garden Wall Inn or camp along the Whitefish Trail at the Whitefish Bike Retreat. Depending on the season, you can walk, hike, bike, snowshoe, or Nordic ski from downtown for miles and miles on paved bicycle and pedestrian paths, scenic country roads, mountain biking tracks, and groomed snow trails.

The town is a stop for three long-distance Adventure Cycling routes: Northern Tier, Great Parks North, and Great Divide Mountain Bike Route. During warm-weather months at Whitefish Mountain Resort, mountain bikers can ride the lifts up to different elevations and let gravity do its thing on nearly 25 miles (40.2 km) of downhill trails. In winter, Whitefish Bike Retreat rents fat-tire bikes and maintains a groomed trail network (free to use, but donations to cover grooming costs are encouraged) for seriously fun fat biking through the snowy wilderness and across frozen lakes.

HUB | *Mountain West United States*

Take a hike through Glacier National Park, just a short drive outside Whitefish.

Big hats are all the rage at Churchill Downs for the annual Kentucky Derby.

Sporting Events

From cliff diving in Portugal to speedway racing in Florida,
these thrilling competitions offer you the chance to play—or watch.

1. THE MASTERS, AUGUSTA, GEORGIA, U.S.

The Masters is as southern as sweet tea and pimento sandwiches (still priced at the tournament's original three dollars). Held the first full week in April at the Augusta National Golf Club, the four-day, 72-hole tournament attracts the world's top players, competing for the official green jacket.

2. RED BULL CLIFF DIVING WORLD CHAMPIONSHIP, SÃO MIGUEL, AZORES, PORTUGAL

Float in an extinct volcano while witnessing death-defying cliff dives at the annual Azores stop of the Red Bull Cliff Diving World Series. Since 2012, one of the most spectacular diving platforms in the seven-event series has been the rocky cliffs on the Islet of Vila Franca do Campo.

3. KENTUCKY DERBY, LOU-ISVILLE, KENTUCKY, U.S.

Held annually on the first Saturday in May, the Kentucky Derby race for three-year-old Thoroughbred horses is the oldest continuously held sporting event in the United States. The race covers 1.25 miles (2 km) around the dirt track at Louisville's legendary Churchill Downs, opened in 1875.

4. DAYTONA 500, DAYTONA, FLORIDA, U.S.

NASCAR zooms into its 36-race season with its most prestigious event: the Daytona 500. Held the third Sunday in February, the 500-mile (805 km), 200-lap race features a field of 40 drivers and a storied history that's on display at the on-site museum and gallery.

5. LUMBERJACK WORLD CHAMPIONSHIPS, HAY-WARD, WISCONSIN, U.S.

With its buzzing chainsaws, flying wood chips, and log-rolling performances, the Lumberjack World Championships showcases the strength, agility, and artistry of 125 talented lumberjacks and lumber-jills from around the world.

6. TOUR DE FRANCE, FRANCE

Typically held the first three weeks in July, the grueling men's cycling race covers some 2,175 miles (3,500 km) over 23 days. Choose a spot on the route to cheer on the passing riders in person—book a trip with Tour de France operators for guaranteed viewing spots.

7. BOSTON MARATHON, MASSACHUSETTS, U.S.

First staged in 1897 and always held on the state's Patriots' Day, the Boston Marathon is the world's oldest consecutively run marathon. Take your try at Heartbreak Hill (mile 20.5) among 30,000 entrants, or go to cheer on runners.

8. THE CHAMPIONSHIPS, WIMBLEDON, LONDON, ENGLAND

Better known as Wimbledon, this Grand Slam tennis tournament is a 14-day event featuring 675 matches—plenty for you to choose from for weekend viewing. A limited number of same-day tickets are available.

9. ROSE BOWL GAME, PAS-ADENA, CALIFORNIA, U.S.

Held annually on New Year's Day since 1916, the Tournament of the Roses game is revered by college football fans. The game is the grand finale of a Rose Bowl New Year's Day parade filled with pageantry and tradition.

10. MELBOURNE CRICKET GROUND, AUSTRALIA

Melbourne Cricket Ground is the world's largest cricket venue. Catch a game of test cricket or watch the Melbourne Stars Big Bash League games, a high-energy family-friendly event.

Harpers Ferry sits between the Potomac and Shenandoah Rivers.

National Treasure
Harpers Ferry National Historical Park, West Virginia, Maryland & Virginia, U.S.

arpers Ferry National Historical Park is steeped in Civil War history and designed to be experienced step by step. Situated at the confluence of the Potomac and Shenandoah Rivers, a junction praised by Thomas Jefferson as "perhaps one of the most stupendous scenes in nature," the 3,600-acre (1,457 ha) national park boasts about 20 miles (32.2 km) of hiking trails. Routes range from easy meanders through fields to a steep climb up Maryland Heights, elevation 1,448 feet (441 m), overlooking the Chesapeake and Ohio Canal and the Potomac.

Although the park is mostly in West Virginia, there are also areas in Maryland and Virginia, making it possible to hike in three states in one weekend. In addition, Harpers Ferry is midway on the 2,178-mile (3,505 km) Appalachian National Scenic Trail (AT). So you can legitimately say you "hiked the AT," even if only for a short stretch. Go car free by taking a train from Baltimore or Washington, D.C., to the station inside the park.

HUB | *Mid-Atlantic United States*

A bridge crosses a creek on a trail in the Beech Mountain woods.

Beech Vacation
Emerald Outback, Beech Mountain, North Carolina, U.S.

early 7 miles (11.3 km) of mountaintop trails, each crossing elevations between 4,700 (1,433 m) and 5,400 feet (1,646 m), make Beech Mountain's Emerald Outback one of the highest adventure trail parks on the East Coast. Open year-round, the North Carolina park is designed to make the summit accessible to hikers, mountain bikers, and trail runners. The park's easy, moderate, and advanced routes are a mix of single-track, double-track, and gravel trails.

Enter through the trailhead in the center of the town of Beech Mountain or at the trailhead near Beech Mountain Resort's Summit Lot parking area. There's no fee to use the park; however, from June to September, you can pay a small fee to ride (and haul your bike) up to the highest elevation trails on the resort chairlift. Beech Mountain Resort offers Hike & Wine and Bike & Brew packages combining lodging, Emerald Outback maps, and tastings at local wineries or breweries.

HUB | *Southeastern United States*

Carefully make your way across coastal rocks on the GR-92.

Coastal Sampler
Costa Brava, Catalonia, Spain

Hike the footpaths of northeastern Spain's "wild coast," the Costa Brava of Catalonia. The rocky region, which stretches from Blanes, 45 miles (72.4 km) northeast of Barcelona and 133 miles (214 km) to the border with France, is sandwiched between the Pyrenees mountain range and the Mediterranean. Running along the coast is the Camino de Ronda, an ancient network of trails connecting the fishing villages of the Costa Brava. Gaps in the old trails are supplemented by the well-marked GR-92, a Grande Randonnée European long-distance route, which overlaps the Camino de Ronda much of the way.

Walking the entire Camino de Ronda takes 10 to 12 days, but the village-hopping structure makes it easy to choose a section to tackle over a weekend. For a Costa Brava sampler—including digging into Catalonian dishes like *suquet de peix* (fishermen's stew) and the region's famous red prawns—walk along beaches and coves and through tunnels and Roman ruins on the paths from Platja d'Aro to Palamós.

HUB | *Northern Spain; Southern Europe*

> "URBAN LOWLAND FOREST INCLUDES TREES UP TO 250 YEARS OLD."

Go Green

Seattle, Washington, U.S.

True to its Emerald City nickname, Seattle is awash in green space. There are more than 485 parks, 200 miles (321.9 km) of shoreline, and an extensive network of recreational trails inside the seaport city. Three national parks—Mount Rainier, Olympic, and North Cascades—are within a two-hour drive. Even downtown, you can skip the main city streets and walk or bike north-south on the Elliott Bay Trail, a paved waterfront rail trail running along Puget Sound.

The city's largest urban oasis, 534-acre (216 ha) Discovery Park, protects tidal beaches, forest groves, meadows, sea cliffs, and sand dunes. From downtown, take the Route 33 Metro bus to the park and hike the round-trip 2.8-mile (4.5 km) Discovery Park Loop Trail, a National Recreational Trail. The route leads through forest and meadows and offers views across Puget Sound of the Seattle skyline and the Cascade and Olympic Mountains in the distance.

The wildest of Seattle's urban parks is Seward, the city's oldest and largest forest. Covering all 300 acres (121 ha) of Bailey Peninsula at the south end of Lake Washington, the park features a 120-acre (49 ha) urban lowland forest, which includes some trees up to 250 years old. A web of dirt and gravel hiking trails leads through the thickly wooded interior of the park, while a 2.4-mile (3.9 km) paved biking and walking loop (Trail 10) parallels the shoreline of the lake. As with all the other parks inside the city, Seward is accessible via public transportation (including the Route 50 Metro bus, as well as the light rail, streetcar, and water taxi).

Also fronting Lake Washington is the free Washington Park Arboretum, 230 acres (93 ha) of gardens, wetlands, and woods, including a nationally recognized collection of oak trees. The arboretum, co-managed by the University of Washington Botanic Gardens and the City of Seattle, has multiple loop trails and garden paths, open to the public daily from 9 a.m. to 5 p.m.

A cherry tree blossoms
on the shore of Lake
Washington in Seward Park.

Snuggle up for warmth
inside a snow-covered suite at
Sweden's Ice Hotel in Kiruna.

Places for Romance

Find that spark again cozying up in these romantic destinations.

1. TANGO IN BUENOS AIRES, ARGENTINA

Let tango be your guide to a smoldering weekend in Buenos Aires. Take a private lesson at Mariposita de San Telmo, catch the Faena Rojo Tango dinner show, and hit the *milonga* circuit.

2. FONDUE IN GRUYÈRES, SWITZERLAND

One of the world's most romantic dishes is Swiss born, and medieval Gruyères is the ideal place to explore that history. Study up at the Fondue Academy, or try as many fondue restaurants as you can. Don't miss Le Chalet.

3. COZY UP IN KIRUNA, SWEDEN

The ripped-from-a-fairy-tale forests of Swedish Lapland harbor the original—and now year-round—Ice Hotel. While the aurora season is extra lovely here, there's no bad time to get cozy in your glittering ice suite.

4. TOAST IN CHAMPAGNE, FRANCE

You could do nothing more than check in to the vineyard-adjacent Royal Champagne Hotel and Spa and still have an absurdly romantic weekend. But you should also sip your way through the region's fabled Champagne houses and caves.

5. FLOAT OVER NEW MEXICO, U.S.

The world's largest ballooning event, October's Albuquerque International Balloon Fiesta, is as ethereal a spectacle as you'll witness. Join in with Rainbow Ryders, which takes spectators up from Balloon Fiesta Park.

6. CAMP IN A TREE HOUSE, SEATTLE, WASHINGTON, U.S.

A Seattle-area forest retreat designed by the stars of *Treehouse Masters,* TreeHouse Point offers all manner of romantic lodgings, but the dreamiest—think private access bridges and Raging River views—may well be the Temple of the Blue Moon.

7. GROOVE IN GUANAJUATO, MEXICO

All winding lanes and colorful facades, colonial Guanajuato is known for its charm—and musicality. So your serenade-for-hire options range from mariachis to *callejoneadas* (intriguingly, minstrels in Renaissance wear). Also: Don't miss a walk through the Alley of the Kiss.

8. SOAK IN TERME DI SATURNIA, ITALY

Find peak romance as you make your way through a series of cascading pools—each filled with ethereal blue thermal water and surrounded by Tuscan countryside. It's not only love you'll be enjoying in these 3,000-year-old springs, but the waters are also known to be antioxidant rich and purifying for mind, body, and spirit.

9. CHASE WATERFALLS IN OREGON, U.S.

The Columbia River Gorge, home to the highest concentration of waterfalls in the United States, makes for a seriously romantic road trip from Portland, Oregon. A few of the must-sees are Bridal Veil (118 feet/36 m tall), Elowah (213 feet/65 m tall), and the larger Multnomah Falls (620 feet/118.9 m tall).

10. CRUISE ZHOUZHUANG, CHINA

The so-called Venice of China dates back almost as far as its Italian counterpart, with plenty of Ming- and Qing-era holdovers lining the canals. Hire the local version of a gondolier to take you around town. Fourteen stone bridges cross the rivers and offer beautiful views of the water town.

"EACH SECTION OF THE
CAPE COD RAIL TRAIL
HAS ITS CHARMS."

Cape Escape

Cape Cod Rail Trail, Yarmouth to Wellfleet, Massachusetts, U.S.

Escape the Cape's notorious Route 6 traffic by pedaling or hiking through the pines on the Cape Cod Rail Trail. The 27.5-mile (44.3 km) relatively flat route follows a 19th-century railroad right-of-way through seven cedar-shingled villages and towns: Yarmouth, Dennis, Harwich, Brewster, Orleans, Eastham, and Wellfleet. Viewing the passing landscape is like watching a highlight reel of quintessential Cape Cod scenery. You'll pass seasonal fried clam and ice-cream stands, restaurants, cranberry bogs, glacier-formed kettle ponds, salt marshes, sandy stretches, access trails to bay and ocean beaches, and other attractions.

There's free parking along the trail at places like the main trailhead on Route 134 in Dennis, Orleans Center, and the Salt Pond Visitor Center at the Cape Cod National Seashore in Eastham. You can camp and park (for a fee) on the route at Nickerson State Park in Brewster, and numerous motels, cottages, and rental properties are within easy walking or biking distance of the trail.

Each section of the Cape Cod Rail Trail has its charms. One of the best entry points for half-day out-and-back trips is the Rail Trail hub town of Orleans. If you want to experience the trail on two wheels, rent a bike (first come, first served) at Orleans Cycle, located near mile 13, and head east toward Wellfleet. Look for the side trail in Eastham leading to the Salt Pond Visitor Center. Stop inside to watch the seashore's orientation movie, *Standing Bold*, and learn about the Cape's glacial, cultural, and natural history, as well as current environmental concerns. From here, follow the Nauset Bike Trail east to the ocean at Coast Guard Beach. Spend time there before heading back to Orleans for lunch, Massachusetts-made Richardson's Farm ice cream, or a signature frozen hot chocolate at the Hot Chocolate Sparrow.

Biking the Cape Cod Rail Trail is a quintessential Massachusetts experience.

For coastal views, hike Indiana's sand dunes.

Sand Castles
Indiana Dunes Country, Chesterton, Indiana, U.S.

Indiana may be better known for corn and car racing, but the state's northwest corner is Dunes Country. Here, 15 miles (24.1 km) of Lake Michigan coastline extend across 2,182-acre (883 ha) Indiana Dunes State Park and, on its east and west side, 13,000-acre (5,261 ha) Indiana Dunes National Park. The national park has more than 50 miles (80.5 km) of trails leading through a variety of habitats, including swamps, black oak savannas, and open dunes. Routes range from the short, wheelchair-accessible Calumet Dunes Trail to the steep Mount Baldy Summit Trail, accessible only on summer weekends on free ranger-led hikes.

In the neighboring state park, there are seven numbered trails covering more than 16 miles (25.7 km). Rugged Trail 8 crosses the summits of the three highest Indiana Dunes, collectively totaling 552 vertical feet (168 m). For a long bike ride, pedal the 8.9-mile (14.3 km) (one way) Oak Savannah rail trail, which partially crosses through Indiana Dunes National Park.

HUB | *Midwestern United States*

Mountain bike through a system of forest trails.

Bike the Ozarks
Fayetteville, Arkansas, U.S.

Biking is king in the rugged Ozarks of Northwest Arkansas. Gravel, soft-surface, and paved trails wind through the region's rock-covered woodlands, hilly terrain, and old-growth forests. The vast network of trails earned Northwest Arkansas worldwide recognition as the first ever International Mountain Bicycling Association (IMBA) Regional Ride Center.

Rookie to expert mountain bikers, recreational riders, and cyclocross (a mountain biking and road racing hybrid) enthusiasts can pedal for miles or days on the trails in and around the region's two IMBA Regional Ride Center cities: Fayetteville, home of the University of Arkansas flagship campus, and neighboring Bentonville, birthplace of Walmart.

Rent a bike at Fayetteville's Phat Tire Bike Shop to tackle challenging routes in nearby Devil's Den State Park or Kessler Mountain Regional Park. For a more leisurely ride, hop on the Northwest Arkansas Razorback Regional Greenway, a 36-mile (57.9 km) paved trail that starts in south Fayetteville.

HUB | *Southeastern or Midwestern United States*

Bear Tracks

Sleeping Bear Dunes National Lakeshore, Michigan, U.S.

Established in 1970, Sleeping Bear is a protected sand-and-freshwater recreational area on the "Third Coast," the nickname given to the eight-state U.S. coastline of the Great Lakes. Of the 100 miles (161 km) of trails on the lakeshore's mainland and two islands (North and South Manitou), some of the most popular stretch across Sleeping Bear's namesake dunes. Hike up the well-trodden Dune Run for a view of Glen Lake, then run or roll back down on the windswept sand.

If you're prepared (carry water and wear sunscreen and hiking shoes for a more strenuous hike), follow the blue-tipped posts of the Dune Trail to Lake Michigan and back. The 3.5-mile (5.6 km) round-trip trek is steep, but the breathtaking dune-and-lake panorama is worth the climb. Summer is the busiest season; however, most mainland trails are open in winter for cross-country skiing and snowshoeing, and rangers regularly lead snowshoe walks in January and February.

HUB | *Midwestern United States*

Look out to the lake far below the top of the sand dunes.

Evolution Lake
reflects the surrounding
mountains at sunset.

PERSPECTIVE

Going the Distance

The National Scenic Trail System Has Forged Memories Foot by Foot

While thru-hiking the entire Appalachian National Scenic Trail, I walked some five million steps. On the Pacific Crest Trail, six million. My current trek, the Continental Divide National Scenic Trail, will require just about seven million. But for each, one of the best steps was the very first. As I took that initial stride from the southern terminus of each of those trails—Springer Mountain, Georgia; Campo, California; and Crazy Cook Monument, New Mexico, respectively—the anxiety of planning and endless checklists evaporated. All that remained was the rush of possibility. With thousands of miles before me and my husband beside me, I could feel that familiar thrill shivering up my spine.

The trail works its magic; footsteps transform from dots on a map and notes in a guidebook into real places. The swimming hole. The campfire under the full moon. The aspen grove. And once passed, those dots and notes are further transfigured into cherished memories.

Hikers are also transformed—and christened anew, with the adoption of a trail name. Early on the Appalachian Trail, I decided to be "Knock on Wood" due to my knee-jerk reaction when others made predictions about the adventures that we would have. To my greenhorn self, bold predictions seemed to tempt fate.

Though I originally took the name as a joke about my fears, I now see it more as a promise to appreciate each day on trail. Against the ponderous time lines of the lands we walk, our human lives seem brief and insubstantial. Each moment on trail is a gift.

I believe we leave behind some part of ourselves on the paths we walk. When I first started on the Appalachian Trail, I was hoping to follow in the footsteps of my cousin Jen, 11 years my senior, who had thru-hiked the AT more than a decade before. A globe-roaming hippie with a tiny pack and a zest for silly puns, Jen has always inspired me to seek adventure. On days when rain pelted down, I imagined Jen undaunted, braving the same storm. In her favorite places, such as Bob Peoples's quirky woodland hostel, Kincora, I felt a new connection between us.

I also felt kinship with those unknown people who had preceded me. I tried to imagine the individuals, their hopes, their stubbed toes, their faces warmed in the sun. Where did their journeys take them?

On the Continental Divide Trail in Colorado, Rollins Pass is covered in rock blinds from which herd animals were once ambushed. They were in use for millennia. I stood among the stones, the wind chilling my bones, and tried to reach back through time to feel something of the ancient hunters who had gathered there.

On the Pacific Crest Trail in California, it was a blisteringly hot afternoon as I staggered up Donner Pass. I loosened my hip belt and fought down nausea. At the ski restaurant we'd stopped at earlier, my husband and I had shoveled down plates of nachos, then added most of a pie and a couple beers to boot. Now I had to sit and rest, and all I could think of was how different my experience was from that of the ill-fated Donner Party, a group of pioneers who had come more than a century and a half before.

I also imagined those who would follow. Who will walk these lands, a day or a century from now?

The National Scenic Trail system is now 52 years old. Congress passed the 1968 act partly to help conserve the Appalachian and Pacific Crest trails. Now the network of government-protected recreational paths numbers 11—including the Natchez Trace Trail, the Florida Trail, and the Potomac Heritage Trail—and encompasses some 18,000 miles (28,968 km). Every year thousands of people hike, bike, and horseback ride through rocky steeps and flat grasslands. They take on entire trails over the course of months—or shorter portions over the course of long weekends.

In another 52 years, may our public lands be just as cherished, our wilderness enduringly preserved. May we still find there that transformative magic.

—**Allie Ghaman** is a backpacker, writer, and illustrator with more than 6,500 trail miles (10,460 km) under her belt.

"A MIX OF PEAT BOGS, LAKES, ROCK-STREWN FIELDS"

Tasmanian Walkabout

Hobart, Tasmania, Australia

Ireland-sized Tasmania, located off Australia's southeastern coast, is the Aussie's only island state. Being detached from the mainland has helped keep Tasmania a largely unspoiled place—one that's best experienced outdoors and on foot.

To inspire people to discover the island one step at a time, Tasmania Parks and Wildlife Service, which manages about half of the state's area, created 60 Great Short Walks. In rugged Tasmania, "short" means any hike that takes less than eight hours, and "walks" range from Grade 1 (flat, even surface, no steps) routes suitable for wheelchair users (with some assistance) to Grade 5 (likely rough, very steep, and unmarked) bushwalking tracks requiring navigation and first aid skills.

Hobart, Tasmania's capital city, is a convenient base for 17 of the Great Short Walks. One of the most popular treks is a 5.7-mile (9.2 km) loop that climbs partway up 4,170-foot (1,271 m) Kunanyi/Mount Wellington and passes beneath the Organ Pipes—formidable hexagonal rock columns towering up to 393 feet (120 m) high. From the Organ Pipes route, you can continue up to Wellington's windswept, boulder-field summit plateau on the aptly named Zig Zag Track. For the pinnacle views without the day-long hike, drive directly to the summit from Hobart and walk less than a mile (1.4 km) on the Zig Zag Track to a glass-encased lookout. From here, in clear weather, you can see Hobart and a wide swath of southeastern Tasmania below.

If leisurely, low-elevation walking is more your speed, follow the 1.6-mile (2.6 km) coastal track from Cornelian Bay to the Royal Tasmanian Botanical Gardens. The route connects to the longer Intercity Cycleway, a biking and walking trail that closely parallels the path of the Derwent River for nearly 10 miles (15.6 km). December to May (summer to fall in Australia) is the best time to take a walking weekend in Hobart. Download the 60 Great Short Walks app to help choose your routes.

HUB | *Southeastern Australia*

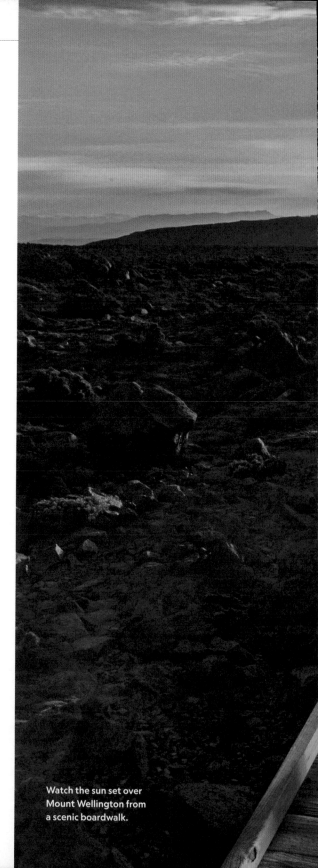

Watch the sun set over Mount Wellington from a scenic boardwalk.

Bergen's numerous trails include cycling Mount Fløyen.

Northern Delights
Bergen, Norway

Bergen, Norway's second city, is situated between seven mountains and is home to a World Heritage site harbor district, Bryggen. So whether you want to hike in the mountains or walk around a compact port city (one of the oldest in northern Europe), center city Bergen is a convenient starting point. May to September, adventure outfitter Base Camp Bergen also rents trekking, road, and e-bikes at the Hanseatic wharf in Bryggen. From there, you can hop on designated bike routes throughout the city.

The closest hiking trails are on 1,050-foot (320 m) Mount Fløyen, easily accessible from the city center via the Fløbanen Funicular. Purchase a one-way ticket for the ride up, where you'll be treated to views of fjords, forested mountains, and the city and harbor below. From the railway station at the top, there are walks leading to a lake and a longer trail to 2,109-foot (643 m) Mount Ulriken, the highest of Bergen's seven summits.

HUB | *Major Western European Cities*

Wild West Trails
Truckee, California, U.S.

Follow trails taken by Native Americans, pioneers (including the infamous Donner Party), and Chinese immigrants who built the transcontinental railroad in and around the Old West–style town of Truckee, California. Located in the Sierra Nevada mountains north of Lake Tahoe and 32 miles (51.5 km) west of Reno, Nevada, Truckee is an all-seasons gateway for miles of walking, hiking, biking, skiing, and snowmobiling trails.

Open to cross-country skiers in winter and cyclists year-round, the paved, 4.4-mile (7.1 km) Truckee River Legacy Trail is a mainly flat route for a leisurely hike or ride. Nearby resorts like Squaw Valley Alpine Meadows and Boreal Mountain have downhill ski trails, and the Truckee area has an extensive network of single-track trail-running and mountain bike trails, such as the 9-mile (14.5 km) Sawtooth Loop featuring two cliff overlooks. Bring a flashlight, and hike through a series of graffiti-gallery railroad tunnels on the Historic Donner Pass Trail, a 5.9-mile (9.5 km) loop.

HUB | *Western United States*

Hike the Grouse Lake Trail to Smith Lake.

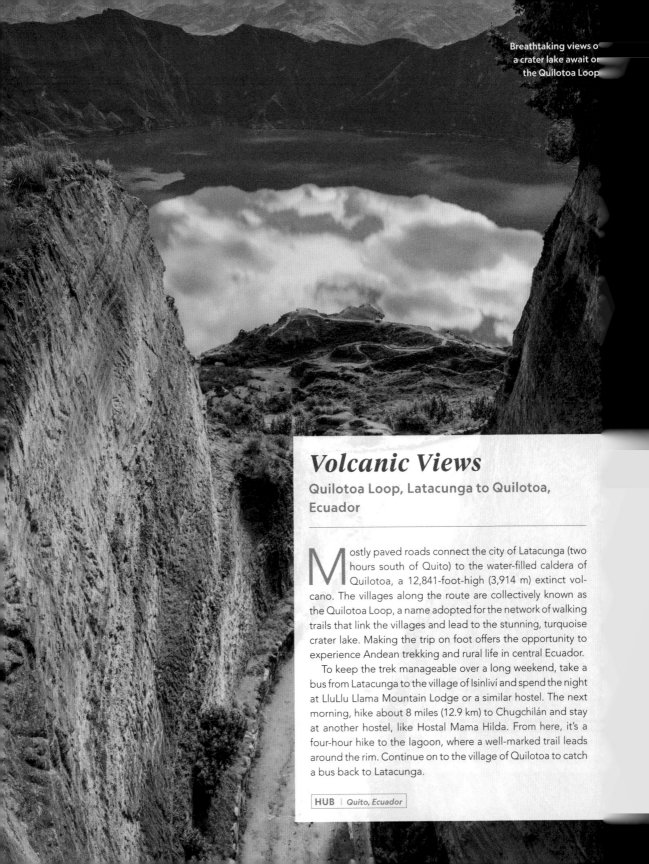

Breathtaking views of
a crater lake await on
the Quilotoa Loop

Volcanic Views

Quilotoa Loop, Latacunga to Quilotoa, Ecuador

Mostly paved roads connect the city of Latacunga (two hours south of Quito) to the water-filled caldera of Quilotoa, a 12,841-foot-high (3,914 m) extinct volcano. The villages along the route are collectively known as the Quilotoa Loop, a name adopted for the network of walking trails that link the villages and lead to the stunning, turquoise crater lake. Making the trip on foot offers the opportunity to experience Andean trekking and rural life in central Ecuador.

To keep the trek manageable over a long weekend, take a bus from Latacunga to the village of Isinliví and spend the night at LluLlu Llama Mountain Lodge or a similar hostel. The next morning, hike about 8 miles (12.9 km) to Chugchilán and stay at another hostel, like Hostal Mama Hilda. From here, it's a four-hour hike to the lagoon, where a well-marked trail leads around the rim. Continue on to the village of Quilotoa to catch a bus back to Latacunga.

HUB | *Quito, Ecuador*

"CONSIDERED ONE OF THE MOST QUINTESSENTIALLY IRISH PLACES IN IRELAND"

Wilde Ireland

Connemara, County Galway, Ireland

Irish poet and playwright Oscar Wilde described Connemara, the wild and rocky northwest corner of County Galway, as "in every way magnificent." The starkly scenic region is shaped by its relationship to the water: the open Atlantic to the west, Killary Harbour to the north, and Galway Bay to the south. Salty sea air regularly hangs damp over the windswept landscape—a mix of peat bogs, lakes, rock-strewn fields bordered by ancient stone walls, sandy beaches, rocky coast, and the quartzite peaks of the Twelve Bens and Maumturk mountains.

Considered one of the most quintessentially Irish places in Ireland, Connemara is home to nearly half of the country's total Gaeltacht, or Gaelic-speaking, population. Walking, biking, and hiking here offer opportunities to hear the lilting Irish language spoken and sung in Connemara's coastal villages and on Clare, Inishbofin, and Inishturk Islands.

Although Connemara looks and feels remote, the region's largest town and unofficial capital, Clifden, is less than 50 miles (80.5 km) away from buzzing Galway City. With its small hotels and bed and breakfasts, Clifden is a logical base for a walking or cycling weekend. Local outfitters, such as Hillwalk Tours and Walk Connemara, offer guided small group and private walks across Connemara, or you can easily set out on your own. To get a feel for the land, a good starting point is the 2.7-mile (4.3 km) Diamond Hill Loop in Connemara National Park.

Clifden also is a cycle hub for County Galway and a popular starting point for cyclists exploring the Wild Atlantic Way, Ireland's 1,553-mile (2,500 km) scenic route spanning six diverse coastal regions. From Clifden, you can choose from several biking routes, including the Sky Road Loop. The 10-mile (16.1 km) ride along a peninsula delivers impressive views of the Atlantic and of Inishturk and Turbot Islands and leads past eerie Clifden Castle, built in the 18th century and abandoned in the 1840s.

HUB | *Galway City, Ireland*

Explore Ireland's Connemara area, including Lough Fee.

Copenhagen's town hall offers free bike rentals to visitors.

Bike Rides

Pedal through countryside villages, lunar landscapes, and mountain trails in these rider-friendly destinations.

1. COPENHAGEN, DENMARK

Routinely named the world's best cycling city by data crunchers, Copenhagen has more bikes than cars (your hotel most likely offers loaners), plus more than 250 miles (402.3 km) of bike lanes and 600 or so miles (965.6 km) of paths in the greater metropolitan area—and countless pedal tours.

2. BOULDER, COLORADO, U.S.

Recently ranked the most bikeable city in the United States, this Rocky Mountain classic has everything from more than 300 miles (482.8 km) of dedicated lanes to a gear vending machine. And there's a major mountain biking bonus: the surrounding foothills. Hit the trails between March and November, when snow is less likely on the ground—though Hall Ranch and Boulder Reservoir trails are often accessible through winter months.

3. MOAB, UTAH, U.S.

With its red rocks, lunar landscapes, and world-renowned Slickrock Bike Trail, this corner of the Utah desert is arguably the most iconic mountain biking getaway in existence. (Keep in mind, Slickrock is just the start; far easier trails abound.)

4. WHISTLER MOUNTAIN, BRITISH COLUMBIA, CANADA

Prefer a bike park? Whistler's has a reputation as the world's best. The Top of the World, which drops almost 5,000 vertical feet (152.4 m), may be the most infamous trail, but you'll find plenty of beginner and intermediate options too.

5. ALPE D'HUEZ, FRANCE

Home of the legendary Megavalanche mountain bike race, this ski resort sees regular Tour de France action too. All kinds of cyclists flock here, and local chalets respond by offering everything from bike tours to repair and cleaning.

6. VERBIER, SWITZERLAND

Another Alpine retreat beloved among mountain bikers, this Swiss ski resort has also started hosting the world's largest e-bike (electric bike) event. Over a long weekend in August, tours, races, and workshops await e-bikers of all skill levels.

7. SACRED VALLEY, PERU

The Sacred Valley of the Inca makes for unquestionably gorgeous mountain biking, but the cultural riches—from ancient ruins to vibrant villages—truly define these trails. Acclaimed operator Habitats Peru will show you the best.

8. TRAVELERS REST, SOUTH CAROLINA, U.S.

To the average cyclist, these Blue Ridge foothills simply make for amazing biking. But to at least one pro, they bear a striking resemblance to Alpine training terrain. Thus, the town's cycling-centric Hotel Domestique, founded by Tour de France veteran George Hincapie.

9. STELLENBOSCH, SOUTH AFRICA

The cycling trails through South Africa's Cape Winelands come with exquisite backdrops—think vineyards, mountains, and centuries-old Cape Dutch architecture. But arguably even better is your post-ride reward: a tasting in any of the world-renowned local wineries.

10. MEKONG DELTA, VIETNAM

Serenity on wheels, a bike ride through Vietnam's Mekong Delta is a mosaic of rice paddies, houses on stilts, and floating markets. The peacefulness feels even more pronounced on a day trip escaping Ho Chi Minh City.

Steep Steps

Namhae Island, South Korea

One of Hallyeo Maritime National Park's nearly 100 islands, Namhae is a rocky yet lushly forested gem just off South Korea's southern coast. Although a suspension bridge and seasonal ferries make for relatively easy connections from the mainland, low-key Namhae is largely off the beaten path.

The island is home to craggy Geumsan (Silk Mountain), elevation 2,234 feet (681 m). Hike the steep trail and stairs to the top to visit exquisite Bori-am Hermitage, a Buddhist temple founded in 683. From the temple and summit overlooks, you're surrounded by sweeping views of the sea, sandy beaches, pine forests, neighboring islands, and the villages below. The most famous Namhae village is Gacheon, better known as Daraengi, where rice paddies stair-step down the steep slopes of Mount Seolheulsan (1,601 feet/488 m). A coastal trail leads to the village, past the flight of terraced fields. On the coast, follow walking paths across boulders and along cliffs, above the crashing waves.

> "YOU'RE SURROUNDED BY SWEEPING VIEWS OF THE SEA, SANDY BEACHES, PINE FORESTS, NEIGHBORING ISLANDS, AND THE VILLAGES BELOW."

HUB | *South Korea; Eastern Asia*

Wooden bridges connect the rocky shores of Daraengi Village on Namhae Island.

Hiking trails lead to scenic overlooks of Squamish Lake and its surrounding old-growth forests.

Sea to Sky
Squamish, British Columbia, Canada

Squamish is arguably West Coast Canada's top outdoor recreation destination. The community sits at the northern tip of Howe Sound, a Pacific fjord teeming with mammoth marine mammals like orcas and whales. Hundreds of walking, hiking, horseback riding, and mountain biking trails weave around the sound and area lakes, through old-growth forests and provincial parks, and up to panoramic viewpoints in the surrounding Coast Mountains.

The extensive Squamish trail network is easily accessible from town. Get free trail maps and expert recommendations, rent bikes and other outdoor gear, and book guided hiking and biking tours at the Squamish Adventure Centre. Among the available tours are environmental nature hikes; rugged treks up Stawamus Chief (or the Chief), the 2,296-foot-high (700 m) granite cliffs looming above town; and kayaking excursions on the Sea to Sky Marine Trail.

HUB | Vancouver, Canada; Pacific Northwest United States

Take the wooded Deeks Lake hike for green views.

The medieval hill town of Follina sits along the Route del Prosecco.

> "THE TERRAIN IS EXHILARATING,
> WITH PUNCHY CLIMBS;
> LONG, LEISURELY DOWNHILLS;
> AND MINIMAL TRAFFIC."

Epic Action Italy

Effervescence Everywhere in Strada del Prosecco

"The power is in the ladies; there are no men," Giovanni Zanon jokes as we power-sip an extra-dry brut from Sorelle Bronca estate. We're halfway into a 32-mile (51.5 km) midmorning cycling loop on a hot Sunday, and this highly regarded prosecco, with hints of honeydew and pear, tastes refreshingly crisp. It's made by Antonella and Ersiliana Bronca, two sisters who took over their father's winery in 1988. The women and their families grow their grapes on a patchwork of 67 acres (27 ha) scattered throughout the region of Valdobbiadene. This, along with the neighboring region of Conegliano, became Italy's 55th UNESCO World Heritage site on July 7, 2019, thanks in part to its aesthetically pleasing checkerboard landscape, where rows of vines grow parallel and vertical to the sloping hills. The resulting prosecco is currently the most popular Italian wine worldwide.

Zanon owns Villa Abbazia, an 18th-century palace converted to a five-star hotel in the village of Follina. It sits across the street from a 12th-century monastery founded by Cistercian monks. Villa Abbazia also houses the only Michelin-starred restaurant in the region. Last night its Puglian chef, Donato Episcopo, prepared us an elaborate, whimsical five-course meal that included trout marinated with citrus fruits for the entrée and ended with tiramisu—the same recipe Zanon's family has used since 1955—and too much grappa.

We dined on an outdoor patio overlooking the grand palace and a garden brimming with lemon trees, rhododendron, and hydrangea, feeling like royalty.

Zanon, the quintessential host, stayed up with guests until 2 a.m., but this morning, his cycling-fanatic side has taken over and he's riding with us on a route of his design that climbs 1,600 feet (487.7 m) through jasmine-scented hills. The terrain is exhilarating, with punchy climbs; long, leisurely downhills; and minimal traffic. We stop every few miles to eat and drink with Zanon's friends. At Pasticceria Villa dei Cedri, a café with pastries that are almost too beautiful to eat, I try the traditional southern Italian cream puff, *tette delle monache*. The name, I later learn, translates to "nuns' breasts." Despite this reminder that Italy is slightly behind the curve in #MeToo political correctness, it's a luscious treat that pairs well with espresso.

It fuels me for our final climb to the new tasting room at Garbara winery, in Cartizze. Cartizze Zero is a light, smooth prosecco known for being so pure that there's no sugar. We sip it while overlooking the verdant vine-covered hills. Only three days in, I'm already wondering how Italy can get any better than this.

—**Stephanie Pearson** is a contributing editor at *Outside* magazine who splits her time between the lakes of northern Minnesota and the deserts of the Southwest.

> "HONG KONG REVEALS ITS QUIETER, NATURAL, WILD SIDE."

Hong Kong, Naturally

Hong Kong

Hong Kong dazzles with its gleaming skyscraper forests, humming night markets, and relentless pace of life. Step just outside the high-tech, high-energy sectors, though, and Hong Kong reveals its quieter, natural, wild side popular with locals seeking respite from 24/7 city life yet still surprising to many visitors.

Mountains, expansive country parks, nature reserves, and marine parks make up most of Hong Kong, which includes Hong Kong Island, Kowloon, the New Territories, and more than 200 outlying islands. No matter where you're staying, the great outdoors is either right outside your door or easily accessible via Hong Kong's superefficient public transportation network. Use the Trip Planner on the Mass Transit Railway (MTR) site to chart a course for a hiking or mountain biking adventure.

For a moderate hike delivering breathtaking views of the South China Sea, tackle rocky Dragon's Back on southeastern Hong Kong Island. The 5-mile (8 km) stone-step and packed-dirt route goes along the spine of the D'Aguilar Peninsula to Big Wave Bay. To venture a bit farther off the beaten path, spend a day hiking in Plover Cove Country Park, located in the northeast New Territories. The main lower elevation route, relatively flat, takes about three to four hours to complete and leads through three diverse settings: forest, high-elevation mountain, and Lai Chi Wo, a centuries-old Hakka (a Han Chinese ethnic subgroup) village.

If adrenaline-pumping trail running or mountain biking is more your speed, run or pedal up to the summit of Tai Mo Shan, Hong Kong's highest peak at elevation 3,140 feet (957 m). One of the most challenging ways to the top is part of the 62-mile (100 km) MacLehose Trail, which winds across the New Territories and passes over mountain peaks and along gorgeous beaches. To see Hong Kong's most iconic panorama, skip the tourist tram and hike the Lung Fu Shan Fitness Trail up to Victoria Peak, Hong Kong Island's highest hill at 1,811 feet (552 m).

Known as a city of steel,
Hong Kong offers a bounty
of nature retreats.

Switzerland's peaks create stunning panoramas.

Alpine Adventures
Les Diablerets, Switzerland

Stay in the Swiss Alpine village of Les Diablerets to play—ski, Nordic walk, snowshoe, snowboard, and hike—at nearby Glacier 3000. The year-round glacier attraction sits 9,842 feet (3,000 m) up in the Vaud Alps, 80 miles (128.7 km) west of Geneva. Ride a cable car to the top to see world-class peaks, such as the 14,691-foot (4,478 m) Matterhorn and the 13,015-foot (3,967 m) Eiger, and to spend the day hiking or skiing trails from the summit.

There are 17 miles (27.4 km) of Glacier 3000 ski runs open October to May and 46 miles (74 km) of marked hiking trails typically open July to September. Hikes range in difficulty from an easy Glacier Walk to the gravity-defying fixed-rope route, Via Ferrata Gemskopf. The shortest hike is the 351-foot-long (107 m) Peak Walk, which leads across the world's only summit-to-summit suspension bridge. For a longer trek, take the 8-mile (12.9 km) Ice and Water hike over the glacier and down to Sanetsch Lake.

HUB | *Geneva, Switzerland*

Presidential Retreat
Veliki Brijun Island, Istria, Croatia

Once the retreat of Yugoslavian leader and communist revolutionary Josip Broz Tito, Veliki Brijun is the largest of the 14 islands making up Brijuni National Park. The car-free island is located only 15 minutes by boat from the small town of Fazana, just off the southwestern coast of Croatia's Istrian Peninsula. Walking and cycling trails wind around most of the island's 2 square miles (5.2 sq km), including through the Safari Zoo and past fascinating archaeological sites, such as the Byzantine castrum, whose earliest finds date to the first century B.C.

The Croatian president maintains a residence here, and there are other government buildings, but most of the island's mix of beaches, forest, meadows, landscaped gardens, and manicured lawns are open to the public. Get the presidential treatment by staying in the historic Hotel Istra-Neptun, popular with socialist dignitaries during Tito's rule. In July and August, the park offers guided swimming and snorkeling tours along an underwater archaeological trail.

HUB | *Zagreb, Croatia*

Visit the ruins along Dobrika Bay's coastline.

Old-World Charm

Echternach, Luxembourg

Nestled in the heart of Luxembourg's hilly Mullerthal, or "Little Switzerland," region, charming Echternach is the start and end point for two of the three loops on the 70-mile (112.7 km) Mullerthal Trail. Spend a weekend hiking the moderate, 22-mile (35.4 km) Route 1 or the more difficult, 23-mile (37 km) Route 2, or combine stages of all three routes, while still beginning and ending in Echternach.

Hiking the trail is the best way to see the region's surreal rock formations, waterfalls, medieval villages, and other cultural treasures, such as the baroque Benedictine Abbey Museum and the Basilica of Saint Willibrord, named for the Catholic patron saint of Luxembourg who founded Echternach, the country's oldest town, in A.D. 698. The region is also part of the German-Luxembourg Nature Park, established in 1964 as Europe's first cross-border nature reserve. Towns along the route offer hiker-friendly lodging, and guided walking tours, suggested itineraries, and baggage transport services are available.

HUB | *Major Western European Cities*

Echternach, also called Little Switzerland, offers one-of-a-kind hiking.

CONTRIBUTORS

ABBIE KOZOLCHYK is an award-winning writer and editor who has contributed to *National Geographic Traveler*, *Travel + Leisure*, the *San Francisco Chronicle*, *Outside*, *World Hum*, *Forbes Traveler*, and many other travel and women's magazines. Her writing has been featured in *The Best Women's Travel Writing* anthology, and she is the author of National Geographic's *The World's Most Romantic Destinations*. When not on the road, she splits her time between California and New York. Find her at abbiekozolchyk.com.

CARRIE MILLER is a traveler, storyteller, and award-winning writer. She has been writing for National Geographic and other publications for more than 20 years. Miller's first book, *100 Dives of a Lifetime: The World's Ultimate Underwater Destinations*, was published by National Geographic in 2019. She is currently writing her second book, based on a 14-month assignment exploring the world's best dive travel destinations. Find her at carrieink.co.nz.

JOE YOGERST has lived and worked as a writer, editor, and photographer on four continents, including stints in South Africa, England, Hong Kong, and Singapore. Among his 40-plus National Geographic projects are the best-selling books *50 States, 5,000 Ideas* and *100 Parks, 5,000 Ideas*, as well as the National Geographic Great Courses video series *The Wonders of America's State Parks*. Yogerst was a longtime contributing editor at *Condé Nast Traveler* and *Islands* magazines and has also written for the *Los Angeles Times*, *Washington Post*, *CNN Travel*, *BBC Travel*, and the *International Herald Tribune* in Paris. His travel books and stories have earned four Lowell Thomas Awards from the Society of American Travel Writers.

KAREN CARMICHAEL is a National Geographic writer, editor, and photographer. Her work has been published in *National Geographic Traveler* and *National Geographic* magazine and more than a dozen National Geographic Travel books, as well as *Budget Travel* and the *Los Angeles Times*. An expedition leader for National Geographic and Los Angeles Times Expeditions, Carmichael has led multiple trips to Spain, Cuba, Ecuador and the Galápagos Islands, Mexico, Myanmar, and Mongolia. She lives in Washington, D.C.

MARYELLEN KENNEDY DUCKETT is a veteran editorial researcher, reporter, and writer who has contributed to National Geographic projects since 1999. Based in East Tennessee near Great Smoky Mountains National Park, she considers a perfect weekend one spent hiking and kayaking, preferably somewhere without Wi-Fi or cell service.

MEGHAN MINER MURRAY is a freelance writer and scuba guide based on Hawaii Island. She's written hundreds of articles about science and travel for both online and print publications and has been a contributing writer and researcher for National Geographic for nearly a decade. This is the seventh National Geographic book in which her work appears.

ALLYSON JOHNSON (INTRODUCTION) is a travel editor for National Geographic Books, where she has worked on such titles as the *New York Times* best-selling *Blue Zones Kitchen*, the award-winning *100 Dives of a Lifetime*, and National Geographic's 5,000 Ideas series. Previously an editor at *Rachael Ray Every Day* magazine, she has been published in *USA Weekend*, The Knot, and Brit + Co, among other publications. She lives with her husband and son in Virginia.

Along with the many other writers who lent their time and talent to this book, *1,000 Perfect Weekends* would not have been possible without the hard work and dedication of our National Geographic books staff. Along with many others, particular thanks go to senior editor Allyson Johnson; art director Sanaa Akkach; photo editors Jill Foley, Whitney Tressel, and Charlie Borst; researcher Lindsay Smith; and senior production editor Judith Klein.

ILLUSTRATIONS CREDITS

Cover, YinYang/Getty Images; Back cover, John Crux/Getty Images; 2-3, Robin Moore; 4, Frank Fell/robertharding.com; 6, Nine OK/Getty Images; 8-9, Christopher Groenhout/Getty Images; 10, Frances Gallogly/TandemStock.com; 11 (UP), Tatsuya Kanabe/Stocksy; 11 (LO), Chris Willson/Alamy Stock; 12-3, John W Banagan/Getty Images; 14 (UP), IrinasCreativePhoto/Getty Images; 14 (LO), GeoStills/Alamy Stock; 15, Gary Bedrosian; 16, Simon Bradfield/Getty Images; 18, Sérgio Nogueira/Alamy Stock; 19 (UP), ben_p/Shutterstock.com; 19 (LO), Christian von Mach/Alamy Stock; 20, Christopher Scott/Alamy Stock; 22-3, Diana Robinson/Getty Images; 24, Mark D Callanan/Getty Images; 26, Toni Anzenberger/Anzenberger/Redux; 27 (UP), stock_colors/Getty Images; 27 (LO), Vladimir Vinogradov/Alamy Stock; 28-9, Nine OK/Getty Images; 30, John Kernick/NG Image Collection; 32 (UP), Kevin McCarthy/Alamy Stock; 32 (LO), Gavin Hellier/JAI/Alamy Stock; 33, Pietro Canali/Sime/eStock Photo; 34-5, Taras Vyshnya/Alamy Stock; 36 (UP), Marc Muench/Alamy Stock; 36 (LO), Michele Falzone/Getty Images; 37, Maurizio Rellini/Sime/eStock Photo; 38-9, Reynaldo Alvarez/Getty Images; 40, David Zentz/Cavan; 42, Seaphotoart/Alamy Stock; 44-5, Giuseppe Greco/Sime/eStock Photo; 46, statikmotion/Alamy Stock; 47 (BOTH), Isibindi Africa Lodges; 48-9, robertharding/NG Image Collection; 50 (UP), Didier Forray/Alamy Stock; 50 (LO), Aerial-motion/Shutterstock; 51, Néstor Rodan/Cavan; 52-3, Jason Langley/Cavan; 54, Stephanie Zell/Getty Images; 55 (UP), Denis Tangney Jr/Getty Images; 55 (LO), Vincent Tullo/The New York Times/Redux; 56, Peter Crosby; 58-9, Spruce Peak; 60 (UP), Windigo SEC; 60 (LO), Arnaud Späni/hemis.fr/Alamy Stock; 61, Aliaume Chapelle/TandemStock.com; 62, Rob Crandall/Alamy Stock; 64, THEPALMER/Getty Images; 66-7, Jenn Ackerman and Tim Gruber/NG Image Collection; 68, Joel Hensler/Shutterstock; 69 (UP), Sean Pavone/Alamy Stock; 69 (LO), Camille Moirenc/hemis.fr/Alamy Stock; 70, Dominic Robinson/Alamy Stock; 72-3, Josh Whalen/TandemStock.com; 74 (UP), Steven St. John; 74 (LO), Nora Bibel/laif/Redux; 75, Mike Cavaroc/TandemStock.com; 76, Henryk Sadura/Getty Images; 78, Jessica Sample/NG Image Collection; 80-81, Roberto Moiola/robertharding/NG Image Collection; 82 (UP), Beverly Joubert; 82 (LO), Craig Lovell/Eagle Visions Photography/Alamy Stock; 83, Christopher Kimmel/robertharding.com; 84, Maridav/Shutterstock; 86, Keith Levit/Design Pics/NG Image Collection; 87 (UP), CSNafzger/Shutterstock; 87 (LO), Leah Nash/The New York Times/Redux; 88-9, Matthew Williams-Ellis/robertharding/NG Image Collection; 90, Wayne Walton/Getty Images; 91 (UP), Gong Bing Xinhua/eyevine/Redux; 91 (LO), Chris Hill; 92-3, Justin Foulkes/Sime/eStock Photo; 94, Bruno Morandi/Sime/eStock Photo; 95 (UP), Michael Runkel/robertharding.com; 95 (LO), Westend61 GmbH/Mareen Fischinger/Alamy Stock; 96, Peter Cain/Sime/eStock Photo; 98 (UP), Alex Mustard/NPL/Minden Pictures; 98 (LO), Paul C./Getty Images; 99, Andrew Watson/Alamy Stock; 100, Steve Vidler/Alamy Stock; 102 (UP), Jerry Monkman/Getty Images; 102 (LO), Gary John Norman/Getty Images; 103, Jill Schneider; 104-5, Andrea Pistolesi/Getty Images; 106, Yamil Lage/AFP via Getty Images; 108, Morgan Heim; 110, Heeb Photos/eStock Photo; 111 (UP), Logan Mock-Bunting/Cavan; 111 (LO), Bertrand Rieger/hemis.fr/Alamy Stock; 112-3, Michael Howard/Sime/eStock Photo; 114, Teryn Wilkes; 116 (UP), Jana Ašenbrennerová; 116 (LO), Karol Kozlowski/AWL Images; 117, Luigi Vaccarella/Sime/eStock Photo; 118, Andia/UIG via Getty Images; 120-21, Clare Fieseler; 122-3, Richard Schultze/Getty Images; 124, Francesco Carovillano/Sime/eStock Photo; 126, Stuart Black/robertharding.com; 127 (UP), Brandon van Son/TandemStock.com; 127 (LO), Alan Copson/robertharding/Alamy Stock; 128-9, Barrett Hedges; 130 (UP), Jesse Estes/TandemStock.com; 130 (LO), Peter Walton/robertharding.com; 131, Marc Muench/TandemStock.com; 132, Jon Bilous/Alamy Stock; 134, Hannele Lahti; 135 (UP), Elenarts/Getty Images; 135 (LO), Chris Murray/Cavan; 136, Ian Trower/robertharding.com; 138-9, Hauke Dressler/robertharding.com; 140 (UP), P. Frischknecht/robertharding.com; 140 (LO), Realimage/Alamy Stock; 141, Francesco Vaninetti/robertharding/NG Image Collection; 142, Alan Majchrowicz/age fotostock/robertharding.com; 144, Frans Lanting/robertharding.com; 145 (UP), Paul Biris/Getty Images; 145 (LO), Brandon Lindblad/Shutterstock; 146-7, Ian Shive/TandemStock.com; 148, Osian Rees/Getty Images; 149 (UP), Ian Dagnall Commercial Collection/Alamy Stock; 149 (LO), AlexG Imagery/Alamy Stock; 150, Scott Stulberg/Getty Images; 152, Mint Images/robertharding.com; 153 (UP), Marco Simoni/robertharding.com; 153 (LO), G & M Therin-Weise/robertharding/NG Image Collection; 154 (UP), fontaineg974/age fotostock; 154 (LO), Michael Runkel/robertharding.com; 155, Carsten Peter/NG Image Collection; 156-7, Georgette Douwma/Getty Images; 158, Manuel Breva Colmeiro/Getty Images; 160, Jürgen & Christine Sohns/imageBROKER/Alamy Stock; 162 (UP), Christian Kober/robertharding.com; 162 (LO), Henry Wismayer/Alamy Stock; 163, Stanislav Moroz/Getty Images; 164-5, AlexGcs/RooM the Agency/Alamy Stock; 166 (UP), Chris Hill; 166 (LO), Matthew Williams-Ellis/robertharding.com; 167, Jon Reaves/robertharding/NG Image Collection; 168-9, Marcel Strelow/Alamy Stock; 170, Education Images/UIG via Getty Images; 172, Jennifer Emerling/NG Image Collection; 174 (UP), Hendrik Holler/robertharding.com; 174 (LO), Calvin Chan Wai Meng/Getty Images; 175, Emily Riddell/Getty Images; 176-7, Jörg Modrow/laif/Redux; 178, Cris Foto/Shutterstock; 180 (UP), Paul Williams-Funkystock/Getty Images; 180 (LO), Juan Vte. Muñoz/Getty Images; 181, Lucas Vallecillos/VWPics/Redux; 182, Ane Aleman Lamothe/FOAP/Getty Images; 184-5, Alan Dyer/VWPics/Redux; 186, Jonas Schoell/EPA/Shutterstock; 188 (UP), Miles Ertman/robertharding/NG Image Collection; 188 (LO), Vitor Marigo/Cavan; 189, Pete McBride; 190-91, Philippe Fleury/Getty Images; 192, Maria Galan/robertharding.com; 194 (UP), Bruno Carrillo Bertens/Getty Images; 194 (LO), Angel Manzano/robertharding.com; 195, F. M. Kearney/Design Pics/NG Image Collection; 196, Peter Eastland/Alamy Stock; 198-9, cinoby/Getty Images; 200, Tatiana Popova/Shutterstock; 201 (UP), Hunter McRae/The New York Times/Redux; 201 (LO), Taylor Glenn/Redux; 202-3, Westend61/Kerstin Bittner/Cavan; 204 (UP), Angelo Cavalli/robertharding.com; 204 (LO), Pietro Canali/Sime/eStock Photo; 205, BISUAL STUDIO/Stocksy; 206-7, AlexAnton/Shutterstock; 208, Imaginechina/Alamy Stock; 210 (UP), Andreas Brandl/robertharding.com; 210 (LO), Stefan Auth/robertharding.com; 211, Westend61/Werner Dieterich/Getty Images; 212-3, Anna Tamila/Shutterstock; 214 (UP), Mark Zhu/Shutterstock.com; 214 (LO), Xinhua/Zhang Cheng/eyevine/Redux; 215, Riccardo

Spila/Sime/eStock Photo; 216, Edwin Remsberg/VW PICS/UIG via Getty Images; 218-9, Jonathan Newton/The Washington Post via Getty Images; 220, Robert Haidinger/laif/Redux; 222 (UP), Mark Henderson/Alamy Stock; 222 (LO), Ben Pipe/robertharding.com; 223, Peter Unger/Getty Images; 224-5, Dane Cronin/TandemStock.com; 226, BISUAL STUDIO/Stocksy; 228, Efrain Padro/Alamy Stock; 230 (UP), Paolo Giocoso/Sime/eStock Photo; 230 (LO), Michael Runkel/robertharding.com; 231, Brian Maranan Pineda; 232-3, Reinhard Schmid/Huber/eStock Photo; 234, Corrado Piccoli/Sime/eStock Photo; 236, RASimon/Getty Images; 238 (UP), Sumith Nunkham/Getty Images; 238 (LO), Karol Kozlowski/robertharding.com; 239, Jordan Banks/Sime/eStock Photo; 240-41, Jonathan Irish/NG Image Collection; 242 (UP), Cosmo Condina/robertharding.com; 242 (LO), David R. Frazier Photolibrary/Alamy Stock; 243, Michael Neelon (tourism)/Alamy Stock; 244, Toni Garca Cano/500px/Getty Images; 246, Adam Woolfitt/robertharding.com; 247 (UP), Frank Fell/robertharding.com; 247 (LO), Richard T. Nowitz/robertharding.com; 248, Prisma/Roland Gerth/Alamy Stock; 250 (UP), Heinz-Dieter Falkenstein/robertharding.com; 250 (LO), Franz Marc Frei/Image Professionals GmbH/Alamy Stock; 251, ronnybas/Alamy Stock; 252-3, camo images/Alamy Stock; 254, travellinglight/Alamy Stock; 256-7, Suzy Bennett/Sime/eStock Photo; 258, World History Archive/age fotostock; 260 (UP), Eric Nathan/robertharding.com; 260 (LO), Bertrand Gardel/hemis.fr/Alamy Stock; 261, JacobH/Getty Images; 262, Nick Bonetti/robertharding.com; 264-5, Sean Pavone/Alamy Stock; 266 (UP), Peter Horree/Alamy Stock; 266 (LO), Craig Lovell/Eagle Visions Photography/Alamy Stock; 267, Jacob Kupferman/Getty Images; 268, apomares/Getty Images; 270, Neil Thomas; 272-3, Jarry/Andia/Alamy Stock; 274, Domingo Leiva/Getty Images; 276-7, Jose Fuste Raga/robertharding.com; 278, Todd Korol/Cavan; 280 (UP), Ihsan Gercelman/Alamy Stock; 280 (LO), Michael Melford; 281, Roy Johnson/dbimages/Alamy Stock; 282-3, Robin Moore; 284 (UP), Luisito Echave/Getty Images; 284 (LO), Robert Haidinger/laif/Redux; 285, Peter Frank Edwards/Redux; 286-7, RMDobson/Getty Images; 288, Michael Nolan/robertharding.com; 289 (UP), Westend61/Kerstin Bittner/Cavan; 289 (LO), Jordan Banks/TandemStock.com; 290, Aurélien Brusini/hemis.fr/Alamy Stock; 292-3, James Whitlow Delano; 294 (UP), Andy Ridder/VISUM/Redux; 294 (LO), Laura Morton/NG Image Collection; 295, Stefano Amantini/Sime/eStock Photo; 296, Andrew Woodley/Alamy Stock; 298-9, Shannon Wild; 300 (UP), Ron Koeberer/TandemStock.com; 300 (LO), Jonathan Irish/NG Image Collection; 301, Jill Schneider; 302-3, Fredo de Luna/VWPics/Redux; 304, Paolo Giocoso/Sime/eStock Photo; 306-7, Frances Gallogly/TandemStock.com; 308 (UP), S-F/Shutterstock; 308 (LO), David Guttenfelder/NG Image Collection; 309, Michael Runkel/robertharding.com/NG Image Collection; 310, ajansen/Getty Images; 312-3, Stefan Klein/imageBROKER/Alamy Stock; 314 (UP), Steve Raymer/NG Image Collection; 314 (LO), Jan Wlodarczyk/robertharding.com; 315, Krista Rossow; 316-7, Alan Marsh/robertharding.com; 318 (UP), Amar and Isabelle Guillen - Guillen Photo LLC/Alamy Stock; 318 (LO), James Shive/TandemStock.com; 319, James Schwabel/Alamy Stock; 320-21, ZUMA Press, Inc./Alamy Stock; 322, Patrick Seeger/picture alliance via Getty Images; 324, 2021 Busch Gardens® Williamsburg; 325 (UP), Yvette Cardozo/Alamy Stock; 325 (LO), Ilene MacDonald/Alamy Stock; 326 (UP), Kazuhiro Nogi/AFP via Getty Images; 326 (LO), Terryfic3D/Getty Images; 327, Arkady/Getty Images; 328-9, Lucy Clark/Alamy Stock; 330-31, Oyen Rodriguez; 332, Woodstock Inn & Resort; 333 (BOTH), Mii amo; 334-5, Diego Fiore/Shutterstock; 336 (UP), The Raj; 336 (LO), David Noton/NPL/Minden Pictures; 337, Elise Hassey; 338, Matthew Wakem/Getty Images; 340-41, © Ron Blunt, courtesy The Greenbrier; 342 (UP), Broken Arrow Lodge; 342 (LO), Juan Jimenez/Cavan; 343, John Athimaritis, courtesy Six Senses Kaplankaya; 344, DEA/A. Dagli Orti/Getty Images; 346 (UP), Ventana Big Sur; 346 (LO), Fogo Island Inn; 347, Monica Donovan/Cavan; 348-9, U.S. Space & Rocket Center; 350, Franck Prignet/Figarophoto/Redux; 352 (UP), Rachel Bovey; 352 (LO), The Red Carnation Hotel Collection; 353, Victor Romero; 354-5, Ashford Castle; 356-7, Jicaro Island Lodge; 358-9, Courtesy of JMKE Photography + Camp Halcyon; 360, Alan Copson/robertharding/NG Image Collection; 362, Christian Goupi/agefotostock/Alamy Stock; 363 (UP), Richard T. Nowitz/age fotostock; 363 (LO), csfotoimages/Getty Images; 364-5, Jacek Sopotnicki/robertharding.com; 366, Cro Magnon/Alamy Stock; 367 (UP), PetrJanJuracka/Shutterstock; 367 (LO), Stephen Alvarez; 368 (UP), Xavier Subias/robertharding.com; 368 (LO), Jeff Clay/TandemStock.com; 369, Roberto Moiola/robertharding.com; 370-71, Jim West/robertharding.com; 372, Joe Mamer/Alamy Stock; 374-5, MOHAMED IMAGES/Alamy Stock; 376, Thomas Linkel/laif/Redux; 378 (UP), Marcos Ferro/Cavan; 378 (LO), Taehoon Kim; 379, Ian Shive/TandemStock.com; 380-81, Richard A. Cooke III; 382 (UP), Alex Messenger/TandemStock.com; 382 (LO), Obie Oberholzer/laif/Redux; 383, Grant Ordelheide/TandemStock.com; 384-5, Bob Corson/Getty Images; 386, Matthew Mahon/Redux; 388 (UP), Will Parson/Chesapeake Bay Program; 388 (LO), Brandon Huttenlocher/Cavan; 389, Brett Holman/TandemStock.com; 390-91, Gonzalo Azumendi/laif/Redux; 392, Imaginechina/Alamy Stock; 394 (UP), Malte Jaeger/laif/Redux; 394 (LO), Lucas Bustamante/NPL/Minden Pictures; 395, IrinaK/Shutterstock.com; 396-7, Markus Thomenius/Alamy Stock; 398 (UP), Zoonar/ImgesByCheri.com/Alamy Stock; 398 (LO), Prisma/Heeb Christian/Alamy Stock; 399, Bob Colley/Alamy Stock; 400-401, HP Huber/Huber/eStock Photo; 402, Walter Bibikow/mauritius images GmbH/Alamy Stock; 404, Michele Westmorland/Getty Images; 405 (BOTH), Stephen Martin; 406, Frans Lanting; 408 (UP), Huttopia; 408 (LO), Nick Fitzhugh; 409, dmodlin01/Getty Images; 410-11, Sépaq; 412, Paul O. Boisvert; 414 (UP), Laurens Kaldeway/Getty Images; 414 (LO), Sean Arbabi/Cavan; 415, Barbara Reddoch/Alamy Stock; 416-7, Jeff Norman/EyeEm/Getty Images; 418 (UP), Kenneth Keifer/500px/Getty Images; 418 (LO), Tentsile Finland; 419, Hoshino Resorts; 420, Marjorie1/Stockimo/Alamy Stock; 422 (UP), d'Olde Kamp; 422 (LO), Dieter Meyrl/Getty Images; 423, Marc Muench/TandemStock.com; 424-5, Carlos G. Lopez/Getty Images; 426, Westend61/Uwe Umstätter/Getty Images; 427 (UP), Sépaq; 427 (LO), Raphael Chapot/Getty Images; 428-9, Aynia Brennan/Shutterstock; 430 (UP), PhotoLatino/eStock Photo; 430 (LO), Olga_Go/Shutterstock; 431, Matthew Williams-Ellis/robertharding/NG Image Collection; 432-3, Paul Van Kan/The New York Times/Redux; 434, Pauline Legay/Getty Images; 436 (UP), Javier Larrea/robertharding.com; 436 (LO), ytyoung/Shutterstock; 437, Zoonar/Dasha Petrenk/age fotostock; 438, Premier Photo/Shutterstock.com; 440, Maike Jessen/Picture Press/Redux; 442-3, Kreangchai Rungfamai/Getty Images; 444 (LO), 2019 PEI Potato Chowder Championship Entry by Chef Terry Nabuurs of the Wheelhouse, Georgetown PEI, photo by Al Douglas; 444 (UP), Kai Schwoerer/Getty Images; 445, Yadid Levy/Anzenberger/Redux; 446 (UP), Kona Coffee Cultural Festival; 446 (LO), Peter Frank Edwards/Redux; 447, Rodrigo Buendia/AFP via Getty Images; 448, David Chapman/Getty Images; 450-51, Alex Craig/Getty Images; 452, Markus Kirchgessner/laif/Redux; 454 (UP), Bertrand Rieger/hemis.fr/Alamy Stock; 454 (LO), H. Mark Weidman/Alamy Stock; 455, Gerard Lacz/FLPA/

Minden Pictures; 456-7, Erich Schlegel/Alamy Stock; 458-9, Obie Oberholzer/laif/Redux; 460 (UP), Timothy Horn; 460 (LO), Walter Bibikow/eStock Photo; 461, Lorenzo Mosica/Archivolatino/Redux; 462-3, Mimi Ditchie/Getty Images; 464, Clara Tuma; 466 (UP), Piotr Redlinski/The New York Times/Redux; 466 (LO), Giorgio Filippini/Sime/eStock Photo; 467, Thomas Linkel/laif/Redux; 468-9, Russell Kord/Alamy Stock; 470, Fabrice Coffrini/AFP via Getty Images; 472-3, Sonja Och/laif/Redux; 474, Antonello D'Agostino; 476 (UP), Tomohiro Ohsumi/Bloomberg via Getty Images; 476 (LO), Hoang Dinh Nam/AFP via Getty Images; 477, James Strachan/robertharding.com; 478, Krista Rossow/NG Image Collection; 480-81, Amiel/Image Professionals GmbH/Alamy Stock; 482, Paola Di Bella/Redux; 483 (UP), Jean-Paul Ferrero/AUSCAPE/Alamy Stock; 483 (LO), Gulliver Theis/laif/Redux; 484-5, Richard Cummins/robertharding.com; 486 (UP), Reinhard Schmid/Huber/eStock Photo; 486 (LO), Bernard Friel/DanitaDelimont/Alamy Stock; 487, Antonio Di Franco; 488, Deb Snelson/Getty Images; 489 (UP), Pat & Chuck Blackley/Alamy Stock; 489 (LO), Michael Melford; 490-91, Yadid Levy/robertharding/Alamy Stock; 492-3, Courtesy Stagecoach Trails Guest Ranch; 494, Karol Kozlowski/robertharding.com; 496-7, Jui-Chi Chan/Alamy Stock; 498 (UP), Carolyn Hebbard/Getty Images; 498 (LO), Education Images/UIG via Getty Images; 499, imageBROKER/Ronny Behnert/Alamy Stock; 500, PhotoAbility/age fotostock; 502-503, Bailey Edelstein; 504, Howard Newcomb/TandemStock.com; 505 (UP), trabantos/Shutterstock.com; 505 (LO), Hung Chung Chih/Shutterstock.com; 506, Matt Stroshane/Disney Cruise Line; 508-9, Goss Images/Alamy Stock; 510 (UP), DBSOCAL/Shutterstock.com; 510 (LO), Beaches® Resorts - Ocho Rios, Jamaica; 511, Westend61/Fotofeeling/Getty Images; 512, lophius/Alamy Stock; 514-5, Andy Gibson/Alamy Stock; 516, Philippe Halle/Dreamstime.com; 517 (UP), Peter McDaniel; 517 (LO), I, you, she or he... by Jaume Plensa. Photo by William J. Hebert; 518, Rachel Royse/Alamy Stock; 519 (UP), Resort at Squaw Creek; 519 (LO), Greg Vaughn/Alamy Stock; 520-21, imageBROKER/Valentin Wolf/Getty Images; 522-3, Likuliku Lagoon Resort, Fiji; 524 (UP), apsimo1/Getty Images; 524 (LO), Julian Haber, courtesy Trout Point Lodge; 525, Robert Gilhooly/Alamy Stock; 526-7, Charles Bergman/Shutterstock; 528, The Asahi Shimbun via Getty Images; 530-31, John De Mello/Alamy Stock; 532, EB Adventure Photography/Shutterstock.com; 533 (UP), Michael Shake/Alamy Stock; 533 (LO), Michael Valigore/Alamy Stock; 534, Micky Hoyle; 536-7, Conor Goulding, Mote Marine Laboratory & Aquarium; 538 (UP), eumelia/Kimberly Powell; 538 (LO), digidreamgrafix/Getty Images; 539, Latitudes/Lucio Rossi/Alamy Stock; 540, Stephen Gorman/Cavan; 542-3, John Warburton-Lee/Alamy Stock; 544, Feng Wei/Getty Images; 546-7, majaiva/Getty Images; 548, Dylan Vaughan; 549 (UP), Thomas Rabsch/laif/Redux; 549 (LO), Oliver Foerstner/Shutterstock.com; 550 (UP), Olas Tulum photo by Natasha Lee; 550 (LO), byvalet/Shutterstock.com; 551, Isla Palenque, The Cayuga Collection; 552, Raul Arboleda/AFP via Getty Images; 554-5, Simon Dux/Getty Images; 556 (UP), Sean Pavone/Alamy Stock; 556 (LO), Courtesy Lapa Rios; 557, Courtesy of Alaska Wildland Adventures; 558-9, Chris Dela Cruz/Getty Images; 560-61, Courtesy Great Plains Conservation; 562-3, chapin31/Getty Images; 564 (UP), Gonzalo Azumendi/Alamy Stock; 564 (LO), Donald Bowers/Shutterstock.com; 565, Courtesy Kaua'i Humane Society; 566, parkerphotography/Alamy Stock; 568-9, REUTERS/Lee Celano/Alamy Stock; 570, Blaine Harrington III/Alamy Stock; 572, Chris Bickford; 573 (UP), Glenn Ruthven/Alamy Stock; 573 (LO), Imke Lass/Redux; 574-5, Tom_Deer/Shutterstock; 576 (UP), Kent C. Horner/Getty Images;

576 (LO), earl_of_omaha/Getty Images; 577, Jeremy Wade Shockley/Cavan; 578-9, dabyg/Getty Images; 580 (UP), Randomphotog/Getty Images; 580 (LO), Valerie Hamilton/dpa/age fotostock; 581, Soloviova Liudmyla/Shutterstock; 582, Gerry Ellis/Globio/Minden Pictures; 584-5, Pgiam/Getty Images; 586, Heather Hansen; 587 (UP), Education Images/UIG via Getty Images; 587 (LO), Hanjo Hellmann/Alamy Stock; 588-9, Jennifer Chase; 590-91, Brian Skerry/NG Image Collection; 592 (UP), Kyle Sparks/Cavan; 592 (LO), Ricardo Ribas/SOPA Images/LightRocket via Getty Images; 593, Richard Taylor/Sime/eStock Photo; 594-5, Louis Arevalo/TandemStock.com; 596 (UP), Cavan/robertharding.com; 596 (LO), Joao Inacio/Getty Images; 597, Rodrigo Friscione/Cultura Creative (RF)/Alamy Stock; 598, Olivier Renck/Cavan; 600-601, Hans-Georg Eiben/Huber/eStock Photo; 602, Nick Ledger/Alamy Stock; 604-5, Photoimagesnz/Getty Images; 606 (UP), Michael Melford/NG Image Collection; 606 (LO), Yvette Cardozo/Alamy Stock; 607, Scott Markewitz/robertharding.com; 608, Yoni Eyal/Getty Images; 610-11, Charly Triballeau/AFP via Getty Images; 612 (UP), ZHPH Production/Stocksy; 612 (LO), Leo Patrizi/Getty Images; 613, Jeff Marsh/Stocksy; 614, Mattias Josefsson/Johnér Images/Alamy Stock; 616, Joel Sheagren/Cavan; 617 (UP), Michael Runkel/robertharding.com; 617 (LO), Keith Ladzinski; 618-9, Mike Theiss; 620, Alfio Finocchiaro/Alamy Stock; 622 (UP), The Washington Post/Getty Images; 622 (LO), Design Pics/Ben Welsh/Getty Images; 623, Justin Bailie/TandemStock.com; 624-5, David Liittschwager/NG Image Collection; 626, Courtesy Galavanta Colombia; 627 (UP), Focus_on_Nature/Getty Images; 627 (LO), Jean-François Ducasse/Alamy Stock; 628-9, Steve Winter/NG Image Collection; 630, Viking/Alamy Stock; 631 (UP), Joel Sartore/NG Image Collection; 631 (LO), Jacquie Ferrato/The Nature Conservancy; 632 (UP), Olivier Parent/Alamy Stock; 632 (LO), Brad Beck/TandemStock.com; 633, Jay Pierstorff; 634-5, Francois Gohier/VWPics/Alamy Stock; 636, Floris van Breugel/NPL/Minden Pictures; 637 (UP), Donna Ikenberry/Art Directors & TRIP/Alamy Stock; 637 (LO), Sean Davey/Cavan; 638-9, Kevin Schafer/Nature Picture Library/Alamy Stock; 640, Ken Geiger/NG Image Collection; 642 (UP), Richard Whitcombe/Shutterstock; 642 (LO), Maurizio Rellini/Sime/eStock Photo; 643, James Hager/robertharding/NG Image Collection; 644, Robert Canis/robertharding; 645 (BOTH), ReefSleep; 646-7, Sylvain Cordier/Getty Images; 648, Michel Hersen/DanitaDelimont.com/Getty Images; 650-51, Mint Images/robertharding.com; 652 (UP), Andrew Stewart/robertharding.com; 652 (LO), Animals and Nature/Shutterstock; 653, Jonathan Kingston; 654-5, Kreg Holt; 656 (UP), Jordan Siemens/Getty Images; 656 (LO), Kreg Holt; 657, Kreg Holt; 658-9, Jordan Siemens/TandemStock.com; 660, Lili Holzer-Glier/Redux; 662 (UP), Walter Bibikow/mauritius images GmbH/Alamy Stock; 662 (LO), KevinClarkArt/Shutterstock.com; 663, Franck Guiziou/hemis.fr/Alamy Stock; 664-5, George Cole/Alamy Stock; 666, Johnathan Ampersand Esper/Cavan; 668-9, Amy Toensing/NG Image Collection; 670 (UP), GALA Images/Alamy Stock; 670 (LO), Marc F. Henning/Alamy Stock; 671, Michelle Laramore/EyeEm/Getty Images; 672, Dmitri Alexander; 674-5, chrissmith731/Getty Images; 676 (UP), Nathaniel Noir/Alamy Stock; 676 (LO), HagePhoto; 677, Jochen Conrad/Alamy Stock; 678-9, Tino Soriano; 680, Zoran Djekic/Stocksy; 682, Michael Mellinger/Getty Images; 683 (UP), Jessica Sample; 683 (LO), Christopher Kimmel/Alpine Edge Photography/Cavan; 684, Kevin Galvin/Alamy Stock; 686-7, Chan Wai Ip/EyeEm/Getty Images; 688 (UP), Giovanni Simeone/Sime/eStock Photo; 688 (LO), Emil Pozar/Alamy Stock; 689, Jeffrey Bos.

INDEX